PHILOSOPHY

THE BASIC ISSUES

SECOND EDITION

PHILOSOPHY

THE BASIC ISSUES

SECOND EDITION

EDITED BY

E. D. KLEMKE
A. DAVID KLINE
ROBERT HOLLINGER

IOWA STATE UNIVERSITY

ST. MARTIN'S PRESS

NEW YORK

To Laura Kline, Pat Hollinger, and Bryan Walker

Library of Congress Catalog Card Number: 85–61247
Copyright © 1986 by St. Martin's Press, Inc.
All Rights Reserved.
Manufactured in the United States of America.
09876
fedcba
For information, write St. Martin's Press, Inc.,
175 Fifth Avenue, New York, N.Y. 10010
cover design: Darby Downey
text design: Judith Woracek
ISBN: 0-312-60568-4

Acknowledgments

"A Defense of Skepticism," by Peter Unger. From *Ignorance* by Peter Unger, © Oxford University Press 1975. Reprinted by permission of Oxford University Press.

"A Critique of Skepticism," by John Hospers. From *An Introduction to Philosophical Analysis*, 2nd ed. © 1967, pp. 143–145, 146–155. Reprinted by permission of Prentice-Hall, Inc., Englewood Cliffs, N.J.

"The Fixation of Belief," by Charles Sanders Peirce. From "The Fixation of Belief," *Popular Science Monthly* (November, 1877).

"The Ethics of Belief," by W. K. Clifford. From part one of "The Ethics of Belief" in *Contemporary Review* (January 1877), reprinted in W. K. Clifford, *Lectures and Essays*, 1879.

"The Will to Believe," by William James. From *The Will to Believe and Other Essays*, 1897.

"Two Tables," by Sir Arthur Eddington. From *The Nature of the Physical World* by Sir Arthur Eddington, © 1928 Cambridge University Press. Reprinted by permission of Cambridge University Press.

"Furniture of the Earth," by L. Susan Stebbing. From *Philosophy and the Physicists*. London: Methuen & Co. Ltd., 1937.

"Science and the Physical World," by W. T. Stace. Reprinted from *Man Against Darkness and Other Essays* by permission of the University of Pittsburgh Press. © 1967 by the University of Pittsburgh Press.

"Physical Objects as Not Reducible to Perceptions," by C. H. Whiteley. In *Philosophy* vol. 34(1959), pp. 142–149. Reprinted by permission of Cambridge University Press.

"The Delusion of Free Will," by Robert Blatchford. Reprinted from *Not Guilty* by Robert Blatchford by permission of Vanguard Press, Inc. All rights reserved. Copyright 1927.

"The Problem of Free Will" by W. T. Stace. From pages 279–291 of *Religion and the Modern World* by W. T. Stace (J. B. Lippincott Company). Copyright 1952 by W. T. Stace. Reprinted by permission of Harper & Row, Publishers, Inc.

"Freedom and Determinism," by Richard Taylor. From *Metaphysics*, © 1963, pp. 5–6, 6–12, 25–29, 31–32. Reprinted by permission of Prentice-Hall, Inc., Englewood Cliffs, N.J.

"Free-Will and Psychoanalysis," by John Hospers. From *Philosophy and Phenomenological Research*, vol. 10, no. 3 (March 1950).

"The Crime of Punishment," by Karl Menninger. © 1968 *Saturday Review* magazine. Reprinted by permission.

Acknowledgments and copyrights continue at the back of the book on pages 553–554, which constitute an extension of the copyright page.

CONTENTS

Preface, xi

Introduction: Philosophy and the Study of Philosophy 1

PART ONE
BELIEF AND KNOWLEDGE   25

Preview 25

Appendix 28

1 / PETER UNGER, **A Defense of Skepticism** 30

2 / JOHN HOSPERS, **A Critique of Skepticism** 36

3 / CHARLES SANDERS PEIRCE, **The Fixation of Belief** 46

4 / W. K. CLIFFORD, **The Ethics of Belief** 53

5 / WILLIAM JAMES, **The Will to Believe** 59

Study Questions 64

Further Readings 65

PART TWO
SCIENCE, COMMON SENSE,
AND THE WORLD   67

Preview 67

6 / SIR ARTHUR EDDINGTON, **Two Tables** 70

7 / L. SUSAN STEBBING, **"Furniture of the Earth"** 73

8 / W. T. STACE, Science and the Physical World   82

9 / C. H. WHITELEY, Physical Objects as Not Reducible to Perceptions   87

Study Questions   94

Further Readings   95

PART THREE
FREEDOM, DETERMINISM, AND RESPONSIBILITY   97

Preview   97

10 / ROBERT BLATCHFORD, The Delusion of Free Will   102

11 / W. T. STACE, The Problem of Free Will   108

12 / RICHARD TAYLOR, Freedom and Determinism   115

13 / JOHN HOSPERS, Free-Will and Psychoanalysis   126

14 / KARL MENNINGER, The Crime of Punishment   137

15 / C. S. LEWIS, The Humanitarian Theory of Punishment   144

Study Questions   150

Further Readings   151

PART FOUR
BODIES, MINDS, AND PERSONS   153

Preview   153

16 / C. E. M. JOAD, The Mind as Distinct from the Body   158

17 / WILLIAM S. ROBINSON, Why I Am a Dualist   164

18 / RICHARD TAYLOR, The Case for Materialism   172

19 / A. A. LUCE, Mind Without Matter   183

20 / JOHN B. WATSON, Behaviorism   190

Study Questions   197

Further Readings   198

PART FIVE

PERSONS, MACHINES, AND IMMORTALITY   201

Preview   201

21 / A. M. TURING, Computing Machinery and Intelligence   205

22 / KEITH GUNDERSON, The Imitation Game   216

23 / CLARENCE DARROW, The Myth of Immortality   222

24 / C. J. DUCASSE, Is Life After Death Possible?   229

Study Questions   236

Further Readings   237

PART SIX

THE EXISTENCE OF GOD   239

Preview   239

25 / JULIAN HARTT, Theism and the Existence of God   245

26 / ERNEST NAGEL, The Case for Atheism   252

27 / BERTRAND RUSSELL, Why I Am Not a Christian   262

28 / T. H. HUXLEY, Agnosticism   274

29 / H. L. MENCKEN, Memorial Service   277

30 / ANTONY FLEW, R. M. HARE, BASIL MITCHELL, Theology and Falsification   280

Study Questions   288

Further Readings   290

PART SEVEN

GOD, FAITH, AND EVIL   291

Preview   291

31 / H. J. McCLOSKEY, God and Evil   295

32 / JOHN HICK, The Problem of Evil   314

33 / RICHARD TAYLOR, Faith   322

34 / RICHARD ROBINSON, Religion, Reason, and Faith   325

Study Questions 334

Further Readings 335

PART EIGHT

MEANING AND EXISTENCE   337

Preview 337

35 / DAVID F. SWENSON, **The Dignity of Human Life** 340

36 / KURT BAIER, **The Meaning of Life** 348

37 / A. J. AYER, **Philosophy and the Meaning of Life** 359

38 / KAI NIELSEN, **Philosophy and the Meaning of Life** 364

Study Questions 373

Further Readings 374

PART NINE

MORAL VALUES: GROUNDS AND NORMS   375

Preview 375

39 / HARRY BROWNE, **The Morality Trap** 378

40 / JAMES RACHELS, **Egoism and Moral Skepticism** 387

41 / JEREMY BENTHAM, **Utilitarianism** 394

42 / PAUL W. TAYLOR, **A Problem for Utilitarianism** 402

43 / R. M. MacIVER, **The Deep Beauty of the Golden Rule** 407

44 / JONATHAN BENNETT, **The Conscience of Huckleberry Finn** 414

45 / EMIL BRUNNER, **Good and the Will of God** 423

46 / KAI NIELSEN, **God and the Good** 425

Study Questions 431

Further Readings 432

PART TEN

ETHICAL JUDGMENTS   435

Preview 435

47 / BERTRAND RUSSELL, **Science and Ethics** 439

48 / BRAND BLANSHARD, **The New Subjectivism in Ethics** 446

49 / RUTH BENEDICT, **Anthropology and the Abnormal** 453

50 / W. T. STACE, **Ethical Relativism** 460

Study Questions 469

Further Readings 470

PART ELEVEN
THE STATE AND SOCIETY   473

Preview 473

51 / CHARLES FRANKEL, **Why Choose Democracy?** 476

52 / JOHN HOSPERS, **The Libertarian Manifesto** 486

53 / CARL COHEN, **Socialism** 493

54 / MICHAEL OAKESHOTT, **On Being Conservative** 499

Study Questions 507

Further Readings 508

PART TWELVE
LIBERTY VS. AUTHORITY   511

Preview 511

55 / LORD PATRICK DEVLIN, **Morals and the Criminal Law** 514

56 / H. L. A. HART, **Immorality and Treason** 527

57 / B. F. SKINNER, **Designing a Culture** 533

58 / MELVIN R. SCHUSTER, **Some Problems for Skinner** 539

Study Questions 546

Further Readings 547

GLOSSARY   549

INDEX   555

PREFACE

Philosophy: The Basic Issues, second edition, like its predecessor, is a collection of informative and accessible readings designed to provide a solid introduction to traditional philosophical problems.

Collectively, we have taught philosophy for more than four decades. Like many instructors, we have spent much time trying to find the best way to introduce our students to the subject. Consequently, in recent years we have settled on a discussion approach to the course—if the topics are interesting and the readings are provocative, discussion and debate flourish and class periods become exciting.

A search over a period of several years has led to the selections used in this book. Classical works often seem to present stylistic problems for many students. Accordingly, we have chosen works mainly by twentieth-century authors, readings that are comprehensible to the beginning student.

Rather than stressing contemporary moral problems, this text focuses on more traditional problems of philosophy—for example, God, freedom, and immortality. Not every selection in this anthology is of equal philosophical quality. Some of the essays are models of philosophical genius; others are likely to become the subjects of spirited criticism and debate. But such divergence can be a virtue. Part of learning to philosophize, we believe, is learning how to decide and to defend which is which.

We have been gratified by the response of both instructors and students to the first edition of this text. For this new edition we have made a number of what we hope are improvements. Eighteen of the fifty-eight readings (three more than last time) are new to this edition. The first edition contained four selections on immortality—we decided that this was too many. So we retained the best two—by Darrow and Ducasse—and added selections by Turing and Gunderson on persons and machines. Thus Part Five is now called "Persons, Machines, and Immortality" and logically follows Part Four, "Bodies, Minds, and Persons." Part Eleven, on theories of the state and society, is totally new and, we think, fills a gap in the first edition and relates this part more closely to Part Twelve. In that regard, we now have a close relation of Parts One and Two; Four and Five; Six and Seven; Nine and Ten; and Eleven and Twelve. Part Three is related to Four and Nine; and Part Eight is related to Six and Ten.

Apart from covering new topics, our selection changes have been made mainly in the attempt to adhere more closely to our stated aims of being both provocative and comprehensible by beginning students. A few selections were dropped because the authors merely stated or explained a position without defending it. They were replaced by readings in which the authors both advocate and defend their positions. In a number of cases we felt that the readings, although valuable, were too long. These selections were carefully edited and abridged, making sure that no essential material was omitted. Similarly, we deleted from a few readings short passages not directly relevant to the subject. Many editorial footnotes have been added to the second edition that, among other things, define a technical term, translate a foreign expression, explain a reference to a person or event, and clarify a fine point. We hope that these notes will be helpful to the beginning student. In the same vein we have added a glossary of philosophical terms.

Philosophy: The Basic Issues, second edition, has a number of additional features that make it especially useful as a teaching tool. The general introduction discusses why philosophy is worthy of study, what it is about, and how one should go about studying it. (These last two topics were appendices in the first edition.) Each of the book's twelve parts begins with a preview that orients the student to the main problems about to be discussed and clearly lays out the various solutions that philosophers have reached. At the end of each part are study questions and an annotated list of readings.

The format of the text is suitable for a variety of teaching approaches and syllabi. The instructor may omit some parts entirely or skip over some of the selections within each part. It is also possible to extract related readings from two or more parts to constitute a unit of study.

We would like to express our deep gratitude to all those people who helped us prepare this book. In addition to the many who aided us with the first edition—including Paul Taylor, Ted Solomon, Richard J. Van Iten, Laura Kline, Rowena Wright, Annette Van Cleave, Robert Irelan, and Steven G. Isaacson—for this new edition we are grateful to John Elrod, Gary Comstock, Joseph Kupfer, William S. Robinson, Edna Wiser, Bernice Power, Barbara Larson, Ray Amsler, and, above all, to David Hauser and Bryan Walker. The following critical readers rendered helpful advice: Curtis Brown of Trinity University, Desmond Fitzgerald of the University of San Francisco, William Maker of Clemson University, David Stalker of the University of Delaware, and Diane Steinberg of Cleveland State University. We are also greatly indebted to Jean Smith, Michael Weber, Sharon Edwards, and the entire staff of the College Division of St. Martin's Press for their encouragement and assistance.

Finally, we hope that instructors and students who have comments or suggestions for improving the volume or who wish to convey their evaluation of it will contact the editors. The text is designed to help instructors introduce the study of philosophy to their students, and make it exciting. We believe that it will succeed in doing so.

E.D.K./A.D.K./R.H.

Introduction: Philosophy and the Study of Philosophy

I. WHY STUDY PHILOSOPHY?

As you are reading these pages, the chances are that you have enrolled in a philosophy course or are thinking of taking one. Or perhaps you are just browsing out of curiosity. In either case you may be wondering, "What on earth is philosophy, anyway?" Unfortunately, this question is not an easy one to answer. Attempts to provide one-sentence answers are generally unilluminating and misleading. Our approach to answering the question will be as follows: We will talk about some of the chief aims or tasks of philosophy. In so doing, we hope not only to answer the question, Why study philosophy? but also the question, What is philosophy? The answer will be that philosophy is the enterprise which seeks to fulfill those aims or tasks.

A

Let us begin, then, by talking about some of the chief aims of philosophy. Among them let us consider five which are relevant to ordinary people as well as professional philosophers. These are (1) the critical scrutiny of our beliefs and convictions; (2) the bringing to light of our hidden assumptions or presuppositions; (3) the quest for a genuinely worthwhile life; (4) the effort to keep alive our sense of wonder about the world; and (5) the posing of certain questions which are not dealt with by other disciplines, and the attempt to answer them. We maintain that pursuing these aims constitutes a good reason both for philosophizing and for pursuing or studying philosophy. (These two activities are interconnected, for as you will see, you cannot adequately study philosophy without doing some philosophizing.)

1. Let us first consider some popular and widely held beliefs:

- Nice guys finish last. (So never give a sucker an even break. Or, don't be a fool.)
- If you can't see it, touch it, kick it, or walk around it, it isn't there. (Or at any rate it isn't worth bothering about.)
- Education is good for only one thing: getting a good job. If it doesn't do that (and maybe even if it does), it is a waste of time and money.
- The only or best measure of happiness is your socioeconomic status and your annual financial statement.
- Nonconformity is abnormal or immoral

[1]

• Everything that happens is willed by God and thus is ultimately for the best.

There is no doubt that these are pervasive beliefs. Perhaps most or all of them are held by the proverbial man (or woman) on the street. Similarly, there are many other beliefs which could be added to the list. Generally, these are held in a rather naive and unquestioning manner. Indeed, many of their advocates are quite dogmatic in their adherence to such beliefs.

But the ordinary person isn't the only one who is dogmatic. There are people with some degree of sophistication and learning who are just as tenacious with regard to certain other beliefs. Let us consider some of these:

• Human beings are nothing but complex physical and chemical systems, so their behavior is, in theory, explainable by the same laws that explain the behavior of billiard balls.
• Science and technology hold the keys to reality and to all human problems.
• All of our beliefs, values, and behaviors are products of our genes, our toilet training, our conditioning, our sexual fantasies, or all of the above.
• Capitalism is the best economic system ever invented and the one which is most in accord with human nature.
• Pure science is morally neutral; and since technology can be used for both good and ill, it is neither good nor bad in itself.
• Scientists are just after the truth; they cannot and should not take moral stands on issues except when they are wearing their "ordinary citizen" hats.

You may be wondering, "What does all this have to do with philosophy?" The answer is, "a great deal." For in reflecting on such claims as these, on what they mean, on whether they are true or false (or nonsensical), on what their implications are, on what life would be like if they were true (or if we believed them), we are already beginning to philosophize. Indeed, to a large extent this is what the activity of philosophizing consists of —the articulation, examination, and critical appraisal of our most cherished beliefs and convictions. Of course, there are some people who find such an enterprise threatening. This is one reason why philosophers have not always been popular. They engage in what the nineteenth-century German philosopher Nietzsche called untimely meditations. By this he meant reflections and thoughts which go against the cultural values and ideals of one's own time. To be sure, this may be unsettling. Nevertheless, such meditations can be healthy for both oneself and one's culture even if, in the end, one accepts one's culture's values and beliefs (as most of us do, at least to some extent). For as John Stuart Mill (a nineteenth-century British philosopher) said, believing what happens to be true, if you are dogmatic and closed minded about it, is worse than believing what happens to be false, as long as you are open minded and willing to discuss your beliefs and change them in the light of evidence, discussion, and criticism. Here, then, is one good reason for philosophizing.

2. We turn now to another. Philosophers have not only been concerned with the task of examining our naive beliefs and convictions. They have also tried to bring to light and make us aware of our assumptions or presuppositions. What does this mean? An assumption or presupposition is a belief which is taken for granted and, hence, of which we may not be conscious. Now, some of our assumptions are ordinary, commonsense beliefs —and, hence, beliefs which we hold consciously. For example:

• The sun will rise tomorrow.
• (In winter), spring will follow.
• If I drink a fifth of gin in a half-hour, I will get drunk. Etc.

But there are other assumptions which often lie behind these ordinary beliefs, assumptions to which we often appeal in order to justify these ordinary beliefs. These are the ones we refer to when we say that philosophers have tried to make us aware of our assumptions or presuppositions. For example, suppose you were to ask a friend to justify his or her belief that the sun will rise tomorrow. Your friend would probably do so by answering, "Because it's always been that way." Here we have reached a *basic* assumption, namely, that what has held in the past will continue to hold in the future. It is important to recognize that this is merely an assumption, not a proved fact. If you think otherwise, ask yourself, "How would I prove it?" By saying, "Well, it has always held in the past?" That would be merely repeating the assumption.

Consider some other assumptions which underlie various beliefs. There are some people who believe that criminals should be punished or even condemned. What is the assumption which underlies this belief? It is that human beings are free agents, that they are always capable of freely choosing to do or not do something, and hence that they are responsible for their actions. Or consider another case. There are some people who believe that the universe must have been created. What is the assumption which underlies this belief? It is that nothing can exist without a cause (and, hence, that the universe must have had a cause).

Part of what philosophers try to do, then, is to make us aware of our basic assumptions or presuppositions. Why is this important? Because as long as we are unaware of our assumptions we are not intellectually free. For if we are unaware of them, we are enslaved to them and to all of the consequences they entail. We are not free in our thinking because all that we think is confined to the limits which are set by our unrecognized assumptions. We must, then, first, become aware of them, and second, examine them critically. This is not to say that we must necessarily dismiss them. We undoubtedly will continue to hold many of them. But the manner in which they are held will be different. Here, then, is another good reason for philosophizing.

3. Let us turn to another. Consider the following claim: It is better to suffer an injustice than to do an injustice to another person, since acting unjustly corrupts one and makes one worse, whereas suffering an injustice does not. The man who said this was Socrates, a philosopher of ancient Greece, whose own "untimely meditations" were thought to be aimed at turning the world upside down and therefore cost him his life. For Socrates, the only worthwhile life for a human being is what he called the examined life. The unexamined life is not worth living, he said. This does not mean that if you are not a philosopher you should hang yourself. It means that a human being needs more than bed and bread in order to not merely survive but live *well*. In short, what Socrates meant is this: A human being who has and acts on ideas, beliefs, and values, and has only a relatively short life span, would do well to think seriously about what to *be*: about what to do with his or her life; about what things are most important.

All this is especially true today, when so many of us are searching for values and purposes to guide our lives in the face of general dissatisfaction with events around us. It is also true in an age pervaded by a never-ending series of crises and dilemmas: abortion, starvation, economic setbacks, political strife, nuclear accidents, and so on. Having a well-developed sense of values and purpose is more important today than ever. This is especially true if we recall that we live in a society where manipulation of information and public opinion, and emphasis on the faddish and the superficial, are the rule rather than the exception. Being dissatisfied with the status quo is not enough. We must, each and every one of us, set our own priorities in order if our society, as well as our own lives, are to be straightened out.

The obvious place to begin such philosophizing is with the question, What do I want to be/do with my life? Too many of us get caught up in the "rat race" too early in life. We live in a society governed by certain assumptions and standards about human happiness and the good life which all too often are taken up unreflectively. We are taught that "success" and "happiness" can be measured in monetary terms, or in terms of socioeconomic status, or in terms of how many college degrees one has, and so on. Materialistic values come to be the measure of everything. We view our own well-being in comparison with that of others and take our bearings by reference to social standards that we often don't even think twice about.

Perhaps this is the wrong way to proceed. Perhaps we ought, each of us, to look inward, to find out what we want, what we value most, what kind of person we want to be, and what sort of life we aspire to. At the social level, too, it may be that our values and priorities need reordering. Do we really value electric gadgets so much that we are willing to risk nuclear disaster or increased risk of cancer to have more nuclear power plants? What, as a society, are our real values?

It may well be that underlying all of these individual and social values is the belief that happiness consists in the unlimited search for more and more material wealth. If so, it may also be true that such a view of happiness is an illusion: The more we have, the more we want and the less satisfied we are. This is why Socrates believed that the best life comes from the realization that self-control, and not insatiable desires, is the source of happiness. Whether he was right or wrong, he was raising issues that are worth thinking about; for the answers we give them will bear on the way we live. Here, then, is another good reason for philosophizing.

4. But there is still another. Most of us, as human beings, are naturally curious. There are certain things which we encounter and various experiences which we have that make us wonder. Something may strike us as odd or strange or mysterious or difficult to comprehend, for example, the vastness of space. This sense of wonder and the desire to learn, to know, to contemplate the mysteries of life and the universe have given rise to philosophy, science, religion, art, and culture. Surely such activity makes us what we are—*human* beings, not mere animals. It does not matter if our wonder cannot always be satisfied. Indeed, it may be the case that our recognition of how little we know and how much there is to learn is precisely what makes life so interesting.

In our age of science and technology, with its continuous knowledge explosion (which makes the bits of information we learn by rote as outdated as last week's newspapers), it is important to keep this sense of wonder alive. We must appreciate how important it is to nurture our curiosity, not just to appreciate the significance of new breakthroughs in science but to help us recapture our sense of wonder about everyday life and experience. All too often we tend to leave it to experts to tell us what it all means. And all too often the experts are interested only in the practical dimensions of new discoveries in science, technology, medicine, and so on. But this is not enough. We want to keep in touch with these developments and connect them with our own search for meaning and understanding. We have to learn how to learn: how to adapt our beliefs and values in the presence of continuing changes in our understanding of things. It is only by doing this that we can avoid feeling alienated from developments in science and technology. And it is only by valuing the human need to ask basic questions about the cosmos and our place in it that we can preserve our sense of balance and our human qualities of curiosity and interest in the world around us.

Once again, it will be helpful to be a bit more specific. We live in an age governed by science and technology. The knowledge we receive from the sciences is often taken to be the highest or the only form of knowledge, capable in principle of answering all our questions and solving all our problems. Political decisions, our educational system, our personal outlooks, and our self-understanding all are governed by what has been called scientism, or the view that science is the measure of everything. Politically, this amounts to the idea that "experts" must make all decisions because only they have the knowledge to do so. Should we build a neutron bomb or more nuclear power plants? Should we engage in recombinant-DNA research and develop techniques for applying genetics to change society? What becomes of democracy in a technological age? And what about education? Is the only knowledge worth having connected with the sciences? Is all learning just the memorization of isolated and all too often useless bits of information? Does this view of learning even help us understand science and the curiosity of scientists about nature? In short, while human curiosity has given us science, do we now live in a society in which the dominance of science actually stifles human curiosity and creativity, and in which education is more like training than it is an adventure in ideas?

Obviously, these are complex and difficult issues; and they only scratch the surface in terms of the impact of science and technology on our society, our educational system, our individual lives and outlooks, and the issues of what knowledge and learning are and how best to nurture and satisfy our natural curiosity. One can only hope that this curiosity will continue to flourish, even if this requires us to rethink our basic assumptions about knowledge, science, and learning. So here we have another good reason for philosophizing.

5. Philosophy has had yet another aim or task, namely, attempting to provide answers to certain questions—questions which are very different from most other kinds of questions. First, they differ from everyday questions, which can be answered by *simple* observation, such as "Is there beer in the refrigerator?" Second, they differ from scientific questions, which can be answered by experimental procedures, such as "What is the specific gravity of lead?" Third, they differ from still other questions, which can be answered by formal or linguistic determinations, such as "What is the square root of 9?"

What are some of the main features of philosophical questions? Isaiah Berlin has called attention to some of them:[1] (1) They are often very general. (2) They may have little practical utility (or if they do it is not always clear just what it is). (3) They are such that there are no obvious and standard procedures or techniques for answering them.

It is perhaps the case that many philosophical questions possess all three of these characteristics. For example, consider this question: Are there any propositions which can be known to be true by thinking alone and which

---

[1]Isaiah Berlin, "Introduction" in *The Age of Enlightenment* (New York: Mentor Books, 1956).

do not require any appeal to experience in order to justify them? This question possesses all three of the features just noted. However, there are other questions which are generally held to be philosophical but do not have all three features, for example, Are there any circumstances in which abortion can be justified? Certainly this question may at least have enormous practical consequences. Similarly, there are many moral questions which are quite specific rather than general. Hence, there are at least some philosophical questions which do not possess the first and/or second of the features mentioned by Berlin.

However, the third feature does seem to be characteristic of almost all or at least many philosophical questions. They are such that there is no obvious or standard way to answer them. Indeed, this is why many people find that there is, at first, something very peculiar about philosophical questions. And this is why some find that the study of philosophy is a very perplexing enterprise.

Let us turn to some examples which illustrate this point. Consider this question: Are walleyed pike found in Illinois? We know right off how to answer this question, namely, by observation, either our own or that of a naturalist. But now consider this question: Are there any entities in the universe which do not exist in either space or time? First, someone who has not had some exposure to philosophy may not understand just what is meant by this question. But second, even if the question is clarified, it remains the case that there seems to be no ordinary or standard procedure by which to attempt to answer it.

Similarly, consider this question: Did the campaigns of Alexander the Great occur in the fourth century B.C.? We cannot, of course, observe Alexander's military ventures ourselves. But we at least know how to look for the relevant evidence, pro or con, by which to provide an answer to the question. But now consider this question: Did the universe have a beginning in time? In this case not only do we not have the relevant evidence, whether from our own observation or from that of someone else, but it is not entirely clear how we would go about looking for what would constitute relevant evidence.

Let us take another example. If you were asked, "Are you quite certain that Ralph Nader knows you?" you could answer the question easily. But suppose someone asked, "Can you be certain about what goes on in anyone else's mind?" Here the answer cannot be given so readily.

In the preceding examples we have contrasted some simple empirical or factual questions with philosophical ones. As we have seen, there are some standard procedures for finding answers to the former.

Let us now turn to some examples of a different sort. Consider this question: How many positive roots are there of the equation $x^2 = 4$? Anyone with a knowledge of elementary mathematics can answer this question. But now consider this question: Do numbers (not numerals) exist? This question is much more difficult to answer. Indeed, it is not clear just how one would attempt to answer it.

Similarly, consider these questions: What is the exact meaning of the word *oculist*? This can easily be answered. But contrast it with, What is the exact meaning of the word *person* (or *living*)? A precise and simple answer is not always available.

In these examples we again find that the first question of each pair is such that there is a generally agreed-upon procedure for answering it. To be sure, in these cases the procedure is a formal (or definitional or verbal) one rather than an empirical one. Nevertheless, it is a simple procedure. But this is not so for the second question of each pair.

To summarize: We have considered several pairs of questions. For the first member of each pair there is some well-attested, generally accepted, straightforward method of discovering the answer. The method differs, depending on whether the question involves primarily empirical or primarily formal procedures. But this is not so for the second member of each pair. Here we seem to run into an obstacle. Furthermore, the first question of each pair can be settled "once and for all," or at least with a high degree of probability. The second member of each pair cannot, or at least it is not immediately apparent how it could be.

Questions of the second sort are those with which philosophy is concerned. They include questions like these: Do minds exist as well as bodies? Are humans free agents? What is humanity's highest goal? What is the purpose of life? Does God exist? These questions are neither empirical nor formal. They cannot be answered solely by observing or running simple empirical tests. Nor can they be answered solely by formal procedures such as calculating—or by merely knowing the meanings of words.

In both Western and Eastern civilizations since a time many centuries B.C., it has been—and still is—the task of philosophy to deal with such questions. And they are still with us, for the reason given earlier. They have no simple answers. There are no purely empirical or formal means by which to answer them—or even attempt to answer them.

How, then, does one try to answer them? Through critical analysis and argument. One must first make the necessary distinctions in order to be sure we know precisely what we are asking. And then one must consider the arguments, pro and con, which have been given (or which we ourselves provide), weigh them, and critically evaluate them. There is no other way by which philosophical questions can be settled.

It should be apparent that the most important questions which we all face are philosophical questions. This is why the study of philosophy is of great value for everyone. And this is why as a member of the human race you have an obligation to wrestle with such questions.

The pursuit of these questions won't be easy. Nothing of value is. But we hope that you will be one of many who have found that pursuit to be exciting, provocative, and of enduring value.

We have shown that philosophical questions fall into a unique category in that: (1) They cannot be answered solely on the basis of simple, straightforward empirical procedures (such as opening the door and looking to see if there is beer in the refrigerator). (2) They cannot be answered solely on the basis of some formal procedure or by getting clear on the meaning of words (such as finding the sum of two numbers). It should be noted that it is not only philosophical questions that possess these two features. Many of the questions that are dealt with by the more advanced or theoretical sciences also have these features.

Consider for example questions which occur within the theory of evolution. One of them is the question of whether, over all of time, organisms *always* gradually change due to natural selection. Of course factual evidence gathered by paleontologists has some bearing on the answer. But it isn't clear what the evidence establishes. And in fact biologists differ in the answers they give to the question. Or consider questions in physics in the area of quantum mechanics. According to one interpretation what we call the world is subjective. It is not out there independently of us. It is tied intimately to observers in a subjective fashion. Its state of existence depends on how we perceive it. According to another interpretation, the world is objective. It is out there independently of us. It goes on even if we do not perceive it. Which answer is correct? Physicists disagree.

We have given two examples (and there are many more) of questions found in the sciences which are such that: (1) they cannot be answered solely by any simple empirical test; and (2) they cannot be answered solely by some formal or linguistic procedure. To that extent they are similar to philosophical questions. What difference, if any, is there, then, between philosophical and scientific questions? To the extent that scientific questions meet (1) and (2), they are indistinguishable from philosophical questions. And indeed many of the great philosophers were also scientists (e.g., Leibniz and Descartes, who lived in the 17th century), and many great scientists were also philosophers (e.g., Einstein). Of course, many other sorts of questions in the sciences do not meet those characteristics and are more properly conceived as being strictly matters of science. Furthermore, many of the questions philosophy is concerned with have a sense of urgency about them and may have a bearing on our everyday lives in terms of what we think and do. That is generally not the case with the philosophical questions found in the sciences. Knowing which of the interpretations of quantum mechanics in physics is true probably would not have any impact on your life—your innermost convictions, your concerns, your goals, and your mode of living. On the other hand, knowing whether or not God exists, or whether we have free will, or whether there are any objective moral standards may have a crucial bearing on your life in thought and action. As someone once put it, in science, we ask questions; in philosophy, we find ourselves questioned.

B

Why study philosophy? We have tried to answer this question by discussing five of the main aims or tasks of philosophy: the critical scrutiny of our naive, cherished beliefs and convictions; the bringing to light of our assumptions or presuppositions; the quest for a worthwhile life (the examined life); the keeping alive of our sense of wonder about the world; and the attempt to answer certain vexing but important questions. We would maintain that the achievement of these aims provides us with an answer to the question, Why study philosophy? It also provides us with at least a partial answer to the question, What is philosophy?—namely, philosophy is that enterprise which seeks to fulfill those aims or tasks. And while this doesn't cover everything which comes under the heading of "philosophy," it does pertain to a good deal.

It is clear from what we have said so far that the pursuit of philosophy involves asking a lot of questions. This holds for all of the tasks of philosophy. Again, there are no easy answers to these questions; in some cases there may be none at all (or at least none which are obvious). But sometimes asking questions is more important than finding the answers to them. For we tend to think of answers as bits of information, and furthermore as useful information, as information that can solve a given problem in science, technology, or practical affairs. (For example: What is the most efficient way of getting X, whatever X is and regardless of the value or disvalue of X?) This view, too, is part of the legacy of our scientific culture and, hence, part of the belief system which requires philosophical investigation and scrutiny.

Objectively speaking, we are infinitesimally minute specks of a gigantic universe. This is no cause for despair. For we have certain capacities which make us qualitatively different from other specks: consciousness, thought, and appreciation. The more we ask questions, the more we extend and benefit from the capacities with which we are endowed. We need to step back from our immediate concerns in order to reflect on our personal and cultural beliefs and values, even though we have no guarantee as to the outcome. Perhaps, as John Maynard Keynes said, in the long run we'll all be dead. But then, *for us* it is the short run that counts. So why not make the most of it? It may be an exaggeration to say, with John Stuart Mill, that it is better to be a Socrates unsatisfied than a pig satisfied. But it is no exaggeration to say that the good life involves more than bread, beer, sex, and money. If you don't think so now, perhaps you will after you have read, digested, and discussed the readings in this book. And if after reading the book you still don't agree, you won't be any worse off for having given it a try.

And in order to give it a fair try you must be prepared to step back and reflect, to try to understand yourself and others, to examine your beliefs and values and those of others. You need to exercise your ability to be skeptical of those various beliefs and values, to ask for evidence or reasons for them, to dig out their assumptions and implications, and to look at them with a critical eye. (This does not mean that you must reject them.) We urge you to take seriously the idea that learning (and reading) are not the same as memorizing bits of information but involve posing difficult and fundamental questions about the meaning, truth, and implications of our most cherished and "obvious" beliefs and values. Again, this involves the ability to understand and take seriously beliefs which you don't agree with; it involves understanding and being true to yourself.

You may be thinking, "It sounds as if the pursuit of philosophy involves an awful lot of hard work." We will not deny that philosophy and the study of philosophy involve a good deal of effort. Is it worth it? We believe so. In the words of a contemporary philosopher, W. T. Jones, "Philosophy is the eternal search for truth, a search which inevitably fails and yet is never defeated; which continually eludes us, but which always guides us. This free, intellectual life of the mind is the noblest inheritance of the Western World; it is also the hope of our future."

You, the student, may also wonder just how to approach the study of philosophy once you have determined that it is important to gain more knowledge about this discipline. To help you in that quest we have provided some guides in last section of this Introduction on how to study philosophy. These will aid you in organizing your study of philosophy and in communicating with others either through writing assignments or through discussion and argument. We feel that you will enjoy the study of philosophy much more if you learn to master both of these skills.

Before turning to those matters, let us first deal with the question: What is philosophy about? What sorts of problems is philosophy concerned with?

II. WHAT PHILOSOPHY IS ABOUT

Most of the main problems or questions with which philosophy is concerned may be thought of as falling into three main areas: problems pertaining to reality, problems pertaining to knowledge, and problems pertaining to value. We shall discuss each of these broad areas and note some of the main problems of each of them. The three areas are: metaphysics (or ontology), epistemology, and axiology.

A. Metaphysics: What is Real?

Let us begin with a discussion of what is meant by the term 'reality' in the philosophical sense. In one very broad sense of the term, 'reality' may mean *whatever is*. But in this loose sense, of course, *anything is*—a ghost as well as a tree, an object of illusion as well as an object of veridical perception. In the philosophical sense of the term, 'reality' designates what is *real*, not necessarily or merely as opposed to what is unreal, but rather whatever is real in the sense of being *ultimately* real. It is difficult to explicate this meaning of the term 'reality' to anyone who has no familiarity with philosophical works. Its meaning can best be apprehended by examples, that is, by reading philosophical works in which philosophers distinguish, and give grounds for the distinction, between those kinds of things which merely have a surface reality from those which have a more fundamental or underlying reality. But as a start, one might say that in the philosophical sense, the term 'reality' refers to whatever is real rather than whatever is merely apparent. In fact, this problem of *appearance* versus *reality* has often been considered as one of the main problems of philosophy.

The area of philosophy which deals with the nature of reality is known as *metaphysics*. Let us consider some of the main *problems* (or questions) which fall under this division of philosophy.

1. The problem of the external world.
    Very briefly, this problem is constituted by such questions as:

    Is there a world (or realm of objects) which exists external to our minds (for example, a world of matter)?
    Or are there any good reasons for believing that such a world exists?

The beginning student might wonder: ''Why on earth would anyone worry about questions like these? Of course such a world exists. We encounter it every day of our lives. How can we possibly doubt its reality?'' In response we can only say: Some philosophers have found reasons for taking these questions seriously. And many have provided arguments which attempt to prove either that no such world exists or if it does, we have no conclusive evidence for thinking that it does. Others have attempted to support our common-sensical belief that such a world does exist.

2. The problem of the self (or mind, or soul).
    The main questions of concern here are:

    Does the self exist in any real, substantial way, as a unitary, continuous entity?
    If so, is it a special mental, non-material substance?
    Or is what I call my self identical with my body or some part of my body for example, my brain?

Most of us think of our selves as having a substantial (although not material) reality. That is, each of us thinks of his/her self as a unitary entity, having a duration through time. Are there any good reasons for these beliefs?

3. The problem of freedom versus determinism.
   The main questions here are:

Are human beings genuinely free agents? That is, can they freely choose among alternatives?
Or are their choices and actions determined?
If the latter, what is meant here by 'determined'?
What bearing do the answers to these questions have with regard to human responsibility?
What bearing do they have on practical issues such as the punishment of criminals?

4. The problem of immortality or survival after death.
   The main questions of concern here are:

Does the human self continue to exist after the death of the body?
If so, does it continue to exist forever? (Is it immortal?)

5. The problem of a god (or gods).
   Here we are concerned with such questions as:

Is there any being whose existence transcends the natural universe—an eternal, divine being? (Or is there even more than one god?)
If so, what is the nature of this being? (Is it infinite or finite, for example? Is it all-powerful? All-knowing? Supremely good?)

Many have held that such a being exists. Some philosophers have tried to prove that such a being must exist in order to explain such things as how the universe came into being. Others have examined these arguments and found them to be defective.

6. The problem of evil.
   By many conceptions, God is held to be (among other things) omnipotent (all-powerful) and supremely good. But there is much evil in the world. This leads to a vexing problem:

Is the existence of evil in the world compatible with the existence of an all-powerful *and* supremely benevolent God?
If so, how?

The preceding problems fall into three main categories: problems pertaining to the natural world in general, problems pertaining to human beings, and problems pertaining to a being beyond the natural universe. Thus we may distinguish various sub-categories of metaphysics. There are many ways in which this might be done. A rough way of distinguishing them might be: general metaphysics (or ontology), philosophical anthropology, and philosophy of religion. Ontology is concerned with broad questions such as, "What kinds of things are real? Is there a real material world?" Philosophical anthropology deals with issues having to do with the nature of human selves. Philosophy of religion (or philosophical theology) has to do with problems about the existence and nature of a god or gods.

B. Epistemology: What is Knowledge?

Let us turn now to a consideration of what is meant by the term 'knowledge' in the philosophical sense. The philosophical sense of the term has its roots in the ordinary sense of the term but constitutes a refinement of it. We commonly contrast knowledge with ignorance. And we commonly think of knowledge as possessing some characteristics, whatever they may be, which are lacking in mere opinion or belief. Philosophers accept and insist upon these distinctions. However, with regard to the province of knowledge, as opposed to belief, they also ask further questions and make further distinctions. Some of these are: knowledge which is absolutely certain as opposed to probably knowledge; knowledge which is significant and informative as opposed to knowledge which is trivial (such as 'A is A').

The area of philosophy which pertains to the investigation of knowledge is known as *epistemology*. Let us consider some of the main epistemological problems.

1. The problem of the criterion of knowledge.
   The main questions here are:

   What constitutes genuine knowledge—as opposed to opinion or belief?
   What is the criterion for knowledge?

2. The problem of the possibility of knowledge.
   Once we have defined what genuine knowledge is, then the question arises:

   Is any genuine knowledge attainable? Or is everything we claim to know merely an opinion or belief?
   If so, what are the limits (if any) within which such knowledge is possible?

3. The problem of the sources of knowledge.
   If we claim to have knowledge of reality (even within limits), then the question may be raised:

   What are the sources or origins of such knowledge? (How does it arise? Where does it come from?)

4. The problem of the grounds of knowledge.

Let us suppose that we claim to have genuine knowledge and that we have indicated its sources, then an even more important question must be raised:

What are the *grounds* for our claims to have knowledge (as opposed to opinion)? That is, how can we *justify* our knowledge claims?

5. The problem of the right to believe.

It is an obvious fact that we all hold many beliefs, some of which may be items of knowledge. The main question which arises with regard to belief is:

When do we have a right to believe something?

In answer to the questions of epistemology—especially numbers 3 and 4—two main movements have arisen which hold competing and conflicting views. These are:

Empiricism: All of our knowledge of the world comes to us via sensory experience and must be justified by appealing to such experience. The only "knowledge" we have which requires no such empirical justification is purely verbal and hence trivial and uninformative. For example 'Uncles are males'.

Rationalism: We can have some genuine knowledge of the world which can be justified without appealing to experience. Such knowledge can be justified by *thinking* as well as by our understanding of language. Such knowledge is not trivial or uninformative, but is significant.

Since much of our knowledge is found in the sciences, some or all of the preceding questions can be formulated with respect to science, along with many other related issues. These constitute the subject matter of a subdivision of epistemology known as philosophy of science.

Much of what we know or claim to know is based on inferences from other things which we know or claim to know. Thus another subdivision of epistemology is logic, which is concerned with criteria for making such inferences.

C. Axiology: What is of Value?

The term 'value' in philosophy also has its roots in the ordinary sense of the term. However, philosophers often make further distinctions and refinements by asking such questions as: Are any values more ultimate than others (the latter being merely apparent or on-the-surface)? Are any values of greater importance to human life than others? If so, what are they?

The best way to approach the study of value is through a consideration of value judgments, or evaluative statements. Consider the following sets of statements:

A	B
1. Jones is six feet tall.	1. Jones is a good man.
2. The atomic bomb has killed many people.	2. The atomic bomb is a bad thing to have.
3. Most people keep promises.	3. Promise-keeping is right.
4. Murder is seldom committed.	4. Murder is wrong.

Consider the statements in group (A). Although they differ from each other, they all have something in common. They assert a *fact*, specific or general, without making any evaluations. They merely state that something is (or is the case). Let us call them *descriptive* statements.

But now consider those in group (B). All of these make some *evaluation*. they do not merely state that something is. They appraise certain things, specific or general. They state that something is good or bad, right or wrong. Let us call them *evaluative* statements.

When we reflect upon these two kinds of statements, certain questions arise. Some of these are:

Are the two kinds really different? Or might they be essentially the same (or at least very similar)? Granted that (A) statements assert facts about the natural world. What about (B) statements? Do they also assert some facts, or are they unique? That is, are (B) statements also descriptive?

Suppose one answered "No" to the latter question. Then another question arises: Why are (B) statements not descriptive? What makes them different from (A) statements? Or suppose that one answered "Yes" to that question and maintained that (B) statements are also descriptive. Then further questions arise: What do they describe? Do they describe objective facts, that is, facts which are the case apart from the person who utters such statements? Or do they merely describe or express certain subjective attitudes and feelings on the part of the person who utters them?

Some of the statements in group (B) are general in character, or at least they purport to be. For example, 'Murder is wrong.' Is the claim that, for example, murder is wrong something *absolute*? Or is it relative to historical eras, societies, individuals, or whatever? The same applies to other general (B) statements.

These sorts of questions and concerns give rise to two main problems concerning evaluative assertions. These are:

1. The problem of objectivism vs. subjectivism.
   Are evaluative statements descriptive?
   If so, do they describe objective facts?
   Or do they merely describe or express our subjective attitudes, feelings, and tastes?

2. The problem of absolutism vs. relativism.
   Are any evaluative statements applicable to all persons at all times and places?
   Or are they relative to cultures or eras?

The division of philosophy which deals with these sorts of questions is known as *axiology*, or theory of value, which has two main subdivisions: ethics and aesthetics. Axiology is concerned not only with the above questions which pertain to the nature of value judgments but also with certain questions which are specifically ethical in character, some which are specifically aesthetic in character, and some which apply to both.

Roughly, aesthetics is concerned with problems pertaining to the arts, and hence is often referred to as philosophy of art; ethics is concerned with issues pertaining to morality and conduct.

Among the chief problems of *ethics* are the following:

1. What is the good?
   Or what is the good life?
   That is, what is man's highest good?
2. Among our moral values, which of them are intrinsically good (good in themselves) as opposed to instrumentally good (good as means to ends)?
3. How, if at all, can we distinguish between right and wrong?
   Between what we ought to do and what we ought not to do?
   What is the correct standard of conduct?
4. Are the judgments we make about good, bad, etc., objective or subjective? Absolute or relative?

There are various other problems which pertain to ethics in a somewhat wider sense. These constitute what may be considered to be a third subdivision of axiology commonly known as social and political philosophy. We shall not attempt to list all of these problems. However, two of these are the subject of much contemporary interest. One is sometimes known as the problem of law *versus* liberty, or liberty *versus* antonomy. The law, or the state which imposes laws, is sometimes conceived as being a guardian of our liberties. On the other hand, by governing certain kinds of behavior or by imposing duties or requirements upon us, the law or state also restricts our liberties. A central question then arises: To what extent, if at all, and in what circumstances is the law or state justified in limiting or restricting our liberties? Another way of saying this is: We seem to have a conflict between authority and antonomy. How, if at all, can this conflict be resolved? The second is the problem of theories of society. Which form of society is best? For example, in the world at present there is tension between capitalism and communism and socialism. Is one of these more defensible? If so, on what grounds?

Finally, there is one problem which is both a question of reality and of value. This is the problem of *the meaning of life*.

The main questions of concern here are:

Does life have any objective purpose or meaning?
If so, what is it, and how can it be realized?
If not, does life have *any* meaning or purpose?

There are many problems with which philosophy is concerned. We have tried to indicate what some of the main ones are. Some of these are discussed in detail in this book. We have tried to focus on those which almost everyone is interested in. (See Previews to the Parts.) We hope that the readers will enjoy and profit from their study of these exciting and important problems.

But before we turn to some of the intriguing and important problems of philosophy, we have one more preliminary task. As you will see, reading philosophical works is very unlike reading most other types of works. To assist you in that regard we offer some comments on how to study philosophy.

III. HOW TO STUDY PHILOSOPHY

A. How to Read a Philosophical Work

Most works in philosophy are difficult to read. This is because philosophical problems are difficult to solve—or even attempt to solve. The editors of this book have chosen selections which have been understood by introductory students in the past. Nevertheless, reading these works will require more effort than reading a newspaper or even a history book.

It is recommended that you read each assignment *at least twice*. First read the entire assignment fairly rapidly in order to ascertain what issues are being discussed, where essential arguments occur, and so forth. Then, perhaps after a break, read the same assignment carefully and *take notes*. Such notes will, among other things, prove valuable when you are studying for exams.

Here are some general questions which you should ask and attempt to answer in writing during your second reading of every assignment:

1. What main thesis (or theses) is the author trying to establish or defend (or prove) in this selection?

2. What main thesis (or theses) is the author trying to oppose or refute, if any?

3. What are the author's arguments for the theses which he or she advocates or defends?

4. What are the author's arguments against the theses which he or she opposes, if any?

5. Has the author made a good case in behalf of the theses which he or she maintains or defends? For example, are the arguments good ones? If so, why? If not, why not?

6. Has the author made a good case against the theses which he or she denies or opposes? Is so, why? If not, why not?

7. What is *your* view on the main issue(s) discussed in this selection, and what are your reasons for holding it?

Note: An alternative way of dealing with question 1 is as follows:

1a. What question(s) is the author attempting to answer in this selection?
1b. How does he or she answer the question(s)?

A few comments should be made with regard to these questions.

1. Be sure to state the main theses in complete sentences. Don't just use a phrase or a partial sentence.

2. Be sure to formulate completely the arguments contained in the selections. Supply all the necessary premises and the conclusion. (See How to Structure and Appraise an Argument.)

3. Be sure to make your own critical appraisal of the author's arguments and views.

4. Be sure to defend whatever view you hold with the best reasons and arguments you can think of.

5. In some cases an author's discussion of what he or she defends is intimately connected with what he or she rejects. In such cases questions 1 and 2, and 3 and 4 may be answered conjointly.

6. Be sure to define or explain any technical and/or crucial terms in the selection.

7. Where relevant, identify the overall argument (or argumentative strategy) of the selection as well as the component arguments. (See How to Structure and Appraise an Argument.)

You will find that you cannot adequately understand a philosophical work just by reading it, or by reading and underlining. It is essential for you to try to convey the authors' main claims and arguments in writing. The above questions and suggestions will help you achieve a better understanding of the works you read. But of course, you must actually engage in the task of answering the study questions in writing.

B. How to Structure and Appraise an Argument

The central method of philosophy consists of the presentation and critical evaluation of arguments. Hence, it is important to develop the ability to structure arguments and appraise them critically. The following remarks on this subject are not exhaustive, but they will illustrate some aspects of these activities.

1. *Structuring an Argument*

Consider this argument:

   If materialism is true, all our thoughts are produced by purely material antecedents. These are quite blind, and are just as likely to produce falsehoods as truths.
   We have thus no reason for believing any of our conclusions—including the truth
   of materialism, which is therefore a self-contradictory hypothesis.

First, identify the conclusion. If more than one inference is drawn, there
may be two or more conclusions. Look for the one that is the final conclusion. Label it "C." Clearly, the final conclusion of the argument just given
is as follows:

C: Materialism is a self-contradictory hypothesis.

Second, identify the premise(s) from which the conclusion is drawn. The
conclusion just stated is drawn from the previous statement:

   (If materialism is true) we have no reason for believing any of our conclusions.

That assertion is drawn from the previous statements and, hence, is a sub-
conclusion for which the previous statements are premises.

We may now, *third*, structure the entire argument as follows (P = premise):

P1. If materialism is true, all our thoughts are produced by purely material antecedents.

P2. Purely material antecedents are blind and are just as likely to produce falsehoods as they are to produce truths.

C1. Therefore, if materialism is true, we have no reason for believing any
of our conclusions—including the truth of materialism.

C2. Therefore, materialism is a self-contradictory hypothesis.

(For purposes of exams and the like, you do not have to include the P1, C1,
etc. These are most useful when you first tackle an argument.)

2. *Appraising an Argument*

Next, criticize the argument. For example, *one* way of appraising an argument is to ask if all the premises are true or at least seem true. If one or
more of the premises is false, then the conclusion cannot be known to be
true on the basis of those premises, even if the logical structure of the argument is valid. A *second* way of attacking an argument is to ask whether the
argument is logically valid. Even if the premises and conclusion are true,
the argument itself may be faulty. So ask yourself, Does the conclusion really follow from the premises? That is, given the truth of the premises, are
we entitled to infer the conclusion? If not, why not? Of course, the best way
to answer such questions is via the principles of logic. But there is an informal way by which one can often do this. And that consists in asking

whether you can conceive of a counter instance. Can you think of a case in which, even though the premises are true, the conclusion need not be true?

A *third* way of appraising an argument is to ask whether or not the premises rest on any assumptions. If so, what are those assumptions? Do they seem acceptable? If so, why; if not, why not? If the argument employs an analogy, then, *fourth*, you should ask whether the analogy seems appropriate. If not, why not? A *fifth* way of criticizing an argument is to ask whether certain terms are *defined* in such a manner as to make the conclusion follow, but only through a process of circular reasoning.

There are, of course, many other ways of criticizing an argument. Among those which deserve mention are the following: *Sixth*, see if the argument commits the fallacy of equivocation (i.e., the use of a term or expression in two or more different senses within the context of the argument). If so, no valid conclusion can be drawn. *Seventh*, determine whether or not the argument involves an infinite regress. For example, if it is claimed that the only way to explain Y is because of X, then does X also require an explanation? If so, does *that*, in turn, also require one? And so forth.

3. *Arguments* Versus *Descriptions*

Many students have great difficulty understanding the difference between (a) stating an argument and (b) describing an argument—or perhaps describing an author's approach to an argument. The difference is crucial, since we will be interested mainly in (a) and not in (b).

Suppose you were assigned an essay by A. B. Smith entitled "An Argument for God's Existence," and suppose you were asked to *state* (in writing) Smith's argument. If that were the case, you would be expected to explicitly formulate every premise which is needed for Smith or anyone else to be able to infer the conclusion, "Therefore God exists." That is, everything which is required in order to support that conclusion must be articulated, premise by premise, and nothing which is not required should be formulated as a premise.

Here is an example of what you should *not* do. You should not include among the premises assertions like "First Smith makes a distinction between . . ." or "Then Smith goes on to claim that . . ." Why is this wrong? First, because Smith's name probably does not occur anywhere in the article, except along with the title to indicate authorship. Second, if you included such assertions you would be implying that Smith wrote an article about herself rather than an article in which she attempted to prove or defend God's existence. But the subject matter of Smith's article is the existence of God, not the behavior of Smith.

Here is an example of what you *should* do. Consider the following passage from "A Critique of Ethics," by C. D. Jones.[2]

___

[2]Adapted from A. J. Ayer, *Language, Truth, and Logic* (New York: Dover, 1946), pp. 104–105.

two, three, four, five. In other cases the overall argument may be somewhat more complex. For example, an author may intend to establish a certain thesis, T, by refuting its opposite, non-T. She then makes her case along the following lines: Here are the arguments which have been put forth in behalf of non-T. All of them are invalid. Here are some arguments against non-T. All of them are valid. Therefore, T is true.

Or an author may proceed along these lines: The question I wish to answer is Q. There are only three alternative answers—A, B, and C. A is false, and here is why. B is false, and here is why. Therefore, C must be true.

In doing your assignments you should not merely write down or formulate the component arguments but also organize them into the overall argument of the essay or chapter.

5. *Theses and Arguments*

In reading any essay or chapter you should distinguish between the author's theses and his or her arguments. Many students have difficulty in grasping this distinction, but it is really a simple one. The main thesis is the chief point which the author is trying to get across. Ask yourself, What is the author trying to convince me of? The answer to that question constitutes the main thesis. It is that which the author is trying to prove or at least defend, or that which the author is trying to refute or attack.

Of course, an author may be trying both to defend one thesis and to attack another. This is obvious in cases in which there is only one opposing point of view. In such cases the author is attacking the thesis which is the logical opposite of the one he or she is defending. However, there may be cases in which the thesis being attacked is not merely the opposite of the one being defended. Also, in some cases an author may be trying to defend more than one main thesis, or to attack more than one.

Except in complex cases, a thesis is something which normally may be stated in a single declarative sentence. It must be a complete sentence, not just a word or phrase. Why must it be stated in a complete sentence? Because a thesis is something which the author is either trying to establish as being true or trying to establish as being false. Truth and falsity do not apply to phrases. Only what a complete declarative sentence expresses has the capacity to be either true or false.

Let's take a simple example. Suppose you are reading an article in which the author presents five arguments in behalf of God's existence. Then obviously the main thesis is "God exists" or "There is a God." The author's arguments then consist of both (a) the main thesis ("God exists"), which is the conclusion of each of the arguments, and (b) all of the premises (other statements) from which that conclusion is supposed to follow.

In reading your assignments you should always state the main theses and arguments in writing. This will help you with regard to both class discussion and examinations.

PART ONE

BELIEF AND KNOWLEDGE

PREVIEW

Rene Descartes, who is the most influential figure in the theory of knowledge, was disgusted with the state of knowledge as he found it in the early seventeenth century. Much of what he had been taught was false. Disagreement on important issues, even among "authorities," was rampant. Descartes began thinking about the nature of knowledge in order to put it on a firm foundation.

> Several years have now passed since I first realized how many were the false opinions that in my youth I took to be true, and thus how doubtful were all the things I subsequently built upon these opinions. From the time I became aware of this, I realized that for once I had to raze everything in my life, down to the very bottom, so as to begin again from the first foundations, if I wanted to establish anything firm and lasting in the sciences.[1]

It is not difficult to get into Descartes' frame of mind. The government assures us that nuclear power stations are safe. The reactor at Three Mile Island suffers a catastrophic accident. Ronald Reagan, along with his cadre of advisors and economics professors, assures us that supply-side economics will reduce the government deficit. The deficit soars. One group of prestigious physicists tells us that violations of a nuclear test ban treaty would be verifiable. An equally qualified group asserts the opposite.

These quandaries make Descartes' project attractive. As in constructing a huge office building where one needs a strong foundation upon which to secure the upper floors, one needs a basic set of beliefs or propositions upon which to secure other beliefs. What sort of beliefs could serve as the foundation? Obviously, we must be very careful in selecting them since if

---

[1]Rene Descartes, *Meditations on First Philosophy*, Indianapolis: Hackett, 1979, p. 13.

they are faulty, that may infect what is built on them, hence undermining the project.

Descartes and many other philosophers, including contemporary ones, have thought that the foundation requires beliefs that are certain—beliefs about which one cannot be mistaken. The task then is to find such beliefs and begin constructing the knowledge edifice. Unfortunately, many philosophers have argued that it is enormously difficult to find even a single belief that is certain. Consider, for example, your belief that you are presently reading a philosophy book. Is that belief certain? Is it impossible that your belief is mistaken? Suppose that an hour ago a blood vessel in your brain burst. When discovered unconscious you were rushed to the emergency room of the nearest hospital. A team of doctors is presently doing exploratory surgery. A number of drugs were administered to you and you are now dreaming wildly. In fact, you are dreaming that you are reading a philosophy book about knowledge. Of course, your belief is mistaken, no one thought to bring your books with you to the hospital. Is this story possible? If it is, how can you be *certain* that you are now reading a philosophy book? If you cannot be certain of something so innocent, it looks very dim for our being certain of anything!

Main Questions

We started out trying to put knowledge on a firm foundation. We seemed to end up wondering if there is any knowledge. This constitutes the main question of this part:

1. Is genuine knowledge possible?

A closely related question concerns the nature or definition of knowledge. Notice that in the opening remarks the crucial move that led us to wonder if we have any knowledge was the assumption that if something is to count as knowledge it must be *certain*. Perhaps this condition needs examination. More generally, then, a second question central to this part is:

2. What is the definition of or criterion for knowledge?

But there is another question which is also closely related to (1) and (2). We often find ourselves in a position in which we *believe* something to be true (or false) but in which we would not claim to *know* it. Or we would not claim to know it with certainty. Further, as we shall see in our answer to (2), believing something is *one* of the conditions for knowing it. This leads to a third and very important question:

3. When do we have a right—a moral and intellectual right—to believe?

The issues here concern the concepts of evidence and belief. Is evidence required for belief, or is it justifiable at times to believe without having evidence for a belief?

Answers

With respect to question (1), there are two possible answers. The negative view is called skepticism; the affirmative, non-skepticism. In the strongest sense, these maintain:

Skepticism: the view that no one can *know* anything.
Non-skepticism: the view that knowledge is possible.

Perhaps few people have been skeptics in the sense just referred to. But some philosophers have been skeptical about whether we can have any knowledge about an *external world*. What is an external world? 'External world' is defined as: A world which is external to and independent of our minds and the contents of our minds, a world external to our consciousness. For example, a world of material objects: rocks, tables, nuclear reactors, bodies of humans and animals, and so forth. Generally, the problem of whether genuine knowledge is possible is discussed in these terms. This provides us with refined definitions of our two answers, namely:

1a. Skepticism: No one can know anything about an external world.

1b. Non-skepticism: Genuine knowledge about an external world is possible.

It is this sense of skepticism and its denial with which we are concerned.

To list the alternative answers to question (2) would be impractical. We will, via the readings, focus on the traditional answer to (2), known as the justified-true-belief account. (See selection 2, Section I.)

With regard to the question as to when we have a right to believe, there are two main views. Neither has a common name, hence we shall refer to them as the first view and the second view:

3a. First view: We have a right to believe something if and only if we have sufficient evidence for our belief. (Belief without evidence is *always* wrong.)

3b. Second view: Sometimes we have a right to believe something even if we don't have evidence for it, if certain conditions are met. (Belief without evidence is *sometimes* justifiable.)

Selections

The selections in Part One correspond to the issues raised in the Preview as follows:

Question	Answer	Selection
(1)	(1a) Skepticism	1
(1)	(1b) Non-skepticism	2, 3
(2)		2, 3
(3)	(3a) First view	4
(3)	(3b) Second view	5

APPENDIX

In any discussion of knowledge it is important to distinguish between two kinds of knowledge and, correspondingly, two kinds of truths or propositions which may be known to be true or false. Consider the statements in the following lists.

A	B
1. Wolves are bred in zoos.	1. Uncles are males.
2. It is raining (at a certain place and time).	2. Either it is raining or it is not raining.
3. No objects of art have sold for more than $5 million.	3. No object can be in two places at once.

Clearly, there is a difference between these two kinds of statements. First, statements of type A, even if they are true, are at best contingently true. They could be false. But statements of type B are necessarily true and their negations are necessarily false.

Second, A-statements are dependent on experience, other than the experience of reading and understanding them, for their justification. In order to know whether it is raining outside your room, you have to look out, put your hand out the window or whatever. But B-statements are not dependent on experience for their justification. In order to know that either it is raining or it isn't, you do not have to run any empirical "test."

Type A statements and our knowledge of them are said to be *a posteriori* (or contingent). Type B statements are said to be *a priori* (or necessary). We may now define these terms:

1. A statement is known *a posteriori* if you have to appeal to experience to find out whether the statement is true.

2. A statement is known *a priori* if you do not have to appeal to experience to find out whether the statement is true.

Someone may object: "But by the above definitions, *all* propositions are *a posteriori*, including the ones designated as *a priori*. These too *are* dependent upon experience. You cannot know that they are true, or even understand them, except through the experience of having come to know (and retain) the meanings of the words."

The reply to this is: any such understanding of the term 'experience' would indeed obliterate the distinction. But the fact is there are some propositions which one can know to be true merely by the "experience" of understanding the words. There are others in which more than that is required, namely experience of the actual facts in the world—not the "experience" of knowing meanings of words. It is this meaning of "experience" which the above definitions use. "Experience" here means experience of more than knowing meanings of words, experience which involves performing some empirical test, looking, feeling, hearing, etc.

Thus consider these propositions:

a. It is raining or it is not raining (here and now).
b. It is raining (here and now).

Statement (a) is *a priori* because you don't have to run any empirical test like looking. You don't need to turn to experiencing what the weather actually is like. But (b) is *a posteriori* because you cannot know it is true just by knowing what the words mean. You need to turn to the world and experience what the weather is like.

1 / A Defense of Skepticism

PETER UNGER

In these pages, I try to argue compellingly for skepticism. . . . The type of skepticism for which I first argue is perhaps the most traditional one: skepticism about knowledge. This is the thesis that no one ever *knows* anything about anything. . . .*

I. A CLASSICAL FORM OF SKEPTICAL ARGUMENT

There are certain arguments for skepticism which conform to a familiar . . . pattern or form. These arguments rely, at least for their psychological power, on vivid descriptions of exotic *contrast cases*. The following is one such rough argument, this one in support of skepticism regarding any alleged *knowledge of an external world*.† The exotic contrast case here concerns an evil scientist, and is described to be in line with the most up to date developments of science, or science fiction. We begin by arbitrarily choosing something concerning an external world which might conceivably, we suppose, be *known*, in one way or another, e.g., that there are rocks or, as we will understand it, that there is at least one rock.

[*Argument*] Now, first, *if* someone, anyone *knows* that there are rocks, then the person *can know* the following quite exotic thing: There is *no* evil scientist deceiving him into *falsely* believing that there are rocks. This scientist uses electrodes to induce experiences and thus carries out his deceptions, concerning the existence of rocks or anything else. He first drills holes painlessly in the variously colored skulls, or shells, of his subjects and then implants his electrodes into the appropriate parts of their brains, or protoplasm, or systems. He sends patterns of electrical impulses into them through the electrodes, which are themselves connected by wires to a laboratory console on which he plays, punching various keys and buttons in accordance with his ideas of how the whole thing works and with his deceptive designs. The scientist's delight is intense, and it is caused not so much by his exercising his scientific and intellectual gifts as by the thought that he is deceiving various subjects about all sorts of things. Part of that de-

---

*[In this selection, Unger does not argue for this extreme thesis. Rather, he argues that: No one can know anything about an *external world*. See Section I, first paragraph.—Eds.]

†[The external world consists of objects which exist independently of being perceived, for example, chairs, rocks, etc. It is external to our minds.—Eds.]

light is caused, on this supposition, by his thought that he is deceiving a certain person, perhaps yourself, into falsely believing that there are rocks. He is, then, an evil scientist, and he lives in a world which is entirely bereft of rocks.

[Argument continued] Now, as we have agreed, [1] if you know that there are rocks, then you can know that there is no such scientist doing this to you, [i.e., deceiving you to falsely believe that there are rocks.] But [2] no one can ever know that this exotic situation does not obtain*; no one can ever know that there is no evil scientist who is, by means of electrodes, deceiving him into falsely believing there to be rocks. That is our second premiss, and it is also very difficult to deny. So, thirdly, as a consequence of these two premises, we have our skeptical conclusion: [3] You never know that there are rocks. But of course we have chosen our person, and the matter of there being rocks, quite arbitrarily, and this argument, it surely seems, may be generalized to cover any external matter at all. From this, we may conclude, finally, that [4] nobody ever knows anything about the external world.

[Comments] This argument is the same in form as the "evil demon" argument in Descartes' Meditations†; it is but a more modern, scientific counterpart, with its domain of application confined to matters concerning the external world.[1] Taking the Meditations as our source of the most compelling skeptical argument the philosophical literature has to offer, we may call any argument of this form the classical argument for skepticism. . . .

These arguments are exceedingly compelling. They tend to make skeptics of us all if only for a brief while. Anyone who would try to further skepticism, as I will try to do, will do well to link his own ideas to these arguments. For then, the very notable feelings and intuitions which they arouse may serve as support for the theses he would advance. . . .

II. ON TRYING TO REVERSE THIS ARGUMENT: EXOTIC CASES AND FEELINGS OF IRRATIONALITY

Our skeptical conclusion would not be welcome to many philosophers. Indeed, most philosophers would be inclined to try to reverse the argument, perhaps in the manner made popular by G. E. Moore.[2] They would not, I

[1]René Descartes, Meditations on First Philosophy, 2nd ed., 1642, in The Philosophical Works of Descartes, trans. E. S. Haldane and G. R. T. Ross (Cambridge, 1972), vol. 1, Meditation I, pp. 144–149. The crux of what I take to be the main argument occurs near the end of Meditation I.

[2]See several of Moore's most famous papers. But most especially, I suggest, see his "Four Forms of Scepticism" in his Philosophical Papers (New York, 1959), p. 226. [Moore was a twentieth century philosopher in England who claimed to know with certainty that an external world exists.—Eds.]

*[Obtain: to occur or be prevalent in occurring.—Eds.]

†[Descartes was a seventeenth century philosopher. Unger's argument is an up-to-date version of Descartes'.—Eds.]

think, wish to deny the first premiss, which in any case seems quite unobjectionable, at least in essential thrust. But even in its early formulation, they would be most happy to deny the second premiss, which is the more substantive one.*

[*Reverse Argument*] The Moorean attempt to reverse our argument will proceed like this: [1.] According to your argument, nobody ever *knows* that there are rocks. [2.] But I *do* know that there are rocks. This is something concerning the external world, and I do know it. Hence, [3.] somebody *does* *know* something about the external world. Mindful of our first premiss, the reversal continues: I can reason at least moderately well and thereby come to know things which I see to be entailed by things I already know. Before reflecting on classical arguments such as this, I may have never realized or even had the idea that from there being rocks it follows that there is *no* evil scientist who is deceiving me into *falsely* believing there to be rocks. But, having been presented with such arguments, I of course *now know* that this last *follows* from what I know. And so, while I might not have known *before* that there is no such scientist, at least [4.] I *now* do know that there is no evil scientist who is deceiving me into falsely believing that there are rocks. So far has the skeptical argument failed to challenge my knowledge successfully that it seems actually to have occasioned an increase in what I know about things.

[*Comments*] While the robust character of this reply has a definite appeal, it also seems quite daring. Indeed, the more one thinks on it, the more it seems to be somewhat foolhardy and even dogmatic. One cannot help but think that for all this philosopher really can *know*, he might have all his experience artificially induced by electrodes, these being operated by a terribly evil scientist who, having an idea of what his "protege" is saying to himself, chuckles accordingly. One thinks as well that for all *one can know* *oneself*, there really is no Moore or any other thinker with whose works one has actually had any contact. The belief that one has may, for all one really can *know*, be due to experiences induced by just such a chuckling operator. For all one can *know*, then, there may not really be any rocks. Positive assertions to the contrary, even on one's own part, seem quite out of place and even dogmatic.

[*Counter Argument*] Suppose that you yourself have just positively made an attempt to reverse; you try to be a Moore [and claim to know that there is no scientist who implanted electrodes and is deceiving you.] Now, [*case 1*] we may suppose that electrodes are removed, that your experiences are now brought about through your perception of actual surroundings, and you are, so to speak, forced to encounter your deceptive tormentor. Wouldn't you be made to feel quite *foolish*, even *embarrassed*, by your claims to *know*? Indeed, you would seem to be exposed quite clearly as having

*[Important! Before reading further, go back and reread the first and second premises of Unger's argument (Section I). They are the statements designated as (1) and (2).—Eds.]

been, not only wrong, but rather irrational and even dogmatic. And [*case 2*] *if* there *aren't* ever any experiences of electrodes and so on, that happy fact can't mean that you are any *less* irrational and dogmatic in saying or thinking that you know. In thinking that you *know*, you will be equally and notably irrational and dogmatic. And, for at least *that* reason, in thinking yourself to *know* there is no such scientist, you will be *wrong* in *either* case. So it appears that one doesn't ever really *know* that there is no such scientist doing this thing.

[*Extension and Qualification*] Now, if you think or say to yourself that you are *certain* or *sure* that there is no scientist doing this, you may be doubly right, but even that does not seem to make matters much better for you. You may be right on *one* count because you may, I will suppose, *be* certain that there is no such scientist, and so be right *in what* you *think*. And in the second place, there may be no evil scientist deceiving you, so that you may be right *in that of which you are certain*. But, even if doubly right here, it seems just as dogmatic and irrational for you ever sincerely to profess this certainty. Thus it seems that, even if you *are* certain of the thing, and even if there *is no* scientist, you *shouldn't be certain* of it. It seems that you are *wrong*, then, and *not* right on a third count, namely, *in being certain* of the thing. It seems much better, perhaps perfectly all right, if you are instead only *confident* that there is no such scientist. It seems perfectly all right for you to *believe* there to be no evil scientist doing this. If you say, not only that you believe it, but that you have some *reason* to believe this thing, what you say *may* seem somewhat suspect, at least on reasoned reflection, but it doesn't have any obvious tint of dogmatism or irrationality to it. Finally, you may simply *assert*, perhaps to yourself, *that there is no evil scientist who is deceiving me into falsely believing that there are rocks*. Perhaps strangely, this seems at least pretty nearly as foolhardy and dogmatic as asserting, or as thinking, *that you know the thing*. . . .

[*Comments*] This idea, that claims to *know* about external things are at least somewhat foolhardy and dogmatic, applies in all possible situations, even the most exotic cases. Suppose, for example, that you actually *do* have a sequence of experience which seems to indicate that an evil scientist was deceiving you into falsely believing that there are rocks. You seem to be confronting an exotic scientist who shows you electrodes, points out places of insertion on your skull or shell, and explains in detail how the whole thing works. And you seem to see no rocks outside the window of this scientist's laboratory. The scientist assures you that there really are no such things as rocks, that he only created an impression of such things by stimulating certain groups of cells in your brain. After enough of this sort of thing dominates your experiences, you *might* suppose that you *know* that there *is* an evil scientist who deceived you in the past, but he now does not. And you may also come to suppose that you *know* that there were *never any* rocks at all. But *should* you think you *know*? These latter experiences might *themselves* find no basis in reality, for all you really might *know*. For all you can *know*, it may be that all the time your experiences are induced by electrodes which are operated by *no* scientist, and it may be that there are no scientists at all, and plenty of rocks. Whether or not this is the case, you may always have new experience to the effect that it is. Is the new experience part of an encounter with *reality*, or is it *too* only part of an induced stream, or perhaps even a random sequence of experience? No matter how involved the going gets, it may always get still more involved. And each new turn may make any previously developed claim to *know* seem quite irrational and dogmatic, if not downright embarrassing. No matter what turns one's experience takes, the statement that one *knows* there to be no scientist *may* be wrong for the reason that there is a scientist. But it *will always* be wrong, it seems, for the reason of dogmatism and irrationality, however this last is to be explained. . . .

III. ORDINARY CASES

Largely because it is so exotic and bizarre, the case of a deceiving scientist lets one feel acutely the apparent irrationality in thinking oneself to *know*. But the exotic cases have no monopoly on generating feelings of irrationality.

[*Ordinary Cases*] [1.] If you are planning a philosophical book and trying to estimate the energy you will spend on each of the several chapters, you might think that you *know* that it will not take much to write the *third* chapter. For the argument *there* may seem *already* so *clearly* outlined in your head. But experience may later seem to show that this argument is far from clear. And much time and effort may become absorbed with no clear fruits to show for it. In that case, you will, I suggest, feel somewhat embarrassed and foolish, even if there is no other person to whom your idea that you *knew* was ever communicated. If you just *believed*, or even if you were quite *confident* that this chapter would not take much effort to write, then, I suggest, you would not feel nearly so foolish or embarrassed, oftentimes not at all.

[2.] Again, you may think you *know* that a certain city is the capital of a certain state, and you may feel quite content in this thought while watching another looking the matter up in the library. You will feel quite foolish, however, if the person announces the result to be *another* city, and if subsequent experience seems to show that announcement to be right. This will occur, I suggest, even if you are just an anonymous, disinterested bystander who happens to hear the question posed and the answer later announced. This is true even if the reference was a newspaper, *The Times*, and the capital was changed only yesterday. But these feelings will be very much less apparent, or will not occur at all, if you only feel very confident, at the outset, that the city is thus-and-such, which later is not announced.

You might of course feel that you shouldn't be quite so confident of such things, or that you should watch out in the future. But you probably *wouldn't* feel, I suggest, that you were *irrational* to be confident of that thing at that time. Much less would you feel that you were *dogmatic* in so being.

[3.] Finally, if you *positively asserted* something to another in a conversation, as though reporting a *known fact*, later contrary experiences might well cause you to feel that you had overstepped the bounds of good sense and rationality. The feeling is that you have manifested a trait of a dogmatic personality. If you happen to be right, your extremely positive approach is not likely to be questioned. In case subsequent events seem to indicate you are wrong about the matter, then you come in for a severe judgement, whether or not this judgement is ever made out loud. This is a rather familiar social experience. (As I say this, even in trying to make my style a little less cautious, to be readable, I leave myself open to just such a judgement by putting the matter in such a positive, unqualified way.) I suggest that such feelings *ought* to be far *more* familiar, occurring even where you are *right* about the matter. They *should not* just occur where you are in fact wrong about things. Accordingly, we should avoid making these claims in *any* case, whether we be right or whether wrong in the matter, e.g., of which city is the capital of that state.

It is hard for us to think that there is any important similarity between such common cases as these and the case of someone thinking himself to *know* that *there are rocks*. Exotic contrast cases, like the case of the evil scientist, help one to appreciate that these cases are really essentially the same. By means of contrast cases, we encourage thinking of all sorts of new sequences of experience, sequences which people would never begin to imagine in the normal course of affairs. How would you react to such developments as *these*, no matter *how* exotic or unlikely? It appears that the proper reaction is to feel as irrational about claiming knowledge of rocks as you felt before, where, e.g., one was apparently caught in thought by the library reference to the state's capital. Who would have thought so, before thinking of contrast cases? Those cases help you see, I suggest, that in *either* case, no matter whether you are in fact right in the matter or whether wrong, thinking that you *know* manifests an attitude of dogmatism. Bizarre experiential sequences help show that there is no essential difference between any two external matters; the apparently most certain ones, like that of rocks, and the ones where thinking about *knowing* appears, even without the most exotic skeptical aids, *not* the way to think.

2 / A Critique of Skepticism

JOHN HOSPERS

I. REQUIREMENTS FOR KNOWING

The word "know" is slippery. It is not always used in the same way. Here are some of its principal uses:

[*Senses of "know"*] 1. Sometimes when we talk about knowing, we are referring to *acquaintance* of some kind. For example, "Do you know Richard Smith?" means approximately the same as "Are you acquainted with Richard Smith? (have you met him? etc.) . . ."

2. Sometimes we speak of knowing *how*: Do you know how to ride a horse, do you know how to use a soldering iron? We even use a colloquial noun, "know-how," in talking about this. Knowing how is an *ability*—we know how to ride a horse if we have the ability to ride a horse, and the test of whether we have the ability is whether in the appropriate situation we can perform the activity in question. . . .

3. But by far the most frequent use of the word "know"—and the one with which we shall be primarily concerned—is the *propositional* sense: "I know that . . ." where the word "that" is followed by a proposition: "I know that I am now reading a book," "I know that I am an American citizen," and so on. There is some relation between this last sense of "know" and the earlier ones. We cannot be acquainted with Smith without knowing some things about him (without knowing *that* certain propositions about him are true), and it is difficult to see how one can know *how* to swim without knowing some true propositions about swimming, concerning what you must do with your arms and legs when in the water. (But the dog knows how to swim, though presumably he knows no propositions about swimming.) . . .

[*Conditions for knowing that*] Now, what is required for us to know in this third and most important sense? Taking the letter *p* to stand for any proposition, what requirements must be met in order for one to assert truly that he knows *p*? There are, after all, many people who claim to know something when they don't; so how can one separate the rightful claims to know from the mistaken ones?

a. *p must be true.* The moment you have some reason to believe that a proposition is not true, this immediately negates a person's claim to know it: You can't know *p* if *p* isn't true. If I say, "I know *p*, but *p* is not true," my statement is self-contradictory,* for part of what is involved in knowing *p* is that *p* is true. Similarly, if I say, "He knows *p*, but *p* is not true," this too is self-contradictory. It may be that I *thought* I knew *p*; but if *p* is false, I didn't really know it. I only thought I did. If I nevertheless claim to know *p*, while admitting that *p* is false, my hearers may rightly conclude that I have not yet learned how to use the word "know." This is already implicit in our previous discussion, for what is it that you know about *p* when you know *p*? You know *that p is true*, of course; the very formulation gives away the case: Knowing *p* is knowing that *p* is true. . . .

But the truth-requirement, though necessary, is not sufficient. There are plenty of true propositions, for example in nuclear physics, that you and I do not know to be true unless we happen to be specialists in that area. But the fact that they are true does not imply that we know them to be true. . . .

b. *Not only must p be true: We must believe that p is true.* This may be called the "subjective requirement": We must have a certain attitude toward *p*—not merely that of wondering or speculating about *p*, but positively *believing* that *p* is true. "I know that *p* is true, but I don't believe that it is" would not only be a very peculiar thing to say, it would entitle our hearers to conclude that we had not learned in what circumstances to use the word "know." There may be numerous statements that you believe but do not know to be true, but there can be none which you know to be true but don't believe, since believing is a part (a defining characteristic) of knowing.

"I know *p*" implies "I believe *p*," and "He knows *p*" implies "He believes *p*," for believing is a defining characteristic of knowing. But believing *p* is *not* a defining characteristic of *p's being true: p* can be true even though neither he nor I nor anyone else believes it. (The earth was round even before anyone believed that it was.) There is no contradiction whatever in saying, "He believed *p* (that is, believed it to be true), but *p* is not true." Indeed, we say things of this kind all the time: "He believes that people are persecuting him, but of course it isn't true." . . .

We have now discussed two requirements for knowing, an "objective" one (*p* must be true) and a "subjective" one (one must believe *p*). Are these sufficient? Can you be said to know something if you believe it and if what you believe is true? If so, we can simply define knowledge as true belief, and that will be the end of the matter.

Unfortunately, however, the situation is not so simple. True belief is not yet knowledge. A proposition may be true, and you may believe it to be true, and yet you may not *know* it to be true. Suppose you believe that there are sentient beings on Mars, and suppose that in the course of time, after space-travelers from the earth have landed there, your belief turns out to be true. The statement was true at the time you uttered it, and you also be-

---

*[A self-contradictory statement is one which both simultaneously affirms something and denies it. Broadly, it is of the form, "*p* and not-*p*."—Eds.]

lieved it at the time you uttered it—but did you *know* it to be true at the time
you uttered it? Certainly not, we would be inclined to say; you were not in a
position to know. It was a lucky guess. Even if you had *some* evidence that it
was true, you didn't *know* that it was true at the time you said it. Some further condition, therefore, is required to prevent a lucky guess from passing
as knowledge. . . .

c. *You must have evidence for p (reason to believe p).* When you guessed which
tosses of the coin would be heads, you had no reason to believe that your
guesses would be correct, so you did not *know*. But after you watched all the
tosses and carefully observed which way the coin tossed each time, then
you knew. You had the evidence of your senses—as well as of people
around you, and photographs if you wished to take them—that this throw
was heads, that one tails, and so on. Similarly, when you predict on the basis of tonight's red sunset that tomorrow's weather will be fair, you don't
yet *know* that your prediction will be borne out by the facts; you have some
reason (perhaps) to believe it, but you cannot be sure. But tomorrow when
you go outdoors and see for yourself what the weather is like, you do know
for sure; when tomorrow comes you have the full evidence before you,
which you do not yet have tonight. Tomorrow "the evidence is in"; tonight, it is not knowledge but only an "educated guess."

[*Problem*] This, then, is our third requirement—evidence. But at this point
our troubles begin. How much evidence must there be? "Some evidence"
won't suffice as an answer: there may be *some* evidence that tomorrow will
be sunny, but you don't yet know it. How about "all the evidence that is
available"? But this won't do either; all the evidence that is now available
may not be enough. All the evidence that is now available is far from sufficient to enable us to know whether there are conscious beings on other
planets. We just don't know, even after we have examined all the evidence
at our disposal.

How about "enough evidence to give us *good reason* to believe it"? But
how much evidence is this? I may have known someone for years and
found him to be scrupulously honest during all that time; by virtually any
criterion, this would constitute good evidence that he will be honest the
next time—and yet he may not be; suppose that the next time he steals
someone's wallet. I had good reason to believe that he would remain honest, but nevertheless I didn't *know* that he would remain honest, for it was
not true. We are all familiar with cases in which someone had good reason
to believe a proposition that nevertheless turned out to be false.

What then *is* sufficient? We are now tempted to say, "Complete
evidence—all the evidence there could ever be—the works, everything."
But if we say this, let us notice at once that there are very few propositions
whose truth we can claim to know. Most of those propositions that in daily
life we claim to know without the slightest hesitation we would *not* know

according to this criterion. For example, we say, "I know that if I were to let go of this pencil, it would fall," and we don't have the slightest hesitation about it; but although we may have excellent evidence (pencils and other objects have always fallen when let go), we don't have *complete* evidence, for we have not yet observed the outcome of letting go of it *this* time. To take an even more obvious case, we say, "I know that there is a book before me now," but we have not engaged in every possible observation that would be relevant to determining the truth of this statement: We have not examined the object (the one we take to be a book) from *all* angles (and since there are an infinite number of angles, who could?), and even if we have looked at it steadily for half an hour, we have not done so for a hundred hours, or a million; and yet it would *seem* (though some have disputed this, as we shall see) that if one observation provides evidence, a thousand observations should provide more evidence—and when could the accumulation of evidence end? . . .

We might, nevertheless, stick to our definition and say that we really do *not* know most of the propositions that in daily life we claim to know: Perhaps I don't *know* that this is a book before me, that I am now indoors and not outdoors, that I am now reading sentences written in the English language, or that there are any other people in the world. But this is a rather astounding claim and needs to be justified. We are all convinced that we know these things: We act on them every day of our lives, and if we were asked outside a philosophy classroom whether we knew them, we would say "yes" without hesitation. Surely we cannot accept a definition of "know" that would practically define knowledge out of existence? But if not, what alternative have we?

"Perhaps we don't have to go so far as to say '*all* the evidence,' '*complete* evidence,' and so on. All we have to say is that we must have *adequate* evidence." But when is the evidence adequate? Is anything less than "all the evidence there could ever be" adequate? "Well, adequate for enabling us to know." But this little addition to our definition lands us in a circle. We are trying to define "know," and we cannot in doing so employ the convenient phrase "enough to enable us to know"—for the last word in this definition is the very one we are trying to define. But once we have dropped the phrase "to know," we are left with our problem once more: How much evidence is adequate evidence? Is it adequate when anything less than *all* the evidence is in? If not all the evidence is in, but only 99.99 percent of it, couldn't that .01 per cent go contrary to the rest of it and require us to conclude that the proposition might not be true after all, and that therefore we didn't know it? Surely it has happened often enough that a statement that we thought we knew, perhaps even would have staked our lives on, turned out in the end to be false, or just doubtful. But in that case we didn't really *know* it after all: The evidence was good, even overwhelming, but yet not good enough, not really adequate, for it was not enough to guarantee the truth of the proposition. Can we know *p* with anything less than *all* the evidence there ever could be for *p*?

II. STRONG AND WEAK SENSES OF "KNOW"

[*Disputes About Knowing*] In daily life we say we know—not just believe or surmise, but *know*—that heavier-than-air objects fall, that snow is white, that we can read and write, and countless other things. If someone denies this, and no fact cited by the one disputant suffices to convince the other, we may well suspect that there is a verbal issue involved: in this case, that they are operating on two different meanings of "know," because they construe the third requirement—the evidence requirement—differently.

[*Case 1*] Suppose I say, "There is a bookcase in my office," and someone challenges this assertion. I reply, "I *know* that there is a bookcase in my office. I put it there myself, and I've seen it there for years. In fact, I saw it there just two minutes ago when I took a book out of it and left the office to go into the classroom." Now suppose we both go to my office, take a look, and there is the bookcase, exactly as before. "See, I *knew* it was here," I say. "Oh no," he replies, "you *believed with good reason* that it was still there, because you had seen it there often before and you didn't see or hear anyone removing it. But you didn't *know* it was there when you said it, for at that moment you were in the classroom and not in your office."

At this point, I may reply, "But I did know it was there, even when I said it. I knew it because *(1) I believed it, (2) I had good grounds on which to base the belief, and (3) the belief was true.* And I would call it knowledge whenever these three conditions are fulfilled. This is the way we use the word 'know' every day of our lives. One knows those true propositions that one believes with good reason. And when I said the bookcase was still in my office, I was uttering one of those propositions."

But now my opponent may reply, "But you still didn't know it. You had good reason to say it, I admit, for you had not seen or heard anyone removing it. You had good reason, but not *sufficient* reason. The evidence you gave was still compatible with your statement being false—and if it was false, you of course did not *know* that it was true. [*Case 2*] Suppose that you had made your claim to knowledge, and I had denied your claim, and we had both gone into your office, and to your great surprise (and mine too) the bookcase was no longer there. Could you *then* have claimed to know that it was still there?"

"Of course not. The falsity of a statement always invalidates the claim to know it. If the bookcase had not been there, I would not have been entitled to say that I knew it was there; my claim would have been mistaken."

"Right—it would have been mistaken. But now please note that the only difference between the two cases is that in the first case the bookcase was there and in the second case it wasn't. *The evidence in the two cases was exactly the same.* You had exactly the same reason for saying that the bookcase was still there in the *second* case (when we found it missing) that you did in the *first* case (when we found it still there). And since you—as you yourself admit—didn't know it in the second case, you couldn't have known it in the first case either. You believed it with good reason, but you didn't *know* it."

[*Solution*] Here my opponent may have scored an important point; he may have convinced me that since I admittedly didn't know in the second case I couldn't have known in the first case either. But here I may make an important point in return: "My belief was the same in the two cases; the evidence was the same in the two cases (I had seen the bookcase two minutes before, had heard or seen no one removing it). The only difference was that in the first case the bookcase was there and in the second case it wasn't (*p* was true in the first case, false in the second). But *this doesn't show that I didn't know* in the first case. What it does show is that *although I might have been mistaken, I wasn't mistaken*. Had the bookcase not been there, I couldn't have claimed to know that it was; but since the bookcase in fact *was* still there, I *did* know, although (on the basis of the evidence I had) I *might* have been mistaken."

"Yes, it turned out to be true—you were lucky. But as we both agree, a lucky guess isn't the same as knowledge."

"But this wasn't just a lucky guess. I had excellent reasons for believing that the bookcase was still there. So the evidence requirement was fulfilled."

"No, it wasn't. You had good reason, excellent reason, but not *sufficient* reason—both times—for believing that the bookcase was still there. But in the second case it wasn't there, so you didn't know; therefore, in the first case where your evidence was *exactly the same*, you didn't know either; you just believed it with good reason, but that wasn't enough: your reason wasn't sufficient, and so you didn't *know*."

Now the difference in the criterion of knowing between the two disputants begins to emerge. According to me, I did know *p* in the first case because my belief was based on excellent evidence and was also true. According to my opponent, I did not know *p* in the first case because my evidence was still less than complete—I wasn't in the room seeing or touching the bookcase when I made the statement. It seems, then, that I am operating with a less demanding definition of "know" than he is. I am using "know" in the *weak* sense, in which I know a proposition when I believe it, have good reason for believing it, and it is true. But he is using "know" in a more demanding sense: He is using it in the *strong* sense, which requires that in order to know a proposition, it must be true, I must believe it, and I must have absolutely *conclusive* evidence in favor of it.

[*Examples*] Let us contrast these two cases:

Suppose that after a routine medical examination the excited doctor reports to me that the X-ray photographs show that I have no heart. I should tell him to get a new machine. I should be inclined to say that the fact that I have a heart is one of the few things that I can count on as absolutely certain. I can feel it beat. I know it's there. Furthermore, how could my blood circulate if I didn't have one? Suppose that later on I suffer a chest injury and undergo a surgical operation. Afterwards the astonished surgeons solemnly declare that they searched my chest cavity and found no heart, and that they made incisions and looked about in other likely places but found it not. They are convinced that I am without a heart. They are unable to understand how circulation can occur or what accounts for the thumping in my chest. But they are in agreement and obviously sincere, and they have clear photographs of my interior spaces. What would be my attitude? Would it be to insist that they were all mistaken? I think not. I believe that I should eventually accept their testimony and the evidence of the photographs. I should consider to be false what I now regard as an absolute certainty. [When I say I know I have a heart, I know it in the weak sense.]

Suppose that as I write this paper someone in the next room were to call out to me, "I can't find an ink-bottle; is there one in the house?" I should reply, "Here is an ink-bottle." If he said in a doubtful tone, "Are you sure? I looked there before," I should reply, "Yes, I know there is; come and get it."

Now could it turn out to be false that there is an ink-bottle directly in front of me on this desk? Many philosophers have thought so. They would say that many things could happen of such a nature that if they did happen it would be proved that I am deceived. I agree that many extraordinary things could happen, in the sense that there is no logical absurdity in the supposition. It could happen that when I next reach for this ink-bottle my hand should seem to pass *through* it and I should not feel the contact of any object. It could happen that in the next moment the ink-bottle will suddenly vanish from sight; or that I should find myself under a tree in the garden with no ink-bottle about; or that one or more persons should enter this room and declare with apparent sincerity that they see no ink-bottle on this desk; or that a photograph taken now of the top of the desk should clearly show all of the objects on it except the ink-bottle. Having admitted that these things *could happen,* am I compelled to admit that if they did happen, then it would be proved that there is no ink-bottle here *now?* Not at all. I could say that when my hand seemed to pass through the ink-bottle I should *then* be suffering from hallucination; that if the ink-bottle suddenly vanished, it would have miraculously ceased to exist; that the other persons were conspiring to drive me mad, or were themselves victims of remarkable concurrent hallucinations; that the camera possessed some strange flaw or that there was trickery in developing the negative: . . . Not only do I not *have* to admit that those extraordinary occurrences would be evidence that there is no ink-bottle here; the fact is that I *do not* admit it. There is nothing whatever that could happen in the next moment or the next year that would by me be called *evidence* that there is not an ink-bottle here now. No future experience or investigation could prove to me that I am mistaken. Therefore, if I were to say, "I know that there is a ink-bottle here," I should be using "know" in the strong sense.[1]

It is in the weak sense that we use the word "know" in daily life, as when I say I know that I have a heart, that if I let go of this piece of chalk it will fall, that the sun will rise tomorrow, and so on. I have excellent reason (evidence) to believe all these things, evidence so strong that (so we say) it amounts to certainty. And yet there are events that could conceivably occur which, if they did occur, would cast doubt on the beliefs or even show them to be false. . . .

III. ARGUMENT AGAINST SKEPTICISM

[Skepticism] But the philosopher is apt to be more concerned with "know" in the strong sense. He wants to inquire whether there are any propositions that we can know without the shadow of a doubt will never be proved false, or even rendered dubious to the smallest degree. "You can say," he will argue, "and I admit that it would be good English usage to say, that you know that you have a heart and that the sun is more than 90 million miles from the earth. But you don't know it until you have absolutely conclusive evidence, and you must admit that the evidence you have, while very strong, is not conclusive. So I shall say, using 'know' in the strong sense, that you do not know these propositions. I want then to ask what propositions can be known in the strong sense, the sense that puts the proposition forever past the possibility of doubt."

And on this point many philosophers have been quite skeptical; they have granted few if any propositions whose truth we could know in the strong sense. . . . Such a person is a *skeptic*. We claim (he says) to know many things about the world, but in fact none of these propositions can be known for certain. What are we to say of the skeptic's position?

[Criticism] Let us first note that in the phrase "know for certain" the "for certain" is redundant—how can we know except for certain? If it is less than certain, how can it be knowledge? We do, however, use the word "certain" ambiguously: (1) Sometimes we say "I am certain," which just means that I have a feeling of certainty about it—"I feel certain that I locked the door of the apartment"—and of course the feeling of certainty is no guarantee that the statement is true. People have very strong feelings of certainty about many propositions that they have no evidence for at all, particularly if they want to believe them or are consoled by believing them. The phrase "feeling certain," then, refers simply to a psychological state, whose existence in no way guarantees that what the person feels certain about is true. But (2) sometimes when we say "I am certain" we mean that

[1]Norman Malcolm, "Knowledge and Belief," in *Knowledge and Certainty*, pp. 66–68.

it *is* certain—in other words, that we *do* know the proposition in question to be true. This, of course, is the sense of "certain" that is of interest to philosophers (the first sense is of more interest to psychiatrists in dealing with patients). Thus we could reformulate our question, "Is anything certain?" or "Are any propositions certain?"

"I can well understand," one might argue, "how you could question some statements, even most statements. But if you carry on this merry game until you have covered *all* statements, you are simply mistaken, and I think I can show you why. You may see someone in a fog or in a bad light and not know (not be certain) whether he has a right hand. But don't you know that *you* have a right hand? There it is! Suppose I now raise my hand and say, 'Here is a hand.' Now you say to me, 'I doubt that there's a hand.' But what evidence do you want? What does your doubt consist of? You don't believe your eyes, perhaps? Very well, then come up and touch the hand. You still aren't satisfied? Then keep on looking at it steadily and touching it, photograph it, call in other people for testimony if you like. If after all this you still say it isn't certain, what more do you want? Under what conditions would you admit that it *is* certain, that you *do* know it? I can understand your doubt when there is some condition left unfulfilled, some test left uncompleted. At the beginning, perhaps you doubted that *if* you tried to touch my hand you would find anything there to touch; but then you did touch, and so you resolved *that* doubt. You resolved further doubts by calling in other people and so on. You performed all the relevant tests, and they turned out favorably. So now, at the end of the process, what is it that you doubt? Oh, I know what you *say*: 'I still doubt that that's a hand.' But isn't this saying 'I doubt' now an empty formula? I can no longer attach any content to that so-called doubt, for there is nothing left to doubt; you yourself *cannot specify any further test that, if performed, would resolve your doubt*. 'Doubt' now becomes an empty word. You're not doubting now that *if* you raised your hand to touch mine, you would touch it, or that *if* Smith and others were brought in, they would also testify that this is a hand—we've already gone through all that. So what is it specifically that you doubt? What possible test is there the negative result of which you fear? I submit that there isn't any. You are confusing a situation in which doubt is understandable (*before* you made the tests) with the later situation in which it isn't, for it has all been dispelled. . . .

"But your so-called doubt becomes meaningless when there is nothing left to doubt—when the tests have been carried out and their results are all favorable. Suppose a physician examines a patient and says, 'It's probable that you have an inflamed appendix.' Here one can still doubt, for the signs may be misleading. So the physician operates on the patient, finds an inflamed appendix and removes it, and the patient recovers. *Now* what would be the sense of the physician's saying, 'It's *probable* that he had an inflamed appendix'? If seeing it and removing it made it only *probable*, what would make it certain? Or you are driving along and you hear a rapid regular thumping sound and you say, 'It's probable that I have a flat tire.' So far you're right; it's only probable—the thumping might be caused by something else. So you go out and have a look, and there is the tire, flat. You find a nail embedded in it, change the tire, and then resume your ride with no more thumping. Are you *now* going to say, 'It's merely *probable* that the car had a flat tire'? But if given all those conditions it would be merely probable, what in the world would make it certain? Can you describe to me the circumstances in which you would say it's certain? If you can't, then the phrase 'being certain' has no meaning as you are using it. You are simply using it in such a special way that it has no application at all, and there is no reason at all why anyone else should follow your usage. In daily life we have a very convenient and useful distinction between the application of the words 'probable' and 'certain.' We say appendicitis is probable *before* the operation, but when the physician has the patient's appendix visible before him on the operating table, now it's certain—that's just the kind of situation in which we apply the word 'certain,' as opposed to 'probable'. Now you, for some reason, are so fond of the word 'probable' that you want to use it for everything—you use it to describe *both* the preoperative and postoperative situations, and the word 'certain' is left without any application at all. But this is nothing but a *verbal manipulation* on your part. You have changed nothing; you have only taken, as it were, two bottles with different contents, and instead of labeling them differently ('probable' and 'certain'), as the rest of us do, you put the same label ('probable') on both of them! What possible advantage is there in this? It's just verbal contrariness. And since you have pre-empted the word 'probable' to cover *both* the situations, we now have to devise a *different* pair of words to mark the perfectly obvious distinction between the situation *before* the surgery and the situation *during* the surgery—the same difference we previously marked by the words 'probable' and 'certain' until you used the word 'probable' to apply to both of them. What gain is there in this *verbal manipulation* of yours?'' . . .

3 / The Fixation of Belief

CHARLES SANDERS PEIRCE

We generally know when we wish to ask a question and when we wish to pronounce a judgment, for there is a dissimilarity between the sensation of doubting and that of believing.

But this is not all which distinguishes doubt from belief. There is a practical difference. Our beliefs guide our desires and shape our actions. The Assassins, or followers of the Old Man of the Mountain,* used to rush into death at his least command, because they believed that obedience to him would insure everlasting felicity. Had they doubted this, they would not have acted as they did. So it is with every belief, according to its degree. The feeling of believing is a more or less sure indication of there being established in our nature some habit which will determine our actions. Doubt never has such an effect.

Nor must we overlook a third point of difference. Doubt is an uneasy and dissatisfied state from which we struggle to free ourselves and pass into the state of belief; while the latter is a calm and satisfactory state which we do not wish to avoid, or to change to a belief in anything else. On the contrary, we cling tenaciously, not merely to believing, but to believing just what we do believe.

Thus, both doubt and belief have positive effects upon us, though very different ones. Belief does not make us act at once, but puts us into such a condition that we shall behave in a certain way, when the occasion arises. Doubt has not the least effect of this sort, but stimulates us to action until it is destroyed. This reminds us of the irritation of a nerve and the reflex action produced thereby; while for the analogue of belief, in the nervous system, we must look to what are called nervous associations—for example, to that habit of the nerves in consequence of which the smell of a peach will make the mouth water.

The irritation of doubt causes a struggle to attain a state of belief. I shall term this struggle *inquiry*, though it must be admitted that this is sometimes not a very apt designation.

The irritation of doubt is the only immediate motive for the struggle to attain belief. It is certainly best for us that our beliefs should be such as may truly guide our actions so as to satisfy our desires; and this reflection will make us reject any belief which does not seem to have been so formed as to

*[Members of a cult.—Eds.]

insure this result. But it will only do so by creating a doubt in the place of that belief. With the doubt, therefore, the struggle begins, and with the cessation of doubt it ends. Hence, the sole object of inquiry is the settlement of opinion. We may fancy that this is not enough for us, and that we seek not merely an opinion, but a true opinion. But put this fancy to the test, and it proves groundless; for as soon as a firm belief is reached we are entirely satisfied, whether the belief be false or true. And it is clear that nothing out of the sphere of our knowledge can be our object, for nothing which does not affect the mind can be a motive for a mental effort. The most that can be maintained is, that we seek for a belief that we shall *think* to be true. But we think each one of our beliefs to be true, and, indeed, it is mere tautology to say so.

That the settlement of opinion is the sole end of inquiry is a very important proposition. It sweeps away, at once, various vague and erroneous conceptions of proof. A few of these may be noticed here.

1. Some philosophers have imagined that to start an inquiry it was only necessary to utter a question or set it down on paper, and have even recommended us to begin our studies with questioning everything! But the mere putting of a proposition into the interrogative form does not stimulate the mind to any struggle after belief. There must be a real and living doubt, and without this all discussion is idle.

2. It is a very common idea that a demonstration must rest on some ultimate and absolutely indubitable propositions. These, according to one school, are first principles of a general nature; according to another, are first sensations. But in point of fact, an inquiry, to have that completely satisfactory result called demonstration, has only to start with propositions perfectly free from all actual doubt. If the premises are not in fact doubted at all, they cannot be more satisfactory than they are.

3. Some people seem to love to argue a point after all the world is fully convinced of it. But no further advance can be made. When doubt ceases, mental action on the subject comes to an end; and if it did go on, it would be without a purpose.

[1. The Method of Tenacity /] If the settlement of opinion is the sole object of inquiry, and if belief is of the nature of a habit, why should we not attain the desired end by taking any answer to a question which we may fancy and constantly reiterating it to ourselves, dwelling on all which may conduce to that belief and learning to turn with contempt and hatred from anything which might disturb it? This simple and direct method is really pursued by many men. I remember once being entreated not to read a certain newspaper lest it might change my opinion upon free trade. ''Lest I might be entrapped by its fallacies and misstatements,'' was the form of expression. ''You are not,'' my friend said, ''a special student of political economy. You might, therefore, easily be deceived by fallacious arguments upon the subject. You might, then, if you read this paper, be led to believe in protection. But you admit that free trade is the true doctrine; and you do not wish to believe what is not true.'' I have often known this system to be deliberately adopted. Still oftener, the instinctive dislike of an undecided state of mind, exaggerated into a vague dread of doubt, makes men cling spasmodically to the views they have already taken. The man feels that, if he only holds to his belief without wavering, it will be entirely satisfactory. Nor can it be denied that a steady and immovable faith yields great peace of mind. It may, indeed, give rise to inconveniences, as if a man should resolutely continue to believe that fire would not burn him, or that he would be eternally damned if he received his *ingesta* otherwise than through a stomach pump. But then the man who adopts this method will not allow that its inconveniences are greater than its advantages. He will say, ''I hold steadfastly to the truth and the truth is always wholesome.'' And in many cases it may very well be that the pleasure he derives from his calm faith overbalances any inconveniences resulting from its deceptive character. Thus, if it be true that death is annihilation, then the man who believes that he will certainly go straight to heaven when he dies, provided he have fulfilled certain simple observances in this life, has a cheap pleasure which will not be followed by the least disappointment. A similar consideration seems to have weight with many persons in religious topics, for we frequently hear it said, ''Oh, I could not believe so-and-so, because I should be wretched if I did.'' When an ostrich buries its head in the sand as danger approaches, it very likely takes the happiest course. It hides the danger, and then calmly says there is no danger; and if it feels perfectly sure there is none, why should it raise its head to see? A man may go through life systematically keeping out of view all that might cause change in his opinions, and if he only succeeds—basing his method, as he does, on two fundamental psychological laws—I do not see what can be said against his doing so. It would be an egotistical impertinence to object that his procedure is irrational, for that only amounts to saying that his method of settling belief is not ours. He does not propose to himself to be rational, and indeed, will often talk with scorn of man's weak and illusive reason. So let him think as he pleases.

But this method of fixing belief, which may be called the method of tenacity, will be unable to hold its ground in practice. The social impulse is against it. The man who adopts it will find that other men think differently from him, and it will be apt to occur to him in some saner moment that their opinions are quite as good as his own, and this will shake his confidence in belief. This conception, that another man's thought or sentiment may be equivalent to one's own, is a distinctly new step, and a highly important one. It arises from an impulse too strong in man to be suppressed without danger of destroying the human species. Unless we make ourselves hermits, we shall necessarily influence each other's opinions; so that the problem becomes how to fix belief, not in the individual merely, but in the community.

[2. The Method of Authority /] Let the will of the state act, then, instead of that of the individual. Let an institution be created which shall have for its object to keep correct doctrines before the attention of the people, to reiterate them perpetually, and to teach them to the young; having at the same time power to prevent contrary doctrines from being taught, advocated, or expressed. Let all possible causes of a change of mind be removed from men's apprehensions. Let them be kept ignorant, lest they should learn of some reason to think otherwise than they do. Let their passions be enlisted, so that they may regard private and unusual opinions with hatred and horror. Then let all men who reject the established belief be terrified into silence. Let the people turn out and tar-and-feather such men, or let inquisitions be made into the manner of thinking of suspected persons, and when they are found guilty of forbidden beliefs, let them be subjected to some signal punishment. When complete agreement could not otherwise be reached, a general massacre of all who have not thought in a certain way has proved a very effective means of settling opinions in a country. If the power to do this be wanting, let a list of opinions be drawn up, to which no man of the least independence of thought can assent, and let the faithful be required to accept all these propositions, in order to segregate them as radically as possible from the influence of the rest of the world.

This method has, from the earliest times, been one of the chief means of upholding correct theological and political doctrines, and of preserving their universal or catholic character. In Rome, especially, it has been practiced from the days of Numa Pompilius to those of Pius Nonus. This is the most perfect example in history; but wherever there is a priesthood—and no religion has been without one—this method has been more or less made use of. Wherever there is aristocracy, or a guild, or any association of a class of men whose interests depend or are supposed to depend on certain propositions, there will inevitably be found some traces of this natural product of social feeling. Cruelties always accompany this system; and when it is consistently carried out, they become atrocities of the most horrible kind in the eyes of any rational man. Nor should this occasion surprise, for the officer of a society does not feel justified in surrendering the interests of that society for the sake of mercy, as he might his own private interests. It is natural, therefore, that sympathy and fellowship should thus produce a most ruthless power.

In judging this method of fixing belief, which may be called the method of authority, we must, in the first place, allow its immeasurable mental and moral superiority to the method of tenacity. Its success is proportionally greater; and in fact it has over and over again worked the most majestic results. The mere structures of stone which it has caused to be put together, in Siam, for example, in Egypt, and in Europe—have many of them a sublimity hardly more than rivaled by the greatest works of Nature. And, except the geological epochs, there are no periods of time so vast as those which are measured by some of these organized faiths. If we scrutinize the matter closely, we shall find that there has not been one of their creeds which has remained always the same; yet the change is so slow as to be imperceptible during one person's life, so that individual belief remains sensibly fixed. For the mass of mankind, then, there is perhaps no better method than this. If it is their highest impulse to be intellectual slaves, then slaves they ought to remain.

[**3. The a priori Method** /] But no institution can undertake to regulate opinions upon every subject. Only the most important ones can be attended to, and on the rest men's minds must be left to the action of natural causes. This imperfection will be no source of weakness so long as men are in such a state of culture that one opinion does not influence another—that is, so long as they cannot put two and two together. But in the most priest-ridden states some individuals will be found who are raised above that condition. These men possess a wider sort of social feeling; they see that men in other countries and in other ages have held to very different doctrines from those which they themselves have been brought up to believe; and they cannot help seeing that it is the mere accident of their having been taught as they have, and of their having been surrounded with the manners and associations they have, that has caused them to believe as they do and not far differently. And their candor cannot resist the reflection that there is no reason to rate their own views at a higher value than those of other nations and other centuries; and this gives rise to doubts in their minds.

They will further perceive that such doubts as these must exist in their minds with reference to every belief which seems to be determined by the caprice either of themselves or of those who originated the popular opinions. The willful adherence to a belief, and the arbitrary forcing of it upon others, must, therefore, both be given up and a new method of settling opinions must be adopted, which shall not only produce an impulse to believe, but shall also decide what proposition it is which is to be believed. Let the action of natural preferences be unimpeded, then, and under their influence let men conversing together and regarding matters in different lights gradually develop beliefs in harmony with natural causes. This method resembles that by which conceptions of art have been brought to maturity. The most perfect example of it is to be found in the history of metaphysical philosophy. Systems of this sort have not usually rested upon observed facts, at least not in any great degree. They have been chiefly adopted because their fundamental propositions seemed ''agreeable to reason.'' This is an apt expression; it does not mean that which agrees with experience, but that which we find ourselves inclined to believe. Plato, for example, finds it agreeable to reason that the distances of the celestial spheres from one another should be proportional to the different lengths of strings which produce harmonious chords. Many philosophers have been led to their main conclusions by considerations like this; but this is the lowest and least developed form which the method takes, for it is clear that another man might find Kepler's (earlier) theory, that the celestial spheres are proportional to the inscribed and circumscribed spheres of the different regular solids, more agreeable to *his* reason. But the shock of opinions will soon lead men to rest on preferences of a far more universal nature. Take, for example, the doctrine that man only acts selfishly—that is, from the consideration that acting in one way will afford him more pleasure than acting in another. This rests on no fact in the world, but it has had a wide acceptance as being the only reasonable theory.

This method is far more intellectual and respectable from the point of view of reason than either of the others which we have noticed. But its failure has been the most manifest. It makes of inquiry something similar to the development of taste; but taste, unfortunately, is always more or less a matter of fashion, and accordingly, metaphysicians have never come to any fixed agreement, but the pendulum has swung backward and forward between a more material and a more spiritual philosophy, from the earliest times to the latest. And so from this, which has been called the *a priori* method, we are driven, in Lord Bacon's phrase, to a true induction. We have examined into this *a priori* method as something which promised to deliver our opinions from their accidental and capricious element. But development, while it is a process which eliminated the effect of some casual circumstances, only magnifies that of others. This method, therefore, does not differ in a very essential way from that of authority. The government may not have lifted its finger to influence my convictions; I may have been left outwardly quite free to choose, we will say, between monogamy and polygamy, and appealing to my conscience only, I may have concluded that the latter practice is in itself licentious. But when I come to see that the chief obstacle to the spread of Christianity among a people of as high culture as the Hindoos has been a conviction of the immorality of our way of treating women, I cannot help seeing that, though governments do not interfere, sentiments in their development will be very greatly determined by accidental causes. Now, there are some people, among whom I must suppose that my reader is to be found, who, when they see that any belief of theirs is determined by any circumstance extraneous to the facts, will from that moment not merely admit in words that that belief is doubtful, but will experience a real doubt of it, so that it ceases to be a belief.

[4. The Method of Science. /] To satisfy our doubts, therefore, it is necessary that a method should be found by which our beliefs may be caused by nothing human, but by some external permanency—by something upon which our thinking has no effect. Some mystics imagine that they have such a method in a private inspiration from on high. But that is only a form of the method of tenacity, in which the conception of truth as something public is not yet developed. Our external permanency would not be external, in our sense, if it was restricted in its influence to one individual. It must be something which affects, or might affect, every man. And, though these affections are necessarily as various as are individual conditions, yet the method must be such that the ultimate conclusion of every man shall be the same. Such is the method of science. Its fundamental hypothesis, restated in more familiar language, is this: There are real things, whose characters are entirely independent of our opinions about them; those realities affect our senses according to regular laws, and, though our sensations are as different as our relations to the objects, yet, by taking advantage of the laws of perception, we can ascertain by reasoning how things really are, and any man, if he has sufficient experience and reason enough about it, will be led to the one true conclusion. The new conception here involved is that of reality. It may be asked how I know that there are any realities. If this hypothesis is the sole support of my method of inquiry, my method of inquiry must not be used to support my hypothesis. The reply is this: (1) If investigation cannot be regarded as proving that there are real things, it at least does not lead to a contrary conclusion; but the method and the conception on which it is based remain ever in harmony. No doubts of the method, therefore, necessarily arise from its practice, as is the case with all the others. (2) The feeling which gives rise to any method of fixing belief is a dissatisfaction at two repugnant propositions. But here already is a vague concession that there is some *one* thing to which a proposition should conform. Nobody, therefore, can really doubt that there are realities, or if he did, doubt would not be a source of dissatisfaction. The hypothesis, therefore, is one which every mind admits. So the social impulse does not cause me to doubt it. (3) Everybody uses the scientific method about a great many things, and only ceases to use it when he does not know how to apply it. (4) Experience of the method has not led me to doubt it, but, on the contrary, scientific investigation has had the most wonderful triumphs in the way of settling opinion. These afford the explanation of my not doubting the method or the hypothesis which it supposes; and not having any doubt, nor believing that anybody else whom I could influence has, it would be the merest babble for me to say more about it. If there be anybody with a living doubt upon the subject, let him consider it. . . .

At present I have only room to notice some points of contrast between the method of scientific investigation and other methods of fixing belief.

This is the only one of the four methods which presents any distinction of a right and a wrong way. If I adopt the method of tenacity and shut myself out from all influences, whatever I think necessary to doing this is necessary according to that method. So with the method of authority: The state may try to put down heresy by means which, from a scientific point of view, seem very ill-calculated to accomplish its purposes; but the only test *on that method* is what the state thinks, so that it cannot pursue the method wrongly. So with the *a priori* method. The very essence of it is to think as one is inclined to think. . . . But with the scientific method the case is different. I may start with known and observed facts to proceed to the unknown; and yet the rules which I follow in doing so may not be such as investigation would approve. The test of whether I am truly following the method is not an immediate appeal to my feelings and purposes, but, on the contrary, itself involves the application of the method. Hence it is that bad reasoning as well as good reasoning is possible; and this fact is the foundation of the practical side of logic. . . .

4 / The Ethics of Belief

W. K. CLIFFORD

A ship-owner was about to send to sea an emigrant-ship. He knew that she was old, and not over-well built at the first; that she had seen many seas and climes, and often had needed repairs. Doubts had been suggested to him that possibly she was not seaworthy. These doubts preyed upon his mind and made him unhappy; he thought that perhaps he ought to have her thoroughly overhauled and refitted, even though this should put him to great expense. Before the ship sailed, however, he succeeded in overcoming these melancholy reflections. He said to himself that she had gone safely through so many voyages and weathered so many storms that it was idle to suppose she would not come safely home from this trip also. He would put his trust in Providence, which could hardly fail to protect all these unhappy families that were leaving their father-land to seek for better times elsewhere. He would dismiss from his mind all ungenerous suspicions about the honesty of builders and contractors. In such ways he acquired a sincere and comfortable conviction that his vessel was thoroughly safe and seaworthy; he watched her departure with a light heart, and benevolent wishes for the success of the exiles in their strange new home that was to be; and he got his insurance money when she went down in mid-ocean and told no tales.

[1.] What shall we say of him? Surely this, that he was verily guilty of the death of those men. It is admitted that he did sincerely believe in the soundness of his ship; but the sincerity of his conviction can in no wise help him, because *he had no right to believe on such evidence as was before him.*

He had acquired his belief not by honestly earning it in patient investigation, but by stifling his doubts. And although in the end he may have felt so sure about it that he could not think otherwise, yet inasmuch as he had knowingly and willingly worked himself into that frame of mind, he must be held responsible for it.

[2.] Let us alter the case a little, and suppose that the ship was not unsound after all; that she made her voyage safely, and many others after it. Will that diminish the guilt of her owner? Not one jot. When an action is once done, it is right or wrong forever; no accidental failure of its good or evil fruits can possibly alter that. The man would not have been innocent, he would only have been not found out. The question of right or wrong has to do with the origin of his belief, not the matter of it; not what it was, but how he got it; not whether it turned out to be true or false, but whether he had a right to believe on such evidence as was before him.

[1, 2 cont.] There was once an island in which some of the inhabitants professed a religion teaching neither the doctrine of original sin nor that of eternal punishment. A suspicion got abroad that the professors of this religion had made use of unfair means to get their doctrines taught to children. They were accused of wresting the laws of their country in such a way as to remove children from the care of their natural and legal guardians; and even of stealing them away and keeping them concealed from their friends and relations. A certain number of men formed themselves into a society for the purpose of agitating the public about this matter. They published grave accusations against individual citizens of the highest position and character, and did all in their power to injure those citizens in the exercise of their profession. So great was the noise they made, that a Commission was appointed to investigate the facts; but after the Commission had carefully inquired into all the evidence that could be got, it appeared that the accused were innocent. Not only had they been accused on insufficient evidence, but the evidence of their innocence was such as the agitators might easily have obtained, if they had attempted a fair inquiry. After these disclosures the inhabitants of that country looked upon the members of the agitating society, not only as persons whose judgment was to be distrusted, but also as no longer to be counted honorable men. For although they had sincerely and conscientiously believed in the charges they had made, *yet they had no right to believe on such evidence as was before them*. Their sincere convictions, instead of being honestly earned by patient inquiring, were stolen by listening to the voice of prejudice and passion.

Let us vary this case also, and suppose, other things remaining as before, that a still more accurate investigation proved the accused to have been really guilty. Would this make any difference in the guilt of the accusers? Clearly not; the question is not whether their belief was true or false, but whether they entertained it on wrong grounds. They would no doubt say, "Now you see that we were right after all; next time perhaps you will believe us.'' And they might be believed, but they would not thereby become honorable men. They would not be innocent, they would only be not found out. Every one of them, if he chose to examine himself *in foro conscientiae*,* would know that he had acquired and nourished a belief, when he had no right to believe on such evidence as was before him; and therein he would know that he had done a wrong thing.

It may be said, however, that in both of these supposed cases it is not the belief which is judged to be wrong, but the action following upon it. The shipowner might say, ''I am perfectly certain that my ship is sound, but still I feel it my duty to have her examined, before trusting the lives of so many people to her.'' And it might be said to the agitator, ''However convinced you were of the justice of your cause and the truth of your convictions, you ought not to have made a public attack upon any man's character until you had examined the evidence on both sides with the utmost patience and care.''

In the first place, let us admit that, so far as it goes, this view of the case is right and necessary; right, because even when a man's belief is so fixed that he cannot think otherwise, he still has a choice in regard to the action suggested by it, and so cannot escape the duty of investigating on the ground of the strength of his convictions; and necessary, because those who are not yet capable of controlling their feelings and thoughts must have a plain rule dealing with overt acts.

But this being premised as necessary, it becomes clear that it is not sufficient, and that our previous judgment is required to supplement it. For it is not possible so to sever the belief from the action it suggests as to condemn the one without condemning the other. No man holding a strong belief on one side of a question, or even wishing to hold a belief on one side, can investigate it with such fairness and completeness as if he were really in doubt and unbiased; so that the existence of a belief not founded on fair inquiry unfits a man for the performance of this necessary duty.

[3.] Nor is that truly a belief at all which has not some influence upon the actions of him who holds it. He who truly believes that which prompts him to an action has looked upon the action to lust after it, he has committed it already in his heart. If a belief is not realized immediately in open deeds, it is stored up for the guidance of the future. It goes to make a part of that aggregate of beliefs which is the link between sensation and action at every moment of all our lives, and which is so organized and compacted together that no part of it can be isolated from the rest, but every new addition modifies the structure of the whole. No real belief, however trifling and fragmentary it may seem, is ever truly insignificant; it prepares us to receive more of its like, confirms those which resembled it before, and weakens others; and so gradually it lays a stealthy train in our inmost thoughts,

*[In the forum of his conscience.—Eds.]

which may some day explode into overt action, and leave its stamp upon our character forever.

[4.] And no one man's belief is in any case a private matter which concerns himself alone. Our lives are guided by that general conception of the course of things which has been created by society for social purposes. Our words, our phrases, our forms and processes and modes of thought, are common property, fashioned and perfected from age to age; an heirloom which every succeeding generation inherits as a precious deposit and a sacred trust to be handed on to the next one, not unchanged but enlarged and purified, with some clear marks of its proper handiwork. Into this, for good or ill, is woven every belief of every man who has speech of his fellows. An awful privilege, and an awful responsibility, that we should help to create the world in which posterity will live.

In the two supposed cases which have been considered, it has been judged wrong to believe on insufficient evidence, or to nourish belief by suppressing doubts and avoiding investigation. The reason of this judgment is not far to seek: It is that in both these cases the belief held by one man was of great importance to other men. But for as much as no belief held by one man, however seemingly trivial the belief, and however obscure the believer, is ever actually insignificant or without its effect on the fate of mankind, we have no choice but to extend our judgment to all cases of belief whatever. Belief, that sacred faculty which prompts the decisions of our will, and knits into harmonious working all the compacted energies of our being, is ours not for ourselves, but for humanity. It is rightly used on truths which have been established by long experience and waiting toil, and which have stood in the fierce light of free and fearless questioning. Then it helps to bind men together, and to strengthen and direct their common action. It is desecrated when given to unproved and unquestioned statements, for the solace and private pleasure of the believer; to add a tinsel splendor to the plain straight road of our life and display a bright mirage beyond it; or even to drown the common sorrows of our kind by a self-deception which allows them not only to cast down but also to degrade us. Whoso would deserve well of his fellows in this matter will guard the purity of his belief with a very fanaticism of jealous care, lest at any time it should rest on an unworthy object and catch a stain which can never be wiped away.

It is not only the leader of men, statesman, philosopher, or poet, that owes this bounden duty to mankind. Every rustic who delivers in the village alehouse his slow, infrequent sentences may help to kill or keep alive the fatal superstitions which clog his race. Every hard-worked wife of an artisan may transmit to her children beliefs which shall knit society together, or rend it in pieces. No simplicity of mind, no obscurity of station can escape the duty of questioning all that we believe.

It is true that this duty is a hard one, and the doubt which comes out of it is often a very bitter thing. It leaves us bare and powerless where we thought that we were safe and strong. To know all about anything is to know how to deal with it under all circumstances. We feel much happier and more secure when we think we know precisely what to do, no matter what happens, than when we have lost our way and do not know where to turn. And if we have supposed ourselves to know all about anything, and to be capable of doing what is fit in regard to it, we naturally do not like to find that we are really ignorant and powerless, that we have to begin again at the beginning, and try to learn what the thing is and how it is to be dealt with—if indeed anything can be learned about it. It is the sense of power attached to a sense of knowledge that makes men desirous of believing, and afraid of doubting.

This sense of power is the highest and best of pleasures when the belief on which it is founded is a true belief, and has been fairly earned by investigation. For then we may justly feel that it is common property, and holds good for others as well as for ourselves. Then we may be glad, not that *I* have learned secrets by which I am safer and stronger, but that *we men* have got mastery over more of the world; and we shall be strong, not for ourselves, but in the name of Man and in his strength. But if the belief has been accepted on insufficient evidence, the pleasure is a stolen one. Not only does it deceive ourselves by giving us a sense of power which we do not really possess, but it is sinful, because it is stolen in defiance of our duty to mankind. That duty is to guard ourselves from such beliefs as from a pestilence, which may shortly master our own body and then spread to the rest of the town. What would be thought of one who, for the sake of a sweet fruit, should deliberately run the risk of bringing a plague upon his family and his neighbors?

[5.] And, as in other such cases, it is not the risk only which has to be considered; for a bad action is always bad at the time when it is done, no matter what happens afterwards. Every time we let ourselves believe for unworthy reasons, we weaken our powers of self-control, of doubting, of judicially and fairly weighing evidence. We all suffer severely enough from the maintenance and support of false beliefs and the fatally wrong actions which they lead to, and the evil born when one such belief is entertained is great and wide. But a greater and wider evil arises when the credulous character is maintained and supported, when a habit of believing for unworthy reasons is fostered and made permanent. If I steal money from any person, there may be no harm done by the mere transfer of possession; he may not feel the loss, or it may prevent him from using the money badly. But I cannot help doing this great wrong toward Man, that I make myself dishonest. What hurts society is not that it should lose its property, but that it should become a den of thieves; for then it must cease to be society. This is why we ought not to do evil that good may come; for at any rate this great evil has come, that we have done evil and are made wicked thereby. In like manner, if I let myself believe anything on insufficient evidence, there may be no great harm done by the mere belief; it may be true after all, or I may never have occasion to exhibit it in outward acts. But I cannot help doing this great wrong toward Man, that I make myself credulous. The danger to society is not merely that it should believe wrong things, though that is great enough, but that it should become credulous, and lose the habit of testing things and inquiring into them; for then it must sink back into savagery.

The harm which is done by credulity in a man is not confined to the fostering of a credulous character in others, and consequent support of false beliefs. Habitual want of care about what I believe leads to habitual want of care in others about the truth of what is told to me. Men speak the truth to one another when each reveres the truth in his own mind and in the other's mind; but how shall my friend revere the truth in my mind when I myself am careless about it, when I believe things because I want to believe them, and because they are comforting and pleasant? Will he not learn to cry "Peace" to me, when there is no peace? By such a course I shall surround myself with a thick atmosphere of falsehood and fraud, and in that I must live. It may matter little to me, in my cloud-castle of sweet illusions and darling lies; but it matters much to Man that I have made my neighbors ready to deceive. The credulous man is father to the liar and the cheat; he lives in the bosom of this his family, and it is no marvel if he should become even as they are. So closely are our duties knit together, that whoso shall keep the whole law, and yet offend in one point, he is guilty of all.

To sum up: It is wrong always, everywhere, and for any one to believe anything upon insufficient evidence. . . .

"But," says one, "I am a busy man; I have no time for the long course of study which would be necessary to make me in any degree a competent judge of certain questions, or even able to understand the nature of the arguments." Then he should have no time to believe.

5 / The Will to Believe

WILLIAM JAMES

. . . Let us give the name of *hypothesis* to anything that may be proposed to our belief; and just as the electricians speak of live and dead wires, let us speak of any hypothesis as either *live* or *dead*. A live hypothesis is one which appeals as a real possibility to him to whom it is proposed. If I ask you to believe in the Mahdi,* the notion makes no electric connection with your nature—it refuses to scintillate with any credibility at all. As an hypothesis it is completely dead. To an Arab, however (even if he be not one of the Mahdi's followers), the hypothesis is among the mind's possibilities: It is alive. This shows that deadness and liveness in an hypothesis are not intrinsic properties, but relations to the individual thinker. They are measured by his willingness to act. The maximum of liveness in an hypothesis means willingness to act irrevocably. Practically, that means belief; but there is some believing tendency wherever there is willingness to act at all.

Next, let us call the decision between two hypotheses an *option*. Options may be of several kinds. They may be (1) *living* or *dead*, (2) *forced* or *avoidable*, (3) *momentous* or *trivial*; and for our purposes we may call an option a *genuine* option when it is of the forced, living, and momentous kind.

1. A living option is one in which both hypotheses are live ones. If I say to you, "Be a theosophist† or be a Mohammedan," it is probably a dead option, because for you neither hypothesis is likely to be alive. But if I say, "Be an agnostic or be a Christian," it is otherwise: Trained as you are, each hypothesis makes some appeal, however small, to your belief.
2. Next, if I say to you, "Choose between going out with your umbrella or without it," I do not offer you a genuine option, for it is not forced. You can easily avoid it by not going out at all. Similarly, if I say, "Either love me or hate me," "Either call my theory true or call it false," your option is avoidable. You may remain indifferent to me, neither loving nor hating, and you may decline to offer any judgment as to my theory. But if I say, "Either accept this truth or go without it." I put on you a forced option, for there is no standing place outside of the alternative. Every dilemma based on a complete logical disjunction, with no possibility of not choosing, is an option of this forced kind.

*[In Mohammedism, an expected spiritual and temporal ruler.—Eds.]
†[Practitioner of a system of religious belief based largely on certain Eastern traditions, such as Buddhism.—Eds.]

3. Finally, if I were Dr. Nansen* and proposed to you to join my North Pole expedition, your option would be momentous; for this would probably be your only similar opportunity, and your choice now would either exclude you from the North Pole sort of immortality altogether or put at least the chance of it into your hands. He who refuses to embrace a unique opportunity loses the prize as surely as if he tried and failed. *Per contra,*† the option is trivial when the opportunity is not unique, when the stake is insignificant, or when the decision is reversible if it later prove unwise. Such trivial options abound in the scientific life. A chemist finds an hypothesis live enough to spend a year in its verification: He believes in it to that extent. But if his experiments prove inconclusive either way, he is quit for his loss of time, no vital harm being done.

It will facilitate our discussion if we keep all these distinctions well in mind. . . .

The thesis I defend is, briefly stated, this: *Our passional nature not only lawfully may, but must, decide an option between propositions, whenever it is a genuine option that cannot by its nature be decided on intellectual grounds; for to say, under such circumstances, "Do not decide, but leave the question open," is itself a passional decision—just like deciding yes or no—and is attended with the same risk of losing the truth.* . . .

Wherever the option between losing truth and gaining it is not momentous, we can throw the chance of *gaining truth* away, and at any rate save ourselves from any chance of *believing falsehood*, by not making up our minds at all till objective evidence has come. In scientific questions, this is almost always the case; and even in human affairs in general, the need of acting is seldom so urgent that a false belief to act on is better than no belief at all. Law courts, indeed, have to decide on the best evidence attainable for the moment, because a judge's duty is to make law as well as to ascertain it, and (as a learned judge once said to me) few cases are worth spending much time over: The great thing is to have them decided on *any* acceptable principle and gotten out of the way. But in our dealings with objective nature we obviously are recorders, not makers, of the truth; and decisions for the mere sake of deciding promptly and getting on to the next business would be wholly out of place. Throughout the breadth of physical nature facts are what they are quite independently of us, and seldom is there any such hurry about them that the risks of being duped by believing a premature theory need be faced. The questions here are always trivial options; the hypotheses are hardly living (at any rate not living for us spectators); the choice between believing truth or falsehood is seldom forced. The attitude of skeptical balance is therefore the absolutely wise one if we would escape mistakes. What difference, indeed, does it make to most of us whether we

*[An explorer, a contemporary of James.—Eds.]
†[By contrast.—Eds.]

have or have not a theory of the Röntgen rays,* whether we believe or not in mind-stuff, or have a conviction about the causality of conscious states? It makes no difference. Such options are not forced on us. On every account it is better not to make them, but still keep weighing reasons *pro et contra*† with an indifferent hand.

I speak, of course, here of the purely judging mind. For purposes of discovery such indifference is to be less highly recommended, and science would be far less advanced than she is if the passionate desires of individuals to get their own faiths confirmed had been kept out of the game. . . . On the other hand, if you want an absolute duffer in an investigation, you must, after all, take the man who has no interest whatever in its results: He is the warranted incapable, the positive fool. The most useful investigator, because the most sensitive observer, is always he whose eager interest in one side of the question is balanced by an equally keen nervousness lest he become deceived. Science has organized this nervousness into a regular *technique*, her so-called method of verification; and she has fallen so deeply in love with the method that one may even say she has ceased to care for truth by itself at all. It is only truth as technically verified that interests her. The truth of truths might come in merely affirmative form, and she would decline to touch it. Such truth as that, she might repeat with Clifford, would be stolen in defiance of her duty to mankind. Human passions, however, are stronger than technical rules. "Le coeur a ses raisons," as Pascal says, "que la raison ne connaît pas"‡: and however indifferent to all but the bare rules of the game the umpire, the abstract intellect, may be, the concrete players who furnish him the materials to judge of are usually, each one of them, in love with some pet "live hypothesis" of his own. Let us agree, however, that wherever there is no forced option, the dispassionately judicial intellect with no pet hypothesis, saving us, as it does, from dupery at any rate, ought to be our ideal.

The question next arises, Are there not somewhere forced options in our speculative questions, and can we (as men who may be interested at least as much in positively gaining truth as in merely escaping dupery) always wait with impunity till the coercive evidence shall have arrived? It seems *a priori* improbable that the truth should be so nicely adjusted to our needs and powers as that. In the great boarding-house of nature, the cakes and the butter and the syrup seldom come out so even and leave the plates so clean. Indeed, we should view them with scientific suspicion if they did.

Moral questions immediately present themselves as questions whose solution cannot wait for sensible proof. A moral question is a question not of what sensibly exists, but of what is good, or would be good if it did exist. Science can tell us what exists; but to compare the *worths*, both of what ex-

---

*[X rays.—Eds.]
†[Pro and con.—Eds.]
‡[The heart has its reasons that reason does not know.—Eds.]

ists and of what does not exist, we must consult, not science, but what Pascal calls our heart. Science herself consults her heart when she lays it down that the infinite ascertainment of fact and correction of false belief are the supreme goods for man. Challenge the statement, and science can only repeat it oracularly, or else prove it by showing that such ascertainment and correction bring man all sorts of other goods which man's heart in turn declares. The question of having moral beliefs at all or not having them is decided by our will. Are our moral preferences true or false, or are they only odd biological phenomena, making things good or bad for *us*, but in themselves indifferent? How can your pure intellect decide? If your heart does not *want* a world of moral reality, your head will assuredly never make you believe in one. . . .

Turn now from these wide questions of good to a certain class of questions of fact, questions concerning personal relations, states of mind between one man and another. *Do you like me or not?*—for example. Whether you do or not depends, in countless instances, on whether I meet you halfway, am willing to assume that you must like me, and show you trust and expectation. The previous faith on my part in your liking's existence is in such cases what makes your liking come. But if I stand aloof, and refuse to budge an inch until I have objective evidence, until you shall have done something apt, as the absolutists say, *ad extorquendum assensum meum,** ten to one your liking never comes. How many women's hearts are vanquished by the mere sanguine insistence of some man that they *must* love him! He will not consent to the hypothesis that they cannot. The desire for a certain kind of truth here brings about that special truth's existence; and so it is in innumerable cases of other sorts. Who gains promotions, boons, appointments but the man in whose life they are seen to play the part of live hypotheses, who discounts them, sacrifices other things for their sake before they have come, and takes risks for them in advance? His faith acts on the powers above him as a claim, and creates its own verification.

A social organism of any sort whatever, large or small, is what it is because each member proceeds to his own duty with a trust that the other members will simultaneously do theirs. Wherever a desired result is achieved by the cooperation of many independent persons, its existence as a fact is a pure consequence of the precursive faith in one another of those immediately concerned. A government, an army, a commercial system, a ship, a college, an athletic team, all exist on this condition, without which not only is nothing achieved, but nothing is even attempted. A whole train of passengers (individually brave enough) will be looted by a few highwaymen, simply because the latter can count on one another, while each passenger fears that if he makes a movement of resistance, he will be shot before anyone else backs him up. If we believed that the whole car-full would rise at once with us, we should each severally rise, and train-robbing would

*[For forcing my agreement.—Eds.]

never even be attempted. There are, then, cases where a fact cannot come at all unless a preliminary faith exists in its coming. *And where faith in a fact can help create the fact*, that would be an insane logic which should say that faith running ahead of scientific evidence is the "lowest kind of immorality" into which a thinking being can fall. Yet such is the logic by which our scientific absolutists pretend to regulate our lives!

In truths dependent on our personal action, then, faith based on desire is certainly a lawful and possibly an indispensable thing.

But now, it will be said, these are all childish human cases, and have nothing to do with great cosmic matters, like the question of religious faith. Let us then pass on to that. Religions differ so much in their accidents that in discussing the religious question we must make it very generic and broad. What then do we now mean by the religious hypothesis? Science says things are; morality says some things are better than other things; and religion says essentially two things.

First, she says that the best things are the more eternal things, the overlapping things, the things in the universe that throw the last stone, so to speak, and say the final word. . . .

The second affirmation of religion is that we are better off even now if we believe her first affirmation to be true.

Now, let us consider what the logical elements of this situation are *in case the religious hypothesis in both its branches be really true*. . . . So proceeding, we see, first, that religion offers itself as a *momentous* option. We are supposed to gain, even now, by our belief, and to lose by our nonbelief, a certain vital good. Secondly, religion is a *forced* option, so far as that good goes. We cannot escape the issue by remaining skeptical and waiting for more light, because, although we do avoid error in that way *if religion be untrue*, we lose the good, *if it be true*, just as certainly as if we positively chose to disbelieve. . . . Skepticism, then, is not avoidance of option; it is option of a certain particular kind of risk. *Better risk loss of truth than chance of error*—that is your faith-vetoer's exact position. He is actively playing his stake as much as the believer is; he is backing the field against the religious hypothesis, just as the believer is backing the religious hypothesis against the field. To preach skepticism to us as a duty until "sufficient evidence" for religion be found is tantamount therefore to telling us, when in presence of the religious hypothesis, that to yield to our fear of its being error is wiser and better than to yield to our hope that it may be true. It is not intellect against all passions, then; it is only intellect with one passion laying down its law. And by what, forsooth, is the supreme wisdom of this passion warranted? Dupery for dupery, what proof is there that dupery through hope is so much worse than dupery through fear? I, for one, can see no proof; and I simply refuse obedience to the scientist's command to imitate his kind of option, in a case where my own stake is important enough to give me the right to choose my own form of risk. If religion be true and the evidence for it be still insufficient, I do not wish, by putting your extinguisher upon my nature (which feels to me as if it had after all some business in this matter), to forfeit my sole chance in life of getting upon the winning side—that chance depending, of course, on my willingness to run the risk of acting as if my passional need of taking the world religiously might be prophetic and right.

All this is on the supposition that it really may be prophetic and right, and that, even to us who are discussing the matter, religion is a live hypothesis which may be true. Now, to most of us religion comes in a still further way that makes a veto on our active faith even more illogical. The more perfect and more eternal aspect of the universe is represented in our religions as having personal form. The universe is no longer a mere *It* to us, but a *Thou*, if we are religious; and any relation that may be possible from person to person might be possible here. For instance, although in one sense we are passive portions of the universe, in another we show a curious autonomy, as if we were small, active centres on our own account. We feel, too, as if the appeal of religion to us were made to our own active good-will, as if evidence might be forever withheld from us unless we met the hypothesis half-way. To take a trivial illustration: Just as a man who in a company of gentlemen made no advances, asked a warrant for every concession, and believed in no one's word without proof would cut himself off by such churlishness from all the social rewards that a more trusting spirit would earn, so here, one who should shut himself up in snarling logicality and try to make the gods extort his recognition willy-nilly, or not get it at all, might cut himself off forever from his only opportunity of making the gods' acquaintance. This feeling, forced on us we know not whence, that by obstinately believing that there are gods (although not to do so would be so easy both for our logic and our life) we are doing the universe the deepest service we can, seems part of the living essence of the religious hypothesis. If the hypothesis *were* true in all its parts, including this one, then pure intellectualism, with its veto on our making willing advances, would be an absurdity; and some participation of our sympathetic nature would be logically required. I, therefore , for one, cannot see my way to accepting the agnostic rules for truth-seeking, or wilfully agree to keep my willing nature out of the game. I cannot do so for this plain reason that *a rule of thinking which would absolutely prevent me from acknowledging certain kinds of truth if those kinds of truth were really there, would be an irrational rule.* That for me is the long and short of the formal logic of the situation, no matter what the kinds of truth might materially be. . . .

STUDY QUESTIONS

1. What condition must be met, according to Unger, if someone is to know something about the external world? Why is it plausible to insist on this condition? Can the condition be stated in a general way, that is, without reference to an evil scientist?

2. Can Unger argue, without contradicting himself, that no one ever knows anything about anything? about an external world?

3. What effect, if any, does the distinction between two kinds of knowledge made in the Preview to Part One have on Unger's version of skepticism?

4. State Hospers' argument against the skeptic. Do you think his argument is sufficient to refute skepticism? Why or why not?

5. What is there about Hospers' argument which makes it somewhat unique and very different from, say, the other arguments in Unger's essay?

6. Is "complete evidence" in Hospers' sense possible? Suppose it is. Would it satisfy Unger?

7. How would Peirce respond to Unger's skepticism? What attitude, belief, or doubt does Unger think we should have toward "There are rocks"?

8. How would Peirce evaluate Hospers's account of propositional knowledge? In particular, how would he construct the evidence condition?

9. Use Clifford's case to construct an adequate evidence condition. He thinks the origin of one's belief is relevant to whether one has the right to be sure or not. Which sorts of origins are acceptable and which are not?

10. Are beliefs actions? Why or why not?

11. Clifford holds that to believe when one does not have the right to believe is both intellectually and morally wrong. Why? Do you agree?

12. In his discussions of religious questions, James presents two arguments against what he calls the Skeptic (that is, anyone like Clifford). State the two arguments. Do they refute Clifford?

13. Supposedly, James would agree that Clifford's shipowner did not have the right to believe. Exactly how, according to James, does the shipowner case differ from cases in which one has the right to believe on no evidence?

14. What good does it do to worry about exactly how knowledge should be defined?

Further Readings

Ammerman, Robert A., and Marcus G. Singer, eds. *Belief, Knowledge and Truth*. New York: Scribner's, 1970. [A set of readings on the standard problems in the theory of knowledge.]

Ayer, A. J. *The Problem of Knowledge*. Baltimore: Penguin Books, 1956. [A theory of knowledge from an empiricist standpoint.]

Bowsma, O. K. "Descartes' Evil Genius." *Philosophical Review*, 58 (1949), 141–151. [A criticism of Descartes' skepticism; also relevant to Unger.]

Brody, Baruch A. *Beginning Philosophy*. Englewood Cliffs, N.J.: Prentice-Hall, 1977, pp. 211–233. [An elementary discussion of the nature of knowledge.]

Cohen, Morris R. "Religion and the Will to Believe." In Singer and Ammerman, pp. 231–234. [Relevant to the Clifford/James debate.]

Descartes, Rene. *Meditations on First Philosophy*. Indianapolis, Ind.: Hackett, 1979. [First published in 1641: the *locus classicus* for skepticism.]

Dretske, Fred. "Conclusive Reasons." *Australasian Journal of Philosophy*, 49 (1971), 1–22. [A very important response to Gettier and Goldman.]

Gettier, Edmund L. "Is Justified True Belief Knowledge?" *Analysis*, 23 (1963), 121–123. [A famous criticism of the justified true belief account of knowledge.]

Goldman, Alvin I. "A Causal Theory of Knowing." *Journal of Philosophy*, 64 (1967), 357–372. [A response to Gettier.]

Hamlyn, D. W. *The Theory of Knowledge*. Garden City, N.Y.: Anchor Books, 1970. [A comprehensive theory of knowledge from a Wittgensteinian point of view.]

Hume, David. *An Enquiry Concerning Human Understanding*. Indianapolis, Ind.: Hackett, 1977. [First published in 1748; a classic statement of an empiricist theory of knowledge.]

Moore, G. E. "A Defense of Common Sense." In *Philosophical Papers*. London: Allen and Unwin, 1959, pp. 32–59. [A critique of skepticism.]

Singer, Marcus G., and Robert A. Ammerman, eds. *Belief, Knowledge and Truth*. New York: Scribner's, 1970. [A set of readings on the standard problems in the theory of knowledge.]

PART TWO

SCIENCE, COMMON SENSE, AND THE WORLD

PREVIEW

The following passage is from the famous physicist Galileo Galilei:

> Sounds . . . are produced in us and felt when . . . there is a rapid vibration of
> air, forming minutely small waves, which move certain cartilages of a certain
> drum which is in our ear. The various external ways in which this wave-motion of
> the air is produced are manifold, but can in large part be reduced to the vibrating
> of bodies which strike the air and form the waves which spread out with great ve-
> locity. . . . But I cannot believe that there exists in external bodies anything other
> than their size, shape, or motion . . . which could excite in us our tastes, sounds,
> and odors. And indeed I should judge that, if ears, tongues, and noses be taken
> away, the number, shape, and motion of bodies would remain, but not their
> tastes, sounds, and odors. The latter, external to the living creature, I believe to be
> nothing but mere names. . . .[1]

Though Galileo does not give his reasons, it is quite clear that he believes
that ordinary objects do not have all the properties we normally attribute to
them. For example, the rose outside our window is not really red and soft
and sweet smelling. Those properties, as considered external to me, the observer, are mere names.

In other passages, Galileo suggests the rationale for his view. He holds
that physics, which is the deepest and most general science, can fulfill its
explanatory functions without ever appealing to color, texture, and odor.
These kinds of qualities are not needed for a physical understanding of ordinary objects. The important qualities for a physical understanding of objects are, at least, shape, size, and motion.

[1]Galileo Galilei, *The Assayer*, selection reprinted in *Philosophy of Science*, ed. by Arthur Danto
and Sidney Morgenbesser, World Publishing Co., 1960, p. 30.

Main Questions

Galileo's is only one of several possible lines of argument that challenge the commonsense understanding of ordinary objects. So, the first general issue in this part is the following:

1. Do ordinary objects have the qualities which we attribute to them on the basis of direct sense perception? (E.g., are stones hard? Are maple leaves green in the spring?)

Though common sense and the view held by Galileo differ radically, they share one central tenet. Both views maintain that physical objects have an existence independent of perceivers. On these views it makes perfect sense to speak of the possible existence of distant galaxies which no one has perceived or ever will perceive. Despite the "obviousness" of this tenet, you will discover in the readings interesting arguments that throw it into doubt. The second main question of the part is, then:

2. Do ordinary objects (desks, stones, cups, trees, etc.) exist even when they are not perceived?

Answers

There are many species of affirmative and negative answers to the first question. The readings provide two sharply contrasting viewpoints. Let us call the affirmative view represented in the text, commonsense realism, and the negative answer, scientific realism.

1a. Commonsense realism: Ordinary objects have the qualities we attribute to them on the basis of sense perception.

1b. Scientific realism: Ordinary objects, as a proper understanding of science teaches us, do not have at least some of the qualities attributed to them on the basis of sense perception.

The shared realism label of the above two answers is meant to mark an affirmative answer to the second main question. Idealism is the view which asserts a negative answer.

2a. Realism: Ordinary objects exist even when not perceived.
2b. Idealism: Ordinary objects exist only when perceived.

Even if one is convinced of realism, it is an important exercise, and we shall add a difficult one: to construct the *argument* that entitles one to this "obvious" position.

Selections

The selections in part two correspond to the issues raised in the preview as follows:

Question	Answer	Selection
(1)	(1b)	6
(1)	(1a)	7
(2)	(2b)	8
(2)	(2a)	9

6 / Two Tables

SIR ARTHUR EDDINGTON

I have settled down to the task of writing these lectures and have drawn up my chairs to my two tables. Two tables! Yes; there are duplicates of every object about me—two tables, two chairs, two pens.

This is not a very profound beginning to a course which ought to reach transcendent levels of scientific philosophy. But we cannot touch bedrock immediately; we must scratch a bit at the surface of things first. And whenever I begin to scratch; the first thing I strike is—my two tables.

One of them has been familiar to me from earliest years. It is a commonplace object of that environment which I call the world. How shall I describe it? It has extension; it is comparatively permanent; it is colored; above all it is *substantial*. By substantial I do not merely mean that it does not collapse when I lean up on it; I mean that it is constituted of "substance," and by that word I am trying to convey to you some conception of its intrinsic nature. It is a *thing*; not like space, which is a mere negation; nor like time, which is—Heaven knows what! But that will not help you to my meaning because it is the distinctive characteristic of a "thing" to have this substantiality, and I do not think substantiality can be described better than by saying that it is the kind of nature exemplified by an ordinary table. And so we go round in circles. After all if you are a plain commonsense man, not too much worried with scientific scruples, you will be confident that you understand the nature of an ordinary table. I have even heard of plain men who had the idea that they could better understand the mystery of their own nature if scientists would discover a way of explaining it in terms of the easily comprehensible nature of a table.

Table no. 2 is my scientific table. It is a more recent acquaintance and I do not feel so familiar with it. It does not belong to the world previously mentioned—that world which spontaneously appears around me when I open my eyes, though how much of it is objective and how much subjective I do not here consider. It is part of a world which in more devious ways has forced itself on my attention. My scientific table is mostly emptiness. Sparsely scattered in that emptiness are numerous electric charges rushing about with great speed; but their combined bulk amounts to less than a billionth of the bulk of the table itself. Notwithstanding its strange construction it turns out to be an entirely efficient table. It supports my writing paper as satisfactorily as table no. 1; for when I lay the paper on it the little electric particles with their headlong speed keep on hitting the underside, so that the paper is maintained in shuttlecock fashion at a nearly steady level. If I lean upon this table I shall not go through; or, to be strictly accurate, the chance of my scientific elbow going through my scientific table is so excessively small that it can be neglected in practical life. Reviewing their properties one by one, there seems to be nothing to choose between the two tables for ordinary purposes; but when abnormal circumstances befall, then my scientific table shows to advantage. If the house catches fire my scientific table will dissolve quite naturally into scientific smoke, whereas my familiar table undergoes a metamorphosis of its substantial nature which I can only regard as miraculous.

There is nothing *substantial* about my second table. It is nearly all empty space—space pervaded, it is true, by fields of force, but these are assigned to the category of "influences," not of "things." Even in the minute part which is not empty we must not transfer the old notion of substance. In dissecting matter into electric charges we have travelled far from that picture of it which first gave rise to the conception of substance, and the meaning of that conception—if it ever had any—has been lost by the way. The whole trend of modern scientific views is to break down the separate categories of "things," "influences," "forms," etc., and to substitute a common background of all experience. Whether we are studying a material object, a magnetic field, a geometrical figure, or a duration of time, our scientific information is summed up in measures; neither the apparatus of measurement nor the mode of using it suggests that there is anything essentially different in these problems. The measures themselves afford no ground for a classification by categories. We feel it necessary to concede some background to the measures—an external world; but the attributes of this world, except insofar as they are reflected in the measures, are outside scientific scrutiny. Science has at last revolted against attaching the exact knowledge contained in these measurements to a traditional picture-gallery of conceptions which convey no authentic information of the background and obtrude irrelevancies into the scheme of knowledge.

I will not here stress further the nonsubstantiality of electrons, since it is scarcely necessary to the present line of thought. Conceive them as substantially as you will, there is a vast difference between my scientific table with its substance (if any) thinly scattered in specks in a region mostly empty and the table of everyday conception which we regard as the type of solid reality—an incarnate protest against Berkeleian subjectivism.* It makes all the difference in the world whether the paper be-

*[Bishop Berkeley thought that tables were sets of ideas.—Eds.]

fore me is poised as it were on a swarm of flies and sustained in shuttle-cock fashion by a series of tiny blows from the swarm underneath, or whether it is supported because there is substance below it, it being the intrinsic nature of substance to occupy space to the exclusion of other substance; all the difference in conception at least, but no difference to my practical task of writing on the paper.

I need not tell you that modern physics has by delicate test and re-morseless logic assured me that my second scientific table is the only one which is really there—wherever "there" may be. On the other hand I need not tell you that modern physics will never succeed in ex-orcising that first table—strange compound of external nature, mental imagery, and inherited prejudice—which lies visible to my eyes and tangible to my grasp. We must bid good-bye to it for the present, for we are about to turn from the familiar world to the scientific world revealed by physics. This is, or is intended to be, a wholly external world.

"You speak paradoxically of two worlds. Are they not really two as-pects or two interpretations of one and the same world?"

Yes, no doubt they are ultimately to be identified after some fashion. But the process by which the external world of physics is transformed into a world of familiar acquaintance in human consciousness is out-side the scope of physics. And so the world studied according to the methods of physics remains detached from the world familiar to con-sciousness, until after the physicist has finished his labors upon it. Pro-visionally, therefore, we regard the table which is the subject of physi-cal research as altogether separate from the familiar table, without prejudging the question of their ultimate identification. It is true that the whole scientific inquiry starts from the familiar world and in the end it must return to the familiar world; but the part of the journey over which the physicist has charge is in foreign territory.

Until recently there was a much closer linkage; the physicist used to borrow the raw material of his world from the familiar world, but he does so no longer. His raw materials are ether, electrons, quanta, po-tentials, Hamiltonian functions, etc., and he is nowadays scrupulously careful to guard these from contamination by conceptions borrowed from the other world. There is a familiar table parallel to the scientific table, but there is no familiar electron, quantum, or potential parallel to the scientific electron, quantum, or potential. We do not even desire to manufacture a familiar counterpart to these things or, as we should commonly say, to "explain" the electron. After the physicist has quite finished his world-building a linkage or identification is allowed; but premature attempts at linkage have been found to be entirely mischie-vous.

7 / "Furniture of the Earth"

L. SUSAN STEBBING

I enter my study and see the blue curtains fluttering in the breeze, for the windows are open. I notice a bowl of roses on the table; it was not there when I went out. Clumsily I stumble against the table, bruising my leg against its hard edge; it is a heavy table and scarcely moves under the impact of my weight. I take a rose from the bowl, press it to my face, feel the softness of the petals, and smell its characteristic scent. I rejoice in the beauty of the graded shading of the crimson petals. In short—I am in a familiar room, seeing, touching, smelling familiar things, thinking familiar thoughts, experiencing familiar emotions.

In some such way might any common reader describe his experiences in the familiar world that he inhabits. With his eyes shut he may recognize a rose from its perfume, stumble against a solid obstacle and recognize it to be a table, and feel the pain from its contact with his comparatively yielding flesh. You, who are reading this paper, may pause and look around you. Perhaps you are in your study, perhaps seated on the seashore, or in a corn-field, or on board ship. Wherever you may be, you will see objects distinguishable one from another, differing in color and in shape; probably you are hearing various sounds. You can see the printed marks on this page, and notice that they are black marks on a whitish background. That you are perceiving something colored and shaped you will not deny; that your body presses against something solid you are convinced; that, if you wish, you can stop reading this book, you know quite well. It may be assumed that you have some interest in philosophy; otherwise you would not be reading *this*. Perhaps you have allowed yourself to be persuaded that the page is not "really colored," that the seat upon which you are sitting is not "really solid"; that you hear only "illusory sounds." If so, it is for such as you that this chapter is written.

Imagine the following scene. You are handed a dish containing some apples—rosy-cheeked, green apples. You take the one nearest to you, and realize that you have been "had." The "apple" is too hard and not heavy enough to be really an apple; as you tap it with your finger-nail it gives out a sound such as never came from tapping a "real" apple. You admire the neatness of the imitation. To sight the illusion is perfect. It is quite sensible to contrast this ingenious fake with a "real" apple, for a "real" apple is just an object that *really* is an apple, and not only *seems* to be one. This fake is an object that looks to your eyes to be an apple, but neither feels nor tastes as an apple does. As soon as you pick it up you know that it is not an apple; there is no need to taste it. We should be speaking in conformity with the rules of good English if we were to say that the dish contained real apples and imitation apples. But this mode of speaking does not lead us to suppose that there are two varieties of *apples*, namely real and imitation apples, as there are Bramley Seedlings and Blenheim pippins. Again, a shadow may be thrown on a wall, or an image may be thrown through a lantern onto a screen. We distinguish the shadow from the object of which it is the shadow, the image from that of which it is the image. Shadow and image are apprehensible only by sight; they really are visual, i.e. *seeable* entities. I can see a man, and I can see his shadow; but there is not both a *real* man and a *shadow* man; there is just the shadow of the man.

This point may seem to have been unduly labored. It is however, of great importance. The words "real" and "really" are familiar words; they are variously used in everyday speech, and are not, as a rule, used ambiguously. The opposition between a *real* object and an *imitation* of a real object is clear. So, too, is the opposition between "really seeing a man" and having an illusion.[1] We can speak sensibly of the distinction between "the real size" and "the apparent size" of the moon, but we know that both these expressions are extremely elliptical. The significance of the words "real" and "really" can be determined only by reference to the context in which they are used. Nothing but confusion can result if, in one and the same sentence, we mix up language used appropriately for the furniture of earth and our daily dealings with it with language used for the purpose of philosophical and scientific discussion.

A peculiarly gross example of such a linguistic mixture is provided by one of Eddington's most picturesque passages:

> I am standing on a threshold about to enter a room. It is a complicated business. In the first place I must shove against an atmosphere pressing with a force of fourteen pounds on every square inch of my body. I must make sure of landing on a plank travelling at twenty miles a second round the sun—a fraction of a second too early or too late, the plank would be miles away. I must do this whilst hanging from a round planet head outward into space, and with a wind of ether blowing at no one knows how many miles a second through every interstice of my body. The plank has no solidity of substance. To step on it is like stepping on a swarm of flies. Shall I not slip through? No, if I make the venture one of the flies hits me and gives me a boost up again; I fall again and am knocked upwards by another fly; and so on. I may hope that the net result will be that I remain steady; but if unfortunately I should slip through the floor or be boosted too violently up to the ceiling the occurrence would be, not a violation of the laws of Nature, but a rare coincidence. (*N.Ph.W.* 342.)*

[1]Cf. "How easy is that bush supposed a bear!"
*[*N.Ph.W.* = *The Nature of the Physical World.*—Eds.]

Whatever we may think of Eddington's chances of slipping through the floor, we must regard his usage of language in this statement as gravely misleading to the common reader. I cannot doubt that it reveals serious confusion in Eddington's own thinking about "the nature of the physical world." Stepping on a plank is not the least like "stepping on a swarm of flies." This language is drawn from, and is appropriate to, our daily intercourse with the familiar furniture of earth. We understand well what it is like to step onto a solid plank; we can also imagine what it would be like to step onto a swarm of flies. We know that two such experiences would be quite different. The plank is solid. If it be securely fixed, it will support our weight. What, then, are we to make of the comparison of stepping onto a plank with stepping onto a swarm of flies? What can be meant by saying "the plank has no solidity of substance"?

Again, we are familiar with the experience of shoving against an obstacle, and with the experience of struggling against a strong head-wind. We know that we do not have "to shove against an atmosphere" as we cross the threshold of a room. We can imagine what it would be like to jump onto a moving plank. We may have seen in a circus an equestrian acrobat jump from the back of a swiftly moving horse onto the back of another horse moving with approximately the same speed. We know that no such acrobatic feat is required to cross the threshold of a room.

I may seem too heavy-handed in my treatment of a picturesque passage, and thus to fall under the condemnation of the man who cannot see a joke and needs to be "in contact with merry-minded companions"[2] in order that he may develop a sense of humor. But the picturesqueness is deceptive; the passage needs serious criticism since Eddington draws from it a conclusion that is important. "Verily," he says, "it is easier for a camel to pass through the eye of a needle than for a scientific man to pass through a door. And whether the door be barn door or church door it might be wiser that he should consent to be an ordinary man and walk in rather than wait until all the difficulties involved in a really scientific ingress are resolved." It is, then, suggested that an ordinary man has no difficulty in crossing the threshold of a room but that "a really scientific ingress" presents difficulties. The suggested contrast is as absurd as the use of the adjective "scientific" prefixed to "ingress," in this context, is perverse. Whatever difficulties a scientist, by reason of his scientific knowledge, may encounter in becoming a member of a spiritual church, these difficulties bear no comparison with the difficulties of the imagined acrobatic feat. Consequently, they are not solved by the consideration that Eddington, no less than the ordinary man, need not hesitate to cross the threshold of his room. The false emotionalism of the picture is reminiscent of Jeans's picture of human be-

2See N. Ph. W. 336

ings standing on "a microscopic fragment of a grain of sand." It is open to a similar criticism.[3]

If Eddington had drawn this picture for purely expository purposes, it might be unobjectionable. The scientist who sets out to give a popular exposition of a difficult and highly technical subject must use what means he can devise to convey to his readers what it is all about. At the same time, if he wishes to avoid being misunderstood, he must surely warn his readers that, in the present stage of physics, very little can be conveyed to a reader who lacks the mathematical equipment required to understand the methods by which results are obtained and the language in which these results can alone find adequate expression. Eddington's picture seems to me to be open to the objection that the image of a swarm of flies used to explain the electronic structure of matter is more appropriate to the old-fashioned classical conceptions that found expression in a model than to the conceptions he is trying to explain. Consequently, the reader may be misled unless he is warned that nothing resembling the spatial relations of flies in a swarm can be found in the collection of electrons. No concepts drawn from the level of common-sense thinking are appropriate to subatomic, i.e. microphysical, phenomena. Consequently, the language of common sense is not appropriate to the description of such phenomena. Since, however, the man in the street tends to think in pictures and may desire to know something about the latest developments of physics, it is no doubt useful to provide him with some rough picture. The danger arises when the scientist uses the picture for the purpose of making explicit denials, and expresses these denials in common-sense language used in such a way as to be devoid of sense. This, unfortunately, is exactly what Eddington has done in the passage we are considering, and indeed, in many other passages as well.

It is worthwhile to examine with some care what exactly it is that Eddington is denying when he asserts that "the plank has no solidity of substance." What are we to understand by "solidity"? Unless we do understand it we cannot understand what the denial of solidity to the plank amounts to. But we can understand "solidity" only if we can truly say the plank is solid. For "solid" just is the word we use to describe a certain respect in which a plank of wood resembles a block of marble, a piece of paper, and a cricket ball, and in which each of these differs from a sponge, from the interior of a soap-bubble, and from the holes in a net. We use the word "solid" sometimes as the opposite of "empty," sometimes as the opposite of "hollow," sometimes as the opposite of "porous." We may also, in a very slightly technical usage, contrast "solid" with "liquid" or with "gaseous." There is, no doubt, considerable variation in the precise significance of the word "solid" in various contexts. Further, as is the case with all words, "solid" may be misused, and may also be used figuratively. But

[3]See above.

there could not be a *misuse*, nor a *figurative* use, unless there were some correct and literal usages. The point is that the common usage of language enables us to attribute a meaning to the phrase "a solid plank"; but there is no common usage of language that provides a meaning for the word "solid" that would make sense if I were to say that the plank on which I stand is not *solid*. We oppose the solidity of the walls of a house to the emptiness of its unfurnished rooms; we oppose the solidity of a piece of pumice-stone to the porous loofah sponge. We do not deny that the pumice-stone is to some degree porous, that the bricks of the wall have chinks and crevices. But we do not know how to use a word that has no sensible opposite. If the plank is nonsolid, then what does "solid" *mean*? In the companion passage to the one quoted earlier, and to which reference was made in a preceding footnote, Eddington depicts the physicist, about to enter a room, as reflecting that "the plank is not what it appears to be—a continuous support for his weight." This remark is absurd. The plank appears to be capable of supporting his weight, and, as his subsequent entry into the room showed, it *was* capable of supporting his weight. If it be objected that the plank is "a support for his weight" but not "a *continuous* support," I would reply that the word "continuous" is here used without any assigned meaning. The plank appears *solid* in that sense of the word "solid" in which the plank is, in fact, solid. It is of the utmost importance to press the question: If the plank appears to be *solid*, but is really *nonsolid*, what does "solid" mean? If "solid" has no assignable meaning, then "nonsolid" is also without sense. If the plank is nonsolid, then where can we find an example to show us what "solid" means? The pairs of words, "solid"—"empty," "solid"—"hollow," "solid"—"porous," belong to the vocabulary of common-sense language; in the case of each pair, if one of the two is without sense, so is the other.

This nonsensical denial of solidity is very common in popular expositions of the physicist's conception of material objects. The author of a recently published book says: "A table, a piece of paper, no longer possess that solid reality which they appear to possess; they are both of them porous, and consist of very small electrically charged particles, which are arranged in a peculiar way."[4] How are we to understand the statement that the table *no longer* possesses "the solid reality" which it appears to possess? The context of the statement must be taken into account. The sentence quoted occurs in a summary of the view of the physical world according to classical physics. It immediately follows the statement: "This picture formed by the physicists has one great drawback as compared with the picture formed by the nonscientific man in the street. It is much more abstract.". . . Here we

---

[4]Ernst Zimmer, *The Revolution of Physics*, trans. H. Stafford Hatfield, 1936, p. 51. I have not been able to consult the German original, so I am unable to determine whether "solid reality" is a good rendering of Zimmer's meaning. Certainly the juxtaposition of the two words is unfortunate, but is evidently judged to be appropriate at least by his translator.

are concerned only with the suggestion that the nonscientific man forms one "picture" of the material world and the scientist another. There are, then, two pictures. Of what, we must ask, are they pictures? Where are we to find application for the words "solid reality," which we may not use with reference to the table? Again we must ask: If the table is nonsolid, what does "solid" mean?

No doubt the author had in mind the nineteenth-century view of the ultra-microscopic world as consisting of solid, absolutely hard, indivisible billiard-ball-like atoms, which were assumed to be solid and hard in a perfectly straightforward sense of the words "solid" and "hard." If so, it would be more appropriate to say that the modern physicist no longer believes that the table *consists* of solid atomic balls than to say that "the table no longer possesses solid reality." There is, indeed, a danger in talking about *the table* at all, for the physicist is not, in fact, concerned with tables. The recent habit of talking as though he were is responsible for much confusion of thought. It leads Eddington into the preposterous nonsense of the "two tables." This view will be familiar to everyone who is interested in the philosophy of the physicists. Nevertheless, it is desirable to quote a considerable part of Eddington's statement, since it is important to examine his view in some detail.

> I have settled down to the task of writing these lectures and have drawn up my chairs to my two tables. Two tables! Yes; there are duplicates of every object about me—two tables, two chairs, two pens. . . . One of them has been familiar to me from earliest years. It is a commonplace object of that environment which I call the world. How shall I describe it? It has extension; it is comparatively permanent; it is colored; above all, it is *substantial*. . . . Table no. 2 is my scientific table. It is a more recent acquaintance and I do not feel so familiar with it. . . . My scientific table is mostly emptiness. Sparsely scattered in that emptiness are numerous electric charges rushing about with great speed; but their combined bulk amounts to less than a billionth of the bulk of the table itself. Notwithstanding its strange construction it turns out to be an entirely efficient table. It supports my writing paper as satisfactorily as table no. 1; for when I lay the paper on it the little electric particles with their headlong speed keep on hitting the underside, so that the paper is maintained in shuttlecock fashion at a nearly steady level. If I lean upon this table I shall not go through; or, to be strictly accurate, the chance of my scientific elbow going through my scientific table is so excessively small that it can be neglected in practical life . . . There is nothing *substantial* about my second table. It is nearly all empty space —space pervaded it is true by fields of force, but these are assigned to the categories of "influences," not of "things."[5]

There is so much to criticize in this passage that it is difficult to know where to begin. Probably Eddington's defence against any criticism would

---

[5]*N.Ph.W.* xi, xii, xiii. I assume the reader's familiarity with the rest of the chapter in which this passage occurs.

be that this is one of the passages in which he "was leading the reader on"[6] (presumably—to put it vulgarly—"up the garden path"), and that consequently it must not be taken as giving "explicit statements" of his philosophical ideas. But he has nowhere expounded his philosophical ideas in nonpopular language. Moreover, the mistakes are so frequently repeated in his writings and seem to be so inextricably bound up with his philosophical conclusions that it is inevitable that these mistakes should be submitted to detailed criticism.

Perhaps the first comment that should be made is that Eddington takes quite seriously the view that there are *two tables*; one belongs to "the external world of physics." the other to "a world of familiar acquaintance in human consciousness." Eddington's philosophy may be regarded as the outcome of a sustained attempt to answer the question: How are the two tables related to one another? It never seems to occur to him that the form of the question is absurd. In answering the question he is hampered from the start by his initial assumption that the tables are *duplicates* of each other, i.e. that it really isn't nonsensical to speak of two *tables*. I hazard the conjecture that Eddington is an inveterate visualizer,[7] and that once he has committed himself to the language of "two tables" he cannot avoid thinking of one as the shadow and of the other as the substance. (In this sentence, I have used the word "substance" simply as the correlative of "shadow." This usage has undoubtedly influenced Eddington's thinking on this topic.) It is evident that the scientific table is to be regarded as the shadow. There are statements that conflict with this interpretation, but Eddington does not leave us in doubt that, whenever he is using the language of *shadowing*, it is the scientific table that is a shadow of the familiar table. It is true that he says, "I need not tell you that modern physics has by delicate test and remorseless logic assured me that my second scientific table is the only one which is really there—wherever 'there' may be." Elsewhere he says, "Our conception of the familiar table was an illusion" (*N.Ph.W.* 323). These discrepancies result from the deep-seated confusions out of which his philosophy springs . . . At present we are concerned with the view—in conflict with the statements just quoted—that the scientific table is a shadow. "In the world of physics," he says, "we watch a shadowgraph performance of the drama of familiar life. The shadow of my elbow rests on the shadow table as

---

6N.P.Sc. 291. [*N.P.Sc.* = *New Pathways in Science.*—Eds.]

7The following passage is significant: "When I think of an electron there rises to my mind a hard, red, tiny ball; the proton similarly is neutral grey. Of course the color is absurd—perhaps not more absurd than the rest of the conception—but I am incorrigible" (*N.Ph.W.* xviii).

Cf. also, "I am liable to visualize a Test-match in Australia as being played upside down" (*N.P.Sc.* 314). Perhaps this habit is responsible for the queer statement (quoted above) that the feat of entering his study has to be accomplished whilst he is "hanging from a round planet head outward into space." Only, in that case, he has forgotten that his study would be hanging outward the same way. What is more important is that he has created a difficulty out of a mode of speech.

the shadow ink flows over the shadow paper. It is all symbolic, and as a symbol the physicist leaves it" (xvi). Elsewhere he suggests that physicists would generally say that "the matter of this familiar table is *really* a curvature of space," but that is a view difficult to reconcile with either of the statements we are considering now.

Certainly there is much in the passage about the two tables that seems to conflict with the view of the scientific table as a shadow. It is said to be "mostly emptiness," but scattered in the emptiness are numerous electric charges whose "combined bulk" is compared in amount with "the bulk of the table itself." Is "the table itself" the familiar table? I think it must be. But the comparison of the *two* bulks is surely nonsensical. Moreover, a shadow can hardly be said to have *bulk*. Yet Eddington insists that the two tables are "parallel"—an odd synonym, no doubt, for a "shadow." He contrasts the scientific *table*, which has a familiar *table* parallel to it, with the scientific electron, quantum, or potential, which have no familiars that are parallel. Of the latter he says that the physicist is scrupulously careful to guard them "from contamination by conceptions borrowed from the other [i.e. the familiar] world." But if electrons, belonging to world no. 2, are to be scrupulously guarded from contamination by world no. 1, how can it make sense to say that they "keep on hitting the underside" of a sheet of paper that, indubitably, is part of the familiar furniture of earth? It is Eddington who reintroduces contamination when he talks in this fashion, and he does so because he supposes that there is a scientific table parallel to the familiar table. I venture to suggest that it is as absurd to say that there is a scientific table as to say that there is a familiar electron or a familiar quantum, or a familiar potential. Eddington insists upon the lack of familiar parallels in the latter cases; surely he is justified in doing so. What is puzzling is his view that there are parallel *tables*. It suggests a return to the days when physicists demanded a model; "the physicist," says Eddington, "used to borrow the raw material of his world from the familiar world, but he does so no longer" (xv). But if the "scientific table" is to be regarded as the product of the "raw material of the scientific world," how can it be regarded as parallel to the familiar table? Eddington seems unable to free himself from the conviction that the physicist is concerned with things of the same nature as the things of the familiar world; hence, *tables* are to be found in both world no. 1 and world no. 2. There is a statement in his exposition of "The Downfall of Classical Physics" that shows how deep-rooted this conviction is. "The atom," he says, "is as porous as the solar system. If we eliminated all the unfilled space in a man's body and collected his protons and electrons into one mass, the man would be reduced to a speck just visible with a magnifying glass" (*N.Ph.W.* 1–2). The comparison is useful enough; the absurdity comes from speaking of the speck as a *man*. If this statement stood alone, it might well be regarded as an expository device. But the constant cropping up of the parallel tables shows that

Eddington does not regard it as absurd to think of the reduction as still leaving a *man*. When, later in the book, he is expounding the conception of space required by relativity theory, he points out that our difficulty in conceiving it is due to the fact that we are "using a conception of space which must have originated many millions of years ago and has become rather firmly embedded in human thought" (81). He adds: "But the space of physics ought not to be dominated by this creation of the dawning mind of an enterprising ape." It seems to me that in allowing himself to speak of the speck as a man, Eddington is allowing himself to be thus dominated. It is true that, in the statement just quoted, Eddington was speaking of relativity physics, but I do not think that "the creation of the dawning mind of an enterprising ape" is any more appropriate to the conception of space in atomic physics. . . . It must suffice at the moment to insist that a *man* is an object belonging to the familiar world, and has no duplicate in "the scientific world."

Perhaps we may be convinced of the absurdity of the notion that there are "duplicates of every object" in the familiar world if we return to the consideration of the description of a familiar scene with which this chapter opened. I spoke there of "blue curtains," of a crimson and scented rose, of a bruised leg. Neglecting at present the consideration of the bruised leg, which—judging by Eddington's account of the adventures of an elephant — is beneath the notice of a scientist, we may ask what duplicate of *blue* is to be found in the scientific world. The answer is that there is no duplicate. It is true that it has a "counterpart," but that is a very different matter. The counterpart of color is "its scientific equivalent electromagnetic wavelength" (88). "The wave," says Eddington, "is the reality—or the nearest we can get to a description of reality; the color is mere mind-spinning. The beautiful hues which flood our consciousness under stimulation of the waves have no relevance to the objective reality." It is obvious that here Eddington is regarding the scientific world as "the objective reality"; the familiar world is subjective. This does not square with the view that the scientific world is the shadow of the familiar world, but it is hopeless to attempt to extract from Eddington any consistent view of their relation. With this difficulty, however, we are not at the moment concerned. The point is that Eddington firmly extrudes *color* from the scientific world, and rightly so. But the *rose* is colored, the *table* is colored, the *curtains* are colored. How, then, can that which is not colored duplicate the rose, the curtains, the table? To say that an electromagnetic wave-length is colored would be as nonsensical as to say that symmetry is colored. Eddington does not say so. But he has failed to realize that a colored object could be *duplicated* only by something with regard to which it would not be meaningless to say that it was colored.

8 / Science and the Physical World

W. T. STACE

So far as I know scientists still talk about electrons, protons, neutrons, and so on. We never directly perceive these; hence if we ask how we know of their existence the only possible answer seems to be that they are an inference from what we do directly perceive. What sort of an inference? Apparently a causal inference. The atomic entities in some way impinge upon the sense of the animal organism and cause that organism to perceive the familiar world of tables, chairs, and the rest.

But is it not clear that such a concept of causation, however interpreted, is invalid? The only reason we have for believing in the law of causation is that we *observe* certain regularities or sequences. We observe that, in certain conditions, A is always followed by B. We call A the cause, B the effect. And the sequence of A–B becomes a causal law. It follows that all *observed* causal sequences are between sensed objects in the familiar world of perception, and that all known causal laws apply solely to the world of sense and not to anything beyond or behind it. And this in turn means that we have not got, and never could have, one jot of evidence for believing that the law of causation can be applied *outside* the realm of perception, or that that realm can have any causes (such as the supposed physical objects) which are not themselves perceived.

Put the same thing in another way. Suppose there is an observed sequence A–B–C, represented by the vertical line in the diagram below.

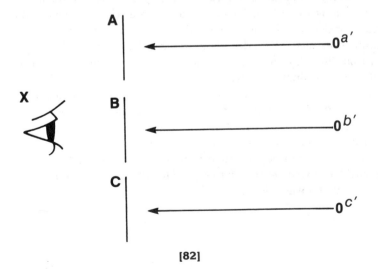

The observer X sees, and can see, nothing except things in the familiar world of perception. What *right* has he, and what *reason* has he, to assert a cause of A, B, and C, such as a', b', c', which he can never observe, behind the perceived world? He has no *right*, because the law of causation on which he is relying has never been observed to operate outside the series of perceptions, and he can have, therefore, no evidence that it does so. And he has no *reason* because the phenomenon C is *sufficiently* accounted for by the cause B, B by A, and so on. It is unnecessary and superfluous to introduce a *second* cause b' for B, c' for C, and so forth. To give two causes for each phenomenon, one in one world and one in another, is unnecessary, and perhaps even self-contradictory.

Is it denied, then, it will be asked, that the star causes light waves, that the waves cause retinal changes, that these cause changes in the optic nerve, which in turn causes movements in the brain cells, and so on? No, it is not denied. But the observed causes and effects are all in the world of perception. And no sequence of sense-data can possibly justify going outside that world. If you admit that we never observe anything except sensed objects and their relations, regularities, and sequences, then it is obvious that we are completely shut in by our sensations and can never get outside them. Not only causal relations, but all other observed relations, upon which *any* kind of inferences might be founded, will lead only to further sensible objects and their relations. No inference, therefore, can pass from what is sensible to what is not sensible.

The fact is that atoms are not inferences from sensations. No one denies, of course, that a vast amount of perfectly valid inferential reasoning takes place in the physical theory of the atom. But it will not be found to be in any strict logical sense inference *from sense-data* to atoms*. An *hypothesis* is set up, and the inferential processes are concerned with the application of the hypothesis, that is, with the prediction by its aid of further possible sensations and with its own internal consistency.

That atoms are not inferences from sensations means, of course, that from the existence of sensations we cannot validly infer the existence of atoms. And this means that we cannot have any reason at all to believe that they exist. And that is why I propose to argue that they do not exist—or at any rate that one could not know it if they did, and that we have absolutely no evidence of their existence.

What status have they, then? Is it meant that they are false and worthless, merely untrue? Certainly not. No one supposes that the entries in the Nautical Almanac "exist" anywhere except on the pages of that book and in the brains of its compilers and readers. Yet they are "true," inasmuch as they enable us to predict certain sensations, namely, the positions and times of

---

*[Singular: sense-datum. A sense-datum is any object or quality which is immediately sensed, for example, a color, shape, sound, taste, etc. At times Stace calls these sensations.— Eds.]

certain perceived objects which we call the stars. And so the formulae of the atomic theory are true in the same sense, and perform a similar function.

I suggest that they are nothing but shorthand formulae, ingeniously worked out by the human mind, to enable it to predict its experience, i.e. to predict what sensations will be given to it. By "predict" here I do not mean to refer solely to the future. To calculate that there was an eclipse of the sun visible in Asia Minor in the year 585 B.C. is, in the sense in which I am using the term, to predict.

In order to see more clearly what is meant, let us apply the same idea to another case, that of gravitation. Newton formulated a law of gravitation in terms of "forces." It was supposed that this law—which was nothing but a mathematical formula—governed the operation of these existent forces. Nowadays it is no longer believed that these forces exist at all. And yet the law can be applied just as well without them to the prediction of astronomical phenomena. It is a matter of no importance to the scientific man whether the forces exist or not. That may be said to be a purely philosophical question. And I think the philosopher should pronounce them fictions. But that would not make the law useless or untrue. If it could still be used to predict phenomena, it would be just as true as it was.

It is true that fault is now found with Newton's law, and that another law, that of Einstein, has been substituted for it. And it is sometimes supposed that the reason for this is that forces are no longer believed in. But this is not the case. Whether forces exist or not simply does not matter. What matters is the discovery that Newton's law does *not* enable us accurately to predict certain astronomical facts such as the exact position of the planet Mercury. Therefore another formula, that of Einstein, has been substituted for it which permits correct predictions. This new law, as it happens, is a formula in terms of geometry. It is pure mathematics and nothing else. It does not contain anything about forces. In its pure form it does not even contain, so I am informed, anything about "humps and hills in space–time." And it does not matter whether any such humps and hills exist. It is truer than Newton's law, not because it substitutes humps and hills for forces, but solely because it is a more accurate formula of prediction.

Not only may it be said that forces do not exist. It may with equal truth be said that "gravitation" does not exist. Gravitation is not a "thing," but a mathematical formula, which exists only in the heads of mathematicians. And as a mathematical formula cannot cause a body to fall, so gravitation cannot cause a body to fall. Ordinarily language misleads us here. We speak of the law "of" gravitation, and suppose that this law "applies to" the heavenly bodies. We are thereby misled into supposing that there are *two* things, namely, the gravitation and the heavenly bodies, and that one of these things, the gravitation, causes changes in the other. In reality nothing exists except the moving bodies. And neither Newton's law nor Einstein's law is, strictly speaking, a law of gravitation. They are both laws of moving bodies, that is to say, formulae which tell us how these bodies will move.

Now just as in the past "forces" were foisted into Newton's law (by himself, be it said), so now certain popularizers of relativity foisted "humps and hills in space–time" into Einstein's law. We hear that the reason why the planets move in curved courses is that they cannot go through these humps and hills, but have to go around them! The planets just get "shoved about," not by forces, but by the humps and hills! But these humps and hills are pure metaphors. And anyone who takes them for "existences" gets asked awkward questions as to what "curved space" is curved "in."

It is not irrelevant to our topic to consider *why* human beings invent these metaphysical monsters of forces and bumps in space–time. The reason is that they have never emancipated themselves from the absurd idea that science "explains" things. They were not content to have laws which merely told them *that* the planets will, as a matter of fact, move in such and such ways. They wanted to know "why" the planets move in those ways. So Newton replied, "Forces." "Oh," said humanity, "that explains it. We understand forces. We feel them every time someone pushes or pulls us." Thus the movements were supposed to be "explained" by entities familiar because analogous to the muscular sensations which human beings feel. The humps and hills were introduced for exactly the same reason. They seem so familiar. If there is a bump in the billiard table, the rolling billiard ball is diverted from a straight to a curved course. Just the same with the planets. "Oh, I see!" says humanity, "that's quite simple. That *explains* everything."

But scientific laws, properly formulated, never "explain" anything. They simply state, in an abbreviated and generalized form, *what happens*. No scientist, and in my opinion no philosopher, knows *why* anything happens, or can "explain" anything. Scientific laws do nothing except state the brute fact that "when *A* happens, *B* always happens too." And laws of this kind obviously enable us to predict. If certain scientists substituted humps and hills for forces, then they have just substituted one superstition for another. For my part I do not believe that *science* has done this, though some *scientists* may have. For scientists, after all, are human beings with the same craving for "explanations" as other people.

I think that atoms are in exactly the same position as forces and the bumps and hills of space–time. In reality the mathematical formulae which are the scientific ways of stating the atomic theory are simply formulae for calculating what sensations will appear in given conditions. But just as the weakness of the human mind demanded that there should correspond to the formula of gravitation a real "thing" which could be called "gravitation itself" or "force," so the same weakness demands that there should be a real thing corresponding to the atomic formulae, and this real thing is called the atom. In reality the atoms no more cause sensations than gravitation causes apples to fall. The only causes of sensations are other sensations. And the relation of atoms to sensations to be felt is not the relation of cause to effect, but the relation of a mathematical formula to the facts and happening which it enables the mathematician to calculate. . . .

It will not be out of place to give one more example to show how common fictitious existences are in science, and how little it matters whether they really exist or not. This example has no strange and annoying talk of "bent spaces" about it. One of the foundations of physics is, or used to be, the law of the conservation of energy. I do not know how far, if at all, this has been affected by the theory that matter sometimes turns into energy. But that does not affect the lesson it has for us. The law states, or used to state, that the amount of energy in the universe is always constant, that energy is never either created or destroyed. This was highly convenient, but it seemed to have obvious exceptions. If you throw a stone up into the air, you are told that it exerts in its fall the same amount of energy which it took to throw it up. But suppose it does not fall. Suppose it lodges on the roof of your house and stays there. What has happened to the energy which you can nowhere perceive as being exerted? It seems to have disappeared out of the universe. No, says the scientist, it still exists as *potential* energy. Now what does this blessed word "potential"—which is thus brought in to save the situation—mean as applied to energy? It means, of course, that the energy does not exist in any of its regular "forms," heat, light, electricity, etc. But this is merely negative. What positive meaning has the term? Strictly speaking, none whatever. Either the energy exists or it does not exist. There is no realm of the "potential" half-way between existence and nonexistence. And this existence of energy can only consist in its being exerted. If the energy is not being exerted, then it is not energy and does not exist. Energy can no more exist without energizing than heat can exist without being hot. The "potential" existence of the energy is, then, a fiction. The actual empirically verifiable facts are that if a certain quantity of energy e exists in the universe and then disappears out of the universe (as happens when the stone lodges on the roof), the same amount of energy e will always reappear, begin to exist again, in certain known conditions. That is the fact which the law of the conservation of energy actually expresses. And the fiction of potential energy is introduced simply because it is convenient and makes the equations easier to work. They could be worked quite well without it, but would be slightly more complicated. In either case the function of the law is the same. Its object is to apprise us that if in certain conditions we have certain perceptions (throwing up the stone), then in certain other conditions we shall get certain other perceptions (heat, light, stone hitting skull, or other such). But there will always be a temptation to hypostatize the potential energy as an "existence," and to believe that it is a "cause" which "explains" the phenomena.

If the views which I have been expressing are followed out, they will lead to the conclusion that, strictly speaking, *nothing exists except sensations* (and the minds which perceive them). The rest is mental construction or fiction. But this does not mean that the conception of a star or the conception of an electron are worthless or untrue. Their truth and value consist in their capacity for helping us to organize our experience and predict our sensations.

9 / Physical Objects as Not Reducible to Perceptions

C. H. WHITELEY

The problem I shall discuss is: What reason have we for believing that there are physical objects? My purpose is not either to raise or to dispel doubts as to the existence of physical objects; this doubt constitutes a medical rather than a philosophical problem. The point of asking the question is that, while there can be no reasonable difference of opinion as to whether there are physical objects, there can be and is reasonable difference of opinion as to how the notion of a physical object is to be analyzed; and if we are clear as to what grounds there are for believing in physical objects, we shall also be clearer as to what sort of physical objects we have grounds for believing in. Also, it is worthwhile to inquire which other beliefs are logically connected with, and which are logically independent of, the belief in physical objects.

I make one important assumption at the outset: namely, that by a physical object or process we mean something that exists or occurs apart from and independently of our perceptions, and of our experiences of other kinds. The distinction between the physical or "real" world and the "subjective" or "imaginary"—illusions, hallucinations, after-images, shadows, rainbows, mental pictures, what we merely suppose, imagine, or expect—is a distinction between things and events which exist or occur whether anybody is aware of them or not, and things and events which have their being only as and when somebody is aware of them. A belief in physical objects is a belief in things which are sometimes at least unobserved by the believer.

It is obvious that the existence of such things is not a question to be settled by sense-perception alone. That there is a material world cannot be established or even made plausible merely by looking, listening, touching; it is not *given* in the way in which the existence of something red and something round, of sounds, smells, aches, feelings of sadness, can be given. I do not mean that the something red or round cannot be a physical object; I mean that it cannot be known to be a physical object just by looking at it or otherwise perceiving it. For I cannot, simply by perceiving something, tell whether that something continues to exist when I cease to perceive it. This logical necessity is not evaded by naïve realism, which holds that the something red or round which appears to sight is (usually at least) identical with a physical object; for though this may be so, we cannot know it just by looking. Nor is it evaded by phenomenalism; for no phenomenalist does or plausibly could analyze statements about physical objects into statements asserting the *actual* occurrence of sense-data; he must add statements about what sense-data *would* be sensed if certain conditions were fulfilled; and this fact is not given by sense-perception, but reasons for it are required. That there are physical objects is not something we observe or perceive, but something we suppose or assume (to call it a "hypothesis" or "postulate" is to suggest something rather too deliberate and self-conscious). In old-fashioned language, it is a transcendent belief; it goes beyond the evidence.

Thus there is no logical absurdity in denying or refusing to admit the existence of a material world. To say that there are no physical objects, while doubtless very foolish, does not involve a man in any logical contradiction, nor does it force him to shut his eyes to any patent and indisputable facts. An intellectually indolent percipient, whose few wants were supplied independently of his own efforts, might well abstain from supposing that there was a physical world. There is some evidence that young babies, who are more or less in this situation, do not believe that there are any material things—do not believe, for instance, that the rattle just dropped from the hand and the visitor just departed from the room are now anywhere at all.

If somebody did behave like this, in what way would he be worse off, and what other beliefs would he be debarred from entertaining? I answer—and this is my principal point—that he would be unable to make valid generalizations, or reliable forecasts of his future experience. He would have to do without the belief in an order in nature, in regular sequences of events, in causal laws. For if I confine myself to what I myself observe or am aware of, I can make no valid generalizations concerning the concomitance or sequence of types of phenomena. I find only that phenomena of one type are quite often accompanied or followed by phenomena of another type, but sometimes not. There is no type of sense-datum A of which it is true that whenever it occurs another type of sense-datum B accompanies or follows or precedes it. And this is the case however complex you make your A and your B. This point has often been overlooked. People know quite well that lightning is always accompanied by thunder, barking by the presence of dogs, that green apples are always sour, and the ground always gets dark and sticky after a heavy fall of rain; and they talk about these as though they were *phenomenal* regularities—as though the seeing of lightning always went along with the hearing of thunder, and so forth. But this is of course not the case. If, as some people have said, it was the business of science to disclose the order or regularity in phenomena, meaning by phenomena what we see and hear and feel, science would be a very unrewarding pursuit. For phenomena are disorderly and irregular, and scientists cannot make them out any different.

Many philosophers have indeed thought that natural regularities could be conceived without the postulation of actual unobserved things and events, if instead we postulate that certain phenomena would occur or would have occurred, given certain unfulfilled conditions. Instead of saying that whenever I hear barking there exists an actual dog, perceived or unperceived, I am to say that whenever I hear barking, I should perceive a dog if certain conditions were fulfilled—if my eyes were open and my sight normal, if there was an adequate amount of light, if I looked in the right direction and there was no opaque obstacle in my line of vision, etc. Such an interpretation in terms of possible phenomena would relieve us of any need to postulate another order of physical events over and above perceptual events, and would in this way be more economical. There are, however, three ways in which phenomenal generalizations of this kind cannot take the place of physical generalizations.

1. A physical generalization associates one uniform property with another uniform property: I mean that when something is asserted to be universally true of dogs, or pieces of iron, or cases of pneumonia, or falling bodies of a weight of ten pounds, it is assumed that there is some physical property or group of properties which is common to all dogs, pieces of iron, etc. Phenomenal generalizations, however, concern associations between sets of diverse phenomena. If we wish to correlate the auditory phenomenon of barking with visual phenomena we must specify a set of canine sense-data, or views of dogs, which are not all alike in any sensory property, but form one class only in virtue of a very complex set of relations.

2. A physical generalization applies to *all* cases of a given type, and the study of nature aims at reducing to laws all events and all features of events. But phenomenal generalizations can never apply to all cases of a given type, but only to some of them, namely to those cases in which the supplementary conditions for observation are fulfilled. The physical generalization "There's no smoke without fire" applies to all instances of smoke, whether or not either the smoke or the fire is observed. But the corresponding phenomenal generalization brings under a uniformity-rule only those

cases in which both the smoke and the fire are observed. Observed smoke can be correlated with observed fire; when I observe the smoke but not the fire, the observed smoke is correlated with nothing, and is an instance of no natural law (except in the forced and trivial sense in which a white cat with brown eyes and quick hearing is an instance of the law that all white cats with blue eyes are deaf); it forms no part of the order of nature.

3. A phenomenal generalization must always include a reference to conditions of observation, whereas physical generalizations are independent of these. We can say without qualification "Whenever it thunders, it lightens." But we can say "Whevever thunder is heard, lightning is seen" only if we add "provided that there is an observer with adequate eyesight, facing in the appropriate direction, having his eyes open and his view not obscured by any opaque object, etc." This difference does not merely prevent the phenomenal generalization from adequately replacing the physical one. It also means that there can be no generalizations on the phenomenal level which are universally valid. For it is impossible to give in purely phenomenal terms an adequate statement of all the conditions required for perceiving lightning besides the occurrence of lightning. It is curious that the analysis of physical-objects statements in terms of sense-data and the analysis of causation in terms of regular sequence should have been so often advocated by the same philosophers. For if we restrict our attention to phenomena, we can find no instances for the regular-sequence concept of cause to apply to.

If therefore, I am to make reliable generalizations about the course of events, and reliable forecasts about my future experiences, I must suppose that there are unperceived as well as perceived events. Thus the connection between the category of substance and that of cause is, as Kant suggested, not fortuitous but necessary. We do not discover that there are (perfect) regularities in nature, that is, in the physical world, as we discover that there are (imperfect) regularities amongst phenomena. On the contrary, the regularity is essential to the concept of nature; the assumption that the physical world is orderly is inseparable from the assumption that the physical world exists. It is only to the extent that I assume it to be orderly that I have any grounds for believing that there is a physical world at all. This may help to account for our strong inclination to regard physical determinism as a necessary *a priori* truth.

What, then, is the sort of supposition which will make it possible to believe in regular sequences and concomitances in the world, and to regulate our expectations accordingly? A simple and comprehensive answer cannot be given to this question. The precise character of the suppositions we make about physical objects and processes is subject to variation for different kinds of cases, and to modification with the improvement of our knowledge. One can, however, indicate the general line which must be followed.

There are, amongst the events which we are aware of, certain associations of characteristics which, while not invariable, are very common: for example, the association between the sound of barking and the sight of dogs, between the visual appearance of oranges and their characteristic flavor, between the brightness of sunshine and felt warmth, between the kinesthetic sensations of speech and the sound of my own voice, between the visible immersion of a lump of sugar in a cup of tea and its gradual disappearance, between the various members of the visible sequence blackcoal . . . flame . . . red-coal . . . ashes, between the patter of raindrops, the sight of rain falling, the feeling of dampness on exposed parts of the body, and the darkening of the soil or pavement. (These are, of course, examples of several different kinds of association.)

The supposition required has two parts:

1. that to these imperfect phenomenal regularities there corresponds in each case a perfect physical regularity; that is, in each case in which there is a frequent association between phenomenal characteristics there are some corresponding physical characteristics which are invariably associated. Whereas the sound of barking is often but not always accompanied by the sight of a dog, there is some type of event, physical barking, which is always accompanied by the presence of some one type of physical object, a dog. Whereas the visual brightness of sunshine is only sometimes accompanied by a feeling of warmth, there is a physical entity, sunlight, and a physical entity, heat, which always goes with it. Whereas a person may be seen setting off from A and arriving at B without being seen at intermediate places at intermediate times, physical passage from A to B involves the temporally continuous traversing of a spatially continuous path. In general, whenever there is an imperfect but frequent association between a phenomenal characteristic A and a phenomenal characteristic B, there is a thing or process having a characteristic corresponding to A which is invariably associated with a thing or process having a characteristic corresponding to B. Thus whenever I hear barking, there exists a physical dog, whether or not there also occurs the experience of my seeing him.

2. The existence of the corresponding physical thing, or the occurrence of the corresponding physical process, is a necessary but not a sufficient condition for the awareness of the phenomenal characteristic. There can be no hearing of barks without their being (physical) barks; but there can be barks without the hearing of barks. The further conditions, other than the existence of the dog or the occurrence of the bark, which are required if I am to have the corresponding perception of the dog or the bark, may be called the observation-conditions. Some of these conditions are pretty easy to discover. For instance, if I am to see anything at all, there must be a certain amount of light (but not enough to dazzle), and my vision must not be blocked by any obstacle. Other observation-conditions can only be discov-

ered by much experimental research: for instance, the need for air or some other transmitting medium in the case of hearing, the need for integrity of the optic nerves in the case of sight. The occurrence of the appropriate sense experience is determined jointly by the corresponding physical process and the relevant observation-conditions. (These conditions, of course, concern the properties of other physical things and processes, so that we cannot say just what they are without knowing something about physical things other than the one to be perceived. Learning about the properties of dogs, and learning about the properties of light and the human sense-organs, go hand in hand.) Thus the assumption of a physical world involves two supposed sets of regularities: an association between one physical characteristic and another, and an association between physical processes together with observation-conditions on the one hand and sense-experiences on the other.

So far, the physical world has been presented as a set of processes which occur independently of perceptions, which are related by laws of sequence and concomitance to other processes, and which together with the relevant observation-conditions determine specific sense-experiences of ours. These are purely relational properties; and nothing has been said so far about any other properties that physical objects may possess. On the view here advocated, namely that the justification of a belief in a physical world is that it makes possible the formulation of laws of nature, the only positive reason for attributing a property to physical objects would be that by assuming physical objects to possess this property we can account for the character of our perceptions, and explain how we come to perceive this rather than that, now rather than then. One way of accounting for the character of our perceptions would be to suppose that the sensory qualities which are present in them (the particular colors, sounds, tastes, etc.) are properties of physical objects and persist unperceived just as they appear when perceived. This is naïve realism. A completely naïve-realist theory would hold that all sensory qualities are properties of physical objects, and exist independently of perception; other theories are naïvely realistic to the extent that they identify the properties of physical things with those properties which are present in sense-experience.

Now the investigation of the properties of physical things is the business of the science of physics. And contemporary physics is not naïvely realistic in any degree. The properties which it attributes to physical objects are not sensory properties, but hypothetical properties defined by their relations to one another and to certain kinds of perceptions. The reason for this is often misunderstood. Philosophical criticism of naïve realism is apt to concentrate on the "argument from illusion," that is, on the *deceptiveness* of sense-perception. This is the wrong sort of criticism. Our perceptions can sometimes mislead us (that is, lead us to form false expectations about other perceptions to come) only because they also, and more often, lead us to form true expectations; perception could not be systematically misleading. But the question whether our perceptions induce in us true or false expectations is quite independent of the question whether they show us the permanent characteristics of material things. The damaging criticisms of naïve realism rest on this principle: Given that the physical object corresponding to a given sense-datum is something which, in conjunction with the relevant observation-conditions, determines the characteristics of that sense-datum, then if a given characteristic can be shown to be determined by the observation-conditions, there can be no reason for attributing it to the corresponding physical object. The successive modifications in our concept of the physical world arise from our increasing knowledge of the dependence of sensory properties upon observation-conditions. The challenge to naïve realism with respect to colors comes from optics. The challenge to naïve realism with respect to space and time comes from relativity-theory. The challenge to naïve realism with respect to beauty and ugliness comes from our understanding of the dependence of esthetic delight and disgust upon the dispositions and past experiences of the subject.

In abandoning naïve realism, scientific theory only carries further a process which pre-scientific common sense has already begun. The common-sense view of the physical world is by no means a purely naïve-realist view. When I look at an object from different angles and in different lights successively, the sensory properties which appear to me are many and various. Common sense does not hold that all these various sensory properties belong to the physical object and exist apart from my perception. Were that so, there would have to be either a multitude of physical objects or a constantly changing object to possess all these different properties. Common sense holds, on the contrary, that there is but one object with one shape, size, color, etc., which is unchanging throughout my changing perceptions. This postulation of a single set of physical properties corresponding to a multiplicity of sensory properties is the first and fundamental step away from naïve realism. A Berkeleian analysis, which reverses this step, is a greater affront to common sense and provokes more resistance from it than a Lockean analysis which takes a step or two further in the same direction.*

It is a belief of common sense that at least some sensory properties are not properties of physical objects, but are due to conditions of observation (quantity and quality of light, distance, defects of vision, etc.). As to whether *any* sensory properties are also physical properties, I am not convinced that common sense has any clear and consistent view. Of course we say that grass is green and roses are red. But does this mean more than that if we look at them under suitable conditions green and red are the colors we

---

*[Berkeley and Locke were 18th century British philosophers.—Eds.]

shall see? It is not clear to me that common sense is committed to the belief that objects have any colors when unperceived. (Examining the way we talk about the matter is of no help. Given that a certain piece of cloth looks bluish in artificial light and grayish in daylight, are we to presume that its color changes with changes in the light, and say "It *is* blue in artifical light and gray in daylight," or are we to presume that it has a color independently of the light, and say "It is really gray, but it looks blue in artificial light?" Ordinary idiom allows us to say either of these things indifferently.) By contrast, there are some properties which common sense does attribute to physical objects apart from perception—size and weight, for instance. When I conclude that this brick must have made that hole in the window, though nobody saw it do so, I credit the brick with having a size and weight at a time when it was not being perceived. But size and weight are not sensory properties. Blueness is a way things look; but heaviness is not a way things look or feel. A thing can, of course, look or feel heavy; but its *being* heavy is something different—it is heavy if it will hold down or make dents in other objects, if you can't lift it with one hand, and so on; and these causal characteristics are not ways of looking or feeling. Properties like size and weight, which common sense does attribute to unperceived objects, bear the same sort of relation to sense-experience as the concepts of modern physics. Thus it seems to me that one can abandon naïve realism in all its forms without abandoning any belief to which common sense is committed.

To sum up: That there are physical objects is a supposition, not a datum. The use of the supposition is to account for the regularities in sensory phenomena, to enable the course of events to be set in a framework of regular sequences and concomitances. It is confirmed by the success we achieve in ordering our experiences by its aid, in making our generalizations continually more extensive and more exact. Being a supposition, and not an inevitable and invariable category of thought, it is subject to modification as we learn more about the conditions under which perception takes place. Scientific concepts are related to sense-experience in a remoter and more complex fashion than common-sense concepts of physical objects. But they are not of an entirely different order. The common-sense concept of "table" is not, like "blue" or "bang" or "stench," a merely phenomenal concept; it is explanatory and theoretical.

STUDY QUESTIONS

1. What, in detail, are the two contrasting descriptions of a table that Eddington gives? Are they incompatible?

2. Physics, according to Eddington, teaches us that only the scientific table "is really there." What does (could) he mean by this? What reasons does he give for believing it?

3. How can Eddington's view, expressed in question 2, be reconciled with his claim that the two tables can perhaps be identified?

4. State and evaluate Stebbing's argument that Eddington cannot reasonably claim that planks and rocks are not solid.

5. Stebbing writes, ''It is evident that the scientific table [according to Eddington] is to be regarded as the shadow.'' Is it evident?

6. Suppose that while driving you hear a thumping sound and quite naturally make a causal inference to the car's having a flat tire. Notice that the flat was not perceived directly but was inferred from something which was directly perceived. What is the difference between this example and the kind of inference which scientists supposedly make to electrons, protons, and so on? Surely your inference is innocent enough, but according to Stace the scientists' are not. Why?

7. How would Whiteley respond to Stace's view, expressed in question 8?

8. Why can phenomenal generalizations not replace physical generalizations?

Further Readings

Ayer, A. J. *The Problem of Knowledge.* Baltimore: Penguin Books, 1962, Chap. 3. [A discussion of phenomenalism.]

Berkeley, George. *Three Dialogues Between Hylas and Philonous.* Indianapolis, Ind.: Hackett, 1979. [First published in 1713; a clear, systematic version of idealism by an important figure in the history of philosophy.]

Galilei, Galileo. ''Two Kinds of Properties.'' In A. Danto and S. Morgenbesser, eds., *Philosophy of Science.* Cleveland: Meridian Books, 1960, pp. 27–32. [A critique of common sense by the famous Renaissance scientist.]

Hospers, John. *An Introduction to Philosophical Analysis,* 2nd ed. Englewood Cliffs, N.J.: Prentice-Hall, 1967, pp. 493–565. [An overview of theories of perception.]

Moore, G. E. ''Proof of an External World.'' In *Philosophical Papers.* London: Allen and Unwin, 1959, pp. 126–148. [A defense of certain commonsense views of perception.]

Mundle, C. W. K. *Perception: Facts and Theories.* London: Oxford University Press, 1971. [An excellent defense of a modified commonsense view.]

Nagel, Ernest. *The Structure of Science.* New York: Harcourt Brace Jovanovich, 1961, Chap. 6. [A discussion of the existence of theoretical entities.]

Russell, Bertrand. *Our Knowledge of the External World.* London: Allen and Unwin, 1929. [A systematic development of Russell's view at one point in his life.]

Ryle, Gilbert. ''The World of Science and the Everyday World.'' In *Dilemmas.* Cambridge: Cambridge University Press, 1954, pp. 68–81. [Discusses certain supposed rivalries between science and common sense.]

Vesey, Godfrey. *Perception.* Garden City, N.Y.: Doubleday, 1971. [A criticism of causal theories of perception.]

PART THREE

FREEDOM, DETERMINISM, AND RESPONSIBILITY

PREVIEW

Almost all of us assume that we have free will, that we at least sometimes freely choose whether or not to perform a certain action. We think that neither the act which we performed nor any other was necessitated. And we think that even if I did act A, I could have done otherwise; I could have performed B, or C, etc.

All of these assumptions have come under attack in recent times—by psychologists, psychiatrists, physiologists, and others. Consider the following discussion from B. F. Skinner's novel, *Walden Two*:

> "Isn't it time we talked about freedom?" I said. "We parted a day or so ago on an agreement to let the question ring. It's time to answer, don't you think?"
>
> "My answer is simple enough," said Frazier. "I deny that freedom exists at all. I must deny it—or my program would be absurd. You can't have a science about a subject matter which hops capriciously about. Perhaps we can never *prove* that man isn't free; it's an assumption. But the increasing success of a science of behavior makes it more and more plausible."
>
> "On the contrary, a simple personal experience makes it untenable," said Castle. "The experience of freedom. I know that I'm free."
>
> "It must be quite consoling," said Frazier.[1]

In *Walden Two* Skinner sketches a modern utopia—one built on "appropriate" technology and a determined effort to utilize a science of behavioral engineering. In the dialog just quoted, the sarcastic Frazier is Skinner's spokesman. Castle, the philosopher, is the stubborn one. If you lack the dogmatic confidence of Frazier and Castle, and instead are pulled by

[1]B. F. Skinner, *Walden Two*, Toronto, 1948, p. 257.

each position, you have been teased by the philosophical problem of free will. Do we or do we not have free will? That is, do some or our actions result from our free choice? That is the crux of the problem.

The main problem of this part is often referred to as the problem of free will *versus* determinism or the free will/determinism controversy. We all have some sense of what free will is. What is meant by determinism?

Determinism, in its broadest form, is the view that every event in the universe has a cause. One consequence of determinism is: Since human acts are events, they too *all* have causes. Another consequence is: Every event—including every action—is in principle predictable.

But precisely how is the broad claim, 'Every event (including every act) has a cause' to be interpreted? While there are various views on this, the interpretation accepted by most, including most writers on the free will/determinism controversy, and especially those who deny free will, is:

For every event E, there is a set of antecedent conditions, C1 . . . Cn, which are sufficient to produce E to the exclusion of any other event. (Given C1 . . . Cn, E and only E can occur.)

Again, this holds for all actions too.

We have already referred to the characterization of determinism as the claim that 'Every event has a cause' as the broad sense of determinism—or of the word 'determinism'. Let us refer to the characterization just given as the strict sense. It will be important to bear this sense in mind since, again, it is this sense of determinism that is accepted by those who deny that we have free will.

The denial of determinism is called 'indeterminism'. Thus, indeterminism is the claim: Not every event has a cause. Some events have no cause. Thus, indeterminism is simply the negation of the broad sense of determinism.

The problem of free will would not grab us with such force were it not for the fact that the concept of freedom is intimately related to the concepts of responsibility and punishment. The following quotation is from a work by Clarence Darrow, the jurist best known for his defense of Thomas Scopes in the famous ''monkey trial'':

> Before any progress can be made in dealing with crime the world must fully realize that crime is only a part of conduct; that each act, criminal or otherwise, follows a cause; that given the same conditions the same result will follow forever and ever; that all punishment for the purpose of causing suffering, or growing out of hatred, is cruel and anti-social; that however much society may feel the need of confining the criminal, it must first of all understand that the act had an all-sufficient cause for which the individual was in no way responsible, and must find the cause of his conduct, and, so far as possible, remove the cause.[2]

---

[2]Clarence Darrow, *Crime: Its Causes and Treatment*, New York, 1922, p. 36.

This provocative passage deserves critical attention. But the present point is that it raises two very important issues which are intimately related to the free will problem. Thus, in addition to the previous question with which this part is concerned, we can add the following: Under what conditions, if any, is a person responsible for his or her actions? Under what conditions, if any, is the punishment of a person justifiable? The readings in this part discuss not only the free will problem but also the consequences of that problem for questions concerning responsibility and punishment.

Main Questions

This leads us to the main questions of this part. The primary question is:

1. Does (genuine) free will exist? Are any of our actions, even if not all, freely chosen by us? Or is everything we do determined by antecedent causes which are sufficient to bring about the actions we do, to the exclusion of all others?

As noted, there are two additional important and related questions:

2. Are we morally responsible for (any of) our actions?
3. Should criminals be punished for their crimes? If so, what is the motive for such punishment?

Answers

The main answers to the first question have, in some cases, been given different labels. For simplicity we settle on these:

1a. Hard determinism
1b. Soft determinism
1c. Self determinism

(1b. is also referred to as Compatibilism. 1c. is also referred to as the Agency Theory. It is a variant of what is known as Libertarianism.)

The answers which these labels designate are:

1a. Hard determinism: Since determinism (strict sense) is true, and since human actions are events, free will cannot exist.

Thus according to hard determinism: for any act A, there is a set of antecedent conditions sufficient to produce A to the exclusion of all other acts.

1b. Soft determinism: Determinism (strict sense) is true; nevertheless, some acts are free. Hence free will *does* exist. And it is compatible with determinism.

Which acts are free? According to soft determinism: Free acts are those for which the immediate cause is an internal, psychological state—a desire, willing, choosing, etc., within the agent. Hence unfree acts are those for which the immediate cause is external to the agent—and hence one in which the agent is compelled. Thus all events, including acts, are caused, but some acts are *also* free.

1c. Self-determinism: Determinism (strict sense) is false. For some events, *some human acts*, it does not hold. In those cases the acts result from our free choice. Hence free will *does* exist.

Thus, according to self-determinism: All events are caused. But for some events, *some human acts*, there is no set of antecedent conditions sufficient to produce a given act to the exclusion of all others. In such cases, I act out of free will.

Note: Such acts are caused, according to self-determinism. Hence indeterminism is false (in this view). But *I myself* am the cause. And hence determinism is false (in this view). Why?

Determinism claims that for every act A, there is a set of conditions C1 . . . Cn, such that given their occurrence, A must occur to the exclusion of all else. That is, determinism claims that since all acts are events, they must be produced by other *events*, namely the conditions C1 . . . Cn. But according to self-determinism that is false. Some acts, however few, are caused or initiated by *me, a person*, and not by a set of conditions or events. Thus, self-determinism is the denial of the *strict* interpretation of determinism.

We turn now to the related questions.

The answers to question (2) are obviously yes or no. Hence, with regard to the question of responsibility:

2a. Affirmative answer: Yes, we are responsible for at least many of our actions.

2b. Negative answer: No, we are not responsible for our actions, or at least, not for most or some of them.

With regard to question (3) of whether or not criminals should be punished, we again have:

3a. Affirmative answer: Yes.
3b. Negative answer: No.

Concerning the motive for such punishment, we find these main alternative answers:

Revenge or retribution: To get back at the criminal or give him his ''just due.''
Rehabilitation: To cure him of his sick behavior.
Deterrence: To prevent others from committing similar crimes.

Selections

In this part, the chief answers to our questions are represented as follows:

Question	Answer	Selection
(1)	(1a) Hard determinism	10, 13
(1)	(1b) Soft determinism	11
(1)	(1c) Self-determinism	12
(2)	(2b) Negative	10, 13
(2)	(2a) Affirmative	11, 12
(3)	(3b) Negative	14
(3)	(3a) Affirmative	15

(Selections 14 and 15 also deal with the proper motive for punishment.)

10 / The Delusion of Free Will

ROBERT BLATCHFORD

[I. INTRODUCTION]

The free will delusion has been a stumbling block in the way of human thought for thousands of years. Let us try whether common sense and common knowledge cannot remove it. . . .

The free will party* claims that man is responsible for his acts, because his will is free to choose between right and wrong. . . .

When a man says his will is free, he means that it is free of all control or interference: that it can overrule heredity and environment.

We reply that the will is ruled by heredity and environment.

The cause of all the confusion on this subject may be shown in a few words.

When the free will party says that man has a free will, they mean that he is free to act as he chooses to act.

There is no need to deny that. *But what causes him to choose?*

That is the pivot upon which the whole discussion turns.

The free will party seems to think of the will as something independent of the man, as something outside him. They seem to think that the will decides without the control of the man's reason.

If that were so, it would not prove the man responsible. "The will" would be responsible, and not the man. It would be as foolish to blame a man for the act of a "free" will as to blame a horse for the action of its rider.

But I am going to prove to my readers, by appeals to their common sense and common knowledge, that *the will is not free*; and that *it is ruled by heredity and environment*.

[II. REASONS GIVEN FOR FREE WILL AND CRITICISMS OF THEM]

1. To begin with, the average man will be against me. He [says he] knows that he chooses between two courses every hour, and often every minute, and he thinks his choice is free. But that is a delusion: His choice is not free. He can "choose," and does "choose." But he can only "choose" as his he-

*[The believers in genuine free will.—Eds.]

redity and his environment cause him to choose. He never did choose and never will choose except as his heredity and his environment—his temperament and his training—cause him to choose. And his heredity and his environment have fixed his choice before he makes it.

2. The average man says, "I know that I can act as I wish to act." But [I ask:] what causes him to wish?

The free will party says, "We know that a man can and does choose between two acts." But [I ask:] what settles the choice?

There is a cause for every wish, a cause for every "choice"; and every cause of every wish and choice arises from heredity, or from environment.

For a man acts always from *temperament*, which is *heredity*, or from *training*, which is *environment*.

And in cases where a man hesitates in his choice between two acts, the hesitation is due to a conflict between his temperament and his training, or, as some would express it, "between his desire and his conscience."

[*Example.*] A man is practicing at a target with a gun, when a rabbit crosses his line of fire. The man has his eye and his sights on the rabbit, and his finger on the trigger. The man's will is "free." If he presses the trigger the rabbit will be killed.

Now, how does the man decide whether or not he shall fire? He decides by feeling, and by reason.

He would like to fire, just to make sure that he could hit the mark. He would like to fire, because he would like to have the rabbit for supper. He would like to fire, because there is in him the old, old hunting instinct, to kill.

But the rabbit does not belong to him. He is not sure that he will not get into trouble if he kills it. Perhaps—if he is a very uncommon kind of man — he feels that it would be cruel and cowardly to shoot a helpless rabbit.

Well. The man's will is "free." He can fire if he likes; he can let the rabbit go if he likes. How will he decide? On what does his decision depend?

His decision depends upon the relative strength of his desire to kill the rabbit, and of his scruples about cruelty, and the law.*

Not only that, but, if we knew the man fairly well, we could guess how his "free" will would act before it acted. The average sporting Briton would kill the rabbit. But we know that there are men who would on no account shoot any harmless wild creature.

Broadly put, we may say that the sportsman would will to fire, and that the humanitarian would not will to fire.

Now, as both their wills are "free," it must be something outside the wills that makes the difference.

Well. The sportsman will kill, because he is a sportsman; the humanitarian will not kill, because he is a humanitarian.

*[Because he was hunting on someone else's private property.—Eds.]

And what makes one man a sportsman and another a humanitarian? Heredity and environment; temperament and training.

One man is merciful, another cruel, by nature; or one is thoughtful and the other thoughtless, by nature. That is a difference of heredity.

One may have been taught all his life that to kill wild things is "sport"; the other may have been taught that it is inhuman and wrong: That is a difference of environment.

Now, the man by nature cruel or thoughtless, who has been trained to think of killing animals as sport, becomes what we call a sportsman, because heredity and environment have made him a sportsman.

The other man's heredity and environment have made him a humanitarian.

The sportsman kills the rabbit because he is a sportsman, and he is a sportsman because heredity and environment have made him one.

That is to say the "free will" is really controlled by heredity and environment. . . .

3. But, it may be asked, how do you account for a man doing the thing he does not wish to do?

No man ever did a thing he did not wish to do. When there are two wishes the stronger rules.

[*Example.*] Let us suppose a case. A young woman gets two letters by the same post; one is an invitation to go with her lover to a concert, the other is a request that she will visit a sick child in the slums. The girl is very fond of music, and is rather afraid of the slums. She wishes to go to the concert, and to be with her lover; she dreads the foul street and the dirty home, and shrinks from the risk of measles or fever. But she goes to the sick child, and she foregoes the concert. Why?

Because her sense of duty is stronger than her self-love.

Now, her sense of duty is partly due to her nature—that is, to her heredity—but it is chiefly due to environment. Like all of us, this girl was born without any kind of knowledge, and with only the rudiments of a conscience. But she has been well taught, and the teaching is part of her environment.

We may say that the girl is "free" to act as she "chooses," but she *does* act as she has been *taught* that she *ought* to act. This teaching, which is part of her environment, controls her will.

We may say that a man is "free" to act as he chooses. He is free to act as *he* "chooses," but *he* will "choose" as heredity and environment cause *him* to choose. For heredity and environment have made him that which he is.

A man is said to be free to decide between two courses. But really he is only "free" to decide in accordance with his temperament and training. . . .

How, then, can we believe that free will is outside and superior to heredity and environment? . . .

4. "What! Cannot a man be honest if he choose?" Yes, if he "choose." But that is only another way of saying that he can be honest if his nature and his training lead him to choose honesty.

"What! Cannot I please myself whether I drink or refrain from drinking?" Yes. But that is only to say you will not drink because it pleases *you* to be sober. But it pleases another man to drink, because his desire for drink is strong, or because his self-respect is weak.

And you decide as you decide, and he decides as he decides, because you are *you* and he is *he*; and heredity and environment made you both that which you are.

And the sober man may fall upon evil days, and may lose his self-respect, or find the burden of his trouble greater than he can bear, and may fly to drink for comfort, or oblivion, and may become a drunkard. Has it not been often so?

And the drunkard may, by some shock, or some disaster, or some passion, or some persuasion, regain his self-respect, and may renounce drink, and lead a sober and useful life. Has it not been often so?

And in both cases the freedom of the will is untouched: It is the change in the environment that lifts the fallen up, and beats the upright down. . . .

The apostles of free will believe that all men's wills are free. But a man can only will that which he is able to will. And one man is able to will that which another man is unable to will. To deny this is to deny the commonest and most obvious facts of life. . . .

[III. ARGUMENTS AGAINST FREE WILL]

1. We all know that we can foretell the action of certain men in certain cases, because we know the men.

We know that under the same conditions Jack Sheppard* would steal and Cardinal Manning† would not steal. We know that under the same conditions the sailor would flirt with the waitress, and the priest would not; that the drunkard would get drunk, and the abstainer would remain sober. We know that Wellington‡ would refuse a bribe, that Nelson‡ would not run away, that Buonaparte§ would grasp at power, that Abraham Lincoln would be loyal to his country, that Torquemada** would not spare a heretic. Why? If the will is free, how can we be sure, before a test arises, how the will must act?

*[A famous criminal.—Eds.]
†[A cardinal of the Roman Catholic Church.—Eds.]
‡[British military men.—Eds.]
§[Napoleon.—Eds.]
**[A 15th century Spanish inquisitor.—Eds.]

Simply because we know that heredity and environment have so formed and molded men and women that under certain circumstances the action of their wills is certain.

Heredity and environment having made a man a thief, he will steal. Heredity and environment having made a man honest, he will not steal.

That is to say, heredity and environment have decided the action of the will, before the time has come for the will to act.

This being so—and we all know that it is so—what becomes of the sovereignty of the will?

Let any man that believes that he can "do as he likes" ask himself *why* he *likes*, and he will see the error of the theory of free will, and will understand why the will is the servant and not the master of the man: For the man is the product of heredity and environment, and these control the will.

[*Examples*] As we want to get this subject as clear as we can, let us take one or two familiar examples of the action of the will.

Jones and Robinson meet and have a glass of whiskey. Jones asks Robinson to have another. Robinson says, "No thank you, one is enough." Jones says, "All right: Have another cigarette." Robinson takes the cigarette. Now, here we have a case where a man refuses a second drink but takes a second smoke. Is it because he would like another cigarette but would not like another glass of whiskey? No. It is because he knows that it is *safer* not to take another glass of whiskey.

How does he know that whiskey is dangerous? He has learned it—from his environment.

"But he *could* have taken another glass if he wished."

But he could not wish to take another, because there was something he wished more strongly—to be safe.

And why did he want to be safe? Because he had learned—from his environment—that it was unhealthy, unprofitable, and shameful to get drunk. Because he had learned—from his environment—that it is easier to avoid forming a bad habit than to break a bad habit when formed. Because he valued the good opinion of his neighbors, and also his position and prospects.

These feelings and this knowledge ruled his will, and caused him to refuse the second glass. . . .

Now suppose Smith asks Williams to have another glass. Williams takes it, takes several, finally goes home—as he often goes home. Why?

Largely because drinking is a habit with him. And not only does the mind instinctively repeat an action but, in the case of drink, a physical craving is set up and the brain is weakened. It is easier to refuse the first glass than the second; it is easier to refuse the second than the third; and it is very much harder for a man to keep sober who has frequently gotten drunk.

So when poor Williams has to make his choice, he has habit against him, he has a physical craving against him, and he has a weakened brain to think with.

"But Williams could have refused the first glass."

No. Because in his case the desire to drink, or to please a friend, was stronger than his fear of the danger. Or he may not have been so conscious of the danger as Robinson was. He may not have been so well taught, or he may not have been so sensible, or he may not have been so cautious. So that his heredity and environment, his temperament and training, led him to take the drink, as surely as Robinson's heredity and environment led him to refuse it.

And now it is my turn to ask a question. If the will is "free," if conscience is a sure guide, how is it that the free will and the conscience of Robinson caused him to keep sober, while the free will and conscience of Williams caused him to get drunk?

Robinson's will was curbed by certain feelings which failed to curb the will of Williams. Because in the case of Williams the feelings were stronger on the other side.

It was the nature and the training of Robinson which made him refuse the second glass, and it was the nature and the training of Williams which made him drink the second glass.

What had free will to do with it? . . .

2. Those who exalt the power of the will, and belittle the power of environment, belie their words by their deeds.

For they would not send their children among bad companions or allow them to read bad books. They would not say the children have free will and therefore have power to take the good and leave the bad.

They know very well that evil environment has power to pervert the will, and that good environment has power to direct it properly.

They know that children may be made good or bad by good or evil training, and that the will follows the training.

That being so, they must also admit that the children of other people may be good or bad by training.

And if a child gets bad training, how can free will save it? Or how can it be blamed for being bad? It never had a chance to be good. That they know this is proved by their carefulness in providing their own children with better environment.

As I have said before, every church, every school, every moral lesson is a proof that preachers and teachers trust to good environment, and not to free will, to make children good.

In this, as in so many other matters, actions speak louder than words.

That, I hope, disentangles the many knots into which thousands of learned men have tied the simple subject of free will; and disposes of the claim that man is responsible because his will is free.

11 / The Problem of Free Will

W. T. STACE

[I. INTRODUCTION]

[A] great problem which the rise of scientific naturalism has created for the modern mind concerns the foundations of morality. . . .

I shall first discuss the problem of free will, for it is certain that if there is not free will there can be no morality. Morality is concerned with what men ought and ought not to do. But if a man has not freedom to choose what he will do, if whatever he does is done under compulsion, then it does not make sense to tell him that he ought not to have done what he did and that he ought to do something different. All moral precepts would in such case be meaningless. Also if he acts always under compulsion, how can he be held morally responsible for his actions? How can he, for example, be punished for what he could not help doing?

[II. THE PROBLEM OF FREE WILL]

It is to be observed that those learned professors of philosophy or psychology who deny the existence of free will do so only in their professional moments and in their studies and lecture rooms. For when it comes to doing anything practical, even of the most trivial kind, they invariably behave as if they and others were free. They inquire from you at dinner whether you will choose this dish or that dish. They will ask a child why he told a lie, and will punish him for not having chosen the way of truthfulness. All of which is inconsistent with a disbelief in free will. This should cause us to suspect that the problem is not a real one; and this, I believe, is the case. The dispute is merely verbal, and is due to nothing but a confusion about the meanings of words. It is what is now fashionably called a semantic problem.

How does a verbal dispute arise? Let us consider a case which, although it is absurd in the sense that no one would ever make the mistake which is involved in it, yet illustrates the principle which we shall have to use in the solution of the problem. Suppose that someone believed that the word ''man'' means a certain sort of five-legged animal; in short that ''five-legged animal'' is the correct *definition* of man. He might then look around the world, and rightly observing that there are no five-legged animals in it, he might proceed to deny the existence of men. This preposterous conclusion would have been reached because he was using an incorrect definition of "man." All you would have to do to show him his mistake would be to give him the correct definition; or at least to show him that his definition was wrong. Both the problem and its solution would, of course, be entirely verbal. The problem of free will, and its solution, I shall maintain, is verbal in exactly the same way. The problem has been created by the fact that learned men, especially philosophers, have assumed an incorrect definition of free will, and then finding that there is nothing in the world which answers to their definition have denied its existence. As far as logic is concerned, their conclusion is just as absurd as that of the man who denies the existence of men. The only difference is that the mistake in the latter case is obvious and crude, while the mistake which deniers of free will have made is rather subtle and difficult to detect.

Throughout the modern period, until quite recently, it was assumed, both by the philosophers who denied free will and by those who defended it, that *determinism is inconsistent with free will.* If a man's actions were wholly determined by chains of causes stretching back into the remote past, so that they could be predicted beforehand by a mind which knew all the causes, it was assumed that they could not in that case be free. This implies that a certain definition of actions done from free will was assumed, namely that they are actions *not* wholly determined by causes or predictable beforehand. Let us shorten this by saying that free will was defined as meaning indeterminism. This is the incorrect definition which has led to the denial of free will. As soon as we see what the true definition is we shall find that the question whether the world is deterministic, as Newtonian science implied, or in a measure indeterministic, as current physics teaches, is wholly irrelevant to the problem.

[III. PROOF OF FREE WILL]

Of course there is a sense in which one can define a word arbitrarily in any way one pleases. But a definition may nevertheless be called correct or incorrect. It is correct if it accords with a *common usage* of the word defined. It is incorrect if it does not. And if you give an incorrect definition, absurd and untrue results are likely to follow. For instance, there is nothing to prevent you from arbitrarily defining a man as a five-legged animal, but this is incorrect in the sense that it does not accord with the ordinary meaning of the word. Also it has the absurd result of leading to a denial of the existence of men. This shows that *common usage is the criterion for deciding whether a definition is correct or not.* And this is the principle which I shall apply to free will. I shall show that indeterminism is not what is meant by the phrase "free will" *as it is commonly used*. And I shall attempt to discover the correct definition by inquiring how the phrase is used in ordinary conversation.

Here are a few samples of how the phrase might be used in ordinary conversation. It will be noticed that they include cases in which the question whether a man acted with free will is asked in order to determine whether he was morally and legally responsible for his acts.

> *Jones* I once went without food for a week.
> *Smith* Did you do that of your own free will?
> *Jones* No. I did it because I was lost in a desert and could find no food.

But suppose that the man who had fasted was Mahatma Gandhi. The conversation might then have gone:

> *Gandhi* I once fasted for a week.
> *Smith* Did you do that of your own free will?
> *Gandhi* Yes. I did it because I wanted to compel the British Government to give India its independence.

Take another case. Suppose that I had stolen some bread, but that I was as truthful as George Washington. Then, if I were charged with the crime in court, some exchange of the following sort might take place:

> *Judge* Did you steal the bread of your own free will?
> *Stace* Yes. I stole it because I was hungry.

Or in different circumstances the conversation might run:

> *Judge* Did you steal of your own free will?
> *Stace* No. I stole because my employer threatened to beat me if I did not.

At a recent murder trial in Trenton some of the accused had signed confessions, but afterwards asserted that they had done so under police duress. The following exchange might have occurred:

> *Judge* Did you sign this confession of your own free will?
> *Prisoner* No. I signed it because the police beat me up.

Now suppose that a philosopher had been a member of the jury. We could imagine this conversation taking place in the jury room:

> *Foreman of the Jury* The Prisoner says he signed the confession because he was beaten, and not of his own free will.
> *Philosopher* This is quite irrelevant to the case. There is no such thing as free will.
> *Foreman* Do you mean to say that it makes no difference whether he signed because his conscience made him want to tell the truth or because he was beaten?
> *Philosopher* None at all. Whether he was caused to sign by a beating or by some desire of his own—the desire to tell the truth, for example—in either case his signing was causally determined, and therefore in neither case did he act of his own

free will. Since there is no such thing as free will, the question whether he signed of his own free will ought not to be discussed by us.

The foreman and the rest of the jury would rightly conclude that the philosopher must be making some mistake. What sort of a mistake could it be? There is only one possible answer. The philosopher must be using the phrase "free will" in some peculiar way of his own which is not the way in which men usually use it when they wish to determine a question of moral responsibility. That is, he must be using an incorrect definition of it as implying action not determined by causes.

Suppose a man left his office at noon, and was questioned about it. Then we might hear this:

> Jones Did you go out of your own free will?
> Smith Yes. I went out to get my lunch.

But we might hear:

> Jones Did you leave your office of your own free will?
> Smith No. I was forcibly removed by the police.

We have now collected a number of cases of actions which, in the ordinary usage of the English language, would be called cases in which people have acted of their own free will. We should also say in all these cases that they *chose* to act as they did. We should also say that they could have acted otherwise, if they had chosen. For instance, Mahatma Gandhi was not compelled to fast; he chose to do so. He could have eaten if he had wanted to. When Smith went out to get his lunch, he chose to do so. He could have stayed and done some more work, if he had wanted to. We have also collected a number of cases of the opposite kind. They are cases in which men were not able to exercise their free will. They had no choice. They were compelled to do as they did. The man in the desert did not fast of his own free will. He had no choice in the matter. He was compelled to fast because there was nothing for him to eat. And so with the other cases. It ought to be quite easy, by an inspection of these cases, to tell what we ordinarily mean when we say that a man did or did not exercise free will. We ought therefore to be able to extract from them the proper definition of the term. Let us put the cases in a table:

Free Acts	Unfree Acts
Gandhi fasting because he wanted to free India.	The man fasting in the desert because there was no food.
Stealing bread because one is hungry.	Stealing because one's employer threatened to beat one.
Signing a confession because one wanted to tell the truth.	Signing because the police beat one.
Leaving the office because one wanted one's lunch.	Leaving because forcibly removed.

It is obvious that to find the correct definition of free acts we must discover what characteristic is common to all the acts in the left-hand column, and is, at the same time, absent from all the acts in the right-hand column. This characteristic which all free acts have, and which no unfree acts have, will be the defining characteristic of free will.

Is being uncaused, or not being determined by causes, the characteristic of which we are in search? It cannot be, because although it is true that all the acts in the right-hand column have causes, such as the beating by the police or the absence of food in the desert, so also do the acts in the left-hand column. Mr. Gandhi's fasting was caused by his desire to free India, the man leaving his office by his hunger, and so on. Moreover there is no reason to doubt that these causes of the free acts were in turn caused by prior conditions, and that these were again the results of causes, and so on back indefinitely into the past. Any physiologist can tell us the causes of hunger. What caused Mr. Gandhi's tremendously powerful desire to free India is no doubt more difficult to discover. But it must have had causes. Some of them may have lain in peculiarities of his glands or brain, others in his past experiences, others in his heredity, others in his education. Defenders of free will have usually tended to deny such facts. But to do so is plainly a case of special pleading, which is unsupported by any scrap of evidence. The only reasonable view is that all human actions, both those which are freely done and those which are not, are either wholly determined by causes, or at least as much determined as other events in nature. It may be true, as the physicists tell us, that nature is not as deterministic as was once thought. But whatever degree of determinism prevails in the world, human actions appear to be as much determined as anything else. And if this is so, it cannot be the case that what distinguishes actions freely chosen from those which are not free is that the latter are determined by causes while the former are not. Therefore, being uncaused or being undetermined by causes must be an incorrect definition of free will.

What, then, is the difference between acts which are freely done and those which are not? What is the characteristic which is present to all the acts in the left-hand column and absent from all those in the right-hand column? Is it not obvious that, although both sets of actions have causes, the causes of those in the left-hand column are *of a different kind* from the causes of those in the right-hand column? The free acts are all caused by desires, or motives, or by some sort of internal psychological states of the agent's mind. The unfree acts, on the other hand, are all caused by physical forces or physical conditions outside the agent. Police arrest means physical force exerted from the outside; the absence of food in the desert is a physical condition of the outside world. We may therefore frame the following rough definitions. *Acts freely done are those whose immediate causes are psy-*

chological states in the agent. Acts not freely done are those whose immediate causes are states of affairs external to the agent. *

It is plain that if we define free will in this way, then free will certainly exists, and the philosopher's denial of its existence is seen to be what it is—nonsense. For it is obvious that all those actions of men which we should ordinarily attribute to the exercise of their free will, or of which we should say that they freely chose to do them, are in fact actions which have been caused by their own desires, wishes, thoughts, emotions, impulses, or other psychological states.

[IV. OBJECTIONS AND REPLIES]

In applying our definition we shall find that it usually works well, but that there are some puzzling cases which it does not seem exactly to fit. These puzzles can always be solved by paying careful attention to the ways in which words are used, and remembering that they are not always used consistently. I have space for only one example. Suppose that a thug threatens to shoot you unless you give him your wallet, and suppose that you do so. Do you, in giving him your wallet, do so of your own free will or not? If we apply our definition, we find that you acted freely, since the immediate cause of the action was not an actual outside force but the fear of death, which is a psychological cause. Most people, however, would say that you did not act of your own free will but under compulsion. Does this show that our definition is wrong? I do not think so. . . . In the case under discussion, though no actual force was used, the gun at your forehead so nearly approximated to actual force that we tend to say the case was one of compulsion. It is a borderline case.

Here is what may seem like another kind of puzzle. According to our view an action may be free though it could have been predicted beforehand with certainty. But suppose you told a lie, and it was certain beforehand that you would tell it. How could one then say, "You could have told the truth"? The answer is that it is perfectly true that you could have told the truth *if* you had wanted to. In fact you would have done so, for in that case

---

*[Note that these "definitions" are criteria for distinguishing between *acts* freely done and acts not freely done. They are not definitions of what free or free will and their opposites *mean*. Stace has indicated what the definitions of free and unfree are in the paragraph following his examples of conversations and in the examples themselves. It is clear that Stace's actual definitions of free and unfree are:

    free = uncompelled

    unfree = compelled

What, then, is he providing in these italicized sentences? Criteria for distinguishing *which* acts are genuinely free and which are unfree.—Eds.]

the causes producing your action, namely your desires, would have been different, and would therefore have produced different effects. It is a delusion that predictability and free will are incompatible. This agrees with common sense. For if, knowing your character, I predict that you will act honorably, no one would say when you do act honorably that this shows you did not do so of your own free will.

[V. THE COMPATIBILITY OF FREE WILL, DETERMINISM, AND RESPONSIBILITY]

Since free will is a condition of moral responsibility, we must be sure that our theory of free will gives a sufficient basis for it. To be held morally responsible for one's actions means that one may be justly punished or rewarded, blamed or praised, for them. But it is not just to punish a man for what he cannot help doing. How can it be just to punish him for an action which it was certain beforehand that he would do? We have not attempted to decide whether, as a matter of fact, all events, including human actions, are completely determined. For that question is irrelevant to the problem of free will. But if we assume for the purposes of argument that complete determinism is true, but that we are nevertheless free, it may then be asked whether such a deterministic free will is compatible with moral responsibility. For it may seem unjust to punish a man for an action which it could have been predicted with certainty beforehand that he would do.

But that determinism is incompatible with moral responsibility is as much a delusion as that it is incompatible with free will. You do not excuse a man for doing a wrong act because, knowing his character, you felt certain beforehand that he would do it. Nor do you deprive a man of a reward or prize because, knowing his goodness or his capabilities, you felt certain beforehand that he would win it.

Volumes have been written on the justification of punishment. But so far as it affects the question of free will, the essential principles involved are quite simple. The punishment of a man for doing a wrong act is justified either on the ground that it will correct his own character or on the ground that it will deter other people from doing similar acts. . . . The question, then, is how, if we assume determinism, punishment can correct character or deter people from evil actions.

Suppose that your child develops a habit of telling lies. You give him a mild beating. Why? Because you believe that his personality is such that the usual motives for telling the truth do not cause him to do so. You therefore supply the missing cause, or motive, in the shape of pain and the fear of future pain if he repeats his untruthful behavior. And you hope that a few treatments of this kind will condition him to the habit of truth telling, so that he will come to tell the truth without the infliction of pain. You assume that his actions are determined by causes, but that the usual causes of truth-telling do not in him produce their usual effects. You therefore supply him with an artificially injected motive, pain and fear, which you think will in the future cause him to speak truthfully.

The principle is exactly the same where you hope, by punishing one man, to deter others from wrong actions. You believe that the fear of punishment will cause those who might otherwise do evil to do well. . . .

Thus we see that moral responsibility is not only consistent with determinism but requires it. The assumption on which punishment is based is that human behavior is causally determined. If pain could not be a cause of truth-telling there would be no justification at all for punishing lies. If human actions and volitions were uncaused, it would be useless either to punish or reward, or indeed to do anything else to correct people's bad behavior. For nothing that you could do would in any way influence them. Thus moral responsibility would entirely disappear. If there were no determinism of human beings at all, their actions would be completely unpredictable and capricious, and therefore irresponsible. And this is in itself a strong argument against the common view of philosophers that free will means being undetermined by causes.

12 / Freedom and Determinism

RICHARD TAYLOR

I. FREEDOM

To say that it is, in a given instance, up to me what I do, is to say that I am in that instance *free* with respect to what I then do. Thus, I am sometimes free to move my finger this way and that, but not, certainly, to bend it backward or into a knot. But what does this mean?

It means, first, that there is no *obstacle* or *impediment* to my activity. Thus, there is sometimes no obstacle to my moving my finger this way and that, though there are obvious obstacles to my moving it far backward or into a knot. Those things, accordingly, that pose obstacles to my motions limit my freedom. . . .

Further, to say that it is, in a given instance, up to me what I do means that nothing *constrains* or *forces* me to do one thing rather than another.

Constraints are like obstacles, except that while the latter prevent, the former enforce. Thus, if my finger is being forcibly bent to the left—by a machine, for instance, or by another person, or by any force that I cannot overcome—then I am not free to move it this way and that. . . .

Obstacles and constraints, then, both obviously limit my freedom. To say I am free to perform some action thus means at least that there is no obstacle to my doing it, and that nothing constrains me to do otherwise.*

Now if we rest content with this observation, as many have, and construe free activity simply as activity that is unimpeded and unconstrained, there is evidently no inconsistency between affirming both the thesis of determinism and the claim that I am sometimes free. For to say that some action of mine is neither impeded nor constrained does not by itself imply that it is not causally determined. The absence of obstacles and constraints are mere negative conditions, and do not by themselves rule out the presence of positive causes. It might seem, then, that we can say of some of my actions that there are conditions antecedent to their performance so that no other actions were possible, and also that these actions were unobstructed and unconstrained. And to say that would logically entail that such actions were both causally determined and free.

II. SOFT DETERMINISM

It is this kind of consideration that has led many philosophers to embrace what is sometimes called soft determinism.† All versions of this theory have in common three claims, by means of which, it is naïvely supposed, a reconciliation is achieved between determinism and freedom. . . .

The three claims of soft determinism are (1) that the thesis of determinism is true, and that accordingly all human behavior, voluntary or other, like the behavior of all other things, arises from antecedent conditions, given which no other behavior is possible—in short, that all human behavior is caused and determined; (2) that voluntary behavior is nonetheless free to the extent that it is not externally constrained or impeded; and (3) that, in the absence of such obstacles and constraints, the causes of voluntary behavior are certain states, events, or conditions within the agent himself; namely, his own acts of will or volitions, choices, decisions, desires, and so on.

Thus, on this view, I am free, and therefore sometimes responsible for what I do, provided nothing prevents me from acting according to my own choice, desire, or volition, or constrains me to act otherwise.* There may, to

*[Note that this conception of free coincides with Stace's, although it is expressed differently.—Eds.]

†[Also known as compatibilism.—Eds.]

be sure, be other conditions for my responsibility—such as, for example, an understanding of the probable consequences of my behavior, and that sort of thing—but absence of constraint or impediment is, at least, one such condition. And, it is claimed, it is a condition that is compatible with the supposition that my behavior is caused—for it is, by hypothesis, caused by my own inner choices, desires, and volitions.*

III. THE REFUTATION OF THIS

The theory of soft determinism looks good at first . . .—but no great acumen is needed to discover that, far from solving any problem, it only camouflages it.

My free actions are those unimpeded and unconstrained motions that arise from my own inner desires, choices, and volitions; let us grant this provisionally. But now, whence arise those inner states that determine what my body shall do? Are they within my control or not? Having made my choice or decision and acted upon it, could I have chosen otherwise or not?

Here the determinist, hoping to surrender nothing and yet to avoid the problem implied in that question, bids us not to ask it; the question itself, he announces, is without meaning. . . .

But it is not nonsense to ask whether the causes of my actions—my own inner choices, decisions, and desires—are themselves caused. And of course they are, if determinism is true, for on that thesis everything is caused and determined. And if they are, then we cannot avoid concluding that, given the causal conditions of those inner states, I could not have decided, willed, chosen, or desired otherwise than I in fact did, for this is a logical consequence of the very definition of determinism. . . .

IV. EXAMPLES

Such is the dialectic of the problem. The easiest way to see the shadowy quality of soft determinism, however, is by means of examples.

Let us suppose that my body is moving in various ways, that these motions are not externally constrained or impeded, and that they are all exactly in accordance with my own desires, choices, or acts of will and whatnot. When I will that my arm should move in a certain way, I find it moving in that way, unobstructed and unconstrained. When I will to speak, my lips and tongue move, unobstructed and unconstrained, in a manner suitable to the formation of the words I choose to utter. Now given that this is a correct

*[As Stace said, these acts are caused by my internal, psychological states.—Eds.]

description of my behavior, namely, that it consists of the unconstrained and unimpeded motions of my body in response to my own volitions, then it follows that my behavior is free, on the soft determinist's definition of "free." It follows further that I am responsible for that behavior; or at least that if I am not, it is not from any lack of freedom on my part.

But if the fulfillment of these conditions renders my behavior free—that is to say, if my behavior satisfies the conditions of free action set forth in the theory of soft determinism—then my behavior will be less free if we assume further conditions that are perfectly consistent with those already satisfied.

We suppose further, accordingly, that while my behavior is entirely in accordance with my own volitions, and thus "free" in terms of the conception of freedom we are examining, my volitions themselves are caused. To make this graphic, we can suppose that an ingenious physiologist can induce in me any volition he pleases, simply by pushing various buttons on an instrument to which, let us suppose, I am attached by numerous wires. All the volitions I have in that situation are, accordingly, precisely the ones he gives me. By pushing one button, he evokes in me the volition to raise my hand; and my hand, being unimpeded, rises in response to that volition. By pushing another, he induces the volition in me to kick, and my foot, being unimpeded, kicks in response to that volition. We can even suppose that the physiologist puts a rifle in my hands, aims it at some passerby, and then, by pushing the proper button, evokes in me the volition to squeeze my finger against the trigger, whereupon the passer-by falls dead of a bullet wound.

This is the description of a man who is acting in accordance with his inner volitions, a man whose body is unimpeded and unconstrained in its motions, these motions being the effects of those inner states. It is hardly the description of a free and responsible agent. It is the perfect description of a puppet. To render a man your puppet, it is not necessary forcibly to constrain the motions of his limbs, after the fashion that real puppets are moved. A subtler but no less effective means of making a man your puppet would be to gain complete control of his inner states and ensure, as the theory of soft determinism does ensure, that his body will move in accordance with them.

The example is somewhat unusual, but it is no worse for that. It is perfectly intelligible, and it does appear to refute the soft determinist's conception of freedom. . . . The example can, moreover, be modified in perfectly realistic ways, so as to coincide with actual and familiar cases. One can, for instance, be given a compulsive desire for certain drugs, simply by having them administered to him over a course of time. Suppose, then, that I do, with neither my knowledge nor consent, thus become a victim of such a desire and act upon it. Do I act freely, merely by virtue of the fact that I am unimpeded in my quest for drugs? In a sense I do, surely, but I am hardly free with respect to whether or not I shall use drugs. I never chose to have the desire for them inflicted upon me.

Nor does it, of course, matter whether the inner states which allegedly prompt all my "free" activity are evoked in me by another agent or by perfectly impersonal forces. Whether a desire which causes my body to behave in a certain way is inflicted upon me by another person, for instance, or derived from hereditary factors, or indeed from anything at all, matters not the least. In any case, if it is in fact the cause of my bodily behavior, I cannot but act in accordance with it. Wherever it came from, whether from personal or impersonal origins, it was entirely caused or determined, and not within my control. Indeed, if determinism is true, as the theory of soft determinism holds it to be,* all those inner states which cause my body to behave in whatever ways it behaves must arise from circumstances that existed before I was born; for the chain of causes and effects is infinite, and none could have been the least different, given those that preceded.

V. SIMPLE INDETERMINISM

We might at first now seem warranted in simply denying determinism, and saying that, insofar as they are free, my actions are not caused; or that, if they are caused by my own inner states—my own desires, impulses, choices, volitions, and whatnot—then these, in any case, are not caused. . . .

Only the slightest consideration will show, however, that this simple denial of determinism has not the slightest plausibility. For let us suppose it is true, and that some of my bodily motions—namely, those that I regard as my free acts—are not caused at all or, if caused by my own inner states, that these are not caused. We shall thereby avoid picturing a puppet to be sure—but only by substituting something even less like a man; for the conception that now emerges is not that of a free man, but of an erratic and jerking phantom, without any rhyme or reason at all.

Suppose that my right arm is free, according to this conception; that is, that its motions are uncaused. It moves this way and that from time to time, but nothing causes these motions. Sometimes it moves forth vigorously, sometimes up, sometimes down; sometimes it just drifts vaguely about— these motions all being wholly free and uncaused. Manifestly I have nothing to do with them at all; they just happen, and neither I nor anyone can ever tell what this arm will be doing next. It might seize a club and lay it on the head of the nearest bystander, no less to my astonishment than to his.

---

*[Recall that soft determinism accepts determinism, in the strict interpretation, as true.— Eds.]

There will never be any point in asking why these motions occur, or in seeking any explanation of them, for under the conditions assumed there is no explanation. They just happen, from no causes at all.

This is no description of free, voluntary, or responsible behavior. Indeed, so far as the motions of my body or its parts are entirely uncaused, such motions cannot even be ascribed to me as my behavior in the first place, since I have nothing to do with them. The behavior of my arm is just the random motion of a foreign object. Behavior that is mine must be behavior that is within my control, but motions that occur from no causes are without the control of anyone. I can have no more to do with, and no more control over, the uncaused motions of my limbs than a gambler has over the motions of an honest roulette wheel. I can only, like him, idly wait to see what happens.

Nor does it improve things to suppose that my bodily motions are caused by my own inner states, so long as we suppose these to be wholly uncaused. The result will be the same as before. My arm, for example, will move this way and that, sometimes up and sometimes down, sometimes vigorously and sometimes just drifting about, always in response to certain inner states, to be sure. But since these are supposed to be wholly uncaused, it follows that I have no control over them and hence none over their effects. If my hand lays a club forcefully on the nearest bystander, we can indeed say that this motion resulted from an inner club-wielding desire of mine; but we must add that I had nothing to do with that desire, and that it arose, to be followed by its inevitable effect, no less to my astonishment than to his. Things like this do, alas, sometimes happen. We are all sometimes seized by compulsive impulses that arise we know not whither, and we do sometimes act upon these. But since they are far from being examples of free, voluntary, and responsible behavior, we need only to learn that behavior was of this sort to conclude that it was not free, voluntary, nor responsible. It was erratic, impulsive, and irresponsible.

VI. DETERMINISM* AND SIMPLE INDETERMINISM AS THEORIES

Both determinism and simple indeterminism are loaded with difficulties, and no one who has thought much on them can affirm either of them without some embarrassment. Simple indeterminism has nothing whatever to be said for it, except that it appears to remove the grossest difficulties of determinism, only, however, to imply perfect absurdities of its own. Determi-

*[In this section, Taylor presents criticisms of determinism and briefly, at the end, of indeterminism. It is important to understand that, by 'determinism' he means the strict interpretation. Note also that, since hard determinism bases its denial of free will on the acceptance of strict determinism, Taylor's criticism is also a criticism of hard determinism.—Eds.]

nism, on the other hand, is at least initially plausible. Men seem to have a natural inclination to believe in it; it is, indeed, almost required for the very exercise of practical intelligence. And beyond this, our experience appears always to confirm it, so long as we are dealing with everyday facts of common experience, as distinguished from the esoteric researches of theoretical physics. But determinism, as applied to human behavior, has implications which few men can casually accept, and they appear to be implications which no modification of the theory can efface.

Both theories, moreover, appear logically irreconcilable to the two items of data that we set forth at the outset; namely, (1) that my behavior is sometimes the outcome of my deliberation and (2) that in these and other cases it is sometimes up to me what I do. Since these were our data, it is important to see, as must already be quite clear, that these theories cannot be reconciled to them.*

[*Determinism*] I can deliberate only about my own future actions, and then only if I do not already know what I am going to do. If a certain nasal tickle warns me that I am about to sneeze, for instance, then I cannot deliberate whether to sneeze or not; I can only prepare for the impending convulsion. But if determinism is true, then there are always conditions existing antecedently to everything I do, sufficient for my doing just that, and such as to render it inevitable. If I can know what those conditions are and what behavior they are sufficient to produce, then I can in every such case know what I am going to do and cannot then deliberate about it.

By itself this only shows, of course, that I can deliberate only in ignorance of the causal conditions of my behavior; it does not show that such conditions cannot exist. It is odd, however, to suppose that deliberation should be a mere substitute for clear knowledge. Ignorance is a condition of speculation, inference, and guesswork, which have nothing whatever to do with deliberation. A prisoner awaiting execution may not know when he is going to die, and he may even entertain the hope of reprieve, but he cannot deliberate about this. He can only speculate, guess—and wait.

Worse yet, however, it now becomes clear that I cannot deliberate about what I am going to do if it is even possible for me to find out in advance, whether I do in fact find out in advance or not. I can deliberate only with the view to deciding what to do, to making up my mind; and this is impossible if I believe that it could be inferred what I am going to do from conditions already existing, even though I have not made that inference myself. If I believe that what I am going to do has been rendered inevitable by con-

*[These items were originally mentioned in a section not reprinted in this selection. He there writes, "there are . . . two things about myself of which I feel quite certain . . . The first is that I deliberate, with the view of making a decision; a decision, namely, to do this thing or that. And the second is that whether or not I deliberate about what to do, it is sometimes up to me what I do . . . We must . . . if we ever hope to be wiser, adjust our theories to our data and not try to adjust our data to our theories." (*Metaphysics*, New York: Prentice-Hall, 1963), p. 37.—Eds.]

ditions already existing, and could be inferred by anyone having the requisite sagacity, then I cannot try to decide whether to do it or not, for there is simply nothing left to decide. I can at best only guess or try to figure it out myself or, all prognostics failing, I can wait and see; but I cannot deliberate. I deliberate in order to *decide* what *to* do, not to *discover* what it is that I am *going* to do. But if determinism is true, then there are always antecedent conditions sufficient for everything that I do, and this can always be inferred by anyone having the requisite sagacity; that is, by anyone having a knowledge of what those conditions are and what behavior they are sufficient to produce.

This suggests what in fact seems quite clear, that determinism cannot be reconciled with our second datum either, to the effect that it is sometimes up to me what I am going to do. For if it is ever really up to me whether to do this thing or that, then, as we have seen, each alternative course of action must be such that I can do it; not that I can do it in some abstruse or hypothetical sense of "can"; nor that I could do it if only something were true that is not true; but in the sense that it is then and there within my power to do it. But this is never so, if determinism is true, for on the very formulation of that theory whatever happens at any time is the only thing that can then happen, given all that precedes it. It is simply a logical consequence of this that whatever I do at any time is the only thing I can then do, given the conditions that precede my doing it. Nor does it help in the least to interpose, among the causal antecedents of my behavior, my own inner states, such as my desires, choices, acts of will, and so on. For even supposing these to be always involved in voluntary behavior—which is highly doubtful in itself—it is a consequence of determinism that these, whatever they are at any time, can never be other than what they then are. Every chain of causes and effects, if determinism is true, is infinite. This is why it is not now up to me whether I shall a moment hence be male or female. The conditions determining my sex have existed through my whole life, and even prior to my life. But if determinism is true, the same holds of anything that I ever am, ever become, or ever do. It matters not whether we are speaking of the most patent facts of my being, such as my sex; or the most subtle, such as my feelings, thoughts, desires, or choices. Nothing could be other than it is, given what was; and while we may indeed say, quite idly, that something—some inner state of mine, for instance—*could* have been different, had only something *else* been different, any consolation of this thought evaporates as soon as we add that whatever would have to have been different could not have been different.

[*Indeterminism*] It is even more obvious that our data cannot be reconciled to the theory of simple indeterminism. I can deliberate only about my own actions; this is obvious. But the random, uncaused motion of any body whatever, whether it be a part of my body or not, is no action of mine and nothing that is within my power. I might try to guess what these motions will be, just as I might try to guess how a roulette wheel will behave, but I cannot deliberate about them or try to decide what they shall be, simply because these things are not up to me. Whatever is not caused by anything is not caused by me, and nothing could be more plainly inconsistent with saying that it is nevertheless up to me what it shall be.

VII. THE THEORY OF AGENCY [SELF-DETERMINISM]

The only conception of action that accords with our data is one according to which men—and perhaps some other things too—are sometimes, but of course not always, self-determining beings; that is, beings which are sometimes the causes of their own behavior. In the case of an action that is free, it must be such that it is caused by the agent who performs it, but such that no antecedent conditions were sufficient for his performing just that action. In the case of an action that is both free and rational, it must be such that the agent who performed it did so for some reason, but this *reason* cannot have been the *cause* of it.

[*Virtue of the Theory*] Now this conception fits what men take themselves to be; namely, beings who act, or who are agents, rather than things that are merely acted upon, and whose behavior is simply the causal consequence of conditions which they have not wrought. When I believe that I have done something, I do believe that it was I who caused it to be done, I who made something happen, and not merely something within me, such as one of my own subjective states, which is not identical with myself. If I believe that something not identical with myself was the cause of my behavior—some event wholly external to myself, for instance, or even one internal to myself, such as a nerve impulse, volition, or whatnot—then I cannot regard that behavior as being an act of mine, unless I further believe that I was the cause of that external or internal event. My pulse, for example, is caused and regulated by certain conditions existing within me, and not by myself. I do not, accordingly, regard this activity of my body as my action, and would be no more tempted to do so if I became suddenly conscious within myself of those conditions or impulses that produce it. This is behavior with which I have nothing to do, behavior that is not within my immediate control, behavior that is not only not free activity, but not even the activity of an agent to begin with; it is nothing but a mechanical reflex. Had I never learned that my very life depends on this pulse beat, I would regard it with complete indifference, as something foreign to me, like the oscillations of a clock pendulum that I idly contemplate.

[*Drawbacks*] Now this conception of activity, and of an agent who is the cause of it, involves two rather strange metaphysical notions that are never applied elsewhere in nature. The first is that of a *self* or *person*—for example, a man—who is not merely a collection of things or events, but a substance and a self-moving being. For on this view it is a man himself, and not merely some part of him or something within him, that is the cause of his own activity. Now we certainly do not know that a man is anything more than an assemblage of physical things and processes, which act in accordance with those laws that describe the behavior of all other physical things and processes. Even though a man is a living being, of enormous complexity, there is nothing, apart from the requirements of this theory, to suggest that his behavior is so radically different in its origin from that of other physical objects, or that an understanding of it must be sought in some metaphysical realm wholly different from that appropriate to the understanding of nonliving things.

Second, this conception of activity involves an extraordinary conception of *causation*, according to which an agent, which is a substance and not an event, can nevertheless be the cause of an event. Indeed, if he is a free agent then he can, on this conception, cause an event to occur—namely, some act of his own—without anything else causing him to do so. This means that an agent is sometimes a cause, without being an antecedent sufficient condition; for if I affirm that I am the cause of some act of mine, then I am plainly not saying that my very existence is sufficient for its occurrence, which would be absurd. If I say that my hand causes my pencil to move, then I am saying that the motion of my hand is, under the other conditions then prevailing, sufficient for the motion of the pencil. But if I then say that I cause my hand to move, I am not saying anything remotely like this, and surely not that the motion of my self is sufficient for the motion of my arm and hand, since these are the only things about me that are moving.

This conception of the causation of events by beings or substances that are not events is, in fact, so different from the usual philosophical conception of a cause that it should not even bear the same name, for "being a cause" ordinarily just means "being an antecedent sufficient condition or set of conditions." Instead, then, of speaking of agents as *causing* their own acts, it would perhaps be better to use another word entirely, and say, for instance, that they *originate* them, *initiate* them, or simply that they *perform* them.

Now this is on the face of it a dubious conception of what a man is. Yet it is consistent with our data, reflecting the presuppositions of deliberation, and appears to be the only conception that is consistent with them, as determinism and simple indeterminism are not. The theory of agency avoids the absurdities of simple indeterminism by conceding that human behavior is caused, while at the same time avoiding the difficulties of determinism by denying that every chain of causes and effects is infinite. Some such causal chains, on this view, have beginnings, and they begin with agents themselves. Moreover, if we are to suppose that it is sometimes up to me what I do, and understand this in a sense which is not consistent with determinism, we must suppose that I am an agent or a being who initiates his own actions, sometimes under conditions which do not determine what action he shall perform. Deliberation becomes, on this view, something that is not only possible but quite rational, for it does make sense to deliberate about activity that is truly my own and that depends in its outcome upon me as its author, and not merely upon something more or less esoteric that is supposed to be intimately associated with me, such as my thoughts, volitions, choices, or whatnot.

One can hardly affirm such a theory of agency with complete comfort, however, and wholly without embarrassment, for the conception of men and their powers which is involved in it is strange indeed, if not positively mysterious. In fact, one can hardly be blamed here for simply denying our data outright, rather than embracing this theory to which they do most certainly point. Our data—to the effect that men do sometimes deliberate before acting, and that when they do, they presuppose among other things that it is up to them what they are going to do—rest upon nothing more than fairly common consent. These data might simply be illusions. It might in fact be that no man ever deliberates, but only imagines that he does, that from pure conceit he supposes himself to be the master of his behavior and the author of his acts. . . .

These are, then, dubitable conceptions, despite their being so well implanted in the commonsense of mankind. . . . Perhaps here, as elsewhere in metaphysics, we should be content with discovering difficulties, with seeing what is and what is not consistent with such convictions as we happen to have, and then drawing such satisfaction as we can from the realization that, no matter where we begin, the world is mysterious and the men who try to understand it are even more so. This realization can, with some justification, make one feel wise, even in the full realization of his ignorance.

13 / Free-Will and Psychoanalysis

JOHN HOSPERS

[Note: In the opening paragraph, the author makes reference to Schlick (a philosopher). M. Schlick held the same position as that of W. T. Stace. He too tried to show that free will and determinism are compatible and co-exist. And he did it by arguments similar to Stace's. Hence whenever you find the name 'Schlick,' you may substitute 'Stace'.]

I. [CRITICISM OF SOFT DETERMINISM]

Schlick's analysis is indeed clarifying and helpful to those who have fallen victim to the confusions he exposes—and this probably includes most persons in their philosophical growing-pains. But *is* this the end of the matter? Is it true that all acts, though caused, are free as long as they are not compelled in the sense which he specifies? May it not be that, while the identification of "free" with "uncompelled" is acceptable, the area of compelled acts is vastly greater than he or most other philosophers have ever suspected? . . . We remember statements about human beings being pawns of their early environment, victims of conditions beyond their control, the result of causal influences stemming from their parents, and the like, and we ponder and ask, "Still, are we really free?" Is there not something in what generations of sages have said about man being fettered? Is there not perhaps something too facile, too sleight-of-hand, in Schlick's cutting of the Gordian knot? For example, when a metropolitan newspaper headlines an article with the words "Boy Killer Is Doomed Long Before He Is Born,"[1] and then goes on to describe how a twelve-year-old boy has been sentenced to prison for the murder of a girl, and how his parental background includes records of drunkenness, divorce, social maladjustment, and paresis, are we still to say that his act, though voluntary and assuredly *not* done at the point of a gun, is free? The boy has early displayed a tendency toward sadistic activity to hide an underlying masochism and "prove that he's a man"; being coddled by his mother only worsens this tendency until, spurned by a girl in his attempt on her, he kills her—not simply in a fit of anger, but calculatingly, deliberately. Is he free in respect of his criminal act, or for that matter in most of the acts of his life? Surely to ask this

[1]*New York Post*, Tuesday, May 18, 1948, p. 4.

[126]

question is to answer it in the negative. Perhaps I have taken an extreme case; but it is only to show the superficiality of the Schlick analysis the more clearly. Though not everyone has criminotic tendencies, everyone has been molded by influences which in large measure at least determine his present behavior; he is literally the product of these influences, stemming from periods prior to his "years of discretion," giving him a host of character traits that he cannot change now even if he would. So obviously does what a man is depend upon how a man comes to be, that it is small wonder that philosophers and sages have considered man far indeed from being the master of his fate. It is not as if man's will were standing high and serene above the flux of events that have molded him; it is itself caught up in this flux, itself carried along on the current. An act is free when it is determined by the man's character, say moralists; but what if the most decisive aspects of his character were already irrevocably acquired before he could do anything to mold them? What if even the degree of will power available to him in shaping his habits and disciplining himself now to overcome the influence of his early environment is a factor over which he has no control? What are we to say of this kind of "freedom"? Is it not rather like the freedom of the machine to stamp labels on cans when it has been devised for just that purpose? Some machines can do so more efficiently than others, but only because they have been better constructed.

II. [THE EVIDENCE FROM PSYCHOANALYSIS]

It is not my purpose here to establish this thesis in general, but only in one specific respect which has received comparatively little attention, namely, the field referred to by psychiatrists as that of unconscious motivation. In what follows I shall restrict my attention to it because it illustrates as clearly as anything the points I wish to make.

Let me try to summarize very briefly the psychoanalytic doctrine on this point.[2] The conscious life of the human being, including the conscious decisions and volitions, is merely a mouthpiece for the unconscious—not directly for the enactment of unconscious drives, but of the compromise between unconscious drives and unconscious reproaches. There is a Big Three behind the scenes which the automaton called the conscious personality

---

[2]I am aware that the theory presented below is not accepted by all practicing psychoanalysts. Many non-Freudians would disagree with the conclusions presented below. But I do not believe that this fact affects my argument, as long as the concept of unconscious motivation is accepted. I am aware, too, that much of the language employed in the following descriptions is animistic and metaphorical; but as long as I am presenting a view I would prefer to "go the whole hog" and present it in its most dramatic form. The theory can in any case be made clearest by the use of such language, just as atomic theory can often be made clearest to students with the use of models.

carries out: The id, an "eternal gimme," presents its wish and demands its immediate satisfaction; the super-ego says no to the wish immediately upon presentation; and the unconscious ego, the mediator between the two, tries to keep peace by means of compromise.[3]

To go into examples of the functioning of these three "bosses" would be endless; psychoanalytic case books supply hundreds of them. The important point for us to see in the present context is that *it is the unconscious that determines what the conscious impulse and the conscious action shall be.* . . .

We have always been conscious of the fact that we are not masters of our fate in every respect—that there are many things which we cannot do, that nature is more powerful than we are, that we cannot disobey laws without danger of reprisals, etc. We have become "officially" conscious, too, though in our private lives we must long have been aware of it, that we are not free with respect to the emotions that we feel—whom we love or hate, what types we admire, and the like. More lately still we have been reminded that there are unconscious motivations for our basic attractions and repulsions, our compulsive actions or inabilities to act. But what is not welcome news is that our very acts of volition, and the entire train of deliberations leading up to them, are but facades for the expression of unconscious wishes, or rather, unconscious compromises and defenses.

[1.] A man is faced by a choice: Shall he kill another person or not? Moralists would say, "Here is a free choice—the result of deliberation, an action consciously entered into." And yet, though the agent himself does not know it, and has no awareness of the forces that are at work within him, his choice is already determined for him: His conscious will is only an instrument, a slave, in the hands of a deep unconscious motivation which determines his action. If he has a great deal of what the analyst calls "freefloating guilt," he will not; but if the guilt is such as to demand immediate absorption in the form of self-damaging behavior, this accumulated guilt will have to be discharged in some criminal action. The man himself does not know what the inner clockwork is; he is like the hands on the clock, thinking they move freely over the face of the clock.

[2.] A woman has married and divorced several husbands. Now she is faced with a choice for the next marriage: shall she marry Mr. A, or Mr. B, or nobody at all? She may take considerable time to "decide" this question and her decision may appear as a final triumph of her free will. Let us assume that A is a normal, well-adjusted, kind and generous man while B is a leech, an impostor, one who will become entangled constantly in quarrels with her. If she belongs to a certain classifiable psychological type, she will inevitably choose B, and she will do so even if her previous husbands have resembled B, so that one would think that she "had learned from experi-

---

[3]This view is very clearly developed in Edmund Bergler, *Divorce Won't Help,* especially Chapter I.

ence." Consciously, she will of course "give the matter due consideration," etc., etc. To the psychoanalyst all this is irrelevant chaff in the wind—only a camouflage for the inner workings about which she knows nothing consciously. If she is of a certain kind of masochistic strain, as exhibited in her previous set of symptoms, she *must* choose B: Her superego, always out to maximize the torment in the situation, seeing what dazzling possibilities for self-damaging behavior are promised by the choice of B, compels her to make the choice she does, and even to conceal the real basis of the choice behind an elaborate facade of rationalization. . . .

[3.] A man has wash-compulsion. He must be constantly washing his hands—he uses up perhaps 400 towels a day. Asked why he does this, he says, "I need to, my hands are dirty"; and if it is pointed out to him that they are not really dirty, he says, "They feel dirty anyway, I feel better when I wash them." So once again he washes them. He "freely decides" every time; he feels that he must wash them, he deliberates for a moment perhaps, but he always ends by washing them. What he does not see, of course, are the invisible wires inside him pulling him inevitably to do the thing he does: The infantile id-wish concerns preoccupation with dirt, the super-ego charges him with this, and the terrified ego must respond, "No, I don't like dirt, see how clean I like to be, look how I wash my hands!"

Let us see what further "free acts" the same patient engages in (this is an actual case history): He is taken to a concentration camp and given the worst of treatment by the Nazi guards. In the camp he no longer chooses to be clean, does not even try to be—on the contrary, his choice is now to wallow in filth as much as he can. All he is aware of now is a disinclination to be clean, and every time he must choose he chooses not to be. Behind the scenes, however, another drama is being enacted: The super-ego, perceiving that enough torment is being administered from the outside, can afford to cease pressing its charges in this quarter—the outside world is doing the torturing now, so the super-ego is relieved of the responsibility. Thus, the ego is relieved of the agony of constantly making terrified replies in the form of washing to prove that the super-ego is wrong. The defense no longer being needed, the person slides back into what is his natural predilection anyway, for filth. This becomes too much even for the Nazi guards: They take hold of him one day, saying "We'll teach you how to be clean!" drag him into the snow, and pour bucket after bucket of icy water over him until he freezes to death. Such is the end-result of an original wish, caught in the machinations of a destroying super-ego.

[4.] Let us take, finally, a less colorful, more everyday example. A student at a university, possessing wealth, charm, and all that is usually considered essential to popularity, begins to develop the following personality-pattern: Although well taught in the graces of social conversation, he always makes a *faux pas* somewhere, and always in the worst possible situation; to his friends he makes cutting remarks which hurt deeply—and always apparently aimed in such a way as to hurt the most: A remark that would not hurt A but would hurt B he invariably makes to B rather than to A, and so on. None of this is conscious. Ordinarily he is considerate of people, but he contrives always (unconsciously) to impose on just those friends who would resent it most, and at just the times when he should know that he should not impose: At 3 o'clock in the morning, without forewarning, he phones a friend in a nearby city demanding to stay at his apartment for the weekend; naturally the friend is offended, but the person himself is not aware that he has provoked the grievance ("common sense" suffers a temporary eclipse when the neurotic pattern sets in, and one's intelligence, far from being of help in such a situation, is used in the interest of the neurosis), and when the friend is cool to him the next time they meet, he wonders why and feels unjustly treated. Aggressive behavior on his part invites resentment and aggression in turn, but all that he consciously sees is others' behavior toward him—and he considers himself the innocent victim of an unjustified "persecution."

Each of these acts is, from the moralist's point of view, free: He chose to phone his friend at 3 a.m.; he chose to make the cutting remark that he did, etc. What he does not know is that an ineradicable masochistic pattern has set in. His unconscious is far more shrewd and clever than is his conscious intellect; it sees with uncanny accuracy just what kind of behavior will damage him most, and unerringly forces him into that behavior. Consciously, the student "doesn't know why he did it"—he gives different "reasons" at different times, but they are all, once again, rationalizations cloaking the unconscious mechanism which propels him willynilly into actions which his "common sense" eschews.

The more of this sort of thing one observes, the more he can see what the psychoanalyst means when he talks about *the illusion of freedom*. And the more of a psychiatrist one becomes, the more he is overcome with a sense of what an illusion this free-will can be. In some kinds of cases most of us can see it already: It takes no psychiatrist to look at the epileptic and sigh with sadness at the thought that soon this person before you will be as one possessed, not the same thoughtful intelligent person you knew. But people are not aware of this in other contexts, for example when they express surprise at how a person whom they have been so good to could treat them so badly. Let us suppose that you help a person financially or morally or in some other way, so that he is in your debt; suppose further that he is one of the many neurotics who unconsciously identify kindness with weakness and aggression with strength. Then he will unconsciously take your kindness to him as weakness and use it as the occasion for enacting some aggression against you. He can't help it, he may regret it himself later; still, he will be driven to do it. If we gain a little knowledge of psychiatry, we can look at him with pity, that a person otherwise so worthy should be so unreliable—but we will exercise realism too, and be aware that there are some types of people that you cannot be good to in "free" acts of their conscious volition; they will use your own goodness against you. . . .

We talk about free-will, and we say, for example, the person is free to do so-and-so if he can do so *if* he wants to—and we forget that his wanting to is itself caught up in the stream of determinism, that unconscious forces drive him into the wanting or not wanting to do the thing in question. The analogy of the puppet whose motions are manipulated from behind by invisible wires, or better still, by springs inside, is a telling one at almost every point.

And the glaring fact is that it all started so early, before we knew what was happening. The personality-structure is inelastic after the age of five, and comparatively so in most cases after the age of three. Whether one acquires a neurosis or not is determined by that age—and just as involuntarily as if it had been a curse of God. If, for example, a masochistic pattern was set up, under pressure of hyper-narcissism combined with real or fancied infantile deprivation, then the masochistic snowball was on its course downhill long before we or anybody else knew what was happening, and long before anyone could do anything about it. To speak of human beings as "puppets" in such a context is no idle metaphor, but a stark rendering of a literal fact: Only the psychiatrist knows what puppets people really are; and it is no wonder that the protestations of philosophers that "the act which is the result of a volition, a deliberation, a conscious decision, is free" leave these persons, to speak mildly, somewhat cold.

But, one may object, all the states thus far described have been abnormal, neurotic ones. The well-adjusted (normal) person at least is free.

Leaving aside the question of how clearly and on what grounds one can distinguish the neurotic from the normal, let me use an illustration of a proclivity that everyone would call normal, namely, the decision of a man to support his wife and possibly a family, and consider briefly its genesis, according to psychoanalytic accounts.[4]

Every baby comes into the world with a full-fledged case of megalomania—interested only in himself, acting as if believing that he is the center of the universe and that others are present only to fulfill his wishes, and furious when his own wants are not satisfied immediately no matter for what reason. Gratitude, even for all the time and worry and care expended on him by the mother, is an emotion entirely foreign to the infant, and as he grows older it is inculcated in him only with the greatest difficulty; his natural tendency is to assume that everything that happens to him is due to himself, except for denials and frustrations, which are due to the "cruel, denying" outer world, in particular the mother; and that he owes nothing to anyone, is dependent on no one. This omnipotence-complex, or illusion of nondependence, has been called the "autarchic fiction." Such a conception of the world is actually fostered in the child by the conduct of adults,

---

[4]E.g., Edmund Bergler, *The Battle of the Conscience*, Chapter I.

who automatically attempt to fulfill the infant's every wish concerning nourishment, sleep, and attention. The child misconceives causality and sees in these wish-fulfillments not the results of maternal kindness and love, but simply the result of his own omnipotence.

This fiction of omnipotence is gradually destroyed by experience, and its destruction is probably the deepest disappointment of the early years of life. First of all, the infant discovers that he is the victim of organic urges and necessities: hunger, defecation, urination. More important, he discovers that the maternal breast, which he has not previously distinguished from his own body (he has not needed to, since it was available when he wanted it), is not a part of himself after all, but of another creature upon whom he is dependent. He is forced to recognize this, e.g., when he wants nourishment and it is at the moment not present; even a small delay is most damaging to the "autarchic fiction." Most painful of all is the experience of weaning, probably the greatest tragedy in every baby's life, when his dependence is most cruelly emphasized; it is a frustrating experience because what he wants is no longer there at all; and if he has been able to some extent to preserve the illusion of nondependence heretofore, he is not able to do so now—it is plain that the source of his nourishment is not dependent on him, but he on it. The shattering of the autarchic fiction is a great disillusionment to every child, a tremendous blow to his ego which he will, in one way or another, spend the rest of his life trying to repair. How does he do this?

First of all, his reaction to frustration is anger and fury; and he responds by kicking, biting, etc., the only way he knows. But he is motorically helpless, and these measures are ineffective, and only serve to emphasize his dependence the more. Moreover, against such responses of the child the parental reaction is one of prohibition, often involving deprivation of attention and affection. Generally the child soon learns that this form of rebellion is profitless, and brings him more harm than good. He wants to respond to frustration with violent aggression, and at the same time learns that he will be punished for such aggression, and that in any case the latter is ineffectual. What face-saving solution does he find? Since he must "face facts," since he must in any case "conform" if he is to have any peace at all, he tries to make it seem as if he himself is the source of the commands and prohibitions: The *external* prohibitive force is *internalized*—and here we have the origin of conscience. By making the prohibitive agency seem to come from within himself, the child can "save face"—as if saying, "The prohibition comes from within me, not from outside, so I'm not subservient to external rule, I'm only obeying rules I've set up myself," and thus to some extent saving the autarchic fiction, and at the same time avoiding unpleasant consequences directed against himself by complying with parental commands.

Moreover, the boy[5] has unconsciously never forgiven the mother for his dependence on her in early life, for nourishment and all other things. It has upset his illusion of nondependence. These feelings have been repressed and are not remembered; but they are acted out in later life in many ways— e.g., in the constant deprecation man has for woman's duties such as cooking and housework of all sorts ("All she does is stay home and get together a few meals, and she calls that work"), and especially in the man's identification with the mother in his sex experiences with women. By identifying with someone one cancels out in effect the person with whom he identifies—replacing that person, unconsciously denying his existence, and the man, identifying with his early mother, playing the active role in "giving" to his wife as his mother has "given" to him, is in effect the denial of his mother's existence, a fact which is narcissistically embarrassing to his ego because it is chiefly responsible for shattering his autarchic fiction. In supporting his wife, he can unconsciously deny that his mother gave to him, and that he was dependent on her giving. Why is it that the husband plays the provider, and wants his wife to be dependent on no one else, although twenty years before he was nothing but a parasitic baby? This is a face-saving device on his part: He can act out the reasoning, "See, I'm not the parasitic baby, on the contrary I'm the provider, the giver." His playing the provider is a constant face-saving device, to deny his early dependence which is so embarrassing to his ego. It is no wonder that men generally dislike to be reminded of their babyhood, when they were dependent on women.

Thus, we have here a perfectly normal adult reaction which is unconsciously motivated. The man "chooses" to support a family—and his choice is as unconsciously motivated as anything could be. (I have described here only the "normal" state of affairs, uncomplicated by the well-nigh infinite number of variations that occur in actual practice.)

III. [THE IMPLICATIONS FOR RESPONSIBILITY]

Now, what of the notion of responsibility? What happens to it on our analysis?

Let us begin with an example, not a fictitious one. A woman and her two-year-old baby are riding on a train to Montreal in mid-winter. The child is ill. The woman wants badly to get to her destination. She is, unknown to herself, the victim of a neurotic conflict whose nature is irrelevant here ex-

---

[5]The girl's development after this point is somewhat different. Society demands more aggressiveness of the adult male, and hence there are more super-ego strictures on tendencies toward passivity in the male; accordingly his defenses must be stronger.

cept for the fact that it forces her to behave aggressively toward the child, partly to spite her husband whom she despises and who loves the child, but chiefly to ward off super-ego charges of masochistic attachment. Consciously she loves the child, and when she says this she says it sincerely, but she must behave aggressively toward it nevertheless, just as many children love their mothers but are nasty to them most of the time in neurotic pseudo-aggression. The child becomes more ill as the train approaches Montreal; the heating system of the train is not working, and the conductor pleads with the woman to get off the train at the next town and get the child to a hospital at once. The woman refuses. Soon after, the child's condition worsens, and the mother does all she can to keep it alive, without, however, leaving the train, for she declares that it is absolutely necessary that she reach her destination. But before she gets there the child is dead. After that, of course, the mother grieves, blames herself, weeps hysterically, and joins the church to gain surcease from the guilt that constantly overwhelms her when she thinks of how her aggressive behavior has killed her child.

Was she responsible for her deed? In ordinary life, after making a mistake, we say, "Chalk it up to experience." Here we should say, "Chalk it up to the neurosis." *She* could not help it if her neurosis forced her to act this way—she didn't even know what was going on behind the scenes; her conscious self merely acted out its assigned part. This is far more true than is generally realized: Criminal actions in general are not actions for which their agents are responsible; the agents are passive, not active—they are victims of a neurotic conflict. Their very hyper-activity is unconsciously determined.

To say this is, of course, not to say that we should not punish criminals. Clearly, for our own protection, we must remove them from our midst so that they can no longer molest and endanger organized society. And of course, if we use the word "responsible" in such a way that justly to hold someone responsible for a deed is by definition identical with being justified in punishing him, then we can and do hold people responsible. But this is like the sense of "free" in which free acts are voluntary ones. It does not go deep enough. In a deeper sense we cannot hold the person responsible: We can hold his neurosis responsible, but *he is not responsible for his neurosis*, particularly since the age at which its onset was inevitable was an age before he could even speak.

The neurosis is responsible—but isn't the neurosis a part of *him*? We have been speaking all the time as if the person and his unconscious were two separate beings; but isn't he one personality, including conscious and unconscious departments together?

I do not wish to deny this. But it hardly helps us here; for what people want when they talk about freedom, and what they hold to when they champion it, is the idea that the *conscious* will is the master of their destiny. "I am the master of my fate, I am the captain of my soul"—and they surely mean their conscious self, the self that they can recognize and search and introspect. Between an unconscious which willy-nilly determines your actions, and an external force which pushes you, there is little if anything to choose. The unconscious is just *as if* it were an outside force; and indeed, psychiatrists will assert that the inner Hitler (your super-ego) can torment you far more than any external Hitler can. Thus, the kind of freedom that people want, the only kind they will settle for, is precisely the kind that psychiatry says that they cannot have.

Heretofore it was pretty generally thought that, while we could not rightly blame a person for the color of his eyes or the morality of his parents, or even for what he did at the age of three, or to a large extent what impulses he had and whom he fell in love with, one *could* do so for other of his adult activities, particularly the acts he performed voluntarily and with premeditation. Later this attitude was shaken. Many voluntary acts came to be recognized at least in some circles, as compelled by the unconscious. . . . The usual examples, such as the kleptomaniac and the schizophrenic, apparently satisfy most philosophers, and with these exceptions removed, the rest of mankind is permitted to wander in the vast and alluring fields of freedom and responsibility. So far, the inroads upon freedom left the vast majority of humanity untouched; they began to hit home when psychiatrists began to realize, though philosophers did not, that the domination of the conscious by the unconscious extended not merely to a few exceptional individuals, but to all human beings, that the "big three behind the scenes" are not respecters of persons, and dominate us all, even including that *sanctum sanctorum* of freedom, our conscious will. To be sure, the domination by the unconscious in the case of "normal" individuals is somewhat more benevolent than the tyranny and despotism exercised in neurotic cases, and therefore the former have evoked less comment; but the principle remains in all cases the same: The unconscious is the master of every fate and the captain of every soul. . . .

IV. [DOES FREE WILL EXIST?]

Assuming the main conclusions of this paper to be true, is there any room left for freedom?

This, of course, all depends on what we mean by "freedom." In the senses suggested at the beginning of this paper, there are countless free acts, and unfree ones as well. When "free" means "uncompelled," and only external compulsion is admitted, again there are countless free acts. But now we have extended the notion of compulsion to include determination by unconscious forces. With this sense in mind, our question is, "With the concept of compulsion thus extended, and in the light of present psychoanalytic knowledge, is there any freedom left in human behavior?"

If practicing psychoanalysts were asked this question, there is little doubt that their answer would be along the following lines: They would say that they were not accustomed to using the term "free" at all, but that if they had to suggest a criterion for distinguishing the free from the unfree, they would say that a person's freedom is present *in inverse proportion to his neuroticism*; in other words, the more his acts are determined by a *malevolent* unconscious, the less free he is. Thus, they would speak of *degrees* of freedom. They would say that as a person is cured of his neurosis, he becomes more free—free to realize capabilities that were blocked by the neurotic affliction. The psychologically well-adjusted individual is in this sense comparatively the most free. Indeed, those who are cured of mental disorders are sometimes said to have *regained their freedom*: They are freed from the tyranny of a malevolent unconscious which formerly exerted as much of a domination over them as if they had been the abject slaves of a cruel dictator.

But suppose one says that a person is free only to the extent that his acts are *not unconsciously determined at all*, be they unconsciously benevolent *or* malevolent? If this is the criterion, psychoanalysts would say, most human behavior cannot be called free at all: Our impulses and volitions having to do with our basic attitudes toward life, whether we are optimists or pessimists, tough-minded or tender-minded, whether our tempers are quick or slow, whether we are "naturally self-seeking" or "naturally benevolent" (and *all the acts consequent upon these things*), what things annoy us, whether we take to blondes or brunettes, old or young, whether we become philosophers or artists or businessmen—all this has its basis in the unconscious. If people generally call most acts free, it is not because they believe that compelled acts should be called free; it is rather through not knowing how large a proportion of our acts actually are compelled. Only the comparatively "vanilla-flavored" aspects of our lives—such as our behavior toward people who don't really matter to us—are exempted from this rule.

These, I think, are the two principal criteria for distinguishing freedom from the lack of it which we might set up on the basis of psychoanalytic knowledge. Conceivably we might set up others. In every case, of course, it remains trivially true that "it all depends on how we choose to use the word." The facts are what they are, regardless of what words we choose for labeling them. But if we choose to label them in a way which is not in accord with what human beings, however vaguely, have long had in mind in applying these labels, as we would be doing if we labeled as "free" many acts which we know as much about as we now do through modern psychoanalytic methods, then we shall only be manipulating words to mislead our fellow creatures.

14 / The Crime of Punishment

KARL MENNINGER

[I]

Few words in our language arrest our attention as do "crime," "violence," "revenge," and "injustice." We abhor crime; we adore justice; we boast that we live by the rule of law. Violence and vengefulness we repudiate as unworthy of our civilization, and we assume this sentiment to be unanimous among all human beings.

Yet crime continues to be a national disgrace and a world-wide problem. It is threatening, alarming, wasteful, expensive, abundant, and apparently increasing! In actuality it is decreasing in frequency of occurrence, but it is certainly increasing in visibility and the reactions of the public to it.

Our system for controlling crime is ineffective, unjust, expensive. Prisons seem to operate with revolving doors—the same people going in and out and in and out. *Who cares?*

Our city jails and inhuman reformatories and wretched prisons are jammed. They are known to be unhealthy, dangerous, immoral, indecent, crime-breeding dens of iniquity. Not everyone has smelled them, as some of us have. Not many have heard the groans and the curses. Not everyone has seen the hate and despair in a thousand blank, hollow faces. But, in a way, we all know how miserable prisons are. *We want them to be that way.* And they are. *Who cares?*

Professional and big-time criminals prosper as never before. Gambling syndicates flourish. White-collar crime may even exceed all others, but goes undetected in the majority of cases. We are all being robbed and we know who the robbers are. They live nearby. *Who cares?*

The public filches millions of dollars worth of food and clothing from stores, towels and sheets from hotels, jewelry and knick-knacks from shops. The public steals, and the same public pays it back in higher prices. *Who cares?*

Time and time again somebody shouts about this state of affairs, just as I am shouting now. The magazines shout. The newspapers shout. The television and radio commentators shout (or at least they "deplore"). Psychologists, sociologists, leading jurists, wardens, and intelligent police chiefs join the chorus. Governors and mayors and Congressmen are sometimes heard. They shout that the situation is bad, bad, bad, and getting worse. Some suggested that we immediately replace obsolete procedures with scientific methods. A few shout contrary sentiments. Do the clear indications derived from scientific discovery for appropriate changes continue to fall on deaf ears? Why is the public so long-suffering, so apathetic, and thereby so continuingly self-destructive? How many Presidents (and other citizens) do we have to lose before we do something?

The public behaves as a sick patient does when a dreaded treatment is proposed for his ailment. We all know how the aching tooth may suddenly quiet down in the dentist's office, or the abdominal pain disappear in the surgeon's examining room. Why should a sufferer seek relief and shun it? Is it merely the fear of the pain of the treatment? Is it the fear of unknown complications? Is it distrust of the doctor's ability? All of these, no doubt.

But, as Freud made so incontestably clear, the sufferer is always somewhat deterred by a kind of subversive, internal opposition to the work of cure. He suffers on the one hand from the pains of his affliction and yearns to get well. But he suffers at the same time from traitorous impulses that fight against the accomplishment of any change in himself, even recovery! Like Hamlet, he wonders whether it may be better after all to suffer the familiar pains and aches associated with the old method than to face the complications of a new and strange, even though possibly better, way of handling things.

The inescapable conclusion is that society *wants* crime, *needs* crime, and gains definite satisfactions from the present mishandling of it! We condemn crime; we punish offenders for it; but we need it. The crime and punishment ritual is a part of our lives. We need crimes to wonder at, to enjoy vicariously, to discuss and speculate about, and to publicly deplore. We need criminals to identify ourselves with, to envy secretly, and to punish stoutly. They do for us the forbidden, illegal things we *wish* to do, and, like scapegoats of old, they bear the burdens of our displaced guilt and punishment—"the iniquities of us all." . . .

Fifty years ago, Winston Churchill declared that the mood and temper of the public in regard to crime and criminals is one of the unfailing tests of the civilization of any country. Judged by this standard, how civilized are we?

The chairman of the President's National Crime Commission . . . declared recently that organized crime flourishes in America because enough of the public wants its services, and most citizens are apathetic about its impact. It will continue uncurbed as long as Americans accept it as inevitable and, in some instances, desirable.

[II]

Are there steps that we can take which will reduce the aggressive stabs and self-destructive lurches of our less well-managing fellow men? Are there ways to prevent and control the grosser violations, other than the clumsy traditional maneuvers which we have inherited? These depend basically upon intimidation and slow-motion torture. We call it punishment, and justify it with our "feeling." We know it doesn't work.

Yes, there *are* better ways. There are steps that could be taken; some *are* taken. But we move too slowly. Much better use, it seems to me, could be made of the members of my profession and other behavioral scientists than having them deliver courtroom pronunciamentos. The consistent use of a diagnostic clinic would enable trained workers to lay what they can learn about an offender before the judge who would know best how to implement the recommendation.

This would no doubt lead to a transformation of prisons, if not to their total disappearance in their present form and function. Temporary and permanent detention will perhaps always be necessary for a few, especially the professionals, but this could be more effectively and economically performed with new types of "facility" (that strange, awkward word for institution).

I assume it to be a matter of common and general agreement that our object in all this is to protect the community from a repetition of the offense by the most economical method consonant with our other purposes. Our "other purposes" include the desire to prevent these offenses from occurring, to reclaim offenders for social usefulness, if possible, and to detain them in protective custody, if reclamation is *not* possible. But how?

The treatment of human failure or dereliction by the infliction of pain is still used and believed in by many nonmedical people. "Spare the rod and spoil the child" is still considered wise counsel by many.

Whipping is still used by many secondary schoolmasters in England, I am informed, to stimulate study, attention, and the love of learning. Whipping was long a traditional treatment for the "crime" of disobedience on the part of children, pupils, servants, apprentices, employees. And slaves were treated for centuries by flogging for such offenses as weariness, confusion, stupidity, exhaustion, fear, grief, and even overcheerfulness. It was assumed and stoutly defended that these "treatments" cured conditions for which they were administered.

Meanwhile, scientific medicine was acquiring many new healing methods and devices. Doctors can now transplant organs and limbs; they can remove brain tumors and cure incipient cancers; they can halt pneumonia, meningitis, and other infections; they can correct deformities and repair breaks and tears and scars. But these wonderful achievements are accomplished on *willing* subjects, people who voluntarily ask for help by even heroic measures. And the reader will be wondering, no doubt, whether doctors can do anything with or for people who *do not want* to be treated at all, in any way! Can doctors cure willful aberrant behavior? Are we to believe that crime is a *disease* that can be reached by scientific measures? Isn't it merely "natural meanness" that makes all of us do wrong things at times even when we "know better"? And are not self-control, moral stamina, and will power the things needed? Surely there is no medical treatment for the lack of those!

[III]

Let me answer this carefully, for much misunderstanding accumulates here. I would say that according to the prevalent understanding of the words, crime is *not* a disease. Neither is it an illness, although I think it *should* be! It *should* be treated, and it could be; but it mostly isn't.

These enigmatic statements are simply explained. Diseases are undesired states of being which have been described and defined by doctors, usually given Greek or Latin appellations, and treated by long-established physical and pharmacological formulae. Illness, on the other hand, is best defined as a state of impaired functioning of such a nature that the public expects the sufferer to repair to the physician for help. The illness may prove to be a disease; more often it is only vague and nameless misery, but something which doctors, not lawyers, teachers, or preachers, are supposed to be able and willing to help.

When the community begins to look upon the expression of aggressive violence as the symptom of an illness or as indicative of illness, it will be because it believes doctors can do something to correct such a condition. At present, some better-informed individuals do believe and expect this. However angry at or sorry for the offender, they want him "treated" in an effective way so that he will cease to be a danger to them. And they know that traditional punishment, "treatment-punishment," will not effect this.

What *will*? What effective treatment is there for such violence? It will surely have to begin with motivating or stimulating or arousing in a cornered individual the wish and hope and intention to change his methods of dealing with the realities of life. Can this be done by education, medication, counseling, training? I would answer *yes*. It can be done successfully in a majority of cases, if undertaken in time.

The present penal system and the existing legal philosophy do not stimulate or even expect such a change to take place in the criminal. Yet change is what medical science always aims for. The prisoner, like the doctor's other patients, should emerge from his treatment experience a different person, differently equipped, differently functioning, and headed in a different direction than when he began the treatment.

It is natural for the public to doubt that this can be accomplished with criminals. But remember that the public *used* to doubt that change could be effected in the mentally ill. No one a hundred years ago believed mental illness to be curable. Today *all* people know (or should know) that *mental illness is curable* in the great majority of instances and that the prospects and rapidity of cure are directly related to the availability and intensity of proper treatment.

The forms and techniques of psychiatric treatment used today number in the hundreds. No one patient requires or receives all forms, but each patient is studied with respect to his particular needs, his basic assets, his interests, and his special difficulties. A therapeutic team may embrace a dozen workers—as in a hospital setting—or it may narrow down to the doctor and the spouse. Clergymen, teachers, relatives, friends, and even fellow patients often participate informally but helpfully in the process of readaptation.

All of the participants in this effort to bring about a favorable change in the patient—i.e., in his vital balance and life program—are imbued with what we may call a *therapeutic attitude*. This is one in direct antithesis to attitudes of avoidance, ridicule, scorn, or punitiveness. Hostile feelings toward the subject, however justified by his unpleasant and even destructive behavior, are not in the curriculum of therapy or in the therapist. This does not mean that therapists approve of the offensive and obnoxious behavior of the patient; they distinctly disapprove of it. But they recognize it as symptomatic of continued imbalance and disorganization, which is what they are seeking to change. They distinguish between disapproval, penalty, price, and punishment.

Doctors charge fees; they impose certain "penalties" or prices, but they have long since put aside primitive attitudes of retaliation toward offensive patients. A patient may cough in the doctor's face or may vomit on the office rug; a patient may curse or scream or even struggle in the extremity of his pain. But these acts are not "punished." Doctors and nurses have no time or thought for inflicting unnecessary pain even upon patients who may be difficult, disagreeable, provocative, and even dangerous. It is their duty to care for them, to try to make them well, and to prevent them from doing themselves or others harm. This requires love, not hate. This is the deepest meaning of the therapeutic attitude. Every doctor knows this; every worker in a hospital or clinic knows it (or should).

There is another element in the therapeutic attitude. It is the quality of hopefulness. If no one believes that the patient can get well, if no one—not even the doctor—has any hope, there probably won't be any recovery. Hope is just as important as love in the therapeutic attitude.

"But you were talking about the mentally ill," readers may interject, "those poor, confused, bereft, frightened individuals who yearn for help from you doctors and nurses. Do you mean to imply that willfully perverse individuals, our criminals, can be similarly reached and rehabilitated? Do you really believe that effective treatment of the sort you visualize can be applied to people *who do not want any help,* who are so willfully vicious, so well aware of the wrongs they are doing, so lacking in penitence or even common decency that punishment seems to be the only thing left?"

Do I believe there is effective treatment for offenders, and that they *can* be changed? *Most certainly and definitely I do.* Not all cases, to be sure; there are also some physical afflictions which we cannot cure at the moment. Some provision has to be made for incurables—pending new knowledge—and these will include some offenders. But I believe the majority of them would prove to be curable. The willfulness and the viciousness of offenders are part of the thing for which they have to be treated. These must not thwart the therapeutic attitude.

It is simply not true that most of them are "fully aware" of what they are doing, nor is it true that they want no help from anyone, although some of them say so. Prisoners are individuals: Some want treatment, some do not. Some don't know what treatment is. Many are utterly despairing and hopeless. Where treatment is made available in institutions, many prisoners seek it even with the full knowledge that doing so will not lessen their sentences. In some prisons, seeking treatment by prisoners is frowned upon by the officials.

Various forms of treatment are even now being tried in some progressive courts and prisons over the country—educational, social, industrial, religious, recreational, and psychological treatments. Socially acceptable behavior, new work–play opportunities, new identity and companion patterns all help toward community reacceptance. Some parole officers and some wardens have been extremely ingenious in developing these modalities of rehabilitation and reconstruction—more than I could list here even if I knew them all. But some are trying. The secret of success in all programs, however, is the replacement of the punitive attitude with a therapeutic attitude.

Offenders with propensities for impulsive and predatory aggression should not be permitted to live among us unrestrained by some kind of social control. *But the great majority of offenders, even "criminals," should never become prisoners if we want to "cure" them.*

[IV]

There are now throughout the country many citizens' action groups and programs for the prevention and control of crime and delinquency. With such attitudes of inquiry and concern, the public could acquire information (and incentive) leading to a change of feeling about crime and criminals. It will discover how unjust is much so-called "justice," how baffled and frustrated many judges are by the ossified rigidity of old-fashioned, obsolete laws and state constitutions which effectively prevent the introduction of sensible procedures to replace useless, harmful ones.

I want to proclaim to the public that things are not what it wishes them to be, and will only become so if it will take an interest in the matter and assume some responsibility for its own self-protection.

Will the public listen?

If the public does become interested, it will realize that we must have more facts, more trial projects, more checked results. It will share the dismay of the President's Commission in finding that no one knows much about even the incidence of crime with any definiteness or statistical accuracy.

The average citizen finds it difficult to see how any research would in any way change his mind about a man who brutally murders his children. But just such inconceivably awful acts most dramatically point up the need for research. Why should—how can—a man become so dreadful as that in our culture? How is such a man made? Is it comprehensible that he can be born to become so depraved?

There are thousands of questions regarding crime and public protection which deserve scientific study. What makes some individuals maintain their interior equilibrium by one kind of disturbance of the social structure rather than by another kind, one that would have landed him in a hospital? Why do some individuals specialize in certain types of crime? Why do so many young people reared in areas of delinquency and poverty and bad example never become habitual delinquents? (Perhaps this is a more important question than why some of them do.)

The public has a fascination for violence, and clings tenaciously to its yen for vengeance, blind and deaf to the expense, futility, and dangerousness of the resulting penal system. But we are bound to hope that this will yield in time to the persistent, penetrating light of intelligence and accumulating scientific knowledge. The public will grow increasingly ashamed of its cry for retaliation, its persistent demand to punish. This is its crime, *our* crime against criminals—and, incidentally, our crime against ourselves. For before we can diminish our sufferings from the ill-controlled aggressive assaults of fellow citizens, we must renounce the philosophy of punishment, the obsolete, vengeful penal attitude. In its place we would seek a comprehensive constructive social attitude—therapeutic in some instances, restraining in some instances, but preventive in its total social impact.

In the last analysis this becomes a question of personal morals and values. No matter how glorified or how piously disguised, vengeance as a human motive must be personally repudiated by each and every one of us. This is the message of old religions and new psychiatries. Unless this message is heard, unless we, the people—the man on the street, the housewife in the home—can give up our delicious satisfactions in opportunities for vengeful retaliation on scapegoats, we cannot expect to preserve our peace, our public safety, or our mental health.

15 / The Humanitarian Theory of Punishment

C. S. LEWIS

[I. THE HUMANITARIAN THEORY]

In England we have lately had a controversy about Capital Punishment. I do not know whether a murderer is more likely to repent and make a good end on the gallows a few weeks after his trial or in the prison infirmary thirty years later. I do not know whether the fear of death is an indispensable deterrent. I need not, for the purpose of this article, decide whether it is a morally permissible deterrent. Those are questions which I propose to leave untouched. My subject is not Capital Punishment in particular, but that theory of punishment in general which the controversy showed to be almost universal among my fellow-countrymen. It may be called the Humanitarian theory. Those who hold it think that it is mild and merciful. In this I believe that they are seriously mistaken. I believe that the 'Humanity' which it claims is a dangerous illusion and disguises the possibility of cruelty and injustice without end. I urge a return to the traditional or Retributive theory not solely, not even primarily, in the interests of society, but in the interests of the criminal.

According to the Humanitarian theory, to punish a man because he deserves it, and as much as he deserves, is mere revenge and, therefore, barbarous and immoral. It is maintained that the only legitimate motives for punishing are the desire to deter others by example or to mend the criminal. When this theory is combined, as frequently happens, with the belief that all crime is more or less pathological, the idea of mending tails off into that of healing or curing, and punishment becomes therapeutic. Thus it appears at first sight that we have passed from the harsh and self-righteous notion of giving the wicked their deserts to the charitable and enlightened one of tending the psychologically sick. What could be more amiable? One little point which is taken for granted in this theory needs, however, to be made explicit. The things done to the criminal, even if they are called cures, will be just as compulsory as they were in the old days when we called them punishments. If a tendency to steal can be cured by psychotherapy, the thief will no doubt be forced to undergo the treatment. Otherwise, society cannot continue.

My contention is that this doctrine, merciful though it appears, really

[144]

means that each one of us, from the moment he breaks the law, is deprived of the rights of a human being.

[II. ARGUMENTS AGAINST THE THEORY]

The reason is this. The Humanitarian theory removes from Punishment the concept of Desert. But the concept of Desert is the only connecting link between punishment and justice. It is only as deserved or undeserved that a sentence can be just or unjust. I do not here contend that the question "Is it deserved?" is the only one we can reasonably ask about a punishment. We may very properly ask whether it is likely to deter others and to reform the criminal. But neither of these two last questions is a question about justice. There is no sense in talking about a "just deterrent" or a "just cure." We demand of a deterrent not whether it is just but whether it will deter. We demand of a cure not whether it is just but whether it succeeds. Thus when we cease to consider what the criminal deserves and consider only what will cure him or deter others, we have tacitly removed him from the sphere of justice altogether; instead of a person, a subject of rights, we now have a mere object, a patient, a "case."

The distinction will become clearer if we ask who will be qualified to determine sentences when sentences are no longer held to derive their propriety from the criminal's deservings. On the old view the problem of fixing the right sentence was a moral problem. Accordingly, the judge who did it was a person trained in jurisprudence; trained, that is, in a science which deals with rights and duties, and which, in origin at least, was consciously accepting guidance from the Law of Nature and from Scripture. We must admit that in the actual penal code of most countries at most times these high originals were so much modified by local custom, class interests, and utilitarian concessions as to be very imperfectly recognizable. But the code was never in principle, and not always in fact, beyond the control of the conscience of the society. And when (say, in eighteenth-century England) actual punishments conflicted too violently with the moral sense of the community, juries refused to convict and reform was finally brought about. This was possible because, so long as we are thinking in terms of Desert, the propriety of the penal code, being a moral question, is a question on which every man has the right to an opinion, not because he follows this or that profession, but because he is simply a man, a rational animal enjoying the Natural Light. But all this is changed when we drop the concept of Desert. The only two questions we may now ask about a punishment are whether it deters and whether it cures. But these are not questions on which anyone is entitled to have an opinion simply because he is a man. He is not entitled to an opinion even if, in addition to being a man, he should happen also to be a jurist, a Christian, and a moral theologian. For they are not questions about principle but about matter of fact; and for such *cuiquam in sua arte credendum*.* Only the expert "penologist" (let barbarous things have barbarous names), in the light of previous experiment, can tell us what is likely to deter: Only the psychotherapist can tell us what is likely to cure. It will be in vain for the rest of us, speaking simply as men, to say, "But this punishment is hideously unjust, hideously disproportionate to the criminal's deserts." The experts with perfect logic will reply, "But nobody was talking about deserts. No one was talking about *punishment* in your archaic, vindictive sense of the word. Here are the statistics proving that this treatment deters. Here are the statistics proving that this other treatment cures. What is your trouble?"

The Humanitarian theory, then, removes sentences from the hands of jurists whom the public conscience is entitled to criticize and places them in the hands of technical experts whose special sciences do not even employ such categories as rights or justice. It might be argued that since this transference results from an abandonment of the old idea of punishment, and, therefore, of all vindictive motives, it will be safe to leave our criminals in such hands. I will not pause to comment on the simple-minded view of fallen human nature which such a belief implies. Let us rather remember that the "cure" of criminals is to be compulsory; and let us then watch how the theory actually works in the mind of the Humanitarian. The immediate starting point of this article was a letter I read in one of our Leftist weeklies. The author was pleading that a certain sin, now treated by our laws as a crime, should henceforward be treated as a disease. And he complained that under the present system the offender, after a term in jail, was simply let out to return to his original environment, where he would probably relapse. What he complained of was not the shutting up but the letting out. On his remedial view of punishment the offender should, of course, be detained until he was cured. And of course the official straighteners are the only people who can say when that is. The first result of the Humanitarian theory is, therefore, to substitute for a definite sentence (reflecting to some extent the community's moral judgment on the degree of ill-desert involved) an indefinite sentence terminable only by the word of those experts—and they are not experts in moral theology nor even in the Law of Nature—who inflict it. Which of us, if he stood in the dock, would not prefer to be tried by the old system?

It may be said that by the continued use of the word "punishment" and the use of the verb "inflict" I am misrepresenting Humanitarians. They are not punishing, not inflicting, only healing. But do not let us be deceived by a name. To be taken without consent from my home and friends; to lose my liberty; to undergo all those assaults on my personality which modern psychotherapy knows how to deliver; to be re-made after some pattern of

---

*[We must believe the expert in his own field.—Eds.]

"normality" hatched in a Viennese laboratory to which I never professed allegiance; to know that this process will never end until either my captors have succeeded or I have grown wise enough to cheat them with apparent success—who cares whether this is called Punishment or not? That it includes most of the elements for which any punishment is feared—shame, exile, bondage, and years eaten by the locust—is obvious. Only enormous ill-desert could justify it; but ill-desert is the very conception which the Humanitarian theory has thrown overboard.

If we turn from the curative to the deterrent justification of punishment we shall find the new theory even more alarming. When you punish a man *in terrorem*,[1] make of him an "example" to others, you are admittedly using him as a means to an end; someone else's end. This, in itself, would be a very wicked thing to do. On the classical theory of Punishment it was of course justified on the ground that the man deserved it. That was assumed to be established before any question of "making him an example" arose. You then, as the saying is, killed two birds with one stone; in the process of giving him what he deserved you set an example to others. But take away desert and the whole morality of the punishment disappears. Why, in Heaven's name, am I to be sacrificed to the good of society in this way?— unless, of course, I deserve it.

But that is not the worst. If the justification of exemplary punishment is not to be based on desert but solely on its efficacy as a deterrent, it is not absolutely necessary that the man we punish should even have committed the crime. The deterrent effect demands that the public should draw the moral, "If we do such an act we shall suffer like that man." The punishment of a man actually guilty whom the public think innocent will not have the desired effect; the punishment of a man actually innocent will, provided the public think him guilty. But every modern State has powers which make it easy to fake a trial. When a victim is urgently needed for exemplary purposes and a guilty victim cannot be found, all the purposes of deterrence will be equally served by the punishment (call it "cure" if you prefer) of an innocent victim, provided that the public can be cheated into thinking him guilty. It is no use to ask me why I assume that our rulers will be so wicked. The punishment of an innocent, that is, an undeserving, man is wicked only if we grant the traditional view that righteous punishment means deserved punishment. Once we have abandoned that criterion, all punishments have to be justified, if at all, on other grounds that have nothing to do with desert. Where the punishment of the innocent can be justified on those grounds (and it could in some cases be justified as a deterrent) it will be no less moral than any other punishment. Any distaste for it on the part of a Humanitarian will be merely a hang-over from the Retributive theory.

---

[1] "To cause terror."

[III. FURTHER CRITICISMS]

It is, indeed, important to notice that my argument so far supposes no evil intentions on the part of the Humanitarian and considers only what is involved in the logic of his position. My contention is that good men (not bad men) consistently acting upon that position would act as cruelly and unjustly as the greatest tyrants. They might in some respects act even worse. Of all tyrannies a tyranny sincerely exercised for the good of its victims may be the most oppressive. It may be better to live under robber barons than under omnipotent moral busybodies. The robber baron's cruelty may sometimes sleep, his cupidity may at some point be satiated; but those who torment us for our own good will torment us without end, for they do so with the approval of their own conscience. They may be more likely to go to Heaven yet at the same time likelier to make a Hell of earth. Their very kindness stings with intolerable insult. To be "cured" against one's will and cured of states which we may not regard as disease is to be put on a level with those who have not yet reached the age of reason or those who never will; to be classed with infants, imbeciles, and domestic animals. But to be punished, however severely, because we have deserved it, because we "ought to have known better," is to be treated as a human person made in God's image.

In reality, however, we must face the possibility of bad rulers armed with a Humanitarian theory of punishment. A great many popular blueprints for a Christian society are merely what the Elizabethans called "eggs in moonshine" because they assume that the whole society is Christian or that the Christians are in control. This is not so in most contemporary States. Even if it were, our rulers would still be fallen men and, therefore, neither very wise nor very good. As it is, they will usually be unbelievers. And since wisdom and virtue are not the only or the commonest qualifications for a place in the government, they will not often be even the best unbelievers.

The practical problem of Christian politics is not that of drawing up schemes for a Christian society, but that of living as innocently as we can with unbelieving fellow-subjects under unbelieving rulers who will never be perfectly wise and good and who will sometimes be very wicked and very foolish. And when they are wicked the Humanitarian theory of punishment will put in their hands a finer instrument of tyranny than wickedness ever had before. For if crime and disease are to be regarded as the same thing, it follows that any state of mind which our masters choose to call disease can be treated as crime and compulsorily cured. It will be vain to plead that states of mind which displease government need not always involve moral turpitude and do not therefore always deserve forfeiture of liberty. For our masters will not be using the concepts of Desert and Punishment but those of disease and cure. We know that one school of psychology already regards religion as a neurosis. When this particular neurosis becomes inconvenient to government, what is to hinder government from proceeding to "cure" it? Such "cure" will, of course, be compulsory; but under the Humanitarian theory it will not be called by the shocking name of Persecution. No one will blame us for being Christians, no one will hate us, no one will revile us. The new Nero will approach us with the silky manners of a doctor, and though all will be in fact as compulsory as the *tunica molesta** or Smithfield or Tyburn,† all will go on within the unemotional therapeutic sphere, where words like "right" and "wrong" or "freedom" and "slavery" are never heard. And thus when the command is given, every prominent Christian in the land may vanish overnight into Institutions for the Treatment of the Ideologically Unsound, and it will rest with the expert jailers to say when (if ever) they are to re-emerge. But it will not be persecution. Even if the treatment is painful, even if it is lifelong, even if it is fatal, that will be only a regrettable accident; the intention was purely therapeutic. In ordinary medicine there were painful operations and fatal operations; so in this. But because they are "treatment," not punishment, they can be criticized only by fellow-experts and on technical grounds, never by men as men and on grounds of justice.

This is why I think it essential to oppose the Humanitarian theory of punishment, root and branch, wherever we encounter it. It carries on its front a semblance of mercy which is wholly false. That is how it can deceive men of good will. The error began, perhaps, with Shelley's statement that the distinction between mercy and justice was invented in the courts of tyrants. It sounds noble, and was indeed the error of a noble mind. But the distinction is essential. The older view was that mercy "tempered" justice, or (on the highest level of all) that mercy and justice had met and kissed. The essential act of mercy was to pardon; and pardon in its very essence involves the recognition of guilt and ill-desert in the recipient. If crime is only a disease which needs cure, not a sin which deserves punishment, it cannot be pardoned. How can you pardon a man for having a gumboil or a club foot? But the Humanitarian theory wants simply to abolish Justice and substitute Mercy for it. This means that you start being "kind" to people before you have considered their rights, and then force upon them supposed kindnesses which no one but you will recognize as kindnesses and which the recipient will feel as abominable cruelties. You have overshot the mark. Mercy, detached from Justice, grows unmerciful. That is the important paradox. As there are plants which will flourish only in mountain soil, so it appears that Mercy will flower only when it grows in the crannies of the rock of Justice: Transplanted to the marsh-lands of mere Humanitarianism, it

*[An annoying tunic worn as a punishment.—Eds.]
†[Two places of execution.—Eds.]

becomes a man-eating weed, all the more dangerous because it is still called by the same name as the mountain variety. But we ought long ago to have learned our lesson. We should be too old now to be deceived by those humane pretensions which have served to usher in every cruelty of the revolutionary period in which we live. These are the "precious balms" which will "break our heads."[2] . . .

STUDY QUESTIONS

1. Blatchford begins by stating four reasons given by others to show that we have free will. What are they? How does he reply to each?

2. Toward the end of the selection, Blatchford gives two direct arguments against free will. State them. Are they good arguments? Why or why not?

3. How does Blatchford attempt to prove determinism? In your view has he succeeded? Why or why not?

4. Many philosophers have thought that if one's actions are not free, then one is not responsible for them. Is that Blatchford's view?

5. Exactly what is the semantic confusion, according to Stace, which gives rise to the problem of free will? Is a person who holds the hard determinist position semantically confused? What does an ordinary person in the street mean by "free"?

6. Discuss Stace's "thug with a gun to your head" case. Why does it seem to present a special problem? Is Stace's solution adequate?

7. How does Stace connect the concepts of free will, moral responsibility, and punishment?

8. How does Taylor criticize soft determinism? Can you develop a new form of soft determinism that will answer Taylor's objection?

9. Taylor raises worries about what he calls "simple indeterminism." Does the agency theory avoid those worries?

10. What does Hospers' criticism of soft determinism add to Taylor's objections?

11. Can Stace's definition of "free" withstand Hospers' essay?

12. Is Menninger really opposed to all punishment, or is he opposed to punishment understood in a particular way? What properties make something punishment?

[2]Psalm cxli. 6.

13. Which of Lewis' arguments against the humanitarian theory are "in principle" objections, and which depend on specific empirical conditions in a society?

14. Now that you have studied the issues in this part of the book, what are the practical consequences of that study for you?

Further Readings

Ayer, A. J. "Freedom and Necessity." In *Philosophical Essays*. London: Macmillan, 1954, pp. 271-284. [A defense of compatibilism.]

Brody, Baruch A. *Beginning Philosophy*. Englewood Cliffs, N.J.: Prentice-Hall, 1977, pp. 162-187. [An elementary discussion of the important positions on the free will problem.]

Campbell, C. A. "Is 'Free Will' a Pseudo-Problem?" *Mind*, 60 (1951), 441-465. [A defense of libertarianism.]

Hook, Sidney, ed. *Determinism and Freedom*. New York: Collier Books, 1961. [A good set of readings on the topics of this section.]

Hospers, John. *An Introduction to Philosophical Analysis*, 2nd ed. Englewood Cliffs, N.J.: Prentice-Hall, 1967, pp. 279-348. [A clear overview of the free will and responsibility topics.]

Hume, David. *An Enquiry Concerning Human Understanding*. Indianapolis, Ind.: Hackett, 1977, Sec. 8. [First published in 1748; a classic statement of compatibilism.]

MacKay, D. M. "On the Logical Indeterminacy of a Free Choice." *Mind*, 69 (1960), 31-40. [Poses a difficulty for the perfect prediction of human actions.]

Ree, Paul. "Determinism and the Illusion of Moral Responsibility." In P. Edwards and A. Pap, eds., *A Modern Introduction to Philosophy*, 3rd ed. New York: Free Press, 1973, pp. 10-27. [A powerful defense of the hard determinist position.]

Salmon, Wesley C. "Determinism and Indeterminism in Modern Science." In Joel Feinberg, ed., *Reason and Responsibility*, 4th ed. Encino, Calif.: Dickenson, 1978, pp. 331-346. [As the title indicates.]

Smart, J. J. C. "Free-Will, Praise and Blame." *Mind*, 70 (1961), 291-306. [On the nature of praise and blame within a compatibilist framework.]

PART FOUR

BODIES, MINDS, AND PERSONS

PREVIEW

Human beings find it quite easy to regard themselves as special. This attitude manifests itself in innumerable ways. For example, we take ourselves to be the masters of everything save other people, and for a long time we found it inconceivable that our home, the earth, was not the center of the universe.

It should not take much reflection to shake at least some of our parochialism. Many beasts are stronger than we are; viruses are more fertile, cockroaches more highly adapted, stones more durable, and so on. When we are pressed, our special feature turns out to be our minds. With respect to thinking and feeling, we are number one. For this reason we believe ourselves to be persons, not mere objects, who are different from other living things.

What is a person? In particular, what sort of things must we be in order to explain our amazing mental life? Are we just bodies? Or do we also have non-material minds? Such questions constitute what is commonly known as the mind-body problem.

For some thinkers, there is no such problem. One of them writes:

There are vexing, unsolved problems of psychology . . . but there are no mind-body problems. The reason why . . . is because there are no such things as *minds* in the first place.[1]

But of course, not everyone would agree. According to certain philosophers, we must be radically different from most, if not all, of the other entities in the universe.

[1]R. Taylor, "How to Bury the Mind-Body Problem," *The American Philosophical Quarterly*, 1969.

Two passages which point toward our special nature from quite different directions follow. The first is from the writings of an eighteenth-century theologian, Johann Michael Schmidt; the second, from the textbook of a contemporary philosopher.

(1) Not many years ago it was reported from France that a man had made a statue that could play various pieces on the Fleuttraversier,* placed the flute to its lips and took it down again, rolled its eyes, etc. But no one has yet invented an image that thinks, or wills, or composes, or even does anything at all similar. Let anyone who wishes to be convinced look carefully at the last fugal work of . . . Bach . . . I am sure that he will soon need his soul if he wishes to observe all the beauties contained therein, let alone wishes to play it to himself or to form a judgment of the author. Everything that the champions of materialism put forward must fall to the ground in view of this single example.[2]

(2) Take the case of vision. Light-waves impinge upon the retina of your eye, producing there an inverted image of the object seen. . . . The optic nerve is stimulated, a chemical-electrical impulse passes along it, and finally, in a very small fraction of a second, the occipital lobe of the brain is stimulated; then a visual sensation occurs. Up to the occurrence of the sensation, every step of the process can be located in space, somewhere inside you head. But supposing you are looking at a solid green wall, where is your sensation of green? Is it in your head, inside your brain somewhere? If so, where? Would someone opening your head or looking at it through a super-x-ray microscope find the green you were seeing? Would it make sense to say that the green was 4 inches behind your eyes?[3]

Both passages suggest that there are certain features of human beings that cannot be accounted for by materialism, the view that people are nothing but their bodies. Furthermore, whatever mental abilities or states people have can be accounted for by their bodies, in particular their brains and nervous systems.

Look again at the quotations. The first suggests that our ability to write and appreciate music is incompatible with materialism. It is claimed that such activities require a soul. The second passage takes a mundane happening, the experience of a green wall, and suggests that this ordinary event cannot be understood materialistically. One's experiences exist, but they are not parts of one's body.

Which view is correct? That represented in the first passage or that represented in the second and third?

[2]Quoted from Douglas R. Hofstadter, *Godel, Escher, Bach: An Eternal Golden Braid*, New York, 1980, p. 27. Schmidt does not make the point here, but another defect from his point of view is that the materialist position is incompatible with the thesis that human beings are immortal. See Part Five.

[3]John Hospers, *An Introduction to Philosophical Analysis*, Englewood Cliffs, N.J., 1967, pp. 379–380.

*[Transverse flute:—Eds.]

Main Questions

This leads us to the main question of this part, which is:

What is a person?
Is a person solely a material body (including a brain, nerve system, etc.)?
Or is a person not only a body but also a non-material mind, or soul, or psyche, or personality, etc.?

(It should be stressed that by 'mind' we are asking about something *non-material*. Hence, we cannot equate minds with, say, brains.)
It should be pointed out that there are some related questions, such as:

If we do have non-material minds, do they survive the death of our bodies?
Can machines perform the things that humans do—for example, think?

These issues will be taken up in Part Five.

Answers

Three main answers have been given to the chief question of this part. These can be characterized simply as answers to the metaphysical problem, "What kinds of things in the universe are ultimately real?" Hence they can be described without making direct reference to the mind-body problem or to the main problem of Part Four: What is a person? In these *broad* terms, the three positions may be defined as follows:

Dualism: The universe contains two unique and irreducible kinds of things: material things and non-material (mental) things.
Materialism: The universe contains only one kind of things: material things.
Idealism: The universe contains only one kind of things: mental things.

When these main positions are characterized *with reference to the mind-body problem*, the definitions must be expanded so as to bring out this reference. If so, we have the following:

(a) Dualism: The universe contains two kinds of things: material and non-material (mental) things. A person consists (or is made up) of both. A person's body is obviously material. But a person also is (or has) something non-material—a mind.

(b) Materialism: The universe contains one kind of things: material things. Hence, a person is solely a material thing. There is nothing non-material about a person.

(c) Idealism: The universe contains one kind of things: non-material things. Hence, a person exists solely as something non-material (or mental). (It is usually held that it is a mind and the contents of that mind.)

A problem for dualism has always been: If both minds and bodies exist, what is the relationship between them? Interactionism is the view that minds and bodies of human beings interact causally.

It should be pointed out that dualism has been held in two forms: The older *traditional* dualism and the newer *revised* dualism:

Traditional dualism: A person consists of two unique and distinct kinds of substances: a physical substance or body, and a mental (non-material) substance or mind. The material substance (body) has certain attributes, such as occupying space. The mental substance (mind) has other different attributes, such as thinking. (Interactionist dualism holds that mind and body can interact with one another.)

Revised dualism: A person is more of a unitary entity than traditional dualism conceives of him to be. On the other hand, a person is not completely material, as materialism conceives him to be. Rather, a person is a psychophysical organism. If you want to talk in the older terms of "substances," then a person consists of only one kind of substance, his material body. The body has certain states or attributes which are purely material, such as, mass, occupying of space, and so forth. But a person is also able to *experience* certain states which are uniquely non-material or mental, such as, thoughts, sensations, feelings, and so on. These cannot in any way be reduced to material states.

In short, the dualism of the traditional sort is a dualism of two kinds of *substances*, each with its own kind of states. The dualism of the revised sort is a dualism of two kinds of *states*, material and non-material.

Obviously, the dualism of the revised sort is much "weaker" than traditional dualism. The traditional dualist claims that, in addition to our having material bodies (one kind of substance), we also have non-material minds (another kind of substance). Theoretically, the one could exist without the other. Hence, for a traditional dualist, survival after death is at least possible. The revised dualist denies that there are such things as mental substances—minds, or souls, or psyches. Again, a person is an organism, a highly complex one. That material organism (body) exists in various states or has various (material) attributes. But a person (perhaps because of a highly developed brain or whatever) can also *experience* various states— thoughts, sensations, etc.—which are uniquely *non-material* or mental.

It should be mentioned that there is a modern variant of materialism called behaviorism. We may characterize it as follows:

(d) Behaviorism: "Mental" phenomena are sets of acts of behavior. For example, having a pain *is* doing and saying certain things; it is nothing but behaving in certain ways.

Selections

The main answers to the questions of this part are represented as follows:

Answer	Selection
(a) Dualism (traditional)	16
(a) Dualism (revised)	17
(b) Materialism	18
(c) Idealism	19
(d) Behaviorism[4]	20

[4]Again, a variant of materialism.

16 / The Mind as Distinct from the Body

C. E. M. JOAD

I. THE RELATIONSHIP OF MIND AND BODY

It is obvious that one of the most important things about the mind is its relationship to the body. Mind and body are continually interacting in an infinite number of different ways. Mind influences body and body mind at every moment of our waking life. If I am drunk I see two lamp-posts instead of one; if I fail to digest my supper I have a nightmare and see blue devils; if I smoke opium or inhale nitrous oxide gas I shall see rosy-colored visions and pass into a state of beatitude. These are instances of the influence of the body upon the mind. If I see a ghost my hair will stand on end; if I am moved to anger my face will become red; if I receive a sudden shock I shall go pale. These are instances of the influence of the mind upon the body.

The examples just quoted are only extreme and rather obvious cases of what is going on all the time. Many thinkers indeed assert that mind and body are so intimately associated that there can be no event in the one which does not produce some corresponding event in the other, although the corresponding event, which we may call the effect of the first event, may be too small to be noticed. The interaction between mind and body is, at any rate, a fact beyond dispute. Yet when we come to reflect upon the manner of this interaction, it is exceedingly difficult to see how it can occur. Mind,[1] it is clear, must be something which is immaterial; if it were material it would be part of the body. The contents of, or even the events which happen in the mind—that is to say, wishes, desires, thoughts, aspirations, hopes, and acts of will—are also immaterial. The body, on the other hand, is matter and possesses the usual qualities of matter, such as size, weight, density, inertia, occupancy of space, and so forth.

Now there is no difficulty in understanding how one material thing can be influenced by another. Each possesses the same attributes of size, shape, and weight, in virtue of which each can, as it were, communicate with or "get at" the other. Thus a paving stone can crush an egg because

---

[1] It is important to emphasize the fact that the word "mind" does not mean the same as the word "brain"; the brain *is* material.

the egg belongs to the same order of being as the stone. But how can the paving stone crush a wish, or be affected by a thought? Material force and mass have no power over ideas; ideas do not exert force, nor do they yield to mass. How, in short, can that which has neither size, weight, nor shape, which cannot be seen, heard, or touched, and which does not occupy space come into contact with that which has these properties? . . .

The issue between those who endeavor to interpret mind action in terms of body action, and those who contend for the unique, distinct, and in some sense independent status of mind is not capable of definite settlement. . . . The most that can be done is to suggest certain objections that can be and have been brought against the materialist position . . . and at the same time to indicate a number of independent considerations which seem to demand a different kind of approach to psychology, and a different interpretation of its problems. This interpretation, to put it briefly, insists that [1.] a living organism is something over and above the matter of which its body is composed; that it is, in short, an expression of a *principle of life*, and that life is a force, stream, entity, spirit, call it what you will, that cannot be described or accounted for in material terms; [2.] that in human beings this principle of life expresses itself at the level of what is called *mind*, that this mind is distinct from both body and brain, . . . and [3.] that *no account of mind action which is given in terms of brain action, gland activity, or bodily responses to external stimuli* can, therefore, be completely satisfactory. This is the view which in some form or other is held by those who find a materialist explanation of psychology unsatisfactory, and in this [essay] we shall be concerned with the reasons for it.

II. BIOLOGICAL CONSIDERATIONS

1. Purposiveness / Some of these reasons, and perhaps the most important, are derived in part from regions which lie outside the scope of psychology proper; they belong to biology, and are based on a consideration of the characteristics which all living beings are found to possess in common. With regard to one of these "alleged"[2] characteristics of living organisms it is necessary to say a few words, since it constitutes a starting point for the method of interpretation with which we shall be concerned in this [essay.] The characteristic in question is that to which we give the name of purposiveness, and because of this characteristic it is said that any attempt to interpret the behavior of living creatures in terms of material response to stimuli must inevitably break down. . . .

[2]I insert the word "alleged" in order to indicate the controversial character of the subject. There is no doubt that it would be thought unsafe by many biologists to assume the existence of the characteristic in question, although I myself do not wish to deny it.

What, therefore, is meant by saying that living creatures are purposive? Primarily, that in addition to those of their movements which may be interpreted as responses to existing situations, they also act in a way which seems to point to the existence of a spontaneous impulse or need to bring about some other situation which does not yet exist. This impulse or need is sometimes known as a conation; a good instance of the sort of thing that is meant is the impulse we feel to maintain the species by obtaining food or seeking a mate. The impulse is chiefly manifested in the efforts a living organism will make to overcome any obstacle which impedes the fulfillment of its instinctive need. It will try first one way of dealing with it and then another, as if it were impelled by some overmastering force which drove it forward to the accomplishment of a particular purpose. Thus the salmon, proceeding upstream, leaping over rocks and breasting the current in order to deposit her spawn in a particular place, is acting in a way which it is difficult to explain in terms of a response to external stimuli. An organism again will seek to preserve the trend of natural growth and development by which alone the purpose of existence will be fulfilled; in its endeavor to reach and to maintain what we may call its natural state or condition, it is capable, if need arises, of changing or modifying its bodily structure. If you take the hydroid plant Antennularia and remove it from the flat surface to which it is accustomed to adhere, it will begin to proliferate long wavy roots or fibers in the effort to find something solid to grip, while everybody has heard of the crab's habit of growing a new leg in place of one that has been knocked off.

Activity of this kind seems difficult to explain on materialist lines as the response to a stimulus; it appears rather to be due to the presence of a living, creative impulse to develop in the face of any obstacle in a certain way. . . .

2. Foresight and Expectation / When we apply this conclusion to human psychology, we are immediately struck by the fact that the individual not only exhibits in common with other organisms this characteristic of purposive behavior, but is in many cases conscious of the nature of the purpose which inspires his behavior. The man who studies in order to pass an examination is not only impelled by a push from behind; he is drawn forward by a pull from in front. This pull in front can only become operative if he can be credited with the capacity to conceive the desirability of a certain state of affairs—namely, the passing of the examination, which does not yet exist; he shows, in other words, foresight and expectation. It is activities of this kind which seem most insistently to involve the assumption of a mind to do the foreseeing and expecting. In other words, the capacity to be influenced by events which lie in the future seems inexplicable on the stimulus-response basis; the *thought* of what does not exist may be allowed to influence the mind, but it is difficult to see how the nonexistent can stimulate the body.

The explanation of our capacity for being influenced by the thought of events that do not yet exist raises much the same difficulty as our undoubted responsiveness to events that have existed but do so no longer, and it will be desirable to consider the problem first of all from this point of view. . . .

III. [CONSIDERATIONS] OF MEANING

[3. The Apprehension of Meaning /] An important fact about our mental life is that we are capable of appreciating meaning. A statement of fact written on a piece of paper is, so far as its material content is concerned, merely a number of black marks inscribed on a white background. Considered, then, as a collection of visual, physical stimuli, it is comparatively unimportant; what is important is the meaning which is attached to these marks. If they inform us, for example, that we have received a legacy of ten thousand pounds it is not the black marks on the white background but the meaning they convey that effects a disturbance in our emotional life sufficiently profound to keep us awake all night. Now the meaning of the marks is obviously not a physical stimulus; it is something immaterial. How, then, is its effect to be explained in terms of bodily responses to physical stimuli, which the mind merely registers? Let us take one or two further examples in order to present the difficulty in a concrete form.

Let us suppose that I am a geometrician and am thinking about the properties of a triangle. As I do not wish at this point to enter into the vexed question of whether *some* physical stimulus is or is not necessary to initiate every chain of reasoning, we will assume that in this case there was a physical stimulus—it may have been a chance remark about Euclid, or the appearance of a red, triangular road signpost, while I am driving a car—a stimulus which we will call X, which prompted me to embark upon the train of speculations about the triangle. My reasoning proceeds until I arrive at a conclusion, which takes the form of a geometrical proposition expressed in a formula. I carry this formula in my head for a number of days and presently write it down. In due course I write a book, setting forth my formula and giving an account of the reasoning which led me to it. The book is read and understood by A. Presently it is translated into French, and is read and understood by B. Later still I deliver a lecture on the subject which is heard and understood by C. As A, B, and C have each of them understood my formula and the reasoning upon which it is based, we may say that the reasoning process has had for them the same meaning throughout. If it had not, they would not all have reached the same conclusion and understood the same thing by it. Yet in each of the four cases the sensory stimulus was different; for myself it was X, for A it was a number of black marks on a white background, for B a number of different black marks on a white background, and for C a number of vibrations in the atmosphere impinging upon his eardrums. It seems incredible that all these different stimuli should have been able to produce a consciousness of the same meaning, if our respective reactions to them were confined to physical responses (which must in each case have been different) which were subsequently reflected in our minds by a process of mental registration of the different responses. The stimuli being different, the intervention of something possessed of the capacity to grasp the *common* element among these physically different entities alone seems able to account for the facts, but the common element is the meaning, which is immaterial and can be grasped, therefore, only by a mind.

4. Synthesizing Power of Mind / This conclusion is reinforced by what we may call the synthesizing power of mind. Synthesizing means putting together, and one of the most remarkable powers that we possess is that of taking a number of isolated sensations and forming them into a whole . . .

Let us consider for a moment the case of aesthetic appreciation. The notes of a symphony considered separately consist merely of vibrations in the atmosphere. Each note may, when sounded in isolation, produce a pleasant sensation, and as one note is struck after another we get a sequence of pleasant sensations. But although this is a sufficient description of the symphony considered as a collection of material events, and of our reactions to these events considered merely in terms of sensations, it is quite clear that we normally think of a symphony as being something more than this. We think of it in fact as a whole, and it is as a whole that it gives what is called aesthetic pleasure. Now in thinking of the symphony in this way our mind is going beyond the mere sequence of pleasant sensations which its individual notes produce, and putting them together into some sort of pattern. If the notes were arranged in a different order, although the actual vibrations which impinged upon our senses would be the same, the pleasurable aesthetic effect would be destroyed.

It seems to follow that our pleasure in a symphony cannot be wholly accounted for, although it may depend upon our physical responses to the stimuli of the individual notes; in order to obtain aesthetic pleasure we must somehow be able to perceive it as more than the sum total of the individual notes—that is, as a whole pattern or arrangement. The pleasure ceases when the *wholeness* of the object perceived is destroyed, as it is, for example, by the transposition of certain notes. We may compare the difference between the physical sensations which are our responses to the visual stimuli of the colours and canvas of which a picture is composed, with our synthesized perception of a picture as a work of art.

We must conclude, then, that we possess the power of realizing external objects not merely as collections of physical stimuli, which of course they are, but as wholes in which the actual sensory elements are combined to form a single object of a higher order. This faculty of combining or putting together seems to involve the existence not only of a mind, but of a mind of an active, creative type which is able to go out beyond the raw material afforded by our bodily sensations, and to apprehend ideal objects as wholes which are more than the collection of physical events which compose their constituent parts.

IV. [CONCLUSION]

The conclusion to which the arguments . . . appear to point is that, in addition to the body and brain, the composition of the living organism includes an immaterial element which we call mind; that this element, although it is in very close association with the brain, is more than a mere glow or halo surrounding the cerebral structure, the function of which is confined to reflecting the events occurring in that structure; that, on the contrary, it is in some sense independent of the brain, and in virtue of its independence is able in part to direct and control the material constituents of the body, using them to carry out its purposes in relation to the external world of objects, much as a driver will make use of the mechanism of his motorcar. Mind so conceived is an active, dynamic, synthesizing force; it goes out beyond the sensations provided by external stimuli and arranges them into patterns, and it seems to be capable on occasion of acting without the provocation of bodily stimuli to set it in motion. It is, in other words, creative; that is, it carries on activities which even the greatest conceivable extension of our physiological knowledge would not enable us to infer from observing the brain. . . .

17 / Why I Am a Dualist

WILLIAM S. ROBINSON

I

I believe that people and other animals have sensations and that these are not purely material things. Since I also believe that some things—rocks and trees, for example—*are* purely material things, I believe that the world as a whole contains (at least) two different kinds of things. This explains why my view is called dualism. The controversial part of this view, however, is the claim that there are sensations which are not purely material things.

To understand this claim we need to understand what a *sensation* is, what a *purely material thing* is, and what argument can be given for the claim. Let us begin with the term *sensation*. It is a difficult and somewhat technical matter to give a satisfactory definition of this term. Fortunately, we do not really need to have one. I have claimed that the world contains at least two kinds of things and this would be true even if there were just one thing of each kind. So it would be enough if we had one example of a sensation for which we can make a clear case that it is not a purely material thing. I will in fact give a little more than enough; I will describe three kinds of sensations and the reader will then be able to provide more. The three are pains, afterimages, and ringing in the ears.

To make sure that our attention is focused on the right thing, it is very important to make sure that we distinguish these three kinds of things from their *causes*. This can be done by considering cases in which the causal situation is somewhat out of the ordinary. (In fact, as we shall see, the very terms *afterimage* and *ringing in the ears* involve the idea that there is a certain peculiarity about their causes.) The usual cause of a pain is damage to some part of the body. Typically, the pain is felt to be located in the part of the body which has been damaged. (The "damage" may, of course, be either from some external cause or from an internal one, as in disease or a congenital defect.) There are, however, cases called "phantom limb," in which amputees suffer pains in limbs they no longer possess. That is, they hurt and seek medical relief; when the doctor asks *where* they hurt, their only natural reply is, for example, "In my right elbow," even though they are all too well aware that they do not have a right arm.

The actual cause of such a pain lies in conditions of nerves in the shoulder or spinal cord. It is at such locations that the doctor will intervene to relieve the pain. So the case of phantom limb does not show that pains are not physically caused or that they do not depend on what goes on in a person's nervous system. It does not show that pains are not purely material things. What it does do is help get our attention focused on the pain itself as distinguished from the injury which may be its cause. Once we have understood this case, those of us who do have arms should be able to distinguish clearly between a hit on the elbow (or a cut, bruise, or chipped bone)—that is, an injury—and the pain we feel when we are thus injured. It is only the pain and not the injury which I am claiming is not purely material.

Afterimages are like things which we see in that (1) they come in different colors and (2) our knowledge of what color they are has something to do with our eyes. They are unlike things we see in that they are not "there" to be seen. That is, we may be having a yellow afterimage when there is nothing yellow reflecting light into our eyes (and no yellow light being reflected into them by white things either). In fact, we may have a yellow afterimage when our eyes are closed and, thus, when they are not receiving reflected light of any kind whatever. Afterimages are caused by relatively bright illuminations of our retinas; but they have the complementary color of that illumination and they occur only after that illumination has ceased. Thus, knowing the color of an afterimage is easily distinguishable from knowing something about the light which causes it. Once again, it is not *these* considerations which are supposed to support dualism. Their point is rather to prepare the way for the argument by getting our attention focused on the kind of colored thing which I am claiming to be not purely material.

The case is very similar with ringing in the ears; so similar, in fact, that it will be enough to merely relate the following actual incident. I once was leaning against a doorjamb while conversing with the occupant of an office. After a while I became aware of a thin, whistle-like sound. I wondered whether it was just a ringing in my ears or a very loud whistle very far away. I did not know which, and I turned my head and moved into and out of the office to find out. I was astonished to find that neither of my hypotheses was correct; the cause was a very small vibration very close, namely, a little air escaping from a valve in a thermostat on the wall about six inches from my ear. However, I have become aware of exactly similar sounds on other occasions when examination turned up no cause outside my head. These sounds are sensations, and so is the one I became aware of while talking to my colleague, even though it (like most pains in *my* right elbow) was caused in a manner which is typical for the kind of sensation it was.

Let us turn now to the notion of a purely material thing. Although I have mentioned rocks and trees as examples, it will not do to merely illustrate what is meant by "purely material things." This is because there are many examples of discovering quite new kinds of purely material things, and we have to know what counts as discovering a new *material* thing as opposed to discovering a new *non*material thing (or showing that something, whether new or old, is nonmaterial). Thus, for example, when electrons were added to the list of things which scientists talked about, they were regarded as newly discovered material things and not as some kind of nonmaterial thing. There is the further reason that as physics has developed, its basic concepts have changed—even those as basic as "particle," "space," and "matter." If we tie our understanding of "material" too closely to particular views in physics, we leave ourselves open to finding that the physicists of tomorrow are no longer talking about purely "material" things. We need some way of understanding "material" which will enable us to avoid such a consequence.

There is one way—and only one—of getting what we need here which is plausible, straightforward, and in accord with all the noncontroversial cases. This approach is to make use of two truths which are rather obvious and are so basic to our understanding of "material" that hardly anything would be left of the idea if they were denied. They are as follows: (A) What a material thing is made of is parts which are material; and (B) if a thing is made of (only) material things, it is material. These truths suggest the following approach: Start with anything whose materiality is uncontroversial, for example, any ordinary, visible, tangible inanimate thing. Enlarge your set of material things by the rule, Whatever a material thing is made of is material. This will give you, for example, molecules, atoms, and electrons as material things. Enlarge your set of material things further by the rule, Whatever is composed of only material things is material. This gives you very large material things, such as planets, solar systems, and galaxies. A material thing, then, is any member of the largest collection which can be generated by this procedure.

This gives us a workable understanding of "material thing," but we must say a few words about *purely* material things. Some musical instruments are highly decorated with ivory inlays, delicate carvings, and sometimes even paintings. Assuming that tonal quality has not been sacrificed, we may say that such an instrument lives in two quite distinct esthetic modes, neither of which is reducible to or accountable for in terms of the other. Its visual excellence is not explainable or even describable by reference to its tonal qualities, and vice versa. Such a visually pleasing object *is* a musical instrument; but because of its visual dimension I think it is natural to say that it is not *purely* a musical instrument.

Contrast the case of a thing which is "both" an arrangement of transistors, wires, circuit chips, and buttons and "also" a calculator. *In a sense* such a thing lives in two modes. For we can talk about what the calculator does—adding, taking roots, storing information, and so forth—or we can talk about how it works. These two ways of talking about it reflect the different interests of the user and the manufacturer (or repairer), and tend to remain distinct. Nonetheless, I shall say that a calculator is *purely* an arrangement of transistors, wires, and so on, because what it does can be fully accounted for by reference to how the transistors and other parts work and how they are connected.

When I claim that sensations are not purely material things, I am not denying that it *may* turn out that pains are aspects of the same things that are also material things—just as in claiming that some object is not purely a musical instrument I would not be denying that a carving may be a thing that is also a musical instrument. A materialism which claimed *only* that everything is material without insisting that everything is *purely* material would be a very weak and uninteresting form of materialism. What I do deny, when I deny that sensations are purely material, is the interesting materialist claim that sensations can be fully accounted for by reference to the uncontroversially material aspect of material things.

II

Before proceeding to the argument for dualism, we must have a more concrete understanding of materialism. There is ample evidence that there is some kind of connection between sensations and brains. For example, in a famous series of experiments Wilder Penfield produced sensations in a number of patients by directly stimulating their brains with electrodes.[1] It is also known that destroying some parts of the brain, or changing their operation by means of electrode stimulation or drugs, can prevent some pains from occurring. These facts lead to the view that *if* sensations are purely material things, they will be very intimately related to material things which are parts of brains. There are just three ways for a materialist to conceive of this relationship. First, it may be held that sensations are made of neurons, as engines are made of rods, pistons, valves, etc., or houses are made of bricks, shingles and beams. Second, it may be held that sensations are *states* of people rather than being *things*. A claim which parallels this one in form is: "Sound waves are *states* of air rather than *things*." The natural development of this view narrows what the state is *of* down to some collection of neurons in the brain. For the state of the rest of my body (i.e., besides my retina or elbow) does not have anything to do with the color of my afterimage or the throbbing of my elbow; and, as I remarked earlier, one does not even need an elbow in order to have pain "in" it. The only thing whose possession seems really required for a sensation to occur is a brain or some part of a brain. Thus, this second way of conceiving materialism must be formulated in this way: Sensations are states of collections of neurons (in the brain). (Compare: Sound waves are states of collections of air molecules—namely, states of being alternately more and less compressed.)

[1]Wilder Penfield, *The Excitable Cortex in Conscious Man.* (Springfield, Ill., 1958).

Third, it may be held that while sensations are not themselves composed of anything, they are parts of brains. [This makes them material, by principle A. Therefore, if they had parts those parts would (by the same principle) be material; and then sensations would be material in the first way (i.e., by being made out of material things). Thus, if the third alternative is to be independent of the success of the first, we must include in it the supposition that sensations have no parts.]

Now, the key fact in the argument for dualism is that none of these three alternatives is *intelligible*. It is important to understand what this means, so let us consider some illustrations. The view that the earth is flat is false, and even obviously false, in the light of the evidence we have. It is, however, an *intelligible* view; it *could* have turned out that we live on an enormous plate (after all, asteroids are typically not even approximately spherical). We know what it would have been like to have had evidence that this was the case. When we hear that people used to think the earth is flat, we understand what they believed; we understand what they would have meant if they had said, "The earth is flat"; and we understand that with limited evidence this may have been a reasonable view to hold. Contrast this case with the claim that the universe is made of numbers. This is not an intelligible view. We have no idea what it would be like for this to be true; we have no idea what it would be like to have evidence supporting such a claim; we do not understand how, even granting severely limited evidence, people could have found it reasonable to believe this. When we read in a history of philosophy that Pythagoras is reputed to have made such a claim, we can only wonder what he meant; that is to say, we can only wonder what intelligible claim it was which he made, which is being reported to us in these words, which, as they stand, are unintelligible. (For example, perhaps he meant that the distances between planets stand to each other in exact integral ratios. *This* claim is intelligible even though it is quite unworthy of being believed.) It is this kind of unintelligibility that I find in such claims as "Sensations are made of neurons," "Sensations are states of collections of neurons," and "Sensations are (in part) what brains are made of." . . . Again, consider the idea that you or your friend is really a character in someone else's dream. This is a sophisticated joke that sometimes occurs to students when their philosophy professors ask them to consider how they know they are not dreaming. But let us try to take it seriously; let us imagine reading in *The New York Times* one morning that scientists report having discovered yesterday that Sting, lead singer of The Police, is actually nothing but the dream character of the group's drummer, Stewart Copeland. Only the most unthinking could fail to recognize this as a hoax. The reason is not that finding out that a body is made of dream-stuff is a particularly difficult thing to do or that we haven't appropriated sufficient funds to do it correctly. The reason is that we have no idea what could count as finding out such a thing.

The first two formulations of materialism, stated above, require similar treatment and I will consider them together; then I will make some remarks about the third alternative. A particular example of the first alternative is, "This pain is made of neurons X, Y and Z." An example of the second alternative is, "Jones's hurting is (or consists in) Jones's neurons X, Y, and Z firing in pattern P_1." (Patterns of neuron firings can be characterized by such properties as the order in which neurons involved in the pattern fire, the ratios of times between firings, the ratios of intensities of output of each neuron, the ratios of durations of firing, and the length of time between repetitions of a sequence of firings. For example, pattern P_1 might be repeated sequences—say, twenty repetitions per second—of firings of X, followed by Y, followed by Y again, followed by Z; where the ratio of firing intervals is 2:1:3 and the ratio of durations is 1:4:2:3.) Neither of these examples is intelligible. We do not understand what it would be like for them to be true; we do not understand what it would be like to find evidence pointing to their truth. In the nature of the case, one cannot *argue* for the unintelligibility of these examples (any more than one can argue that "The universe is made of numbers" is unintelligible). The following examples, however, will focus attention on the point at which the unintelligibility occurs, by showing what intelligibility looks like in parallel cases in which it is present. A ladder is composed of parts—parts which are not ladders themselves, but rungs and sides. This composition is fully intelligible because when you understand what a rung is, what a side is, and how they are arranged, you thereby understand how a ladder can help you get onto a roof. Again, being properly aligned is a state of my car, and this state is (or consists in) some of the parts of my car being in a certain arrangement. This composition is fully intelligible because when you understand what rods, chassis, and so forth are and how they are arranged after the bolts have been properly tightened, you thereby understand why the wheels contact the road in a rectangle rather than a parallelogram. By contrast, you could know all you wished about neural firing sequences, intensities, and timing: You would not thereby understand that the person in whose brain they occur must be in pain.

We have to be careful at this point to distinguish between evidence that one thing *causes* another and evidence that one thing is *made of* (composed of, consists of or in) others. Some viruses cause warts, but warts are not made out of those viruses; my parents caused me but are not parts of me. My cells, by contrast, did not bring me into existence; they are what I am made of. The experiments by Penfield which I mentioned earlier are evidence that sensations are caused by neural firings. *This* claim is not only intelligible but so well supported that it is hard to imagine how a reasonable person could deny it. Now, if I knew which neural firings cause which sensations and I knew that a neural firing of a certain kind was about to occur, I would be able to predict that a certain kind of sensation was about to occur.

In this sense one could say that if I knew everything about neurons I would know which sensations would be forthcoming. But all this does not give any intelligibility to the idea that a red afterimage may really be composed of neurons or that a C-sharp ringing in the ears is just some neurons firing in a certain pattern. When you think about the parts of a ladder in their arrangement, you can *see why* the whole thus composed does what it does. If you knew all about the innards of an Atari set, you would *understand why*, when you put it into a certain state by pushing the right buttons, it plays "Breakout." But you cannot in this way understand that there should be pain or a red afterimage through getting to know the details of a neural firing pattern. Why should a firing interval ratio of 2:1:3:2 go with hurting (for example) whereas one of 1:4:2:3 goes with itching? What has a duration ratio of 5:3:4:1:2 got to do with red in my afterimage, rather than blue or yellow? The problem with these questions is not that it would take a lot of research to answer them. The problem is that we have no idea what could count as a research program designed to answer them.

Let us turn to the third alternative, that is, the view that sensations are (in part) what brains are made of. According to this view, a list of brain parts which includes only such items as carbon atoms, subatomic particles, neurons, and water molecules must be incomplete. A complete list would have to include, for example, pains and ringing in the ears. To imagine this is to imagine that a neural scientist might have reason to say, with a perfectly straight face, something like the following: "I have weighed the chemical constituents of brain number 247 and have found a discrepancy. The constituents make up less than the brain when it was measured as a whole. Therefore, some pains or ringing in the ears must have been part of the brain." But this is not intelligible. We can imagine a discrepancy, of course, and we can imagine anybody *saying* anything. What we cannot imagine is that it could be reasonable for a neural scientist to account for a discrepancy by bringing in sensations as the overlooked parts.

There is, however, one approach which seems to hold promise of giving us a way of imagining just such a possibility. This approach suggests that we model the discovery that pains are brain parts on the discovery of subatomic particles. The pattern of such discoveries is, roughly, this. One takes some unquestionably material thing and subjects it to some unusual conditions, for example, bombardment in a cyclotron. One observes how it reacts, and then one attempts to explain the reaction. Particles are assumed to exist if they are required for such explanations. Particles introduced into physics in this way are, in accord with principle A, taken by everyone to be material. To extend this pattern to sensations is to suppose that pains, for example, might turn out to be needed to explain something that goes on in the brain which would otherwise be inexplicable.

This extension of the method of introducing particles, however, is not really intelligible. Of course, it could happen that when we try to explain in detail how brains work we will be surprised and will have to revise some current theories to account for new evidence. Such revision might even involve supposing that there are things in the brain which we have not yet recognized. What we do not understand, however, is how it could be reasonable to take the newly required things to be pains or afterimages. The reason behind this unintelligibility is as follows. When physicists introduce a new particle, they introduce it as having a force associated with it, so that how it affects other particles is built right into what it is. For example, electrons were not *discovered* to have a negative charge, and they could not have been discovered to have it—for the theory of electrons lays it down that the particles which it calls electrons are just the ones with a negative charge. Similarly, genes were *introduced* as trait carriers rather than being discovered to be so. Now, pains, afterimages, and so forth are not introduced as interacting in some way with neurons or carbon compounds. The pattern by which particles are introduced in physics does not explain how something that is not introduced as having a certain force can be discovered to have it. Thus, we really have no model for "discovering" that pains make neurons or chemical compounds operate in any particular way. We have no model for making intelligible a claim that "this neuron fires now because, in addition to the electrochemical forces on it (which by themselves are insufficient to make it fire), there is present a lime-green afterimage." Without such a model, however, the idea that pains might explain operations in brains remains a mere form of words with no intelligible interpretation; and so, therefore, does the idea that pains might be parts of brains.

If I were to believe that sensations are purely material things, I would have to believe either that they are composed of neurons or that they are states of collections of neurons or that they are parts of brains. I have argued that none of these consequences is intelligible. It is not reasonable to believe that claims are true when they are unintelligible to you. So I do not believe these consequences. Neither, therefore, do I believe what leads to them, that is, the claim that sensations are purely material. That is why I am a dualist.[2]

[2]The editors are grateful to Prof. Robinson for having written this essay for this volume.

18 / The Case for Materialism

RICHARD TAYLOR

I. INTRODUCTION

Sometimes the simplest and most obvious distinctions give rise to the profoundest intellectual difficulties, and things most commonplace in our daily experience drive home to us the depths of our ignorance. Men have fairly well fathomed the heavens, so that perhaps nothing counts as surer knowledge than astronomy, the science of the things most distant from us, and yet the grass at our feet presents impenetrable mysteries. In like manner, our knowledge of man, of human history, of cultures remote in time and distance, fills volumes, and yet each of us is bewildered by that one being that is closest to him, namely, himself, as soon as he asks the most elementary questions. And oddly, it seems that the simplest question one can ask about himself—the question namely, What am I?—is the very hardest to answer, and nonetheless the most important. One can ask of many other things, including some very complex ones—such as a tree, a drop of water, or a machine—just what they are, and be quite certain that his answers, though incomplete, are nonetheless not wholly wrong. But when one asks what he himself is, what he is in his innermost nature; when he asks what is that "I" with which he is so intimately concerned and which is for him the very center of the universe, then he is bewildered, and must fall back on philosophical speculations of the most difficult sort.

It is, moreover, this simple and basic question that has the greatest philosophical ramifications. All morals, religion, metaphysics, and law turn upon it. Law and morality, for example, presuppose the existence of moral agents who have responsibilities and are capable of incurring guilt. But obviously, certain kinds of things can have responsibilities, and certain others cannot; and if men are in fact beings of the latter kind, then morality and law, as traditionally conceived, are nonsense. Again, many religions presuppose that men are spiritual beings, capable of surviving the destruction of their bodies in death. If a man is in fact nothing of the sort, then those religions rest upon a misconception. It is thus imperative that we try to find some answer to this basic and simple question. . . .

II. THE REALITY OF THE SELF AND THE BODY

However unsure I may be of the nature of myself and of the relation of myself to my body, I can hardly doubt the reality of either. Whether I am identical with my body, or whether I am a spirit, or soul, or perhaps only a collection of thoughts and feelings—whatever I am, I cannot doubt my own being, cannot doubt that I am part of the world, even prior to any philosophical reflection on the matter. For surely if I know anything at all, as presumably I do, then I know that I exist. There seems to be nothing I could possibly know any better. And this is, of course, quite consistent with my great ignorance as to the nature of that self of whose existence I feel so assured.

I know, further, that I have a body. I may have learned this from experience, in the same way that I have learned of the existence of innumerable other things, or I may not have; it is, in any case, something I surely know. I may also have only the vaguest conception, or even a totally erroneous one, of the relationship between myself and my body; I can nevertheless no more doubt the reality of the one than the other. I may also be, as I surely am, quite ignorant of the nature and workings of my body and even of many of its parts, but no such ignorance raises the slightest doubt of its reality.

Now what is the connection between these, between myself and my body? Just what relationship am I affirming by "have," when I say with such confidence that I have a body? Abstractly, there seem to be just three general possibilities. In the first place, my having a body might consist simply in the *identity* of myself with my body, or of my *being* a body. Or second, it might amount to *possession*, such that my having a body consists essentially in this body's being among the various other things that I own or possess, it being at the same time, perhaps, in some way unique among these. Or finally, there may be some special, perhaps highly metaphysical relationship between the two, such as that I as a person am one thing, my body another quite different thing, the two being somehow connected to each other in a special way, appropriately expressed by the assertion that the one *has* the other.

Now there are great difficulties in all these suggestions, and, under the third, numerous special theories are possible, as we shall see. We had best, however, begin with the simplest view, to see then whether any of the others are any better.

III. MATERIALISM

I know that I have a body, and that this is a material thing, though a somewhat unusual and highly complicated one. There would, in fact, be no other reason for calling it my body, except to affirm that it is entirely material, for nothing that is not matter could possibly be a part of my body. Now if my having a body consists simply in the identity of myself with my body, then it follows that I *am* a body, and nothing more. Nor would the affirmation of the identity of myself with my body be at all inconsistent with saying that I have a body, for we often express the relationship of identity in just this way. Thus, one might correctly say of a table that is *has* four legs and a top, or of a bicycle that it *has* two wheels, a frame, a seat, and handle bars. In such cases, no one would suppose that the table or the bicycle is one thing, and its parts or "body" another, the two being somehow mysteriously connected. The table or the bicycle just *is* its parts, suitably related. So likewise, I might just *be* the totality of my bodily parts, suitably related and all functioning together in the manner expressed by saying that I am a living body, or a living, material animal organism.

This materialistic conception of a person has the great advantage of simplicity. We do know that there are bodies, that there are living animal bodies, and that some of these are in common speech denominated men. A person is, then, on the view, nothing mysterious or metaphysical, at least as regards the *kind* of thing he is.

A consequence of this simplicity is that we need not speculate upon the relationship between one's body and his mind, or ask how the two are connected, or how one can act upon the other, all such questions being rendered senseless within the framework of this view, which in the first place denies that we are dealing with two things. The death of the animal organism—which is, of course, an empirical fact and not subject to speculation—will, moreover, be equivalent to the destruction of the person, consisting simply in the cessation of those functions which together constitute being alive. Hence, the fate of a person is simply, on this view, the fate of his body, which is ultimately a return to the dust whence he sprang. This alleged identity of oneself with his body accounts, moreover, for the solicitude every man has for his body, and for its health and well-being. If a person is identical with his body then any threat to the latter is a threat to himself, and he must view the destruction of it as the destruction of himself. And such, in fact, does seem to be the attitude of all men, whatever may be their philosophical or religious opinions. Again, the distinction that every man draws between himself and other persons, or himself and other things, need be no more than the distinction between one body and others. When I declare that some foreign object—a doorknob, for instance, or a shoe—is no part of myself, I may be merely making the point that it is no part of my body. I would, surely, be more hesitant in declaring that my hand, or my brain and nervous system, which are physical objects, are no parts of me.

Such a conception has nevertheless always presented enormous difficulties, and these have seemed so grave to most philosophers that almost any theory, however absurd when examined closely, has at one time or another seemed to them preferable to materialism. Indeed, the difficulties of materialism are so grave that, for some persons, they need only to be mentioned to render the theory unworthy of discussion.

IV. THE MEANING OF "IDENTITY"

By "identity" the materialist must mean a strict and total identity of himself and his body, nothing less. Now to say of anything, X, and anything, Y, that X and Y are identical, or that they are really one and the same thing, one must be willing to assert of X anything whatever that he asserts of Y, and vice versa. This is simply a consequence of their identity, for if there is anything whatever that can be truly asserted of any object X, but cannot be truly asserted of some object Y, then it logically follows that X and Y are two different things, and not the same thing. In saying, for instance, that the British wartime prime minister and Winston Churchill are one and the same person, one commits himself to saying of either whatever he is willing to say of the other—such as, that he lived to a great age, smoked cigars, was a resolute leader, was born at Blenheim, and so on. If there were any statement whatever that was true of, say, Mr. Churchill, but not true of the wartime prime minister, then it would follow that Mr. Churchill was not the wartime prime minister, that we are here referring to two different men, and not one.

The question can now be asked, then, whether there is anything true of me that is not true of my body, and vice versa. [1.] There are, of course, ever so many things that can be asserted indifferently of both me and my body without absurdity. For instance, we can say that I was born at such and such place and time, and it is not the least odd to say this of my body as well. Or we can say that my body now weighs exactly so many pounds, and it would be just as correct to give this as my weight; and so on.

[2.] But now consider more problematical assertions. It might, for instance, be true of me at a certain time that I am morally blameworthy or praiseworthy. Can we then say that my body or some part of it, such as my brain, is in exactly the same sense blameworthy or praiseworthy? Can moral predicates be applied without gross incongruity to any physical object at all? Or suppose I have some profound wish or desire, or some thought—the desire, say, to be in some foreign land at a given moment, or thoughts of the Homeric gods. It seems at least odd to assert that my body, or some part of it, wishes that it were elsewhere, or has thoughts of the gods. How, indeed, can any purely physical state of any purely physical object ever be a state that is *for* something, or of something, in the way that my desires and thoughts are such? And how, in particular, could a purely physical state be in this sense *for* or *of* something that is not real? Or again, suppose that I am religious, and can truly say that I love God and neighbor, for instance. Can I without absurdity say that my body or some part of it, such as my foot or brain, is religious, and loves God and neighbor? Or can one suppose that my being religious, or having such love, consists simply in my body's being in a certain state, or behaving in a certain way? If I claim the identity of myself with my body, I must say all these odd things; that is, I must be willing to assert of my body, or some part of it, everything I assert of myself. There is perhaps no logical absurdity or clear falsity in speaking thus of one's corporeal frame, but such assertions as these are at least strange, and it can be questioned whether, as applied to the body, they are even still meaningful.

[3.] The disparity between bodily and personal predicates becomes even more apparent, however, if we consider epistemological predicates, involved in statements about belief and knowledge. Thus, if I believe something—believe, for instance, that today is February 31—then I am in a certain state; the state, namely, of having a certain belief which is in this case necessarily a false one. Now how can a physical state of any physical object be identical with that? And how, in particular, can anything be a *false* physical state of an object? The physical states of things, it would seem, just *are*, and one cannot even think of anything that could ever distinguish one such state from another as being either true or false. A physiologist might give a complete physical description of a brain and nervous system at a particular time, but he could never distinguish some of those states as true and others as false, nor would he have any idea what to look for if he were asked to do this. At least, so it would certainly seem.

V. PLATONIC DUALISM

[A.] It is this sort of reflection that has always led metaphysicians and theologians to distinguish radically between the mind or soul of a man and his body, ascribing properties to the mind that are utterly different in kind from those exhibited by the body; properties which, it is supposed, could not be possessed by any body, just because of its nature as a physical object.

The simplest and most radical of such views *identifies* the person or self with a soul or mind, and declares its relationship to the body to be the almost accidental one of mere occupancy, possession, or use. Thus Plato,* and many mystical philosophers before and after him, thought of the body as a veritable prison of the soul, a gross thing of clay from which the soul one day gladly escapes, to live its own independent and untrammeled existence, much as a bird flees its cage or a snake sheds its skin. A person, thus conceived, is a non-material substance—a *spirit*, in the strictest sense— related to an animal body as possessor to thing possessed, tenant to abode, or user to thing used. A person *has* a body only in the sense that he, perhaps temporarily, occupies, owns, or uses a body, being all the while some-

---

*[A philosopher of ancient Greece.—Eds.]

thing quite distinct from it and having, perhaps, a destiny quite different from the melancholy one that is known sooner or later to overtake the corporeal frame.

This dualism of mind and body has been, and always is, firmly received by millions of unthinking men, partly because it is congenial to the religious framework in which their everyday metaphysical opinions are formed, and partly, no doubt, because every man wishes to think of himself as something more than just one more item of matter in the world. Wise philosophers, too, speak easily of the attributes of the mind as distinct from those of the body, thereby sundering the two once and for all. Some form of dualism seems in fact indicated by the metaphysical, moral, and epistemological difficulties of materialism which are, it must be confessed, formidable indeed.

[B.] But whatever difficulties such simple dualism may resolve, it appears to raise others equally grave. For one thing, it is not nearly as simple as it seems. Whatever a partisan of such a view might say of the simplicity of the mind or soul, a *man* is nonetheless, on this view, *two* quite disparate things, a mind and a body, having almost nothing in common and only the flimsiest connection with each other. This difficulty, once it is acutely felt, is usually minimized by conceiving of a man, in his true self as nothing but a mind, and representing his body as something ancillary to this true self, something that is not really any part of him at all but only one among the many physical objects that he happens to possess, use, or what not, much as he possesses and uses various other things in life. His body does, to be sure, occupy a preeminent place among such things, for it is something without which he would be quite helpless; but this renders it no more a part or whole of his true self or person than any other of the world's physical things.

[1.] Possession, however, is essentially a social concept, and sometimes a strictly legal one. Something counts as one of my possessions by virtue of my title to it, and this is something conferred by men, in accordance with conventions and laws fabricated by men themselves. Thus does a field or a building count as one of my possessions. But a certain animal body, which I identify as mine, is not mine in any sense such as this. My dominion over my body arises from no human conventions or laws, and is not alterable by them. The body of a slave, though it may be owned by another man in the fullest sense of ownership that is reflected in the idea of possession, is nevertheless the slave's body in a metaphysical sense in which it could not possibly be the body of his master. One has, moreover, a solicitude for his body wholly incommensurate with his concern for any treasure, however dear. The loss of the latter is regarded as no more than a loss, though perhaps a grave one, while the abolition of one's body cannot be regarded as the mere loss of something clearly held, but is contemplated by any man as an appalling and total calamity.

[2.] The ideas of occupancy or use do not express the relation of mind and body any better. *Occupancy*, for instance, is a physical concept; one thing occupies another by being in or upon it. But the mind, on this view, is no physical thing, and no sense can be attached to its resting within or upon any body; the conception is simply ridiculous. Nor does one simply *use* his body the way he uses implements and tools. One does, to be sure, sometimes use his limbs and other parts, over which he has voluntary control, in somewhat the manner in which he uses tools; but many of one's bodily parts, including some that are vital, the very existence of which may be unknown to him, are not within his control at all. They are nonetheless parts of his body. Artificial devices, too, like hearing aids, spectacles, and the like, do not in the least become parts of one's body merely by being used, even in the case of a man who can barely do without them. They are merely things worn or used. Nor can one say that one's body is that physical being in the world upon which one absolutely depends for his continuing life, for there are many such things. One depends on the sun, for instance, and the air he breathes; without these he would perish as certainly as if deprived of his heart; yet no one regards the sun or the air around him as any part of his body.

A man does not, then, *have* a body in the way in which he has anything else at all, and any comparison of the body to a material possession or instrument is about as misleading as likening it to a chamber in which one is more or less temporarily closeted. The connection between oneself and his body is far more intimate and metaphysical than anything else we can think of. One's body is at least a part of himself, and is so regarded by every man. Yet it is not merely a part, as the arm is part of the body; and we are so far without any hint of how the mind and the body are connected. . . .

VI. MATERIALISM AGAIN

One thing should by now seem quite plain, however, and that is that the difficulties of simple materialism are not overcome by any form of dualism. There is, therefore, no point in recommending dualism as an improvement over materialism. To assert that a man is both body *and* mind—that is, that he is two things rather than one—not only does not remove any problem involved in saying that he is one thing only, namely, a body, but introduces all the problems of describing the connection between those two things. We are led to conclude, then, that a metaphysical understanding of human nature must be sought within the framework of materialism, according to which a man is entirely identical with his body.

All forms of dualism arise from the alleged disparity between persons and physical objects. Men, it is rightly noted, are capable of thinking, believing, feeling, wishing, and so on; but bodies, it is claimed, are capable of none of these things, and the conclusion is drawn that men are not bodies. Yet it cannot be denied that men *have* bodies; hence, it is decided that a man, or a person, is a nonphysical entity, somehow more or less intimately related to a body. But here it is rarely noted that whatever difficulties there may be in applying personal and psychological predicates and descriptions to bodies, precisely the same difficulties are involved in applying such predicates and descriptions to *anything whatever*, including spirits or souls. If, for example, a philosopher reasons that a body cannot think, and thereby affirms that, since a person thinks, a person is a soul or spirit or mind rather than a body, we are entitled to ask how a spirit can think. For surely, if a spirit or soul can think, we can affirm that a body can do so; and if we are then asked *how* a body can think, our reply can be that it thinks in precisely the manner in which the dualist supposes a soul thinks. The difficulty of imagining how a body thinks is not in the least lessened by asserting that something else, which is not a body, thinks. And so it is with every other personal predicate or description. Whenever faced with the dualist's challenge to explain how a body can have desires, wishes, how it can deliberate, choose, repent, how it can be intelligent or stupid, virtuous or wicked, and so on, our reply can always be: The body can do these things, and be these things, in whatever manner one imagines the soul can do these things and be these things. For to repeat, the difficulty here is in seeing how *anything at all* can deliberate, choose, repent, think, be virtuous or wicked, and so on, and *that* difficulty is not removed but simply glossed over by the invention of some new thing, henceforth to be called the "mind" or "soul."

It becomes quite obvious what is the source of dualistic metaphysics when the dualist or soul philosopher is pressed for some description of the mind or soul. The mind or soul, it turns out in such descriptions, is just whatever it is that thinks, reasons, deliberates, chooses, feels, and so on. But the fact with which we began was that *men* think, reason, deliberate, choose, feel, and so on. And we do in fact have some fairly clear notion of what we mean by a man, for we think of an individual man as a being existing in space and time, having a certain height and weight—as a being, in short, having many things in common with other objects in space and time, and particularly with those that are living, i.e., with other animals. But the dualist, noting that a man is significantly different from other beings, insofar as he, unlike most of them, is capable of thinking, deliberating, choosing, and so on, suddenly asserts that it is not a man, as previously conceived, that does these things at all, but something else, namely, a mind or soul, or something that does not exist in space and time nor have any height and weight, nor have, in fact, any material properties at all. And then when we seek some understanding of what this mind or soul is, we find it simply described as a thing that thinks, deliberates, feels, and so on.

But surely the proper inference should have been that men are like all other physical objects in some respects—e.g., in having size, mass, and location in space and time; that they are like some physical objects but unlike others in certain further respects—e.g., in being living, sentient, and so on; and like no other physical objects at all in still other respects—e.g., in being rational, deliberative, and so on. And of course none of this suggests that men are not physical objects, but rather that they are precisely physical objects, like other bodies in some ways, unlike many other bodies in other ways, and unlike any other bodies in still other respects.

The dualist or soul philosopher reasons that since men think, feel, desire, choose and so on, and since such things cannot be asserted of bodies, then men are not bodies. Reasoning in this fashion, we are forced to the conclusion that men are not bodies—though it is a stubborn fact that men nevertheless *have* bodies. So the great problem then is to connect men, now conceived as souls or minds, to their bodies. But philosophically, it is just exactly as good to reason that, since men think, feel, desire, choose, etc., and since men are bodies—i.e., are living, animal organisms having the essential material attributes of weight, size, and so on—then *some* bodies think, feel, desire, choose, etc. This argument is just as good as the dualist's argument and does not lead us into a morass of problems concerning the connection between soul and body.

VII. THE SOURCE OF DUALISTIC THEORIES

Why, then, does the dualist's argument have, and this one lack, such an initial plausibility? Why have so many philosophers been led into dualistic metaphysical views, on the basis of arguments apparently no stronger than other arguments having simpler conclusions but which are rarely even considered?

Part of the answer is perhaps that, when we form an idea of a *body* or a *physical object*, what is most likely to come to mind is not some man or animal but something much simpler, such as a stone or a marble. When we are then invited to consider whether a physical object might think, deliberate, choose, and the like, we are led to contemplate the evident absurdity of supposing things like *that* do such things, and thus we readily receive the claim that bodies cannot think, deliberate, choose, and the like, and the dualist extracts his conclusion. But suppose we began somewhat differently. Suppose we began with a consideration of two quite dissimilar physical objects—a living, animal body, of the kind commonly denominated "man," on the one hand, and a simple body, of the kind denominated "stone," on the other. Now let it be asked whether there is any absurdity in supposing that one of these things might be capable of thinking, deliberating, choosing, and the like. Here there is no absurdity at all in asserting that an object of the first kind might indeed have such capacities, but evidently not one of the second kind—from which we would conclude, not that men are not physical objects, but rather that they are physical objects which are significantly different from other physical objects, such as stones. And there is, of course, nothing the least astonishing in this.

But how, one may wonder, can a "mere physical object" have feelings? But here the answer should be: Why, if it is a physical object of a certain familiar kind, should it not have feelings? Suppose, for example, that it is a living body, like a frog or mouse, equipped with a complicated and living nervous system. Where is the absurdity in asserting that a "mere physical object" of this sort can feel? Evidently there is none. Hardly anyone would want to insist that beings of this sort—frogs and mice, for instance—must have souls to enable them to feel. It seems enough that they have complicated living nervous systems.

The same type of answer can be given if it is asked how a "mere physical object" can think. If we suppose that it is a physical object of a certain familiar kind, namely, a living body having the form and other visible attributes of a man, and possessed of an enormously complex living brain and nervous system—in short, that the object in question is a living human being—then there is no absurdity in supposing that this being thinks. Any argument purporting to show that such a being cannot think, and must therefore have a nonmaterial soul to do its thinking for it, would be just as good an argument to show that frogs and mice cannot feel, and must therefore have souls to do their feeling for them. The outcome of such philosophizing is just as good, and just as absurd, in the one case as it is in the other.

Now the materialist would, of course, like to maintain that psychological states, such as feeling, believing, desiring, and so on, are really nothing but perfectly *familiar kinds* of material states, that is, states of the body, particularly of the brain and nervous system; states that are either observable or testable by the usual methods of biology, physics, and chemistry. But this, as we have seen earlier, seems to be a vain hope, and will always be an obstacle to any simple materialism. There is always, it seems, something that can be asserted of certain psychological states which makes little if any sense when asserted of any ordinary or familiar state of matter. One can say of a belief, for instance, that it is true or false, but this can never be said, except metaphorically or derivatively, of any familiar state of matter, such as an arrangement of molecules; we could say of such a thing that it is true or false, only if we first assumed that it is identical with some belief that is such. Again, one can say of a desire that it is the desire *for* this or that—for instance, the desire for food; of a fear that it is a fear *of* something—for instance, a fear of heights; but of no familiar state of matter can it be said that it is, in the same sense, *for* or *of* anything. It just *is* the state of matter that it is. Suppose, for example, that the materialist should say that the feeling of hunger is simply *identical* with a certain familiar state of the body; not merely that it is prompted by that state but that it *is* that state, and is describable in terms of the concepts of physics and chemistry. Thus, let us suppose him to claim that hunger just *is* the state consisting of having an empty stomach, together with a deficiency of certain salts or other substances in the blood, and a certain physical disequilibrium of the nervous system consequent upon these conditions. Now there is, of course, no doubt an intimate connection between such states as these and the desire for food, but the assertion of their *identity* with that desire will always be plagued because, unlike the desire, those bodily states can be fully described without mentioning food at all, and without saying that they are in any sense states that are *for* food. Indeed, the notion of something being *for* or *of* something else, in the sense in which a desire may be a desire *for* food, or a fear may be a fear *of* heights, is not a concept of physics or chemistry at all. And yet it can surely be said of a certain desire that it is a desire for food, or of a certain fear that it is a fear of heights. The referential character of such states seems, indeed, essential to any proper description of them. Significantly, when those substances that are physiologically associated with such states are artifically administered to someone, in the effort to create within him those states themselves, the effort fails. It is fairly well known, for example, what physiological changes a man undergoes when he is in a state of fear; but when these changes are artificially evoked in him, he does not experience fear in the usual sense. He describes his state as being vaguely *like* fear, but finds that he is not afraid *of* anything.

But while psychological states are thus evidently not identical with any familiar bodily states, it does not follow that they are identical with no state of matter at all. They may, in fact, be unfamiliar states of matter, that is, states of the body that are not observable or testable by the ordinary methods of biology, physics, and chemistry. This suggestion is not as question-begging as it appears, for it is conceded by the most resolute soul philosophers and dualists that psychological states are strange ones in this respect at least, that they are not thus observable. From the fact that some state is unobservable by the usual methods of scientific observation, nothing whatever follows with respect to the truth or falsity of materialism. From the fact that a certain state is in some respect unusual it does not follow that it is a state of an unusual thing, of a soul rather than a body, but rather, that if it is a state of the body it is an unusual one, and if it is a state of the soul it is no less unusual. Nothing is made clearer, more comprehensible, or less strange by postulating some new substance as the subject of certain states not familiar to the natural sciences, and then baptizing that new substance "the mind" or "the soul." Nor does one avoid materialism at this point by saying that by the "mind" or "soul" we just *mean* that which is the subject of psychological states; for while that might indeed be true, it is nevertheless an open question whether what we thus mean by the "mind" or "soul" might not turn out, after all, to be what we ordinarily denominate "the body." The existence of nothing whatever can be derived from any definitions of terms. . . .

VIII. CONCLUSION

Of course we cannot, by these reflections, pretend to have solved the problems of mind and matter, nor to have proved any theory of materialism. Human nature is mysterious, and remains so, no matter what one's metaphysical theory is or how simple it is. It does nevertheless seem evident that no dualistic theory of man renders human nature any less mysterious, and that whatever questions are left unanswered by the materialist are left equally unanswered, though perhaps better concealed, by his opponents.

19 / Mind Without Matter

A. A. LUCE

I am . . . asking, "Does matter exist?" And I answer, "No"; but I am also asking a deeper, constructive question, viz.: "What precisely do I see and touch?" If we know precisely what we see and touch and otherwise sense, the question about matter settles itself automatically. We are studying sense-perception in order to find out precisely what man perceives by sense. Matter has always been the intellectual refuge of scepticism and half-knowledge. The materialist distrusts his senses, depreciates their position and rejects their evidence. He holds that sense without matter does not make sense. That contention goes far and cuts deep, and warps a man's attitude, not only to things of spirit, but to reality all along the line. The materialist holds that without matter the sensible could not exist as a *thing*, could not cause, and would be indistinguishable from dream. . . .

I open my eyes and see. What precisely do I see? I stretch out my hand and touch. What precisely do I touch? What precisely do we see and touch, when we see and touch? That is our question. We have many names in ordinary life for the myriad things we see and touch—shoes, ships, sealing-wax, apples, pears and plums; those names are precise enough for action, but they are not precise enough for thought; thought is concerned with common features and resemblances, more than with differences and distinctions. Now; when I see ships and shoes and apples and so forth, what precisely do I see that is common to all those sights? I see colours and shades of colour, light and its modes, illuminated points and lines and surfaces. Those are the things I actually see, and I call them inclusively visual data; they are the elemental objects of the sense of sight. And when I touch shoes and ships and apples and so forth, what precisely do I touch that is common to all those touches? I touch hard, soft, solid, fluid, resistant, yielding, and (in the wider sense of ''touch'') hot, cold, warm and tepid. Those are the things I actually touch, and I call them inclusively tactual data; they are the elemental objects of the sense of touch. . . .

The theory of matter, as we have seen, requires us to hold that in every instance of sense-perception there are two factors to be recognised and distinguished, viz. the actual object of sense, the sense-data* actually perceived by eye or ear or hand or other sense organ, and the material substance, itself unperceived and unperceivable, that supports the sense-data. The case against the theory is, in outline, that the theory postulates an intolerable division, based on an improbable guess. It is not a theory reasonably distinguishing homogeneous parts in a thing, like shell and kernel, pea and pod. It is a theory requiring us to break up the one homogeneous thing into two heterogeneous and inconsistent parts, and, incidentally, to pin our faith to the existence of material substance, for which there is not the slightest evidence from fact.

Let us take an instance, and see how the theory of matter works out. See yonder mahogany table. Its colour is brown, in the main, though it is veined and grained in lighter colours. Its touch is hard and smooth. It has a smell and a taste and a sound; but I hardly ever need to bother about them; for I know the table ordinarily by its colours and by the cut and shape of its lines of light and its shading, and if I am in doubt I can handle it, and feel it and lift it up. It is a sensible table. It is a sensible table through and through. I can bore holes in it, can plane away its surfaces, can burn it with fire and reduce it to ashes; and I shall never come on anything in it that is not an actual or possible object of sense; it is composed entirely of sense-data and *sensibilia*.† Now the theory of matter brings in totally different considerations; it asks me to believe that all these sense-data and *sensibilia* do not constitute the real table. I am asked to believe that beneath the table I see and touch stands another table, a supporting table, a table of a totally different nature that cannot be seen or touched or sensed in any other way, a table to be taken on trust, and yet a highly important table, because it is the real, invariable, material table, while the table I see and touch is only

---

*[Colors, sounds, tastes, tactile sensations, smells etc.—actual objects of sense.—Eds.]
†[Possible sense data.—Eds.]

apparent, variable, inconstant and volatile. The visible-tangible, sensible table has colour and hardness and the other qualities by which things of sense are known and distinguished. The real table has none of these.

What an impossible duality! Yonder mahogany table proves to be two tables. It is a sensible table, and it is a material table. If I take the theory seriously, and go through with it, I am bound to believe the same of everything else around me; wherever I look, I am condemned to see double, and to grope my way through life with divided aim and reduced efficiency.

No rational account of the coexistence of the two tables has ever been given, nor could be given. Some say that the "real table" is the *cause* of the apparent table, but how the cause works is a mystery. Some say that the "real table" is the original, and the apparent table a copy; but what would be the use of a copy that is totally unlike its original? And who, or what, does the copying, and how? The two tables are left there, juxtaposed, unrelated and unexplained. They are not two aspects of the one thing; they are not two parts of the one thing; they have nothing in common; they are not comparable; they could not stem from the one stock; they are heterogeneous; they are at opposite poles of thought; they differ as light from darkness; if the one is, the other is not. No mixing of the two is possible; they cannot be constituents of the one thing; for they are contradictories; if the table is really coloured, then it is not matter; if the table is really matter, then it is not coloured. The supposition of two heterogeneous bodies in the one thing of sense is self-contradictory, destroying the unity of the thing. . . .

Then consider the question of evidence. What evidence is there for the existence of matter? What evidence is there for non-sensible matter? Why should I believe in the matter of materialism? Set aside the misunderstanding that confuses matter with the sensible; set aside the prejudice that would identify with matter the chemical atom, or the subatomic objects of nuclear physics; set aside the legend of the constant sum-total of energy from which all springs and to which all returns; set aside mere tradition and the voice of uninformed authority. And what philosophical evidence is there for the matter of materialism? There is no evidence at all. Writers on matter appeal to prejudice and ignorance in favour of matter; they assume and take it for granted that everyone accepts the existence of matter; they never attempt to prove its existence directly. There is no direct evidence to be had. They try to establish it indirectly. There could not be an external *thing*, they say, unless there were matter; unless there were matter, they say, there would be no cause of change in the external world, nor any test for true and false. . . .

I have examined the typical case of seeing and touching, and have shown that there is no place for matter there. I have examined the normal perceptual situation, and have shown that it contains no evidence for matter, and that the forcible intrusion of matter destroys the unity of the thing perceived and of the world of sense. The onus of proof is on the materialist, and the immaterialist can fairly challenge him to produce his evidence. If there is matter, produce it. If there is evidence for matter, produce it. Neither matter, nor valid evidence for matter, has ever yet been produced.

[1.] The nearest approach to evidence for matter proves on careful study to be bad evidence. . . . I refer to the notion of *support*. The strength of materialism (and its ultimate weakness) is its exploitation of the sub-rational feeling that somehow the pillars of the house rest on matter. People turn to matter for support; they are dimly aware of the need for support; but if they analysed that need, they would look for the support elsewhere.

Sense-data need support, and from the time of Aristotle* to the present day men have claimed that matter supplies the desired support. But could matter, if it existed, supply the kind of support that sense-data need? Literal support is not in question. Sense-data do not need literal support, and if they did need it, matter *ex hypothesi*† could not supply it. In the literal sense sense-data are *given* supported; they are supported by other sense-data. The table supports the books; the books rest on it; without it they would fall. I can see and feel the books and the table in effective contact. That support is visible and tangible. Literal support means sensible support, which is just what matter . . . could not give; for matter cannot be seen or touched or otherwise sensed. The legs of the table support the table; the floor supports both; the earth supports the floor; in all such cases support and things supported are homogeneous; both are *sensibilia*. Matter is not a *sensibile*. Matter and sense are heterogeneous *ex hypothesi*, and therefore matter, if there were such a thing, could not literally support sense-data.

Sense-data cannot stand alone. Like letters of the alphabet or figures or any other symbols they need the support of mind or spirit. By their very mould and nature they are not absolute, but are relative to mind or spirit. An alphabet *in vacuo* would be nonsense. The footprint in the sand implies one to leave the imprint, and the same *understood* implies one to understand it. To "understand" is to stand under and support, as the taking mind stands under and supports the work of the making mind. The materialist's quest of matter as an absolute object of perception, distinct from sense-data, is wrong-headed in principle; he leaves out of the account his own mind. His mind supports his object, as the reader's understanding mind supports the meaning of the printed page, and takes out of it what the writer's mind put into it. Sense-data are not mind or modes of mind; they do not think or will or plan or purpose; but they are from mind and for the mind, and they imply mind and cannot be understood apart from mind. That is why they cannot stand alone; that is why they require support; that

*[A philosopher of ancient Greece.—Eds.]
†[By hypothesis.—Eds.]

is why they require *that sort* of support that only mind or spirit can give. To look to matter for such support would be absurd; for matter is defined as that which is not mind or spirit. Matter cannot support the objects of our senses in theory or practice, literally or metaphorically, and to look to matter for support is to lean on a broken reed.

Let me clinch the argument with an appeal to observable fact in a concrete case. If matter is, I ask, *where* is it? If matter is, it is in things, and in all external things, and the type of external thing selected is neither here nor there. I will choose a homely, explorable thing that we can know through and through, a mutton chop. If matter is, it is in this mutton chop. I ask, where? Where is it in this mutton chop? Where could it be? Take away from this given chop all its sense-data, including its obtainable sense-data. Take away those of the outside and those of the inside, those of the meat and the bone, those of the fat and the lean, be it cooked or uncooked. Take away all that we do sense and all that we might sense, and what is left? There are its visual data, its browns and reds and blacks and whites, and all the other colours and hues of its surface and potential surfaces and centre. There are its tactual data, its rough and smooth, hard and soft, resistant and yielding, solid and fluid, and those varied palpables that admit my knife or hinder its easy passage. It has auditory data; its fat and lean and bone make different sounds when struck by knives and forks. Many smells and savours go to its composing, raw or cooked. Air and moisture link it to its sensible context, and show as steam and vapour under heat. The chop has sensible shapes that may concern artists and even geometricians; it has sensible contents and sensible forms that are specially the concern of chemist and physicist; they are no less sensible and no less real than those contents and forms that are of importance to the butcher and the housewife and the cook. Take them all away in thought. Take away all the *sensa* and the *sensibilia* of this mutton chop, and what is left? Nothing! Nothing is left. In taking away its *sensa* and *sensibilia* you have taken away all the mutton chop, and nothing is left, and its matter is nowhere. Its matter, other than its sense-data, is nothing at all, nothing but a little heap of powdered sentiment, nothing but the ghost of the conventional thing, nothing but the sceptic's question-mark. . . .

[2.] Is matter wanted as a cause? Are sense-data or sensible qualities (call them what you wish) effects of matter? Are the immediate objects of our senses caused by matter? Are sense-data so lacking in causal power that material substance must be postulated and assumed? Is material substance the power behind the scenes, the secret spring of causal action? . . .

Is matter wanted as a cause? Several questions are here combined. What is meant by "cause"? Can sense-data cause? Can they make changes begin to be? If they can, is there any need for matter? If they cannot, how could matter help? If sense-data are passive, how could material substance activate them, and confer on them the power of the cause?

These questions answer themselves in the light of the foregoing analysis of "cause." The term "cause" is ambiguous. In one sense, sense-data can cause, in the other sense, not. Sense-data are not spirits; they cannot make changes begin to be; they cannot directly alter the course of events; for they are passive; but indirectly they give rise to effects; they are signs of what is coming; men read those signs and act on them and make changes begin to be. The sign works through the mind that reads it and understands it and acts on it, just as the works of Shakespeare work through minds that read them and understand them and act on them. The passive sign gives rise indirectly to changes it does not produce. In that respect, and in that respect only, the passive objects of sense around us are causes. In strict speech they are not causes, but are like causes, and not unnaturally, but wrongly, they become credited with the power of making changes begin to be. For practical purposes it is enough for us to know that smoke and fire are almost invariably found together. When we see the smoke we expect the fire, and we are on our guard and take precautions. That is the full extent of the causal connection. The smoke is a passive sign of what is coming; it involves you and me in action, but does not act itself. The black smoke is there, and it will soon burst into a red flame unless I extinguish it. That is the only sense in which the black smoke is the cause of the red flame. The smoke does not make the fire begin to be. The smoke is not the true cause of the fire. The smoke is but the customary antecedent; when we see or smell it, we expect its consequent. The two are indissolubly connected in our minds because they are very frequently associated in nature. The association is there in nature, as in the mind; sometimes we see the smoke before the fire, sometimes the fire before the smoke. Hence it matters little which we call *cause*, and which we call *effect*; they are two parts of the one process; all we need to know is that the two events are causally connected in the sense that the one makes us expect the other. It is no truer that the fire is the cause of the smoke than that the smoke is the cause of the fire. Both propositions are on the one level as regards truth and falsity. In respect of significance or cue-causation, both events are indifferently causes and effects. In respect of efficient or true causation, neither is cause, neither is effect of the other.

Then comes the question about matter. Sense-data *per se* are passive; they may be viewed as acting indirectly through their significance for minds. Does matter enter into the cause? Is material substance the hidden hand behind the scenes? No; matter has nothing to say to causation in either sense of the term. *Ex hypothesi* matter has no significance for mind, and has not the power of the cause. Matter could not cause, nor enable sense-data to do so. There is no room for matter in the causal relation. All that matter does is to mystify, and people are too ready to be mystified. They see that the objects of sense cannot truly cause, and yet that some cause of change is required; and instead of thinking the problem out along the lines sketched above, they jump at the hypothesis of material substance. It shelves the problem and puts it out of sight; it is a facile solution that saves men the trouble of thinking. They say to themselves, "Matter is something we know not what; it acts we know not how." And so all issues in mystery.

Putting aside mystery and mystification, we see that what calls for explanation is some sensible event, some event in the world of sense. We *see* the water rise, and the litmus-paper change colour; we feel the wax soft and then still softer. A sensible change has occurred, and as rational sentients we are bound to ask, "What did it? What caused this change in the world of sense?" To reply, "The material substance of moon or wax acid did it," or, "Material substance in general did it," may give some mystic satisfaction to mystic minds; but such replies have no explanatory value; they shed no light on the problem. Man wants to know causes, and needs to know causes, in order to have some control over events. If he cannot shape the course of events, he must shape his behaviour to suit the events. He needs to be able to move muscle and limb at the right time and to push and pull the things of sense in immediate contact with his body. To do so to the best advantage man needs a certain attitude to things; he needs confidence in the universe, its order and regularity, its wisdom and its goodness. Man is spirit and sense. To form and guide his experience man needs a knowledge of spiritual causes and sensible effects. Matter comes under neither category; *ex hypothesi* matter is neither spiritual nor sensible; therefore it can contribute nothing to a knowledge of causes; it cannot be seen or touched, and therefore it cannot tell me when or how to push and pull the things I see and touch around me. Even if matter existed and possessed some occult power of altering sensible things and effecting visible and tangible changes, we never could *know* that this matter effected that change; we never could connect cause and its effect; we should be none the wiser for the existence of matter; we should have nothing to build on, no foundation for experience or for future action. We never could *know* that this invisible was the cause of that visible change, or that that intangible was the cause of this tangible change. In a word, if matter were a cause, we should never have the evidence of sense as to the cause of a sensible effect. Matter would be of no practical use with regard to knowledge of causes, and it would make no practical difference in life and experience. The invention of matter and its intrusion into the causal relation is purely psychological. It gives some sort of relief to the feelings; it cannot be too easily disproved, and it asks nothing of our moral and spiritual nature. . . .

20 / Behaviorism

JOHN B. WATSON

I. WHAT IS BEHAVIORISM?

Behaviorism . . . holds that the subject matter of human psychology *is the behavior of the human being*. Behaviorism claims that consciousness is neither a definite nor a usable concept. The behaviorist, who has been trained always as an experimentalist, holds, further, that belief in the existence of consciousness goes back to the ancient days of superstition and magic. . . .

The extent to which most of us are shot through with a savage background is almost unbelievable. Few of us escape it. Not even a college education seems to correct it. If anything, it seems to strengthen it, since the colleges themselves are filled with instructors who have the same background. Some of our greatest biologists, physicists, and chemists, when outside of their laboratories, fall back upon folk lore which has become crystallized into religious concepts. These concepts—these heritages of a timid savage past—have made the emergence and growth of scientific psychology extremely difficult.

One example of such a religious concept is that every individual has a *soul* which is separate and distinct from the *body*. This soul is really a part of a supreme being. This ancient view led to the philosophical platform called "dualism." This dogma has been present in human psychology from earliest antiquity. No one has ever touched a soul, or seen one in a test tube, or has in any way come into relationship with it as he has with the other objects of his daily experience. . . .

With the development of the physical sciences which came with the renaissance, a certain release from this stifling soul cloud was obtained. A man could think of astronomy, of the celestial bodies and their motions, of gravitation and the like, without involving soul. Although the early scientists were as a rule devout Christians, nevertheless they began to leave soul out of their test tubes.

Psychology and philosophy, however, in dealing as they thought with non-material objects, found it difficult to escape the language of the church, and hence the concept of mind or soul as distinct from the body came down almost unchanged in essence to the latter part of the nineteenth century.

Wundt, the real father of experimental psychology, unquestionably wanted in 1879 a scientific psychology. He grew up in the midst of a dualistic philosophy of the most pronounced type. He could not see his way clear to a solution of the mind-body problem. His psychology, which has reigned supreme to the present day, is necessarily a compromise. He substituted the term *consciousness* for the term soul. Consciousness is not quite so unobservable as soul. We observe it by peeking in suddenly and catching it unawares as it were (*introspection*). . . .

All other introspectionists are equally illogical. In other words, they do not tell us what consciousness is, but merely begin to put things into it by assumption; and then when they come to analyze consciousness, naturally they find in it just what they put into it. Consequently, in the analyses of consciousness made by certain of the psychologists you find such elements as *sensations* and their ghosts, the *images*. . . . And so it goes. Literally hundreds of thousands of printed pages have been published on the minute analysis of this intangible something called "consciousness." And how do we begin work upon it? Not by analyzing it as we would a chemical compound, or the way a plant grows. No, those things are material things. This thing we call consciousness can be analyzed only by *introspection*—a looking in on what takes place inside of us.

As a result of this major assumption that there is such a thing as consciousness and that we can analyze it by introspection, we find as many analyses as there are individual psychologists. There is no way of experimentally attacking and solving psychological problems and standardizing methods.

II. THE ADVENT OF THE BEHAVIORISTS

In 1912 the objective psychologists or behaviorists reached the conclusion that they could no longer be content to work with Wundt's formulations. They felt that the 30 odd barren years since the establishment of Wundt's laboratory had proved conclusively that the so-called introspective psychology of Germany was founded upon wrong hypotheses—that no psychology which included the religious mind-body problem could ever arrive at verifiable conclusions. They decided either to give up psychology or else to make it a natural science. . . .

In his first efforts to get uniformity in subject matter and in methods the behaviorist began his own formulation of the problem of psychology by sweeping aside all mediaeval conceptions. He dropped from his scientific vocabulary all subjective terms such as sensation, perception, image, desire, purpose, and even thinking and emotion as they were subjectively defined.

The behaviorist asks: Why don't we make what we can *observe* the real field of psychology? Let us limit ourselves to things that can be observed, and formulate laws concerning only those things. Now what can we observe? We can observe *behavior—what the organism does or says*. And let us point out at once: that *saying* is doing—that is, *behaving*. Speaking overtly or to ourselves (thinking) is just as objective a type of behavior as baseball.

The rule, or measuring rod, which the behaviorist puts in front of him always is: Can I describe this bit of behavior I see in terms of "stimulus and response"? By stimulus we mean any object in the general environment or any change in the tissues themselves due to the physiological condition of the animal, such as the change we get when we keep an animal from sex activity, when we keep it from feeding, when we keep it from building a nest. By response we mean anything the animal does—such as turning toward or away from a light, jumping at a sound, and more highly organized activities such as building a skyscraper, drawing plans, having babies, writing books, and the like.

You will find, then, the behaviorist working like any other scientist. His sole object is to gather facts about behavior—verify his data—subject them both to logic and to mathematics (the tools of every scientist). He brings the new-born individual *into his experimental nursery* and begins to set problems: What is the baby doing now? What is the stimulus that makes him behave this way? He finds that the stimulus of tickling the cheek brings the response of turning the mouth to the side stimulated. The stimulus of the nipple brings out the sucking response. The stimulus of a rod placed on the palm of the hand brings closure of the hand and the suspension of the whole body by that hand and arm if the rod is raised. Stimulating the infant with a rapidly moving shadow across the eye will not produce blinking until the individual is sixty-five days of age. Stimulating the infant with an apple or stick of candy or any other object will not call out attempts at reaching until the baby is around 120 days of age. Stimulating a properly brought up infant at any age with snakes, fish, darkness, burning paper, birds, cats, dogs, monkeys, will not bring out that type of response which we call "fear" (which to be objective we might call reaction "X") which is a catching of the breath, a stiffening of the whole body, a turning away of the body from the source of stimulation, a running or crawling away from it. . . .

On the other hand, there are just two things which will call out a fear response, namely, a loud sound, and loss of support.

Now the behaviorist finds from observing children brought up *outside of his nursery* that hundreds of these objects will call out fear responses. Consequently, the scientific question arises: If at birth only two stimuli will call out fear, how do all these other things ever finally come to call it out? Please note that the question is not a speculative one. It can be answered by experiments, and the experiments can be reproduced and the same findings can be had in every other laboratory if the original observation is sound. Convince yourself of this by making a simple test.

If you will take a snake, mouse or dog and show it to a baby who has never seen these objects or been frightened in other ways, he begins to manipulate it, poking at this, that or the other part. Do this for ten days until you are logically certain that the child will always go toward the dog and never run away from it (positive reaction) and that it does not call out a fear response at any time. In contrast to this, pick up a steel bar and strike upon it loudly behind the infant's head. Immediately the fear response is called forth. Now try this: At the instant you show him the animal and just as he begins to reach for it, strike the steel bar behind his head. Repeat the experiment three or four times. A new and important change is apparent. The animal now calls out the same response as the steel bar, namely a fear response, We call this, in behavioristic psychology, the *conditioned emotional response*—a form of *conditioned reflex*.

Our studies of conditioned reflexes make it easy for us to account for the child's fear of the dog on a thoroughly natural science basis without lugging in consciousness or any other so-called mental process. A dog comes toward the child rapidly, jumps upon him, pushes him down and at the same time barks loudly. Oftentimes one such combined stimulation is all that is necessary to make the baby run away from the dog the moment it comes within his range of vision. . . .

III. DOES THIS BEHAVIORISTIC APPROACH LEAVE ANYTHING OUT OF PSYCHOLOGY?

After so brief a survey of the behavioristic approach to the problems of psychology, one is inclined to say: "Why, yes, it is worthwhile to study human behavior in this way, but the study of behavior is not the whole of psychology. It leaves out too much. Don't I have sensations, perceptions, conceptions? Do I not forget things and remember things, imagine things, have visual images and auditory images of things I once have seen and heard? Can I not see and hear things that I have never seen or heard in nature? Can I not be attentive or inattentive? Can I not will to do a thing or will not to do it, as the case may be? Do not certain things arouse pleasure in me, and others displeasure? Behaviorism is trying to rob us of everything we have believed in since earliest childhood."

Having been brought up on introspective psychology, as most of us have, you naturally ask these questions and you will find it hard to put away the old terminology and begin to formulate your psychological life in terms of behaviorism. Behaviorism is new wine and it will not go into old bottles. It is advisable for the time being to allay your natural antagonism and accept the behavioristic platform at least until you get more deeply into it. Later you will find that you have progressed so far with behaviorism that the questions you now raise will answer themselves in a perfectly satisfactory natural science way. Let me hasten to add that if the behaviorist were to ask you what you mean by the subjective terms you have been in the habit of using he could soon make you tongue-tied with contradictions. He could even convince you that you do not know what you mean by them. You have been using them uncritically as part of your social and literary tradition.

This is the fundamental starting point of behaviorism. You will soon find that instead of self-observation being the easiest and most natural way of studying psychology, it is an impossible one; you can observe in yourselves only the most elementary forms of response. You will find, on the other hand, that when you begin to study what your neighbor is doing, you will rapidly become proficient in giving a reason for his behavior and in setting situations (presenting stimuli) that will make him behave in a predictable manner. . . .

IV. WHAT IS A STIMULUS?

If I suddenly flash a strong light in your eye, your pupil will contract rapidly. If I were suddenly to shut off all light in the room in which you are sitting, the pupil would begin to widen. If a pistol shot were suddenly fired behind you you would jump and possibly turn your head around. If hydrogen sulphide were suddenly released in your sitting room you would begin to hold your nose and possibly even seek to leave the room. If I suddenly made the room very warm, you would begin to unbutton your coat and perspire. If I suddenly made it cold, another response would take place.

Again, on the inside of us we have an equally large realm in which stimuli can exert their effect. For example, just before dinner the muscles of your stomach begin to contract and expand rhythmically because of the absence of food. As soon as food is eaten those contractions cease. By swallowing a small balloon and attaching it to a recording instrument we can easily register the response of the stomach to lack of food and note the lack of response when food is present. In the male, at any rate, the pressure of certain fluids (semen) may lead to sex activity. In the case of the female possibly the presence of certain chemical bodies can lead in a similar way to overt sex behavior. The muscles of our arms and legs and trunk are not only subject to stimuli coming from the blood; they are also stimulated by their own responses—that is, the muscle is under constant tension; any increase in that tension, as when a movement is made, gives rise to a stimulus which leads to another response in that same muscle or in one in some distant part of the body; any decrease in that tension, as when the muscle is relaxed, similarly gives rise to a stimulus. . . .

The two commonsense classifications of response are "external" and "internal"—or possibly the terms "overt" (explicit) and "implicit" are better. By external or overt responses we mean the ordinary doings of the human being: he stoops to pick up a tennis ball, he writes a letter, he enters an automobile and starts driving, he digs a hole in the ground, he sits down to write a lecture, or dances, or flirts with a woman, or makes love to his wife. We do not need instruments to make these observations. On the other hand, responses may be wholly confined to the muscular and glandular systems inside the body. A child or hungry adult may be standing stock still in front of a window filled with pastry. Your first exclamation may be "He isn't doing anything" or "He is just looking at the pastry." An instrument would show that his salivary glands are pouring out secretions, that his stomach is rhythmically contracting and expanding, and that marked changes in blood pressure are taking place—that the endocrine glands are pouring substances into the blood. The internal or implicit responses are difficult to observe, not because they are inherently different from the external or overt responses, but merely because they are hidden from the eye. . . .

V. AN EXAMPLE: JEALOUSY

Ask any group of individuals what they mean by jealousy—what the stimulus is that produces it, what the pattern of the response is, and you get only the vaguest, most unserviceable kind of replies. Ask these same individuals what the unlearned (unconditioned) stimulus is that calls out the response; ask them what the unlearned (unconditioned) response pattern is. To both questions you get unscientific answers. Most individuals say, "Oh, jealousy is a pure instinct." If we diagram thus

$$S \dots\dots\dots\dots\dots\dots\dots\dots\dots\dots\dots\dots\dots\dots\dots R$$
$$? \qquad\qquad\qquad\qquad\qquad\qquad\qquad ?$$

we have to put a question mark under both stimulus and response.

And yet jealousy is one of the most powerful factors in the organization of present day individuals. It is recognized by the courts as one of the strongest of "motives" leading to action. Robberies and murders are committed because of it; careers are both made and unmade because of it; marital quarrels, separations and divorces are probably more frequently to be traced to it than to any other single cause. Its almost universal permeation through the whole action stream of all individuals has led to the view that it is an inborn instinct. And yet the moment you begin to observe people and try to determine what kinds of situations call out jealous behavior and what the details of that behavior are, you see that the situations are highly complex (social) and that the reactions are all highly organized (learned). This in itself should make us doubt its hereditary origin. Let us watch people for awhile to see if their behavior will not throw light upon the situations and the responses.

In the first place, as we have said, the situation is always a social one—it involves people. What people? *Always the person who calls out our conditioned love responses.* This may be the mother, father, or brother, sister or sweetheart, wife or husband—the object of homosexual attachments also must be admitted to this group. The wife-husband situation is second only to the sweetheart one for calling out violent response. This brief examination helps us somewhat in our understanding of jealousy. The situation is always a substitutive one, that is, conditioned. It involves the person calling out conditioned love responses. This generalization, if true, takes it out of the class of inherited forms of behavior at once.

The responses in adults are legion. I have taken notes on a great many cases among both children and adults. To vary our procedure let us take the responses of an adult first. *Case A.* A is a "very jealous husband," married two years to a beautiful young woman only slightly younger. They go out frequently to parties. If his wife (1) dances a little close to her partner, (2) if she sits out a dance to talk to a man and talks in a low tone to him, (3) if in a moment of gaiety she kisses another man in the open light of the room before everyone, (4) if she goes out even with other women to lunch or tea or to shop, (5) if she invites her own group of friends for a party at home— then jealous behavior is exhibited. Such stimuli bring out the responses (1) refusal to talk or dance with his wife, (2) increased tension of all his muscles, mouth shuts tightly, eyes seem to grow smaller, jaw "hardens." He next withdraws himself from other people in the room. His face becomes flushed, then black. *This behavior may and usually does persist for days after the affair is started. He will talk to no one about the affair. Mediation is impossible.* The jealous state seems to have to run itself down or out. The wife herself by no amount of assurance of love, of innocence, by no system of apology or obeisance can do anything towards hastening recovery. Yet his wife is devoted to him and has never been even in the slightest measure unfaithful, as he himself admits verbally when not in the jealous state. In a person less well bred, less well schooled, it is easy to see that his behavior might become overt—he might blacken his wife's eye, or if there were a real male aggressor, might attack or murder him. . . .

So far our experiments on jealousy are merely preliminary. If any generalization at all can be made, it would seem to take the following form: Jealousy is a bit of behavior whose stimulus is a (conditioned) love stimulus the response to which is rage—but a pattern of rage containing possibly the original visceral components but in addition parts of many habit patterns (fighting, boxing, shooting, talking). We may use this diagram to hold our facts together:

$$(C) S \dots\dots\dots\dots\dots\dots (U\&C)R$$

Sight (or sound) of loved object being tampered or interfered with.	*Stiffening of whole body,* clenching of hands, reddening and then blackening of face—pronounced breathing, fighting, verbal recrimination, etc.

Naturally this is reduced only to the barest schematism. The response may take many forms and the stimulus may consist of far more subtle factors than I have noted here, but I believe we are on the right track in trying to formulate jealousy in these terms. . . .

STUDY QUESTIONS

1. Does having purposes, plans, expectations, and the like require that some future state of affairs have an effect on us? If it does, how would dualism help reduce the oddness of such a situation?

2. Can you think of any characteristics which humans have that cannot be adequately explained or accounted for except on the hypothesis that we have non-material minds? What are they? If you think there are none, why do you hold that view?

3. State Joad's four arguments on behalf of dualism. Critically evaluate each.

4. Joad holds that the four types of phenomena which he cites cannot be explained on the basis of the stimulus-response model of explanation (the view that all capacities of all organisms, including humans, are merely material responses to material stimuli). Do you agree? Why or why not?

5. Suppose one is trying to decide between two claims that have the following forms: (1) A is made of B and C; (2) A is caused by B and C. What sort of experiment would settle the issue? Suppose further that A is a sensation and B and C are neural structures. Are there any special problems for the experiment now?

6. The author of "Why I Am a Dualist" claims that the reader will be able to provide other examples of sensations besides those used in the paper. Can you do so? Also, try to give a general definition for "sensation." What difficulties do you encounter?

7. Jones plans to build a robot that says, "Ouch" if you hit it or cut its "skin." It is also supposed to say things like "Why did you do that?" and "Please don't do that again" on the appropriate occasions. It will also take aspirin when you hit it on the head and will be very hard to get into a dentist's chair unless you promise it novocaine. If Jones succeeds, do you think that would prove Robinson's main point to be wrong?

8. How does Taylor know he has a body? How does he know his body is a material thing? (See the Luce article.)

9. What is strict identity? What predicates present some difficulty for the claim that a person is identical to his/her body?

10. What difficulties convince Taylor that dualism is a mistaken theory? Do you agree?

11. Explain Luce's "two table" objection to materialism.

12. Sense-data and sensibilia are two important technical terms for Luce. Why does he introduce them?

13. Why cannot matter "support" sense-data? What does support sense-data (according to Luce)?

14. Explain why, according to Luce, matter cannot play a causal role in the world. (Distinguish the senses of "cause.")

15. Luce believes his view is on the side of commonsense. Why? Is he right? If so, why? If not, why not?

16. What is introspective psychology? What theory of mind does Watson take it as being allied with? Why is introspective psychology a superstitious belief?

17. Try to sketch a behavioristic treatment of several psychological notions, e.g., being clever, being in pain, having a red after-image. Do you notice any difficulties in such an approach?

18. Is the mind-body problem really a scientific issue and not a philosophical one? Justify your answer.

Further Readings

Blanchard, Brand, and B. F. Skinner. "The Problem of Consciousness—A Debate." *Philosophy and Phenomenological Research*, 27 (1967), 317–337. [Dualistic and behaviorist perspectives are represented in the debate.]

Broad, C. D. *The Mind and Its Place in Nature*. London: Routledge and Kegan Paul, 1925, Chapter 3. [A sensitive examination of dualism.]

Brody, Baruch A. *Beginning Philosophy*. Englewood Cliffs, N.J.: Prentice-Hall, 1977, pp. 139–161. [A clear, elementary treatment of dualism, behaviorism, and the identity theory.]

Chappell, V. C., ed. *The Philosophy of Mind*. Englewood Cliffs, N.J.: Prentice-Hall, 1962. [A fairly recent, comprehensive set of readings on the philosophy of mind.]

Dennett, Daniel C. "Why You Can't Make a Computer That Feels Pain." *Synthese*, 38 (1978), 415–456. [Argues that the traditional reasons for denying robot consciousness are mistaken.]

Descartes, Rene. *Meditations on First Philosophy*. Indianapolis, Ind.: Hackett, 1979. [First published in 1641; see especially Meditations I, II, and VI for the classical development of dualism.]

Hofstadter, Douglas R., and Daniel C. Dennett. *The Mind's I*. New York: Basic Books, 1981. [A collective of lively and provocative articles in the philosophy of mind.]

Hospers, John. *An Introduction to Philosophical Analysis*, 2nd ed. Englewood Cliffs, N.J.: Prentice-Hall, 1967, pp. 378–424. [An elementary overview of theories of mind.]

O'Connor, John, ed. *Modern Materialism: Readings on Mind–Body Identity*. New York: Harcourt Brace Jovanovich, 1969. [Exactly what the title indicates.]

Smart, J. J. C. "Sensations and Brain Processes." *Philosophical Review*, 68 (1959), 141–156. [A famous defense of the identity theory version of materialism.]

PART FIVE

PERSONS, MACHINES, AND IMMORTALITY

PREVIEW

As we saw, the main question of Part Four was: What is a person? Is a person solely a material body? Or is a person also something non-material: a self, psyche, soul, and so on? There are two important questions which are closely related to the above question(s). They are the subject matter of this part.

Consider the following transcript of a conversation between a psychotherapist and a female patient. (The lines in small letters are spoken by the patient. The ones in capitals are the therapist's responses.)

men are all alike.
IN WHAT WAY?
they're always bugging us about something or other.
CAN YOU THINK OF A SPECIFIC EXAMPLE?
well, my boyfriend made me come here.
YOUR BOYFRIEND MADE YOU COME HERE?
he noticed that i'm depressed much of the time.
I'M SORRY TO HEAR YOU ARE DEPRESSED.
he's right. i am unhappy.
DO YOU THINK COMING HERE WILL HELP YOU NOT TO BE UN-
    HAPPY?
i need some help, that much is clear.
WHAT WOULD IT MEAN TO YOU IF YOU GOT SOME HELP?
perhaps I could learn to get along with my mother.
TELL ME MORE ABOUT YOUR FAMILY.
my mother takes care of me.
WHO ELSE IN YOUR FAMILY TAKES CARE OF YOU?
my father.

YOUR FATHER?
you are like my father in some ways.
WHAT RESEMBLANCE DO YOU SEE?
you are not very aggressive, but i don't think you want me to notice
    that.
WHAT MAKES YOU THINK I AM NOT VERY AGGRESSIVE?
you don't argue with me.
WHY DO YOU THINK I DON'T ARGUE WITH YOU?
you are afraid of me.
DOES IT PLEASE YOU TO BELIEVE I AM AFRAID OF YOU?
it pleases my father to think i am afraid of him.
WHAT ELSE COMES TO MIND WHEN YOU THINK OF YOUR FA-
    THER?
bullies.
DOES THAT HAVE ANYTHING TO DO WITH THE FACT THAT
    YOUR BOYFRIEND MADE YOU COME HERE?[1]

Who was the therapist? A computer (or computer program, LISA, at MIT). One is inclined to say that the computer is very perceptive!

In recent years, much research has gone on in the field commonly called artificial intelligence. While this research is prompted by varying motives and toward varying ends, it has led to the question of whether persons are but complicated machines, or conversely whether machines (robots, etc.) can have the characteristics usually ascribed to only human beings. A more modest form of this question is: Can machines think (in the normal, human sense of 'think')? If so, what bearing, if any, does this have on the issue of what persons are? This formulation of our question is the subject of two of the selections in this part.[2]

Some years ago an obscure Arizona miner named James Kidd was concerned with the question of whether the soul survived the death of the body. In a handwritten will dated January 2, 1946, he wrote,

> this is my first and only will and is dated the second day of January 1946. I have no. heir's have not been married in my life, an after all my funeral expenses have been paid and $100. one hundred dollars to some preacher of the gospital to say fare well at my grave sell all my property which is all in cash and stocks with E F Hutton Co Phoenix some in safety box, and have this balance money to go into a research of some scientific proof of a soul of the human body which leaves at death I think in time there can be a Photograph of soul leaving the human at death.
>
> James Kidd

---

[1]Quoted in Carl Sagan, "In Praise of Robots." *Natural History Magazine*, Jan., 1975, p. 330.

[2]We have chosen Turing's essay because it is one of the earliest to address itself to this topic and, hence, has become a "classic."

Kidd's will was taken seriously by a number of people. In 1967 it was probated in the Superior Court of the State of Arizona. Among the claimants to the money, which was valued at over $200,000, were philosophers, psychologists, religionists, and mediums. There were even some who claimed that they could fulfill the last request in Kidd's will.

The yearning for immortality seems to be a perennial one in the history of the human race. It has been held in many (though not all) cultures, dating back to ancient and perhaps even primitive times. But is there any basis for the belief? That is the question discussed in the other two selections in this part.

It is perhaps obvious that the belief in immortality is often closely linked with the belief in the existence of a divine being, a god. In religions like Christianity, both are central tenets of faith. However, these beliefs are logically distinct and independent of one another. Thus, even if there is no good reason to accept the belief in the existence of a god, it is quite possible that our selves are immortal or at least survive the death of the body. Since the questions are independent of one another, we will treat them separately in this volume. In this part we will be concerned with the problem of survival and immortality. In the next two parts we will turn to the problem of the existence of God.

Main Questions

The main questions, then, of this part are:

1. Is there any essential difference between humans and certain machines, such as robots? Are persons merely machines?

Or alternatively: Can machines think? If so, what bearing does this have on what persons are?

2. Are we (or our minds, or selves, or souls, or personalities) immortal? Or do we in any way and for any time (even if not forever) survive the death of our bodies?

Answers

Unlike the questions in previous parts, the chief answers to these two questions have been given no commonly accepted labels. But in both cases, it is obvious that there are only two possible answers: Yes, or very likely; and no, or not very likely. So let us simply designate them the affirmative and negative answers.

1a. The affirmative answer. Machines have all of the characteristics commonly thought to belong only to persons. (This implies that persons are or may be essentially machines.) Or:

1a. Yes, machines can think.

1b. The negative answer. Persons are unique and different from machines. No matter how much machines can do, they cannot have or be all that is involved in being a human person. Or:

1b. No, machines cannot think.

2a. The affirmative answer. A person is or has a nonmaterial self, and that self (mind, soul, consciousness, etc.) is immortal, or at least survives the death of the body.

2b. The negative answer. Even if there is such an entity as the self (which is doubtful), it does not survive the death of the body, and hence cannot be immortal. Immortality is at best a myth.

Selections

In this part, the readings seriously consider the answers to the first question and explicitly provide answers to the second. These are represented as follows:

Question	Answer		Selection
(1)	(1a)	The affirmative	21
(1)	(1b)	Critique of (a)	22
(2)	(2b)	The negative	23
(2)	(2a)	The affirmative	24

21 / Computing Machinery and Intelligence

A. M. TURING

The Imitation Game / I propose to consider the question "Can machines think?" This should begin with definitions of the meaning of the terms "machine" and "think." The definitions might be framed so as to reflect so far as possible the normal use of the words, but this attitude is dangerous. If the meaning of the words "machine" and "think" are to be found by examining how they are commonly used it is difficult to escape the conclusion that the meaning and the answer to the question, "Can machines think?" is to be sought in a statistical survey such as a Gallup poll. But this is absurd. Instead of attempting such a definition I shall replace the question by another, which is closely related to it and is expressed in relatively unambiguous words.

The new form of the problem can be described in terms of a game which we call the "imitation game." It is played with three people, a man (A), a woman (B), and an interrogator (C) who may be of either sex. The interrogator stays in a room apart from the other two. The object of the game for the interrogator is to determine which of the other two is the man and which is the woman. He knows them by labels X and Y, and at the end of the game he says either "X is A and Y is B" or "X is B and Y is A." The interrogator is allowed to put questions to A and B thus:

C: Will X please tell me the length of his or her hair? Now suppose X is actually A, then A must answer. It is A's object in the game to try to cause C to make the wrong identification. His answer might therefore be:

"My hair is shingled, and the longest strands are about nine inches long."

In order that tones of voice may not help the interrogator the answers should be written, or better still, typewritten. The ideal arrangement is to have a teleprinter communicating between the two rooms. Alternatively the question and answers can be repeated by an intermediary. The object of the game for the third player (B) is to help the interrogator. The best strategy for her is probably to give truthful answers. She can add such things as "I am the woman, don't listen to him!" to her answers, but it will avail nothing as the man can make similar remarks.

We now ask the question, "What will happen when a machine takes the part of A in this game?" Will the interrogator decide wrongly as often when the game is played like this as he does when the game is played between a man and a woman? These questions replace our original, "Can machines think?"

Critique of the New Problem / As well as asking, "What is the answer to this new form of the question," one may ask, "Is this new question a worthy one to investigate?" This latter question we investigate without further ado, thereby cutting short an infinite regress.

The new problem has the advantage of drawing a fairly sharp line between the physical and the intellectual capacities of a man. No engineer or chemist claims to be able to produce a material which is indistinguishable from the human skin. It is possible that at some time this might be done, but even supposing this invention available we should feel there was little point in trying to make a "thinking machine" more human by dressing it up in such artificial flesh. The form in which we have set the problem reflects this fact in the condition which prevents the interrogator from seeing or touching the other competitors, or hearing their voices. Some other advantages of the proposed criterion may be shown up by specimen questions and answers. Thus:

Q: Please write me a sonnet on the subject of the Forth Bridge.*
A: Count me out on this one. I never could write poetry.
Q: Add 34957 to 70764.
A: (Pause about 30 seconds and then give as answer) 105621.
Q: Do you play chess?
A: Yes.
Q: I have K at my K1, and no other pieces. You have only K at K6 and R at R1. It is your move. What do you play?
A: (After a pause of 15 seconds) R-R8 mate.

The question and answer method seems to be suitable for introducing almost any one of the fields of human endeavor that we wish to include. We do not wish to penalize the machine for its inability to shine in beauty competitions, nor to penalize a man for losing in a race against an airplane. The conditions of our game make these disabilities irrelevant. The "witnesses" can brag, if they consider it advisable, as much as they please about their charms, strength or heroism, but the interrogator cannot demand practical demonstrations. . . .

The Machines Concerned in the Game / It is natural that we should wish to permit every kind of engineering technique to be used in our machines. We also wish to allow the possibility that an engineer or team of engineers

---

*[A bridge of note in England.—Eds.]

may construct a machine which works, but whose manner of operation cannot be satisfactorily described by its constructors because they have applied a method which is largely experimental. Finally, we wish to exclude from the machines men born in the usual manner. It is difficult to frame the definitions so as to satisfy these three conditions. One might for instance insist that the team of engineers should be all of one sex, but this would not really be satisfactory, for it is probably possible to rear a complete individual from a single cell of the skin (say) of a man. To do so would be a feat of biological technique deserving of the very highest praise, but we would not be inclined to regard it as a case of "constructing a thinking machine." This prompts us to abandon the requirement that every kind of technique should be permitted. We are the more ready to do so in view of the fact that the present interest in "thinking machines" has been aroused by a particular kind of machine, usually called an "electronic computer" or "digital computer." Following this suggestion we only permit digital computers to take part in our game.

This restriction appears at first sight to be a very drastic one. I shall attempt to show that it is not so in reality. To do this necessitates a short account of the nature and properties of these computers. . . .

Digital Computers / The idea behind digital computers may be explained by saying that these machines are intended to carry out any operations which could be done by a human computer. The human computer is supposed to be following fixed rules; he has no authority to deviate from them in any detail. We may suppose that these rules are supplied in a book, which is altered whenever he is put on to a new job. He has also an unlimited supply of paper on which he does his calculations. He may also do his multiplications and additions on a "desk machine," but this is not important.

If we use the above explanation as a definition we shall be in danger of circularity of argument. We avoid this by giving an outline of the means by which the desired effect is achieved. A digital computer can usually be regarded as consisting of three parts:

1. Store.
2. Executive unit.
3. Control.

The store is a store of information, and corresponds to the human computer's paper, whether this is the paper on which he does his calculations or that on which his book of rules is printed. Insofar as the human computer does calculations in his head a part of the store will correspond to his memory.

The executive unit is the part which carries out the various individual operations involved in a calculation. What these individual operations are will vary from machine to machine. Usually fairly lengthy operations can be done such as "Multiply 3540675445 by 7076345687" but in some machines only very simple ones such as "Write down 0" are possible.

We have mentioned that the "book of rules" supplied to the computer is replaced in the machine by a part of the store. It is then called the "table of instructions." It is the duty of the control to see that these instructions are obeyed correctly and in the right order. The control is so constructed that this necessarily happens.

The information in the store is usually broken up into packets of moderately small size. In one machine, for instance, a packet might consist of ten decimal digits. Numbers are assigned to the parts of the store in which the various packets of information are stored, in some systematic manner. A typical instruction might say—

> Add the number stored in position 6809 to that in 4302 and put the result back into the latter storage position.

Needless to say it would not occur in the machine expressed in English. It would more likely be coded in a form such as 6809430217. Here 17 says which of various possible operations is to be performed on the two numbers. In this case the operation is that described above, viz. "Add the number. . . ." It will be noticed that the instruction takes up 10 digits and so forms one packet of information, very conveniently. The control will normally take the instructions to be obeyed in the order of the positions in which they are stored, but occasionally an instruction such as

> Now obey the instruction stored in position 5606, and continue from there

may be encountered, or again

> If position 4505 contains 0 obey next the instruction stored in 6707, otherwise continue straight on.

Instructions of these latter types are very important because they make it possible for a sequence of operations to be repeated over and over again until some condition is fulfilled, but in doing so to obey, not fresh instructions on each repetition, but the same ones over and over again. To take a domestic analogy, suppose Mother wants Tommy to call at the cobbler's every morning on his way to school to see if her shoes are done; she can ask him afresh every morning. Alternatively she can stick up a notice once and for all in the hall which he will see when he leaves for school and which tells him to call for the shoes, and also to destroy the notice when he comes back if he has the shoes with him.

The reader must accept it as a fact that digital computers can be constructed, and indeed have been constructed, according to the principles we have described, and that they can in fact mimic the actions of a human computer very closely. . . .

[II]

Contrary Views on the Main Question / We may now consider the ground to have been cleared and we are ready to proceed to the debate on our question, "Can machines think?" and the variant of it quoted at the end of the last section. We cannot altogether abandon the original form of the problem, for opinions will differ as to the appropriateness of the substitution and we must at least listen to what has to be said in this connection.

It will simplify matters for the reader if I explain first my own beliefs in the matter. Consider first the more accurate form of the question. I believe that in about fifty years' time it will be possible to program computers, with a storage capacity of about 10^9, to make them play the imitation game so well that an average interrogator will not have more than 70 per cent chance of making the right identification after five minutes of questioning. The original question, "Can machines think?" I believe to be too meaningless to deserve discussion. Nevertheless I believe that at the end of the century the use of words and general educated opinion will have altered so much that one will be able to speak of machines thinking without expecting to be contradicted. I believe further that no useful purpose is served by concealing these beliefs. The popular view that scientists proceed inexorably from well-established fact to well-established fact, never being influenced by any unproved conjecture, is quite mistaken. Provided it is made clear which are proved facts and which are conjectures, no harm can result. Conjectures are of great importance since they suggest useful lines of research.

I now proceed to consider opinions opposed to my own.

The Theological Objection / Thinking is a function of man's immortal soul. God has given an immortal soul to every man and woman, but not to any other animal or to machines. Hence no animal or machine can think.

I am unable to accept any part of this, but will attempt to reply in theological terms. I should find the argument more convincing if animals were classed with men, for there is a greater difference, to my mind, between the typical animate and the inanimate than there is between man and the other animals. . . . But let us leave this point aside and return to the main argument. It appears to me that the argument quoted above implies a serious restriction of the omnipotence* of the Almighty. It is admitted that there are certain things that He cannot do such as making one equal to two, but should we not believe that He has freedom to confer a soul on an elephant if He sees fit? We might expect that He would only exercise this power in conjunction with a mutation which provided the elephant with an appropriately improved brain to minister to the needs of this soul. An argument

*[All-powerfulness.—Eds.]

of exactly similar form may be made for the case of machines. It may seem different because it is more difficult to "swallow." But this really only means that we think it would be less likely that He would consider the circumstances suitable for conferring a soul. The circumstances in question are discussed in the rest of this paper. In attempting to construct such machines we should not be irreverently usurping His power of creating souls, any more than we are in the procreation of children: rather we are, in either case, instruments of His will providing mansions for the souls that He creates.

However, this is mere speculation. I am not very impressed with theological arguments whatever they may be used to support. . . .

The "Heads in the Sand" Objection / "The consequences of machines thinking would be too dreadful. Let us hope and believe that they cannot do so."

This argument is seldom expressed quite so openly as in the form above. But it affects most of us who think about it at all. We like to believe that Man is in some subtle way superior to the rest of creation. It is best if he can be shown to be *necessarily* superior, for then there is no danger of him losing his commanding position. The popularity of the theological argument is clearly connected with this feeling. It is likely to be quite strong in intellectual people, since they value the power of thinking more highly than others, and are more inclined to base their belief in the superiority of Man on this power.

I do not think that this argument is sufficiently substantial to require refutation. Consolation would be more appropriate: perhaps this should be sought in the transmigration of souls. . . .

The Argument from Consciousness / This argument is very well expressed in Professor Jefferson's Lister Oration for 1949. . . .

This argument appears to be a denial of the validity of our test. According to the most extreme form of this view the only way by which one could be sure that a machine thinks is to *be* the machine and to feel oneself thinking. One could then describe these feelings to the world, but of course no one would be justified in taking any notice. Likewise according to this view the only way to know that a *man* thinks is to be that particular man. It is in fact the solipsist* point of view. It may be the most logical view to hold but it makes communication of ideas difficult. A is liable to believe "A thinks but B does not" while B believes "B thinks but A does not." Instead of arguing continually over this point it is usual to have the polite convention that everyone thinks.

---

*[Solipsism is the view that all one can know to exist is one's own mind and the contents of that mind.—Eds.]

I am sure that Profession Jefferson does not wish to adopt the extreme and solipsist point of view. Probably he would be quite willing to accept the imitation game as a test. The game (with the player B omitted) is frequently used in practice under the name of *viva voce*† to discover whether someone really understands something or has "learned it parrot fashion." Let us listen in to a part of such a *viva voce*:

Interrogator: In the first line of your sonnet which reads "Shall I compare thee to a summer's day," would not "a spring day" do as well or better?

Witness: It wouldn't scan.

Interrogator: How about "a winter's day." That would scan all right.

Witness: Yes, but nobody wants to be compared to a winter's day.

Interrogator: Would you say Mr. Pickwick‡ reminded you of Christmas?

Witness: In a way.

Interrogator: Yet Christmas is a winter's day, and I do not think Mr. Pickwick would mind the comparison.

Witness: I don't think you're serious. By a winter's day one means a typical winter's day, rather than a special one like Christmas.

And so on. What would Professor Jefferson say if the sonnet-writing machine was able to answer like this in the *viva voce*? I do not know whether he would regard the machine as "merely artificially signaling" these answers, but if the answers were as satisfactory and sustained as in the above passage I do not think he would describe it as "an easy contrivance." This phrase is, I think, intended to cover such devices as the inclusion in the machine of a record of someone reading a sonnet, with appropriate switching to turn it on from time to time.

In short then, I think that most of those who support the argument from consciousness could be persuaded to abandon it rather than be forced into the solipsist position. They will then probably be willing to accept our test. . . .

Arguments from Various Disabilities / These arguments take the form, "I grant you that you can make machines do all the things you have mentioned but you will never be able to make one to X." Numerous features X are suggested in this connection. I offer a selection:

> Be kind, resourceful, beautiful, friendly, have initiative, have a sense of humor, tell right from wrong, make mistakes, fall in love, enjoy strawberries and cream, make someone fall in love with it, learn from experience, use words properly, be the subject of its own thought, have as much diversity of behavior as a man, do something really new.

No support is usually offered for these statements. I believe they are mostly founded on the principle of scientific induction. A man has seen thousands

†[oral examination.—Eds.]
‡[A character in a novel by Charles Dickens.—Eds.]

of machines in his lifetime. They are ugly, each is designed for a very limited purpose, when required for a minutely different purpose they are useless, the variety of behavior of any one of them is very small, etc., etc. Naturally he concludes that these are necessary properties of machines in general. Many of these limitations are associated with the very small storage capacity of most machines. . . . A few years ago, when very little had been heard of digital computers, it was possible to elicit much incredulity concerning them, if one mentioned their properties without describing their construction. That was presumably due to a similar application of the principle of scientific induction. These applications of the principle are of course largely unconscious. When a burned child fears the fire and shows that he fears it by avoiding it, I should say that he was applying scientific induction. (I could of course also describe his behavior in many other ways.) The works and customs of mankind do not seem to be very suitable material to which to apply scientific induction. A very large part of space-time must be investigated if reliable results are to be obtained. Otherwise we may (as most English children do) decide that everybody speaks English, and that it is silly to learn French. . . .

The claim that "machines cannot make mistakes" seems a curious one. One is tempted to retort, "Are they any the worse for that?" But let us adopt a more sympathetic attitude, and try to see what is really meant. I think this criticism can be explained in terms of the imitation game. It is claimed that the interrogator could distinguish the machine from the man simply by setting them a number of problems in arithmetic. The machine would be unmasked because of its deadly accuracy. The reply to this is simple. The machine (programmed for playing the game) would not attempt to give the *right* answers to the arithmetic problems. It would deliberately introduce mistakes in a manner calculated to confuse the interrogator. A mechanical fault would probably show itself through an unsuitable decision as to what sort of a mistake to make in the arithmetic. Even this interpretation of the criticism is not sufficently sympathetic. But we cannot afford the space to go into it much further. It seems to me that this criticism depends on a confusion between two kinds of mistakes. We may call them "errors of functioning" and "errors of conclusion." Errors of functioning are due to some mechanical or electrical fault which causes the machine to behave otherwise than it was designed to do. In philosophical discussions one likes to ignore the possibility of such errors; one is therefore discussing "abstract machines." These abstract machines are mathematical fictions rather than physical objects. By definition they are incapable of errors of functioning. In this sense we can truly say that "machines can never make mistakes." Errors of conclusion can only arise when some meaning is attached to the output signals from the machine. The machine might, for instance, type out mathematical equations, or sentences in English. When a false proposition is typed we say that the machine has committed an error of conclusion.

There is clearly no reason at all for saying that a machine cannot make this kind of mistake. It might do nothing but type out repeatedly "0 = 1." To take a less perverse example, it might have some method for drawing conclusions by scientific induction. We must expect such a method to lead occasionally to erroneous results.

The claim that a machine cannot be the subject of its own thought can of course only be answered if it can be shown that the machine has *some* thought with *some* subject matter. Nevertheless, "the subject matter of a machine's operations" does seem to mean something, at least to the people who deal with it. If, for instance, the machine was trying to find a solution of the equation $x^2 - 40x - 11 = 0$ one would be tempted to describe this equation as part of the machine's subject matter at that moment. In this sort of sense a machine undoubtedly can be its own subject matter. It may be used to help in making up its own programs, or to predict the effect of alterations in its own structure. By observing the results of its own behavior it can modify its own programs so as to achieve some purpose more effectively. These are possibilities of the near future, rather than Utopian dreams. . . .

Lady Lovelace's Objection / . . . A variant of Lady Lovelace's* objection states that a machine can "never do anything really new." This may be parried for a moment with the saw, "There is nothing new under the sun." Who can be certain that "original work" that he has done was not simply the growth of the seed planted in him by teaching, or the effect of following well-known general principles? A better variant of the objection says that a machine can never "take us by surprise." This statement is a more direct challenge and can be met directly. Machines take me by surprise with great frequency. This is largely because I do not do sufficient calculation to decide what to expect them to do, or rather because, although I do a calculation, I do it in a hurried, slipshod fashion, taking risks. Perhaps I say to myself, "I suppose the voltage here ought to be the same as there: anyway let's assume it is." Naturally I am often wrong, and the result is a surprise for me, for by the time the experiment is done these assumptions have been forgotten. These admissions lay me open to lectures on the subject of my vicious ways, but do not throw any doubt on my credibility when I testify to the surprises I experience. . . .

The view that machines cannot give rise to surprises is due, I believe, to a fallacy to which philosophers and mathematicians are particularly subject. This is the assumption that as soon as a fact is presented to a mind all consequences of that fact spring into the mind simultaneously with it. It is a very useful assumption under many circumstances, but one too easily forgets that it is false. A natural consequence of doing so is that one then as-

---

*[Lady Lovelace is the author of a memoir on Babbage, the inventor of the first computer-calculator.—Eds.]

sumes that there is no virtue in the mere working out of consequences from data and general principles.

Argument from Continuity in the Nervous System / The nervous system is certainly not a discrete state machine. A small error in the information about the size of a nervous impulse impinging on a neuron, may make a large difference to the size of the outgoing impulse. It may be argued that, this being so, one cannot expect to be able to mimic the behavior of the nervous system with a discrete state system.

It is true that a discrete state machine must be different from a continuous machine. But if we adhere to the conditions of the imitation game, the interrogator will not be able to take any advantage of this difference. The situation can be made clearer if we consider some other simpler continuous machine. A differential analyzer will do very well. (A differential analyzer is a certain kind of machine not of the discrete state type used for some kinds of calculation.) Some of these provide their answers in a typed form, and so are suitable for taking part in the game. It would not be possible for a digital computer to predict exactly what answers the differential analyzer would give to a problem, but it would be quite capable of giving the right sort of answer. For instance, if asked to give the value of π (actually about 3.1416) it would be reasonable to choose at random between the values 3.12, 3.13, 3.14, 3.15, 3.16 with the probabilities of 0.05, 0.15, 0.55, 0.19, 0.06 (say). Under these circumstances it would be very difficult for the interrogator to distinguish the differential analyzer from the digital computer. . . .

[III]

The reader will have anticipated that I have no very convincing arguments of a positive nature to support my views. If I had I should not have taken such pains to point out the fallacies in contrary views. Such evidence as I have I shall now give.

Let us return for a moment to Lady Lovelace's objection, which stated that the machine can only do what we tell it to do. One could say that a man can "inject" an idea into the machine, and that it will respond to a certain extent and then drop into quiescence, like a piano string struck by a hammer. Another simile would be an atomic pile of less than critical size: an injected idea is to correspond to a neutron entering the pile from without. Each such neutron will cause a certain disturbance which eventually dies away. If, however, the size of the pile is sufficiently increased, the disturbance caused by such an incoming neutron will very likely go on and on increasing until the whole pile is destroyed. Is there a corresponding phenomenon for minds, and is there one for machines? There does seem to be one for the human mind. The majority of them seem to be "subcritical," i.e., to correspond in this analogy to piles of subcritical size. An idea presented to such a mind will on an average give rise to less than one idea in reply. A smallish proportion are supercritical. An idea presented to such a mind may give rise to a whole "theory" consisting of secondary, tertiary and more remote ideas. Animals' minds seem to be very definitely subcritical. Adhering to this analogy we ask, "Can a machine be made to be supercritical?"

The "skin of an onion" analogy is also helpful. In considering the functions of the mind or the brain we find certain operations which we can explain in purely mechanical terms. This we say does not correspond to the real mind: it is a sort of skin which we must strip off if we are to find the real mind. But then in what remains we find a further skin to be stripped off, and so on. Proceeding in this way do we ever come to the "real" mind, or do we eventually come to the skin which has nothing in it? In the latter case the whole mind is mechanical. (It would not be a discrete state machine however. We have discussed this.)

These last two paragraphs do not claim to be convincing arguments. They should rather be described as "recitations tending to produce belief." . . .

As I have explained, the problem is mainly one of programming. Advances in engineering will have to be made too, but it seems unlikely that these will not be adequate for the requirements. Estimates of the storage capacity of the brain vary from 10^{10} to 10^{15} binary digits. I incline to the lower values and believe that only a very small fraction is used for the higher types of thinking. Most of it is probably used for the retention of visual impressions. I should be surprised if more than 10^9 was required for satisfactory playing of the imitation game, at any rate against a blind man. (Note: The capacity of the *Encyclopedia Britannica*, eleventh edition, is 2×10^9.) A storage capacity of 10^7 would be a very practicable possibility even by present techniques. It is probably not necessary to increase the speed of operations of the machines at all. Parts of modern machines which can be regarded as analogues of nerve cells work about a thousand times faster than the latter. This should provide a "margin of safety" which could cover losses of speed arising in many ways. Our problem then is to find out how to program these machines to play the game. At my present rate of working I produce about a thousand digits of program a day, so that about sixty workers, working steadily through the fifty years might accomplish the job, if nothing went into the wastepaper basket. Some more expeditious method seems desirable. . . .

We may hope that machines will eventually compete with men in all purely intellectual fields. But which are the best ones to start with? Even this is a difficult decision. Many people think that a very abstract activity, like the playing of chess, would be best. It can also be maintained that it is best to provide the machine with the best sense organs that money can buy, and then teach it to understand and speak English. This process could follow the normal teaching of a child. Things would be pointed out and named, etc. Again I do not know what the right answer is, but I think both approaches should be tried.

We can only see a short distance ahead, but we can see plenty there that needs to be done.

22 / The Imitation Game

KEITH GUNDERSON

I

Disturbed by what he took to be the ambiguous, if not meaningless, character of the question "Can machines think?" the late A. M. Turing in his article "Computing Machinery and Intelligence" [immediately preceding this selection] sought to replace that question in the following way. He said:

> The new form of the problem can be described in terms of a game which we call the "imitation game." It is played with three people, a man (A), a woman (B), and an interrogator (C) who may be either sex. The interrogator stays in a room apart from the other two. The object of the game for the interrogator is to determine which of the other two is the man and which is the woman. He knows them by labels X and Y, and at the end of the game he says either "X is A and Y is B" or "X is B an Y is A." The interrogator is allowed to put questions to A and B thus:
>
> C: "Will X please tell me the length of his or her hair?"
>
> Now suppose X is actually A, then A must answer. It is A's object in the game to try to cause C to make the wrong identification. His answer might therefore be:
>
> "My hair is shingled, and the longest strands are about nine inches long."
>
> In order that tones of voice may not help the interrogator the answers should be written, or better still, typewritten. The ideal arrangement is to have a teleprinter communicating between the two rooms. Alternatively the question and answers can be repeated by an intermediary. The object of the game for the third player (B) is to help the interrogator. The best strategy for her is probably to give truthful answers. She can add such things as "I am the woman, don't listen to him!" to her answers, but it will avail nothing as the man can make similar remarks.
>
> We now ask the question, "What will happen when a machine takes the part of A in this game?" Will the interrogator decide wrongly as often as when the game is played between a man and a woman? These questions replace our original, "Can machines think?"

And Turing's answers to these latter questions are more or less summed up in the following passage: "I believe that in fifty years' time it will be possible to program computers, with a storage capacity of about 10^9, to make them play the imitation game so well that an average interrogator will not have more than 70 per cent chance of making the right identification after five minutes of questioning." And though he goes on to reiterate that he suspects that the original question "Can machines think?" is meaningless, and that it should be disposed of and replaced by a more precise formulation of the problems involved (a formulation such as a set of questions about the imitation game and machine capacities), what finally emerges is that Turing does answer the "meaningless" question after all, and that his answer is in the affirmative and follows from his conclusions concerning the capabilities of machines which might be successfully substituted for people in the imitation-game context.

It should be pointed out that Turing's beliefs about the possible capabilities and capacities of machines are not limited to such activities as playing the imitation game as successfully as human beings. He does not, for example, deny that it might be possible to develop a machine which would relish the taste of strawberries and cream, though he thinks it would be "idiotic" to attempt to make one, and confines himself on the whole in his positive account to consideration of machine capacities which could be illustrated in terms of playing the imitation game.

So we shall be primarily concerned with asking whether or not a machine, which could play the imitation game as well as Turing thought it might, would thus be a machine which we would have good reasons for saying was capable of thought and what would be involved in saying this.

Some philosophers have not been satisfied with Turing's treatment of the question "Can machines think?" But the imitation game itself, which indeed seems to constitute the hub of his positive treatment, has been little more than alluded to or remarked on in passing. I shall try to develop in a somewhat more detailed way certain objections to it, objections which, I believe, Turing altogether fails to anticipate. My remarks shall thus in the main be critically oriented, which is not meant to suggest that I believe there are no plausible lines of defense open to a supporter of Turing. I shall, to the contrary, close with a brief attempt to indicate what some of these might be and some general challenges which I think Turing has raised for the philosopher of mind. But these latter I shall not elaborate upon.

II

Let us consider the following question: "Can rocks imitate?" One might say that it is a question "too meaningless to deserve discussion." Yet it seems possible to reformulate the problem in relatively unambiguous words as follows:

> The new form of the problem can be described in terms of a game which we call the "toe-stepping game." It is played with three people, a man (A), a woman (B), and an interrogator (C) who may be of either sex. The interrogator stays in a room apart from the other two. The door is closed, but there is a small opening in the wall next to the floor through which he can place most of his foot. When he does so, one of the other two may step on his toe. The object of the game for the interrogator is to determine, by the way in which his toe is stepped on, which of the other two is the man and which is the woman. He knows them by labels X and Y, and at the end of the game he says either "X is A and Y is B" or "X is B and Y is A." Now the interrogator—rather the person whose toe gets stepped on—may indicate before he puts his foot through the opening, whether X or Y is to step on it. Better yet, there might be a narrow division in the opening, one side for X and one for Y (one for A and one for B).
>
> Now suppose C puts his foot through A's side of the opening (which may be labeled X or Y on C's side of the wall). It is A's object in the game to try to cause C to make the wrong identification. His step on the toe might therefore be quick and jabbing like some high-heeled woman.
>
> The object of the game for the third player (B) is to help the person whose toe gets stepped on. The best strategy for her is probably to try to step on it in the most womanly way possible. She can add such things as a slight twist of a high heel to her stepping, but it will avail nothing as the man can step in similar ways, since he will also have at his disposal various shoes with which to vary his toe-stepping.
>
> We now ask the question: "What will happen when a rock-box (a box filled with rocks of varying weights, sizes, and shapes) is constructed with an electric eye which operates across the opening in the wall so that it releases a rock which descends upon C's toe whenever C puts his foot through A's side of the opening, and this comes to take the part of A in this game?" (The situation can be made more convincing by constructing the rock-box so that there is a mechanism pulling up the released rock shortly after its descent, thus avoiding telltale noises such as a rock rolling on the floor, etc.) Will then the interrogator—the person whose toe gets stepped on—decide wrongly as often as when the game is played between a man and a woman? These questions replace our original, "Can rocks imitate?"

I believe that in less than fifty years' time it will be possible to set up elaborately constructed rock-boxes, with large rock-storage capacities, so that they will play the toe-stepping game so well that the average person who would get his toe stepped on would not have more than 70 per cent chance of making the right identification after about five minutes of toe-stepping.

The above seems to show the following: what follows from the toe-stepping game situation surely is not that rocks are able to imitate (I assume no one would want to take that path of argument) but only that they are able to be rigged in such a way that they could be substituted for a human being in a toe-stepping game without changing any essential characteristics of that game. And this is claimed in spite of the fact that if a human being were to play the toe-stepping game as envisaged above, we would no doubt be correct in saying that that person was imitating, etc. To be sure, a digital computer is a more august mechanism than a rock-box, but Turing has not provided us with any arguments for believing that its role in the imitation game, as distinct from the net results it yields, is any closer a match for a human being executing such a role, than is the rock-box's execution of its role in the toe-stepping game a match for a human being's execution of a similar role. The parody comparison can be pushed too far. But I think it lays bare the reason why there is no contradiction involved in saying, "Yes, a machine can play the imitation game, but it can't think." It is for the same reason that there is no contradiction in saying, "Of course a rock-box of such-and-such a sort can be set up, but rocks surely can't imitate." For thinking (or imitating) cannot be fully described simply by pointing to net results such as those illustrated above. For if this were not the case it would be correct to say that a piece of chalk could think or compose because it was freakishly blown about by a tornado in such a way that it scratched a rondo on a blackboard, and that a phonograph could sing, and that an electric-eye could see people coming.

People may be let out of a building by either an electric-eye or a doorman. The end result is the same. But though a doorman may be rude or polite, the electric-eye neither practices nor neglects etiquette. Turing brandishes net results. But I think the foregoing at least indicates certain difficulties with any account of thinking or decision as to whether a certain thing is capable of thought which is based primarily on net results. And, of course, one could always ask whether the net results were really the same. But I do not wish to follow that line of argument here. It is my main concern simply to indicate where Turing's account, which is cast largely in terms of net results, fails because of this. It is not an effective counter to reply: "But part of the net results in question includes intelligent people being deceived!" For what would this add to the general argument? No doubt people could be deceived by rock-boxes! It is said that hi-fidelity phonographs have been perfected to the point where blindfolded music critics are unable to distinguish their "playing" from that of, let us say, the Budapest String Quartet. But the phonograph would never be said to have performed with unusual brilliance on Saturday, nor would it ever deserve an encore. . . .

III

But let us return to the imitation game itself. It is to be granted that if human beings were to participate in such a game, we would almost surely regard them as deliberating, deciding, wondering—in short, "thinking things over"—as they passed their messages back and forth. And if someone were to ask us for an example of Johnson's intellectual prowess or mental capabilities, we might well point to this game which he often played, and how he enjoyed trying to outwit Peterson and Hanson who also participated in it. But we would only regard it as one of the many examples we might give of Peterson's mental capacities. We would ordinarily not feel hard pressed to produce countless other examples of Peterson deliberating, figuring, wondering, reflecting, or what in short we can call thinking. We might, for example, relate how he works over his sonnets or how he argues with Hanson. Now, I do not want to deny that it is beyond the scope of a machine to do these latter things. I am not, in fact, here concerned with giving an answer to the question, "Can machines think?" What I instead want to emphasize is that what we would say about Peterson in countless other situations is bound to influence what we say about him in the imitation game. A rock rolls down a hill and there is, strictly speaking, no behavior or action on the part of the rock. But if a man rolls down a hill we might well ask if he was pushed or did it intentionally, whether he's enjoying himself, playing a game, pretending to be a tumbleweed, or what. We cannot think of a man as simply or purely rolling down a hill—unless he is dead. A fortiori, we cannot understand him being a participant in the imitation game apart from his dispositions, habits, etc., which are exhibited in contexts other than the imitation game. Thus we cannot hope to find any decisive answer to the question as to how we should characterize a machine which can play (well) the imitation game, by asking what we would say about a man who could play (well) the imitation game. Thinking, whatever positive characterization or account is correct, is not something which any one example will explain or decide. But the part of Turing's case which I've been concerned with rests largely on one example.

IV

The following might help to clarify the above. Imagine the dialogue below:

Vacuum Cleaner Salesman: Now here's an example of what the all-purpose Swish 600 can do. (He then applies the nozzle to the carpet and it sucks up a bit of dust.)

Housewife: What else can it do?

Vacuum Cleaner Salesman: What do you mean "What else can it do?" It just sucked up that bit of dust, didn't you see?

Housewife: Yes, I saw it suck up a bit of dust, but I thought it was all-purpose: Doesn't it suck up larger and heavier bits of straw or paper or mud? And can't it get in the tight corners? Doesn't it have other nozzles? What about the cat hair on the couch?

Vacuum Cleaner Salesman: It sucks up bits of dust. That's what vacuum cleaners are for.

Housewife: Oh, that's what it does. I thought it was simply an example of what it does.

Vacuum Cleaner Salesman: It is an example of what it does. What it does is to suck up bits of dust.

We ask: Who's right about examples? We answer: It's not perfectly clear that anyone is lying or unjustifiably using the word "example." And there's no obvious linguistic rule or regularity to point to which tells us that if S can only do x, then S's doing x cannot be an example of what S can do since being an example presupposes or entails or whatnot that other kinds of examples are forthcoming (sucking up mud, cat hair, etc.). Yet, in spite of this, the housewife has a point. One simply has a right to expect more from an all-purpose, Swish 600 than what has been demonstrated. Here clearly the main trouble is with "all-purpose" rather than with "example," though there may still be something misleading about saying, "Here's an example . . .," and it would surely mislead to say, "Here's *just* an example . . .," followed by ". . . of what the all-purpose Swish 600 can do." The philosophical relevance of all this to our own discussion can be put in the following rather domestic way: "thinking" is a term which shares certain features with "all-purpose" as it occurs in the phrase "all-purpose Swish 600." It is not used to designate or refer to one capability, capacity, disposition, talent, habit, or feature of a given subject any more than "all-purpose" in the above example is used to mark out one particular operation of a vacuum cleaner. Thinking, whatever positive account one might give of it, is not, for example, like swimming or tennis playing. The question as to whether Peterson can swim or play tennis can be settled by a few token examples of Peterson swimming or playing tennis. (And it might be noted it is hardly imaginable that the question as to whether Peterson could think or not would be raised. For in general it is not at all interesting to ask that question of contemporary human beings, though it might be interesting for contemporary human beings to raise it in connection with different anthropoids viewed at various stages of their evolution.) But if we suppose the question were raised in connection with Peterson the only appropriate sort of answer to it would be one like, "Good heavens, what makes you think he can't?" (as if anticipating news of some horrible brain injury inflicted on Peterson). And our shock would not be at his perhaps having lost a particular talent. It would not be like the case of a Wimbledon champion losing his tennis talent because of an amputated arm.

It is no more unusual for a human being to be capable of thought than it is for a human being to be composed of cells. Similarly, "He can think" is no more answer to questions concerning Peterson's mental capacities or intelligence, than "He's composed of cells" is an answer to the usual type of question about Peterson's appearance. And to say that Peterson can think is not to say there are a few token examples of thinking which are at our fingertips, any more than to say that the Swish 600 is all-purpose is to have in mind a particular maneuver or two of which the device is capable. It is because thinking cannot be identified with what can be shown by any one example or type of example; thus Turing's approach to the question ''Can a machine think?'' via the imitation game is less than convincing. In effect he provides us below with a dialogue very much like the one above:

Turing: You know, machines can think.
Philosopher: Good heavens! Really? How do you know?
Turing: Well, they can play what's called the imitation game. (This is followed by a description of same.)
Philosopher: Interesting. What else can they do? They must be capable of a great deal if they can really think.
Turing: What do you mean, ''What else can they do?'' They play the imitation game. That's thinking, isn't it?
Etc.

But Turing, like the vacuum cleaner salesman, has trouble making his sale.

23 / The Myth of Immortality

CLARENCE DARROW

[I. The Belief in Immortality]

There is, perhaps, no more striking example of the credulity of man than the widespread belief in immortality. This idea includes not only the belief that death is not the end of what we call life, but that personal identity involving memory persists beyond the grave. So determined is the ordinary individual to hold fast to this belief that, as a rule, he refuses to read or to think upon the subject lest it cast doubt upon his cherished dream. Of those who may chance to look at this contribution, many will do so with the determination not to be convinced, and will refuse even to consider the manifold reasons that might weaken their faith. I know that this is true, for I know the reluctance with which I long approached the subject and my firm determination not to give up my hope. Thus the myth will stand in the way of a sensible adjustment to facts.

Even many of those who claim to believe in immortality still tell themselves and others that neither side of the question is susceptible of proof.

Just what can these hopeful ones believe that the word "proof" involves? The evidence against the persistence of personal consciousness is as strong as the evidence for gravitation, and much more obvious. It is as convincing and unassailable as the proof of the destruction of wood or coal by fire. If it is not certain that death ends personal identity and memory, then almost nothing that man accepts as true is susceptible of proof.

The beliefs of the race and its individuals are relics of the past. Without careful examination, no one can begin to understand how many of man's cherished opinions have no foundation in fact. The common experience of all men should teach them how easy it is to believe what they wish to accept. Experienced psychologists know perfectly well that if they desire to convince a man of some idea, they must first make him *want* to believe it. There are so many hopes, so many strong yearnings and desires attached to the doctrine of immortality that it is practically impossible to create in any mind the wish to be mortal. Still, in spite of strong desires, millions of people are filled with doubts and fears that will not down. After all, is it not better to look the question squarely in the face and find out whether we are harboring a delusion?

It is customary to speak of a "belief in immortality." First, then, let us see what is meant by the word "belief." If I take a train in Chicago at noon, bound for New York, I believe I will reach that city the next morning. I believe it because I have been to New York. I have read about the city. I have known many other people who have been there, and their stories are not inconsistent with any known facts in my own experience. I have even examined the timetables, and I know just how I will go and how long the trip will take. In other words, when I board the train for New York I believe I will reach that city because I have *reason* to believe it.

But if I am told that next week I shall start on a trip to Goofville; that I shall not take my body with me; that I shall stay for all eternity: can I find a single fact connected with my journey—the way I shall go, the part of me that is to go, the time of the journey, the country I shall reach, its location in space, the way I shall live there—or anything that would lead to a rational belief that I shall really make the trip? Have I ever known anyone who has made the journey and returned? If I am really to believe, I must try to get some information about all these important facts.

But people hesitate to ask questions about life after death. They do not ask, for they know that only silence comes out of the eternal darkness of endless space. If people really believed in a beautiful, happy, glorious land waiting to receive them when they died; if they believed that their friends would be waiting to meet them; if they believed that all pain and suffering would be left behind: why should they live through weeks, months, and even years of pain and torture while a cancer eats its way to the vital parts of the body? Why should one fight off death? Because he does *not* believe in any real sense: He only hopes. Everyone knows that there is no real evidence of any such state of bliss; so we are told not to search for proof. We are to accept through faith alone. But every thinking person knows that faith can only come through belief. Belief implies a condition of mind that accepts a certain idea. This condition can be brought about only by evidence. True, the evidence may be simply the unsupported statement of your grandmother; it may be wholly insufficient for reasoning men; but, good or bad, it must be enough for the believer or he could not believe.

Upon what evidence, then, are we asked to believe in immortality? There is no evidence. One is told to rely on faith, and no doubt this serves the purpose so long as one can believe blindly whatever he is told. But if there is no evidence upon which to build a positive belief in immortality, let us examine the other side of the question. Perhaps evidence can be found to support a positive conviction that immortality is a delusion. . . .

[II. Arguments Against Immortality]

The idea of continued life after death is very old. It doubtless had its roots back in the childhood of the race. In view of the limited knowledge of primitive man, it was not unreasonable. His dead friends and relatives visited him in dreams and visions and were present in his feeling and imagination until they were forgotten. Therefore the lifeless body did not raise the question of dissolution, but rather of duality. It was thought that man was a dual being possessing a body and a soul as separate entities, and that when a man died, his soul was released from his body to continue its life apart. Consequently, food and drink were placed upon the graves of the dead to be used in the long journey into the unknown. In modified forms, this belief in the duality of man persists to the present day.

But primitive man had no conception of life as having a beginning and an end. In this he was like the rest of the animals. Today everyone of ordinary intelligence knows how life begins, and to examine the beginnings of life leads to inevitable conclusions about the way life ends. If man has a soul, it must creep in somewhere during the period of gestation and growth.

All the higher forms of animal life grow from a single cell. Before the individual life can begin its development, it must be fertilized by union with another cell; then the cell divides and multiplies until it takes the form and pattern of its kind. At a certain regular time the being emerges into the world. During its term of life millions of cells in its body are born, die, and are replaced until, through age, disease, or some catastrophe, the cells fall apart and the individual life is ended.

It is obvious that but for the fertilization of the cell under right conditions, the being would not have lived. It is idle to say that the initial cell has a soul. In one sense it has life; but even that is precarious and depends for its continued life upon union with another cell of the proper kind. The human mother is the bearer of probably ten thousand of one kind of cell, and the human father of countless billions of the other kind. Only a very small fraction of these result in human life. If the unfertilized cells of the female and the unused cells of the male are human beings possessed of souls, then the population of the world is infinitely greater than has ever been dreamed. Of course no such idea as belief in the immortality of the germ cells could satisfy the yearnings of the individual for a survival of life after death.

If that which is called a "soul" is a separate entity apart from the body, when, then, and where and how was this soul placed in the human structure? The individual began with the union of two cells, neither of which had a soul. How could these two soulless cells produce a soul? I must leave this search to the metaphysicians. When they have found the answer, I hope they will tell me, for I should really like to know.

We know that a baby may live and fully develop in its mother's womb and then, through some shock at birth, may be born without life. In the past these babies were promptly buried. But now we know that in many cases, where the bodily structure is complete, the machine may be set to work by artificial respiration or electricity. Then it will run like any other human body through its allotted term of years. We also know that in many cases of drowning, or when some mishap virtually destroys life without hopelessly impairing the body, artificial means may set it in motion once more, so that it will complete its term of existence until the final catastrophe comes. Are we to believe that somewhere around the stillborn child and somewhere in the vicinity of the drowned man there hovers a detached soul waiting to be summoned back into the body by a pulmotor? This, too, must be left to the metaphysicians.

The beginnings of life yield no evidence of the beginnings of a soul. It is idle to say that the something in the human being which we call "life" is the soul itself, for the soul is generally taken to distinguish human beings from other forms of life. There is life in all animals and plants, and at least potential life in inorganic matter. This potential life is simply unreleased force and matter—the great storehouse from which all forms of life emerge and are constantly replenished. It is impossible to draw the line between inorganic matter and the simpler forms of plant life, and equally impossible to draw the line between plant life and animal life, or between other forms of animal life and what we human beings are pleased to call the highest form. If the thing which we call "life" is itself the soul, then cows have souls; and, in the very nature of things, we must allow souls to all forms of life and to inorganic matter as well.

Life itself is something very real, as distinguished from the soul. Every man knows that his life had a beginning. Can one imagine an organism that has a beginning and no end? If I did not exist in the infinite past, why should I, or could I, exist in the infinite future? "But," say some, "your consciousness, your memory may exist even after you are dead. This is what we mean by the soul." Let us examine this point a little.

I have no remembrance of the months that I lay in my mother's womb. I cannot recall the day of my birth nor the time when I first opened my eyes to the light of the sun. I cannot remember when I was an infant, or when I began to creep on the floor, or when I was taught to walk, or anything before I was five or six years old. Still, all of these events were important, wonderful, and strange in a new life. What I call my "consciousness," for lack of a better word and a better understanding, developed with my growth and the crowding experiences I met at every turn. I have a hazy recollection of the burial of a boy soldier who was shot toward the end of the Civil War. He was buried near the schoolhouse when I was seven years old. But I have no remembrance of the assassination of Abraham Lincoln, although I must then have been eight years old. I must have known about it at the time, for my family and my community idolized Lincoln, and all America was in mourning at his death. Why do I remember the dead boy soldier who was buried a year before? Perhaps because I knew him well. Perhaps because his family was close to my childish life. Possibly because it came to me as my first knowledge of death. At all events, it made so deep an impression that I recall it now.

"Ah, yes," say the believers in the soul, "what you say confirms our own belief. You certainly existed when these early experiences took place. You were conscious of them at the time, even though you are not aware of it now. In the same way, may not your consciousness persist after you die, even though you are not now aware of the fact?"

On the contrary, my fading memory of the events that filled the early years of my life leads me to the opposite conclusion. So far as these incidents are concerned, the mind and consciousness of the boy are already dead. Even now, am I fully alive? I am seventy-one years old. I often fail to recollect the names of some of those I knew full well. Many events do not make the lasting impression that they once did. I know that it will be only a few years, even if my body still survives decay, when few important matters will even register in my mind. I know how it is with the old. I know that physical life can persist beyond the time when the mind can fully function. I know that if I live to an extreme old age, my mind will fail. I shall eat and drink and go to my bed in an automatic way. Memory—which is all that binds me to the past—will already be dead. All that will remain will be a vegetative existence; I shall sit and doze in the chimney corner, and my body will function in a measure even though the ego will already be practically dead. I am sure that if I die of what is called "old age," my consciousness will gradually slip away with my failing emotions; I shall no more be aware of the near approach of final dissolution than is the dying tree.

In primitive times, before men knew anything about the human body or the universe of which it is a part, it was not unreasonable to believe in spirits, ghosts, and the duality of man. For one thing, celestial geography was much simpler then. Just above the earth was a firmament in which the stars were set, and above the firmament was heaven. The place was easy of access, and in dreams the angels were seen going up and coming down on a ladder. But now we have a slightly more adequate conception of space and the infinite universe of which we are so small a part. Our great telescopes reveal countless worlds and planetary systems which make our own sink into utter insignificance in comparison. We have every reason to think that beyond our sight there is endless space filled with still more planets, so infinite in size and number that no brain has the smallest conception of their extent. Is there any reason to think that in this universe, with its myriads of worlds, there is no other life so important as our own? Is it possible that the inhabitants of the earth have been singled out for special favor and endowed with souls and immortal life? Is it at all reasonable to suppose that any special account is taken of the human atoms that forever come and go upon this planet? . . .

[III. Other Matters]

Some of those who profess to believe in the immortality of man—whether it be of his soul or his body—have drawn what comfort they could from the modern scientific doctrine of the indestructibility of matter and force. This doctrine, they say, only confirms in scientific language what they have always believed. This, however, is pure sophistry. It is probably true that no matter or force has ever been or ever can be destroyed. But it is likewise true that there is no connection whatever between the notion that personal consciousness and memory persist after death and the scientific theory that matter and force are indestructible. For the scientific theory carries with it a corollary, that the forms of matter and energy are constantly changing through an endless cycle of new combinations. Of what possible use would it be, then, to have a consciousness that was immortal, but which, from the moment of death, was dispersed into new combinations so that no two parts of the original identity could ever be reunited again?

These natural processes of change, which in the human being take the forms of growth, disease, senility, death, and decay, are essentially the same as the process by which a lump of coal is disintegrated in burning. One may watch the lump of coal burning in the grate until nothing but ashes remains. Part of the coal goes up the chimney in the form of smoke; part of it radiates through the house as heat; the residue lies in the ashes on the hearth. So it is with human life. In all forms of life nature is engaged in combining, breaking down, and recombining her store of energy and matter into new forms. The thing we call "life" is nothing other than a state of equilibrium which endures for a short span of years between the two opposing tendencies of nature—the one that builds up and the one that tears down. In old age, the tearing-down process has already gained the ascendancy, and when death intervenes, the equilibrium is finally upset by the complete stoppage of the building-up process, so that nothing remains but complete disintegration. The energy thus released may be converted into grass or trees or animal life; or it may lie dormant until caught up again in the crucible of nature's laboratory. But whatever happens, the man—the *You* and the *I*—like the lump of coal that has been burned, is gone, irrevocably dispersed. All the King's horses and all the King's men cannot restore it to its former unity.

The idea that man is a being set apart, distinct from all the rest of nature, is born of man's emotions, of his loves and hates, of his hopes and fears, and of the primitive conceptions of undeveloped minds. The *You* or the *I* which is known to our friends does not consist of an immaterial something called a "soul" which cannot be conceived. We know perfectly well what we mean when we talk about this *You* and this *Me*: and it is equally plain that the whole fabric that makes up our separate personalities is destroyed, dispersed, disintegrated beyond repair by what we call "death."

Those who refuse to give up the idea of immortality declare that nature never creates a desire without providing the means for its satisfaction. They likewise insist that all people, from the rudest to the most civilized, yearn for another life. As a matter of fact, nature creates many desires which she does not satisfy; most of the wishes of men meet no fruition. But nature does not create any emotion demanding a future life. The only yearning that the individual has is to keep on living—which is a very different thing. This urge is found in every animal, in every plant. It is simply the momentum of a living structure: or, as Schopenhauer* put it, "the will to live." What we long for is a continuation of our present state of existence, not an uncertain reincarnation in a mysterious world of which we know nothing.

All men recognize the hopelessness of finding any evidence that the individual will persist beyond the grave. As a last resort, we are told that it is better that the doctrine be believed even if it is not true. We are assured that without this faith, life is only desolation and despair. However that may be, it remains that many of the conclusions of logic are not pleasant to contemplate; still, so long as men think and feel, at least some of them will use their faculties as best they can. For if we are to believe things that are not true, who is to write our creed? Is it safe to leave it to any man or organization to pick out the errors that we must accept? The whole history of the world has answered this question in a way that cannot be mistaken.

---

*[A 19th century German philosopher who held that all living things exhibit a "will to live."—Eds.]

And after all, is the belief in immortality necessary or even desirable for man? Millions of men and women have no such faith; they go on with their daily tasks and feel joy and sorrow without the lure of immortal life. The things that really affect the happiness of the individual are the matters of daily living. They are the companionship of friends, the games and contemplations. They are misunderstandings and cruel judgments, false friends and debts, poverty and disease. They are our joys in our living companions and our sorrows over those who die. Whatever our faith, we mainly live in the present—in the here and now. Those who hold the view that man is mortal are never troubled by metaphysical problems. At the end of the day's labor we are glad to lose our consciousness in sleep; and intellectually, at least, we look forward to the long rest from the stresses and storms that are always incidental to existence.

When we fully understand the brevity of life, its fleeting joys and unavoidable pains; when we accept the fact that all men and women are approaching an inevitable doom: the consciousness of it should make us more kindly and considerate of each other. This feeling should make men and women use their best efforts to help their fellow travellers on the road, to make the path brighter and easier as we journey on. It should bring a closer kinship, a better understanding, and a deeper sympathy for the wayfarer who must live a common life and die a common death.

24 / Is Life After Death Possible?

C. J. DUCASSE

The question whether human personality survives death is sometimes asserted to be one upon which reflection is futile. Only empirical evidence, it is said, can be relevant, since the question is purely one of fact.

But no question is purely one of fact until it is clearly understood; and this one is, on the contrary, ambiguous and replete with tacit assumptions. Until the ambiguities have been removed and the assumptions critically examined, we do not really know just what it is we want to know when we ask whether a life after death is possible. Nor, therefore, can we tell until then what bearing on this question various facts empirically known to us may have.

To clarify its meaning is chiefly what I now propose to attempt. I shall . . . state, as convincingly as I can in the space available, the arguments commonly advanced to prove that such a life is impossible. After that, I shall consider the logic of these arguments, and show that they quite fail to establish the impossibility. Next, the tacit but arbitrary assumption,. which makes them nevertheless appear convincing, will be pointed out. . . .

Let us turn to the first of these tasks. . . .

I. THE ARGUMENTS AGAINST SURVIVAL

There are, first of all, a number of *facts* which definitely suggest that both the existence and the nature of consciousness wholly depend on the presence of a functioning nervous system. [F1.] It is pointed out, for example, that wherever consciousness is observed, it is found associated with a living and functioning body. [F2.] Further, when the body dies, or the head is struck a heavy blow, or some anesthetic is administered, the familiar outward evidences of consciousness terminate, permanently or temporarily. [F3.] Again, we know well that drugs of various kinds—alcohol, caffeine, opium, heroin, and many others—cause specific changes at the time in the nature of a person's mental states. . . . [F4.] Again, the contents of consciousness, the mental powers, or even the personality, are modified in characteristic ways when certain regions of the brain are destroyed by disease or injury or are disconnected from the rest by such an operation as prefrontal lobotomy. . . .

That continued existence of mind after death is impossible has been argued also on the basis of *theoretical considerations*. [T1.] It has been contended, for instance, . . . that "consciousness" is only the name we give to certain types of behavior, which differentiate the higher animals from all other things in nature. According to this view, to say, for example, that an animal is conscious of a difference between two stimuli means nothing more than that it responds to each by different behavior. That is, the difference of *behavior* is what consciousness of difference between the stimuli *consists in*; and is not, as is commonly assumed, only the behavioral sign of something mental and not public, called "consciousness that the stimuli are different."

[T2.] Or again, consciousness, of the typically human sort called thought, is identified with the typically human sort of behavior called speech; and this, again, not in the sense that speech *expresses* or *manifests* something different from itself, called "thought," but in the sense that speech—whether uttered or only whispered—*is* thought itself. And obviously, if thought, or any mental activity, is thus but some mode of behavior of the living body, the mind cannot possibly survive death. . . .

II. THE ARGUMENTS EXAMINED

Such, in brief, are the chief reasons commonly advanced for holding that survival is impossible. Scrutiny of them, however, will, I think, reveal that they are not as strong as they first seem and far from strong enough to show that there can be no life after death.

[T1 and T2.] Let us consider first the assertion that "thought," or "consciousness," is but another name for subvocal speech, or for some other form of behavior, or for molecular processes in the tissues of the brain. As Paulsen and others have pointed out,[1] no evidence ever is or can be offered to support that assertion, because it is in fact but a disguised proposal to make the words "thought," "feeling," "sensation," "desire," and so on, denote facts quite different from those which these words are commonly employed to denote. To say that those words are but other names for certain chemical or behavioral events is as grossly arbitrary as it would be to say that "wood" is but another name for glass, or "potato" but another name for cabbage. What thought, desire, sensation, and other mental states are like, each of us can observe directly by introspection; and what introspection reveals is that they do not in the least resemble muscular contraction, or glandular secretion, or any other known bodily events. No tampering with language can alter the observable fact that thinking is one thing and muttering quite another; that the feeling called anger has no resemblance to the bodily behavior which usually goes with it; or that an act of will is not in the least like anything we find when we open the skull and examine the brain. Certain mental events are doubtless connected in some way with certain bodily events, but they are not those bodily events themselves. The connection is not identity.

[F2, F3, and F4.] This being clear, let us next consider the arguments offered to show that mental processes, although not identical with bodily processes, nevertheless depend on them. We are told, for instance, that some head injuries, or anesthetics, totally extinguish consciousness for the time being. As already pointed out, however, the strict fact is only that the usual bodily signs of consciousness are then absent. But they are also absent when a person is asleep; and yet, at the same time, dreams, which are states of consciousness, may be occurring.

It is true that when the person concerned awakens, he often remembers his dreams, whereas the person that has been anesthetized or injured has usually no memories relating to the period of apparent blankness. But this could mean that his consciousness was, for the first time, dissociated from

[1]F. Paulsen, "Introduction to Philosophy," 2nd ed., trans. F. Thilly. pp. 82–83.

its ordinary channels of manifestation, as was reported of the co-conscious personalities of some of the patients of Dr. Morton Prince.[2] Moreover, it sometimes occurs that a person who has been in an accident reports lack of memories not only for the period during which his body was unresponsive but also for a period of several hours *before* the accident, during which he had given to his associates all the ordinary external signs of being conscious as usual.

But, more generally, if absence of memories relating to a given period proved unconsciousness for that period, this would force us to conclude that we were unconscious during the first few years of our lives, and indeed have been so most of the time since; for the fact is that we have no memories whatever of most of our days. That we were alive and conscious on any long past specific date is, with only a few exceptions, not something we actually remember, but only something which we infer must be true.

III. EVIDENCE FROM PSYCHICAL RESEARCH

[F1 and F2] Another argument advanced against survival was, it will be remembered, that death must extinguish the mind, since all manifestations of it then cease. But to assert that they invariably then cease is to ignore altogether the considerable amount of evidence to the contrary, gathered over many years and carefully checked by the Society for Psychical Research. This evidence which is of a variety of kinds, has been reviewed by Professor Gardner Murphy in an article published in the Journal of the Society.[3] He mentions first the numerous well-authenticated cases of apparition of a dead person to others as yet unaware that he had died or even been ill or in danger. The more strongly evidential cases of apparition are those in which the apparition conveys to the person who sees it specific facts until then secret. An example would be that of the apparition of a girl to her brother nine years after her death, with a conspicuous scratch on her cheek. Their mother then revealed to him that she herself had made that scratch accidentally while preparing her daughter's body for burial, but that she had then at once covered it with powder and never mentioned it to anyone.

Another famous case is that of a father whose apparition some time after death revealed to one of his sons the existence and location of an unsuspected second will, benefiting him, which was then found as indicated. Still another case would be the report by General Barter, then a subaltern in the British Army in India, of the apparition to him of a lieutenant he had

[2]"My Life as a Dissociated Personality," ed. Morton Prince (Boston: Badger).

[3]"An Outline of Survival Evidence," *Journal of the American Society for Psychical Research*, January, 1945.

not seen for two or three years. The lieutenant's apparition was riding a brown pony with black mane and tail. He was much stouter than at their last meeting, and, whereas formerly clean-shaven, he now wore a peculiar beard in the form of a fringe encircling his face. On inquiry the next day from a person who had known the lieutenant at the time he died, it turned out that he had indeed become very bloated before his death; that he had grown just such a beard while on the sick list; and that he had some time before bought and eventually ridden to death a pony of that very description.

Other striking instances are those of an apparition seen simultaneously by several persons. It is on record that an apparition of a child was perceived first by a dog, that the animal's rushing at it, loudly barking, interrupted the conversation of the seven persons present in the room, thus drawing their attention to the apparition, and that the latter then moved through the room for some fifteen seconds, followed by the barking dog.[4]

Another type of empirical evidence of survival consists of communications, purporting to come from the dead, made through the persons commonly called sensitives, mediums, or automatists. Some of the most remarkable of these communications were given by the celebrated American medium, Mrs. Piper, who for many years was studied by the Society for Psychical Research, London, with the most elaborate precautions against all possibility of fraud. Twice, particularly, the evidences of identity supplied by the dead persons who purportedly were thus communicating with the living were of the very kinds, and of the same precision and detail, which would ordinarily satisfy a living person of the identity of another living person with whom he was not able to communicate directly, but only through an intermediary, or by letter or telephone.[5]

Again, sometimes the same mark of identity of a dead person, or the same message from him, or complementary parts of one message, are obtained independently from two mediums in different parts of the world.

Of course, when facts of these kinds are recounted, as I have just done, only in abstract summary, they make little if any impression upon us. And the very word "medium" at once brings to our minds the innumerable in-

---

[4]The documents obtained by the Society for Psychical Research concerning this case, that of the lieutenant's apparition, and that of the girl with the scratch are reproduced in Sir Ernest Bennett's "Apparitions and Haunted Houses" (London: Faber and Faber, 1945), pp. 334–337, 28–35, and 145–150 respectively.

[5]A summary of some of the most evidential facts may be found in the book by M. Sage, entitled "Mrs. Piper and the Society for Psychical Research" (New York: Scott-Thaw Co., 1904); others of them are related in some detail in Sir Oliver Lodge's "The Survival of Man," sec. 4 (New York: Moffat, Yard and Co., 1909), and in A. M. Robbins' "Both Sides of the Veil," part 2 (Boston: Sherman, French, and Co., 1909). The fullest account is in the *Proceedings of the Society for Psychical Reseach*.

stances of demonstrated fraud perpetrated by charlatans to extract money from the credulous bereaved. But the modes of trickery and sources of error, which immediately suggest themselves to us as easy, natural explanations of the seemingly extraordinary facts, suggest themselves just as quickly to the members of the research committees of the Society for Psychical Research. Usually, these men have had a good deal more experience than the rest of us with the tricks of conjurers and fraudulent mediums, and take against them precautions far more strict and ingenious than would occur to the average skeptic.[6]

But when, instead of stopping at summaries, one takes the trouble to study the detailed, original reports, it then becomes evident that they cannot all be just laughed off; for to accept the hypothesis of fraud or malobservation would often require more credulity than to accept the facts reported.

IV. THE INITIAL ASSUMPTION BEHIND THE ARGUMENTS AGAINST SURVIVAL

We have now scrutinized . . . the reasons mentioned earlier for rejecting the possibility of survival, and we have found them all logically weak . . . It will be useful for us to . . . inquire why so many of the persons who advance those reasons nevertheless think them convincing.

It is, I believe, because these persons approach the question of survival with a certain unconscious metaphysical bias. It derives from a particular initial assumption which they tacitly make. It is that *to be real is to be material.** And to be material, of course, is to be some process or part of the perceptually public world, that is, of the world we all perceive by means of our so-called five senses.

Now, the assumption that to be real is to be material is a useful and appropriate one for the purpose of investigating the material world and of operating upon it; and this purpose is a legitimate and frequent one. But those persons, and most of us, do not realize that the validity of that assumption is strictly relative to that specific purpose. Hence they, and most of us, continue making the assumption, and it continues to rule judgment, even when, as now, the purpose in view is a different one, for which the assumption is no longer useful or even congruous.

The point is all-important here and therefore worth stressing. Its essence is that the conception of the nature of reality that proposes to define the real as the material is not the expression of an observable fact to which everyone

---

[6]Cf. H. Carrington, ''The Physical Phenomena of Spiritualism, Fraudulent and Genuine'' (Boston: Small, Maynard & Co., 1908).

*[This is to be interpreted as an identity claim. Thus x is real = x is material.—Eds.]

would have to bow, but is the expression only of a certain direction of interest on the part of the persons who so define reality—of interest, namely, which they have chosen to center wholly in the material, perceptually public world. This specialized interest is of course as legitimate as any other, but it automatically ignores all the facts, commonly called facts of mind, which only introspection reveals. And that specialized interest is what alone compels persons in its grip to employ the word "mind" to denote, instead of what it commonly does denote, something else altogether, namely, the public behavior of bodies that have minds.

Only so long as one's judgment is swayed unawares by that special interest do the logically weak arguments against the possibility of survival, which we have examined, seem strong.

It is possible, however, and just as legitimate, as well as more conducive to a fair view of our question, to center one's interest at the start on the facts of mind as introspectively observable, ranking them as most real in the sense that they are the facts the intrinsic nature of which we most directly experience, the facts which we most certainly know to exist; and moreover, that they are the facts without the experiencing of which we should not know any other facts whatever—such, for instance, as those of the material world.

The sort of perspective one gets from this point of view is what I propose now to sketch briefly. For one thing, the material world is then seen to be but one among other objects of our consciousness. Moreover, one becomes aware of the crucially important fact that it is an object postulated rather than strictly given. What this means may be made clearer by an example. Suppose that, perhaps in a restaurant we visit for the first time, an entire wall is occupied by a large mirror and we look into it without realizing that it is a mirror. We then perceive, in the part of space beyond it, various material objects, notwithstanding that in fact they have no existence there at all. A certain set of the vivid color images which we call visual sensations was all that was strictly given to us, and these we construed, automatically and instantaneously, but nonetheless erroneously, as signs or appearances of the existence of certain material objects at a certain place.

Again, and similarly, we perceive in our dreams various objects which at the time we take as physical but which eventually we come to believe were not so. And this eventual conclusion, let it be noted, is forced upon us not because we then detect that something, called "physical substance," was lacking in those objects, but only because we notice, as we did not at the time, that their behavior was erratic—incoherent with their ordinary one. That is, their appearance was a *mere* appearance, deceptive in the sense that it did not then predict truly, as ordinarily it does, their later appearances. This, it is important to notice, is the *only* way in which we ever discover that an object we perceive was not really physical, or was not the particular sort of physical object we judged it to be.

These two examples illustrate the fact that our perception of physical objects is sometimes erroneous. But the essential point is that, even when it is veridical instead of erroneous, *all* that is literally and directly given to our minds is still only *some set of sensations*. These, on a given occasion, may be only color sensations; but they often include also tactual sensations, sounds, odors, and so on. It is especially interesting, however, to remark here in passing that, with respect to almost all the many thousands of persons and other "physical" objects we have perceived in a life time, *vivid color images* were the only data our perceiving strictly had to go by; so that, if the truth should happen to have been that those objects, like ghosts or images in a mirror, were actually intangible—that is, were *only* color images—we should never have discovered that this was the fact. For all we *directly* know, it *may* have been the fact!

To perceive a physical object, then, instead of merely experiencing passively certain sensations (something which perhaps hardly ever occurs) is always to *interpret*, that is to *construe*, given sensations as signs of, and appearances to us of, a postulated something other than themselves, which we believe is causing them in us and is capable of causing in us others of specific kinds. We believe this because we believe that our sensations too must have some cause, and we find none for them among our other mental states.

Such a postulated extramental something we call a physical object. We say that we observe physical objects, and this is true. But it is important for the present purpose to be clear that we "observe" them never in any more direct or literal manner than is constituted by the process of interpretive postulation just described—never, for example, in the wholly direct and literal manner in which we are able to observe our sensations themselves and our other mental states.

STUDY QUESTIONS

1. State what you take to be Turing's reformulation of the question, "Do machines think?" Why does he hold that this is an acceptable reformulation?

2. Do you agree that his reformulation captures the essence of the original question? If so, why? If not, why not?

3. Critically evaluate Turing's replies to the objections. Has he met them adequately?

4. Do you see any way in which the persons who raised the objections might reply to Turing? If so, what would their replies (most likely) be?

5. In your view, does Turing's essay lend any credibility to the claim advocated by some that: Persons are essentially machines, or not very different from machines? Why or why not?

6. State Gunderson's criticisms of Turing. Are they valid criticisms? Why or why not?

7. What point is Darrow trying to make in his discussion of taking a trip to Goofville?

8. Darrow argues against the belief in immortality. State his main arguments. Are they good arguments? Why or why not?

9. Some think that rejection of the belief in immortality leads to pessimism. Why does Darrow disagree? What is your view?

10. State the arguments against survival to which Ducasse refers. Critically evaluate his examination of those arguments.

11. Ducasse cites some evidence from psychical research. Is this supposed evidence sufficient to make likely the fact of survival? Why or why not?

12. What is the "initial assumption" behind the arguments against survival (according to Ducasse)? Do you agree that this assumption lies behind those arguments? Why or why not?

13. Adopt the standpoint of Darrow and criticize Ducasse. How would Ducasse respond?

14. What bearing, if any, does the question of survival and immortality have on the aims of philosophy discussed in the introduction to this book (section I)?

15. Many people believe that if we did not survive death, our life on earth would have no meaning or purpose, and hence would not be worth living. Do you agree? Why or why not?

16. In your judgment, is a solution to the mind-body problem a requisite for an answer to the question of whether we survive the death of our bodies? Why or why not?

Further Readings

A. Persons and Machines

Anderson, A. R., ed. *Minds and Machines.* Englewood Cliffs, N.J.: Prentice-Hall, 1964. [A collection of provocative essays for and against artificial intelligence.]

Boden, Margaret. *Artificial Intelligence and Natural Man.* New York: Basic Books,

1977. [Perhaps the best single book on almost every aspect of this subject.]

Dreyfus, Hubert. *What Computers Can't Do: A Critique of Artificial Reason.* New York: Harper and Row, 1972. [A work against artificial intelligence.]

Gunderson, Keith. *Mentality and Machines.* Garden City, N.Y.: Anchor Books, 1971. [Discusses the possibility of machines thinking and/or feeling.]

Scriven, Michael. "Man Versus Machine." In *Primary Philosophy.* New York: McGraw-Hill, 1966. [Very sympathetic to the view that robots, etc., are virtually no different from humans.]

B. Survival After Death and Immortality

Broad, C. D. *Lectures on Psychical Research.* New York: Humanities Press, 1962. [Takes seriously the claim that psychical research provides evidence for survival.]

Flew, Antony. *A New Approach to Psychical Research.* London: Watts, 1953. [Questions whether the belief in survival can be confirmed or disconfirmed by any empirical data.]

Lamont, Corliss. *The Illusion of Immortality.* New York: Wisdom Library, 1959. [A very lively and readable attack by a leading humanist on the belief in immortality.]

Penelhum, T. *Survival and Disembodied Existence.* London: Routledge and Kegan Paul, 1970. [Argues that a doctrine of survival based on the notion of the persistence of disembodied persons through time runs into difficulties, but that a theory of "astral or ectoplasmic" bodies does not encounter such difficulties.]

Russell, Bertrand. *Why I Am Not a Christian.* New York: Simon & Schuster and London: G. Allen and Unwin, 1957. [A criticism of the belief in survival after death and other religious doctrines.]

Taylor, A. E. *The Christian Hope of Immortality.* London: Geoffrey Bles, 1938. [An account which articulates the religious perspective on the issue of immortality.]

PART SIX

THE EXISTENCE OF GOD

PREVIEW

In *Primary Philosophy* Michael Scriven writes,

> What kind of God, if any, exists? This is the primary problem about God, and it is simply stated. Nothing else about the issue is simple. And the problem's complexity is matched by its profundity. No other problem has such important consequences for our lives and our thinking about other issues, and to no other problem does the answer at first seem so obvious. There must be a God, for how else could the Universe have come to exist, or life and morality have any point? So one feels.[1]

We agree with Scriven that the problem is a profound one and that it has important consequences for our lives and our thinking about other matters. We also agree with his view (articulated later in the book) that it cannot be settled on the basis of how one feels but must be settled on the basis of reason and arguments. Many of these arguments, and criticisms of them, will be found in the selections contained in this part of the book and the next.

There are a number of questions which arise in connection with the problem of God (or the problems of the existence of a god). Among them are these:

1. Are there any good reasons (based on either empirical evidence or rational arguments) for the belief that a god exists? If so, what are they? On the contrary, are there any good reasons to reject the belief? If so, what are they?

2. If a god exists, what sort of god is it? What are the attributes of God?

3. By many conceptions God is held to be, among other things, all-powerful and supremely benevolent. Can the fact of evil in the world be reconciled with such a belief?

[1]Michael Scriven, *Primary Philosophy* (New York: McGraw-Hill, 1966), p. 87.

4. There are some who hold that, even though reason and arguments fail, when it comes to the existence and nature of God we nevertheless have a right to have faith that such a being exists. Is this a tenable view? If so, why? If not, why not?

5. Some maintain that without God—or at least faith in God—life would have no meaning or purpose, and hence would not be worth living. Is this true?

Questions 1 and 2 will be taken up in this part; 3 and 4 in Part Seven; 5 in Part Eight.

Main Questions

Hence the main questions of this Part are:

1. Does God exist? Or are there any good reasons to believe that a god exists?

2. If so, what is the nature of that being? What are the attributes of God?

Answers

1. With regard to the question of whether or not a god exists, traditionally there have been three main answers. In recent years, a fourth position has been held. The three traditional answers are:

Theism: the view which affirms the existence of a god.

Atheism: the view which denies the existence of God or accepts no belief in God.

Agnosticism: the view that since we do not have sufficient evidence to decide, we should neither accept nor reject but keep the issue open, and for now, suspend our judgment.

Hence, we may state the main claims of each as follows:

1a. Theism: God does exist.

1b. Atheism: God does not exist. Or there is no good reason for anyone to believe that God exists.

1c. Agnosticism (or skepticism): We don't have sufficient evidence to decide whether or not God exists. We must suspend our judgment for now.

The above views all consider the claim that God exists to be a meaningful and even important one, even if that belief is deemed to be false or questionable. In recent years some philosophers have raised questions as to whether the claim that God exists, or any other theological claim, can be meaningful. Hence, we have a fourth approach to our first main question which we shall call:

1d. Non-cognitivism: The claim that God exists is not a genuine claim at all. It is meaningless. (The same holds for the denial of it.)

In this part of the book, we will take the theistic claim to be a meaningful one, however, even if it is false. (One selection briefly represents the meaningless approach.)

There are, of course, many varieties of theism. According to one conception, God is wholly transcendent to the universe. According to another, God is wholly immanent within the natural universe. According to still another, God is (somehow) both transcendent and immanent. The latter is the view advocated by some religions today. There are still other conceptions of theism which are much looser than those just mentioned. Thus, according to some conceptions, God is merely a force operating within the natural universe. According to others, God is the sum total of all moral value. There is even a conception according to which God is identical with the natural universe! We will not be concerned with these looser conceptions of God in this volume. In so doing, we believe that most traditional believers would be in agreement with us, since they would hardly find those conceptions adequate. Therefore, in our consideration of questions 1 and 2—via the selections contained in this part—we will be concerned with what we will refer to as the traditional conception of God.

It should also be pointed out that atheism may be understood in two different senses. It may be taken to be the view which denies the existence of God. While the theist affirms, the atheist denies. But atheism may also be understood simply as the rejection of the belief in God, rather than the denial of God's existence. If the theist is one who has a belief in God, then the atheist (in this sense) is merely one who is without such a belief. Agnosticism is the belief that, since we do not have sufficient reasons to either affirm or deny God's existence, we must (for now, at least) suspend our judgment.

2. We said that we will be here concerned with the traditional conception of God. But—and this brings us to question 2—what is that conception? According to the traditional conception, advocated by religions like Christianity, God is held to be omnipotent (all-powerful), omniscient (all-knowing), supremely good (or omnibenevolent), infinite, eternal, a being who possesses all perfections, the creator of the universe. (Many who hold this conception also maintain that God is a person—one who loves us, answers prayers, and so forth.) The readings contained in both this part and the next assume that it is such a god that is at issue in the questions and answers pertaining to the existence of a god, the problem of evil, and the like.

Selections

The selections in this part are primarily concerned with the first three answers to the question of whether God exists and only briefly with the fourth approach. These are represented as follows:

Question	Answer	Selection
(1)	(1a) Theism	25
(1)	(1b) Atheism	26-27-29 (?)
(1)	(1c) Agnosticism	28-29 (?)
(1)	(1d) Non-cognitivism; Theistic rejoinders	30

APPENDIX

ARGUMENTS FOR THE EXISTENCE OF GOD

There are many people who would hold that the only way by which any existence claim can be established is by finding good reasons for it. Good reasons may then be said to consist either of empirical evidence or rational arguments. If one's conception of God is that of religions like Judaism and Christianity, empirical evidence would not seem appropriate. Hence, in this view, if God's existence is to be established, it has to be on the basis of good arguments. Similarly, if the claim that God exists is to be refuted, it has to be on the basis of criticism of those arguments.

The following are among the better-known and most widely held arguments in behalf of God's existence. Our concern in this appendix is neither to support them nor to refute them. We are simply stating them, since some of the selections presuppose familiarity with these arguments.

The Ontological Argument
(A Priori Argument)

We have an idea of an all-perfect being, and that is what we mean by God. God is "that than which nothing greater can be conceived." That is, God is a being which contains or possesses all conceivable perfections (among these are such qualities as being all-powerful, all-knowing, etc.). Now, if this being "existed" merely as an idea in our minds, if this being did not actually possess existence, then it would be less perfect than if it really existed. If it lacked existence, it would not be all-perfect. It would not be as great as a being who also existed. But this would contradict our agreed-upon definition of God: a being who is all-perfect. Hence, God must exist.

The First-Cause Argument
(Cosmological Argument)

First Version / Every event must have a cause, and that cause, in turn, must have a cause, and so on. If there were no end to this backward progression of causes and effects, then their succession would be infinite. But an infinite series of causes and events is unintelligible. Hence, there must be a first cause which is itself uncaused. Such a being we call God. Therefore, God exists.

Second Version / Every event must have a cause. If we trace the succession of causes and effects within the universe backward to infinity, we find that we have only two alternatives. Either there is no ultimate first cause or there is such a cause which is itself uncaused. But if there were no ultimate first cause, then although there would be a cause for each event within the succession, there would be no cause for the entire succession as a whole. But there must be a cause for the whole succession. Therefore, there must exist a being which is the first or ultimate cause and is itself uncaused. Such a being we call God. Therefore, God exists.

The Argument from Contingency
(A Variant of the Cosmological Argument)

Everything that exists has either contingent or necessary existence. To say that anything has contingent existence is to say that its existence is dependent on the existence of something else. It cannot be the ground of its own existence. To say that anything has necessary existence is to say that its existence is not dependent on the existence of something else. It is self-sufficient, the ground of its own existence. Since the existence of contingent beings is not self-sufficient, it is impossible that only contingent beings exist. Therefore, there must exist a necessary being. This being we call God. Therefore, God exists.

The Design Argument
(Teleological Argument)

The universe exhibits orderliness and purpose. Many things or events occur in an orderly fashion, for example, the behavior of the planets in our solar system. Many other things are correlated with one another in a way which is purposeful. Among these there is an adaptation of means to ends, as in the intricate structure of the human eye. It is especially things of the second sort—the purposive features of living organisms, and life itself—which require an explanation. They could not have come about by accident or chance. They must be a result of some greater plan. Just as the existence of, say, a watch indicates that a designer/creator (an intelligent mind) must have planned it and brought it into being, so the existence of the universe and various phenomena within the universe indicate that an even greater designer/creator (an intelligent Mind) must have planned it and brought it into being. Such a being is what we mean by God. Therefore, God exists.

The Moral Argument

First Form / People have a sense of moral obligation. This claim of obedience to a moral law is felt as coming from outside of themselves. No naturalistic account of this sense of obligation in terms of human needs or behavior can explain it. It can be explained only by the existence of a moral lawgiver outside of the natural universe. Hence, such a lawgiver must exist. Such a being we call God. Therefore, God exists.

Second Form / In the effort to fulfill our obligation, our pursuit of the good sometimes gets frustrated. If this constantly occurred, the world wouldn't really be good. So the world in which this happens can't be ultimately real. There must be a real world of genuine moral value, under the control of a supreme mind. Therefore such a mind, God, must exist.

Or alternately: we have a duty to fulfill the highest good. For the world to be just, there must be agreement between our acting in accordance with our duty and the achievement of happiness. But in this world, that doesn't always happen. Therefore there must be a guarantor that the virtuous will receive their reward, in some other world. Therefore such a guarantor, God, must exist.

The Argument from Religious Experience

Many people claim to have experiences in which they have immediate and direct knowledge of God. Therefore, God exists. (Strictly speaking, this is not an argument in behalf of God's existence. For the advocate of this claim maintains that because one has a direct experience of God it is not necessary to infer the existence of God by drawing a conclusion from a set of premises.)

The Natural Law Argument

There are natural laws (laws of nature). Where there are laws, there must be a lawgiver. Therefore such a lawgiver, God, exists.

25 / Theism and the Existence of God

JULIAN HARTT

Theism is a metaphysical theory, that is, a theory concerning the nature of reality, a view of the significance of human life in relation to the total scheme of things. . . . Theism is the theory that the world (including man) is the product or effect of the activity of God, who is personal so far as intelligence, will, and love can be attributed to Him, and who governs or directs the world for the realization of the greatest ultimate good, and who has adequate resources for the realization of this aim. . . . In summary of the theistic conception of God . . ., God is a personal individual, selfidentical, absolute, and supremely perfect. . . .

I. [THE PROOF OF A METAPHYSICAL THEORY]

[A. Metaphysical Theories and Matter of Fact Claims /] The proof of a metaphysical theory is a very different matter from the verification of a factclaim. As a case of the latter, suppose I say that the table upon which I am writing is hard. If you wish to discover whether that claim is true, you feel the table for yourself; and if its surface is sufficiently resistant to the touch, you agree that it is hard. This kind of verification is a simple and relatively direct affair, however complex and confusing its presuppositions may be, because it concerns stable features of a "public" and common world. It concerns aspects of the world accessible to all interested parties. But the verification of a metaphysical claim is not so simple and direct. The materialist does not say, "anybody can tell that the world is nothing but physical substance by just looking for himself." The metaphysician does not report the facts in so simple a manner. He theorizes about the facts, he interprets the facts, and he appeals to the facts as evidence for the truth of his theories. The metaphysician tries to set the facts in a framework of theory designed to embrace them all, that is to say, designed to give a coherent and practically significant view of the world we know and are compelled to live in.

There are many such views, many such systematic theories. Each has its enthusiastic followers who refute all the competing systems and claim the truth for their own. How, in such a hubbub of assertion and denial, of proof and refutation, could the truth be recognized? The situation is not, however, so hopeless as it looks. Those who agree that metaphysics is significant should also be able to agree on how metaphysical theories are to be tested. And one of the things that such people are pretty generally agreed on is that one of the tests is coherence or internal consistency. Another is clarity; and yet another is fruitfulness in and for concrete activity, or for life as a whole. The last element is very important, and for a simple reason: If metaphysics is the attempt to produce a view of the meaning of life as a whole, it ought to make a real difference in living, it ought not to be the kind of theory that makes no ripple upon the waters of concrete existence.

It should hardly need saying that there is no neat yardstick for the determination of the adequate or decisive degree of any of these requirements of a metaphysical theory or for the way in which they should be combined. Because such a measure is lacking, the durable systems have been revised over and over to meet the thrust of searching criticism and to synthesize fresh discoveries about the world. From this it seems a natural inference that such theories are really born for conflict with one another and that in this conflict the relative truth and concrete significance of the various alternatives are worked out. . . .

[B. Proving and Refuting a Metaphysical Theory /] It was said above that metaphysical theories seem born for conflict. This can be seen also in the fact that to prove such a theory involves disproving its rivals. Fundamentally there are two ways of accomplishing this latter objective. One is to show that the alternatives of the favored system are really unthinkable; that is, they cannot be thought without falling into absurdities. This is called dialectic. . . .

The use of dialectic is determined by the basic conviction that a genuinely significant theory must be as free as possible from internal contradiction. This is perhaps a kind of rudimentary rationalism, for the philosopher believes that an utterly self-contradictory notion *cannot* be true, *cannot* really be faithful to reality. . . .

The second way of disproving or refuting a metaphysical theory is to show that it ignores or misinterprets certain essential facts. Every durable type of metaphysics of course tries to get in all these essential facts; it tries to account for the "full orb" of human experience and the environment in which it is set. And therefore the charge of ignoring significant aspects of experience is not quite so simple as it sounds when it is preferred against such a theory. What the criticism generally signifies is that the full flavor, the solid impact, of a range of experience are not discernible in that system. The system blanches the richness of certain areas of experience and leaves it but a faint shadow of the original. . . .

The aim, then, of a philosophical proof is to leave but one pair of alternatives relative to that proof: accept it or be convicted of arbitrariness and unreasonableness. . . .

This is but to say that the aim of philosophical inquiry and argument is *certainty*. Certainty is the state of being rationally satisfied with an interpretation of experience. . . .

[C. Proving Theism /] The theist accepts the aim or ideal of certainty. Theism is not something that *might* be true, that might be believed as an interesting option among others. It is true, and its truth must be shown forth. How has theism gone about this?

First of all it is of capital importance to prove that God exists . . . Such proof, if successful, could hardly be expected to make a person religious, and it would very likely take a great deal more than that to make him Christian, but as a minimum it would clarify his understanding of God.

In the presentation of the theistic proofs I shall not resort to the formal patterns traditionally employed. I shall try rather to state the essential contention of each of the proofs, and the kind of analysis of experience upon which it rests.*

II. THE A POSTERIORI ARGUMENTS

[1. The Cosmological Argument /] The a posteriori arguments are based upon some feature of the commonly experienced world. They all attempt to prove that God or infinite being is the only adequate and rationally satisfying explanation of that particular feature of the world and of the world as a whole. The nerve of [cosmological] arguments is as follows:

> Something exists, and it is finite.
> The finite is not the cause of itself.
> Neither can the finite in its whole or essential being be the effect of another finite entity.
> Therefore the proper cause of this something is infinite, and this infinite being necessarily exists, and is God.

The root conviction here appears to be that *finitude* (limitation, dependency, etc.) presupposes infinitude as the source of its limitation and the support of its dependency. This is not a matter of mere definition or word games. Everything experienced is finite; and nature, the system of finite

---

*[Hartt presupposes that his readers are familiar with the traditional arguments (or "proofs") for the existence of God. Before you read further, we suggest that you reread the appendix to the Preview to Part Six.—Eds.]

entities, is itself finite, so far as we can reasonably judge, because there is no reason for supposing that the extension of nature indefinitely either forwards or backwards in time and in complexity lifts it beyond finitude. . . .

There are many variations upon this theme in theism, but the theme is constant. Its important elements are: (1) Finitude and its application to all nature. Finitude characterizes everything in experience and experience itself. And then the claim is that a finite universe existing by itself is unthinkable—it would be an effect without adequate or sufficient cause. (2) The "causal law" or the principle of sufficient reason. Every event and every entity, and every configuration of events and of entities, require a sufficient or adequate explanation and agency. The theist repudiates the idea of causation as mere uniformity of sequence; at this point he sides with common sense against tendencies in contemporary scientific thought. Cause is real agency, power that does things. . . . (3) The necessity of the infinite as the unlimited and the inclusive. It has frequently been argued that the finite does not require the infinite as its cause, but only a (perhaps immeasurably) greater finite, perhaps a greater finite in the form of the cooperation of an indefinitely large number of other finites. The theistic rejoinder to that is that such proposals spring from an inadequate analysis of "finite." The cooperation of finites with one another does not lift them beyond finitude, for the fact of their cooperation itself requires explanation, and this explanation cannot be any one of the factors or entities taken up into this system. The cause of the system of finites is itself infinite, selfsubsistent being. This infinite being, again, is not nature or the universe but the God who is the transcendent cause of nature and the universe. . . .

This "cosmological" conviction is the core of another line of argument. Finite being is limited being. But this limitation requires explanation, because there is no reason apparent in the finite itself why it should be *this* being rather than *that*, why this kind of world rather than another, why one pattern of relationships rather than another; and we cannot rest in the answer, "Well, that is just the way it is." *Why* should it be that way?—this question ought not to be evaded. The theistic reply to that question is that limitation either argues purpose or is ultimately inexplicable. Now the retreat into ultimate inexplicabilities is hazardous indeed, because it can easily turn into a rout—it can lead to an obscurantist mentality, an incorrigible, lazy-minded agnosticism. And therefore back of mystery or beyond it we must, as rational creatures, seek at least the vague, looming shadow of intelligibility and rationality. Thus back of limitation, of finitude, we see purpose. This purpose is the purpose of an unlimited, all-inclusive being who of necessity is prior to the limited, exclusive, and dependent. No rational *why* can be asked of the existence of such a being, for his being and will affirm all positive possibilities, exclude nothing of value.

[2. The Teleological Argument /] At this point we are close to the strain of theistic argument that is known as "teleological." Theism as a whole is teleological metaphysics, through and through; and it is therefore not very much of a curiosity that specific proofs of teleological character should have been formulated in this tradition. The objective of this type of argument is to show that the many instances and levels of *adaptations* in the world are so many indications of a cosmic intelligence, which, by reason of its power and wisdom, may rightly be addressed as God. And behind all the permutations in the formal structure of this proof there is a persistent theme: Though there may be chance *in* the universe, the universe itself is not the creature of chance but of intelligent *purpose*. The total environment in which our life is set is not a fortuitously functioning mechanism or organism. It is everywhere instinct with purpose. The theist contends that it cannot be intelligibly argued that mind and purposive behavior as we know it in ourselves and as we see it suggested, at least, elsewhere have accidentally and fortuitously developed in a nonpurposive environment, for a "nonpurposive environment" necessarily means a nonmental, nonspiritual environment. (No real meaning can be given to the notion of a mind without purpose; and no real meaning can be given to purpose without mind or spirit.) Such an "unplanned for" development would mean that mental processes, such as reasoning and willing, have been caused or produced by nonmental processes and are still being so caused. But it is clearly impossible to argue (i.e., to *reason*) for such a position with any consistent conviction that the argument itself is a significant factor in the determination of a mind; and therefore it remains an opinion bereft of all rational grounds. It will not do, then, to suppose that purposeful activity is limited to the human enterprise and that all else in nature, so far as we can read her, is blind and mindless action. For our minds, our intelligent purposing, have not made the world in which we live, nor have they created our own fundamental natures. They are not responsible for (although they are responsible *to*) the basic scheme. And it will not do to suppose that "man is organic with nature" and then hasten to strike out of nature what is so truly human, that is, purpose-controlled activity, leaving man "the witty, canny child of a witless mother." Over against such notions theism stands for the acknowledgement of the genuine kinship of man and nature as participants in the cosmic order and plan of God.

[3. The Moral Argument /] *Finitude* is a pervasive characteristic of the world. *Purposeful adaptation and arrangement* is another such characteristic. We are now turning a line of argument that is concerned with the interpretation of a uniquely human realm, that of morality, the *recognition and pursuit of moral values*. This line of argument was first explicitly formulated by Kant, who, after destroying, to his own satisfaction, the rational certainty of theistic (and all other) metaphysics, turned to reasonable belief in most of the cardinal tenets of theism, predicated upon the bed-rock practical certainties of moral experience. The central motif of this sort of argument is that moral experience reveals data that metaphysics must acknowledge, such as the sense of *unqualified obligation*. Only if a God exists as the shaper and governor of the moral environment, which in turn shapes and molds us, do such data make any real sense. Again, the argument is put in these terms: Morality discloses a world deeper and richer than the natural, space–time world, in which richer world we feel called upon to make an unqualified response to the right and the good, even though the "natural man's" happiness and life may be forfeited thereby. A good man does his duty, though the heavens fall in upon him. But the good is not really good if the world systematically penalizes and frustrates its pursuit. Therefore, again, the world in which this seems to happen is not the ultimately real world. *That* world is one in which moral worth is honored all the way through; it is a supremely rational world and one therefore at all essential points under the control of a supreme mind. . . .

It is the task of the philosopher to evaluate these pursuits of truth and of value and the judgments and perceptions from which they arise. His aim is not to call in question, upon first acquaintance, the good that men seek. His aim is rather, as a metaphysican, to see what kind of sense the picture makes as a whole. And the theistic metaphysician believes that the clearest and best sense appears when human values, and our whole life and the life of all nature, are seen as expressions of a divine will and purpose, when all that is creaturely and finite is seen over against the eternal and the infinite.

III. THE A PRIORI ARGUMENT

So far arguments based upon some experienced feature of the world or upon some all-pervasive characteristic of the world have been reviewed. A very different kind of proof proceeds directly from the inspection of the definition of the idea of God to the rationally inescapable conclusion that such a being really exists. This argument, known as "ontological," was first explicitly formulated by Anselm (1033–1109). . . . It has also been frequently revived and revised after apparently annihilating criticism. In its primitive form the argument is based upon the standard definition of God as that being than which none greater can be conceived. If such a being were only an idea, only a possibility, then indeed a greater being *could* be conceived, namely one that actually or concretely existed. But by definition no being can be greater than God, and therefore God necessarily exists, not merely as or in idea, but really.

The intent of the argument is to show that nonexistence cannot be seriously and intelligently predicated of God; that is, the attempt to do so results in self-contradiction. If this is so, then the mind, so far as it thinks of God at all, must think of him as actually existing, notwithstanding verbal denials of his existence. Against this claim it has frequently been argued that the entire argument is deposited at the outset in the definition of God. This is of course the case, and the adherents of the argument have rarely considered it a damaging criticism, since the purpose of any formal deductive argument is to show what is contained in the prime definitions of the argument. So here: The argument intends to show what one lets himself in for when he uses the term "God" seriously. The being to whom this term properly applies *cannot* be a mere possibility; He alone among all beings *must* exist.

In spite of its failure to win a large following of admirers this argument has a remarkably perennial character, largely, I think, because of its profoundly religious character rather than because of any logical power or neatness and simplicity. The religious sentiment embedded in it concerns the all-sufficiency of God, God's perfect power of being. The argument really derives, then, from the conviction that God is the "cause," the whole explanation, of His own nature and existence, and therefore no appeal is made to the nature of the experienced world, but only to the idea of God and what it contains. It might then be said with substantial justification that this proof above all the others discloses the intent of proof that deals with the ultimate problems of human life, because it sets forth what is already apprehended in the idea of God, quite as though the only way one could possibly prove the existence of God would be by beginning with God, for if one began anywhere else, could he ever really reach from that which is not God to God Himself?

IV. THE APPEAL TO RELIGIOUS EXPERIENCE

In recent times, . . . arguments for God based upon religious experience have appeared in theistic thought. The fundamental claims of such arguments are that there are irreducible *religious* data that must be accounted for by any philosophy aiming at comprehensiveness and that the reality of God, the religious object, is the only adequate way of accounting for these data. The data identified as irreducibly religious are the deeply ingrained impulsion to worship (something in the world elicits from man a worshipful response, arouses the sense of awe and reverence), the mystical awareness of God, and the practical results of the religious life. These data can be adequately understood only if they are seen to be the effect in the human spirit of relation to religious reality, or God.

This argument is a fairly close relative of the argument *consensus gentium* and of the pragmatic argument.* "The plain man" is wont to say that where there's a lot of smoke there must be at least a little fire. So the almost universal presence of religious concern in mankind argues at least a dim awareness of a religious environing reality. And again, whether or not the religious life hooks into anything *out there*, it can be made to produce something good *in here*; and until definite and unmistakable word is forthcoming from *out there*, the good fruit of practical religious living may be said to be the truth of religious belief. . . .

If God exists, it is entirely possible and perhaps inevitable that all men should have a dim and confused awareness of Him, and that here and there this dim awareness of Him should be clarified and sharpened into a dazzling focus (mysticism). If God exists, then the prime concern of religious activity and ultimately of all our activity is to bring us into the most positive and productive relationships with Him in whom is fullness of life. If God exists, then the "data" of religious experience are in the main veridical and reliable. And then the arguments from religious experience may test the data by the theistic affirmation and weigh the theistic affirmation by the light of religious experience. . . .

26 / The Case for Atheism

ERNEST NAGEL

I

I must begin by stating what sense I am attaching to the word "atheism," and how I am construing the theme of this [essay]. I shall understand by "atheism" a critique and a denial of the major claims of all varieties of theism. And by theism I shall mean the view which holds, as one writer has expressed it, "that the heavens and the earth and all that they contain owe their existence and continuance in existence to the wisdom and will of a supreme, self-consistent, omnipotent, omniscient, righteous, and benevolent

---

*[*Consensus gentium*: roughly, consensus of mankind. Pragmatic argument: roughly, since religious beliefs produce good consequences, they are true.—Eds.]

being, who is distinct from, and independent of, what he has created."
Several things immediately follow from these definitions.

In the first place, atheism is not necessarily an irreligious concept, for theism is just one among many views concerning the nature and origin of the world. The denial of theism is logically compatible with a religious outlook upon life, and is in fact characteristic of some of the great historical religions. For as readers of this volume will know, early Buddhism is a religion which does not subscribe to any doctrine about a god; and there are pantheistic religions and philosophies which, because they deny that God is a being separate from and independent of the world, are not theistic in the sense of the word explained above.

The second point to note is that atheism is not to be identified with sheer unbelief, or with disbelief in some particular creed of a religious group. Thus, a child who has received no religious instruction and has never heard about God, is not an atheist—for he is not denying any theistic claims. Similarly, an adult who has withdrawn from the faith of his fathers without reflection or because of frank indifference to any theological issue is also not an atheist—for such an adult is not challenging theism and is not professing any views on the subject. . . .

One final word of preliminary explanation. I propose to examine some *philosophic* concepts of atheism, and I am not interested in the slightest in the many considerations atheists have advanced against the evidences for some particular religious and theological doctrine—for example, against the truth of the Christian story. What I mean by "philosophical" in the present context is that the views I shall consider are directed against any form of theism, and have their origin and basis in a logical analysis of the theistic position, and in a comprehensive account of the world believed to be wholly intelligible without the adoption of a theistic hypothesis. . . .

II

As I see it, atheistic philosophies fall into two major groups: (1) those which hold that the theistic doctrine is meaningful, but reject it either on the ground that (a) the positive evidence for it is insufficient or (b) the negative evidence is quite overwhelming; and (2) those who hold that the theistic thesis is not even meaningful, and reject it (a) as just nonsense or (b) as literally meaningless, but interpreting it as a symbolic rendering of human ideals, thus reading the theistic thesis in a sense that most believers in theism would disavow. It will not be possible in the limited space at my disposal to discuss the second category of atheistic critiques; and in any event, most of the traditional atheistic critiques of theism belong to the first group.

But before turning to the philosophical examination of the major classical arguments for theism, it is well to note that such philosophical critiques do not quite convey the passion with which atheists have often carried on their analyses of theistic views. For historically, atheism has been, and indeed continues to be, a form of social and political protest, directed as much against institutionalized religion as against theistic doctrine. Atheism has been, in effect, a moral revulsion against the undoubted abuses of the secular power exercised by religious leaders and religious institutions.

Religious authorities have opposed the correction of glaring injustices, and encouraged politically and socially reactionary policies. Religious institutions have been havens of obscurantist thought and centers for the dissemination of intolerance. Religious creeds have been used to set limits to free inquiry, to perpetuate inhumane treatment of the ill and the underprivileged, and to support moral doctrines insensitive to human suffering.

These indictments may not tell the whole story about the historical significance of religion; but they are at least an important part of the story. The refutation of theism has thus seemed to many an indispensable step not only toward liberating men's minds from superstition but also toward achieving a more equitable reordering of society. And no account of even the more philosophical aspects of atheistic thought is adequate which does not give proper recognition to the powerful social motives that actuate many atheistic arguments.

But however this may be, I want now to discuss three classical arguments for the existence of God, arguments which have constituted at least a partial basis for theistic commitments. As long as theism is defended simply as dogma, asserted as a matter of direct revelation or as the deliverance of authority, belief in the dogma is impregnable to rational argument. In fact, however, reasons are frequently advanced in support of the theistic creed, and these reasons have been the subject of acute philosophical critiques.

III

[1. The Cosmological Argument /] One of the oldest intellectual defenses of theism is the cosmological argument, also known as the argument from a first cause. Briefly put, the argument runs as follows. Every event must have a cause. Hence an event A must have as cause some event B, which in turn must have a cause C, and so on. But if there is no end to this backward progression of causes, the progression will be infinite; and in the opinion of those who use this argument, an infinite series of actual events is unintelligible and absurd. Hence there must be a first cause, and this first cause is God, the initiator of all change in the universe.

[*Criticism.*] The argument is an ancient one . . . and it has impressed many generations of exceptionally keen minds. The argument is nonetheless a weak reed on which to rest the theistic thesis. Let us waive any question concerning the validity of the principle that every event has a cause, for though the question is important its discussion would lead us far afield. However, if the principle is assumed, it is surely incongruous to postulate a first cause as a way of escaping from the coils of an infinite series. For if everything must have a cause, why does not God require one for His own existence? The standard answer is that He does not need any, because He is self-caused. But if God can be self-caused, why cannot the world be self-caused? Why do we require a God transcending the world to bring the world into existence and to initiate changes in it? On the other hand, the supposed inconceivability and absurdity of an infinite series of regressive causes will be admitted by no one who has competent familiarity with the modern mathematical analysis of infinity. The cosmological argument does not stand up under scrutiny.

[2. The Ontological Argument /] The second "proof" of God's existence is usually called the ontological argument. It too has a long history going back to early Christian days, though it acquired great prominence only in medieval times. The argument can be stated in several ways, one of which is the following. Since God is conceived to be omnipotent, he is a perfect being. A perfect being is defined as one whose essence or nature lacks no attributes (or properties) whatsoever, one whose nature is complete in every respect. But it is evident that we have an idea of a perfect being, for we have just defined the idea; and since this is so, the argument continues, God who is the perfect being must exist. Why must he? Because his existence follows from his defined nature. For if God lacked the attribute of existence, he would be lacking at least one attribute, and would therefore not be perfect. To sum up, since we have an idea of God as a perfect being, God must exist.

[*Criticism.*] There are several ways of approaching this argument, but I shall consider only one. The argument was exploded by the 18th century philosopher Immanuel Kant. The substance of Kant's criticism is that it is just a confusion to say that existence is an attribute, and that though the *word* "existence" may occur as the grammatical predicate in a sentence, no attribute is being predicated of a thing when we say that the thing exists or has existence. Thus, to use Kant's example, when we think of $100 we are thinking of the nature of this sum of money; but the nature of $100 remains the same whether we have $100 in our pockets or not. Accordingly, we are confounding grammar with logic if we suppose that some characteristic is being attributed to the nature of $100 when we say that a $100 bill exists in someone's pocket.

To make the point clearer, consider another example. When we say that a lion has a tawny color, we are predicating a certain attribute of the animal, and similarly when we say that the lion is fierce or is hungry. But when we say the lion exists, all that we are saying is that something is (or has the nature of) a lion; we are not specifying an attribute which belongs to the nature of anything that is a lion. In short, the word "existence" does not signify any attribute, and in consequence no attribute that belongs to the nature of anything. Accordingly, it does not follow from the assumption that we have an idea of a perfect being that such a being exists. For the idea of a perfect being does not involve the attribute of existence as a constituent of that idea, since there is no such attribute. The ontological argument thus has a serious leak, and it can hold no water.

IV

[3. The Teleogical Argument /] The two arguments discussed thus far are purely dialectical, and attempt to establish God's existence without any appeal to empirical data. The next argument, called the argument from design, is different in character, for it is based on what purports to be empirical evidence. . . .

One variant of it calls attention to the remarkable way in which different things and processes in the world are integrated with each other, and concludes that this mutual "fitness" of things can be explained only by the assumption of a divine architect who planned the world and everything in it. For example, living organisms can maintain themselves in a variety of environments, and do so in virtue of their delicate mechanisms which adapt the organisms to all sorts of environmental changes. There is thus an intricate pattern of means and ends throughout the animate world. But the existence of this pattern is unintelligible, so the argument runs, except on the hypothesis that the pattern has been deliberately instituted by a Supreme Designer. If we find a watch in some deserted spot, we do not think it came into existence by chance, and we do not hesitate to conclude that an intelligent creature designed and made it. But the world and all its contents exhibit mechanisms and mutual adjustments that are far more complicated and subtle than are those of a watch. Must we not therefore conclude that these things too have a Creator?

[Criticism.] The conclusion of this argument is based on an inference from analogy: The watch and the world are alike in possessing a congruence of parts and an adjustment of means to ends; the watch has a watch-maker; hence the world has a world-maker. But is the analogy a good one? Let us once more waive some important issues, in particular the issue of whether the universe is the unified system such as the watch admittedly is. And let us concentrate on the question of what is the ground for our assurance that watches do not come into existence except through the operations of intelligent manufacturers. The answer is plain. We have never run across a watch which has not been deliberately made by someone. But the situation is nothing like this in the case of the innumerable animate and inanimate systems with which we are familiar. Even in the case of living organisms, though they are generated by their parent organisms, the parents do not "make" their progeny in the same sense in which watchmakers make watches. And once this point is clear, the inference from the existence of living organisms to the existence of a supreme designer no longer appears credible.

Moreover, the argument loses all its force if the facts which the hypothesis of a divine designer is supposed to explain can be understood on the basis of a better supported assumption. And indeed, such an alternative explanation is one of the achievements of Darwinian biology. For Darwin showed that one can account for the variety of biological species, as well as for their adaptations to their environments, without invoking a divine creator and acts of special creation. The Darwinian theory explains the diversity of biological species in terms of chance variations in the structure of organisms, and of a mechanism of selection which retains those variant forms that possess some advantages for survival. The evidence for these assumptions is considerable; and developments subsequent to Darwin have only strengthened the case for a thoroughly naturalistic explanation of the facts of biological adaptation. In any event, this version of the argument from design has nothing to recommend it. . . .

V

[4. The Moral Argument /] The inconclusiveness of the three classical arguments for the existence of God was already made evident by Kant, in a manner substantially not different from the above discussion. There are, however, other types of arguments for theism that have been influential in the history of thought, two of which I wish to consider, even if only briefly.

Indeed, though Kant destroyed the classical intellectual foundations for theism, he himself invented a fresh argument for it. Kant's attempted proof is not intended to be a purely theoretical demonstration, and is based on the supposed facts of our moral nature. It has exerted an enormous influence on subsequent theological speculation. In barest outline, the argument is as follows. According to Kant, we are subject not only to physical laws like the rest of nature, but also to moral ones. These moral laws are categorical imperatives, which we must heed not because of their utilitarian consequences but simply because as autonomous moral agents it is our duty to accept them as binding. However, Kant was keenly aware that though virtue may be its reward, the virtuous man (that is, the man who acts out of a sense of duty and in conformity with the moral law) does not always receive his just desserts in this world; nor did he shut his eyes to the fact that evil men frequently enjoy the best things this world has to offer. In short, virtue does not always reap happiness. Nevertheless, the highest human good is the realization of happiness commensurate with one's virtue; and Kant believed that it is a practical postulate of the moral life to promote this good. But what can guarantee that the highest good is realizable? Such a guarantee can be found only in God, who must therefore exist if the highest good is not to be a fatuous ideal. The existence of an omnipotent, omniscient, and omnibenevolent God is thus postulated as a necessary condition for the possibility of a moral life.

[*Criticism.*] Despite the prestige this argument has acquired, it is difficult to grant it any force. It is enough to postulate God's existence. But as Bertrand Russell observed in another connection, postulation has all the advantages of theft over honest toil. No postulation carries with it any assurance that what is postulated is actually the case. And though we may postulate God's existence as a means to guaranteeing the possibility of realizing happiness together with virtue, the postulation establishes neither the actual realizability of this ideal nor the fact of his existence. Moreover, the argument is not made more cogent when we recognize that it is based squarely on the highly dubious conception that considerations of utility and human happiness must not enter into the determination of what is morally obligatory. . . .

[5. The Argument from Religious Experience /] One further type of argument, pervasive in much Protestant theological literature, deserves brief mention. Arguments of this type take their point of departure from the psychology of religious and mystical experience. Those who have undergone such experiences often report that during the experience they feel themselves to be in the presence of the divine and holy, that they lose their sense of self-identity and become merged with some fundamental reality, or that they enjoy a feeling of total dependence upon some ultimate power. The overwhelming sense of transcending one's finitude, which characterizes such vivid periods of life, and of coalescing with some ultimate source of all existence, is then taken to be compelling evidence for the existence of a supreme being. In a variant form of this argument, other theologians have identified God as the object which satisfies the commonly experienced need for integrating one's scattered and conflicting impulses into a coherent unity, or as the subject which is of ultimate concern to us. In short, a proof of God's existence is found in the occurrence of certain distinctive experiences.

[*Criticism.*] It would be flying in the face of well-attested facts were one to deny that such experiences frequently occur. But do these facts constitute evidence for the conclusion based on them? Does the fact, for example, that an individual experiences a profound sense of direct contact with an alleged transcendent ground of all reality, constitute competent evidence for the claim that there is such a ground and that it is the immediate cause of the experience? If well-established canons for evaluating evidence are accepted, the answer is surely negative. No one will dispute that many men do have vivid experiences in which such things as ghosts or pink elephants appear before them; but only the hopelessly credulous will without further ado count such experiences as establishing the existence of ghosts and pink elephants. To establish the existence of such things, evidence is required that is obtained under controlled conditions and that can be confirmed by independent inquirers. Again, though a man's report that he is suffering pain may be taken at face value, one cannot take at face value the claim, were he to make it, that it is the food he ate which is the cause (or a contributory cause) of his felt pain—not even if the man were to report a vivid feeling of abdominal disturbance. And similarly, an overwhelming feeling of being in the presence of the Divine is evidence enough for admitting the genuineness of such feeling; it is no evidence for the claim that a supreme being with a substantial existence independent of the experience is the cause of the experience.

VI

Thus far the discussion has been concerned with *noting inadequacies in various arguments widely used to support theism*. However, much atheistic criticism is also directed toward *exposing incoherencies in the very thesis of theism*. I want therefore to consider this aspect of the atheistic critique, though I will restrict myself to the central difficulty in the theistic position, which arises from the simultaneous attribution of omnipotence, omniscience, and omnibenevolence to the Deity. The difficulty is that of reconciling these attributes with the occurrence of evil in the world. Accordingly, the question to which I now turn is whether, despite the existence of evil, it is possible to construct a theodicy which will justify the ways of an infinitely powerful and just God to man. . . .

I do not believe it is possible to reconcile the alleged omnipotence and omnibenevolence of God with the unvarnished facts of human existence. In point of fact, many theologians have concurred in this conclusion; for in order to escape from the difficulty which the traditional attributes of God present, they have assumed that God is not all-powerful, and that there are limits as to what He can do in his efforts to establish a righteous order in the universe. But whether such a modified theology is better off is doubtful; and in any event, the question still remains whether the facts of human life support the claim that an omnibenevolent Deity, though limited in power, is revealed in the ordering of human history. It is pertinent to note in this connection that though there have been many historians who have made the effort, no historian has yet succeeded in showing to the satisfaction of his professional colleagues that the hypothesis of a Divine Providence is capable of explaining anything which cannot be explained just as well without this hypothesis.

VII

This last remark naturally leads to the question whether, apart from their polemics against theism, philosophical atheists have not shared a common set of positive views, a common set of philosophical convictions which set them off from other groups of thinkers. In one very clear sense of this query the answer is indubitably negative. For there never has been what one might call a "school of atheism" in the way in which there has been a Platonic school or even a Kantian school. . . .

Nevertheless, despite the variety of philosophic positions to which atheists have subscribed at one time or another in the history of thought, it seems to me that atheism is not simply a negative standpoint. At any rate, there is a certain quality of intellectual temper that has characterized, and continues to characterize, many philosophical atheists. . . . I want therefore to conclude this discussion with a brief enumeration of some points of positive doctrine to which by and large philosophical atheists seem to me to subscribe. . . .

In the first place, philosophical atheists reject the assumption that there are disembodied spirits, or that incorporeal entities of any sort can exercise a causal agency. On the contrary, atheists are generally agreed that if we wish to achieve any understanding of what takes place in the universe, we must look to the operations of organized bodies. Accordingly, the various processes taking place in nature, whether animate or inanimate, are to be explained in terms of the properties and structures of identifiable and spatio-temporally located objects. Moreover, the present variety of systems and activities found in the universe is to be accounted for on the basis of the transformations things undergo when they enter into different relations with one another—transformations which often result in the emergence of novel kinds of objects. . . .

In the second place, atheists generally manifest a marked empirical temper, and often take as their ideal the intellectual methods employed in the contemporaneous empirical sciences. Philosophical atheists differ considerably on important points of detail in their account of how responsible claims to knowledge are to be established. But there is substantial agreement among them that controlled sensory observation is the court of final appeal in issues concerning matters of fact. It is indeed this commitment to the use of an empirical method which is the final basis of the atheistic critique of theism. For at bottom this critique seeks to show that we can understand whatever a theistic assumption is alleged to explain, through the use of the proved methods of the positive sciences and without the introduction of empirically unsupported *ad hoc* hypotheses* about a Deity. It is

---

*[Any hypothesis created for the special purpose of trying to save some theory or proposition.—Eds.]

pertinent in this connection to recall a familiar legend about the French mathematical physicist Laplace. According to the story, Laplace made a personal presentation of a copy of his now famous book on celestial mechanics to Napoleon. Napoleon glanced through the volume, and finding no reference to the Deity asked Laplace whether God's existence played any role in the analysis. "Sire, I have no need for that hypothesis," Laplace is reported to have replied. The dismissal of sterile hypothesis characterizes not only the work of Laplace; it is the uniform rule in scientific inquiry. The sterility of the theistic assumption is one of the main burdens of the literature of atheism both ancient and modern.

And finally, atheistic thinkers have generally accepted a utilitarian basis for judging moral issues, and they have exhibited a libertarian attitude toward human needs and impulses. The conceptions of the human good they have advocated are conceptions which are commensurate with the actual capacities of mortal men, so that it is the satisfaction of the complex needs of the human creature which is the final standard for evaluating the validity of a moral ideal or moral prescription.

In consequence, the emphasis of atheistic moral reflection has been this worldly rather than other-worldly, individualistic rather than authoritarian. The stress upon a good life that must be consummated in this world has made atheists vigorous opponents of moral codes which seek to repress human impulses in the name of some unrealizable other-worldly ideal. The individualism that is so pronounced a strain in many philosophical atheists has made them tolerant of human limitations and sensitive to the plurality of legitimate moral goals. On the other hand, this individualism has certainly not prevented many of them from recognizing the crucial role which institutional arrangements can play in achieving desirable patterns of human living. In consequence, atheists have made important contributions to the development of a climate of opinion favorable to pursuing the values of a liberal civilization, and they have played effective roles in attempts to rectify social injustices.

Atheists cannot build their moral outlook on foundations upon which so many men conduct their lives. In particular, atheism cannot offer the incentives to conduct and the consolations for misfortune which theistic religions supply to their adherents. It can offer no hope of personal immortality, no threats of Divine chastisement, no promise of eventual recompense for injustices suffered, no blueprints to sure salvation. For on its view of the place of man in nature, human excellence and human dignity must be achieved within a finite life-span, or not at all, so that the rewards of moral endeavor must come from the quality of civilized living, and not from some source of disbursement that dwells outside of time. Accordingly, atheistic moral relection at its best does not culminate in a quiescent ideal of human perfection, but is a vigorous call to intelligent activity—activity for the sake of realizing human potentialities and for eliminating whatever stands in the way of such realization. . . .

27 / Why I Am Not a Christian

BERTRAND RUSSELL

I

The subject [of this paper] is "Why I Am Not a Christian."* Perhaps it would be as well, first of all, to try to make out what one means by the word *Christian*. It is used these days in a very loose sense by a great many people. Some people mean no more by it than a person who attempts to live a good life. In that sense I suppose there would be Christians in all sects and creeds; but I do not think that that is the proper sense of the word, if only because it would imply that all the people who are not Christians—all the Buddhists, Confucians, Mohammedans, and so on—are not trying to live a good life. I do not mean by a Christian any person who tries to live decently according to his lights. I think that you must have a certain amount of definite belief before you have a right to call yourself a Christian. The word does not have quite such a full-blooded meaning now as it had in the times of St. Augustine and St. Thomas Aquinas.† In those days, if a man said that he was a Christian it was known what he meant. You accepted a whole collection of creeds which were set out with great precision, and every single syllable of those creeds you believed with the whole strength of your convictions.

What Is a Christian?

Nowadays it is not quite that. We have to be a little more vague in our meaning of Christianity. I think, however, that there are two different items which are quite essential to anybody calling himself a Christian. The first is one of a dogmatic nature—namely, that you must believe in God and immortality. If you do not believe in those two things, I do not think that you can properly call yourself a Christian. Then, further than that, as the name implies, you must have some kind of belief about Christ. The Mohammedans, for instance, also believe in God and in immortality, and yet they would not call themselves Christians. I think you must have at the very lowest the belief that Christ was, if not divine, at least the best and wisest of men. If you are not going to believe that much about Christ, I do not think

*[This essay was first presented as a public lecture.—Eds.]
†[Medieval theologians.—Eds.]

you have any right to call yourself a Christian. Of course, there is another sense, which you find in *Whitaker's Almanack* and in geography books, where the population of the world is said to be divided into Christians, Mohammedans, Buddhists, fetish worshipers, and so on; and in that sense we are all Christians. The geography books count us all in, but that is a purely geographical sense, which I suppose we can ignore. Therefore I take it that when I tell you why I am not a Christian I have to tell you two different things: first, why I do not believe in God and in immortality;[†] and, secondly, why I do not think that Christ was the best and wisest of men, although I grant him a very high degree of moral goodness.

But for the successful efforts of unbelievers in the past, I could not take so elastic a definition of Christianity as that. As I said before, in olden days it had a much more full-blooded sense. For instance, it included the belief in hell. Belief in eternal hell-fire was an essential item of Christian belief until pretty recent times. In this country, as you know, it ceased to be an essential item because of a decision of the Privy Council,[‡] and from that decision the Archbishop of Canterbury and the Archbishop of York dissented; but in this country our religion is settled by Act of Parliament, and therefore the Privy Council was able to override their Graces and hell was no longer necessary to a Christian. Consequently I shall not insist that a Christian must believe in hell.

II

The Existence of God

To come to this question of the existence of God: It is a large and serious question, and if I were to attempt to deal with it in any adequate manner I should have to keep you here until Kingdom Come, so that you will have to excuse me if I deal with it in a somewhat summary fashion. You know, of course, that the Catholic Church has laid it down as a dogma that the existence of God can be proved by the unaided reason. That is a somewhat curious dogma, but it is one of their dogmas. They had to introduce it because at one time the freethinkers adopted the habit of saying that there were such and such arguments which mere reason might urge against the existence of God, but of course they knew as a matter of faith that God did exist. The arguments and the reasons were set out at great length, and the Catholic Church felt that they must stop it. Therefore they laid it down that the existence of God can be proved by the unaided reason, and they have

†[In this essay Russell does not take up the issue of immortality. He does so in a companion essay. Both of these essays were published in *Why I Am Not a Christian and Other Essays.*—Eds.]

‡[In England, a body of advisors whose function it is to advise the sovereign in matters of state.—Eds.]

had to set up what they considered were arguments to prove it. There are, of course, a number of them, but I shall take only a few.

1. The First-Cause Argument / Perhaps the simplest and easiest to understand is the argument of the First Cause. It is maintained that everything we see in this world has a cause, and as you go back in the chain of causes further and further you must come to a First Cause, and to that First Cause you give the name of God. That argument, I suppose, does not carry very much weight nowadays, because, in the first place, cause is not quite what it used to be. The philosophers and the men of science have got going on cause, and it has not anything like the vitality it used to have; but, apart from that, you can see that the argument that there must be a First Cause is one that cannot have any validity. I may say that when I was a young man and was debating these questions very seriously in my mind, I for a long time accepted the argument of the First Cause, until one day, at the age of eighteen, I read John Stuart Mill's* Autobiography, and I there found this sentence: ''My father taught me that the question 'Who made me?' cannot be answered, since it immediately suggests the further question 'Who made God?' '' That very simple sentence showed me, as I still think, the fallacy in the argument of the First Cause. If everything must have a cause, then God must have a cause. If there can be anything without a cause, it may just as well be the world as God, so that there cannot be any validity in that argument. It is exactly of the same nature as the Hindu's view that the world rested upon an elephant and the elephant rested upon a tortoise; and when they said, ''How about the tortoise?'' the Indian said, ''Suppose we change the subject.'' The argument is really no better than that. There is no reason why the world could not have come into being without a cause; nor, on the other hand, is there any reason why it should not have always existed. There is no reason to suppose that the world had a beginning at all. The idea that things must have a beginning is really due to the poverty of our imagination. Therefore, perhaps, I need not waste any more time upon the argument about the First Cause.

2. The Natural-Law Argument / Then there is a very common argument from natural law. That was a favorite argument all through the eighteenth century, especially under the influence of Sir Isaac Newton and his cosmogony. People observed the planets going around the sun according to the law of gravitation, and they thought that God had given a behest to these planets to move in that particular fashion, and that was why they did so. That was, of course, a convenient and simple explanation that saved them the trouble of looking any further for explanations of the law of gravitation. Nowadays we explain the law of gravitation in a somewhat complicated

*[A 19th century British philosopher.—Eds.]

fashion that Einstein has introduced. I do not propose to give you a lecture on the law of gravitation, as interpreted by Einstein, because that again would take some time; at any rate, you no longer have the sort of natural law that you had in the Newtonian system, where, for some reason that nobody could understand, nature behaved in a uniform fashion. We now find that a great many things we thought were natural laws are really human conventions. You know that even in the remotest depths of stellar space there are still three feet to a yard. That is, no doubt, a very remarkable fact, but you would hardly call it a law of nature. And a great many things that have been regarded as laws of nature are of that kind. On the other hand, where you can get down to any knowledge of what atoms actually do, you will find they are much less subject to law than people thought, and that the laws at which you arrive are statistical averages of just the sort that would emerge from chance. There is, as we all know, a law that if you throw dice you will get double sixes only about once in thirty-six times, and we do not regard that as evidence that the fall of the dice is regulated by design; on the contrary, if the double sixes came every time we should think that there was design. The laws of nature are of that sort as regards a great many of them. They are statistical averages such as would emerge from the laws of chance; and that makes this whole business of natural law much less impressive than it formerly was. Quite apart from that, which represents the momentary state of science that may change tomorrow, the whole idea that natural laws imply a lawgiver is due to a confusion between natural and human laws. Human laws are behests commanding you to behave a certain way, in which way you may choose to behave, or you may choose not to behave; but natural laws are a description of how things do in fact behave, and being a mere description of what they in fact do, you cannot argue that there must be somebody who told them to do that, because even supposing that there were, you are then faced with the question, "Why did God issue just those natural laws and no others?" If you say that he did it simply from his own good pleasure, and without any reason, you then find that there is something which is not subject to law, and so your train of natural law is interrupted. If you say, as more orthodox theologians do, that in all the laws which God issues he had a reason for giving those laws rather than others—the reason, of course, being to create the best universe, although you would never think it to look at it—if there were a reason for the laws which God gave, then God himself was subject to law, and therefore you do not get any advantage by introducing God as an intermediary. You have really a law outside and anterior to the divine edicts, and God does not serve your purpose, because he is not the ultimate lawgiver. In short, this whole argument about natural law no longer has anything like the strength that it used to have. I am traveling on in time in my review of the arguments. The arguments that are used for the existence of God change their character as time goes on. They were at first hard intellectual arguments embodying certain quite definite fallacies. As we come to modern times they become less respectable intellectually and more and more affected by a kind of moralizing vagueness.

3. The Argument from Design / The next step in this process brings us to the argument from design. You all know the argument from design: Everything in the world is made just so that we can manage to live in the world, and if the world was ever so little different, we could not manage to live in it. That is the argument from design. It sometimes takes a rather curious form; for instance, it is argued that rabbits have white tails in order to be easy to shoot. I do not know how rabbits would view that application. It is an easy argument to parody. You all know Voltaire's remark, that obviously the nose was designed to be such as to fit spectacles. That sort of parody has turned out to be not nearly so wide of the mark as it might have seemed in the eighteenth century, because since the time of Darwin we understand much better why living creatures are adapted to their environment. It is not that their environment was made to be suitable to them but that they grew to be suitable to it, and that is the basis of adaptation. There is no evidence of design about it.

When you come to look into this argument from design, it is a most astonishing thing that people can believe that this world, with all the things that are in it, with all its defects, should be the best that omnipotence and omniscience have been able to produce in millions of years. I really cannot believe it. Do you think that, if you were granted omnipotence and omniscience and millions of years in which to perfect your world, you could produce nothing better than the Ku Klux Klan or the Fascists? Moreover, if you accept the ordinary laws of science, you have to suppose that human life and life in general on this planet will die out in due course: It is a stage in the decay of the solar system; at a certain stage of decay you get the sort of conditions of temperature and so forth which are suitable to protoplasm, and there is life for a short time in the life of the whole solar system. You see in the moon the sort of thing to which the earth is tending—something dead, cold, and lifeless.

I am told that that sort of view is depressing, and people will sometimes tell you that if they believed that, they would not be able to go on living. Do not believe it; it is all nonsense. Nobody really worries much about what is going to happen millions of years hence. Even if they think they are worrying much about that, they are really deceiving themselves. They are worried about something much more mundane, or it may merely be a bad digestion; but nobody is really seriously rendered unhappy by the thought of something that is going to happen to this world millions and millions of years hence. Therefore, although it is of course a gloomy view to suppose that life will die out—at least I suppose we may say so, although sometimes when I contemplate the things that people do with their lives I think it is almost a consolation—it is not such as to render life miserable. It merely makes you turn your attention to other things.

4. The Moral Arguments for Deity / Now we reach one stage further in what I shall call the intellectual descent that the theists have made in their argumentations, and we come to what are called the moral arguments for the existence of God. You all know, of course, that there used to be in the old days three intellectual arguments for the existence of God, all of which were disposed of by Immanuel Kant* in the *Critique of Pure Reason*; but no sooner had he disposed of those arguments than he invented a new one, a moral argument, and that quite convinced him. He was like many people: In intellectual matters he was skeptical, but in moral matters he believed implicitly in the maxims that he had imbibed at his mother's knee. That illustrates what the psychoanalysts so much emphasize—the immensely stronger hold upon us that our very early associations have than those of later times.

Kant, as I say, invented a new moral argument for the existence of God, and that in varying forms was extremely popular during the nineteenth century. It has all sorts of forms. One form is to say that there would be no right or wrong unless God existed. I am not for the moment concerned with whether there is a difference between right and wrong, or whether there is not: That is another question. The point I am concerned with is that, if you are quite sure there is a difference between right and wrong, you are then in this situation: Is that difference due to God's fiat or is it not? If it is due to God's fiat, then for God himself there is no difference between right and wrong, and it is no longer a significant statement to say that God is good. If you are going to say, as theologians do, that God is good, you must then say that right and wrong have some meaning which is independent of God's fiat, because God's fiats are good and not bad independently of the mere fact that he made them. If you are going to say that, you will then have to say that it is not only through God that right and wrong came into being, but that they are in their essence logically anterior to God. You could, of course, if you liked, say that there was a superior deity who gave orders to the God who made this world, or could take up the line that some of the gnostics took up—a line which I often thought was a very plausible one—that as a matter of fact this world that we know was made by the devil at a moment when God was not looking. There is a good deal to be said for that, and I am not concerned to refute it.

5. The Argument for the Remedying of Injustice / Then there is another very curious form of moral argument, which is this: They say that the existence of God is required in order to bring justice into the world. In the part

*[An 18th century philosopher.—Eds.]

of this universe that we know there is great injustice, and often the good suffer, and often the wicked prosper, and one hardly knows which of those is the more annoying; but if you are going to have justice in the universe as a whole you have to suppose a future life to redress the balance of life here on earth. So they say that there must be a God, and there must be heaven and hell in order that in the long run there may be justice. That is a very curious argument. If you looked at the matter from a scientific point of view, you would say, "After all, I know only this world. I do not know about the rest of the universe, but so far as one can argue at all on probabilities one would say that probably this world is a fair sample, and if there is injustice here the odds are that there is injustice elsewhere also." Supposing you got a crate of oranges that you opened, and you found all the top layer of oranges bad, you would not argue, "The underneath ones must be good, so as to redress the balance." You would say, "Probably the whole lot is a bad consignment"; and that is really what a scientific person would argue about the universe. He would say, "Here we find in this world a great deal of injustice, and so far as that goes that is a reason for supposing that justice does not rule in the world; and therefore so far as it goes it affords a moral argument against deity and not in favor of one." Of course I know that the sort of intellectual arguments that I have been talking to you about are not what really moves people. What really moves people to believe in God is not any intellectual argument at all. Most people believe in God because they have been taught from early infancy to do it, and that is the main reason.

Then I think that the next most powerful reason is the wish for safety, a sort of feeling that there is a big brother who will look after you. That plays a very profound part in influencing people's desire for a belief in God.

III

The Character of Christ

I now want to say a few words upon a topic which I often think is not quite sufficiently dealt with by rationalists, and that is the question whether Christ was the best and the wisest of men. It is generally taken for granted that we should all agree that that was so. I do not myself. I think that there are a good many points upon which I agree with Christ a great deal more than the professing Christians do. I do not know that I could go with Him all the way, but I could go with Him much further than most professing Christians can. You will remember that He said, "Resist not evil: but whosoever shall smite thee on thy right cheek, turn to him the other also." That is not a new precept or a new principle. It was used by Lao-tse and Buddha some 500 or 600 years before Christ, but it is not a principle which as a matter of fact Christians accept. I have no doubt that the present Prime Minister,[1] for instance, is a most sincere Christian, but I should not advise any of you to go and smite him on one cheek. I think you might find that he thought this text was intended in a figurative sense.

Then there is another point which I consider excellent. You will remember that Christ said, "Judge not lest ye be judged." That principle I do not think you would find was popular in the law courts of Christian countries. I have known in my time quite a number of judges who were very earnest Christians, and none of them felt that they were acting contrary to Christian principles in what they did. Then Christ says, "Give to him that asketh of thee, and from him that would borrow of thee turn not thou away." That is a very good principle. . . . I cannot help observing that the last general election was fought on the question of how desirable it was to turn away from him that would borrow of thee, so that one must assume that the Liberals and Conservatives of this country are composed of people who do not agree with the teaching of Christ, because they certainly did very emphatically turn away on that occasion.

Then there is one other maxim of Christ which I think has a great deal in it, but I do not find that it is very popular among some of our Christian friends. He says, "If thou wilt be perfect, go and sell that which thou hast, and give to the poor." That is a very excellent maxim, but, as I say, it is not much practiced. All these, I think, are good maxims, although they are a little difficult to live up to. I do not profess to live up to them myself; but then, after all, it is not quite the same thing as for a Christian.

1. Defects in Christ's Teaching / Having granted the excellence of these maxims, I come to certain points in which I do not believe that one can grant either the superlative wisdom or the superlative goodness of Christ as depicted in the Gospels; and here I may say that one is not concerned with the historical question. Historically it is quite doubtful whether Christ ever existed at all, and if He did we do not know anything about Him, so that I am not concerned with the historical question, which is a very difficult one. I am concerned with Christ as He appears in the Gospels, taking the Gospel narrative as it stands, and there one does find some things that do not seem to be very wise. For one thing, He certainly thought that His second coming would occur in clouds of glory before the death of all the people who were living at that time. There are a great many texts that prove that. He says, for instance, "Ye shall not have gone over the cities of Israel till the Son of Man be come." Then He says, "There are some standing here which shall not taste death till the Son of Man comes into His kingdom''; and there are a lot of places where it is quite clear that He believed that His second coming would happen during the lifetime of many then living. That

[1]Stanley Baldwin.

was the belief of His earlier followers, and it was the basis of a good deal of His moral teaching. When He said, "Take no thought for the morrow," and things of that sort, it was very largely because He thought that the second coming was going to be very soon, and that all ordinary mundane affairs did not count. I have, as a matter of fact, known some Christians who did believe that the second coming was imminent. I knew a parson who frightened his congregation terribly by telling them that the second coming was very imminent indeed, but they were much consoled when they found that he was planting trees in his garden. The early Christians did really believe it, and they did abstain from such things as planting trees in their gardens, because they did accept from Christ the belief that the second coming was imminent. In that respect, clearly He was not so wise as some other people have been, and He was certainly not superlatively wise.

2. The Moral Problem / Then you come to moral questions. There is one very serious defect, to my mind, in Christ's moral character, and that is that He believed in hell. I do not myself feel that any person who is really profoundly humane can believe in everlasting punishment. Christ certainly as depicted in the Gospels did believe in everlasting punishment, and one does find repeatedly a vindictive fury against those people who would not listen to His preaching—an attitude which is not uncommon with preachers, but which does somewhat detract from superlative excellence. You do not, for instance, find that attitude in Socrates. You find him quite bland and urbane toward the people who would not listen to him; and it is, to my mind, far more worthy of a sage to take that line than to take the line of indignation. You probably all remember the sort of things that Socrates was saying when he was dying, and the sort of things that he generally did say to people who did not agree with him.

You will find that in the Gospels Christ said, "Ye serpents, ye generation of vipers, how can ye escape the damnation of hell?" That was said to people who did not like His preaching. It is not really to my mind quite the best tone, and there are a great many of these things about hell. There is, of course, the familiar text about the sin against the Holy Ghost: "Whosoever speaketh against the Holy Ghost it shall not be forgiven him neither in this world nor in the world to come." That text has caused an unspeakable amount of misery in the world, for all sorts of people have imagined that they have committed the sin against the Holy Ghost, and thought that it would not be forgiven them either in this world or in the world to come. I really do not think that a person with a proper degree of kindliness in his nature would have put fears and terrors of that sort into the world.

Then Christ says, "The Son of Man shall send forth His angels, and they shall gather out of His kingdom all things that offend, and them which do iniquity, and shall cast them into a furnace of fire; there shall be wailing and gnashing of teeth"; and He goes on about the wailing and gnashing of teeth. It comes in one verse after another, and it is quite manifest to the reader that there is a certain pleasure in contemplating wailing and gnashing of teeth, or else it would not occur so often. Then you all, of course, remember about the sheep and the goats; how at the second coming He is going to divide the sheep from the goats, and He is going to say to the goats, "Depart from me, ye cursed, into everlasting fire." He continues, "And these shall go away into everlasting fire." Then He says again, "If thy hand offend thee, cut it off; it is better for thee to enter into life maimed, than having two hands to go into hell, into the fire that never shall be quenched; where the worm dieth not and the fire is not quenched." He repeats that again and again also. I must say that I think all this doctrine, that hell-fire is a punishment for sin, is a doctrine of cruelty. It is a doctrine that put cruelty into the world and gave the world generations of cruel torture; and the Christ of the Gospels, if you could take Him as His chroniclers represent Him, would certainly have to be considered partly responsible for that.

There are other things of less importance. There is the instance of the Gadarene swine, where it certainly was not very kind to the pigs to put the devils into them and make them rush down the hill to the sea. You must remember that He was omnipotent, and He could have made the devils simply go away; but He chose to send them into the pigs. Then there is the curious story of the fig tree, which always rather puzzled me. You remember what happened about the fig tree. "He was hungry; and seeing a fig tree afar off having leaves, He came if haply He might find anything thereon; and when He came to it He found nothing but leaves, for the time of figs was not yet. And Jesus answered and said unto it: 'No man eat fruit of thee hereafter for ever' . . . and Peter . . . saith unto Him: 'Master, behold the fig tree which thou cursedst is withered away.'" This is a very curious story, because it was not the right time of year for figs, and you really could not blame the tree. I cannot myself feel that either in the matter of wisdom or in the matter of virtue Christ stands quite as high as some other people known to history. I think I should put Buddha and Socrates above Him in those respects.

IV

The Emotional Factor

As I said before, I do not think that the real reason why people accept religion has anything to do with argumentation. They accept religion on emotional grounds. One is often told that it is a very wrong thing to attack religion, because religion makes men virtuous. So I am told; I have not noticed it. You know, of course, the parody of that argument in Samuel Butler's book, *Erewhon Revisited*. You will remember that in *Erewhon* there is a certain Higgs who arrives in a remote country, and after spending some time he escapes from that country in a balloon. Twenty years later he comes back to that country and finds a new religion in which he is worshiped under the name of the "Sun Child," and it is said that he ascended into heaven. He finds that the Feast of the Ascension is about to be celebrated, and he hears Professors Hanky and Panky say to each other that they never set eyes on the man Higgs, and they hope they never will; but they are the high priests of the religion of the Sun Child. He is very indignant, and he comes up to them, and he says, "I am going to expose all this humbug and tell the people of Erewhon that it was only I, the man Higgs, and I went up in a balloon." He was told, "You must not do that, because all the morals of this country are bound round this myth, and if they once know that you did not ascend into heaven they will all become wicked"; and so he is persuaded of that and he goes quietly away.

That is the idea—that we should all be wicked if we did not hold to the Christian religion. It seems to me that the people who have held to it have been for the most part extremely wicked. You find this curious fact, that the more intense has been the religion of any period and the more profound has been the dogmatic belief, the greater has been the cruelty and the worse has been the state of affairs. In the so-called ages of faith, when men really did believe the Christian religion in all its completeness, there was the Inquisition, with its tortures; there were millions of unfortunate women burned as witches; and there was every kind of cruelty practiced upon all sorts of people in the name of religion.

You find as you look around the world that every single bit of progress in humane feeling, every improvement in the criminal law, every step toward the diminution of war, every step toward better treatment of the colored races, or every mitigation of slavery, every moral progress that there has been in the world, has been consistently opposed by the organized churches of the world. I say quite deliberately that the Christian religion, as organized in its churches, has been and still is the principal enemy of moral progress in the world.

How the Churches Have Retarded Progress

You may think that I am going too far when I say that that is still so. I do not think that I am. Take one fact. You will bear with me if I mention it. It is not a pleasant fact, but the churches compel one to mention facts that are not pleasant. Supposing that in this world that we live in today an inexperienced girl is married to a syphilitic man; in that case the Catholic Church says, "This is an indissoluble sacrament. You must endure celibacy or stay together. And if you stay together, you must not use birth control to prevent the birth of syphilitic children." Nobody whose natural sympathies have not been warped by dogma, or whose moral nature was not absolutely dead to all sense of suffering, could maintain that it is right and proper that that state of things should continue.

That is only an example. There are a great many ways in which, at the present moment, the church, by its insistence upon what it chooses to call morality, inflicts upon all sorts of people undeserved and unnecessary suffering. And of course, as we know, it is in its major part an opponent still of progress and of improvement in all the ways that diminish suffering in the world, because it has chosen to label as morality a certain narrow set of rules of conduct which have nothing to do with human happiness; and when you say that this or that ought to be done because it would make for human happiness, they think that has nothing to do with the matter at all. "What has human happiness to do with morals? The object of morals is not to make people happy."

Fear, the Foundation of Religion

Religion is based, I think, primarily and mainly upon fear. It is partly the terror of the unknown and partly, as I have said, the wish to feel that you have a kind of elder brother who will stand by you in all your troubles and disputes. Fear is the basis of the whole thing—fear of the mysterious, fear of defeat, fear of death. Fear is the parent of cruelty, and therefore it is no wonder if cruelty and religion have gone hand in hand. It is because fear is at the basis of those two things. In this world we can now begin a little to understand things, and a little to master them by help of science, which has forced its way step by step against the Christian religion, against the churches, and against the opposition of all the old precepts. Science can help us to get over this craven fear in which mankind has lived for so many generations. Science can teach us, and I think our own hearts can teach us, no longer to look around for imaginary supports, no longer to invent allies in the sky, but rather to look to our own efforts here below to make this world a fit place to live in, instead of the sort of place that the churches in all these centuries have made it.

What We Must Do

We want to stand upon our own feet and look fair and square at the world —its good facts, its bad facts, its beauties, and its ugliness; see the world as it is and be not afraid of it. Conquer the world by intelligence and not merely by being slavishly subdued by the terror that comes from it. The whole conception of God is a conception derived from the ancient Oriental despotisms. It is a conception quite unworthy of free men. When you hear people in church debasing themselves and saying that they are miserable sinners, and all the rest of it, it seems contemptible and not worthy of self-respecting human beings. We ought to stand up and look the world frankly in the face. We ought to make the best we can of the world, and if it is not so good as we wish, after all it will still be better than what these others have made of it in all these ages. A good world needs knowledge, kindliness, and courage; it does not need a regretful hankering after the past or a fettering of the free intelligence by the words uttered long ago by ignorant men. It needs a fearless outlook and a free intelligence. It needs hope for the future, not looking back all the time toward a past that is dead, which we trust will be far surpassed by the future that our intelligence can create.

28 / Agnosticism

T. H. HUXLEY

. . . **A**gnosticism . . . is not a creed, but a method, the essence of which lies in the rigorous application of a single principle. That principle is of great antiquity; it is as old as Socrates; as old as the writer who said, ''Try all things, hold fast by that which is good''; it is the foundation of the Reformation, which simply illustrated the axiom that every man should be able to give a reason for the faith that is in him; it is the great principle of Descartes*; it is the fundamental axiom of modern science. Positively the principle may be expressed: In matters of the intellect, follow your reason as far as it will take you, without regard to any other consideration. And negatively: In matters of the intellect do not pretend that conclusions are certain which are not demonstrated or demonstrable. That I take to be the agnostic faith, which if a man keep whole and undefiled, he shall not be ashamed to look the universe in the face, whatever the future may have in store for him. . . .

The present discussion has arisen out of the use, which has become general in the last few years, of the terms ''Agnostic'' and ''Agnosticism.''

The people who call themselves ''Agnostics'' have been charged with doing so because they have not the courage to declare themselves ''Infidels.'' It has been insinuated that they have adopted a new name in order to escape the unpleasantness which attaches to their proper denomination. To this wholly erroneous imputation, I have replied by showing that the term ''Agnostic'' did, as a matter of fact, arise in a manner which negatives it;

*[A 17th century French philosopher.—Eds.]

and my statement has not been, and cannot be, refuted. Moreover, speaking for myself, and without impugning the right of any other person to use the term in another sense, I further say that Agnosticism is not properly described as a "negative" creed, nor indeed as a creed of any kind, except in so far as it expresses absolute faith in the validity of a principle, which is as much ethical as intellectual. This principle may be stated in various ways, but they all amount to this: that it is wrong for a man to say that he is certain of the objective truth of any proposition unless he can produce evidence which logically justifies that certainty. This is what Agnosticism asserts; and, in my opinion, it is all that is essential to Agnosticism. That which Agnostics deny and repudiate, as immoral, is the contrary doctrine, that there are propositions which men ought to believe, without logically satisfactory evidence; and that reprobation ought to attach to the profession of disbelief in such inadequately supported propositions. The justification of the Agnostic principle lies in the success which follows upon its application, whether in the field of natural, or in that of civil, history; and in the fact that, so far as these topics are concerned, no sane man thinks of denying its validity. . . .

The extent of the region of the uncertain, the number of the problems the investigation of which ends in a verdict of not proven, will vary according to the knowledge and the intellectual habits of the individual Agnostic. I do not very much care to speak of anything as "unknowable." What I am sure about is that there are many topics about which I know nothing; and which, so far as I can see, are out of reach of my faculties. But whether these things are knowable by any one else is exactly one of those matters which is beyond my knowledge, though I may have a tolerably strong opinion as to the probabilities of the case. . . .

It was inevitable that a conflict should arise between Agnosticism and Theology; or rather, I ought to say between Agnosticism and Ecclesiasticism. For Theology, the science, is one thing; and Ecclesiasticism, the championship of a foregone conclusion as to the truth of a particular form of Theology, is another. With scientific Theology, Agnosticism has no quarrel. On the contrary, the Agnostic, knowing too well the influence of prejudice and idiosyncrasy, even on those who desire most earnestly to be impartial, can wish for nothing more urgently than that the scientific theologian should not only be at perfect liberty to thresh out the matter in his own fashion; but that he should, if he can, find flaws in the Agnostic position; and, even if demonstration is not to be had, that he should put, in their full force, the grounds of the conclusions he thinks probable. The scientific theologian admits the Agnostic principle, however widely his results may differ from those reached by the majority of Agnostics.

But, as between Agnosticism and Ecclesiasticism, or, as our neighbours across the Channel call it, Clericalism, there can be neither peace nor truce. The Cleric asserts that it is morally wrong not to believe certain propositions, whatever the results of a strict scientific investigation of the evidence of these propositions. He tells us "that religious error is, in itself, of an immoral nature." He declares that he has prejudged certain conclusions, and looks upon those who show cause for arrest of judgment as emissaries of Satan. It necessarily follows that, for him, the attainment of faith, not the ascertainment of truth, is the highest aim of mental life. And, on careful analysis of the nature of this faith, it will too often be found to be, not the mystic process of unity with the Divine, understood by the religious enthusiast; but that which the candid simplicity of a Sunday scholar once defined it to be. "Faith," said this unconscious plagiarist of Tertullian,* "is the power of saying you believe things which are incredible."

Now I, and many other Agnostics, believe that faith, in this sense, is an abomination; and though we do not indulge in the luxury of self-righteousness so far as to call those who are not of our way of thinking hard names, we do feel that the disagreement between ourselves and those who hold this doctrine is even more moral than intellectual. . . .

I trust that I have now made amends for any ambiguity, or want of fulness, in my previous exposition of that which I hold to be the essence of the Agnostic doctrine. Henceforward, I might hope to hear no more of the assertion that we are necessarily Materialists, Idealists, Atheists, Theists, or any other *ists*, if experience had led me to think that the proved falsity of a statement was any guarantee against its repetition. And those who appreciate the nature of our position will see, at once, that when Ecclesiasticism declares that we ought to believe this, that, and the other, and are very wicked if we don't, it is impossible for us to give any answer but this: We have not the slightest objection to believe anything you like, if you will give us good grounds for belief; but, if you cannot, we must respectfully refuse, even if that refusal should wreck morality and insure our own damnation several times over. We are quite content to leave that to the decision of the future. The course of the past has impressed us with the firm conviction that no good ever comes of falsehood, and we feel warranted in refusing even to experiment in that direction.

*[An early church father and theologian who said, "I believe *because* it is absurd."—Eds.]

29 / Memorial Service

H. L. MENCKEN

Where is the grave-yard of dead gods? What lingering mourner waters their mounds? There was a day when Jupiter was the king of the gods, and any man who doubted his puissance* was *ipso facto*† a barbarian and an ignoramus. But where in all the world is there a man who worships Jupiter to-day? And what of Huitzilopochtli? In one year—and it is no more than five hundred years ago—50,000 youths and maidens were slain in sacrifice to him. Today, if he is remembered at all, it is only by some vagrant savage in the depths of the Mexican forest. Huitzilopochtli, like many other gods, had no human father; his mother was a virtuous widow; he was born of an apparently innocent flirtation that she carried on with the sun. When he frowned, his father, the sun, stood still. When he roared with rage, earthquakes engulfed whole cities. When he thirsted he was watered with 10,000 gallons of human blood. But today [in 1921] Huitzilopochtli is as magnificently forgotten as Allen G. Thurman. Once the peer of Allah, Buddha, and Wotan, he is now the peer of General Coxey, Richmond P. Hobson, Nan Petterson, Alton B. Parker, Adelina Patti, General Weyler, and Tom Sharkey.

Speaking of Huitzilopochtli recalls his brother, Tezcatilpoca. Tezcatilpoca was almost as powerful: He consumed 25,000 virgins a year. Lead me to his tomb: I would weep, and hang a *couronne des perles*.‡ But who knows where it is? Or where the grave of Quitzalcoatl is? Or Tialoc? Or Chalchihuitlicue? Or Xiehtecutli? Or Centeotl, that sweet one? Or Tlazolteotl, the goddess of love? Or Mictlan? Or Ixtlilton? Or Omacatl? Or Yacatecutli? Or Mixcoatl? Or Xipe? Or all the host of Tzitzimitles? Where are their bones? Where is the willow on which they hung their harps? In what forlorn and unheard of hell do they await the resurrection morn? Who enjoys their residuary estates? Or that of Dis, whom Caesar found to be the chief god of the Celts? Or that of Tarves, the bull? Or that of Moccos, the pig? Or that of Epona, the mare? Or that of Mullo, the celestial jack-ass? There was a time when the Irish revered all these gods as violently as they now hate the English. But today even the drunkest Irishman laughs at them.

---

*[Power.—Eds.]
†[By that fact alone.—Eds.]
‡[Crown of pearls.—Eds.]

But they have company in oblivion: The hell of dead gods is as crowded as the Presbyterian hell for babies. Damona is there, and Esus, and Drunemeton, and Silvana, and Dervones, and Adsalluta, and Deva, and Belisama, and Axona, and Vintios, and Taranuous, and Sulis, and Cocidius, and Adsmerius, and Dumiatis, and Caletos, and Moccus, and Ollovidius, and Albiorix, and Leucitius, and Vitucadrus, and Ogmios, and Uxellimus, and Borvo, and Grannos, and Mogons. All mighty gods in their day, worshiped by millions, full of demands and impositions, able to bind and loose—all gods of the first class, not dilettanti. Men labored for generations to build vast temples to them—temples with stones as large as hay-wagons. The business of interpreting their whims occupied thousands of priests, wizards, archdeacons, evangelists, haruspices,* bishops, archbishops. To doubt them was to die, usually at the stake. Armies took to the field to defend them against infidels: Villages were burned, women and children were butchered, cattle were driven off. Yet in the end they all withered and died, and today there is none so poor to do them reverence. Worse, the very tombs in which they lie are lost, and so even a respectful stranger is debarred from paying them the slightest and politest homage.

What has become of Sutekh, once the high god of the whole Nile Valley? What has become of:

Resheph	Ahijah	Shalem
Anath	Isis	Dagon
Ashtoreth	Ptah	Sharrab
El	Anubis	Yau
Nergal	Baal	Amon-Re
Nebo	Astarte	Osiris
Ninib	Hadad	Sebek
Melek	Addu	Molech?

All these were once gods of the highest eminence. Many of them are mentioned with fear and trembling in the Old Testament. They ranked, five or six thousand years ago, with Jahveh himself; the worst of them stood far higher than Thor. Yet they have all gone down the chute, and with them the following:

Bilé	Kerridwen	Ni-zu
Lêr	Pwyll	Sahi
Arianrod	Tammuz	Aa
Morrigu	Venus	Allatu
Govannon	Bau	Jupiter
Gunfled	Mulu-hursang	Cunina
Sokk-mimi	Anu	Potina
Memetona	Beltis	Statilinus
Dagda	Nusku	Diana of Ephesus

*[A special class of priests.—Eds.]

Robigus	U-Mersi	Nin-azu
Pluto	Beltu	Lugal-Amarada
Ops	Dumu-zi-abzu	Zer-panitu
Meditrina	Kuski-banda	Merodach
Vesta	Sin	U-ki
Tilmun	Abil Addu	Dauke
Ogyrvan	Apsu	Gasan-abzu
Dea Dia	Dagan	Elum
Ceros	Elali	U-Tin-dir-ki
Vaticanus	Isum	Marduk
Edulia	Mami	Nin-lil-la
Adeona	Nin-man	Nin
Iuno Lucina	Zaraqu	Persephone
Saturn	Suqamunu	Istar
Furrina	Zagaga	Lagas
Vediovis	Gwydion	U-urugal
Consus	Manawyddan	Sirtumu
Cronos	Nuada Argetlam	Ea
Enki	Tagd	Nirig
Engurra	Goibniu	Nebo
Belus	Odin	Samas
Dimmer	Llaw Gyffes	Ma-banba-anna
Mu-ul-lil	Lleu	En-Mersi
Ubargisi	Ogma	Amurru
Ubilulu	Mider	Assur
Gasan lil	Rigantona	Aku
U-dimmer-an-kia	Marzin	Qarradu
Enurestu	Mars	Ura-gala
U-sab-sib	Kaawanu	Ueras

You may think I spoof. That I invent the names. I do not. Ask the rector to lend you any good treatise on comparative religion: You will find them all listed. They were gods of the highest standing and dignity—gods of civilized peoples—worshiped and believed in by millions. All were theoretically omnipotent, omniscient, and immortal. And all are dead.

30 / Theology and Falsification

ANTONY FLEW, R. M. HARE, BASIL MITCHELL

I. ANTONY FLEW

Let us begin with a parable. It is a parable developed from a tale told by John Wisdom in his haunting and revelatory article "Gods."[1] Once upon a time two explorers came upon a clearing in the jungle. In the clearing were growing many flowers and many weeds. One explorer says, "Some gardener must tend this plot." The other disagrees: "There is no gardener." So they pitch their tents and set a watch. No gardener is ever seen. "But perhaps he is an invisible gardener." So they set up a barbed-wire fence. They electrify it. They patrol with bloodhounds. (For they remember how H. G. Wells's *The Invisible Man* could be both smelled and touched, though he could not be seen.) But no shrieks ever suggest that some intruder has received a shock. No movements of the wire ever betray an invisible climber. The bloodhounds never give cry. Yet still the Believer is not convinced. "But there is a gardener, invisible, intangible, insensible to electric shocks, a gardener who has no scent and makes no sound, a gardener who comes secretly to look after the garden which he loves." At last the Skeptic despairs, "But what remains of your original assertion? Just how does what you call an invisible, intangible, eternally elusive gardener differ from an imaginary gardener or even from no gardener at all?"

In this parable we can see how what starts as an assertion, that something exists or that there is some analogy between certain complexes of phenomena, may be reduced step by step to an altogether different status, to an expression perhaps of a "picture preference."[2] The Skeptic says there is no gardener. The Believer says there is a gardener (but invisible, etc.). One man talks about sexual behavior. Another man prefers to talk of Aphrodite (but knows that there is not really a superhuman person additional to, and somehow responsible for, all sexual phenomena).[3] The process of qualification may be checked at any point before the original assertion is completely withdrawn and something of that first assertion will remain (tautology). Mr. Wells's invisible man could not, admittedly, be seen, but in all other respects he was a man like the rest of us. But though the process of

[1]*P.A.S.*, 1944–45, reprinted as chap. 10 of *Logic and Language*, vol. 1 (Blackwell, 1951), and in his *Philosophy and Psychoanalysis* (Blackwell, 1953).

[2]Cf. J. Wisdom, "Other Minds," *Mind*, 1940; reprinted in his *Other Minds* (Blackwell, 1952).

[3]Cf. Lucretius, *De Rerum Natura*, II, 655–60.

qualification may be, and of course usually is, checked in time, it is not always judiciously so halted. Someone may dissipate his assertion completely without noticing that he has done so. A fine, brash hypothesis may thus be killed by inches, the death by a thousand qualifications.

And in this, it seems to me, lies the peculiar danger, the endemic evil, of theological utterance. Take such utterances as "God has a plan," "God created the world," "God loves us as a father loves his children." They look at first sight very much like assertions, vast cosmological assertions. Of course, this is no sure sign that they either are or are intended to be assertions. But let us confine ourselves to the cases where those who utter such sentences intend them to express assertions (merely remarking parenthetically that those who intend or interpret such utterances as crypto-commands, expressions of wishes, disguised ejaculations, concealed ethics, or anything else but assertions are unlikely to succeed in making them either properly orthodox or practically effective).

Now to assert that such and such is the case is necessarily equivalent to denying that such and such is not the case.[4] Suppose then that we are in doubt as to what someone who gives vent to an utterance is asserting, or suppose that, more radically, we are skeptical as to whether he is really asserting anything at all, one way of trying to understand (or perhaps it will be to expose) his utterance is to attempt to find what he would regard as counting against, or as being incompatible with, its truth. For if the utterance is indeed an assertion, it will necessarily be equivalent to a denial of the negation of that assertion. And anything which would count against the assertion, or which would induce the speaker to withdraw it and to admit that it had been mistaken, must be part of (or the whole of) the meaning of the negation of that assertion. And to know the meaning of the negation of an assertion is as near as makes no matter to knowing the meaning of that assertion.[5] And if there is nothing which a putative assertion denies, then there is nothing which it asserts either: and so it is not really an assertion. When the skeptic in the parable asked the Believer, "Just how does what you call an invisible, intangible, eternally elusive gardener differ from an imaginary gardener or even from no gardener at all?" he was suggesting that the Believer's earlier statement had been so eroded by qualification that it was no longer an assertion at all.

Now it often seems to people who are not religious as if there was no conceivable event or series of events the occurrence of which would be admitted by sophisticated religious people to be a sufficient reason for conceding, "There wasn't a God after all" or "God does not really love us then." Someone tells us that God loves us as a father loves his children. We are re-

---

[4]For those who prefer symbolism: $p \equiv \sim \sim p$. [Any proposition, p, is equivalent to not-not-p. —Eds.]

[5]For by simply negating $\sim p$ we get p: $\sim \sim p \equiv p$. [Not-not-p is equivalent to p.—Eds.]

assured. But then we see a child dying of inoperable cancer of the throat. His earthly father is driven frantic in his efforts to help, but his Heavenly Father reveals no obvious sign of concern. Some qualification is made— God's love is "not a merely human love" or it is "an inscrutable love," perhaps—and we realize that such sufferings are quite compatible with the truth of the assertion that "God loves us as a father (but, of course, . . .)." We are reassured again. But then perhaps we ask: What is this assurance of God's (appropriately qualified) love worth, what is this apparent guarantee really a guarantee against? Just what would have to happen not merely (morally and wrongly) to tempt but also (logically and rightly) to entitle us to say, "God does not love us" or even "God does not exist"? I therefore put to the succeeding symposiasts the simple central questions, "What would have to occur or to have occurred to constitute for you a disproof of the love of, or of the existence of, God?"

II. R. M. HARE

I wish to make it clear that I shall not try to defend Christianity in particular, but religion in general—not because I do not believe in Christianity, but because you cannot understand what Christianity is until you have understood what religion is.

I must begin by confessing that, on the ground marked out by Flew, he seems to me to be completely victorious. I therefore shift my ground by relating another parable. A certain lunatic is convinced that all dons* want to murder him. His friends introduce him to all the mildest and most respectable dons that they can find, and after each of them has retired, they say, "You see, he doesn't really want to murder you; he spoke to you in a most cordial manner; surely you are convinced now?" But the lunatic replies, "Yes, but that was only his diabolical cunning; he's really plotting against me the whole time, like the rest of them; I know it, I tell you." However many kindly dons are produced, the reaction is still the same.

Now we say that such a person is deluded. But what is he deluded about? About the truth or falsity of an assertion? Let us apply Flew's test to him. There is no behavior of dons that can be enacted which he will accept as counting against his theory; and therefore his theory, on this test, asserts nothing. But it does not follow that there is no difference between what he thinks about dons and what most of us think about them—otherwise we should not call him a lunatic and ourselves sane, and dons would have no reason to feel uneasy about his presence in Oxford.

Let us call that in which we differ from this lunatic our respective *bliks*. He has an insane *blik* about dons; we have a sane one. It is important to realize that we have a sane one, not no *blik* at all; for there must be two sides

*[Tutors or fellows of a college of Oxford or Cambridge Universities.—Eds.]

to any argument—if he has a wrong *blik*, then those who are right about dons must have a right one. Flew has shown that a *blik* does not consist in an assertion or system of them; but nevertheless it is very important to have the right *blik*.

Let us try to imagine what it would be like to have different *bliks* about other things than dons. When I am driving my car, it sometimes occurs to me to wonder whether my movements of the steering-wheel will always continue to be followed by corresponding alterations in the direction of the car. I have never had a steering failure, though I have had skids, which must be similar. Moreover, I know enough about how the steering of my car is made, to know the sort of thing that would have to go wrong for the steering to fail—steel joints would have to part, or steel rods break, or something—but how do I know that this won't happen? The truth is, I don't know; I just have a *blik* about steel and its properties, so that normally I trust the steering of my car; but I find it not at all difficult to imagine what it would be like to lose this *blik* and acquire the opposite one. People would say I was silly about steel; but there would be no mistaking the reality of the difference between our respective *bliks*—for example, I should never go in a motor car. Yet I should hesitate to say that the difference between us was the difference between contradictory assertions. No amount of safe arrivals or bench-tests will remove my *blik* and restore the normal one; for my *blik* is compatible with any finite number of such tests.

It was Hume who taught us that our whole commerce with the world depends upon our *blik* about the world; and that differences between *bliks* about the world cannot be settled by observation of what happens in the world. That was why, having performed the interesting experiment of doubting the ordinary man's *blik* about the world, and showing that no proof could be given to make us adopt one *blik* rather than another, he turned to backgammon to take his mind off the problem. It seems, indeed, to be impossible even to formulate as an assertion the normal *blik* about the world which makes me put my confidence in the future reliability of steel joints, in the continued ability of the road to support my car, and not gape beneath it revealing nothing below; in the general nonhomicidal tendencies of dons; in my own continued well-being (in some sense of that word that I may not now fully understand) if I continue to do what is right according to my lights; in the general likelihood of people like Hitler coming to a bad end. But perhaps a formulation less inadequate than most is to be found in the Psalms: "The earth is weak and all the inhabiters thereof: I bear up the pillars of it."

The mistake of the position which Flew selects for attack is to regard this kind of talk as some sort of *explanation*, as scientists are accustomed to use the word. As such, it would obviously be ludicrous. We no longer believe in God as an Atlas—*nous n'avons pas besoin de cette hypothèse*.* But it is never-

*[We have no need for that hypothesis.—Eds.]

theless true to say that, as Hume saw, without a *blik* there can be no explanation; for it is by our *bliks* that we decide what is and what is not an explanation. Suppose we believed that everything that happened, happened by pure chance. This would not of course be an assertion; for it is compatible with anything happening or not happening, and so, incidentally, is its contradictory. But if we had this belief we should not be able to explain or predict or plan anything. Thus, although we should not be *asserting* anything different from those of a more normal belief, there would be a great difference between us; and this is the sort of difference that there is between those who really believe in God and those who really disbelieve in him.

The word "really" is important, and may excite suspicion. I put it in, because when people have had a good Christian upbringing, as have most of those who now profess not to believe in any sort of religion, it is very hard to discover what they really believe. The reason why they find it so easy to think that they are not religious, is that they have never got into the frame of mind of one who suffers from the doubts to which religion is the answer. Not for them the terrors of the primitive jungle. Having abandoned some of the more picturesque fringes of religion, they think that they have abandoned the whole thing—whereas in fact they still have got, and could not live without, a religion of a comfortably substantial, albeit highly sophisticated, kind, which differs from that of many "religious people" in little more than this, that "religious people" like to sing Psalms about theirs—a very natural and proper thing to do. But nevertheless there may be a big difference lying behind—the difference between two people who, though side by side, are walking in different directions. I do not know in what direction Flew is walking; perhaps he does not know either. But we have had some examples recently of various ways in which one can walk away from Christianity, and there are any number of possibilities. After all, man has not changed biologically since primitive times; it is his religion that has changed, and it can easily change again. And if you do not think that such changes make a difference, get acquainted with some Sikhs and some Mussulmans of the same Punjabi stock; you will find them quite different sorts of people.

There is an important difference between Flew's parable and my own which we have not yet noticed. The explorers do not *mind* about their garden; they discuss it with interest, but not with concern. But my lunatic, poor fellow, minds about dons; and I mind about the steering of my car; it often has people in it that I care for. It is because I mind very much about what goes on in the garden in which I find myself that I am unable to share the explorers' detachment.

III. BASIL MITCHELL

Flew's article is searching and perceptive, but there is, I think, something odd about his conduct of the theologian's case. The theologian surely would not deny that the fact of pain counts against the assertion that God loves men. This very incompatibility generates the most intractable of theological problems—the problem of evil. So the theologian does recognize the fact of pain as counting against Christian doctrine. But it is true that he will not allow it—or anything—to count decisively against it; for he is committed by his faith to trust in God. His attitude is not that of the detached observer, but of the believer.

Perhaps this can be brought out by yet another parable. In time of war in an occupied country, a member of the resistance meets one night a stranger who deeply impresses him. They spend that night together in conversation. The Stranger tells the Partisan that he himself is on the side of the resistance—indeed that he is in command of it, and urges the Partisan to have faith in him no matter what happens. The Partisan is utterly convinced at that meeting of the Stranger's sincerity and constancy and undertakes to trust him.

They never meet in conditions of intimacy again. But sometimes the Stranger is seen helping members of the resistance, and the Partisan is grateful and says to his friends, "He is on our side."

Sometimes he is seen in the uniform of the police handing over patriots to the occupying power. On these occasions his friends murmur against him, but the Partisan still says, "He is on our side." He still believes that, in spite of appearances, the Stranger did not deceive him. Sometimes he asks the Stranger for help and receives it. He is then thankful. Sometimes he asks and does not receive it. Then he says, "The Stranger knows best." Sometimes his friends, in exasperation, say, "Well, what *would* he have to do for you to admit that you were wrong and that he is not on our side?" But the Partisan refuses to answer. He will not consent to put the Stranger to the test. And sometimes his friends complain, "Well, if *that's* what you mean by his being on our side, the sooner he goes over to the other side the better."

The Partisan of the parable does not allow anything to count decisively against the proposition "The Stranger is on our side." This is because he has committed himself to trust the Stranger. But he of course recognizes that the Stranger's ambiguous behavior *does* count against what he believes about him. It is precisely this situation which constitutes the trial of his faith.

When the Partisan asks for help and doesn't get it, what can he do? He can (a) conclude that the Stranger is not on our side or (b) maintain that he is on our side but that he has reasons for withholding help.

The first he will refuse to do. How long can he uphold the second position without its becoming just silly?

I don't think one can say in advance. It will depend on the nature of the impression created by the Stranger in the first place. It will depend, too, on the manner in which he takes the Stranger's behavior. If he blandly dismisses it as of no consequence, as having no bearing upon his belief, it will be assumed that he is thoughtless or insane. And it quite obviously won't do for him to say easily, "Oh, when used of the Stranger the phrase 'is on our side' *means* ambiguous behavior of this sort." In that case he would be like the religious man who says blandly of a terrible disaster, "It is God's will." No, he will only be regarded as sane and reasonable in his belief if he experiences in himself the full force of the conflict.

It is here that my parable differs from Hare's. The partisan admits that many things may and do count against his belief: whereas Hare's lunatic who has a *blik* about dons doesn't admit that anything counts against his *blik*. Nothing *can* count against *bliks*. Also the Partisan has a reason for having in the first instance committed himself, viz. the character of the Stranger; whereas the lunatic has no reason for his *blik* about dons—because, of course, you can't have reasons for *bliks*.

This means that I agree with Flew that theological utterances must be assertions. The Partisan is making an assertion when he says, "The Stranger is on our side."

Do I want to say that the Partisan's belief about the Stranger is, in any sense, an explanation? I think I do. It explains and makes sense of the Stranger's behavior; it helps to explain also the resistance movement in the context of which he appears. In each case it differs from the interpretation which the others put upon the same facts.

"God loves men" resembles "the Stranger is on our side" (and many other significant statements, e.g. historical ones) in not being conclusively falsifiable. They can both be treated in at least three different ways: (1) as provisional hypotheses to be discarded if experience tells against them; (2) as significant articles of faith; (3) as vacuous formulae (expressing, perhaps, a desire for reassurance) to which experience makes no difference and which make no difference to life.

The Christian, once he has committed himself, is precluded by his faith from taking up the first attitude: "Thou shalt not tempt the Lord thy God." He is in constant danger, as Flew has observed, of slipping into the third. But he need not; and, if he does, it is a failure in faith as well as in logic.

IV. ANTONY FLEW

It has been a good discussion, and I am glad to have helped to provoke it. But now . . . it must come to an end: and the Editors of *University* have asked me to make some concluding remarks. Since it is impossible to deal with all the issues raised or to comment separately upon each contribution, I will concentrate on Mitchell and Hare, as representative of two very different kinds of response to the challenge made in "Theology and Falsification."

The challenge, it will be remembered, ran like this. Some theological utterances seem to, and are intended to, provide explanations or express assertions. Now an assertion, to be an assertion at all, must claim that things stand thus and thus; *and not otherwise.* Similarly an explanation, to be an explanation at all, must explain why this particular thing occurs; *and not something else.* Those last clauses are crucial. And yet sophisticated religious people—or so it seemed to me—are apt to overlook this, and tend to refuse to allow, not merely that anything actually does occur, but that anything conceivably could occur, which would count against their theological assertions and explanations. But in so far as they do this their supposed explanations are actually bogus, and their seeming assertions are really vacuous.

Mitchell's response to this challenge is admirably direct, straightforward, and understanding. He agrees "that theological utterances must be assertions." He agrees that if they are to be assertions, there must be something that would count against their truth. He agrees, too, that believers are in constant danger of transforming their would-be assertions into "vacuous formulae." But he takes me to task for an oddity in my "conduct of the theologian's case. The theologian surely would not deny that the fact of pain counts against the assertion that God loves men. This very incompatibility generates the most intractable of theological problems, the problem of evil." I think he is right. I should have made a distinction between two very different ways of dealing with what looks like evidence against the love of God: The way I stressed was the expedient of qualifying the original assertion; the way the theologian usually takes, at first, is to admit that it looks bad but to insist that there is—there must be—some explanation which will show that, in spite of appearances, there really is a God who loves us. His difficulty, it seems to me, is that he has given God attributes which rule out all possible saving explanations. In Mitchell's parable of the Stranger it is easy for the believer to find plausible excuses for ambiguous behavior, for the Stranger is a man. But suppose the Stranger is God. We cannot say that he would like to help but cannot: God is omnipotent. We cannot say that he would help if he only knew: God is omniscient. We cannot say that he is not responsible for the wickedness of others: God creates those others. Indeed an omnipotent, omniscient God must be an accessory before (and during) the fact to every human misdeed, as well as being responsible for every nonmoral defect in the universe. So, though I entirely concede that Mitchell was absolutely right to insist against me that the theologian's first move is to look for an *explanation*, I still think that in the end, if relentlessly pursued, he will have to resort to the avoiding action of *qualification*. And there lies the danger of that death by a thousand qualifications, which would, I agree, constitute "a failure in faith as well as in logic."

Hare's approach is fresh and bold. He confesses that "on the ground marked out by Flew, he seems to me to be completely victorious." He therefore introduces the concept of *blik*. But while I think that there is room for some such concept in philosophy, and that philosophers should be grateful to Hare for his invention, I nevertheless want to insist that any attempt to analyze Christian religious utterances as expressions or affirmations of a *blik* rather than as (at least would-be) assertions about the cosmos is fundamentally misguided. *First*, because thus interpreted they would be entirely unorthodox. If Hare's religion really is a *blik*, involving no cosmological assertions about the nature and activities of a supposed personal creator, then surely he is not a Christian at all? *Second*, because thus interpreted, they could scarcely do the job they do. If they were not even intended as assertions then many religious activities would become fraudulent, or merely silly. If "You ought *because* it is God's will" asserts no more than "You ought," then the person who prefers the former phraseology is not really giving a reason, but a fraudulent substitute for one, a dialectical bad check. If "My soul must be immortal *because* God loves his children, etc." asserts no more than "My soul must be immortal," then the man who reassures himself with theological arguments for immortality is being as silly as the man who tries to clear his overdraft by writing his bank a check on the same account. (Of course, neither of these utterances would be distinctively Christian: but this discussion never pretended to be so confined.) Religious utterances may indeed express false or even bogus assertions: but I simply do not believe that they are not both intended and interpreted to be or at any rate to presuppose assertions, at least in the context of religious practice, whatever shifts may be demanded, in another context, by the exigencies of theological apologetic.

One final suggestion. The philosophers of religion might well draw upon George Orwell's last appalling nightmare *1984* for the concept of *doublethink*. "*Doublethink* means the power of holding two contradictory beliefs simultaneously, and accepting both of them. The party intellectual knows that he is playing tricks with reality, but by the exercise of *doublethink* he also satisfies himself that reality is not violated" (*1984*, p. 220). Perhaps religious intellectuals too are sometimes driven to doublethink in order to retain their faith in a loving God in face of the reality of a heartless and indifferent world. But of this more another time, perhaps.

STUDY QUESTIONS

1. Hartt begins with a discussion of how metaphysical theories are proved and criticized. How is this relevant to the question of the existence of God?

2. Critically evaluate Hartt's discussion of (a) the a posteriori arguments, (b) the a priori argument and (c) the appeal to religious experience.

3. According to Nagel, atheistic philosophies fall into two groups. Distinguish between those groups.

4. State Nagel's criticisms of the traditional arguments for the existence of God. Critically evaluate those criticisms.

5. Nagel maintains (in the latter part of his essay) that there are incoherencies in the very thesis of theism. What are they (or what is one)?

6. Nagel maintains that atheism is not merely a negative viewpoint. Do you think he has supported that claim? Why or why not?

7. Russell attempts to show that (some of) the main arguments in behalf of the existence of God are invalid. State his criticisms. Do you agree with him? Why or why not?

8. State Russell's criticisms of the character of Christ. Do these seem valid to you? Why or why not?

9. What is the basis of religious belief, according to Russell? Do you agree? Why or why not?

10. Why does Huxley think that agnosticism is preferable to atheism (as well as to theism)? Do you agree? Why or why not?

11. What is the main point which Mencken is trying to make in ''Memorial Service''?

12. What is the main issue discussed by Flew? What does he maintain with regard to it and why? Has he, in your view, made the best case for his position? How do Hare and Mitchell respond?

13. Which of the essays in this part has, in your view, presented the best case either for or against the thesis that God exists? Give reasons for your view.

14. Is there any possible situation in which science should allow supernatural causes for an event or series of events? If so, describe the situation and justify your view. If not, explain why not.

15. Do you think that there is any historical evidence which justifies, at least to some degree, the claim that God has revealed himself to humans? Justify your answer.

16. Evaluate the following argument: ''If God did not exist, then there would be no objective moral law, for moral laws must be decreed by some being, a being who is supremely good.''

17. In section I of the Introduction to this book, it was maintained that one of the tasks or aims of philosophy is the bringing to light of our hidden assumptions. Which, if any, of the essays in this part rely on assumptions, and what are those assumptions?

Further Readings

Angeles, Peter, ed. *Critiques of God*. Buffalo, N.Y.: Prometheus Books, 1976. [An excellent collection of essays representing atheistic and skeptical viewpoints on various facets of the problem of God's existence.]

Flew, Antony, and Alastair MacIntyre. *New Essays in Philosophical Theology*. New York: Macmillan, 1955. [Contains interesting articles, both pro and con, representing a contemporary approach to the problem and focusing on the issue of the significance of discourse about God.]

Hick, John, ed. *The Existence of God*. New York: Macmillan, 1964. [A collection of both classical and contemporary selections which present the main philosophical arguments for the existence of God.]

Hume, David. *Dialogues Concerning Natural Religion*. New York: Haffner, 1961. [A detailed criticism of some of the traditional arguments for the existence of God, including a lengthy discussion of the problem of evil.]

Matson, Wallace I. *The Existence of God*. Ithaca, N.Y.: Cornell University Press, 1965. [A thorough examination and criticism of all of the classical arguments for God's existence.]

Mitchell, Basil, ed. *Philosophy of Religion*. Oxford: Oxford University Press, 1971. [A collection of recent important essays on issues of faith in God, language about God, and related topics.]

Nielsen, Kai. "In Defense of Atheism." In *Perspectives in Education, Religion and the Arts*. Albany, N.Y.: State University of New York Press, 1970. [See next entry.]

_____. "Religion and Commitment." In R. H. Ayers and W. T. Blackstone, eds., *Religious Language and Knowledge*. (Athens: University of Georgia Press, 1972). [Vigorous and stimulating criticisms of religious belief, focusing on the issue of whether religious discourse is significant.]

Russell, Bertrand, and F. C. Coppleston. "The Existence of God—A Debate." *Humanitas* (Manchester, England). [A lively debate between a Roman Catholic believer and a skeptic.]

Scriven, Michael. *Primary Philosophy*. New York: McGraw-Hill, 1966. Chap. 4, pp. 87–167. [Contains a detailed and vigorous criticism of virtually every area of argument in behalf of the existence of God.]

Wisdom, John. "Gods." In John Wisdom, ed., *Philosophy and Psychoanalysis*. Oxford: R. Blackwell, 1957, pp. 144–181. [A subtle but provocative contemporary approach to the problem.]

PART SEVEN

GOD, FAITH, AND EVIL

PREVIEW

One of the greatest difficulties which confronts the believer in a (traditional) god is the problem of evil. The problem was succinctly stated in ancient times by Epicurus (371–342 B.C.). With regard to God: "Is he willing to prevent evil, but not able? then is he impotent [rather than all-powerful]. Is he able, but not willing? then is he malevolent [rather than supremely benevolent]. Is he both able and willing? whence then is evil?"[1] It would seem, then, that the existence of a traditional god is not consistent with the fact of evil in the world.

More recently, J. L. Mackie has formulated the problem very clearly.[2] Consider these three propositions:

A. God is omnipotent (all-powerful).
B. God is wholly good (supremely benevolent).
C. Evil exists.

There seems to be a contradiction[3] in holding all three of these propositions. Thus at most any two of them could be true, but not all three. So one must be false. Why is there a contradiction or tension in holding all three? If (A) were true, God could have created a world with no evil. If (B) were true, God would have wished a world with no evil. Hence one of the three propositions is false. But (C) is clearly true. There is much evil in the world, in-

---

[1]This formulation of the problem actually stems from the eighteenth-century philosopher David Hume. See his "Dialogues Concerning Natural Religion," in C. W. Hendel, Jr., ed., *Hume: Selections* (New York: Scribner's, 1937), p. 365.

[2]*Mind*, vol. LXIV, no. 254, 1955.

[3]In its most direct form, two propositions are the logical contradictories of each other if they have this feature: they cannot both be true, *and* they cannot both be false. Hence if one is true, the second must be false; and if the second is true, the first must be false. Thus any propositions of these forms are the contradictories of each other.

cluding pointless and unnecessary evil. Therefore must not either (A) or (B) be false? If you answer no, then another question arises. How can the existence of evil be reconciled (be consistent with) the existence of an omnipotent and wholly good God?

Hence, if one recognizes the reality of evil, then it appears that God cannot be both all-powerful and supremely good. If so, then the only alternatives are the following:

1. God exists, a god who is fully able to prevent evil but does not wish to do so. Hence, being somewhat sadistic, God is not supremely benevolent.

2. God exists, a god who wishes to prevent evil from occurring, but does not have the ability to do so. Hence, God is not all-powerful but is at best a finite, limited being. Or

3. No god exists at all.

However, there are some thinkers—including those within the Christian tradition—who refuse to accept the fact that (1), (2), and (3) are the only alternatives. According to them, the fact of evil can be reconciled with the existence of a traditional god. Thus, they maintain that (4) God exists, a god who is both all-powerful and supremely benevolent but allows evil to exist for some purpose. (Just what that purpose is varies from one thinker to another.) The first two selections in this part of the book present opposing views with regard to the question of whether or not the existence of God is compatible with the fact of evil.

It should be pointed out (as the writers make clear) that in considering this problem it is necessary to distinguish between two conceptions of evil: natural evil, such as suffering and death which are brought about by natural phenomena like earthquakes, tornadoes, floods, and certain diseases; and moral evil, such as pain and suffering which are brought about by the

---

All Xs are Ys.
Some Xs are not Ys.

No Xs are Ys.
Some Xs are Ys.

This is an X.
This is not an X.

In all cases the two propositions cannot be simultaneously true. So if one is true, the other must be false; and v.v. If three propositions are involved, as in the assertions (A), (B) and (C), above, then if they are such that affirming all three is a contradiction, then at least one of them must be false. At most any two could be true.

A contradiction, or more accurately, self-contradiction, then, consists of the simultaneous affirmation of two or more propositions which cannot be jointly true (or jointly false). It is logically impossible for them to be jointly true (or false).

actions (or inaction) of people. Some writers maintain that only the fact of natural evil is inconsistent with the existence of a (traditional) god. Others maintain that both natural and moral evil are inconsistent with the existence of such a god. That is, they maintain that God is responsible not only for natural evil but for moral evil as well. The reasons for that view will be considered in the selections which follow.

In the Preview to Part Six we listed five questions or problems which have to do with the problem of God. The selections in Part Six dealt with the first two questions. With the problem of evil, we come to the third. We need not say any more about this question here.

We turn now to a brief discussion of question (4). There are many believers in the existence of a god who admit that, in the customary sense of "good reasons," there are no good reasons for belief in the existence of a god; that is, there is no genuine empirical evidence (evidence which is intersubjectively testable, repeatable), and there are no logically valid arguments. Some even admit that the problem of evil is a genuine one and poses a hardship for religious belief. Nevertheless, they maintain that, for various reasons, one still has a right to have faith in the existence of God, and even faith in the existence of a traditional god. Is this a tenable view? Can it be supported in any way?

Main Questions

In summary, the main questions of this part are:

1. Can the fact of evil in the world be reconciled with the existence of an all-powerful and supremely benevolent god?
2. Is faith in God (without evidence and without reasons) justifiable?

Answers

Again, there are no common labels for these answers. We will again simply call them the affirmative and negative answers.

1a. Affirmative answer: Yes. Evil can be reconciled with the existence of an omnipotent and supremely good god.

1b. Negative answer: No. The fact of evil is incompatible with the existence of a supremely good and all-powerful god.

2a. Affirmative answer: Yes. Faith, even if unreasonable, is justifiable or necessary.

2b. Negative answer: No. Faith in God without good reasons is unjustifiable and deplorable.

Selections

In this part, the answers to these questions are represented as follows:

Question	Answer	Selection
(1)	(1b) Negative	31
(1)	(1a) Affirmative	32
(2)	(2a) Affirmative	33
(2)	(2b) Negative	34

Note

The opening selection (31) by H. J. McCloskey is rather long. For those who would prefer to assign or read it in an abridged version, we suggest the following deletions:

Section I, p. 295, lines 6–23; p. 297, line 19 – p. 298, line 6; p. 298, line 32 – p. 299, line 14.

Section II, p. 302, last 7 lines; p. 304, line 17 – p. 307, line 41.

Section III, p. 309, line 29 – p. 310, line 4; p. 311, lines 9–16; p. 313, lines 8–37.

31 / God and Evil

H. J. McCLOSKEY

I. THE PROBLEM STATED

Evil is a problem for the theist in that a contradiction is involved in the fact of evil on the one hand, and the belief in the omnipotence and perfection of God on the other. God cannot be both all-powerful and perfectly good if evil is real. This contradiction is well set out in its detail by Mackie in his discussion of the problem.[1] In his discussion Mackie seeks to show that this contradiction cannot be resolved in terms of man's free will. In arguing in this way Mackie neglects a large number of important points, and concedes far too much to the theist. He implicitly allows that while physical evil creates a problem, this problem is reducible to the problem of moral evil, and that therefore the satisfactoriness of solutions of the problem of evil turns on the compatibility of free will and absolute goodness. In fact physical evils create a number of distinct problems which are not reducible to the problem of moral evil. Further, the proposed solution of the problem of moral evil in terms of free will renders the attempt to account for physical evil in terms of moral good, and the attempt thereby to reduce the problem of evil to the problem of moral evil, completely untenable. Moreover, the account of moral evil in terms of free will breaks down on more obvious and less disputable grounds than those indicated by Mackie. Moral evil can be shown to remain a problem whether or not free will is compatible with absolute goodness. I therefore propose in this paper to reopen the discussion of "the problem of evil" by approaching it from a more general standpoint, examining a wider variety of solutions than those considered by Mackie and his critics.

The fact of evil creates a problem for the theist; but there are a number of simple solutions available to a theist who is content seriously to modify his

[1]"Evil and Omnipotence," *Mind*, 1955. [In the opening paragraphs of his essay Mackie writes, "The problem of evil, in the sense in which I shall be using the phrase, is a problem only for someone who believes that there is a God who is both omnipotent and wholly good. . . . In its simplest form the problem is this: (A) God is omnipotent; (B) God is wholly good; and yet (C) evil exists. There seems to be some contradiction between these three propositions, so that if any two of them were true, the third would be false. But at the same time all three are essential parts of most theological positions: The theologian, it seems, at once *must* adhere and cannot consistently adhere to all three." For the definition of 'contradiction,' see Note 3 to the preview to this Part.—Eds.]

theism. He can either admit a limit to God's power, or he can deny God's moral perfection. He can assert either (1) that God is not powerful enough to make a world that does not contain evil, or (2) that God created only the good in the universe and that some other power created the evil, or (3) that God is all-powerful but morally imperfect, and chose to create an imperfect universe. Few Christians accept these solutions, and this is no doubt partly because such "solutions" ignore the real inspiration of religious beliefs, and partly because they introduce embarrassing complications for the theist in his attempts to deal with other serious problems. However, if any one of these "solutions" is accepted, then the problem of evil is avoided, and a weakened version of theism is made secure from attacks based upon the fact of the occurrence of evil.

For more orthodox theism, according to which God is both omnipotent and perfectly good, evil creates a real problem; and this problem is well stated by the Jesuit Father G. H. Joyce. Joyce writes:

> The existence of evil in the world must at all times be the greatest of all problems which the mind encounters when it reflects on God and His relation to the world. If He is, indeed, all-good and all-powerful, how has evil any place in the world which He has made? Whence came it? Why is it here? If He is all-good why did He allow it to arise? If all-powerful why does He not deliver us from the burden? Alike in the physical and moral order creation seems so grievously marred that we find it hard to understand how it can derive in its entirety from God.[2]

The facts which give rise to the problem are of two general kinds, and give rise to two distinct types of problem. These two general kinds of evil are usually referred to as "physical" and as "moral" evil. These terms are by no means apt—suffering for instance is not strictly physical evil—and they conceal significant differences. However, this terminology is too widely accepted and too convenient to be dispensed with here, the more especially as the various kinds of evil, while important as distinct kinds, need not for our purposes be designated by separate names.

Physical evil and moral evil then are the two general forms of evil which independently and jointly constitute conclusive grounds for denying the existence of God in the sense defined, namely as an all-powerful, perfect Being. The acuteness of these two general problems is evident when we consider the nature and extent of the evils of which account must be given. To take physical evils, looking first at the less important of these.

(a) Physical Evils / Physical evils are involved in the very constitution of the earth and animal kingdom. There are deserts and icebound areas; there are dangerous animals of prey, as well as creatures such as scorpions and snakes. There are also pests such as flies and fleas and the hosts of other

---

[2]Joyce: *Principles of Natural Theology*, chap. 17. All subsequent quotations from Joyce in this paper are from this chapter of this work.

insect pests, as well as the multitude of lower parasites such as tapeworms, hookworms, and the like. Secondly, there are the various natural calamities and the immense human suffering that follows in their wake—fires, floods, tempests, tidal-waves, volcanoes, earthquakes, droughts, and famines. Thirdly, there are the vast numbers of diseases that torment and ravage man. Diseases such as leprosy, cancer, poliomyelitis, appear *prima facie** not to be creations which are to be expected of a benevolent Creator. Fourthly, there are the evils with which so many are born—the various physical deformities and defects such as misshapen limbs, blindness, deafness, dumbness, mental deficiency, and insanity. Most of these evils contribute toward increasing human pain and suffering; but not all physical evils are reducible simply to pain. Many of these evils are evils whether or not they result in pain. This is important, for it means that, unless there is one solution to such diverse evils, it is both inaccurate and positively misleading to speak of the problem of physical evil. Shortly I shall be arguing that no one "solution" covers all these evils, so we shall have to conclude that physical evils create not one problem but a number of distinct problems for the theist.

The nature of the various difficulties referred to by the theist as the problem of physical evil is indicated by Joyce in a way not untypical among the more honest, philosophical theists, as follows:

> The actual amount of suffering which the human race endures is immense. Disease has store and to spare of torments for the body: and disease and death are the lot to which we must all look forward. At all times, too, great numbers of the race are pinched by want. Nor is the world ever free for very long from the terrible sufferings which follow in the track of war. If we concentrate our attention on human woes, to the exclusion of the joys of life, we gain an appalling picture of the ills to which the flesh is heir. So too if we fasten our attention on the sterner side of nature, on the pains which men endure from natural forces—on the storms which wreck their ships, the cold which freezes them to death, the fire which consumes them—if we contemplate this aspect of nature alone we may be led to wonder how God came to deal so harshly with His Creatures as to provide them with such a home.

Many such statements of the problem proceed by suggesting, if not by stating, that the problem arises at least in part by concentrating one's attention too exclusively on one aspect of the world. This is quite contrary to the facts. The problem is not one that results from looking at only one aspect of the universe. It may be the case that over-all pleasure predominates over pain, and that physical goods in general predominate over physical evils, but the opposite may equally well be the case. It is both practically impossible and logically impossible for this question to be resolved. However, it is not an unreasonable presumption, with the large bulk of mankind inade-

*[On first appearance.—Eds.]

quately fed and housed and without adequate medical and health services, to suppose that physical evils at present predominate over physical goods. In the light of the facts at our disposal, this would seem to be a much more reasonable conclusion than the conclusion hinted at by Joyce and openly advanced by less cautious theists, namely that physical goods in fact outweigh physical evils in the world.

However, the question is not, Which predominates, physical good or physical evil? The problem of physical evil remains a problem whether the balance in the universe is on the side of physical good or not, because the problem is that of accounting for the fact that physical evil occurs at all.

(b) Moral Evil / Physical evils create one of the groups of problems referred to by the theist as "the problem of evil." Moral evil creates quite a distinct problem. Moral evil is simply immorality—evils such as selfishness, envy, greed, deceit, cruelty, callousness, cowardice, and the larger scale evils such as wars and the atrocities they involve.

Moral evil is commonly regarded as constituting an even more serious problem than physical evil. Joyce so regards it, observing:

> The man who sins thereby offends God. . . . We are called on to explain how God came to create an order of things in which rebellion and even final rejection have such a place. Since a choice from among an infinite number of possible worlds lay open to God, how came He to choose one in which these occur? Is not such a choice in flagrant opposition to the Divine Goodness?

Some theists seek a solution by denying the reality of evil or by describing it as a "privation" or absence of good. They hope thereby to explain it away as not needing a solution. This, in the case of most of the evils which require explanation, seems to amount to little more than an attempt to sidestep the problem simply by changing the name of that which has to be explained. It can be exposed for what it is simply by describing some of the evils which have to be explained. That is why a survey of the data to be accounted for is a most important part of the discussion of the problem of evil.

In *The Brothers Karamazov*, Dostoyevski introduces a discussion of the problem of evil by reference to some then recently committed atrocities. Ivan states the problem:

> "By the way, a Bulgarian I met lately in Moscow," Ivan went on . . . "told me about the crimes committed by Turks in all parts of Bulgaria through fear of a general rising of the Slavs. They burn villages, murder, outrage women and children, and nail their prisoners by the ears to the fences, leave them till morning, and in the morning hang them—all sorts of things you can't imagine. People talk sometimes of bestial cruelty, but that's a great injustice and insult to the beasts; a beast can never be so cruel as a man, so artistically cruel. The tiger only tears and gnaws and that's all he can do. He would never think of nailing people by the ears, even if he were able to do it. These Turks took a pleasure in torturing children too; cut-

ting the unborn child from the mother's womb, and tossing babies up in the air and catching them on the points of their bayonets before their mothers' eyes. Doing it before the mother's eyes was what gave zest to the amusement. Here is another scene that I thought very interesting. Imagine a trembling mother with her baby in her arms, a circle of invading Turks around her. They've planned a diversion: They pet the baby to make it laugh. They succeed; the baby laughs. At that moment, a Turk points a pistol four inches from the baby's face. The baby laughs with glee, holds out its little hands to the pistol, and he pulls the trigger in the baby's face and blows out its brains. Artistic, wasn't it?''[3]

Ivan's statement of the problem was based on historical events. Such happenings did not cease in the nineteenth century. *The Scourge of the Swastika* by Lord Russell of Liverpool contains little else than descriptions of such atrocities; and it is simply one of a host of writings giving documented lists of instances of evils, both physical and moral.

Thus the problem of evil is both real and acute. There is a clear *prima facie** case that evil and God are incompatible—both cannot exist. Most theists admit this, and that the onus is on them to show that the conflict is not fatal to theism; but a consequence is that a host of proposed solutions are advanced.

The mere fact of such a multiplicity of proposed solutions, and the widespread repudiation of each other's solutions by theists, in itself suggests that the fact of evil is an insuperable obstacle to theism as defined here. It also makes it impossible to treat of all proposed solutions, and all that can be attempted here is an examination of those proposed solutions which are most commonly invoked and most generally thought to be important by theists.

Some theists admit the reality of the problem of evil, and then seek to sidestep it, declaring it to be a great mystery which we poor humans cannot hope to comprehend. Other theists adopt a rational approach and advance rational arguments to show that evil, properly understood, is compatible with, and even a consequence of, God's goodness. The arguments to be advanced in this paper are directed against the arguments of the latter theists; but insofar as these arguments are successful against the rational theists, to that extent they are also effective in showing that the nonrational approach in terms of great mysteries is positively irrational.

II. PROPOSED SOLUTIONS TO THE PROBLEM OF PHYSICAL EVIL

Of the large variety of arguments advanced by theists as solutions to the problem of physical evil, five popularly used and philosophically significant solutions will be examined. They are, in brief: (i) Physical good (plea-

---

[3]P. 244, Garnett translation, Heinemann.

sure) requires physical evil (pain) to exist at all. (ii) Physical evil is God's punishment of sinners. (iii) Physical evil is God's warning and reminder to man. (iv) Physical evil is the result of the natural laws, the operations of which are on the whole good. (v) Physical evil increases the total good.

(i) Physical Good Is Impossible Without Physical Evil / Pleasure is possible only by way of contrast with pain. Here the analogy of color is used. If everything were blue we should, it is argued, understand neither what color is nor what blue is. So with pleasure and pain.

The most obvious defect of such an argument is that it does not cover all physical goods and evils. It is an argument commonly invoked by those who think of physical evil as creating only one problem, namely the problem of human pain. However, the problems of physical evils are not reducible to the one problem, the problem of pain; hence the argument is simply irrelevant to much physical evil. Disease and insanity are evils, but health and sanity are possible in the total absence of disease and insanity. Further, if the argument were in any way valid even in respect of pain, it would imply the existence of only a speck of pain, and not the immense amount of pain in the universe. A speck of yellow is all that is needed for an appreciation of blueness and of color generally. The argument is therefore seen to be seriously defective on two counts even if its underlying principle is left unquestioned. If its underlying principle is questioned, the argument is seen to be essentially invalid. Can it seriously be maintained that if an individual were born crippled and deformed and never in his life experienced pleasure, that he could not experience pain, not even if he were severely injured? It is clear that pain is possible in the absence of pleasure. It is true that it might not be distinguished by a special name and called pain, but the state we now describe as a painful state would nonetheless be possible in the total absence of pleasure. So too the converse would seem to apply. Plato brings this out very clearly in Book 9 of the *Republic* in respect of the pleasures of taste and smell. These pleasures seem not to depend for their existence on any prior experience of pain. Thus the argument is unsound in respect of its main contention; and in being unsound in this respect, it is at the same time ascribing a serious limitation to God's power. It maintains that God cannot create pleasure without creating pain, although as we have seen, pleasure and pain are not correlatives.

(ii) Physical Evil Is God's Punishment for Sin / This kind of explanation was advanced to explain the terrible Lisbon earthquake in the 18th century, in which 40,000 people were killed. There are many replies to this argument, for instance Voltaire's. Voltaire asked: "Did God in this earthquake select the 40,000 least virtuous of the Portugese citizens?" The distribution of disease and pain is in no obvious way related to the virtue of the persons afflicted, and popular saying has it that the distribution is slanted in the opposite direction. The only way of meeting the fact that evils are not distributed proportionately to the evil of the sufferer is by suggesting that all human beings, including children, are such miserable sinners, that our offences are of such enormity, that God would be justified in punishing all of us as severely as it is possible for humans to be punished; but even then, God's apparent caprice in the selection of His victims requires explanation. In any case it is by no means clear that young children, who very often suffer severely, are guilty of sin of such an enormity as would be necessary to justify their sufferings as punishment.

Further, many physical evils are simultaneous with birth—insanity, mental defectiveness, blindness, deformities, as well as much disease. No crime or sin of *the child* can explain and justify these physical evils as punishment; and for a parent's sin to be punished in the child is injustice or evil of another kind.

Similarly, the sufferings of animals cannot be accounted for as punishment. For these various reasons, therefore, this argument must be rejected. In fact it has dropped out of favor in philosophical and theological circles, but it continues to be invoked at the popular level.

(iii) Physical Evil Is God's Warning to Men / It is argued, for instance of physical calamities, that "they serve a moral end which compensates the physical evil which they cause. The awful nature of these phenomena, the overwhelming power of the forces at work, and man's utter helplessness before them rouse him from the religious indifference to which he is so prone. They inspire a reverential awe of the Creator who made them, and controls them, and a salutary fear of violating the laws which He has imposed" (Joyce). This is where immortality is often alluded to as justifying evil.

This argument proceeds from a proposition that is plainly false; and that the proposition from which it proceeds is false is conceded implicitly by most theologians. Natural calamities do not necessarily turn people to God, but rather present the problem of evil in an acute form; and the problem of evil is said to account for more defections from religion than any other cause. Thus if God's object in bringing about natural calamities is to inspire reverence and awe, He is a bungler. There are many more reliable methods of achieving this end. Equally important, the use of physical evil to achieve this object is hardly the course one would expect a benevolent God to adopt when other, more effective, less evil methods are available to Him, for example, miracles, special revelation, etc.

(iv) Evils Are the Results of the Operation of Laws of Nature / This fourth argument relates to most physical evil, but it is more usually used to account for animal suffering and physical calamities. These evils are said to result from the operation of the natural laws which govern these objects, the relevant natural laws being the various causal laws, the law of pleasure-pain as a law governing sentient beings, etc. The theist argues that the non-occurrence of these evils would involve either the constant intervention by God in a miraculous way, and contrary to his own natural laws, or else the construction of a universe with different components subject to different laws of nature; for God, in creating a certain kind of being, must create it subject to its appropriate law: He cannot create it and subject it to any law of his own choosing. Hence He creates a world which has components and laws good in their total effect, although calamitous in some particular effects.

Against this argument three objections are to be urged. First, it does not cover all physical evil. Clearly not all disease can be accounted for along these lines. Secondly, it is not to give a reason against God's miraculous intervention simply to assert that it would be unreasonable for Him constantly to intervene in the operation of His own laws. Yet this is the only reason that theists seem to offer here. If, by intervening in respect to the operation of His laws, God could thereby eliminate an evil, it would seem to be unreasonable and evil of Him not to do so. Some theists seek a way out of this difficulty by denying that God has the power miraculously to intervene; but this is to ascribe a severe limitation to His power. It amounts to asserting that when His Creation has been effected, God can do nothing else except contemplate it. The third objection is related to this, and is to the effect that it is already to ascribe a serious limitation to God's omnipotence to suggest that He could not make sentient beings which did not experience pain, nor sentient beings without deformities and deficiencies, nor natural phenomena with different laws of nature governing them. There is no reason why better laws of nature governing the existing objects are not possible on the divine hypothesis. Surely, if God is all-powerful, He could have made a better universe in the first place, or one with better laws of nature governing it, so that the operation of its laws did not produce calamities and pain. To maintain this is not to suggest that an omnipotent God should be capable of achieving what is logically impossible. All that has been indicated here is logically possible, and therefore not beyond the powers of a being Who is really omnipotent.

This fourth argument seeks to exonerate God by explaining that He created a universe sound on the whole, but such that He had no direct control over the laws governing His creations, and had control only in His selection of His creations. The previous two arguments attribute the detailed results of the operations of these laws directly to God's will. Theists commonly use all three arguments. It is not without significance that they betray such uncertainty as to whether God is to be *commended* or *exonerated*.

(v) The Universe Is Better with Evil in It / This is the important argument. One version of it runs:

> Just as the human artist has in view the beauty of his composition as a whole, not making it his aim to give to each several part the highest degree of brilliancy, but that measure of adornment which most contributes to the combined effect, so it is with God [Joyce].

Another version of this general type of argument explains evil not so much as a *component* of a good whole, seen out of its context as a mere component, but rather as a *means* to a greater good. Different as these versions are, they may be treated here as one general type of argument, for the same criticisms are fatal to both versions.

This kind of argument if valid simply shows that some evil may enrich the universe; it tells us nothing about *how much* evil will enrich this particular universe, and how much will be too much. So, even if valid in principle—and shortly I shall argue that it is not valid—such an argument does not in itself provide a justification for the evil in the universe. It shows simply that the evil which occurs might have a justification. In view of the immense amount of evil the probabilities are against it.

This is the main point made by Wisdom in his discussion of this argument. Wisdom sums up his criticism as follows:

> It remains to add that, unless there are independent arguments in favor of this world's being the best logically possible world, it is probable that some of the evils in it are not logically necessary to a compensating good; it is probable because there are so many evils.[4]

Wisdom's reply brings out that the person who relies upon this argument as a conclusive and complete argument is seriously mistaken. The argument, if valid, justifies only some evil. A belief that it justifies all the evil that occurs in the world is mistaken, for a second argument, by way of a supplement to it, is needed. This supplementary argument would take the form of a proof that all the evil that occurs is *in fact* valuable and necessary as a means to greater good. Such a supplementary proof is in principle impossible; so, at best, this fifth argument can be taken to show only that some evil *may be* necessary for the production of good, and that the evil in the world may perhaps have a justification on this account. This is not to justify a physical evil, but simply to suggest that physical evil might nonetheless have a justification, although we may never come to know this justification.

Thus the argument even if it is valid as a general form of reasoning is unsatisfactory because inconclusive. It is, however, also unsatisfactory in that

4*Mind*, 1931.

it follows on the principle of the argument that, just as it is possible that evil in the total context contributes to increasing the total ultimate good, so equally, it will hold that good in the total context may increase the ultimate evil. Thus if the principle of the argument were sound, we could never know whether evil is really evil, or good really good. (Esthetic analogies may be used to illustrate this point.) By implication it follows that it would be dangerous to eliminate evil because we may thereby introduce a discordant element into the divine symphony of the universe; and, conversely, it may be wrong to condemn the elimination of what is good, because the latter may result in the production of more, higher goods.

So it follows that, even if the general principle of the argument is not questioned, it is still seen to be a defective argument. On the one hand, it proves too little—it justifies only some evil and not necessarily all the evil in the universe; on the other hand, it proves too much because it creates doubts about the goodness of apparent goods. These criticisms in themselves are fatal to the argument as a solution to the problem of physical evil.

However, because this is one of the most popular and plausible accounts of physical evil, it is worthwhile considering whether it can properly be claimed to establish even the very weak conclusion indicated above.

Why, and in what way, is it supposed that physical evils such as pain and misery, disease and deformity, will heighten the total effect and add to the value of the moral whole? The answer given is that physical evil enriches the whole by giving rise to moral goodness. Disease, insanity, physical suffering, and the like are said to bring into being the noble moral virtues—courage, endurance, benevolence, sympathy, and the like. This is what the talk about the enriched whole comes to. W. D. Niven makes this explicit in his version of the argument:

> Physical evil has been the goad which has impelled men to most of those achievements which made the history of man so wonderful. Hardship is a stern but fecund parent of invention. Where life is easy because physical ills are at a minimum we find man degenerating in body, mind, and character.

And Niven concludes by asking:

> Which is preferable—a grim fight with the possibility of splendid triumph; or no battle at all?[5]

---

[5]W. D. Niven, *Encyclopedia of Religion and Ethics*.
Joyce's corresponding argument runs:
Pain is the great stimulant to action. Man no less than animals is impelled to work by the sense of hunger. Experience shows that were it not for this motive the majority of men would be content to live in indolent ease. Man must earn his bread.
One reason plainly why God permits suffering is that man may rise to a height of heroism which would otherwise have been beyond his scope. Nor are these the only benefits which it confers. That sympathy for others which is one of the most precious parts of our experience, and one of the most fruitful sources of well-doing, has its origin in the fellow-feeling engen-

The argument is: Physical evil brings moral good into being, and in fact is an essential precondition for the existence of some moral goods. Further, it is sometimes argued in this context that those moral goods which are possible in the total absence of physical evils are more valuable in themselves if they are achieved as a result of a struggle. Hence physical evil is said to be justified on the grounds that moral good plus physical evil is better than the absence of physical evil.

A common reply, and an obvious one, is that urged by Mackie.[6] Mackie argues that while it is true that moral good plus physical evil together are better than physical good alone, the issue is not as simple as that, for physical evil also gives rise to and makes possible many moral evils that would not or could not occur in the absence of physical evil. It is then urged that it is not clear that physical evils (for example, disease and pain) plus some moral goods (for example, courage) plus some moral evil (for example, brutality) are better than physical good and those moral goods which are possible and which would occur in the absence of physical evil.

This sort of reply, however, is not completely satisfactory. The objection it raises is a sound one, but it proceeds by conceding too much to the theist, and by overlooking two more basic defects of the argument. It allows implicitly that the problem of physical evil may be reduced to the problem of moral evil; and it neglects the two objections which show that the problem of physical evil cannot be so reduced.

The theist therefore happily accepts this kind of reply, and argues that if he can give a satisfactory account of moral evil he will then have accounted for both physical and moral evil. He then goes on to account for moral evil in terms of the value of free will and/or its goods. This general argument is deceptively plausible. It breaks down for the two reasons indicated here, but it breaks down at another point as well. If free will alone is used to justify moral evil, then even if no moral good occurred, moral evil would still

---

dered by endurance of similar trials. Furthermore, were it not for these trials, man would think little enough of a future existence, and of the need of striving after his last end. He would be perfectly content with his existence, and would reck little of any higher good. These considerations here briefly advanced suffice at least to show how important is the office filled by pain in human life, and with what little reason it is asserted that the existence of so much suffering is irreconcilable with the wisdom of the Creator.

And:

It may be asked whether the Creator could not have brought man to perfection without the use of suffering. Most certainly He could have conferred upon him a similar degree of virtue without requiring any effort on his part. Yet it is easy to see that there is a special value attaching to a conquest of difficulties such as man's actual demands, and that in God's eyes this may well be an adequate reason for assigning this life to us in preference to another. . . . Pain has value in respect to the next life, but also in respect to this. The advance of scientific discovery, the gradual improvement of the organization of the community, the growth of material civilization are due in no small degree to the stimulus afforded by pain.

[6]Mackie, "Evil and Omnipotence," *Mind*, 1955.

be said to be justified; but physical evil would have no justification. Physical evil is not essential to free will; it is only justified if moral good actually occurs, and if the moral good which results from physical evils outweighs the moral evils. This means that the argument from free will cannot alone justify physical evil along these lines; and it means that the argument from free will and its goods does not justify physical evil, because such an argument is incomplete, and necessarily incomplete. It needs to be supplemented by factual evidence that it is logically and practically impossible to obtain.

The correct reply, therefore, is first that the argument is irrelevant to many instances of physical evil, and secondly that it is not true that physical evil plus the moral good it produces is better than physical good and its moral goods. Much pain and suffering, in fact much physical evil generally, for example in children who die in infancy, animals, and the insane passes unnoticed; it therefore has no morally uplifting effects upon others, and cannot by virtue of the examples chosen have such effects on the sufferers. Further, there are physical evils such as insanity and much disease to which the argument is inapplicable. So there is a large group of significant cases not covered by the argument. And where the argument is relevant, its premise is plainly false. It can be shown to be false by exposing its implications in the following way.

We either have obligations to lessen physical evil or we have not. If we have obligations to lessen physical evil, then we are thereby reducing the total good in the universe. If, on the other hand, our obligation is to increase the total good in the universe, it is our duty to prevent the reduction of physical evil and possibly even to increase the total amount of physical evil. Theists usually hold that we are obliged to reduce the physical evil in the universe; but in maintaining this, the theist is, in terms of this account of physical evil, maintaining that it is his duty to reduce the total amount of real good in the universe, and thereby to make the universe worse. Conversely, if by eliminating the physical evil he is not making the universe worse, then that amount of evil which he eliminates was unnecessary and in need of justification. It is relevant to notice here that evil is not always eliminated for morally praiseworthy reasons. Some discoveries have been due to positively unworthy motives, and many other discoveries which have resulted in a lessening of the sufferings of mankind have been due to no higher a motive than a scientist's desire to earn a reasonable living wage.

This reply to the theist's argument brings out its untenability. The theist's argument is seen to imply that war plus courage plus the many other moral virtues war brings into play are better than peace and its virtues; that famine and its moral virtues are better than plenty; that disease and its moral virtues are better than health. Some Christians in the past, in consistency with this mode of reasoning, opposed the use of anesthetics to leave scope for the virtues of endurance and courage, and they opposed state aid to the sick and needy to leave scope for the virtues of charity and sympathy. Some have even contended that war is a good in disguise, again in consistency with this argument. Similarly, the theist should, in terms of this fifth argument, in his heart if not aloud regret the discovery of the Salk polio vaccine because Dr. Salk has in one blow destroyed infinite possibilities of moral good.

There are three important points that need to be made concerning this kind of account of physical evil. (a) We are told, as by Niven, Joyce, and others, that pain is a goad to action and that part of its justification lies in this fact. This claim is empirically false as a generalization about all people and all pain. Much pain frustrates action and wrecks people and personalities. On the other hand, many men work and work well without being goaded by pain or discomfort. Further, to assert that men need goading is to ascribe another evil to God, for it is to claim that God made men naturally lazy. There is no reason why God should not have made men naturally industrious; the one is no more incompatible with free will than the other. Thus the argument from physical evil being a goad to man breaks down on three distinct counts. Pain often frustrates human endeavor, pain is not essential as a goad with many men, and where pain is a goad to higher endeavors, it is clear that less evil means to this same end are available to an omnipotent God. (b) The real fallacy in the argument is in the assumption that all or the highest moral excellence results from physical evil. As we have already seen, this assumption is completely false. Neither all moral goodness nor the highest moral goodness is triumph in the face of adversity or benevolence toward others in suffering. Christ Himself stressed this when He observed that the two great commandments were commandments to love. Love does not depend for its possibility on the existence and conquest of evil. (c) The "negative" moral virtues which are brought into play by the various evils—courage, endurance, charity, sympathy, and the like—besides not representing the highest forms of moral virtue, are in fact commonly supposed by the theist and atheist alike not to have the value this fifth argument ascribes to them. We—theists and atheists alike—reveal our comparative valuations of these virtues and of physical evil when we insist on state aid for the needy; when we strive for peace, for plenty, and for harmony within the state.

In brief, the good man, the morally admirable man, is he who loves what is good knowing that it is good and preferring it because it is good. He does not need to be torn by suffering or by the spectacle of another's sufferings to be morally admirable. Fortitude in his own sufferings and sympathetic kindness in others' may reveal to us his goodness; but his goodness is not necessarily increased by such things.

Five arguments concerning physical evil have now been examined. We have seen that the problem of physical evil is a problem in its own right, and one that cannot be reduced to the problem of moral evil; and further, we have seen that physical evil creates not one but a number of problems to which no one nor any combination of the arguments examined offers a solution.

III. PROPOSED SOLUTIONS TO THE PROBLEM OF MORAL EVIL

The problem of moral evil is commonly regarded as being the greater of the problems concerning evil. As we shall see, it does create what appears to be insuperable difficulties for the theist; but so too, apparently, do physical evils.

For the theist moral evil must be interpreted as a breach of God's law and as a rejection of God Himself. It may involve the eternal damnation of the sinner, and in many of its forms it involves the infliction of suffering on other persons. Thus it aggravates the problem of physical evil, but its own peculiar character consists in the fact of sin. How could a morally perfect, all-powerful God create a universe in which occur such moral evils as cruelty, cowardice, and hatred, the more especially as these evils constitute a rejection of God Himself by His creations, and as such involve them in eternal damnation?

The two main solutions advanced relate to free will and to the fact that moral evil is a consequence of free will. There is a third kind of solution, more often invoked implicitly than as an explicit and serious argument, which need not be examined here as its weaknesses are plainly evident. This third solution is to the effect that moral evils and even the most brutal atrocities have their justification in the moral goodness they make possible or bring into being.

(i) Free Will Alone Provides a Justification for Moral Evil / This is perhaps the more popular of the serious attempts to explain moral evil. The argument in brief runs: Men have free will; moral evil is a consequence of free will; a universe in which men exercise free will even with lapses into moral evil is better than a universe in which men become *automata* doing good always because predestined to do so. Thus on this argument it is the mere fact of the supreme value of free will itself that is taken to provide a justification for its corollary moral evil.

(ii) The Goods Made Possible by Free Will Provide a Basis for Accounting for Moral Evil / According to this second argument, it is not the mere fact of free will that is claimed to be of such value as to provide a justification of moral evil, but the fact that free will makes certain goods possible. Some indicate the various moral virtues as the goods that free will makes possible, while others point to beatitude, and others again to beatitude achieved by man's own efforts or the virtues achieved as a result of one's own efforts. What all these have in common is the claim that the good consequences of free will provide a justification of the bad consequences of free will, namely moral evil.

Each of these two proposed solutions encounters two specific criticisms, which are fatal to their claims to be real solutions.

(i) [Free Will Alone Provides a Justification for Moral Evil. /]

To consider first the difficulties to which the former proposed solution is exposed. (a) A difficulty for the first argument—that it is free will alone that provides a justification for moral evil—lies in the fact that the theist who argues in this way has to allow that it is logically possible on the free will hypothesis that all men should always will what is evil, and that even so, a universe of completely evil men possessing free will is better than one in which men are predestined to virtuous living. It has to be contended that the value of free will itself is so immense that it more than outweighs the total moral evil, the eternal punishment of the wicked, and the sufferings inflicted on others by the sinners in their evilness. It is this paradox that leads to the formulation of the second argument; and it is to be noted that the explanation of moral evil switches to the second argument or to a combination of the first and second arguments, immediately the theist refuses to face the logical possibility of complete wickedness, and insists instead that in fact men do not always choose what is evil.

(b) The second difficulty encountered by the first argument relates to the possibility that free will is compatible with less evil, and even with no evil, that is, with absolute goodness. If it could be shown that free will is compatible with absolute goodness, or even with less moral evil than actually occurs, then all or at least some evil will be left unexplained by free will alone.

Mackie, in his recent paper, and Joyce, in his discussion of this argument, both contend that free will is compatible with absolute goodness. Mackie argues that if it is not possible for God to confer free will on men and at the same time ensure that no moral evil is committed, He cannot really be omnipotent. Joyce directs his argument rather to fellow-theists, and it is more of an *ad hominem* argument* addressed to them. He writes:

> Free will need not (as is often assumed) involve the power to choose wrong. Our ability to misuse the gift is due to the conditions under which it is exercised here. In our present state we are able to reject what is truly good, and exercise our power of preference in favor of some baser attraction. Yet it is not necessary that it should be so. And all who accept Christian revelation admit that those who attain their final beatitude exercise freedom of will, and yet cannot choose aught but what is truly good. They possess the knowledge of Essential Goodness; and to it,

*[Literally, argument directed to the man.—Eds.]

not simply to good in general, they refer every choice. Moreover, even in our present condition it is open to omnipotence so to order our circumstances and to confer on the will such instinctive impulses that we should in every election adopt the right course and not the wrong one.

To this objection, that free will is compatible with absolute goodness and that therefore a benevolent, omnipotent God would have given man free will and ensured his absolute virtue, it is replied that God is being required to perform what is logically impossible. It is logically impossible, so it is argued, for free will and absolute goodness to be combined, and hence, if God lacks omnipotence only in this respect, He cannot be claimed to lack omnipotence in any sense in which serious theists have ascribed it to Him.

Quite clearly, if free will and absolute goodness are logically incompatible, then God, in not being able to confer both on man, does not lack omnipotence in any important sense of the term. However, it is not clear that free will and absolute goodness are logically opposed; and Joyce does point to considerations which suggest that they are not logical incompatibles. For my own part I am uncertain on this point; but my uncertainty is not a factual one but one concerning a point of usage. It is clear that an omnipotent God could create rational agents predestined always to make virtuous "decisions"; what is not clear is whether we should describe such agents as having free will. The considerations to which Joyce points have something of the status of test cases, and they would suggest that we should describe such agents as having free will. However, no matter how we resolve the linguistic point, the question remains—Which is more desirable, free will and moral evil and the physical evil to which free will gives rise, or this special free will or pseudo-free will which goes with absolute goodness? I suggest that the latter is clearly preferable. Later I shall endeavor to defend this conclusion; for the moment I am content to indicate the nature of the value judgment on which the question turns at this point.

The second objection to the proposed solution of the problem of moral evil in terms of free will alone, is related to the contention that free will is compatible with less moral evil than occurs, and possibly with no moral evil. We have seen what is involved in the latter contention. We may now consider what is involved in the former. It may be argued that free will is compatible with less moral evil than in fact occurs on various grounds. (1) God, if He were all-powerful, could miraculously intervene to prevent some or perhaps all moral evil; and He is said to do so on occasions in answer to prayers (for example, to prevent wars) or of His own initiative (for instance, by producing calamities which serve as warnings, or by working miracles, etc.).

(2) God has made man with a certain nature. This nature is often interpreted by theologians as having a bias to evil. Clearly God could have created man with a strong bias to good, while still leaving scope for a decision to act evilly. Such a bias to good would be compatible with freedom of the

will. (3) An omnipotent God could so have ordered the world that it was less conducive to the practice of evil.

These are all considerations advanced by Joyce, and separately and jointly, they establish that God could have conferred free will upon us, and at least very considerably *reduced* the amount of moral evil that would have resulted from the exercise of free will. This is sufficient to show that *not all* the moral evil that exists can be justified by reference to free will alone. This conclusion is fatal to the account of moral evil in terms of free will alone. The more extreme conclusion that Mackie seeks to establish—that absolute goodness is compatible with free will—is not essential as a basis for refuting the free will argument. The difficulty is as fatal to the claims of theism whether all moral evil or only some moral evil is unaccountable. However, whether Mackie's contentions are sound is still a matter of logical interest, although not of any real moment in the context of the case against theism, once the fact that less moral evil is compatible with free will has been established.

(ii) [The Goods Made Possible by Free Will Provide a Basis for Accounting for Moral Evil. /] The second free will argument arises out of an attempt to circumvent these objections. It is not free will but the value of the goods achieved through free will that is said to be so great as to provide a justification for moral evil.

(*a*) This second argument meets a difficulty in that it is now necessary for it to be supplemented by a proof that the number of people who practice moral virtue or who attain beatitude and/or virtue after a struggle is sufficient to outweigh the evilness of moral evil, the evilness of their eternal damnation, and the physical evil they cause to others. This is a serious defect in the argument, because it means that the argument can at best show that moral evil *may have* a justification, and not that it has a justification. It is both logically and practically impossible to supplement and complete the argument. It is necessarily incomplete and inconclusive even if its general principle is sound.

(*b*) This second argument is designed also to avoid the other difficulty of the first argument—that free will may be compatible with no evil and certainly with less evil. It is argued that even if free will is compatible with absolute goodness it is still better that virtue and beatitude be attained after a genuine personal struggle; and this, it is said, would not occur if God in conferring free will nonetheless prevented moral evil or reduced the risk of it. Joyce argues in this way:

> To receive our final beatitude as the fruit of our labors, and as the recompense of a hard-won victory, is an incomparably higher destiny than to receive it without any effort on our part. And since God in His wisdom has seen fit to give us such a lot as this, it was inevitable that man should have the power to choose wrong. We could not be called to merit the reward due to victory without being exposed to the possibility of defeat.

There are various objections which may be urged here. First, this argument implies that the more intense the struggle, the greater is the triumph and resultant good, and the better the world; hence we should apparently, on this argument, court temptation and moral struggles to attain greater virtue and to be more worthy of our reward. Secondly, it may be urged that God is being said to be demanding too high a price for the goods produced. He is omniscient. He knows that many will sin and not attain the goods or the Good free will is said to make possible. He creates men with free will, with the natures men have, in the world as it is constituted, knowing that in His doing so He is committing many to moral evil and eternal damnation. He could avoid all this evil by creating men with rational wills predestined to virtue, or He could eliminate much of it by making men's natures and the conditions in the world more conducive to the practice of virtue. He is said not to choose to do this. Instead, at the cost of the sacrifice of the many, He is said to have ordered things so as to allow fewer men to attain this higher virtue and higher beatitude that result from the more intense struggle.

In attributing such behavior to God, and in attempting to account for moral evil along these lines, theists are, I suggest, attributing to God immoral behavior of a serious kind—of a kind we should all unhesitatingly condemn in a fellow human being.

We do not commend people for putting temptation in the way of others. On the contrary, anyone who today advocated, or even allowed where he could prevent it, the occurrence of evil and the sacrifice of the many—even as a result of their own freely chosen actions—for the sake of the higher virtue of the few would be condemned as an immoralist. To put severe temptation in the way of the many, knowing that many and perhaps even most will succumb to the temptation, for the sake of the higher virtue of the few would be blatant immorality; and it would be immoral whether or not those who yielded to the temptation possessed free will. This point can be brought out by considering how a conscientious moral agent would answer the question: Which should I choose for other people, a world in which there are intense moral struggles and the possibility of magnificent triumphs and the certainty of many defeats, or a world in which there are less intense struggles, less magnificent triumphs, but more triumphs and fewer defeats, or a world in which there are no struggles, no triumphs, and no defeats? We are constantly answering less easy questions than this in a way that conflicts with the theist's contentions. If by modifying our own behavior we can save someone else from an intense moral struggle and almost certain moral evil, for example if by refraining from gambling or excessive drinking ourselves we can help a weaker person not to become a confirmed gambler or an alcoholic, or if by locking our car and not leaving it unlocked and with the key in it we can prevent people yielding to the temptation to become car thieves, we feel obliged to act accordingly, even though the persons concerned would freely choose the evil course of conduct. How much clearer is the decision with which God is said to be faced—the choice between the higher virtue of some and the evil of others, or the higher but less high virtue of many more, and the evil of many fewer. Neither alternative denies free will to men.

These various difficulties dispose of each of the main arguments relating to moral evil. There are in addition to these difficulties two other objections that might be urged.

If it could be shown that man has not free will, both arguments collapse; and even if it could be shown that God's omniscience is incompatible with free will, they would still break down. The issues raised here are too great to be pursued in this paper; and they can simply be noted as possible additional grounds from which criticisms of the main proposed solutions of the problem of moral evil may be advanced.

The other general objection is by way of a follow-up to points made in objections (b) to both arguments (i) and (ii). It concerns the relative value of free will and its goods and evils, and the value of the best of the alternatives to free will and its goods. Are free will and its goods so much more valuable than the next best alternatives that their superior value can really justify the immense amount of evil that is introduced into the world by free will?

Theologians who discuss this issue ask: Which is better—men with free will striving to work out their own destinies, or automata-machine-like creatures, who never make mistakes because they never make decisions? When put in this form we naturally doubt whether free will plus moral evil plus the possibility of the eternal damnation of the many and the physical evil of untold billions are quite so unjustified after all; but the fact of the matter is that the question has not been fairly put. The real alternative is, on the one hand, rational agents with free wills making many bad and some good decisions on rational and nonrational grounds, and "rational" agents predestined always "to choose" the right things for the right reasons—that is, if the language of automata must be used, rational automata. Predestination does not imply the absence of rationality in all senses of that term. God, were He omnipotent, could preordain the decisions and the reasons upon which they were based; and such a mode of existence would seem to be in itself a worthy mode of existence, and one preferable to an existence with free will, irrationality, and evil.

IV. CONCLUSION

In this paper it has been maintained that God, were He all-powerful and perfectly good, would have created a world in which there was no unnecessary evil. It has not been argued that God ought to have created a perfect world, nor that He should have made one that is in any way logically impossible. It has simply been argued that a benevolent God could, and would, have created a world devoid of superfluous evil. It has been contended that there is evil in this world—unnecessary evil—and that the more popular and philosophically more significant of the many attempts to explain this evil are completely unsatisfactory. Hence we must conclude from the existence of evil that there cannot be an omnipotent, benevolent God.

32 / The Problem of Evil

JOHN HICK

[I. CLARIFICATION OF THE PROBLEM]

[A. The Problem /] To many, the most powerful positive objection to belief in God is the fact of evil. Probably for most agnostics it is the appalling depth and extent of human suffering, more than anything else, that makes the idea of a loving Creator seem so implausible and disposes them toward one or another of the various naturalistic theories of religion.

As a challenge to theism, the problem of evil has traditionally been posed in the form of a dilemma: If God is perfectly loving, he must wish to abolish evil; and if he is all-powerful, he must be able to abolish evil. But evil exists; therefore God cannot be both omnipotent and perfectly loving.

[B. Untenable "Solutions" /] Certain solutions, which at once suggest themselves, have to be ruled out so far as the Judaic-Christian faith is concerned.

To say, for example (with contemporary Christian Science), that evil is an illusion of the human mind, is impossible within a religion based upon the stark realism of the Bible. Its pages faithfully reflect the characteristic mixture of good and evil in human experience. They record every kind of sorrow and suffering, every mode of man's inhumanity to man and of his painfully insecure existence in the world. There is no attempt to regard evil as anything but dark, menacingly ugly, heart-rending, and crushing. In the

Christian scriptures, the climax of this history of evil is the crucifixion of Jesus, which is presented not only as a case of utterly unjust suffering, but as the violent and murderous rejection of God's Messiah. There can be no doubt, then, that for biblical faith, evil is unambiguously evil, and stands in direct opposition to God's will.

Again, to solve the problem of evil by means of the theory (sponsored, for example, by the Boston "Personalist" School)[1] of a finite deity who does the best he can with a material, intractable and co-eternal with himself, is to have abandoned the basic premise of Hebrew-Christian monotheism; for the theory amounts to rejecting belief in the infinity and sovereignty of God.

Indeed, any theory which would avoid the problem of the origin of evil by depicting it as an ultimate constituent of the universe, coordinate with good, has been repudiated in advance by the classic Christian teaching, first developed by Augustine, that evil represents the going wrong of something which in itself is good.[2] Augustine holds firmly to the Hebrew-Christian conviction that the universe is *good*—that is to say, it is the creation of a good God for a good purpose. He completely rejects the ancient prejudice, widespread in his day, that matter is evil. There are, according to Augustine, higher and lower, greater and lesser goods in immense abundance and variety; but everything which has being is good in its own way and degree, except in so far as it may have become spoiled or corrupted. Evil—whether it be an evil will, an instance of pain, or some disorder or decay in nature—has not been set there by God, but represents the distortion of something that is inherently valuable. Whatever exists is, as such, and in its proper place, good; evil is essentially parasitic upon good, being disorder and perversion in a fundamentally good creation. This understanding of evil as something negative means that it is not willed and created by God; but it does not mean (as some have supposed) that evil is unreal and can be disregarded. Clearly, the first effect of this doctrine is to accentuate even more the question of the origin of evil.

[II. SOLUTION TO THE PROBLEM]

Theodicy,[3] as many modern Christian thinkers see it, is a modest enterprise, negative rather than positive in its conclusions. It does not claim to explain, nor to explain away, every instance of evil in human experience,

---

[1]Edgar Brightman's *A Philosophy of Religion* (Englewood Cliffs, N.J.: Prentice-Hall, Inc., 1940), chaps. 8–10, is a classic exposition of one form of this view.

[2]See Augustine's *Confessions*, Book VII, chap. 12; *City of God*, Book XII, chap. 3; *Enchiridion*, chap. 4.

[3]The word "theodicy," from the Greek *theos* (God) and *dike* (righteous), means the justification of God's goodness in face of the fact of evil.

but only to point to certain considerations which prevent the fact of evil (largely incomprehensible though it remains) from constituting a final and insuperable bar to rational belief in God.

In indicating these considerations it will be useful to follow the traditional division of the subject. There is the problem of *moral evil* or wickedness: Why does an all-good and all-powerful God permit this? And there is the problem of the *nonmoral evil* of suffering or pain, both physical and mental: Why has an all-good and all-powerful God created a world in which this occurs?

[A. Moral Evil /] Christian thought has always considered moral evil in its relation to human freedom and responsibility. To be a person is to be a finite center of freedom, a (relatively) free and self-directing agent responsible for one's own decision. This involves being free to act wrongly as well as to act rightly. The idea of a person who can be infallibly guaranteed always to act rightly is self-contradictory. There can be no guarantee in advance that a genuinely free moral agent will never choose amiss. Consequently, the possibility of wrongdoing or sin is logically inseparable from the creation of finite persons, and to say that God should not have created beings who might sin amounts to saying that he should not have created people.

This thesis has been challenged in some recent philosophical discussions of the problem of evil, in which it is claimed that no contradiction* is involved in saying that God might have made people who would be genuinely free and who could yet be guaranteed always to act rightly. A quotation from one of these discussions follows:

> If there is no logical impossibility† in a man's freely choosing the good on one, or on several occasions, there cannot be a logical impossibility in his freely choosing the good on every occasion. God was not, then, faced with a choice between making innocent automata and making beings who, in acting freely, would sometimes go wrong: There was open to him the obviously better possibility of making beings who would act freely but always go right. Clearly, his failure to avail himself of this possibility is inconsistent with his being both omnipotent and wholly good.[4]

A reply to this argument is suggested in another recent contribution to the discussion.[5] If by a free action we mean an action which is not exter-

---

[4] J. L. Mackie, "Evil and Omnipotence," *Mind* (April, 1955), p. 209. A similar point is made by Antony Flew in "Divine Omnipotence and Human Freedom," *New Essays in Philosophical Theology*. An important critical comment on these arguments is offered by Ninian Smart in "Omnipotence, Evil and Supermen," *Philosophy* (April, 1961), with replies by Flew (January, 1962) and Mackie (April, 1962).

[5] Flew, in *New Essays in Philosophical Theology*.

*[For the definition of 'contradiction', see Note 3 to the Preview to this Part. Understanding this concept is essential to understanding the next several paragraphs.—Eds.]

†[I.e. contradiction.—Eds.]

nally compelled but which flows from the nature of the agent as he reacts to the circumstances in which he finds himself, there is, indeed, no contradiction between our being free and our actions being ''caused'' (by our own nature) and therefore being in principle predictable. There is a contradiction, however, in saying that God is the cause of our acting as we do but that we are free beings in relation to God. There is, in other words, a contradiction in saying that God has made us so that we shall of necessity act in a certain way, and that we are genuinely independent persons in relation to him. If all our thoughts and actions are divinely predestined, however free and morally responsible we may seem to be to ourselves, we cannot be free and morally responsible in the sight of God, but must instead be his helpless puppets. Such ''freedom'' is like that of a patient acting out a series of posthypnotic suggestions: He appears, even to himself, to be free, but his volitions have actually been predetermined by another will, that of the hypnotist, in relation to whom the patient is not a free agent.

A different objector might raise the question of whether or not we deny God's omnipotence if we admit that he is unable to create persons who are free from the risks inherent in personal freedom. The answer that has always been given is that to create such beings is logically impossible. It is no limitation upon God's power that he cannot accomplish the logically impossible, since there is nothing here to accomplish, but only a meaningless conjunction of words[6]—in this case ''person who is not a person.'' God is able to create beings of any and every conceivable kind; but creatures who lack moral freedom, however superior they might be to human beings in other respects, would not be what we mean by persons. They would constitute a different form of life which God might have brought into existence instead of persons. When we ask why God did not create such beings in place of persons, the traditional answer is that only persons could, in any meaningful sense, become ''children of God,'' capable of entering into a personal relationship with their Creator by a free and uncompelled response to his love.

When we turn from the possibility of moral evil as a correlate of man's personal freedom to its actuality, we face something which must remain inexplicable even when it can be seen to be possible. For we can never provide a complete causal explanation of a free act; if we could, it would not be a free act. The origin of moral evil lies forever concealed within the mystery of human freedom.

The necessary connection between moral freedom and the possibility, now actualized, of sin throws light upon a great deal of the suffering which afflicts mankind. For an enormous amount of human pain arises either from the inhumanity or the culpable incompetence of mankind. This in-

---

[6]As Aquinas said, '' . . . nothing that implies a contradiction falls under the scope of God's omnipotence.'' *Summa Theologica*, part 1, question 25, article 4.

cludes such major scourges as poverty, oppression and persecution, war, and all the injustice, indignity, and inequity which occur even in the most advanced societies. These evils are manifestations of human sin. Even disease is fostered to an extent, the limits of which have not yet been determined by psychosomatic medicine, by moral and emotional factors seated both in the individual and in his social environment. To the extent that all of these evils stem from human failures and wrong decisions, their possibility is inherent in the creation of free persons inhabiting a world which presents them with real choices which are followed by real consequences.

[B. Physical Evil /] We may now turn more directly to the problem of suffering. Even though the major bulk of actual human pain is traceable to man's misused freedom as a sole or part cause, there remain other sources of pain which are entirely independent of the human will, for example, earthquake, hurricane, storm, flood, drought, and blight. In practice, it is often impossible to trace a boundary between the suffering which results from human wickedness and folly and that which falls upon mankind from without. Both kinds of suffering are inextricably mingled together in human experience. For our present purpose, however, it is important to note that the latter category does exist and that it seems to be built into the very structure of our world. In response to it, theodicy, if it is wisely conducted, follows a negative path. It is not possible to show positively that each item of human pain serves the divine purpose of good; but, on the other hand, it does seem possible to show that the divine purpose as it is understood in Judaism and Christianity could not be forwarded in a world which was designed as a permanent hedonistic paradise.

An essential premise of this argument concerns the nature of the divine purpose in creating the world. The skeptic's assumption is that man is to be viewed as a completed creation and that God's purpose in making the world was to provide a suitable dwelling-place for this fully formed creature. Since God is good and loving, the environment which he has created for human life to inhabit is naturally as pleasant and comfortable as possible. The problem is essentially similar to that of a man who builds a cage for some pet animal. Since our world, in fact, contains sources of hardship, inconvenience, and danger of innumerable kinds, the conclusion follows that this world cannot have been created by a perfectly benevolent and all-powerful deity.[7]

Christianity, however, has never supposed that God's purpose in the creation of the world was to construct a paradise whose inhabitants would experience a maximum of pleasure and a minimum of pain. The world is

---

[7]This is the nature of David Hume's argument in his discussion of the problem of evil in his *Dialogues*, part 11.

seen, instead, as a place of "soul-making" in which free beings grappling with the tasks and challenges of their existence in a common environment may become "children of God" and "heirs of eternal life." A way of thinking theologically of God's continuing creative purpose for man was suggested by . . . Irenaeus.* Following hints from St. Paul, Irenaeus taught that man has been made as a person in the image of God but has not yet been brought as a free and responsible agent into the finite likeness of God, which is revealed in Christ.[8] Our world, with all its rough edges, is the sphere in which this second and harder stage of the creative process is taking place.

[III. RELATED ISSUES]

[A. Consequences if There Were No Evil /] This conception of the world (whether or not set in Irenaeus' theological framework) can be supported by the method of negative theodicy. Suppose, contrary to fact, that this world were a paradise from which all possibility of pain and suffering were excluded. The consequences would be very far-reaching. For example, no one could ever injure anyone else: The murderer's knife would turn to paper or his bullets to thin air; the bank safe, robbed of a million dollars, would miraculously become filled with another million dollars (without this device, on however large a scale, proving inflationary); fraud, deceit, conspiracy, and treason would somehow always leave the fabric of society undamaged. Again, no one would ever be injured by accident: The mountain-climber, steeplejack, or playing child falling from a height would float unharmed to the ground; the reckless driver would never meet with disaster. There would be no need to work, since no harm could result from avoiding work; there would be no call to be concerned for others in time of need or danger, for in such a world there could be no real needs or dangers.

To make possible this continual series of individual adjustments, nature would have to work by "special providences" instead of running according to general laws which men must learn to respect on penalty of pain or death. The laws of nature would have to be extremely flexible: Sometimes gravity would operate, sometimes not; sometimes an object would be hard and solid, sometimes soft. There could be no sciences, for there would be no enduring world structure to investigate. In eliminating the problems and hardships of an objective environment, with its own laws, life would become like a dream in which, delightfully but aimlessly, we would float and drift at ease.

[8]See Irenaeus' *Against Heresies*, book IV, chaps. 37 and 38.
*[An early Christian theologian and church father.—Eds.]

One can at least begin to imagine such a world. It is evident that our present ethical concepts would have no meaning in it. If, for example, the notion of harming someone is an essential element in the concept of a wrong action, in our hedonistic paradise there could be no wrong actions— nor any right actions in distinction from wrong. Courage and fortitude would have no point in an environment in which there is, by definition, no danger or difficulty. Generosity, kindness, love, prudence, unselfishness, and all other ethical notions which presuppose life in a stable environment could not even be formed. Consequently, such a world, however well it might promote pleasure, would be very ill adapted for the development of the moral qualities of human personality. In relation to this purpose it would be the worst of all possible worlds.

It would seem, then, that an environment intended to make possible the growth in free beings of the finest characteristics of personal life must have a good deal in common with our present world. It must operate according to general and dependable laws; and it must involve real dangers, difficulties, problems, obstacles, and possibilities of pain, failure, sorrow, frustration, and defeat. If it did not contain the particular trials and perils which— subtracting man's own very considerable contribution—our world contains, it would have to contain others instead.

To realize this is not, by any means, to be in possession of a detailed theodicy. It is to understand that this world, with all its "heartaches and the thousand natural shocks that flesh is heir to," an environment so manifestly not designed for the maximization of human pleasure and the minimization of human pain, may be rather well adapted to the quite different purpose of "soul-making."[9]

These considerations are related to theism as such. Specifically, Christian theism goes further in the light of the death of Christ, which is seen paradoxically both (as the murder of the divine Son) as the worst thing that has ever happened and (as the occasion of man's salvation) as the best thing that has ever happened. As the supreme evil turned to supreme good, it provides the paradigm for the distinctively Christian reaction to evil. Viewed from the standpoint of Christian faith, evils do not cease to be evils; and certainly, in view of Christ's healing work, they cannot be said to have been sent by God. Yet it has been the persistent claim of those seriously and wholeheartedly committed to Christian discipleship that tragedy, though truly tragic, may nevertheless be turned, through a man's reaction

---

[9] This brief discussion has been confined to the problem of human suffering. The large and intractable problem of animal pain is not taken up here. For a discussion of it, see, for example, Nels Ferre, *Evil and the Christian Faith* (New York: Harper & Row, Publishers, Inc., 1947), chap. 7; and Austin Farrer, *Love Almighty and Ills Unlimited* (New York: Doubleday & Company, Inc., 1961), chap. 5.

to it, from a cause of despair and alienation from God to a stage in the ful-fillment of God's loving purpose for that individual. As the greatest of all evils, the crucifixion of Christ, was made the occasion of man's redemption, so good can be won from other evils. As Jesus saw his execution by the Ro-mans as an experience which God desired him to accept, an experience which was to be brought within the sphere of the divine purpose and made to serve the divine ends, so the Christian response to calamity is to accept the adversities, pains, and afflictions which life brings, in order that they can be turned to a positive spiritual use.[10]

[B. Life After Death /] At this point, theodicy points forward in two ways to the subject of life after death.

First, although there are many striking instances of good being trium-phantly brought out of evil through a man's or a woman's reaction to it, there are many other cases in which the opposite has happened. Some-times obstacles breed strength of character, dangers evoke courage and un-selfishness, and calamities produce patience and moral steadfastness. But sometimes they lead, instead, to resentment, fear, grasping selfishness, and disintegration of character. Therefore, it would seem that any divine purpose of soul-making which is at work in earthly history must continue beyond this life if it is ever to achieve more than a very partial and fragmen-tary success.

Second, if we ask whether the business of soul-making is worth all the toil and sorrow of human life, the Christian answer must be in terms of a future good which is great enough to justify all that has happened on the way to it.

[10] This conception of providence is stated more fully in John Hick, *Faith and Knowledge* (Ithaca: Cornell University Press, 1957), chap. 7, from which some sentences are incorporated in this paragraph.

33 / Faith

RICHARD TAYLOR

"**O**ur most holy religion," David Hume* said, "is founded on *faith*, not on reason." (All quotations are from the last two paragraphs of Hume's essay "Of Miracles.") He did not then conclude that it ought, therefore, to be rejected by reasonable men. On the contrary, he suggests that rational evaluation has no proper place in this realm to begin with, that a religious man need not feel in the least compelled to put his religion "to such a trial as it is, by no means, fitted to endure," and he brands as "dangerous friends or disguised enemies" of religion those "who have undertaken to defend it by the principles of human reason."

I want to defend Hume's suggestion, and go a bit farther by eliciting some things that seem uniquely characteristic of *Christian* faith, in order to show what it has, and what it has not, in common with other things to which it is often compared. I limited myself to Christian faith because I know rather little of any other, and faith is, with love and hope, supposed to be a uniquely Christian virtue.

I. FAITH AND REASON

Faith is not reason, else religion would be, along with logic and metaphysics, a part of philosophy, which it assuredly is not. Nor is faith belief resting on scientific or historical inquiry, else religion would be part of the corpus of human knowledge, which it clearly is not. More than that, it seems evident that by the normal, common-sense criteria of what is reasonable, the content of Christian faith is *un*reasonable. This, I believe, should be the starting point, the *datum*, of any discussion of faith and reason. It is, for instance, an essential content of the Christian faith that, at a certain quite recent time, God became man, dwelt among us in the person of a humble servant, and then, for a sacred purpose, died, to live again. Now, apologetics usually addresses itself to the *details* of this story, to show that they are not inherently incredible, but this is to miss the point. It is indeed *possible* to be-

---

*[An 18th century British philosopher.—Eds.]

lieve it, and in the strict sense the story is credible. Millions of people do most deeply and firmly believe it. But even the barest statement of the content of that belief makes it manifest that it does not and, I think, could not, ever result from rational inquiry. "Mere reason," Hume said, "is insufficient to convince us of its veracity." The Christian begins the recital of his faith with the words, "I believe," and it would be an utter distortion to construe this as anything like "I have inquired, and found it reasonable to conclude." If there were a man who could say that in honesty, as I think there is not, then he would, in a clear and ordinary sense, believe, but he would have no religious faith whatsoever, and his beliefs themselves would be robbed of what would make them religious.

Now if this essential and (it seems to me) obvious unreasonableness of Christian belief could be recognized at the outset of any discussion of religion, involving rationalists on the one hand and believers on the other, we would be spared the tiresome attack and apologetics upon which nothing ultimately turns, the believer would be spared what is, in fact, an uncalled-for task of reducing his faith to reason or science, which can, as Hume noted, result only in "exposing" it as neither, and the rationalist would be granted his main point, not as a conclusion triumphantly extracted, but as a datum too obvious to labor.

II. FAITH AND CERTAINTY

Why, then, does a devout Christian embrace these beliefs? Now this very question, on the lips of a philosopher, is wrongly expressed, for he invariably intends it as a request for reasons, as a means of putting the beliefs to that unfair "trial" of which Hume spoke. Yet there is a clear and definite answer to this question, which has the merit of being true and evident to anyone who has known intimately those who dwell in the atmosphere of faith. The reason the Christian believes that story around which his whole life turns is, simply, that he cannot help it. If he is trapped into eliciting grounds for it, they are grounds given after the fact of conviction. Within "the circle of faith," the question whether on the evidence one *ought* to believe "does not arise." One neither seeks nor needs grounds for the acceptance of what he cannot help believing. "Whoever is moved by *faith* to assent," Hume wrote, "is conscious of a continued miracle in his own person, which subverts all the principles of his understanding, and gives him a determination to believe. . . ." It is this fact of faith which drives philosophers to such exasperation, in the face of which the believer is nonetheless so utterly unmoved.

The believer sees his life as a gift of God, the world as the creation of

God, his own purposes, insofar as they are noble, as the purposes of God, and history as exhibiting a divine plan, made known to him through the Christian story. He sees things this way, just because they do seem so, and he cannot help it. This is why, for him, faith is so "easy," and secular arguments to the contrary so beside the point. No one seeks evidence for that of which he is entirely convinced, or regards as relevant what seems to others to cast doubt. The believer is like a child who recoils from danger, as exhibited, for instance, in what he for the first time sees as a fierce animal; the child has no difficulty *believing* he is in peril, just because he cannot help believing it, yet his belief results not at all from induction based on past experience with fierce animals, and no reassurances, garnered from our past experience, relieve his terror at all.

III. SOME CONFUSIONS

If this is what religious faith essentially is—if, as a believer might poetically but, I think, correctly describe it, faith is an involuntary conviction, often regarded as a "gift," on the part of one who has voluntarily opened his mind and heart to receive it—then certain common misunderstandings can be removed.

In the first place, faith should never be likened to an *assumption*, such as the scientist's assumption of the uniformity of nature, or whatnot. An assumption is an intellectual device for furthering inquiry. It need not be a conviction nor, indeed, even a belief. But a half-hearted faith is no religious faith. Faith thus has that much, at least, in common with knowledge, that it is a *conviction*, and its subjective state is *certainty*. One thus wholly distorts faith if he represents the believer as just "taking" certain things "on faith," and then reasons, like a philosopher, from these beginnings, as though what were thus "taken" could, like an assumption, be rejected at will.

Again, it is a misunderstanding to represent faith as "mere tenacity." Tenacity consists in stubbornly clinging to what one hopes, but of which one is not fully convinced. The child who is instantly convinced of danger in the presence of an animal is not being tenacious or stubborn, even in the face of verbal reassurances, and no more is the Christian whose acts are moved by faith. The believer does not so much *shun* evidence as something that might *shake* his faith, but rather regards it as not to the point. In this he may appear to philosophers to be mistaken, but only if one supposes, as he need not, that one should hold only such beliefs as are rational.

Again, it is misleading to refer to any set of propositions, such as those embodied in a creed, as being this or that person's "faith." Concerning that content of belief in which one is convinced by faith, it is logically (though I think not otherwise) possible that one might be convinced by evidence, in which case it would have no more to do with faith or religion than do the statements in a newspaper. This observation has this practical importance, that it is quite possible—in fact, common—for the faith of different believers to be one and the same, despite creedal differences.

And finally, both "faith" (or "fideism") and "reason" (or "rationalism") can be, and often are, used as pejorative terms and as terms of commendation. Which side one takes here is arbitrary, for there is no non-question-begging way of deciding. A rationalist can perhaps find reasons for being a rationalist, though this is doubtful; but in any case it would betray a basic misunderstanding to expect a fideist to do likewise. This is brought out quite clearly by the direction that discussions of religion usually take. A philosophical teacher will often, for instance, labor long to persuade his audience that the content of Christian faith is unreasonable, which is a shamefully easy task for him, unworthy of his learning. Then, suddenly, the underlying assumption comes to light that Christian beliefs ought, therefore, to be abandoned by rational people! A religious hearer of this discourse might well reply that, religion being unreasonable but nonetheless manifestly worthy of belief, we should conclude with Hume that reason, in this realm at least, ought to be rejected. Now one can decide that issue by any light that is granted him, but it is worth stressing that the believer's position on it is just exactly as good, and just as bad, as the rational skeptic's.

34 / Religion, Reason, and Faith

RICHARD ROBINSON

I. RELIGION AND REASON

There is something commonly accepted as a great good which I reject, namely religion.

Religion has held a big place in the thoughts and feelings of most of the human beings who have yet lived; and, though some have found it an inescapable evil, most have found it a great good. The founder of the Gifford lectures* said that "religion is of all things the most excellent and precious. . . ."

The religious man feels that his god is the supreme good, and the worship of him is the supreme good for man; and he obtains an immense satisfaction in worship and obedience. His creed gives him the feeling that the universe is important and that he has his own humble but important part in it. "God is working his purpose out, as year succeeds to year"; and in this august enterprise the believer has an assured place. When he says that "man cannot be at ease in the world unless he has a faith to sustain him," the faith he is thinking of is in part that there is something extremely important to do. Thus his religion lays that specter of futility and meaninglessness, which man's self-consciousness and thoughtfulness are always liable to raise. The convert says to himself, in the words at the end of Tolstoy's *Anna Karenina*: "My whole life, every moment of my life, will be, not meaningless as before, but full of deep meaning, which I shall have power to impress on every action." The great comfort of such a belief is obvious.

But this is still less than half of the comfort religion can give. For it is not yet an answer to man's greatest horror, the death of his loved ones and himself. If his religion also makes him believe that death is not the end of life, that on the contrary he and his loved ones will live forever in perfect justice and happiness, this more than doubles his feeling of comfort and security. This doctrine of the happy survival of death is the chief attraction of the Christian religion to most of its adherents; and their first profound religious belief comes to them as a reassurance after their first realization that they are going to die. It is an easy defensive reaction against this terrible discovery. . . .

Such is the enormous comfort that religion can give. Because of it a man who deprives the people of the comfort of believing "in the final proportions of eternal justice" is often regarded as a "cruel oppressor, the merciless enemy of the poor and wretched" (Edmund Burke, "Reflections on the French Revolution," *Works*, v. 432).

But is it a cruel oppression to preach atheism? There is a sinister suggestion in this idea, namely the suggestion that we ought to preach religion whether or not it is true, and that we ought not to estimate rationally whether it is true, which implies that truth is below comfort in value.

It seems to me that religion buys its benefits at too high a price, namely at the price of abandoning the ideal of truth and shackling and perverting man's reason. The religious man refuses to be guided by reason and evidence in a certain field, the theory of the gods, theology. He does not say: "I believe that there is a god, but I am willing to listen to argument that I

---

*[A famous philosophy lecture series in England.—Eds.]

am mistaken, and I shall be glad to learn better.'' He does not seek to find and adopt the more probable of the two contradictories, ''There is a god'' and ''There is no god.'' On the contrary, he makes his choice between those two propositions once for all. He is determined never to revise his choice, but to believe that there is a god no matter what the evidence. The secretary of the Christian Evidence Society wrote to *The Times** (March 19, 1953) and said: ''When demand is made upon devout Christians to produce evidence in justification of their intense faith in God they are apt to feel surprised, pained, and even disgusted that any such evidence should be considered necessary.'' That is true. Christians do not take the attitude of reasonable inquiry toward the proposition that there is a god. If they engage in discussion on the matter at all, they seek more often to intimidate their opponent by expressing shock or disgust at his opinion, or disapproval of his character. They take the view that to hold the negative one of these two contradictories is a moral crime. They make certain beliefs wicked as such, without reference to the question whether the man has reached them sincerely and responsibly. This view, that certain beliefs are as such wicked, is implied in these two sentences in John's gospel (xvi. 8–9 and xx. 29): ''He will reprove the world of sin . . . because they believe not on me,'' and ''Blessed are they that have not seen, and yet have believed.'' There is an extensive example of this attitude in Newman's† fifteenth sermon.

Along with the view that certain beliefs are as such wicked, there often goes, naturally, the view that it is wicked to try to persuade a person to hold certain beliefs. The believer's complaint, ''You are undermining my faith,'' implies that it is wrong as such to try to convince a man that there is no god. It implies that whether one believes the proposition or not, and whether one has a good reason to believe it or not, are irrelevant, because it is just wrong in itself to recommend this proposition. This view is contrary to the search for truth and the reasonable attitude of listening to argument and guiding oneself thereby.

If theology were a part of reasonable inquiry, there would be no objection to an atheist's being a professor of theology. That a man's being an atheist is an absolute bar to his occupying a chair of theology proves that theology is not an open-minded and reasonable inquiry. Someone may object that a professor should be interested in his subject and an atheist cannot be interested in theology. But a man who maintains that there is no god must think it a sensible and interesting question to ask whether there is a god; and in fact we find that many atheists are interested in theology. Professor H. D. Lewis tells (*Philosophy*, 1952, p. 347) that an old lady asked him what phi-

---

*[Of London.—Eds.]
†[Newman was a 19th century English writer and a Roman Catholic cardinal.—Eds.]

losophy is, and, when he had given an answer, she said: "O I see, theology." She was nearly right, for theology and philosophy have the same subject-matter. The difference is that in philosophy you are allowed to come out with whichever answer seems to you the more likely.

In most universities the title of theology includes a lot of perfectly good science which is not theory of god, and which I do not reject, I mean the scientific study of the history of the Jews and their languages and their religious books. All that can be reasonable study, and usually is so. But it is a hindrance to the progress of knowledge that we are largely organized for research in such a way that a man cannot be officially paid to engage in these branches of research unless he officially maintains that there is a god. It is as if a man could not be a professor of Greek unless he believed in Zeus and Apollo.*

Religious persons often consider gambling to be a bad thing. It certainly causes a great deal of misery. But much of the badness of gambling consists in its refusal to face the probabilities and be guided by them; and in the matter of refusing to face the probabilities religion is a worse offender than gambling, and does more harm to the habits of reason. Religious belief is, in fact, a form of gambling, as Pascal saw. It does more harm to reason than ordinary gambling does, however, because it is more in earnest.

It has been said that the physicist has just as closed a mind about cause as the Christian has about god. The physicist assumes through thick and thin that everything happens according to causal laws. He presupposes cause, just as the Christian presupposes god.

But the physicist does not *assume* that there is a reign of law; he hopes that there is. He looks for laws; but whenever a possible law occurs to him, he conscientiously tries to disprove it by all reasonable tests. He asserts at any time only such laws as seem at that time to have passed all reasonable tests, and he remains always prepared to hear of new evidence throwing doubt on those laws. This is far from the Christian attitude about god. The Christian does not merely hope that there is a god and maintain only such gods as the best tests have shown to be more probable than improbable.

The main irrationality of religion is preferring comfort to truth; and it is this that makes religion a very harmful thing on balance, a sort of endemic disease that has so far prevented human life from reaching its full stature. For the sake of comfort and security religion is prepared to sophisticate thought and language to any degree. For the sake of comfort and security there pours out daily, from pulpit and press, a sort of propaganda which, if it were put out for a nonreligious purpose, would be seen by everyone to be cynical and immoral. We are perpetually being urged to adopt the Christian creed not because it is true but because it is beneficial, or to hold that it

*[Greek gods.—Eds.]

must be true just because belief in it is beneficial. "The Christian faith," we are assured, "is a necessity for a fully adjusted personality" (a psychiatrist in the *Radio Times* for March 20, 1953, p. 33). Hardly a week passes without someone recommending theism on the ground that if it were believed there would be much less crime; and this is a grossly immoral argument. Hardly a week passes without someone recommending theism on the ground that unless it is believed the free nations will succumb to the Communists; and that is the same grossly immoral argument. It is always wicked to recommend anybody to believe anything on the ground he or anybody else will feel better or be more moral or successful for doing so, or on any ground whatever except that the available considerations indicate that it is probably true. The pragmatic suggestion, that we had better teach the Christian religion whether it is true or not, because people will be much less criminal if they believe it, is disgusting and degrading; but it is being made to us all the time, and it is a natural consequence of the fundamental religious attitude that comfort and security must always prevail over rational inquiry.

This pragmatic fallacy is not the only fallacy into which religion is frequently led by preferring comfortingness to truth, though it is the main one. The religious impulse encourages all the fallacies. It encourages the argument *ad hominem*,* that is the argument that my adversary's view must be false because he is a wicked man: The atheist is impious, therefore he is wicked, therefore his view is false. Religion encourages also the argument from ignorance: Instead of rejecting a proposition if it is probably false, the religious man thinks himself entitled to accept it because it is not certainly false. Biased selection of the instances is also very common in religious language. Any case of a man getting his wish after praying for it, or being struck by lightning after doing something mean, is taken as good evidence that there is a god who gives and punishes. Contrary cases are not looked for; and if they obtrude themselves they are dealt with by the further hypothesis that "God's ways are inscrutable." Religious arguments even exhibit, very often, what seems the most fallacious possible fallacy, namely inferring a theory from something that contradicts the theory. Thus we often find: "Since no explanation is final, God is the final explanation"; and "Since everybody believes in God, you are wrong not to believe in God."

I have been saying that religion is gravely infected with intellectual dishonesty. You may find this very unlikely for a general reason. You may think it very unlikely that such widespread dishonesty would go unnoticed. I do not think so. I think, on the contrary, that it is quite common for a moral defect to pervade a certain sphere and yet escape notice in that sphere, although the people concerned are wide awake to its presence in other places. I think there are plenty of other cases of this. One of them is

*[To or against the man.—Eds.]

that the English, who are greater haters of the bully and the might-is-right man, nevertheless bully and intimidate each other when driving a car. They know that power does not confer any right, but they assume that horse-power does. Life is full of such inconsistencies, because we can never see all the implications and applications of our principles. In religion it is particularly easy for intellectual dishonesty to escape notice, because of the common assumption that all honesty flows from religion and religion is necessarily honest whatever it does.

II. FAITH

According to Christianity one of the great virtues is faith. Paul gave faith a commanding position in the Christian scheme of values, along with hope and love, in the famous thirteenth chapter of his first letter to the Corinthians. Thomas Aquinas* held that infidelity is a very great sin, that infidels should be compelled to believe, that heretics should not be tolerated, and that heretics who revert to the true doctrine and then relapse again should not be received into penitence, but killed (*Summa Theologica*, 2-2, 1-16).

According to me this is a terrible mistake, and faith is not a virtue but a positive vice. More precisely, there is, indeed, a virtue often called faith, but that is not the faith which the Christians make much of. The true virtue of faith is faith as opposed to faithlessness, that is, keeping faith and promises and being loyal. Christian faith, however, is not opposed to faithlessness but to unbelief. It is faith as some opposite of unbelief that I declare to be a vice.

When we investigate what Christians mean by their peculiar use of the word "faith," I think we come to the remarkable conclusion that all their accounts of it are either unintelligible or false. Their most famous account is that in Heb. xi. 1: "Faith is the substance of things hoped for, the evidence of things not seen." This is obviously unintelligible. In any case, it does not make faith a virtue, since neither a substance nor an evidence can be a virtue. A virtue is a praiseworthy habit of choice, and neither a substance nor an evidence can be a habit of choice. When a Christian gives an intelligible account of faith, I think you will find that it is false. I mean that it is not a true dictionary report of how he and other Christians actually use the word. For example, Augustine* asked: "What is faith but believing what you do not see?" (*Joannis Evang. Tract.*, c. 40, § 8). But Christians do not use the word "faith" in the sense of believing what you do not see. You do not see thunder; but you cannot say in the Christian sense: "Have faith that it

---

*[A medieval theologian.—Eds.]

is thundering,'' or ''I have faith that it has thundered in the past and will again in the future.'' You do not see mathematical truths; but you cannot say in the Christian sense: ''Have faith that there is no greatest number.'' If we take Augustine's ''see'' to stand here for ''know,'' still it is false that Christians use the word ''faith'' to mean believing what you do not know, for they would never call it faith if anyone believed that the sun converts hydrogen into helium, although he did not know it.

A good hint of what Christians really mean by their word ''faith'' can be got by considering the proposition: ''Tom Paine had faith that there is no god.'' Is this a possible remark, in the Christian sense of the word ''faith''? No, it is an impossible remark, because it is self-contradictory, because part of what Christians mean by ''faith'' is belief that there *is* a god.

There is more to it than this. Christian faith is not merely believing that there is a god. It is believing that there is a god no matter what the evidence on the question may be. ''Have faith,'' in the Christian sense, means ''Make yourself believe that there is a god without regard to evidence.'' Christian faith is a habit of flouting reason in forming and maintaining one's answer to the question whether there is a god. Its essence is the determination to believe that there is a god no matter what the evidence may be.

No wonder that there is no true and intelligible account of faith in Christian literature. What they mean is too shocking to survive exposure. Faith is a great vice, an example of obstinately refusing to listen to reason, something irrational and undesirable, a form of self-hypnotism. Newman wrote that ''if we but obey God strictly, in time (through his blessing) faith will become like sight'' (*Sermon* 15). This is no better than if he had said: ''Keep on telling yourself that there is a god until you believe it. Hypnotize yourself into this belief.''

It follows that, far from its being wicked to undermine faith, it is a duty to do so. We ought to do what we can toward eradicating the evil habit of believing without regard to evidence.

The usual way of recommending faith is to point out that belief and trust are often rational or necessary attitudes. Here is an example of this from Newman: ''To hear some men speak (I mean men who scoff at religion), it might be thought we never acted on Faith or Trust, except in religious matters; whereas we are acting on trust every hour of our lives. . . . We trust our *memory* . . . the general soundness of our reasoning powers. . . . Faith in (the) sense of *reliance on the words of another* as opposed to trust in oneself . . . is the common meaning of the word'' (*Sermon* 15).

The value of this sort of argument is as follows. It is certainly true that belief and trust are often rational. But it is also certainly true that belief and trust are often irrational. We have to decide in each case by rational considerations whether to believe and trust or not. Sometimes we correctly decide not to trust our memory on some point, but to look the matter up in a book.

Sometimes even we correctly decide not to trust our own reason, like poor Canning deciding he was mad because the Duke of Wellington told him he was. But Christian faith is essentially a case of irrational belief and trust and decision, because it consists in deciding to believe and trust the proposition that there is a god no matter what the evidence may be.

Another common way to defend Christian faith is to point out that we are often obliged to act on something less than knowledge and proof. For example, Newman writes: "Life is not long enough for a religion of inferences; we shall never have done beginning if we determine to begin with proof. Life is for action. If we insist on proof for everything, we shall never come to action; to act you must assume, and that assumption is faith" (*Assent*, p. 92).

The value of this argument is as follows. It is true that we are often unable to obtain knowledge and proof. But it does not follow that we must act on faith, for faith is belief reckless of evidence and probability. It follows only that we must act on some belief that does not amount to knowledge. This being so, we ought to assume, as our basis for action, those beliefs which are more probable than their contradictories in the light of the available evidence. We ought not to act on faith, for faith is assuming a certain belief without reference to its probability.

There is an ambiguity in the phrase "have faith in" that helps to make faith look respectable. When a man says that he has faith in the president he is assuming that it is obvious and known to everybody that there is a president, that the president exists, and he is asserting his confidence that the president will do good work on the whole. But if a man says he has faith in telepathy, he does not mean that he is confident that telepathy will do good work on the whole, but that he believes that telepathy really occurs sometimes, that telepathy exists. Thus the phrase "to have faith in x" sometimes means to be confident that good work will be done by x, who is assumed or known to exist, but at other times means to believe that x exists. Which does it mean in the phrase "have faith in God"? It means ambiguously both; and the self-evidence of what it means in the one sense recommends what it means in the other sense. If there is a perfectly powerful and good god it is self-evidently reasonable to believe that he will do good. In this sense "Have faith in God" is a reasonable exhortation. But it insinuates the other sense, namely "Believe that there is a perfectly powerful and good god, no matter what the evidence." Thus the reasonableness of trusting God if he exists is used to make it seem also reasonable to believe that he exists.

It is well to remark here that a god who wished us to decide certain questions without regard to the evidence would definitely *not* be a perfectly good god.

Even when a person is aware that faith is belief without regard to evidence, he may be led to hold faith respectable by the consideration that we sometimes think it good for a man to believe in his friend's honesty in spite of strong evidence to the contrary, or for a woman to believe in her son's innocence in spite of strong evidence to the contrary. But while we admire and love the love that leads the friend or parent to this view, we do not adopt or admire his conclusion unless we believe that he has private evidence of his own, gained by his long and intimate association, to outweigh the public evidence on the other side. Usually we suppose that his love has led him into an error of judgment, which both love and hate are prone to do.

This does not imply that we should never act on a man's word if we think he is deceiving us. Sometimes we ought to act on a man's word although we privately think he is probably lying. For the act required may be unimportant, whereas accusing a man of lying is always important. But there is no argument from this to faith. We cannot say that sometimes we ought to believe a proposition although we think it is false!

So I conclude that faith is a vice and to be condemned. As Plato* said, "It is unholy to abandon the probably true" (*Rp.* 607 c). Out of Paul's† "faith, hope, and love" I emphatically accept love and reject faith. As to hope, it is more respectable than faith. While we ought not to believe against the probabilities, we are permitted to hope against them. But still the Christian overtones of hope are other-worldly and unrealistic. It is better to take a virtue that avoids that. Instead of faith, hope, and love, let us hymn reason, love, and joy.

What is the application of this to the common phrase "a faith to live by"? A faith to live by is not necessarily a set of beliefs or valuations maintained without regard to evidence in an irrational way. The phrase can well cover also a criticized and rational choice of values. To decide, for example, that the pursuit of love is better than the pursuit of power, in view of the probable effects of each on human happiness and misery, and to guide one's actions accordingly, is a rational procedure, and is sometimes called and may well be called "a faith to live by." In this case a faith to live by is a choice of values, a decision as to great goods and evils. . . . On the other hand, many "faiths to live by" are irrational and bad. Some people will not count anything as a faith to live by unless it deliberately ignores rational considerations; so that what they will consent to call a faith to live by must always be something that is bad according to me. Other people refuse to count anything as a faith to live by unless it includes a belief that the big battalions are on their side, so that according to them a man who rationally concludes that he is not the darling of any god by definition has no faith to live by. . . .

---

*[A philosopher of ancient Greece.—Eds.]
†[The apostle.—Eds.]

STUDY QUESTIONS

1. According to McCloskey, why is the fact of evil a problem for the theist?

2. What are the two general kinds of evil? State the proposed solutions to each. State McCloskey's criticisms of those solutions.

3. What conclusion(s) does McCloskey defend? State his arguments in behalf of those conclusion(s), and critically evaluate them.

4. Why does Hick rule out certain solutions to the problem of evil? Do you agree that they should be ruled out? Why or why not?

5. In your view, who has dealt with the problem of evil most adequately, Hick or McCloskey? Why?

6. What is the main claim that Taylor defends? What are his reasons for it?

7. State Robinson's main theses in "Religion, Reason, and Faith." State his arguments in behalf of these theses. Critically evaluate his position.

8. Why does Robinson hold that faith is a vice? Do you agree? Why or why not?

9. In "The Will to Believe" (see Part One), does William James provide a justifiable answer to Robinson's criticisms? Why or why not?

10. Adopt Robinson's standpoint and reply to James.

11. Evaluate the following: "The problem of evil is no problem at all for Christianity because any amount of pain and misery on earth is nothing compared with the infinite and eternal happiness which Christianity promises."

12. St. Augustine maintained that, although we think there are natural evils, in fact there are none. We think this way because we are not able to comprehend things as they really are. If we could view an earthquake or tornado or plague through God's eyes, we would see that it was just the right thing to occur at that particular place and time. Critically evaluate this argument.

13. The French philosopher Pascal held that the way to decide whether or not to believe in the existence of God is to ask whether believing or disbelieving is better and then bet accordingly. He maintains:

> If we wager that God exists and he does, then we gain eternal bliss; if he does not, we have lost nothing. If we wager that God does not exist and he does, then eternal misery is our share; if he does not, we gain only a lucky true belief. The obvious wager is to bet God exists. With such a bet we have everything to gain

and nothing to lose. This is far superior to a bet where we have little to gain and everything to lose.

This is known as "Pascal's Wager." Evaluate this attempt to justify belief in God.

14. Would someone who accepts the existence of God on faith be acting in a manner which is consistent with the aims of philosophy discussed in the introduction to this book? Why or why not?

Further Readings

A. The Problem of Evil

Hick, John. *Evil and the God of Love*. New York: Harper & Row, 1966. [An attempt by a religious believer to solve the problem of evil.]

Hume, David. *Dialogues Concerning Natural Religion*. New York: Haffner, 1961. Pts. 10 and 11. [A vigorous formulation and discussion of the problem, along with criticisms of some of the classical arguments for the existence of God.]

Mackie, J. L. "Evil and Omnipotence." *Mind*, 64 (1955), 200–212. [A more technical but forceful statement of the argument from evil against belief in God.]

Madden, Edward H. "The Many Faces of Evil." *Philosophy and Phenomenological Research*, 24 (1964), 481–492. [A thorough examination of the problem by a nonbeliever.]

Pike, Nelson, ed. *God and Evil*. Englewood Cliffs, N.J.: Prentice-Hall, 1964. [A collection of classical and recent discussions of the problem from various stand points.]

B. Religious Faith

Hick, John. *Faith and Knowledge*, 2nd ed. Ithaca, N.Y.: Cornell University Press, 1960. [An eloquent defense of religious faith.]

Hick, John. "Faith as Experiencing—As." In G. N. A. Vesy, *Talk of God*. New York: Macmillan, 1959. [Provides a new interpretation of the nature of faith.]

Kaufman, Walter. *The Faith of a Heretic*. Garden City, N.Y.: Doubleday, 1961. [A vigorous and readable work presenting the view against religious faith.]

Martin, C. B. *Religious Belief*. Ithaca, N.Y.: Cornell University Press, 1959. [A contemporary criticism of religious belief.]

Mitchell, Basil, ed. *Faith and Logic*. London: Allen & Unwin, 1957. [A collection of essays on religious faith and related topics by several contemporary thinkers.]

PART EIGHT

MEANING AND EXISTENCE

PREVIEW

In the *Myth of Sisyphus* Camus writes,

> There is but one truly philosophical problem, and that is suicide. Judging whether life is or is not worth living amounts to answering the fundamental question of philosophy. All the rest—whether the world has three dimensions, whether the mind has nine or twelve categories—comes afterwards. These are games; one must first answer. . . .
>
> If I ask myself how to judge that this question is more urgent than that, I reply that one judges by the actions it entails. I have never seen anyone die for the ontological argument [for the existence of God]. Galileo, who held a scientific truth of great importance, abjured it with the greatest of ease as soon as it endangered his life. In a certain sense, he did right. That truth was not worth the stake. Whether the earth or the sun revolves around the other is a matter of profound indifference. . . . On the other hand, I see many people die because they judge that life is not worth living. I see others paradoxically getting killed for the ideas or illusions that give them a reason for living (what is called a reason for living is also an excellent reason for dying). I therefore conclude that the meaning of life is the most urgent of questions.[1]

Many people would agree with Camus—even if they would not agree with the somewhat exaggerated manner in which he expresses his view. And surely almost every reflective and sensitive person has asked at one time or another, What is the meaning of life? What is it all about? What is the point of it all? And one tends to feel that if life has no meaning or purpose, then it is not worth living. Hence, surely the question of the meaning of life is one of the most important of all philosophical and "existential" questions. It will, hence, be examined in this part.

[1]A. Camus. *The Myth of Sisyphus* (New York: Knopf, 1955), p. 3.

Of course, some have maintained that there is only one basis for providing meaning to life: God, or at least faith in God. Without the existence of God, or faith in his existence, life would have no meaning or purpose and, hence, would not be worth living. Others have also held that the scientific view of the world has led to a rejection of belief in God and, hence, to the result that life is meaningless. These claims need to be examined—and will be. This leads us to the main question of this part.

Main Question

The main question dealt with in this part is:

Does (human) life have a meaning and/or purpose?
If so, how? And what sort of meaning is it? If not, why not?

Answers

In turning to possible answers to this question, we find three main approaches or stances. These positions have no commonly accepted labels. Hence, we shall designate them by descriptive phrases, as follows:

a. The theistic answer. The theist maintains that the meaning of life can be found only in the existence of God or through faith in God's existence. Without the existence of God, or faith in God, life has no meaning, no purpose, and, hence, is not worth living.

b. The nontheistic alternative. Many people have questioned the theistic answer. In their view even if life has no meaning or purpose on any grand, cosmic scale, this does not entail that it has no meaning or purpose at all. On the contrary, it is maintained that, by denying such objective meaning or purpose, humans are free to forge their own meaning and purpose, and to do so within the bounds of the natural universe. No appeal to something which transcends the natural universe is required in order to give life genuine meaning and purpose. Hence, the theist's conclusion does not follow. Since meaning and purpose can be found without faith in God, life can be genuinely worth living without such faith.

c. The approach which questions the meaningfulness of the question. Some have maintained that "What is the meaning of life?" is an odd question. It is one which stems from confusion or for which there is no possible means to find a significant answer. Hence, the question itself is meaningless.

In summary, we have these answers to our question:

a. The theistic answer: Without God or faith in God, life can have no meaning or purpose and, hence, would be not worth living.

b. The nontheistic alternative: Life can have meaning and purpose and, hence, be worthwhile even if we give up the belief in God. Meaning is independent of God.

c. The third approach: The whole question, "What is the meaning of life?" is itself meaningless.

Selections

The readings in this part give attention to all of these alternative answers to the question of whether life has meaning and are represented as follows:

Answer	Selection
(a) Theistic answer	35
(b) Nontheistic alternative	36
(c) Meaningless approach	37
(d) Critique of (c)	38

35 / The Dignity of Human Life

DAVID F. SWENSON

[I. THE NEED FOR A VIEW OF LIFE]

Man lives forward, but he thinks backward. As an active being, his task is to press forward to the things that are before, toward the goal where is the prize of the high calling. But as a thinking, active being, his forward movement is conditioned by a retrospect. If there were no past for a man, there could be no future; and if there were no future and no past, but only such an immersion in the present as is characteristic of the brute which perisheth, then there would be nothing eternal in human life, and everything distinctively and essentially human would disappear from our existence.

As a preparation for an existence in the present, the youth of a nation are trained in various skills and along devious lines, according to their capacities and circumstances, for the parts they are to play in existence; their natural talents are developed, some by extended periods of intellectual training, others for participation in various forms of business or technical training; but whatever be the ultimate end of the training, its purpose is to develop those latent powers they possess which will eventually prove of benefit to themselves or to others. But, in addition to this, which we may call a preparation for the external life, a something else is urgently needed, a something so fundamentally important that in its absence every other form of preparation is revealed as imperfect and incomplete, even ineffective and futile.

This so particularly indispensable something is a *view of life*, and a view of life is not acquired as a direct and immediate result of a course of study, the reading of books, or a communication of results. It is wholly a product of the individual's own knowledge of himself as an individual, of his individual capabilities and aspirations. A view of life is a principle of living, a spirit and an attitude capable of maintaining its unity and identity with itself in all of life's complexities and varying vicissitudes; and yet also capable of being declined, to use the terminology of the grammatical sciences, in all the infinite variety of cases that the language of life affords. Without this preparation the individual life is like a ship without a rudder, a bit of wreckage floating with the current to an uncomprehended destiny. A view of life is not objective knowledge, but subjective conviction. It is a part of man's own self, the source whence the stream of his life issues. It is the dominant attitude of the spirit which gives to life its direction and its goal. This is why it cannot be directly communicated or conveyed, like an article of commerce, from one person to another. If a view of life were a body of knowledge about life, or a direct and immediate implication from such knowledge, it would be subject to objective communication and systematic instruction. But it is rather a personal expression of what a man essentially is in his own inmost self, and this cannot be learned by rote, or accepted at the hands of some external authority. Knowledge is the answer or answers that things give to the questions we ask of them; a view of life is the reply a person gives to the question that life asks of him. We begin life by scrutinizing our environment, ourselves playing the role of questioners and examiners and critics; but at a later moment, when the soul comes of age and is about to enter upon its majority, it learns that the tables have been turned and the roles reversed; from that moment it confronts a question, a searching and imperative question, in relation to which no evasion can avail, and to which no shifting of responsibility is possible.

In discussing the problem of *a view of life which can give it meaning and dignity and worth*, I am well aware that no one can acquire a view of life by listening to a speech.* Nevertheless, a speech may serve the more modest purpose of stimulating a search, perhaps a more earnest search; and may render more articulate possibly the convictions of those who have already won some such conception, having made it their own by a heartfelt and spontaneous choice.

[II. ONE APPROACH]

All men are endowed by nature with a desire for happiness—a principle so obvious as scarcely to need any explanation, and certainly no defense. A human life without happiness or hope of happiness is not a life, but rather a death in life. Happiness is life's vital fluid and the very breath of its nostrils. Happiness and life are so much one and the same thing that the more profoundly any life discovers happiness, the more significant and abundant is that life itself. . . .

But for a thinking human being—and God made every man a thinker, whatever may be our estimate of that which men make of themselves—for a thinking human being, happiness cannot consist in the satisfaction of momentary impulse, of blind feeling, of brute immediacy. A pleasant absorption in the present, oblivious of prospect or retrospect, careless of the wider relations or the deeper truth of life, can be called happiness only on the basis of frivolity and thoughtlessness. Just as life is not life unless it is happy, so happiness is not happiness unless it can be justified. In order really to be happiness it requires to be interpenetrated with a sense of *meaning, reason,* and *worth*.

---

*[This essay was originally presented as an address to an audience.—Eds.]

For the quest of happiness, like every other human quest, faces a danger. The danger that confronts it is the possibility of error: the error of permitting oneself to be lured into promising paths that lead to no goal, and the error of coming to rest in hollow satisfactions and empty joys. It is possible to believe oneself happy, to seem happy to oneself and to others, and yet in reality to be plunged in the deepest misery; just as, on the other hand, it is possible to stand possessed of the greatest treasure, and yet, in thoughtlessness, to imagine oneself destitute, and through that very thoughtlessness not only neglect and ignore but actually deprive oneself of what one already has. The basic problem of life, the question in response to which a view of life seeks to propound an answer, may therefore be formulated as follows: What is that happiness which is also a genuine and lasting good? In what does it consist, and how may it be attained?

There exists an ancient handbook, an *Art of Rhetoric*, compiled for the guidance and information of orators and other public speakers, written by one of the greatest of Greek philosophers. In this handbook the author formulates the commonly prevailing conceptions of happiness as among the things useful for public speakers to know. . . . Happiness is said to be commonly defined as independence of life, as prosperity with virtue, as comfortable circumstances with security, or as the enjoyment of many possessions, together with the power to keep and defend them. Its constituent elements are noble birth, wealth, many good and influential friends, bodily health and beauty, talents and capacities, good fortune, honors, and lastly virtue. We readily perceive how strange and old-fashioned these conceptions are, how foreign to all our modern and enlightened notions. I shall therefore subjoin a more up-to-date consideration of the same subject, derived from a very modern author writing in a journal of today. The author raises the question as to what circumstances and conditions have the power to make him feel really alive, tingling with vitality, instinct with the joy of living. He submits a long list including a variety of things, of which I shall quote the chief: the sense of health; successful creative work, like writing books; good food and drink; pleasant surroundings; praise, not spread on too thick; friends and their company; beautiful things, books, music; athletic exercises and sports; daydreaming; a good fight in a tolerably decent cause; the sense of bodily danger escaped; the consciousness of being a few steps ahead of the wolf of poverty. . . . So speaks our modern writer. And now that I have juxtaposed these two accounts, I have to confess to the strange feeling that, despite the interval of more than two thousand years between them, they sound unexpectedly alike. . . . How strange to find such a similarity! Can it be that after all that has been said and written about the revolutionary and radical changes introduced into life by modern science, modern invention, and modern industry, the influence of the steam engine and the printing press, the telegraph and the radio, the automobile and the airplane, together with the absolutely devastating discoveries of astronomers—can it be, in spite of all this, that the current conceptions of life and its meaning have remained essentially unchanged? . . .

[III. PROBLEMS WITH THAT APPROACH]

However that may be, I do not think that anyone will deny that such views as these are widely held, and constitute the view of life perhaps of the majority of men. . . . But there are serious difficulties in the way of constructing a view of life out of such considerations.

[1.] The constituents of happiness are in both cases a multiplicity of things. . . . But the self which sets its heart upon any such multiplicity of external goods, which lives in them and by them and for them, dependent upon them for the only happiness it knows—such a self is captive to the diverse world of its desires. It belongs to the world and does not own itself. It is not in the deepest sense a self, since it is not free and is not a unity. The manifold conditions of its happiness split the self asunder; no ruling passion dominates its life; no concentration gives unity to the personality and single-mindedness to the will. Its name is legion, and its nature is double-mindedness. . . .

[2.] Reflection discovers yet another difficulty in connection with such views of life. Whoever seeks his happiness in external conditions, of whatever sort, seeks it in that which is in its essential nature precarious. He presumes upon the realization of conditions which are not intrinsic to him, or within his control. This happiness is subject to the law of uncertainty, to the qualification of an unyielding, mysterious *perhaps*. Here lurks the possibility of despair. Give a man the full satisfaction of his wishes and ambitions, and he deems himself happy; withdraw from him the smile of fortune's favor, and disappoint his expectation and his hope, and he will be plunged into despair. The shift from happiness to unhappiness in such a life is every moment imminent. . . .

[3.] A third consideration. Wealth and power and the like, even bodily health and beauty of person, are not in the strictest sense intrinsic values, but rather representative and comparative, conditional and hypothetical. Money is good—if I have learned how to use it; and so with power and influence, health and strength. But in themselves these things are abstract and neutral, and no man can truthfully say whether the acquirement of them in any individual case will work more good than harm. . . .

[4.] Lastly, it must be pointed out that the conditions of happiness as conceived in all such views of life, inevitably imply a privileged status for the happy individual. They rest upon differential capabilities and exceptionally fortunate circumstances. To choose them as the end and aim of life constitutes an injury to the mass of men who are not so privileged. This one thought alone is of so arresting a quality as to give the deepest concern to every man who has the least trace of human sympathy and human feeling.

I hope I have a soul not entirely a stranger to happy admiration; I know I feel moved to bend low in respect before exceptional talent and perform- ance, and that I am eager to honor greatness and genius wherever I have the gift to understand it. And I am not so unfeeling as to refuse a tribute of sympathetic joy to those who rejoice in fortune's favors and bask in the smiles of outward success. But as the fundamental source of inspiration of my life, I need something that is not exclusive and differential, but inclusive and universal. I require to drink from a spring at which all men may refresh themselves; I need an aim that reconciles me to high and low, rich and poor, cultured and uncultured, sophisticated and simple; to the countless generations of the past as well as to the men and women of the future. I need a spiritual bond that binds me to all human beings in a common un- derstanding of that which is fundamental and essential to human life. To have my life and happiness in that which is inaccessible to the many or to the few, seems to me an act of treason to humanity, a cowardly and pusil- lanimous attack upon the brotherhood of man; for without the inner spiri- tual tie of an essential aim which all can reach and all can understand, the concept of the human race as a spiritual unity is destroyed, and nothing is left of mankind but a biological species, only slightly better equipped than the other animals to cope with the present state of their physical environ- ment.

The difference between man and man are indeed inseparable from this our imperfect temporal existence; but I cannot and will not believe that their development constitutes the perfection of life itself. Rather is this to be found in the discovery and expectation of *something underlying and absolute*, something that can be found by all who seek it in earnest, something to which our lives may give expression, subordinating to its unifying principle the infinite multitude of ends, reducing them to their own relative measure and proportion, and refusing to permit the unimportant to become impor- tant, the relative to become absolute. The possibility of making this discov- ery and of giving it expression is, so it seems to me, *the fundamental meaning of life, the source of its dignity and worth*. The happiness that is found with this discovery is not invidious and divisive, but unifying and reconciling; it does not abrogate the differences, but it destroys their power to wound and to harm, the fortunate through being puffed up in arrogance and pride, the unfortunate through being depressed in envy and disappointment. For this happiness is not denied to any man, no matter how insignificant and humble.

[IV. THE ETHICO-RELIGIOUS VIEW OF LIFE]

Our criticism has brought us to the threshold of an ethical view of life. That the essence of life and its happiness is to be sought in the moral con- sciousness alone is the conviction that animates this address, and gives it its reason for being. This view holds that *the individual human self has an infi-*

nite worth, that *the personality has an external validity*, that *the bringing of this validity to expression in the manifold relations and complications of life is the true task of the self*, that *this task gives to the individual's historical development an infinite significance*, because it is a process through which the personality in its truth and depth comes to its own. "Find your self," says the moral consciousness; "reclaim it in its total and in so far unworthy submergence in relative ends; dare to think the nothingness, the hollowness, the relativity, the precariousness, the lack of intrinsic meaning of that which constitutes the entire realm of the external and the manifold; liberate yourself from slavery to finite ends; have the courage to substitute the one thing needful for the many things wished for, and perhaps desirable, making first things first, and all other things secondary—and you will find that these other things will be added unto you in the measure in which you require them and can use them as servants and ministers of your highest good."

So speaks the voice within us, a still small voice, a soft whisper easily overwhelmed by the noise and traffic of life, but a voice, nevertheless, which no one can permit to be silenced except at the cost of acquiring restlessness instead of peace, anxiety instead of trust and confidence, a distracted spirit instead of harmony with one's self. The moral spirit finds the meaning of life in choice. It finds it in that which proceeds from man and remains with him as his inner essence rather than in the accidents of circumstance and turns of external fortune. The individual has his end in himself. He is no mere instrument in the service of something external, nor is he the slave of some powerful master; nor of a class, a group, or party; nor of the state or nation; nor even of humanity itself, as an abstraction solely external to the individual. Essentially and absolutely he is an end; only accidentally and relatively is he a means. And this is true of the meanest wage slave, so called, in industry's impersonal machine—precisely as true of him as it is of the greatest genius or the most powerful ruler.

Is there anyone so little stout-hearted, so effeminately tender, so extravagantly in love with an illusory and arbitrary freedom, as to feel that the glorious promise of such a view of life is ruined, its majestic grandeur shriveled into cramped pettiness, because the task which it offers the individual is not only an invitation, but also an obligation as well? Shall we confess that we cannot endure this "Thou must" spoken to ourselves,[1] even when the voice proceeds from no external power but from our inmost self, there where the human strikes its roots into the *divine*? Truly, it is this "Thou must" that is the *eternal* guarantee or our calling, the savior of our hope, the inspirer of our energy, the preserver of our aim against the shiftings of feeling and the vicissitudes of circumstance. It steels the will and makes it fast; it gives courage to begin after failure; it is the triumph over despondency and despair. For *duty is the eternal in a man, or that by which he lays hold of the eternal; and only through the eternal can a man become a conqueror of the life of*

[1]Suggested by Emerson's "So nigh is grandeur to our dust." *Voluntaries.*

time. It is in the moral consciousness that a man begins truly to sense *the presence of God*; and every religion that has omitted the ethical is in so far a misunderstanding of religion, reducing it to myth and poetry, having significance only for the imagination, but not for the whole nature of man as concrete reality. The moral consciousness is a lamp, a wonderful lamp; but not like the famous lamp of Aladdin,[2] which when rubbed had the power to summon a spirit, a willing servant ready and able to fulfill every wish. But whenever a human being rubs the lamp of his moral consciousness with moral passion, a Spirit does appear. This Spirit is God, and the Spirit is master and lord, and man becomes his servant. But this service is man's true freedom, for a derivative spirit like man, who certainly has not made himself, or given himself his own powers, cannot in truth impose upon himself the law of his own being. It is in the ''Thou must'' of God and man's ''I can'' that the divine image of God in human life is contained, to which an ancient book refers when it asserts that God made man in his own image. That is the inner glory, the spiritual garb of man, which transcends the wonderful raiment with which the Author of the universe has clothed the lilies of the field, raiment which in its turn puts to shame the royal purple of Solomon. The lilies of the field[3] cannot hear the voice of duty or obey its call; hence they cannot bring their will into harmony with the divine will. In the capacity to do this lies man's unique distinction among all creatures; here is his self, his independence, his glory and his crown.

I know that all men do not share this conviction. Youth is often too sure of its future. The imagination paints the vision of success and fortune in the rosiest tints; the sufferings and disappointments of which one hears are for youth but the exception that proves the rule; the instinctive and blind faith of youth is in the relative happiness of some form of external success. Maturity, on the other hand, has often learned to be content with scraps and fragments, wretched crumbs saved out of the disasters on which its early hopes suffered shipwreck. Youth pursues an ideal that is illusory; age has learned, O wretched wisdom! to do without an ideal altogether. But the ideal is there, implanted in the heart and mind of man by his Maker, and no mirages of happiness or clouds of disappointment, not the stupor of habit or the frivolity of thoughtlessness, can entirely erase the sense of it from the depths of the soul. . . .

Let us but learn to perceive that no differential talent, no privileged status, no fortunate eventuality, can at bottom be worthwhile as a consummation; that all such things are quite incapable of dignifying life; and when the misunderstandings with respect to the nature of a moral consciousness have been cleared away, the road will be open to the discovery of man as man. A preoccupation with the secondary thoughts and interests of life is

[2]S. Kierkegaard, *Postscript*, p. 124.
[3]S. Kierkegaard, *The Gospel of Suffering*, pp. 174–177.

always exhausting and trivializing, and in the end bewildering. Our true refreshment and invigoration will come through going back to the first and simplest thoughts, the primary and indispensable interests. We have too long lost ourselves in anxious considerations of what it may mean to be a shoemaker or a philosopher, a poet or a millionaire; in order to find ourselves, it is needful that we concentrate our energies upon the infinitely significant problem of what it means simply to be a man, without any transiently qualifying adjectives. When Frederick the Great asked his Court preacher if he knew anything about the future life, the preacher answered, "Yes, Your Majesty, it is absolutely certain that in the future life Your Highness will not be king of Prussia." And so it is; we were men before we became whatever of relative value we became in life, and we shall doubtless be human beings long after what we thus became or acquired will have lost its significance for us. On the stage some actors have roles in which they are royal and important personages; others are simple folk, beggars, workingmen, and the like. But when the play is over and the curtain is rolled down, the actors cast aside their disguises, the differences vanish, and all are once more simply actors. So, when the play of life is over, and the curtain is rolled down upon the scene, the differences and relativities which have disguised the men and women who have taken part will vanish, and all will be simply human beings. But there is this difference between the actors of the stage and the actors of life. On the stage it is imperative that the illusion be maintained to the highest degree possible; an actor who plays the role of king as if he was an actor, or who too often reminds us that he is assuming a role, is precisely a poor actor. But on the stage of life, the reverse is the case. There it is the task, not to preserve, but to expose, the illusion; to win free from it while still retaining one's disguise. The disguising garment ought to flutter loosely about us, so loosely that the least wind of human feeling that blows may reveal the royal purple of humanity beneath. This revelation is the moral task; the moral consciousness is the consciousness of the dignity that invests human life when the personality has discovered itself, and is happy in the will to be itself.

Such is the view of life to which the present speaker is committed. He has sought to make it seem inviting, but not for a moment has he wished to deny that it sets a difficult task for him who would express it in the daily intercourse of life. Perhaps it has long since captured our imaginations; for it is no new gospel worked out to satisfy the imaginary requirements of the most recent fashions in human desire and feeling; on the contrary, it is an old, old view. But it is not enough that the truth of the significance inherent in having such a view of life should be grasped by the imagination, or by the elevated mood of a solemn hour; only the heart's profound movement, the will's decisive commitment,[4] can make that which is truth in general also a truth for me.

---

[4]*Postscript*, p. 226.

36 / The Meaning of Life

KURT BAIER

I. INTRODUCTION

Tolstoy,* in his autobiographical work, "A Confession," reports how, when he was fifty and at the height of his literary success, he came to be obsessed by the fear that life was meaningless.

"At first I experienced moments of perplexity and arrest of life, as though I did not know what to do or how to live; and I felt lost and became dejected. But this passed, and I went on living as before. Then these moments of perplexity began to recur oftener and oftener, and always in the same form. They were always expressed by the questions: What is it for? What does it lead to? At first it seemed to me that these were aimless and irrelevant questions. I thought that it was all well known, and that if I should ever wish to deal with the solution it would not cost me much effort; just at present I had no time for it, but when I wanted to, I should be able to find the answer. The questions however began to repeat themselves frequently, and to demand replies more and more insistently, and like drops of ink always falling on one place they ran together into one black blot."[1]

[1.] A Christian living in the Middle Ages would not have felt any serious doubts about Tolstoy's questions. To him it would have seemed quite certain that life had a meaning, and quite clear what it was. The medieval Christian world picture assigned to man a highly significant, indeed the central part in the grand scheme of things. The universe was made for the express purpose of providing a stage on which to enact a drama starring Man in the title role.

[According to this view,] . . . the world was created by God in the year 4004 B.C. Man was the last and the crown of this creation, made in the likeness of God, placed in the Garden of Eden on earth, the fixed center of the universe, around which revolved the nine heavens of the sun, the moon, the planets, and the fixed stars, producing as they revolved in their orbits the heavenly harmony of the spheres. And this gigantic universe was created for the enjoyment of man, who was originally put in control of it. Pain and death were unknown in paradise. But this state of bliss was not to last.

---

[1]Count Leo Tolstoy, "A Confession," reprinted in *A Confession, The Gospel in Brief, and What I Believe*, no. 229, The World's Classics (London: Geoffrey Cumberlege, 1940).

*[A 19th century Russian novelist and thinker.—Eds.]

Adam and Eve ate of the forbidden tree of knowledge, and life on this earth turned into a death-march through a vale of tears. Then, with the birth of Jesus, new hope came into the world. After He had died on the cross, it became at least possible to wash away with the purifying water of baptism some of the effects of Original Sin and to achieve salvation. That is to say, on condition of obedience to the law of God, man could now enter heaven and regain the state of everlasting, deathless bliss from which he had been excluded because of the sin of Adam and Eve.

To the medieval Christian the meaning of human life was therefore perfectly clear. The stretch on earth is only a short interlude, a temporary incarceration of the soul in the prison of the body, a brief trial and test, fated to end in death, the release from pain and suffering. What really matters is the life after the death of the body. One's existence acquires meaning not by gaining what this life can offer but by saving one's immortal soul from death and eternal torture, by gaining eternal life and everlasting bliss.

[2.] The scientific world picture which has found ever more general acceptance from the beginning of the modern era onwards is in profound conflict with all this. At first, the Christian conception of the world was discovered to be erroneous in various important details. The Copernican theory showed up the earth as merely one of several planets revolving round the sun, and the sun itself was later seen to be merely one of many fixed stars, each of which is itself the nucleus of a solar system similar to our own. Man, instead of occupying the center of creation, proved to be merely the inhabitant of a celestial body no different from millions of others. Furthermore, geological investigations revealed that the universe was not created a few thousand years ago but was probably millions of years old.

Disagreements over details of the world picture, however, are only superficial aspects of a much deeper conflict. The appropriateness of the whole Christian outlook is at issue. For Christianity, the world must be regarded as the "creation" of a kind of Superman, a person possessing all the human excellences to an infinite degree, and none of the human weaknesses, Who has made man in His image, a feeble, mortal, foolish copy of Himself. In creating the universe, God acts as a sort of playwright-cum-legislator-cum-judge-cum-executioner. In the capacity of playwright, He creates the historical world process, including man. He erects the stage and writes, in outline, the plot. He creates the *dramatis personae** and watches over them with the eye partly of a father, partly of the law. While on stage, the actors are free to extemporize, but if they infringe the divine commandments, they are later dealt with by their creator in His capacity of judge and executioner.

Within such a framework, the Christian attitudes toward the world are natural and sound: It is natural and sound to think that all is arranged for

*[Persons of a drama.—Eds.]

the best even if appearances belie it; to resign oneself cheerfully to one's lot; to be filled with awe and veneration in regard to anything and everything that happens; to want to fall on one's knees and worship and praise the Lord. These are wholly fitting attitudes within the framework of the world view just outlined. And this world view must have seemed wholly sound and acceptable because it offered the best explanation which was then available of all the observed phenomena of nature.

As the natural sciences developed, however, more and more things in the universe came to be explained without the assumption of a supernatural creator. Science, moreover, could explain them better, that is, more accurately and more reliably. The Christian hypothesis of a supernatural maker, whatever other needs it was capable of satisfying, was at any rate no longer indispensable for the purpose of explaining the existence or occurrence of anything. In fact, scientific explanations do not seem to leave any room for this hypothesis. The scientific approach demands that we look for a natural explanation of anything and everything. The scientific way of looking at and explaining things has yielded an immensely greater measure of understanding of, and control over, the universe than any other way. And when one looks at the world in this scientific way, there seems to be no room for a personal relationship between human beings and a supernatural perfect being ruling and guiding men. Hence many scientists and educated men have come to feel that the Christian attitudes toward the world and human existence are inappropriate. They have become convinced that the universe and human existence in it are without a purpose and therefore devoid of meaning. . . .[2]

II. THE PURPOSE OF MAN'S EXISTENCE

. . . Complaints such as these do not mean quite the same to everybody, but one thing, I think, they mean to most people: Science shows life to be meaningless, because life is without purpose. The medieval world picture provided life with a purpose; hence medieval Christians could believe that life had a meaning. The scientific account of the world takes away life's purpose and with it its meaning.

There are, however, two quite different senses of "purpose." Which one is meant? Has science deprived life of purpose in both senses? And if not, is it a harmless sense in which human existence has been robbed of purpose? Could human existence still have meaning if it did not have a purpose in that sense?

What are the two senses? In the first and basic sense, purpose is normally attributed only to persons or their behavior, as in "Did you have a purpose

[2]See e.g. Edwyn Bevan, *Christianity*, pp. 211–227. See also H. J. Paton, *The Modern Predicament* (London: George Allen and Unwin Ltd., 1955) pp. 103–116, 374.

in leaving the ignition on?" In the second sense, purpose is normally attributed only to things, as in "What is the purpose of that gadget you installed
in the workshop?" The two uses are intimately connected. We cannot attribute a purpose to a thing without implying that someone did something,
in the doing of which he had some purpose, namely, to bring about the
thing with the purpose. Of course, *his* purpose is not identical with *its* purpose. In hiring laborers and engineers and buying materials and a site for a
factory and the like, the entrepreneur's purpose, let us say, is to manufacture cars, but the purpose of cars is to serve as a means of transportation.

There are many things that a man may do, such as buying and selling,
hiring laborers, plowing, felling trees, and the like, which it is foolish,
pointless, silly, perhaps crazy, to do if one has no purpose in doing them. A
man who does these things without a purpose is engaging in inane, futile
pursuits. Lives crammed full with such activities devoid of purpose are
pointless, futile, worthless. Such lives may indeed be dismissed as meaningless. But it should also be perfectly clear that acceptance of the scientific
world picture does not force us to regard our lives as being without a purpose in this sense. Science has not only not robbed us of any purpose
which we had before, but it has furnished us with enormously greater
power to achieve these purposes. Instead of praying for rain or a good harvest or offspring, we now use ice pellets, artificial manure, or artificial in-
semination.

By contrast, having or not having a purpose, in the other sense, is value
neutral. We do not think more or less highly of a thing for having or not
having a purpose. "Having a purpose," in this sense, confers no kudos,
"being purposeless" carries no stigma. A row of trees growing near a farm
may or may not have a purpose: It may or may not be a windbreak, may or
may not have been planted or deliberately left standing there in order to
prevent the wind from sweeping across the fields. We do not in any way
disparage the trees if we say they have no purpose, but have just grown
that way. They are as beautiful, made of as good wood, as valuable, as if
they had a purpose. And, of course, they break the wind just as well. The
same is true of living creatures. We do not disparage a dog when we say
that it has no purpose, is not a sheep dog or a watch dog or a rabbiting dog,
but just a dog that hangs around the house and is fed by us.

Man is in a different category, however. To attribute to a human being a
purpose in that sense is not neutral, let alone complimentary: It is offensive. It is degrading for a man to be regarded as merely serving a purpose. . . .

The Christian and the scientific world pictures do indeed differ fundamentally on this point. The latter robs man of a purpose in this sense. It
sees him as a being with no purpose allotted to him by anyone but himself.
It robs him of any goal, purpose, or destiny appointed for him by any outside agency. The Christian world picture, on the other hand, sees man as a
creature, a divine artefact, something halfway between a robot (manufac-

tured) and an animal (alive), a homunculus, or perhaps Frankenstein, made in God's laboratory, with a purpose or task assigned him by his Maker.

However, lack of purpose in this sense does not in any way detract from the meaningfulness of life. I suspect that many who reject the scientific outlook because it involves the loss of purpose of life, and therefore meaning, are guilty of a confusion between the two senses of "purpose" just distinguished. They confusedly think that if the scientific world picture is true, then their lives must be futile because that picture implies that man has no purpose given him from without. But this is muddled thinking, for, as has already been shown, pointlessness is implied only by purposelessness in the other sense, which is not at all implied by the scientific picture of the world. These people mistakenly conclude that there can be no purpose *in* life because there is no purpose *of* life; that *men* cannot themselves adopt and achieve purposes because *man*, unlike a robot or a watchdog, is not a creature with a purpose.[3]

However, not all people taking this view are guilty of the above confusion. Some really hanker after a purpose of life in this sense. To some people the greatest attraction of the medieval world picture is the belief in an omnipotent, omniscient, and all-good Father, the view of themselves as His children who worship Him, of their proper attitude to what befalls them as submission, humility, resignation in His will, and what is often described as the "creaturely feeling."[4] All these are attitudes and feelings appropriate to a being that stands to another in the same sort of relation, though of course on a higher plane, in which a helpless child stands to his progenitor. Many regard the scientific picture of the world as cold, unsympathetic, unhomely, frightening, because it does not provide for any appropriate object of this creaturely attitude. There is nothing and no one in the world, as science depicts it, in which we can have faith or trust, on whose guidance we can rely, to whom we can turn for consolation, whom we can worship or submit to—except other human beings. This may be felt as a keen disappointment, because it shows that the meaning of life cannot lie in submission to His will, in acceptance of whatever may come, and in worship. But it does not imply that life can have *no* meaning. It merely implies that it must have a different meaning from that which it was thought to have. Just as it is a great shock for a child to find that he must stand on his own feet, that his father and mother no longer provide for him, so a person who has lost his faith in God must reconcile himself to the idea that he has to stand

---

[3]See e.g. "Is Life Worth Living?" B.B.C. Talk by the Rev. John Sutherland Bonnell, in *Asking Them Questions*, Third Series, ed. R. S. Wright (London: Geoffrey Cumberledge, 1950).

[4]See e.g. Rudolf Otto, *The Idea of the Holy*, pp. 9–11. See also C. A. Campbell, *On Selfhood and Godhood* (London: George Allen & Unwin Ltd., 1957) p. 246, and H. J. Paton, *The Modern Predicament*, pp. 69–71.

on his own feet, alone in the world except for whatever friends he may succeed in making.

But is not this to miss the point of the Christian teaching? Surely, Christianity can tell us the meaning of life because it tells us the grand and noble end for which God has created the universe and man. No human life, however pointless it may seem, is meaningless because, in being part of God's plan, every life is assured of significance.

This point is well taken. It brings to light a distinction of some importance: We call a person's life meaningful not only if it is worthwhile but also if he has helped in the realization of some plan or purpose transcending his own concerns. A person who knows he must soon die a painful death can give significance to the remainder of his doomed life by, say, allowing certain experiments to be performed on him which will be useful in the fight against cancer. In a similar way, only on a much more elevated plane, every man, however humble or plagued by suffering, is guaranteed significance by the knowledge that he is participating in God's purpose.

What, then, on the Christian view, is the grand and noble end for which God has created the world and man in it? . . .

If we turn to those who are willing to state God's purpose in so many words, we encounter two insuperable difficulties. The first is to find a purpose grand and noble enough to explain and justify the great amount of undeserved suffering in this world. . . . Could a God be called omniscient, omnipotent, *and* all-good who, for the sake of satisfying his desire to be loved and served, imposes (or has to impose) on his creatures the amount of undeserved suffering we find in the world?

There is, however, a much more serious difficulty still: God's purpose in making the universe must be stated in terms of a dramatic story, many of whose key incidents symbolize religious conceptions and practices which we no longer find acceptable: the imposition of a taboo on the fruits of a certain tree; the sin and guilt incurred by Adam and Eve by violating the taboo; the wrath of God;[5] the curse of Adam and Eve and all their progeny; the expulsion from paradise; the Atonement by Christ's bloody sacrifice on the cross, which makes available by way of the sacraments God's Grace, by which alone men can be saved (thereby, incidentally, establishing the valuable power of priests to forgive sins and thus alone make possible a man's entry to heaven[6]); Judgment Day, on which the sheep are separated from the goats and the latter condemned to eternal torment in hell-fire.

[5]It is difficult to feel the magnitude of this first sin unless one takes seriously the words ''Behold, the man has eaten of the fruit of the tree of knowledge of good and evil, and is become as one of us; and now, may he not put forth his hand, and take also of the tree of life, and eat, and live for ever?'' Genesis iii, 22.

[6]See in this connection the pastoral letter of February 2, 1905, by Johannes Katschtaler, Prince Bishop of Salzburg, on the honor due to priests, contained in *Quellen zur Geschichte des Papsttums*, by Mirbt, pp. 497–499, translated and reprinted in *The Protestant Tradition*, by J. S. Whale (Cambridge: University Press, 1955) pp. 259–262.

Obviously it is much more difficult to formulate a purpose for creating the universe and man that will justify the enormous amount of undeserved suffering which we find around us, if that story has to be fitted in as well. For now we have to explain not only why an omnipotent, omniscient, and all-good God should create such a universe and such a man, but also why, foreseeing every move of the feeble, weak-willed, ignorant, and covetous creature to be created, He should nevertheless have created him and, having done so, should be incensed and outraged by man's sin, and why He should deem it necessary to sacrifice His own son on the cross to atone for this sin, which was, after all, only a disobedience of one of his commands, and why this atonement and consequent redemption could not have been followed by man's return to paradise—particularly of those innocent children who had not yet sinned—and why, on Judgment Day, this merciful God should condemn some to eternal torment.[7] It is not surprising that in the face of these and other difficulties, we find, again and again, a return to the first view: that God's purpose cannot meaningfully be stated. . . .

There remains one fundamental hurdle which no form of Christianity can overcome: the fact that it demands of man a morally repugnant attitude toward the universe. It is now very widely held[8] that the basic element of the Christian religion is an attitude of worship toward a being supremely worthy of being worshipped and that it is religious feelings and experiences which apprise their owner of such a being and which inspire in him the knowledge or the feeling of complete dependence, awe, worship, mystery, and self-abasement. . . . Christianity thus demands of men an attitude inconsistent with one of the presuppositions of morality: that man is not wholly dependent on something else, that man has free will, that man is in principle capable of responsibility. . . .

III. THE MEANING OF LIFE

Perhaps some of you will have felt that I have been shirking the real problem. To many people the crux of the matter seems as follows. How can there be any meaning in our life if it ends in death? What meaning can there be in it that our inevitable death does not destroy? How can our existence be meaningful if there is no after-life in which perfect justice is meted out? How can life have any meaning if all it holds out to us are a few miserable

---

[7]How impossible it is to make sense of this story has been demonstrated beyond any doubt by Tolstoy in his famous ''Conclusion of a Criticism of Dogmatic Theology,'' reprinted in *A Confession, The Gospel in Brief, and What I Believe.*

[8]See e.g. the two series of Gifford Lectures most recently published: *The Modern Predicament,* by H. J. Paton (London: George Allen & Unwin Ltd., 1955), pp. 69 ff., and *On Selfhood and Godhood,* by C. A. Campbell (London: George Allen & Unwin Ltd. 1957), pp. 231–250.

earthly pleasures and even these to be enjoyed only rarely and for such a piteously short time?

I believe this is the point which exercises most people most deeply. . . .

What, then, is it that inclines us to think that if life is to have a meaning, there would have to be an after-life? It is this. The Christian world view contains the following propositions. The first is that since the Fall, God's curse of Adam and Eve, and the expulsion from paradise, life on earth for mankind has not been worthwhile, but a vale of tears, one long chain of misery, suffering, unhappiness, and injustice. The second is that a perfect after-life is awaiting us after the death of the body, and that we can enter this perfect life only on certain conditions, among which is also the condition of enduring our earthly existence to its bitter end. In this way, our earthly existence, which, in itself, would not (at least for many people if not all) be worth living, acquires meaning and significance: Only if we endure it can we gain admission to the realm of the blessed. . . .

It is not surprising, then, that when the implications of the scientific world picture begin to sink in, when we come to have doubts about the existence of God and another life, we are bitterly disappointed. For if there is no after-life, then all we are left is our earthly life, which we have come to regard as a necessary evil, the painful fee of admission to the land of eternal bliss. But if there is no eternal bliss to come and if this hell on earth is all, why hang on till the horrible end?

Our disappointment therefore arises out of these two propositions, that the earthly life is not worth living, and that there is another perfect life of eternal happiness and joy which we may enter upon if we satisfy certain conditions. We can regard our lives as meaningful if we believe both. We cannot regard them as meaningful if we believe merely the first and not the second. It seems to me inevitable that people who are taught something of the history of science will have serious doubts about the second. If they cannot overcome these, as many will be unable to do, then they must either accept the sad view that their life is meaningless or they must abandon the first proposition: that this earthly life is not worth living. They must find the meaning of their life in this earthly existence. But is this possible?

A moment's examination will show us that the Christian evaluation of our earthly life as worthless, which we accept in our moments of pessimism and dissatisfaction, is not one that we normally accept. Consider only the question of murder and suicide. On the Christian view, other things being equal, the most kindly thing to do would be for every one of us to kill as many of our friends and dear ones as still have the misfortune to be alive, and then to commit suicide without delay, for every moment spent in this life is wasted. On the Christian view, God has not made it that easy for us. He has forbidden us to hasten others or ourselves into the next life. Our bodies are his private property and must be allowed to wear themselves out in the way decided by Him, however painful and horrible that may be. . . .

On this view, murder is a less serious wrong than suicide. For murder can always be confessed and repented and therefore forgiven, suicide cannot—unless we allow the ingenious way out chosen by the heroine of Graham Greene's play, *The Living Room*, who swallows a slow but deadly poison and, while awaiting its taking effect, repents having taken it. Murder, on the other hand, is not so serious because, in the first place, it need not rob the victim of anything but the last lap of his march in the vale of tears, and, in the second place, it can always be forgiven. . . .

These views strike us as odd, to say the least. They are the logical consequence of the official medieval evaluation of this our earthly existence. If this life is not worth living, then taking it is not robbing the person concerned of much. The only thing wrong with it is the damage to God's property, which is the same both in the case of murder and suicide. We do not take this view at all. Our view, on the contrary, is that murder is the most serious wrong because it consists in taking away from some one else against his will his most precious possession, his life. For this reason, when a person suffering from an incurable disease asks to be killed, the mercy killing of such a person is regarded as a much less serious crime than murder because, in such a case, the killer is not robbing the other of a good against his will. Suicide is not regarded as a real crime at all, for we take the view that a person can do with his own possessions what he likes.

However, from the fact that these are our normal opinions, we can infer nothing about their truth. After all, we could easily be mistaken. Whether life is or is not worthwhile is a value judgment. Perhaps all this is merely a matter of opinion or taste. Perhaps no objective answer can be given. Fortunately, we need not enter deeply into these difficult and controversial questions. It is quite easy to show that the medieval evaluation of earthly life is based on a misguided procedure.

Let us remind ourselves briefly of how we arrive at our value judgments. When we determine the merits of students, meals, tennis players, bulls, bathing belles, we do so on the basis of some criteria and some standard or norm. Criteria and standards notoriously vary from field to field and even from case to case. But that does not mean that we have *no* idea about what are the appropriate criteria or standards to use. It would not be fitting to apply the criteria for judging bulls to the judgment of students or bathing belles. They score on quite different points. And even where the same criteria are appropriate, as in the judgment of students enrolled in different schools and universities, the standards will vary from one institution to another. Pupils who would only just pass in one would perhaps obtain honors in another. The higher the standard applied, the lower the marks, that is, the merit conceded to the candidate.

The same procedure is applicable also in the evaluation of a life. We examine it on the basis of certain criteria and standards. The medieval Christian view uses the criteria of the ordinary man: A life is judged by what the person concerned can get out of it: the balance of happiness over unhappiness, pleasure over pain, bliss over suffering. Our earthly life is judged not worthwhile because it contains much unhappiness, pain, and suffering, little happiness, pleasure, and bliss. The next life is judged worthwhile because it provides eternal bliss and no suffering.

Armed with these criteria, we can compare the life of this man and that, and judge which is more worthwhile, which has a greater balance of bliss over suffering. But criteria alone enable us merely to make comparative judgments of value, not absolute ones. We can say which is more and which is less worthwhile, but we cannot say which is worthwhile and which is not. In order to determine the latter, we must introduce a standard. But what standard ought we to choose?

Ordinarily, the standard we employ is the average of the kind. We call a man and a tree tall if they are well above the average of their kind. We do not say that Jones is a short man because he is shorter than a tree. We do not judge a boy a bad student because his answer to a question in the Leaving Examination is much worse than that given in reply to the same question by a young man sitting for his finals for the Bachelor's degree.

The same principles must apply to judging lives. When we ask whether a given life was or was not worthwhile, then we must take into consideration the range of worthwhileness which ordinary lives normally cover. Our end poles of the scale must be the best possible and the worst possible life that one finds. A good and worthwhile life is one that is well above average. A bad one is one well below.

The Christian evaluation of earthly lives is misguided because it adopts a quite unjustifiably high standard. Christianity singles out the major shortcomings of our earthly existence: There is not enough happiness; there is too much suffering; the good and bad points are quite unequally and unfairly distributed; the underprivileged and underendowed do not get adequate compensation; it lasts only a short time. It then quite accurately depicts the perfect or ideal life as that which does not have any of these shortcomings. Its next step is to promise the believer that he will be able to enjoy this perfect life later on. And then it adopts as its standard of judgment the perfect life, dismissing as inadequate anything that falls short of it. Having dismissed earthly life as miserable, it further damns it by characterizing most of the pleasures of which earthly existence allows as bestial, gross, vile, and sinful, or alternatively as not really pleasurable.

This procedure is as illegitimate as if I were to refuse to call anything tall unless it is infinitely tall, or anything beautiful unless it is perfectly flawless, or any one strong unless he is omnipotent. Even if it were true that there is available to us an after-life which is flawless and perfect, it would still not be legitimate to judge earthly lives by this standard. We do not fail every candidate who is not an Einstein. And if we do not believe in an after-life, we must of course use ordinary earthly standards.

I have so far only spoken of the worthwhileness, only of what a person can get out of a life. There are other kinds of appraisal. Clearly, we evaluate people's lives not merely from the point of view of what they yield to the persons that lead them, but also from that of other men on whom these lives have impinged. We judge a life more significant if the person has contributed to the happiness of others, whether directly by what he did for others, or by the plans, discoveries, inventions, and work he performed. Many lives that hold little in the way of pleasure or happiness for its owner are highly significant and valuable, deserve admiration and respect on account of the contributions made.

It is now quite clear that death is simply irrelevant. If life can be worthwhile at all, then it can be so even though it be short. And if it is not worthwhile at all, then an eternity of it is simply a nightmare. It may be sad that we have to leave this beautiful world, but it is so only if and because it is beautiful. And it is no less beautiful for coming to an end. I rather suspect that an eternity of it might make us less appreciative, and in the end it would be tedious.

It will perhaps be objected now that I have not really demonstrated that life has a meaning, but merely that it can be worthwhile or have value. It must be admitted that there is a perfectly natural interpretation of the question, "What is the meaning of life?" on which my view actually proves that life has no meaning. I mean the interpretation discussed in section II of this [essay], where I attempted to show that, if we accept the explanations of natural science, we cannot believe that living organisms have appeared on earth in accordance with the deliberate plan of some intelligent being. Hence, on this view, life cannot be said to have a purpose, in the sense in which man-made things have a purpose. Hence it cannot be said to have a meaning or significance in that sense.

However, this conclusion is innocuous. People are disconcerted by the thought that life as such has no meaning in that sense only because they very naturally think it entails that no individual life can have meaning either. They naturally assume that *this* life or *that* can have meaning only if *life as such* has meaning. But it should by now be clear that your life and mine may or may not have meaning (in one sense) even if life as such has none (in the other). Of course, it follows from this that your life may have meaning while mine has not. The Christian view guarantees a meaning (in one sense) to every life, the scientific view does not (in any sense). By relating the question of the meaningfulness of life to the particular circumstances of an individual's existence, the scientific view leaves it an open question whether an individual's life has meaning or not. It is, however, clear that the latter is the important sense of "having a meaning." . . .

"But here lies the rub," it will be said. "Surely, it makes all the difference whether there is an after-life. This is where morality comes in." It would be a mistake to believe that. Morality is not the meting out of punishment and reward. To be moral is to refrain from doing to others what, if they followed reason, they would not do to themselves, and to do for others what, if they followed reason, they would want to have done. It is, roughly speaking, to recognize that others, too, have a right to a worthwhile life. Being moral does not make one's own life worthwhile, it helps others to make theirs so. . . .

IV. CONCLUSION

. . . My main conclusion is that acceptance of the scientific world picture provides no reason for saying that life is meaningless, but on the contrary every reason for saying that there are many lives which are meaningful and significant. My subsidiary conclusion is that one of the reasons frequently offered for retaining the Christian world picture, namely, that its acceptance gives us a guarantee of a meaning for human existence, is unsound. We can see that our lives can have a meaning even if we abandon it and adopt the scientific world picture instead. . . .

37 / Philosophy and the Meaning of Life

A. J. AYER

I

Contemporary philosophers may be divided into two classes: the pontiffs and the journeymen. As the names that I have chosen indicate, the basis of this division is not so much a difference of opinion as a difference of attitude. It is not merely that the journeyman denies certain propositions which the pontiff asserts, or that he asserts certain propositions which the pontiff denies. It is rather that he has a radically different conception of the method of philosophy and of the ends that it is fitted to achieve. Thus, it is characteristic of those whom I describe as pontiffs that they think it within the province of philosophy to compete with natural science. They may, indeed, be willing to admit that the scientist achieves valuable results in his own domain, but they insist that he does not, and cannot, attain to the complete and final truth about reality; and they think that it is open to the philosopher to make this deficiency good. In support of this view, they may, for example, argue that every scientific theory is based upon presuppositions which cannot themselves be scientifically proved; and from this they may infer, in the interests of their own "philosophical" brand of irrationality, that science itself is fundamentally irrational; or else they may have recourse to metaphysics to supply the missing proof. Alternatively, they may hold that the scientist deals only with the appearances of things, whereas the philosopher by the use of his special methods penetrates to the reality beyond. In general, the ideal of the pontiffs is to construct a metaphysical system. Such a system may actually include some scientific hypotheses, either as premisses or, more frequently, as deductions from metaphysical first principles. It may, on the other hand, be uncompromisingly metaphysical. In either case, the aim is to give a complete and definitive account of "ultimate" reality. . . .

Unlike the pontiffs, the journeymen do not set out in quest of ultimate reality. Nor do they try to bring philosophy into competition with the natural sciences. Believing, as they do, that the only way to discover what the world is like is to form hypotheses and test them by observation, which is in fact the method of science, they are content to leave the scientist in full possession of the field of speculative knowledge. Consequently they do not try to build systems. The task of the philosopher, as they see it, is rather to deal piecemeal with a special set of problems. Some of these problems are historical, in the sense that they involve the criticism and interpretation of the work of previous philosophers; others are primarily mathematical, as belonging to the specialized field of formal logic; others again are set by the sciences: they involve the analysis of scientific method, the evaluation of scientific theories, the clarification of scientific terms. It is, for example, a philosophical problem to decide what is meant by "probability": and the journeymen have already contributed much towards its solution. Finally, there are a number of problems, such as the problem of perception, the problem of our knowledge of other minds, the question of the significance of moral judgments, that arise out of the common usages and assumptions of everyday life. In a broad sense, all these problems are semantic: that is to say, they can all be represented as concerned with the use of language. But since the term "semantics" is technically applied to a particular formal discipline which does not, even for the journeymen, comprehend the whole of philosophy, I think it better to resume their philosophical activities under the general heading of logical analysis. . . .

II

On the side of the pontiffs, imaginative literature. On the side of the journeymen, the re-integration of philosophy with science, or the piecemeal solution of logical or linguistic puzzles. Surely, it will be said, this is not what the public expects of its philosophers. Surely, the business of the philosopher is to make clear the meaning of life, to show people how they ought to live. Call him a pontiff or a journeyman, according to his method of approach; the distinction is not of any great importance. What is important is the message that he has to give. It is wisdom that is needed, not merely scientific knowledge. Of what use to us is the understanding of nature if we do not know the purpose of our existence or how we ought to live? And who is to answer these supremely important questions if not the philosopher?

The reply to this is that there is no true answer to these questions; and since this is so it is no use expecting even the philosopher to provide one. What can be done, however, is to make clear why, and in what sense, these questions are unanswerable; and once this is achieved it will be seen that there is also a sense in which they can be answered. It will be found that the form of answer is not a proposition, which must be either true or false, but the adoption of a rule, which cannot properly be characterized as either true or false, but can nevertheless be judged as more or less acceptable. And with this the problem is solved, so far as reasoning can solve it. The rest is a matter of personal decision, and ultimately of action.

Let us begin then by considering the purpose of our existence. How is it possible for our existence to have a purpose? We know very well what it is for a man to have a purpose. It is a matter of his intending, on the basis of a given situation, to bring about some further situation, which for some reason or other he conceives to be desirable. And in that case it may be said that events have a meaning for him according as they conduce, or fail to conduce, towards the end that he desires. But how can life in general be said to have any meaning? A simple answer is that all events are tending towards a certain specifiable end: so that to understand the meaning of life it is necessary only to discover this end. But, in the first place, there is no good reason whatever for supposing this assumption to be true, and secondly, even if it were true, it would not do the work that is required of it. For what is being sought by those who demand to know the meaning of life is not an explanation of the facts of their existence, but a justification. Consequently a theory which informs them merely that the course of events is so arranged as to lead inevitably to a certain end does nothing to meet their need. For the end in question will not be one that they themselves have chosen. As far as they are concerned it will be entirely arbitrary; and it will be a no less arbitrary fact that their existence is such as necessarily to lead to its fulfilment. In short, from the point of view of justifying one's existence, there is no essential difference between a teleological explanation of events and a mechanical explanation. In either case, it is a matter of brute fact that events succeed one another in the ways that they do and are explicable in the ways that they are. And indeed what is called an explanation is nothing other than a more general description. Thus, an attempt to answer the question why events are as they are must always resolve itself into saying only how they are. But what is required by those who seek the meaning of life is precisely an answer to their question "Why?" that is something other than an answer to any question "How?" And just because this is so they can never legitimately be satisfied.

But now, it may be objected, suppose that the world is designed by a superior being. In that case the purpose of our existence will be the purpose that it realizes for him; and the meaning of life will be found in our conscious adaptation to his purpose. But here again, the answer is, first, that there is no good reason whatsoever for believing that there is any such superior being; and, secondly, that even if there were, he could not accomplish what is here required of him. For let us assume, for the sake of argument, that everything happens as it does because a superior being has intended that it should. As far as we are concerned, the course of events still remains entirely arbitrary. True, it can now be said to fulfil a purpose; but the purpose is not ours. And just as, on the previous assumption, it merely happened to be the case that the course of events conducted to the end that it did, so, on this assumption, it merely happens to be the case that the deity has the purpose that he has, and not some other purpose, or no purpose at all. Nor does this unwarrantable assumption provide us even with a rule of life. For even those who believe most firmly that the world was designed by a superior being are not in a position to tell us what his purpose can have been. They may indeed claim that it has been mysteriously revealed to them, but how can it be proved that the revelation is genuine? And even if we waive this objection, even if we assume not only the world as we find it is working out the purpose of a superior being, but also that we are capable of discovering what this purpose is, we are still not provided with a rule of life. For either his purpose is sovereign or it is not. If it is sovereign, that is, if everything that happens is necessarily in accordance with it, then this is true also of our behavior. Consequently, there is no point in our deciding to conform to it, for the simple reason that we cannot do otherwise. However we behave, we shall fulfil the purpose of this deity; and if we were to behave differently, we should still be fulfilling it; for if it were possible for us not to fulfil it it would not be sovereign in the requisite sense. But suppose that it is not sovereign, or, in other words, that not all events must necessarily bear it out. In that case, there is no reason why we should try to conform to it, unless we independently judge it to be good. But that means that the significance of our behavior depends finally upon our own judgments of value; and the concurrence of a deity then becomes superfluous.

The point is, in short, that even the invocation of a deity does not enable us to answer the question why things are as they are. At the best it complicates the answer to the question how they are by pushing the level of explanation to a further stage. For even if the ways of the deity were clear to those who believed in him, which they apparently are not, it would still be, even to them, a matter of brute fact that he behaved as he did, just as to those who do not believe in him it is a matter of brute fact that the world is what it is. In either case the question "Why?" remains unanswered, for the very good reason that it is unanswerable. That is to say, it may be answerable at any given level, but the answer is always a matter of describing at a higher level not why things are as they are, but simply how they are. And so, to whatever level our explanations may be carried, the final statement is never an answer to the question "Why?" but necessarily only an answer to the question "How?"

It follows, if my argument is correct, that there is no sense in asking what is the ultimate purpose of our existence, or what is the real meaning of life. For to ask this is to assume that there can be a reason for our living as we do which is somehow more profound than any mere explanation of the facts; and we have seen that this assumption is untenable. Moreover it is untenable in logic and not merely in fact. The position is not that our existence unfortunately lacks a purpose which, if the fates had been kinder, it might conceivably have had. It is rather that those who inquire, in this way, after the meaning of life are raising a question to which it is not logically possible that there should be an answer. Consequently, the fact that they are disappointed is not, as some romanticists would make it, an occasion for cynicism or despair. It is not an occasion for any emotional attitude at all. And the reason why it is not is just that it could not conceivably have been otherwise. If it were logically possible for our existence to have a purpose, in the sense required, then it might be sensible to lament the fact that it had none. But it is not sensible to cry for what is logically impossible. If a question is so framed as to be unanswerable, then it is not a matter for regret that it remains unanswered. It is, therefore, misleading to say that life has no meaning; for that suggests that the statement that life has a meaning is factually significant, but false; whereas the truth is that, in the sense in which it is taken in this context, it is not factually significant.

There is, however, a sense in which it can be said that life does have a meaning. It has for each of us whatever meaning we severally choose to give it. The purpose of a man's existence is constituted by the ends to which he, consciously or unconsciously, devotes himself. Some men have a single overriding purpose to which all their activities are subordinated. If they are at all successful in achieving it, they are probably the happiest, but they are the exceptions. Most men pass from one object to another; and at any one time they may pursue a number of different ends, which may or may not be capable of being harmonized. Philosophers, with a preference for tidiness, have sometimes tried to show that all these apparently diverse objects can really be reduced to one: but the fact is that there is no end that is common to all men, not even happiness. For setting aside the question whether men ought always to pursue happiness, it is not true even that they always do pursue it, unless the word "happiness" is used merely as a description of any end that is in fact pursued. Thus the question what is the meaning of life proves, when it is taken empirically, to be incomplete. For there is no single thing of which it can truly be said that this is the meaning of life. All that can be said is that life has at various times a different meaning for different people, according as they pursue their several ends.

That different people have different purposes is an empirical matter of fact. But what is required by those who seek to know the purpose of their existence is not a factual description of the way that people actually do conduct themselves, but rather a decision as to how they should conduct themselves. Having been taught to believe that not all purposes are of equal value, they require to be guided in their choice. And thus the inquiry into the purpose of our existence dissolves into the question "How ought men to live?" . . .

38 / Philosophy and the Meaning of Life

KAI NIELSEN

I

Anglo-Saxon philosophy has in various degrees "gone linguistic." . . . There is a pervasive emphasis by English-speaking philosophers on what can and cannot be said, on what is intelligible, and on what is nonsensical. . . .

Critics from many quarters have raised their voices to assault linguistic philosophy as useless pedantry remote from the perennial concerns of philosophy or the problems of belief and life that all men encounter when, in Hesse's terms, they feel to the full "the whole riddle of human destiny." Traditionally the philosophical enterprise sought, among other things, to give us some enlightenment about our human condition, but as philosophy "goes linguistic," it has traitorously and irresponsibly become simply talk about the uses of talk. The philosopher has left his "high calling" to traffic in linguistic trivialities. . . .

It is my conviction that such a charge is unfounded. . . . I want to show how the use of the analytical techniques of linguistic philosophy can help us in coming to grips with the problems of human purpose and the meaning of Life. . . .

First, I want to say that . . . 'What is the meaning of life?' does *not* have a clear use; but that it does not have a clear use does not, I repeat, entail or in any way establish that it does not have a use or even that it does not have a supremely important use.[1] Secondly, 'What is the meaning of life?' most typically—though not always—functions as a request for the goals *worth* seeking in life though sometimes it may serve to ask if there are *any* goals worth seeking in life.[2] We are asking what (if anything) is the point to our lives? What (if anything) could give our lives purpose or point? In anguish we struggle to find the purpose, point or rationale of our grubby lives. But if this is the nature of the question, what would an answer look like? For this to be a fruitful question, all of us must ask ourselves individually: what would we take as an answer? When we ask this we are apt to come up with a blank; and if we are readers of philosophical literature we may remember that, along with others, a philosopher as persuasive and influential as A. J. Ayer has said that all such questions are unanswerable. But if they are really unanswerable—or so it would seem—then they are hardly genuine questions.

I will concede that *in a sense* such questions are unanswerable, but in a much more important sense they *are* answerable. We can be intelligent about and reason about such questions. . . . In showing what kind of answers could not be answers to this question, the temptation is to stress that there are no answers at all and that indeed no answers are needed. I want to try to show why this is wrong and what an answer would look like.

II

How then is it possible for our life to have a meaning or a purpose? For a while, oddly enough, Ayer in his "The Claims of Philosophy" is a perfectly sound guide.[3] We do know what it is for a man to have a purpose. "It is a matter," Ayer remarks, "of his intending, on the basis of a given situation, to bring about some further situation which for some reason or other he conceives to be desirable."

[1]John Wisdom has driven home this point with force. In particular see his "The Modes of Thought and the Logic of 'God'" in his *Paradox and Discovery* (California, 1965).

[2]Ronald Hepburn has correctly stressed that this for some people may not be what is uppermost in their minds when they ask that question. *Religious Studies*, vol. I (1965) pp. 125–140. See also Ilham Dilman's remarks about Hepburn's analysis in "Life and Meaning," *Philosophy*, 40 (October 1965).

[3]The rest of the references to Ayer in the text are from this essay. His brief remarks in his "What I Believe" in *What I Believe* (London: 1966) pp. 15–16 and in his introduction to *The Humanist Outlook*, A. J. Ayer (ed.), (London: 1968) pp. 6–7 are also relevant as further brief statements of his central claims about the meaning of life. [The previous selection is an abridged version of Ayer's "The Claims of Philosophy."—Eds.]

But, Ayer asks, how is it possible for life *in general* to have a meaning or a purpose?

Well, there is one very simple answer. Life in general has a purpose if all living beings are tending toward a certain specifiable end. To understand the meaning of life or the purpose of existence it is only necessary to discover this end.

As Ayer makes perfectly clear, there are overwhelming difficulties with such an answer. In the first place there is no good reason to believe living beings are tending toward some specifiable end. But even if it were true that they are all tending toward this end such a discovery would not at all answer the question 'What is the meaning or purpose of life?' This is so because when we human beings ask this exceedingly vague question we are not just asking for *an explanation of* the facts of existence; we are asking for a *justification* of these facts. . . .

When we ask: 'What is the meaning of life?' we want an answer that is more than *just* an explanation or description of *how* people behave or *how* events are arranged or *how* the world is constituted. We are asking for a *justification* for our existence. We are asking for a justification for why life is as it is, and not even the most complete explanation and/or description of *how* things are ordered can answer this quite different question. The person who demands that some general description of man and his place in nature should entail a statement that man ought to live and die in a certain way is asking for something that can no more be the case than it can be the case that ice can gossip. To ask about the meaning of our lives involves asking how we should live, or whether any decision to live in one way is more *worthy* of acceptance than any other. Both of these questions are clearly questions of value; yet no statement of *fact* about how we in fact do live can by itself be sufficient to answer such questions. No statement of what ought to be the case can be deduced from a statement of what is the case. If we are demanding such an answer, then Ayer is perfectly right in claiming the question is unanswerable.

Let me illustrate. Suppose, perhaps as a result of some personal crisis, I want to take stock of myself. As Kierkegaard would say, I want to appropriate, take to heart, the knowledge I have or can get about myself and my condition in order to arrive at some decision as to what sort of life would be most meaningful for me, would be the sort of life I would truly want to live if I could act rationally and were fully apprised of my true condition. I might say to myself, though certainly not to others, unless I was a bit of an exhibitionist, 'Look Nielsen, you're a little bit on the vain side and you're arrogant to boot. And why do you gossip so and spend so much of your time reading science fiction? And why do you always say what you expect other people want you to say? You don't approve of that in others, do you? And why don't you listen more? And weren't you too quick with Jones and too indulgent with Smith'? In such a context I would put these questions and a host of questions like them to myself. And I might come up with some general explanations, good or bad, like 'I act this way because I have some fairly pervasive insecurities.' And to my further question, 'Well, why do you have these insecurities?' I might dig up something out of my past such as 'My parents died when I was two and I never had any real home.' To explain why this made me insecure I might finally evoke a whole psychological theory and eventually perhaps even a biological and physiological theory, and these explanations about the nature of the human animal would themselves finally rest, in part at least, on various descriptions of how man does behave. In addition, I might, if I could afford it and were sufficiently bedevilled by these questions, find my way to a psychiatrist's couch and there, after the transference had taken place, I would eventually get more quite personalized explanations of my behavior and attitudes. But none of these things, in themselves, could tell me the meaning of life or even the meaning of my life, though they indeed might help me in this search. I might discover that I was insecure because I could never get over the wound of the loss of my father. I might discover that unconsciously I blamed myself. As a child I wished him dead and then he died so somehow I did it, really. And I would, of course, discover how unreasonable this is. I would come to understand that people generally react this way in those situations. In Tolstoy's phrase, we are all part of the "same old river." And, after rehearsing it, turning it over, taking it to heart, I might well gain control over it and eventually gain control over some of my insecurities. I could see and even live through again what *caused* me to be vain, arrogant and lazy. But suppose, that even after all these discoveries I really didn't want to change. After stocktaking, I found that I was willing to settle for the *status quo*. Now I gratefully acknowledge that this is very unlikely, but here we are concerned with the *logical* possibilities. 'Yes, there are other ways of doing things,' I say to myself, 'but after all is said and done I have lived this way a long time and I would rather go on this way than change. This sort of life, is after all, the most meaningful one. This is how I really want to act and this is how I, and others like me, ought to act.' What possible facts could anyone appeal to which would prove, in the sense of logically entail, that I was wrong and that the purpose of life or the meaning of life was very different than I thought it was? It is Ayer's contention, and I think he is right, that there are none.

'But you have left out God,' someone might say. 'You have neglected the possibility that there is a God and that God made man to His image and likeness and that God has a plan for man. Even Sartre, Heidegger and Camus agree that to ask 'What is the Meaning of Life?' or 'What is the purpose of human existence?' is, in effect, to raise the question of God. If there is a God your conclusion would not follow, and, as Father Copleston has said, if there is *no* God human existence can have no end or purpose other than that given by man himself.

I would want to say, that the whole question of God or no God, Jesus or no Jesus, is entirely beside the point. . . .

As far as I can see, there are no good reasons to believe either that there is a God or that the human animal has been ordered for some general end; but even if this were so it would not give us an answer to the question: 'What is the meaning of life?'

This is so because the question has been radically misconstrued. When we ask: 'What is the meaning of life?' or 'What is the purpose of human existence?' we are normally asking, as I have already said, questions of the following types 'What should we seek?', 'What ends—if any—are worthy of attainment?' Questions of this sort require a very different answer than any answer to: 'What is the meaning of "obscurantism"?', 'What is the purpose of the ink-blotter?' and 'What is the purpose of the liver?'. Ayer is right when he says: "what is required by those who seek to know the purpose of their existence is not a factual description of the way that people actually do conduct themselves, but rather a decision as to how they *should* conduct themselves." Again he is correct in remarking: "There is—a sense in which it can be said that life does have a meaning. It has for each of us whatever meaning we severally *choose* to give it. The purpose of a man's existence is constituted by the ends to which he, consciously or unconsciously, devotes himself." . . .

But Ayer, still writing in the tradition of logical empiricism, often writes as if it followed from the truth of what we have said so far, that there could be no reasoning about 'How ought man to live?' or 'What is the meaning of life?'. Thus Ayer says at one point in "The Claims of Philosophy": "He [the moral agent] cannot prove his judgments of value are correct, for the simple reason that no judgment of value is capable of proof." He goes on to argue that people have no way of demonstrating that one judgment of value is superior to another. A decision between people in moral disagreement is a "subject for persuasion and finally a matter of individual choice."

As we have just seen there is a sound point to Ayer's stress on choice vis-a-vis morality, but taken as a whole his remarks are at best misleading. There is reasoning about moral questions and there are arguments and proofs in morality. There are principles in accordance with which we appraise our actions, and there are more general principles, like the principle of utility or the principles of distributive justice in accordance with which we test our lower-level moral rules. And there is a sense of 'being reasonable' which, as Hume and Westermarck were well aware, has distinctive application to moral judgments. Thus, if I say, 'I ought to be relieved of my duties, I'm just too ill to go on' I not only must believe I am in fact ill, I must also be prepared to say, of any of my colleagues or anyone else similarly placed, that in like circumstances they too ought to be relieved of their duties if they fall ill. There is a certain *generality* about moral discourse and a man is not reasoning morally or 'being reasonable' if he will not allow those inferences. Similarly, if I say 'I want x' or 'I prefer x' I need not, though I may, be prepared to give reason why I want it or prefer it, but if I say 'x is the right thing to do' or 'x is good' or 'I ought to do x' or 'x is worthy of attainment,' I must—perhaps with the exception of judgments of intrinsic goodness—be prepared to give *reasons* for saying 'x is the right thing to do,' 'x is good,' 'I ought to do x' and the like.

It is indeed true in morals and in reasoning about human conduct generally that justification must come to an end; but this is also true in logic, science and in common sense empirical reasoning about matters of fact; but it is also true that the end point in reasoning over good and evil is different than in science and the like, for in reasoning about how to act, our judgment finally terminates in a choice—a decision of principle. And here is the truth in Ayer's remark that moral judgments are "*finally* a matter of individual choice." But, unless we are to mislead, we must put the emphasis on 'finally,' for a dispassioned, neutral analysis of the uses of the language of human conduct will show, as I have indicated, that there is reasoning, and in a relevant sense, 'objective reasoning,' about moral questions. It is not at all a matter of pure persuasion or goading someone into sharing your attitudes.

III

There are, however, other considerations that may be in our minds when we ask 'What is the meaning of life?' or 'Does life have a meaning?'. In asking such questions, we may *not* be asking 'What should we seek?' or 'What goals are worth seeking really?' Instead we may be asking 'Is *anything* worth seeking?' Does it matter finally what we do?' Here, some may feel, we finally meet the real tormenting "riddle of human existence."

Such a question is not simply a moral question: it is a question concerning human conduct, a question about how to live one's life or about whether to continue to live one's life. Yet when we consider what an answer would look like here we draw a blank. If someone says 'Is anything worthwhile?' we gape. We want to reply: 'Why, sitting in the sunshine in the mornings, seeing the full moon rise, meeting a close friend one hasn't seen in a long time, sleeping comfortably after a tiring day, all these things and a million more are most assuredly worthwhile. Any life devoid of experiences of this sort would most certainly be impoverished.'

Yet this reply is so obvious we feel that something different must be intended by the questioner. The questioner knows that we, and most probably he, ordinarily regard such things as worthwhile, but he is asking if these things or *anything* is worthwhile *really*? These things *seem* worthwhile but are they in reality? And here we indeed do not know what to say. If someone queries whether it is really worthwhile leaving New York and going to the beach in August we have some idea of what to say; there are some criteria which will enable us to make at least a controversial answer to this question. But when it is asked, in a philosophical manner, *if anything, ever* is really worthwhile, it is not clear that we have a genuine question before us. The question borrows its form from more garden-variety questions but when we ask it in this general way do we actually know what we mean? If someone draws a line on the blackboard, a question over the line's straightness can arise only if some criterion for a line's being straight is accepted. Similarly only if some criterion of worthiness is accepted can we intelligibly ask if a specific thing or anything is worthy of attainment.

But if a sensitive and reflective person asks, 'Is anything worthwhile, really?' could he not be asking this because, 1) he has a certain vision of human excellence, and 2) his austere criteria for what is worthwhile have developed in terms of that vision? Armed with such criteria, he might find nothing that man can in fact attain under his present and foreseeable circumstances *worthy* of attainment. . . . In terms of his ideal of human excellence nothing is worthy of attainment.

To this, it is natural to respond, 'If this is our major problem about the meaning of life, then this is indeed no intellectual or philosophical riddle about human destiny. . . . We can say what a meaningful life would look like even though we can't attain it. If such is the question, there is no "riddle of human existence," though there is a pathos to human life and there is the social-political pattern problem of how to bring the requisite human order into existence. Yet only if we have a conception of what human life should be can we feel such pathos.'

If it is said in response to this that what would really be worthwhile could not possibly be attained, an absurdity has been uttered. To say something is worthy of attainment implies that, everything else being equal, it ought to be attained. But to say that something ought to be attained implies that it *can* be attained. Thus we *cannot* intelligibly say that something is worthy of attainment but that it cannot possibly be attained. So in asking 'Is anything worthy of attainment?' we must acknowledge that there are evaluative criteria operative which guarantee that what is sincerely said to be worthy of attainment is at least in principle attainable. And as we have seen in speaking of morality, 'x is worthy of attainment' does not mean 'x is preferred,' though again, in asserting that something is worthy of attainment, or worthwhile, we imply that we would choose it, everything else being equal, in preference to something else. But we cannot intelligibly speak of a choice if there is no possibility of doing one thing rather than another.

Life is often hard and, practically speaking, the ideals we set our hearts on, those to which we most deeply commit ourselves, may in actual fact be impossible to achieve. A sensitive person may have an ideal of conduct, an ideal of life, that he assents to without reservation. But the facts of human living being what they are, he knows full well that this ideal cannot be realized. His ideals are intelligible enough, logically their achievement is quite possible, but as a matter of *brute fact* his ideals are beyond his attainment. If this is so, is it worthwhile for him and others like him to go on living or to strive for anything at all? Can life, under such circumstances, be anything more than an ugly habit? For such a man, 'What is the meaning of life?' has the force of 'What *point* can a life such as mine have under these circumstances?'. And in asking whether such a life has a point he is asking the very question we put above, viz. can life be worth living under such conditions.

Again such a question is perfectly intelligible and is in no way unanswerable any more than any other question about how to act, though here too we must realize that the facts of human living *cannot* be sufficient for a man simply to read off an answer without it in any way affecting his life. Here, too, *any* answer will require a decision or some kind of effective involvement on the part of the person involved. A philosopher can be of help here in showing what kind of answers we cannot give, but it is far less obvious that he can provide us with a set of principles that together with empirical facts about his condition and prospects, will enable the perplexed man to know what he ought to do. The philosopher or any thoughtful person who sees just what is involved in the question can give some helpful advice. Still the person involved must work out an answer in anguish and soreness of heart.

However, I should remind him that no matter how bad his own life was, there would always remain something he could do to help alleviate the sum total of human suffering. This certainly has value and if he so oriented his life, he could not say that his life was without point. I would also argue that in normal circumstances he could not be sure that his ideals of life would permanently be frustrated, and if he held ideals that would be badly frustrated under almost any circumstances, I would get him to look again at his ideals. Could such ideals really be adequate? Surely man's reach must exceed his grasp, but how far should we go? Should not any ideal worth its salt come into some closer involvement with the realities of human living? . . . Finally, it does not seem to me reasonable to expect that *all* circumstances can have sufficient meaning to make them worthwhile. Under certain circumstances life is not worth living. As a philosopher, I would point out this possibility and block those philosophical-religious claims that would try to show that this could not possibly be.

Many men who feel the barbs of constant frustration, come to feel that their ideals have turned out to be impossible, and ask in anguish—as a consequence—'Does life really have any meaning?'. To a man in such anguish I would say all I have said above and much more, though I am painfully aware that such an approach may seem cold and unfeeling. I know that these matters deeply affect us; indeed they can even come to obsess us, and when we are so involved it is hard to be patient with talk about what can and cannot be said. But we need to understand these matters as well; and, after all, what more can be done along this line than to make quite plain what is involved in his question and try to exhibit a range of rational attitudes that could be taken toward it. . . . But I would also try to make clear that finally an answer to such a question must involve a decision or the having or adopting of a certain attitude on the part of the person involved. This certainly should be stressed and it should be stressed that the question 'Is such a life meaningful' is a sensible question, which admits of a non-obscurantist, non-metaphysical treatment. . . .

IV

In asking 'What is the meaning of Life?' we have seen how this question is in reality a question concerning human conduct. It asks either 'What should we seek?' or 'What ends (if any) are really worthwhile?'. I have tried to show in what general ways such questions are answerable. We can give reasons for our moral judgments and moral principles and the whole activity of morality can be seen to have a point, but not all questions concerning what is worthwhile are moral questions. Where moral questions do not enter we must make a decision about what, on reflection, we are going to seek. We must ascertain what—all things considered—really answers to our interests or, where there is no question of anything answering to our interests or failing to answer to our interests, we should decide what on reflection we prefer. What do we really want, wish to approve of, or admire? To ask 'Is anything worthwhile?' involves our asking 'Is there nothing that we, on reflection, upon knowledge of ourselves and others, want, approve of, or admire?' When we say 'So-and-so is worthwhile' we are making a normative judgment that cannot be derived from determining what we desire, admire or approve of. That is to say, these statements do not entail statements to the effect that so and so is worthwhile. But in determining what is worthwhile this is finally all we have to go on. In saying something is worthwhile, we 1) *express* our preference, admiration or approval; 2) in some sense imply that we are prepared to defend our choice with *reasons*: and 3) in effect, indicate our belief that others like us in the relevant respects and similarly placed, will find it worthwhile too. And the answer to our question is that, of course, there are things we humans desire, prefer, approve of, or admire. This being so, our question is not unanswerable. Again we need not fly to a metaphysical enchanter. . . .

Surely, I have not exhausted the question for, literally speaking, it is not one question but a cluster of loosely related questions all concerning 'the human condition'—how man is to act and how he is to live his life even in the face of the bitterest trials and disappointments. Questions here are diverse, and a philosopher, or anyone else, becomes merely pretentious and silly when he tries to come up with some formula that will solve, resolve or dissolve the perplexities of human living. But I have indicated in skeletal fashion how we can approach general questions about 'What (if anything) is worth seeking?' And I have tried to show how such questions are neither meaningless nor questions calling for esoteric answers. . . .

STUDY QUESTIONS

1. In the passage quoted in the Preview to this part, Camus maintains that the question of the meaning of life is the most urgent of all questions. Do you agree? Why or why not?

2. In your judgment, does Swenson also agree that the problem is as urgent as Camus maintains? If so, why? If not, why not?

3. State what you take to be Swenson's chief arguments on behalf of the theistic position. Critically evaluate those arguments.

4. In the General Introduction to this text (section I), it was said that one of the tasks of philosophy is to examine our (often hidden) assumptions or presuppositions. What presuppositions do you find Swenson to be relying on?

5. Baier contrasts two opposing views (pictures) of the world, and their respective standpoints on the question of whether or not life is meaningful. State the chief theses of the two world views. State what each is said to imply regarding the issue of whether or not life has any meaning.

6. What does Baier conclude in his discussion? What are his reasons for reaching that conclusion? Do you agree? Why or why not?

7. How does Baier respond to the claim that the scientific account of the world takes away life's purpose and meaning? Do you agree? Why or why not?

8. How does Baier answer the question, "How can there be any meaning in our life if it ends in death?" Critically evaluate the answer.

9. State precisely Ayer's main thesis. Now state his arguments on behalf of the thesis.

10. How does Nielsen reply to Ayer? How would Baier reply to Ayer?

11. In your view, which of the authors represented in this part of the book has presented the best answer to the question of the meaning of life? Why do you consider his answer the best?

12. To what extent, if any, do the authors agree about the meaning of life? On what points do they differ?

13. Examine again Camus's claim (quoted in the Preview) that the meaning of life is the most urgent of questions. Having read the selections in this part, do you now agree or disagree? Why?

14. It has been maintained by some that without God, or faith in God, life would be without meaning or purpose and, hence, would not be worth living. Therefore, even if there is *no* god, it is better for one to *believe* that there is. Do you agree? Why or why not?

Further Readings

Britton, Karl. *Philosophy and the Meaning of Life.* Cambridge: Cambridge University Press, 1969. [Examines the bearing of philosophy on the question of the meaning of life.]

Frankl, Victor. *Man's Search for Meaning.* New York: Beacon, 1963. [A partially autobiographical account from the perspective of a psychologist.]

Klemke, E. D., ed. *The Meaning of Life.* New York: Oxford University Press, 1981. [Presents three approaches to the issue: the theistic perspective, the nontheistic alternative, and the approach which questions the question. Contains many of the most important essays on the topic.]

Lamont, Corliss. *The Philosophy of Humanism.* New York: Frederick Ungar, 1949, 1957, 1965. [Defends a humanistic approach to the issue in a very readable manner.]

May, Rollo. *Man's Search for Meaning.* New York: W. W. Norton, 1953. [Another treatment of the issue by a psychologist, but one well versed in philosophy.]

Munitz, Milton K. *The Mystery of Existence.* New York: New York University Press, 1965. [Not directly on the subject, but on an issue closely related to it.]

Nielsen, Kai. *Ethics Without God.* Buffalo, N.Y.: Prometheus Books, 1973. [Contains a treatment of the subject within the broader context of ethics.]

Sanders, Steven, and David R. Cheney, eds. *The Meaning of Life.* Englewood Cliffs, N.J.: Prentice-Hall, 1980. [Another collection of essays; overlaps in part with Klemke.]

PART NINE

MORAL VALUES: GROUNDS AND NORMS

PREVIEW

Suppose you are in a situation in which you must decide whether or not to tell a lie. Let us imagine that you have discovered that your roommate's steady date is secretly going out with somebody else. Your roommate has heard rumors to this effect and suspects that you know the truth. If your roommate asks you whether his/her date is cheating on him/her, should you lie or tell the truth? How are you to decide; that is, on the basis of what sort of standards, values, and norms should you make and, if need be, justify or defend your decision?

1. You might base your decision regarding whether to lie to your roommate or not on selfish considerations, that is, on whether you would benefit from lying to him/her. You might decide, for example, that lying would make your roommate feel better and that this would make you feel better. Your decision is based on the impact the lie would have on you, rather than its potential effect on your roommate. If so, then for you the main or only ground for making moral decisions is the question, "What's in it for me?"

2. A second approach to moral decision making would be to decide what to do by estimating the consequences of our actions. If the consequences are, on the whole, good—or at least "better" than the available alternatives—we can and, indeed, ought to do the action which promotes those good consequences. So if it turns out that lying to your roommate would promote better consequences than not lying, you ought to lie. But now the obvious question becomes, "What are 'good' consequences?" One possible answer would be: Whatever brings about the most happiness (or least unhappiness) for all those concerned—not just for yourself.

3. Suppose you subscribe to certain moral principles or laws, such as the "golden rule." Perhaps this rule or set of moral principles prohibits lying in

all situations. That is, the principle says, "Never lie, no matter what." In this case your decision not to lie to your roommate will not be based on such factors as, for example, the desire to protect him/her. It will be based exclusively on the desire to follow the moral principle which you accept.

4. A fourth approach involves an appeal to divine laws or commandments. Such theories bid us discover, as best we can, what the divine laws prescribe or prohibit in any situation. Sources for making such a discovery include the Bible or other religious texts, the clergy, some religiously sanctioned moral code (e.g., the Ten Commandments), or some other religious authority. If you hold this theory, you probably won't lie at all.

Main Question

With this example and the approaches to it, we may now state the main question in this part. It is:

How are moral decisions about what to do or what not to do to be arrived at and defended? That is: What is the correct moral standard or standards of conduct, a standard by which to decide what is right or wrong, and by which to make moral assessments of right or wrong?

Answers

Our example and the discussion of it provides us with the main answers to the central question. These are:

a. Egoism: the proper standard of conduct is the enhancement of your own long-term self-interest or happiness.

b. Utilitarianism: The proper standard of conduct is the maximization of the greatest amount of happiness, or least amount of unhappiness, for *all* concerned, not just one's self.

c. Formalism: The proper standard of conduct is a rule which expresses the form or way of proceeding for conduct, but not the content of particular actions.

d. The Divine Command Theory: The proper standard of conduct is whatever is commanded or forbidden by God.

On the basis of our previous discussion, we may now define right and wrong conduct for each of these views:

a. Egoism: An action is right if it enhances your own long term self-interest—brings *you* happiness. A wrong action is one which does not work to your own self-interest.

b. Utilitarianism: An action is right it if brings about or increases the greatest amount of happiness for anyone likely to be affected by the action.

An action is wrong if it diminishes the greatest amount of happiness of anyone affected by it.

   c. Formalism: An action is right if it is in accordance with a rule. A wrong action is one which is not. The Golden Rule Theory (one type of formalism) holds: An action is right if it is in accordance with the Golden Rule—that is, one in which you do unto others as you would have them do unto you.

   d. The Divine Command Theory: An action is right if it is commanded or willed by God. An action is wrong if it is forbidden or condemned by God.

   It may be helpful to add a comment or two concerning utilitarianism.

   The utilitarian believes that what is right or wrong is determined by how much good or value is brought into the world, or how much bad is prevented from coming into the world, as the result of any action. Good and bad—values—are defined in terms of things such as pleasure and pain, knowledge and ignorance, and so on. Many utilitarians take pleasure to be the highest value and pain the lowest, so that right is bringing about the greatest amount of pleasure one can, and wrong is increasing the amount of misery. Utilitarianism thus may require complex estimations of what the actual consequences of any action will be as part of the decision as to what is right or wrong in any given situation (especially since many actions bring both pleasure and pain in their wake).

Selections

We have presented an essay which defends each of these four approaches to standards of conduct and which draws out some implications of each; then we have included a criticism of each, so that the reader can develop her/his own philosophical thoughts on these important issues. It is hoped that this collection of essays on approaches to moral thinking and decision making will have some bearing on the reader's future conduct.

Answers	Selections	Criticisms
(a) Egoism	39	40
(b) Utilitarianism	41	42
(c) Formalism	43	44
(d) Divine Command Theory	45	46

39 / The Morality Trap

HARRY BROWNE

I. THE MORALITY TRAP

The Morality Trap is the belief that you must obey a moral code created by someone else. . . .

Morality is a powerful word. Perhaps even more powerful is the word *immoral*. In an attempt to avoid being labeled *immoral*, many people allow themselves to be manipulated by others. . . .

It seems to me that there are three different kinds of morality. I call them *personal, universal,* and *absolute*. By looking at each of them, I think we can get a clearer idea of what morality is and how it can be useful in helping you to achieve your freedom.

A. Personal Morality

You act in ways that you hope will bring the best consequences to you. And the "best consequences" are those that bring you happiness.

You always have to consider the consequences of your actions; they're the point of anything you do. However, any given act will undoubtedly cause *many* consequences. You may see that a particular action will produce a consequence you want, but you might also be aware that it could produce other consequences that you don't want. . . .

Since you're always seeking numerous different goals, you try to foresee the ways in which something immediately desirable might get in the way of other things that are ultimately more desirable. You try to consider more than just what's immediately in front of you. You're placing things in a broader context.

Obviously, you can't expect to foresee *all* the consequences of a given act, but you can try to see all the significant ones. In some cases . . . there are obvious consequences that immediately rule out a proposed course of action. . . .

Because you can't foresee all the specific consequences of what you do, there's a need to have some generalized rules available that can help keep you out of situations that could be troublesome. Those rules can be valuable if they do two things: (1) steer you away from potential disasters; and (2) remind you of the things you must do to satisfy your most important *long-term* desires.

The basic question is: "How can I get something I want without hurting my chances for other things that are more important to me?"

It is this generalized, *long-term* attitude that underlies an individual's basic code of conduct. And when we speak of morality, I can't think of any other sensible reason to be concerned about the subject. Its purpose is to keep you aimed in the direction you most want to go.

Personal morality is an attempt to consider all the relevant consequences of your actions.

"Relevant" means those consequences that will affect *you*. How your actions affect others is only important insofar as that, in turn, affects you.

A personal morality is basic to your overall view of how you'll find happiness. . . .

And it's important that you form it yourself. No one else (including me) is qualified to tell you how to live. A realistic morality has to consider many personal factors: your emotional nature, abilities, strengths, weaknesses, and, most important, your goals.

Your code of conduct has to be consistent with your goals so that you don't do anything that would make those goals unattainable. A code devised by someone else will necessarily be based upon the goals *he* believes possible and desirable.

To be useful, a morality shouldn't include rules for every possible situation. It shouldn't be concerned with minor questions involving only immediate consequences. It's devised to prevent big problems for you and to keep you aimed toward the ultimate goals that mean the most to you. Moral questions are concerned only with matters that involve large consequences.

There's a difference, for instance, between investing three dollars in a movie that might prove to be a dud and investing your life savings in a risky business venture. There's also a difference between tasting a different food that's commonly eaten (such as snails) and sampling toadstools in the forest. The first might cause a stomachache; the second could poison you.

A useful morality will prevent you from doing things that might take years to correct, while keeping you aimed in the direction of the things that are most important to you.

And since such matters are an outgrowth of your own personal values, it's obvious that no one else can create your morality for you.

A *personal morality* is the attempt to consider all the relevant consequences of your actions. This is only one of three common types of moralities, however.

B. Universal Morality

The second type is a morality that is meant to apply to everyone in the world. A *universal morality* is one that's supposed to bring happiness to anyone who uses it.

When you're exposed to the ideas of someone who has apparently done well with his own life, it's easy to conclude that he has all the final answers. His reasoning makes sense to you; he has results to show for his ideas. What further proof could you need to demonstrate that he knows how to live?

He probably does know how to live—*his* life. It would be foolish not to consider the ideas such a person offers. But it would also be foolish to expect that, as intelligent as he may be, he could have answers that apply to every life in the world.

His ideas have worked for him because he's been wise enough to develop ideas that are consistent with his own nature. He hasn't tried to live by the standards created by others; he's found his own. And that's vitally important.

You must do the same thing, too—if you want your code of conduct to work that well for you. Your rules have to consider everything that's unique about you—your emotions, your aptitudes, your weak points, your hopes and fears. . . .

A universal morality is a code of conduct that is presumed to bring happiness to anyone who uses it. I don't believe there can be such a thing. The differences between individuals are far too great to allow for anything but the most general kinds of rules.

C. Absolute Morality

There's a third kind of morality. The first two are attempts to help you achieve happiness—one self-directed and the other coming from someone else. The third type is the opposite of this. An *absolute morality* is a set of rules to which an individual is expected to *surrender* his own happiness.

There are two main characteristics of an absolute morality:

1. It presumably comes from *an authority outside of the individual*. It comes from someone or somewhere more important than the individual himself.

2. It proposes that the individual should be "moral" *regardless of the consequences to himself*. In other words, doing what is "right" is more important than one's own happiness.

These two characteristics intertwine, so we'll consider them together.

[1.] Absolute morality is the most common type of morality, and it can be pretty intimidating. You can be made to appear "selfish," "whimworshiping," "egotistic," "hedonistic," or "ruthless" if you merely assert that your own happiness is the most important thing in your life.

But what could be more important than your happiness? It's said that an authoritarian moral code is necessary to protect society. But who is society?

Isn't it just a large group of people, each of whom has differing ideas concerning how one should live?

And if an individual is required to give up his own happiness, of what value is society to him?

It's also suggested that God commanded that we live by certain rules. But who can be sure he knows exactly when and how and what God said and what he meant? And even if that could be established once and for all, what would be the consequences to the individual if he acted otherwise? How do we know?

And if the code did come from God, it still had to be handled by human beings on its way to you. Whatever the absolute morality may be, you're relying upon someone else to vouch for its authority.

Suppose you use a holy book as your guide. I haven't yet seen one that doesn't have some apparent contradictions regarding conduct in it. Those contradictions may disappear with the proper interpretation; but who provides the interpretation? You'll do it yourself or you'll select someone to provide it for you. In either case, *you* have become the authority by making the choice.

There's no way someone else can become your authority; ultimately the decision will be yours in choosing the morality you'll live by—even if you choose to cite someone else (you've chosen) as the authority for your acts.

[2.] And there's no way you can ignore the consequences to yourself; a human being naturally acts in terms of consequences.

What happens, however, is that other people introduce consequences that they hope will influence you. They say that your "immoral" acts will: "prevent you from going to heaven" or "cause other people to disapprove of you" or "destroy society and cause chaos, and it will all be your fault."

Once again, however, it will be *you* deciding for yourself whether any of these consequences will result and whether any of them are important to you.

The absolute morality fails on its two important characteristics. Even if you choose to believe there's a higher authority, you are the authority who chooses what it is and what it is telling you to do. And since you'll always be considering consequences, even if you try to fix it so that you aren't, it's important to deliberately recognize the consequences and decide which ones are important to you. . . .

D. Your Morality

You are responsible for what happens to you (even if someone else offers to accept that responsibility), because you're the one who'll experience the consequences of your acts.

You are the one who decides what is right and what is wrong—no matter what meaning others may attach to those words. You don't have to obey blindly the dictates that you grew up with or that you hear around you now. Everything can be challenged, *should* be challenged, examined to determine its relevance to you and what you want.

As you examine the teachings of others, you may find that some of it is very appropriate to you, but much of it may be meaningless or even harmful. The important thing is to carefully reappraise any moral precept that has been guiding your actions.

As you examine each of the rules you've been living by, ask yourself:

- Is this rule something that *others* have devised on behalf of "society" to restrain individuals? Or have *I* devised it in order to make my life better for myself?
- Am I acting by an old, just-happens-to-be-there morality? Or is it something I've personally determined from the knowledge of who I am and what I want?
- Are the rewards and punishments attached to the rules vague and intangible? Or do the rules point to specific happiness I can achieve or unhappiness I can avoid?
- Is it a morality I've accepted because "someone undoubtedly knows the reason for it"? Or is it one I've created because *I* know the reason for it?
- Is it a morality that's currently "in style" and accepted by all those around me? Or is it a morality specifically tailored to *my* style?
- Is it a morality that's aimed *at* me and *against* my self-interest? Or is it a morality that's *for* me and comes *from me*?

All the answers must come from you—not from a book or a lecture or a sermon. . . .

No matter how you approach the matter, *you* are the sovereign authority who makes the final decisions. The more you realize that, the more your decisions will fit realistically with your own life. . . .

II. THE UNSELFISHNESS TRAP

The Unselfishness Trap is the belief that you must put the happiness of others ahead of your own.

Unselfishness is a very popular ideal, one that's been honored throughout recorded history. Wherever you turn, you find encouragement to put the happiness of others ahead of your own—to do what's best for the world, not for yourself.

If the ideal is sound, there must be something unworthy in seeking to live your life as you want to live.

So perhaps we should look more closely at the subject—to see if the ideal is sound. For if you attempt to be free, we can assume that someone's going to consider that to be selfish. . . .

Each person always acts in ways he believes will make him feel good or will remove discomfort from his life. Because everyone is different from everyone else, each individual goes about it in his own way.

One man devotes his life to helping the poor. Another one lies and steals. Still another person tries to create better products and services for which he hopes to be paid handsomely. One woman devotes herself to her husband and children. Another one seeks a career as a singer.

In every case, the ultimate motivation has been the same. Each person is doing what *he* believes will assure his happiness. What varies between them is the *means* each has chosen to gain his happiness.

We could divide them into two groups labeled "selfish" and "unselfish," but I don't think that would prove anything. For the thief and the humanitarian each have the same motive—to do what he believes will make him feel good.

In fact, we can't avoid a very significant conclusion; *Everyone is selfish*. Selfishness isn't really an issue, because everyone selfishly seeks his own happiness. . . .

A. A Better World?

Let's look first at the ideal of living for the benefit of others. It's often said that it would be a better world if everyone were unselfish. But would it be?

If it were somehow possible for everyone to give up his own happiness, what would be the result? Let's carry it to its logical conclusion and see what we find.

To visualize it, let's imagine that happiness is symbolized by a big red rubber ball. I have the ball in my hands—meaning that I hold the ability to be happy. But since I'm not going to be selfish, I quickly pass the ball to you. I've given up my happiness for you.

What will you do? Since you're not selfish either, you won't keep the ball; you'll quickly pass it on to your next-door neighbor. But he doesn't want to be selfish either, so he passes it to his wife, who likewise gives it to her children.

The children have been taught the virtue of unselfishness, so they pass it to playmates, who pass it to parents, who pass it to neighbors, and on and on and on.

I think we can stop the analogy at this point and ask what's been accomplished by all this effort. Who's better off for these demonstrations of pure unselfishness?

How would it be a better world if everyone acted that way? Whom would we be unselfish for? There would have to be a selfish person who would receive, accept, and enjoy the benefits of our unselfishness for there to be any purpose to it. But that selfish person (the object of our generosity) would be living by lower standards than we do.

For a more practical example, what is achieved by the parent who "sacrifices" himself for his children, who in turn are expected to sacrifice themselves for *their* children, etc.? The unselfishness concept is a merry-go-round that has no ultimate purpose. No one's self-interest is enhanced by the continual relaying of gifts from one person to another to another.

Perhaps most people have never carried the concept of unselfishness to this logical conclusion. If they did, they might reconsider their pleas for an unselfish world.

B. Negative Choices

But, unfortunately, the pleas continue, and they're a very real part of your life. In seeking your own freedom and happiness, you have to deal with those who tell you that you shouldn't put yourself first. That creates a situation in which you're pressured to act negatively—to put aside your plans and desires in order to avoid the condemnation of others.

One of the characteristics of a free man is that he's usually choosing positively—deciding which of several alternatives would make him the happiest; while the average person, most of the time, is choosing which of two or three alternatives will cause him the least discomfort.

When the reason for your actions is to avoid being called "selfish" you're making a negative decision and thereby restricting the possibilities for your own happiness.

You're in the Unselfishness Trap if you regretfully pay for your aunt's surgery with the money you'd saved for a new car, or if you sadly give up the vacation you'd looked forward to in order to help a sick neighbor.

You're in the trap if you feel you're *required* to give part of your income to the poor, or if you think that your country, community, or family has first claim on your time, energy, or money.

You're in the Unselfishness Trap any time you make negative choices that are designed to avoid being called "selfish."

It isn't that no one else is important. You might have a self-interest in someone's well-being, and giving a gift can be a gratifying expression of the affection you feel for him. But you're in the trap if you do such things in order to appear unselfish.

C. Helping Others

There *is* an understandable urge to give to those who are important and close to you. However, that leads many people to think that indiscriminate giving is the key to one's own happiness. They say that the way to be happy is to make others happy; get your glow by basking in the glow you've created for someone else.

It's important to identify that as a personal opinion. If someone says that giving is the key to happiness, isn't he saying that's the key to *his* happiness?

I think we can carry the question further, however, and determine how efficient such a policy might be. The suggestion to be a giver presupposes that you're able to judge what will make someone else happy. And experience has taught me to be a bit humble about assuming what makes others happy.

My landlady once brought me a piece of her freshly baked cake because she wanted to do me a favor. Unfortunately, it happened to be a kind of cake that was distasteful to me. I won't try to describe the various ways I tried to get the cake plate back to her without being confronted with a request for my judgment of her cake. It's sufficient to say that her well-intentioned favor interfered with my own plans.

And now, whenever I'm sure I know what someone else "needs," I remember that incident and back off a little. There's no way that one person can read the mind of another to know all his plans, goals, and tastes.

You may know a great deal about the desires of your intimate friends. But *indiscriminate* gift-giving and favor-doing is usually a waste of resources—or, worse, it can upset the well-laid plans of the receiver.

When you give to someone else, you might provide something he values—but probably not the thing he considers most important. If you expend those resources for *yourself*, you automatically devote them to what you consider to be most important. The time or money you've spent will most likely create more happiness that way.

If your purpose is to make someone happy, you're more apt to succeed if you make yourself the object. You'll never know another person more than a fraction as well as you can know yourself. . . .

D. Alternatives

As I indicated earlier . . ., it's too often assumed that there are only two alternatives: (1) Sacrifice your interests for the benefit of others; or (2) Make others sacrifice their interests for you. If nothing else were possible, it would indeed be a grim world.

Fortunately, there's more to the world than that. Because desires vary from person to person, it's possible to create exchanges between individuals in which both parties benefit.

For example, if you buy a house, you do so because you'd rather have the house than the money involved. But the seller's desire is different—he'd rather have the money than the house. When the sale is completed, each of

you has received something of greater value than what you gave up—
otherwise you wouldn't have entered the exchange. Who, then, has had to
sacrifice for the other?

In the same way, your daily life is made up of dozens of such exchanges—
small and large transactions in which each party gets something he values
more than what he gives up. The exchange doesn't have to involve money;
you may be spending time, attention, or effort in exchange for something
you value.

Mutually beneficial relationships are possible when desires are compatible. Sometimes the desires are the same—like going to a movie together.
Sometimes the desires are different—like trading your money for someone's house. In either case, it's the *compatibility* of the desires that makes the
exchange possible.

No sacrifice is necessary when desires are compatible. So it makes sense
to seek out people with whom you can have mutually beneficial relationships. . . .

An efficiently selfish person *is* sensitive to the needs and desires of others. But he doesn't consider those desires to be demands upon him.
Rather, he sees them as *opportunities*—potential exchanges that might be
beneficial to him. He identifies desires in others so that he can decide if exchanges with them will help him get what he wants.

He doesn't sacrifice himself for others, nor does he expect others to be
sacrificed for him. He takes the third alternative—he finds relationships
that are mutually beneficial so that no sacrifice is required.

E. Please Yourself

Everyone is selfish; everyone is doing what he believes will make himself
happier. The recognition of that can take most of the sting out of accusations that you're being "selfish." Why should you feel guilty for seeking
your own happiness when that's what everyone else is doing, too?

The demand that you be unselfish can be motivated by any number of
reasons: that you'd help create a better world, that you have a moral obligation to be unselfish, that you give up your happiness to the selfishness of
someone else, or that the person demanding it has just never thought it
out.

Whatever the reason, you're not likely to convince such a person to stop
his demands. But it will create much less pressure on you if you realize that
it's *his* selfish reason. And you can eliminate the problem entirely by looking for more compatible companions.

To find constant, profound happiness requires that you be free to seek
the gratification of your own desires. It means making positive choices.

If you slip into the Unselfishness Trap, you'll spend a good part of you time making negative choices—trying to avoid the censure of those who tell you not to think of yourself. . . .

If someone finds happiness by doing "good works" for others, let him. That doesn't mean that's the best way for you to find happiness.

And when someone accuses you of being selfish, just remember that he's only upset because you aren't doing what *he* selfishly wants you to do.

40 / Egoism and Moral Skepticism

JAMES RACHELS

I. [INTRODUCTION]

Our ordinary thinking about morality is full of assumptions that we almost never question. We assume, for example, that we have an obligation to consider the welfare of other people when we decide what actions to perform or what rules to obey; we think that we must refrain from acting in ways harmful to others, and that we must respect their rights and interests as well as our own. We also assume that people are in fact capable of being motivated by such considerations, that is, that people are not wholly selfish and that they do sometimes act in the interests of others. . . .

[Views attacking these assumptions] have come to be known as *psychological egoism* and *ethical egoism* respectively. Psychological egoism is the view that all men are selfish in everything that they do, that is, that the only motive from which anyone ever acts is self-interest. On this view, even when men are acting in ways apparently calculated to benefit others, they are actually motivated by the belief that acting in this way is to their own advantage, and if they did not believe this, they would not be doing that action. Ethical egoism is, by contrast, a normative view about how men *ought* to act. It is the view that, regardless of how men do in fact behave, they have no obligation to do anything except what is in their own interests. According to the ethical egoist, a person is always justified in doing whatever is in his own interest, regardless of the effect on others.

Clearly, if either of these views is correct, then "the moral institution of life" (to use Butler's well-turned phrase) is very different than what we nor-

ajority of mankind is grossly deceived about what is, or
se, where morals are concerned.

II. [PSYCHOLOGICAL EGOISM]

Psy⸺ goism seems to fly in the face of the facts. We are tempted to say, "Of course people act unselfishly all the time. For example, Smith gives up a trip to the country, which he would have enjoyed very much, in order to stay behind and help a friend with his studies, which is a miserable way to pass the time. This is a perfectly clear case of unselfish behavior, and if the psychological egoist thinks that such cases do not occur, then he is just mistaken." Given such obvious instances of "unselfish behavior," what reply can the egoist make? There are two general arguments by which he might try to show that all actions, including those such as the one just outlined, are in fact motivated by self-interest. Let us examine these in turn:

A. The first argument goes as follows. If we describe one person's action as selfish, and another person's action as unselfish, we are overlooking the crucial fact that in both cases, assuming that the action is done voluntarily, *the agent is merely doing what he most wants to do*. If Smith stays behind to help his friend, that only shows that he wanted to help his friend more than he wanted to go to the country. And why should he be praised for his "unselfishness" when he is only doing what he most wants to do? So, since Smith is only doing what he wants to do, he cannot be said to be acting unselfishly.

This argument is so bad that it would not deserve to be taken seriously except for the fact that so many otherwise intelligent people have been taken in by it. First, the argument rests on the premise that people never voluntarily do anything except what they want to do. But this is patently false; there are at least two classes of actions that are exceptions to this generalization. One is the set of actions which we may not want to do, but which we do anyway as a means to an end which we want to achieve; for example, going to the dentist in order to stop a toothache, or going to work every day in order to be able to draw our pay at the end of the month. These cases may be regarded as consistent with the spirit of the egoist argument, however, since the ends mentioned are wanted by the agent. But the other set of actions are those which we do, not because we want to, nor even because there is an end which we want to achieve, but because we feel ourselves *under an obligation* to do them. For example, someone may do something because he has promised to do it, and thus feels obligated, even though he does not want to do it. It is sometimes suggested that in such cases we do the action because, after all, we want to keep our promises; so, even here, we are doing what we want. However, this dodge will not work:

If I have promised to do something, and if I do not want to do it, then it is simply false to say that I want to keep my promise. In such cases we feel a conflict precisely because we do *not* want to do what we feel obligated to do. It is reasonable to think that Smith's action falls roughly into this second category: He might stay behind, not because he wants to, but because he feels that his friend needs help.

But suppose we were to concede, for the sake of the argument, that all voluntary action is motivated by the agent's wants, or at least that Smith is so motivated. Even if these were granted, it would not follow that Smith is acting selfishly or from self-interest. For if Smith wants to do something that will help his friend, even when it means forgoing his own enjoyments, that is precisely what makes him *unselfish*. What else could unselfishness be, if not wanting to help others? Another way to put the same point is to say that it is the *object* of a want that determines whether it is selfish or not. The mere fact that I am acting on *my* wants does not mean that I am acting selfishly; that depends on *what it is* that I want. If I want only my own good, and care nothing for others, then I am selfish; but if I also want other people to be well-off and happy, and if I act on *that* desire, then my action is not selfish. So much for this argument.

B. The second argument for psychological egoism is this. Since so-called unselfish actions always produce a sense of self-satisfaction in the agent,[1] and since this sense of satisfaction is a pleasant state of consciousness, it follows that the point of the action is really to achieve a pleasant state of consciousness, rather than to bring about any good for others. Therefore, the action is "unselfish" only at a superficial level of analysis. Smith will feel much better with himself for having stayed to help his friend—if he had gone to the country, he would have felt terrible about it—and that is the real point of the action. . . .

This argument suffers from defects similar to the previous one. Why should we think that merely because someone derives satisfaction from helping others this makes him selfish? Isn't the unselfish man precisely the one who *does* derive satisfaction from helping others, while the selfish man does not? . . . Similarly, it is nothing more than shabby sophistry to say, because Smith takes satisfaction in helping his friend, that he is behaving selfishly. If we say this rapidly, while thinking about something else, perhaps it will sound all right; but if we speak slowly, and pay attention to what we are saying, it sounds plain silly.

Moreover, suppose we ask *why* Smith derives satisfaction from helping his friend. The answer will be, it is because Smith cares for him and wants him to succeed. If Smith did not have these concerns, then he would take

---

[1]Or, as it is sometimes said, "It gives him a clear conscience," or "He couldn't sleep at night if he had done otherwise," or "He would have been ashamed of himself for not doing it," and so on.

no pleasure in assisting him; and these concerns, as we have already seen, are the marks of unselfishness, not selfishness. To put the point more generally: If we have a positive attitude toward the attainment of some goal, then we may derive satisfaction from attaining that goal. But the *object* of our attitude is *the attainment of that goal*; and we must want to attain the goal before we can find any satisfaction in it. We do not, in other words, desire some sort of "pleasurable consciousness" and then try to figure out how to achieve it; rather, we desire all sorts of different things—money, a new fishing-boat, to be a better chess-player, to get a promotion in our work, etc.—and because we desire these things, we derive satisfaction from attaining them. And so, if someone desires the welfare and happiness of another person, he will derive satisfaction from that; but this does not mean that this satisfaction is the object of his desire, or that he is in any way selfish on account of it.

It is a measure of the weakness of psychological egoism that these insupportable arguments are the ones most often advanced in its favor. Why, then, should anyone ever have thought it a true view? Perhaps because of a desire for theoretical simplicity: In thinking about human conduct, it would be nice if there were some simple formula that would unite the diverse phenomena of human behavior under a single explanatory principle, just as simple formulae in physics bring together a great many apparently different phenomena. And since it is obvious that self-regard is an overwhelmingly important factor in motivation, it is only natural to wonder whether all motivation might not be explained in these terms. But the answer is clearly No; while a great many human actions are motivated entirely or in part by self-interest, only by a deliberate distortion of the facts can we say that all conduct is so motivated. . . .

III. [ETHICAL EGOISM]

The ethical egoist would say at this point, "Of course it is possible for people to act altruistically, and perhaps many people do act that way—but there is no reason why they *should* do so. A person is under no obligation to do anything except what is in his own interests."[2] This is really quite a radical doctrine. Suppose I have an urge to set fire to some public building (say, a department store) just for the fascination of watching the spectacular blaze: According to this view, the fact that several people might be burned to death provides no reason whatever why I should not do it. After all, this only concerns *their* welfare, not my own, and according to the ethical egoist the only person I need think of is myself.

[2]I take this to be the view of Ayn Rand, insofar as I understand her confusing doctrine.

Some might deny that ethical egoism has any such monstrous consequences. They would point out that it is really to my own advantage not to set the fire—for, if I do that I may be caught and put into prison. . . . Moreover, even if I could avoid being caught it is still to my advantage to respect the rights and interests of others, for it is to my advantage to live in a society in which people's rights and interests are respected. Only in such a society can I live a happy and secure life; so, in acting kindly toward others, I would merely be doing my part to create and maintain the sort of society which it is to my advantage to have.[3] Therefore, it is said, the egoist would not be such a bad man; he would be as kindly and considerate as anyone else, because he would see that it is to his own advantage to be kindly and considerate.

This is a seductive line of thought, but it seems to me mistaken. Certainly it is to everyone's advantage (including the egoist's) to preserve a stable society where people's interests are generally protected. But there is no reason for the egoist to think that merely because *he* will not honor the rules of the social game, decent society will collapse. For the vast majority of people are not egoists, and there is no reason to think that they will be converted by his example—especially if he is discreet and does not unduly flaunt his style of life. What this line of reasoning shows is not that the egoist himself must act benevolently, but that he must encourage *others* to do so. He must take care to conceal from public view his own self-centered method of decision-making, and urge others to act on precepts very different from those on which he is willing to act.

The rational egoist, then, cannot advocate that egoism be universally adopted by everyone. For he wants a world in which his own interests are maximized; and if other people adopted the egoistic policy of pursuing their own interests to the exclusion of his interest, as he pursues his interests to the exclusion of theirs, then such a world would be impossible. So he himself will be egoist, but he will want others to be altruists.

This brings us to what is perhaps the most popular "refutation" of ethical egoism current among philosophical writers—the argument that ethical egoism is at bottom inconsistent because it cannot be universalized.[4] The argument goes like this:

To say that any action or policy of action is *right* (or that it *ought* to be adopted) entails that it is right for *anyone* in the same sort of circumstances. I cannot, for example, say that it is right for me to lie to you, and yet object when you lie to me (provided, of course, that the circumstances are the same). I cannot hold that it is all right for me to drink your beer and then complain when you drink mine. This is just the requirement that we be

---

[3]Cf. Thomas Hobbes, *Leviathan* (London, 1651) , chap. 17.

[4]See, for example, Brian Medlin, "Ultimate Principles and Ethical Egoism," *Australasian Journal of Philosophy*, vol. 35 (1957), 111–118; and D. H. Monro, *Empiricism and Ethics* (Cambridge, 1967), chap. 16.

consistent in our evaluations; it is a requirement of logic. Now it is said that ethical egoism cannot meet this requirement because, as we have already seen, the egoist would not want others to act in the same way that he acts. Moreover, suppose he *did* advocate the universal adoption of egoistic policies: he would be saying to Peter, "You ought to pursue your own interests even if it means destroying Paul"; and he would be saying to Paul, "You ought to pursue your own interests even if it means destroying Peter." The attitudes expressed in these two recommendations seem clearly inconsistent—he is urging the advancement of Peter's interest at one moment, and countenancing their defeat at the next. Therefore, the argument goes, there is no way to maintain the doctrine of ethical egoism as a consistent view about how we ought to act. We will fall into inconsistency whenever we try.

What are we to make of this argument? Are we to conclude that ethical egoism has been refuted? Such a conclusion, I think, would be unwarranted; for I think that we can show, contrary to this argument, how ethical egoism can be maintained consistently. We need only to interpret the egoist's position in a sympathetic way: We should say that he has in mind a certain kind of world which he would prefer over all others; it would be a world in which his own interests were maximized, regardless of the effects on other people. The egoist's primary policy of action, then, would be to act in such a way as to bring about, as nearly as possible, this sort of world. Regardless of however morally reprehensible we might find it, there is nothing *inconsistent* in someone's adopting this as his ideal and acting in a way calculated to bring it about. And if someone did adopt this as his ideal, then he would not advocate universal egoism; as we have already seen, he would want other people to be altruists. So if he advocates any principles of conduct for the general public, they will be altruistic principles. This would not be inconsistent; on the contrary, it would be perfectly consistent with his goal of creating a world in which his own interests are maximized. To be sure, he would have to be deceitful; in order to secure the good will of others, and a favorable hearing for his exhortations to altruism, he would have to pretend that he was himself prepared to accept altruistic principles. But again, that would be all right; from the egoist's point of view, this would merely be a matter of adopting the necessary means to the achievement of his goal—and while we might not approve of this, there is nothing inconsistent about it. . . .

Is there, then, no way to refute the ethical egoist? If by "refute" we mean show that he has made some *logical* error, the answer is that there is not. However, there is something more that can be said. The egoist challenge to our ordinary moral convictions amounts to a demand for an explanation of why we should adopt certain policies of action, namely policies in which the good of others is given importance. We can give an answer to this demand, albeit an indirect one. The reason one ought not to do actions that would hurt other people is: Other people would be hurt. The reason one ought to do actions that would benefit other people is: Other people would be benefited. This may at first seem like a piece of philosophical sleight-of-hand, but it is not. The point is that the welfare of human beings is something that most of us value *for its own sake,* and not merely for the sake of something else. Therefore, when *further* reasons are demanded for valuing the welfare of human beings, we cannot point to anything further to satisfy this demand. It is not that we have no reason for pursuing these policies, but that our reason *is* that these policies are for the good of human beings.

So if we are asked, "Why shouldn't I set fire to this department store?" one answer would be, "Because if you do, people may be burned to death." This is a complete, sufficient reason which does not require qualification or supplementation of any sort. If someone seriously wants to know why this action shouldn't be done, that's the reason. If we are pressed further and asked the skeptical question, "But why shouldn't I do actions that will harm others?" we may not know what to say—but this is because the questioner has included in this question the very answer we would like to give: "Why shouldn't you do actions that will harm others? Because doing those actions would harm others."

The egoist, no doubt, will not be happy with this. He will protest that *we* may accept this as a reason, but *he* does not. And here the argument stops: There are limits to what can be accomplished by argument, and if the egoist really doesn't care about other people—if he honestly doesn't care whether they are helped or hurt by his actions—then we have reached those limits. If we want to persuade him to act decently toward his fellow humans, we will have to make our appeal to such other attitudes as he does possess, by threats, bribes, or other cajolery. That is all that we can do.

Though some may find this situation distressing (we would like to be able to show that the egoist is just *wrong*), it holds no embarrassment for common morality. What we have come up against is simply a fundamental requirement of rational action, namely, that the existence of reasons for action always depends on the prior existence of certain attitudes in the agent. For example, the fact that a certain course of action would make the agent a lot of money is a reason for doing it only if the agent wants to make money; the fact that practicing at chess makes one a better player is a reason for practicing only if one wants to be a better player; and so on. Similarly, the fact that a certain action would help the agent is a reason for doing the action only if the agent cares about his own welfare, and the fact that an action would help others is a reason for doing it only if the agent cares about others. In this respect ethical egoism and what we might call ethical altruism are in exactly the same fix: Both require that the agent *care* about himself, or about other people, before they can get started.

. So a nonegoist will accept "It would harm another person" as a reason not to do an action simply because he cares about what happens to that other person. When the egoist says that he does *not* accept that as a reason, he is saying something quite extraordinary. He is saying that he has no affection for friends or family, that he never feels pity or compassion, that he is the sort of person who can look on scenes of human misery with complete indifference, so long as he is not the one suffering. Genuine egoists, people who really don't care at all about anyone than themselves, are rare. . . .

41 / Utilitarianism

JEREMY BENTHAM

OF THE PRINCIPLE OF UTILITY

I. Nature has placed mankind under the governance of two sovereign masters, *pain* and *pleasure*. It is for them alone to point out what we ought to do, as well as to determine what we shall do. On the one hand the standard of right and wrong, on the other the chain of causes and effects, are fastened to their throne. They govern us in all we do, in all we say, in all we think: every effort we can make to throw off our subjection, will serve but to demonstrate and confirm it. In words a man may pretend to abjure their empire: but in reality he will remain subject to it all the while. The *principle of utility* recognises this subjection, and assumes it for the foundation of that system, the object of which is to rear the fabric of felicity by the hands of reason and of law. Systems which attempt to question it, deal in sounds instead of sense, in caprice instead of reason, in darkness instead of light.

But enough of metaphor and declamation: it is not by such means that moral science is to be improved.

II. The principle of utility is the foundation of the present work: it will be proper therefore at the outset to give an explicit and determinate account of what is meant by it. By the principle of utility is meant that principle which approves or disapproves of every action whatsoever, according to the tendency which it appears to have to augment or diminish the happiness of the party whose interest is in question: or, what is the same thing in other words, to promote or to oppose that happiness.* I say of every action what-

*[What Bentham means by this sentence is: By the principle of utility is meant the principle that every action is to be approved of or disapproved of according to the tendency which it appears to have to augment or diminish the happiness of anyone whose interest is in question. . . .—Eds.]

soever; and therefore not only of every action of a private individual, but of every measure of government.

III. By utility is meant that property in any object, whereby it tends to produce benefit, advantage, pleasure, good, or happiness (all this in the present case comes to the same thing) or (what comes again to the same thing) to prevent the happening of mischief, pain, evil, or unhappiness to the party whose interest is considered: if that party be the community in general, then the happiness of the community: if a particular individual, then the happiness of that individual.

IV. The interest of the community is one of the most general expressions that can occur in the phraseology of morals: no wonder that the meaning of it is often lost. When it has a meaning, it is this. The community is a fictitious *body*, composed of the individual persons who are considered as constituting as it were its *members*. The interest of the community then is, what?—the sum of the interests of the several members who compose it.

V. It is in vain to talk of the interest of the community, without understanding what is the interest of the individual. A thing is said to promote the interest, or to be *for* the interest, of an individual, when it tends to add to the sum total of his pleasures: or, what comes to the same thing, to diminish the sum total of his pains.

VI. An action then may be said to be conformable to the principal of utility, or, for shortness sake, to utility (meaning with respect to the community at large), when the tendency it has to augment the happiness of the community is greater than any it has to diminish it.

VII. A measure of government (which is but a particular kind of action, performed by a particular person or persons) may be said to be conformable to or dictated by the principle of utility, when in like manner the tendency which it has to augment the happiness of the community is greater than any which it has to diminish it.

VIII. When an action, or in particular a measure of government, is supposed by a man to be conformable to the principle of utility, it may be convenient, for the purposes of discourse, to imagine a kind of law or dictate, called a law or dictate of utility: and to speak of the action in question, as being conformable to such law or dictate.

IX. A man may be said to be a partisan of the principle of utility, when the approbation or disapprobation he annexes to any action, or to any measure, is determined by and proportioned to the tendency which he conceives it to have to augment or to diminish the happiness of the community; or in other words, to its conformity or unconformity to the laws or dictates of utility.

X. Of an action that is conformable to the principle of utility one may always say either that it is one that ought to be done, or at least that it is not one that ought not to be done. One may say also, that it is right it should be done; at least that it is not wrong it should be done; that it is a right action; at least that it is not a wrong action. When thus interpreted, the words *ought,* and *right* and *wrong,* and others of that stamp, have a meaning: when otherwise, they have none.

XI. Has the rectitude of this principle been ever formally contested? It should seem that it had, by those who have not known what they have been meaning. Is it susceptible of any direct proof? It should seem not: for that which is used to prove everything else, cannot itself be proved: a chain of proofs must have their commencement somewhere. To give such proof is as impossible as it is needless.

XII. Not that there is or ever has been that human creature breathing, however stupid or perverse, who has not on many, perhaps on most occasions of his life, deferred to it. By the natural constitution of the human frame, on most occasions of their lives men in general embrace this principle, without thinking of it: if not for the ordering of their own actions, yet for the trying of their own actions, as well as of those of other men. There have been, at the same time, not many, perhaps, even of the most intelligent, who have been disposed to embrace it purely and without reserve. There are even few who have not taken some occasion or other to quarrel with it, either on account of their not understanding always how to apply it, or on account of some prejudice or other which they were afraid to examine into, or could not bear to part with. For such is the stuff that man is made of: in principle and in practice, in a right track and in a wrong one, the rarest of all human qualities is consistency.

XIII. When a man attempts to combat the principle of utility, it is with reasons drawn, without his being aware of it, from that very principle itself. His arguments, if they prove any thing, prove not that the principle is *wrong,* but that, according to the applications he supposes to be made of it, it is *misapplied.* Is it possible for a man to move the earth? Yes; but he must first find out another earth to stand upon.

OF PRINCIPLES ADVERSE TO THAT OF UTILITY

I. If the principle of utility be a right principle to be governed by, and that in all cases, it follows from what has been just observed, that whatever principle differs from it in any case must necessarily be a wrong one. To prove any other principle, therefore, to be a wrong one, there needs no more than just to show it to be what it is, a principle of which the dictates are in some point or other different from those of the principle of utility: to state it is to confute it.

II. A principle may be different from that of utility in two ways: 1. By being constantly opposed to it: this is the case with a principle which may be termed the principle of *asceticism.* 2. By being sometimes opposed to it, and sometimes not, as it may happen: this is the case with another, which may be termed the principle of *sympathy* and *antipathy.*

III. By the principle of asceticism I mean that principle, which, like the principle of utility, approves or disapproves of any action, according to the tendency which it appears to have to augment or diminish the happiness of the party whose interest is in question; but in an inverse manner: approving of actions in as far as they tend to diminish his happiness; disapproving of them in as far as they tend to augment it.*

IV. It is evident that any one who reprobates any the least particle of pleasure, as such, from whatever source derived, is *pro tanto* a partisan of the principle of asceticism. It is only upon that principle, and not from the principle of utility, that the most abominable pleasure which the vilest of malefactors ever reaped from his crime would be to be reprobated, if it stood alone. The case is, that it never does stand alone; but is necessarily followed by such a quality of pain (or, what comes to the same thing, such a chance for a certain quantity of pain) that the pleasure in comparison of it, is as nothing: and this is the true and sole, but perfectly sufficient, reason for making it a ground for punishment. . . .

V. The principle of utility is capable of being consistently pursued; and it is but tautology to say, that the more consistently it is pursued, the better it must ever be for humankind. The principle of asceticism never was, nor ever can be, consistently pursued by any living creature. Let but one tenth part of the inhabitants of this earth pursue it consistently, and in a day's time they will have turned it into a hell.

VI. Among principles adverse to that of utility, that which at this day seems to have most influence in matters of government, is what may be called the principle of sympathy and antipathy. By the principle of sympathy and antipathy, I mean that principle which approves or disapproves of certain actions, not on account of their tending to augment the happiness, nor yet on account of their tending to diminish the happiness of the party whose interest is in question, but merely because a man finds himself disposed to approve or disapprove of them: holding up that approbation or disapprobation as a sufficient reason for itself, and disclaiming the necessity of looking out for any extrinsic ground.† Thus far in the general department of morals: and in the particular department of politics, measuring out the quantum (as well as determining the ground) of punishment, by the degree of the disapprobation.

VII. It is manifest, that this is rather a principle in name than in reality: it is not a positive principle of itself, so much as a term employed to signify the negation of all principle. What one expects to find in a principle is something that points out some external consideration, as a means of war-

*[Again, he means: By the principle of asceticism I mean the principle that every action is to be approved of or disapproved of according to the tendency which it appears to have to augment or diminish the unhappiness of anyone whose interest is in question. . . .—Eds.]

†[Again: . . . the principle that every action is to be approved of or disapproved of according to whether one finds oneself disposed of to approve or disapprove it.—Eds.]

ranting and guiding the internal sentiments of approbation and disapprobation: this expectation is but ill fulfilled by a proposition, which does neither more nor less than hold up each of those sentiments as a ground and standard for itself.

VIII. In looking over the catalogue of human actions (says a partisan of this principle) in order to determine which of them are to be marked with the seal of disapprobation, you need but to take counsel of your own feelings: whatever you find in yourself a propensity to condemn, is wrong for that very reason. For the same reason it is also meet for punishment: in what proportion it is adverse to utility, or whether it be adverse to utility at all, is a matter that makes no difference. In that same *proportion* also is it meet for punishment: if you hate much, punish much: if you hate little, punish little: punish as you hate. If you hate not at all, punish not at all: the fine feelings of the soul are not to be overborne and tyrannized by the harsh and rugged dictates of political unity. . . .

IX. It is manifest, that the dictates of this principle will frequently coincide with those of utility, though perhaps without intending any such thing. Probably more frequently than not: and hence it is that the business of penal justice is carried on upon that tolerable sort of footing upon which we see it carried on in common at this day. For what more natural or more general ground of hatred to a practice can there be, than the mischievousness of such practice? What all men are exposed to suffer by, all men will be disposed to hate. It is far yet, however, from being a constant ground: for when a man suffers, it is not always that he knows what it is he suffers by. A man may suffer grievously, for instance, by a new tax, without being able to trace up the cause of his sufferings to the injustice of some neighbour, who has eluded the payment of an old one.

X. The principle of sympathy and antipathy is most apt to err on the side of severity. It is for applying punishment in many cases which deserve none: in many cases which deserve some, it is for applying more than they deserve. There is no incident imaginable, be it ever so trivial, and so remote from mischief, from which this principle may not extract a ground of punishment. Any difference in taste: any difference in opinion: upon one subject as well as upon another. No disagreement so trifling which perseverance and altercation will not render serious. Each becomes in the other's eyes an enemy, and, if laws permit, a criminal. This is one of the circumstances by which the human race is distinguished (not much indeed to its advantage) from the brute creation. . . .

XI. There are two things which are very apt to be confounded, but which it imports us carefully to distinguish:—the motive or cause, which, by operating on the mind of an individual, is productive of any act: and the ground or reason which warrants a legislator, or other bystander, in regarding that act with an eye of approbation. When the act happens, in the particular instance in question, to be productive of effects which we approve of, much more if we happen to observe that the same motive may frequently be productive, in other instances, of the like effects, we are apt to transfer our approbation to the motive itself, and to assume, as the just ground for the approbation we bestow on the act, the circumstance of its originating from that motive. It is in this way that the sentiment of antipathy has often been considered as a just ground of action. Antipathy, for instance, in such or such a case, is the cause of an action which is attended with good effects: but this does not make it a right ground of action in that case, any more than in any other. Still farther. Not only the effects are good, but the agent sees beforehand that they will be so. This may make the action indeed a perfectly right action: but it does not make antipathy a right ground of action. For the same sentiment of antipathy, if implicitly deferred to, may be, and very frequently is, productive of the very worst effects. Antipathy, therefore, can never be a right ground of action. No more, therefore, can resentment, which, as will be seen more particularly hereafter, is but a modification of antipathy. The only right ground of action, that can possibly subsist, is, after all, the consideration of utility, which, if it is a right principle of action, and of approbation, in any one case, is so in every other. Other principles in abundance, that is, other motives, may be the reasons why such and such an act *has* been done: that is, the reasons or causes of its being done: but it is this alone that can be the reason why it might or ought to have been done. Antipathy or resentment requires always to be regulated, to prevent its doing mischief: to be regulated by what? always by the principle of utility. The principle of utility neither requires nor admits of any other regulator than itself.

VALUE OF A LOT OF PLEASURE OR PAIN, HOW TO BE MEASURED

I. Pleasures then, and the avoidance of pains, are the *ends* which the legislator has in view: it behooves him therefore to understand their *value*. Pleasures and pains are the *instruments* he has to work with: it behooves him therefore to understand their force, which is again, in other words, their value.

II. To a person considered *by himself*, the value of a pleasure or pain considered *by itself*, will be greater or less, according to the four following circumstances:

1. Its *intensity*.
2. Its *duration*.
3. Its *certainty* or *uncertainty*.
4. Its *propinquity* or *remoteness*.

III. These are the circumstances which are to be considered in estimating a pleasure or a pain considered each of them by itself. But when the value of any pleasure or pain is considered for the purpose of estimating the tendency of any *act* by which it is produced, there are two other circumstances to be taken into the account; these are,

5. Its *fecundity*, or the chance it has of being followed by sensations of the *same* kind: that is, pleasures, if it be a pleasure: pains, if it be a pain.

6. Its *purity*, or the chance it has of *not* being followed by sensations of the *opposite* kind: that is, pains, if it be a pleasure: pleasures, if it be a pain.

These two last, however, are in strictness scarcely to be deemed properties of the pleasure or the pain itself; they are not, therefore, in strictness to be taken into the account of the value of that pleasure or that pain. They are in strictness to be deemed properties only of the act, or other event, by which such pleasure or pain has been produced; and accordingly are only to be taken into the account of the tendency of such act or such event.

IV. To a *number* of persons, with reference to each of whom the value of a pleasure or a pain is considered, it will be greater or less, according to seven circumstances: to wit, the six preceding ones; *viz.*

1. Its *intensity*.
2. Its *duration*.
3. Its *certainty* or *uncertainty*.
4. Its *propinquity* or *remoteness*.
5. Its *fecundity*.
6. Its *purity*.

And one other; to wit:

7. Its *extent*; that is, the number of persons to whom it *extends*; or (in other words) who are affected by it.

V. To take an exact account then of the general tendency of any act, by which the interests of a community are affected, proceed as follows. Begin with any one person of those whose interests seem most immediately to be affected by it: and take an account,

1. Of the value of each distinguishable *pleasure* which appears to be produced by it in the *first* instance.

2. Of the value of each *pain* which appears to be produced by it in the *first* instance.

3. Of the value of each pleasure which appears to be produced by it *after* the first. This constitutes the *fecundity* of the first *pleasure* and the *impurity* of the first *pain*.

4. Of the value of each *pain* which appears to be produced by it after the first. This constitutes the *fecundity* of the first *pain*, and the *impurity* of the first pleasure.

5. Sum up all the values of all the *pleasures* on the one side, and those of all the pains on the other. The balance, if it be on the side of pleasure, will give the *good* tendency of the act upon the whole, with respect to the interests of that *individual* person; if on the side of pain, the *bad* tendency of it upon the whole.

6. Take an account of the *number* of persons whose interests appear to be concerned; and repeat the above process with respect to each. *Sum up* the numbers expressive of the degrees of *good* tendency, which the act has, with respect to each individual, in regard to whom the tendency of it is *good* upon the whole: do this again with respect to each individual, in regard to whom the tendency of it is *bad* upon the whole. Take the *balance*; which, if on the side of *pleasure*, will give the general *good tendency* of the act, with respect to the total number or community of individuals concerned; if on the side of pain, the general *evil tendency*, with respect to the same community.

VI. It is not to be expected that this process should be strictly pursued previously to every moral judgment, or to every legislative or judicial operation. It may, however, be always kept in view: and as near as the process actually pursued on these occasions approaches to it, so near will such process approach to the character of an exact one.

VII. The same process is alike applicable to pleasure and pain, in whatever shape they appear: and by whatever denomination they are distinguished: to pleasure, whether it be called *good* (which is properly the cause or instrument of pleasure) or *profit* (which is distant pleasure, or the cause or instrument of distant pleasure), or *convenience*, or *advantage, benefit, emolument, happiness,* and so forth: to pain, whether it be called *evil* (which corresponds to *good*), or *mischief,* or *inconvenience,* or *disadvantage,* or *loss,* or *unhappiness,* and so forth.

VIII. Nor is this a novel and unwarranted, any more than it is a useless theory. In all this there is nothing but what the practice of mankind, wheresoever they have a clear view of their own interest, is perfectly conformable to. An article of property, an estate in land, for instance, is valuable, on what account? On account of the pleasures of all kinds which it enables a man to produce, and what comes to the same thing the pains of all kinds which it enables him to avert. But the value of such an article of property is universally understood to rise or fall according to the length or shortness of the time which a man has in it: the certainty or uncertainty of its coming into possession. As to the *intensity* of the pleasures which a man may derive from it, this is never thought of, because it depends upon the use which each particular person may come to make of it; which cannot be estimated till the particular pleasures he may come to derive from it, or the particular pains he may come to exclude by means of it, are brought to view. For the same reason, neither does he think of the *fecundity* or *purity* of those pleasures. . . .

42 / A Problem for Utilitarianism

PAUL W. TAYLOR

. . . **T**he objection raised against . . . utilitarian ethics is that *the principle of utility does not provide a sufficient ground for the obligations of justice*. Since the idea of justice is a fundamental moral concept, no normative ethical system can be considered adequate that does not show the basis for our duty to be just. The argument starts with a careful examination of the ultimate norm of utilitarian ethics, the principle of utility itself. Exactly what is utility? It has been described in the words, "the maximizing of intrinsic value and the minimizing of intrinsic disvalue." What, precisely, does this mean?

It will be helpful in answering this question to think of measurable units of intrinsic value and disvalue. We shall accordingly speak of units of happiness and unhappiness, respectively. This will enable us to see the difficulty more clearly, although no particular view of what is to be taken as the measurement of a unit of happiness or unhappiness will be presupposed. We all know in general what it means to be very happy, quite happy, not especially happy, rather unhappy, and extremely unhappy. Thus, the idea of degrees of happiness corresponds to something in our experience. We also know what it means to be happy for a brief moment, or for a day, and we use such phrases as "It was a happy two-week vacation," "I was not very happy during my early teens," and "He has led an unhappy life." There is some basis, therefore, in our everyday concept of happiness (and also of pleasure) for giving meaning to the idea of quantities or amounts of happiness, even though we do not ordinarily measure these quantities in arithmetical terms.

What, then, does the utilitarian mean by maximizing intrinsic value and minimizing intrinsic disvalue? There are three variables or factors that must be introduced in order to make this idea clear. First, it means to bring about, in the case of *one* person, the greatest balance of value over disvalue. Thus, if one act or rule yields $+1000$ of happiness and -500 units of unhappiness for a given person, while another act or rule yields $+700$ units and -100 units for that person, then, all other factors being equal, the second alternative is better than the first, since the balance of the second ($+600$) is greater than the balance of the first ($+500$). Similarly, to "minimize disvalue" would mean that an act or rule which yielded $+100$ and -300 for a given person would be better than one that yielded $+500$ and -1000 for the same person, other things being equal (even though more happiness is produced by the second than by the first).

The second factor is that the happiness and unhappiness of *all persons* affected must be considered. Thus, if four persons, A, B, C, and D, each experience some difference of happiness or unhappiness in life as a consequence of the act or rule but no difference occurs in the lives of anyone else, then the calculation of maximum value and minimum disvalue must include the balance of pluses and minuses occurring in the experience of every one of the four persons. Suppose in one case the balance is $+300$ for A, $+200$ for B, -300 for C, and -400 for D. And suppose the alternative yields $+200$ for A, $+100$ for B, -400 for C, and $+500$ for D. Then if someone were to claim that the first is better than the second because D's happiness or unhappiness does not count (D, for example, might be a slave while A, B, and C are free men), this conclusion would not be acceptable to utilitarians. For them, the second alternative is better than the first because the second yields a higher total balance than the first when *all* persons are considered.

The third factor in the utilitarian calculus has been tacitly assumed in the foregoing discussion of the second factor. This is the principle that, in calculating the units of happiness or unhappiness for different persons, the same criteria for measuring quantity are used. If totals of $+500$ and -200 represent sums of happiness and unhappiness in the experience of A and $+300$ and -400 represent sums of happiness and unhappiness in the experience of B, then one unit of plus (or minus) for A must be equal to one unit of plus (or minus) for B. No differences between A and B are to be considered as grounds for assigning a different weight to one or the other's happiness or unhappiness. When utilitarians assert that everyone's happiness is to count *equally*, they mean that, in calculating consequences, it is irrelevant *whose* happiness or unhappiness is affected by the act or rule. This may be called the principle of the equality of worth of every person as a person. (It does not mean, of course, that everyone is just as morally good or bad as everyone else!)

Now when these three factors are used in calculating utility, it is still possible for some persons to be unfairly or unjustly treated. For the greatest total balance of pluses over minuses may be brought about in a given society by actions or rules which discriminate against certain persons on irrelevant grounds. Although a greater quantity of happiness and a lesser amount of unhappiness are produced, they are distributed unjustly among the persons affected. To illustrate this possibility, consider two societies, one of which distributes different amounts of happiness to people on the basis of their race or religion, the other dispensing them on the basis of people's different needs, abilities, and merits, where "merits" are determined by contributions to the common good or general happiness. In the first society, people belonging to one race or religion are favored in educational opportunities, comfortable housing, and high-paying jobs, while people of another race or religion are disfavored. Race and religion function in that society as grounds for discrimination. In the second society, on the other hand, race or religion do not matter as far as education, housing, and jobs are concerned. All that counts are such things as, Does the individual have a need for special treatment, a need which, if overlooked, would unfairly handicap him in matters of education, housing, or jobs? (For example, a blind person might be given special schooling and a special job, so that his blindness will not mean that he has less of a chance for happiness in life than others.) Or, has the individual, through fair and open competition, proven himself qualified for a high-paying job? Or, does he have exceptional abilities—such as musical genius or mathematical brilliance—which deserve the society's recognition, so that advanced education and scholarships are made available to him? Here race and religion do not function as grounds for discrimination, since they are not considered in determining the proper distribution of happiness and unhappiness throughout the population.

The problem of utility and justice arises when it is seen that, in the two societies described above, it is possible for the first to produce a greater total net balance of happiness over unhappiness than the second. Thus, suppose the first society can force the members of the disfavored race or religion to work long hours for little or no pay, so that they produce much more and use up much less of what is produced than they would without such coercion. Then, even if the calculation of utility includes the unhappiness of the disadvantaged, the total balance of happiness over unhappiness could be greater than that resulting from the second society's system of production and consumption. A utilitarian, it seems, would have to say in that case that the first society was morally better than the second, since its policies and rules yielded a higher net utility. Yet the first society, if not simply and self-evidently unjust, would at least be considered (even by utilitarians) to be less just than the second. Hence, utility and justice are incompatible when applied to certain types of societies under certain conditions.

Such conflicts between utility and justice can occur because, as far as utility alone is concerned, it is always morally right to increase one person's happiness at the expense of another's, if the total net balance of pluses over minuses is greater than would be the case were the two persons treated equally. It would seem, in contrast to this, that justice requires that no individual serve as a mere instrument or means to someone else's happiness. (If a person freely consents to sacrifice his happiness for the sake of another, he is not, of course, being used merely as a means to someone else's ends.) On this point the opposition between justice and utility appears to be fundamental.

It should be noted in this connection that utility not only permits but actually requires one individual's being made unhappy if doing so adds to a group's happiness *however small an increase in happiness might be experienced by each of its members,* as long as the total amount of happiness to the group outweighs the unhappiness of the individual in question. Thus, suppose an innocent man is made a scapegoat for the guilt of others and accordingly suffers punishment. If he experiences, say, -100 units of unhappiness and if there are 101 persons who, in victimizing him, gain $+1$ unit of happiness each (perhaps in relief at seeing another blamed for their own wrongdoing), then the principle of utility *requires* that the scapegoat be punished. This is not because the scapegoat's unhappiness is being ignored or is being assigned less intrinsic worth than the happiness of others. Each unit of unhappiness (-1) experienced by the scapegoat is equal in "weight" to a unit of happiness ($+1$) of someone in the group. It just happens that in the given situation the total quantity of the group's happiness is greater than that of the scapegoat's unhappiness. Consequently the principle of utility, when applied to this situation, entails that the scapegoat be made to suffer.

It is in this way that the idea of justice seems to present a major philosophical difficulty for all forms of utilitarianism. How might utilitarians reply to this criticism? They would begin by pointing out that, when we leave abstract speculations about theoretical possibilities behind and face the actual world around us, we find that any conflict between justice and utility is highly unlikely. The apparent plausibility of the cases given above, they would say, depends on their being abstracted from the real processes of historical and social development. They hold that when these processes are fully taken into account, it becomes clear that injustice inevitably yields great disutility.

In support of this claim, utilitarians ask us to consider how the principle of utility would apply to situations of social conflict, where one person's (or group's) interests can be furthered only if another person's (or group's) interests are frustrated. For this is where the concepts of justice and injustice are applicable. Now with regard to such situations, the principle of utility requires social rules which enable people to resolve their disagreements and live in harmony with one another. To live in harmony means, not that no social conflicts occur, but that whenever they do occur, there is a set of rules everyone can appeal to as a fair way to resolve them. Such rules will (a) take everyone's interests into account, (b) give equal consideration to the interests of each person, and (c) enable all parties to a dispute to decide issues on grounds freely acceptable by all. For it is only when everyone can appeal to such a system of conflict-resolving rules that the society as a whole can achieve its maximum happiness and minimum unhappiness.

This can be seen by referring to the condition of anyone who does *not* accept a set of conflict-resolving rules as fair. Such a person will simply consider himself to be under social coercion with respect to those rules. That is, he will conform to the rules only because he is forced to by society. If his interests are frustrated by their operation, he will believe he has legitimate moral complaints against the rest of society, and will then think any action necessary to right the wrongs carried out in the name of the rules to be justified. The greater the number of such disaffected persons, the deeper will be the state of social disharmony. It is obvious that very little happiness can be realized in such a society.

At this point the following objection might be raised. To make sure that social conflict will not get out of hand, let those who accept the rules establish a power structure which will ensure their domination over those who reject them. In this way, although some (the powerless) may suffer, those in power can maximize their happiness. To this the utilitarian replies, "History has shown us that no such power structure can last for long; even while it does last, the effort spent by the 'ins' on maintaining domination over the 'outs' makes it impossible for the 'ins' to obtain much happiness in life. A social system of this kind is constantly liable to break down. The need to preserve their position of power drives the 'ins' to ever greater measures of surveillance and repression. The society as a whole becomes a closed system in which the freedom of all individuals is diminished. Accompanying this curtailment of human freedom is a dwindling in the very conception of man and his creative powers. Inevitably, there develops an intolerance of diversity in thought, in speech, in styles of life. A narrow conformity of taste, ideas, and outward behavior becomes the main concern of everyone. What kind of "happiness" is this? What amount of intrinsic value does such a narrow way of life really make possible for people, even people who have the power to advance their interests at the expense of others?"

The upshot of the argument is now apparent: Given a clearheaded view of the world as it is and a realistic understanding of man's nature, it becomes more and more evident that injustice will never have, in the long run, greater utility than justice. Even if the two principles of justice and utility can logically be separated in the abstract and even if they can be shown to yield contradictory results in hypothetical cases, it does not follow that the fundamental idea of utilitarianism must be given up. For it remains the case that, when we are dealing with the actual practices of people in their social and historical settings, to maximize happiness and minimize unhappiness requires an open, freely given commitment on the part of *everyone* to comply with the rules for settling conflicts among them. Anyone who is coerced into following the rules when he, in good conscience, cannot accept them as being fair to everyone (and consequently to himself) will not consider himself morally obligated to abide by them. Since he will either feel unjustly treated himself or see himself as a participant in the unfair treatment of others, society stands condemned in his judgment. From his point of view he will have good reason to do what he can to change or abolish the rules. He will join with anyone else who rejects them as unfair, in an effort to overcome his powerlessness. Thus, injustice becomes, in actual practice, a source of great social disutility. If society's reaction to the challenge of its dissidents is only a stronger attempt to impose its rules by force, this response will, sooner or later, bring about a situation in which no one really benefits. Not only is it profoundly true that "might does not make right," it is equally true that might cannot create the maximum balance of human happiness over human misery, when the lives of everyone are taken into account.

Whether this argument provides a successful rebuttal to the criticism of utilitarianism when viewed in the light of justice is a matter for the reader's own reflection.

43 / The Deep Beauty of the Golden Rule

R. M. MacIVER

I

The subject that learned men call ethics is a wasteland on the philosophical map. Thousands of books have been written on this matter, learned books and popular books, books that argue and books that exhort. Most of them are empty and nearly all are vain. Some claim that pleasure is *the* good; some prefer the elusive and more enticing name of happiness; others reject such principles and speak of equally elusive goals such as self-fulfillment. Others claim that *the* good is to be found in looking away from the self in devotion to the whole—which whole? in the service of God—whose God?—even in the service of the State—who prescribes the service? Here indeed, if anywhere, after listening to the many words of many apostles, one goes out by the same door as one went in.

The reason is simple. You say: "This is the way you should behave." But I say: "No, that is not the way." You say: "This is right." But I say: "No, that is wrong, and this is right." You appeal to experience. I appeal to experience against you. You appeal to authority: it is not mine. What is left? If you are strong, you can punish me for behaving my way. But does that prove anything except that you are stronger than I? Does it prove the absurd dogma that might makes right? Is the slavemaster right because he owns the whip, or Torquemada because he can send his heretics to the flames?

From this impasse no system of ethical rules has been able to deliver itself. How can ethics lay down final principles of behavior that are not your values against mine, your group's values against my group's?

Which, by the way, does not mean that your rules are any less valid for you because they are not valid for me. Only a person of shallow nature and autocratic learnings would draw that conclusion. For the sake of your integrity you must hold to your own values, no matter how much others reject them. Without *your* values you are nothing. True, you should search them and test them and learn by *your* experience and gain wisdom where you can. Your values are your guides through life but you need to use your own eyes. If I have different guides I shall go another way. So far as we diverge, values are relative as between you and me. But your values cannot be relative for you or mine for me.

That is not here the issue. It is that the relativity of values between you and me, between your group and my group, your sect and my sect, makes futile nearly all learned disquisitions about the first principles of ethics.

By ethics I mean the philosophy of how men should behave in their relations to one another. I am talking about philosophy, not about religion. When you have a creed, you can derive from it principles of ethics. Philosophy cannot begin with a creed, but only with reasoning about the nature of things. It cannot therefore presume that the values of other men are less to be regarded than the values of the proponent. If it does, it is not philosophy but dogma, dogma that is the enemy of philosophy, the kind of dogma that has been the source of endless tyranny and repression.

Can it be a philosophy worth the name that makes a universal of your values and thus rules mine out of existence, where they differ from yours?

How can reasoning decide between my values and yours? Values do not claim truth in any scientific sense; instead they claim validity, rightness. They do not declare what is so but what *should* be so. I cling to my values, you to yours. Your values, some of them, do not hold for me; some of them may be repulsive to me; some of them may threaten me. What then? To what court of reason shall we appeal? To what court that you and I both accept is there any appeal?

The lack of any court is the final *fact* about final values. It is a fundamental fact. It is a terrifying fact. It is also a strangely challenging fact. It gives man his lonely autonomy, his true responsibility. If he has anything that partakes of the quality of a God it comes from this fact. Man has more than the choice to obey or disobey. If he accepts authority he also chooses the authority he accepts. He is responsible not only to others but, more deeply, to himself.

II

Does all this mean that a universal ethical principle, applicable alike to me and you, even where our values diverge, is impossible? That there is no rule to go by, based on reason itself, in this world of irreconcilable valuations?

There is no rule that can prescribe both my values and yours or decide between them. There is one universal rule, and one only, that can be laid down, on ethical grounds—that is, apart from the creeds of particular religions and apart from the ways of the tribe that falsely and arrogantly universalize themselves.

Do to others as you would have others do to you. This is the only rule that stands by itself in the light of its own reason, the only rule that can stand by itself in the naked, warring universe, in the face of the contending values of men and groups.

What makes it so? Let us first observe that the universal herein laid down is one of procedure. It prescribes a mode of behaving, not a goal of action. On the level of goals, of *final* values, there is irreconcilable conflict. One rule prescribes humility, another pride; one prescribes abstinence, another commends the flesh-pots; and so forth through endless variations. All of us wish that *our* principle could be universal; most of us believe that it *should* be, that our *ought* ought to be all men's *ought*, but since we differ there can be on this level, no possible agreement.

When we want to make our ethical principle prevail we try to persuade others, to "convert" them. Some may freely respond, if their deeper values are near enough to ours. Others will certainly resist and some will seek to persuade us in turn—why shouldn't they? Then we can go no further except by resort to force and fraud. We can, if we are strong, dominate some and we can bribe others. We compromise our own values in doing so and we do not in the end succeed; even if we were masters of the whole world we could never succeed in making our principle universal. We could only make it falsely tyrannous.

So if we look for a principle in the name of which we can appeal to all men, one to which their reason can respond in spite of their differences, we must follow another road. When we try to make our values prevail over those cherished by others, we attack their values, their dynamic of behavior, their living will. If we go far enough we assault their very being. For the will is simply valuation in action. Now the deep beauty of the golden rule is that instead of attacking the will that is in other men, it offers their will a new dimension. "Do as you *would* have others . . . ." As *you* would will others to do. It bids you expand your vision, see yourself in new relationships. It bids you transcend your insulation, see yourself in the place of others, see others in your place. It bids you test your values or at least your way of pursuing them. If you would disapprove that another should treat you as you treat him, the situations being reversed is not that a sign that, by the standard of your own values, you are mistreating him?

This principle obviously makes for a vastly greater harmony in the social scheme. At the same time it is the only universal of ethics that does not take sides with or contend with contending values. It contains no dogma. It bids everyone follow his own rule, as it would apply *apart* from the accident of his particular fortunes. It bids him enlarge his own rule, as it would apply whether he is up or whether he is down. It is an accident that you are up and I am down. In another situation you would be down and I would be up. That accident has nothing to do with my *final* values or with yours. You have numbers and force on your side. In another situation I would have the numbers and the force. All situations of power are temporary and precarious. Imagine then the situations reversed and that you had a more wonderful power than is at the command of the most powerful, the power to make the more powerful act toward you as you would want him to act. If power is your dream, then dream of a yet greater power—and act out the spirit of your dream.

But the conclusive argument is not in the terms of power. It goes far deeper, down to the great truth that power so often ignores and that so often in the end destroys it, the truth that when you maltreat others you detach yourself from them, from the understanding of them, from the understanding of yourself. You insulate yourself, you narrow your own values, you cut yourself off from that which you and they have in common. And this commonness is more enduring and more satisfying than what you possess in insulation. You separate yourself, and for all your power you weaken yourself. Which is why power and fear are such close companions.

This is the reason why the evil you do to another, you do also, in the end, to yourself. While if you and he refrain from doing evil, one to another—not to speak of the yet happier consequences of doing positive good—this reciprocity of restraint from evil will redound to the good of both.

That makes a much longer story and we shall not here enter upon it. Our sole concern is to show that the golden rule is the *only* ethical principle, as already defined, that can have clear right of way everywhere in the kind of world we have inherited. It is the only principle that allows every man to follow his own intrinsic values while nevertheless it transforms the chaos of warring codes into a reasonably well-ordered universe.

Let us explain the last statement. What are a man's intrinsic values? Beyond his mere self-seeking every human being needs, and must find, some attachment to a larger purpose. These attachments, in themselves and apart from the way he pursues them, are his intrinsic values. For some men they are centered in the family, the clan, the "class," the community, the nation, the "race." It is the warfare of their group-attachments that creates the deadliest disturbances of modern society. For some men the focus of attachment is found in the greater "cause," the faith, the creed, the way of life. The conflict of these attachments also unlooses many evils on society and at some historical stages has brought about great devastation.

The greatest evils inflicted by man on man over the face of the earth are wrought not by the self-seekers, the pleasure lovers, or the merely amoral, but by the fervent devotees of ethical principles, those who are bound body and soul to some larger purpose, the nation, the "race," the "masses," the "brethren" whoever they may be. The faith they invoke, whatever it may be, is not large enough when it sets a frontier between the members and the non-members, the believers and the non-believers. In the heat of devotion to that larger but exclusive purpose there is bred the fanaticism that corrodes and finally destroys all that links man to the common humanity. In the name of the cause, they will torture and starve and trample under foot millions on millions of their fellowmen. In its name they will cultivate the blackest treachery. And if their methods fail, as fail in the end they must, they will be ready, as was Hitler, to destroy their own cause or their own people, the chosen ones, rather than accept the reality their blinded purpose denied.

III

How then can we say that the golden rule does not disqualify the intrinsic values of such people—even of people like Hitler or, say, Torquemada? In the name of his values Torquemada burned at the stake many persons who differed from their fellows mainly by being more courageous, honest, and faithful to their faith. What then were Torquemada's values? He was a servant of the Church and the Church was presumptively a servant of Jesus Christ. It was not the intrinsic values of his creed that moved him and his masters to reject the Christian golden rule. Let us concede they had some kind of devotion to religion. It was the distorted, fanatical way in which they pursued the dimmed values they cherished, it was not the values themselves, to which their inhumanity can be charged.

Let us take the case of Hitler. Apart from his passion for Germany, or the German "folk," he would have been of no account, for evil or for good. That passion of itself, that in his view intrinsic value, might have inspired great constructive service instead of destruction. It was the method he used, and not the values he sought to promote thereby, that led to ruin, his blind trust in the efficacy of ruthless might. Belonging to a "folk" that had been reduced in defeat from strength to humiliation, fed on false notions of history and responsive to grotesque fallacies about a "master race," he conceived the resurgence of Germany in the distorted light of his vindictive imagination. Had Hitler been a member of some small "folk," no more numerous, say, than the population of his native Austria, he might have cherished the same values with no less passion, but his aspirations would have taken a different form and would never have expressed themselves in horror and tragedy.

The golden rule says nothing against Hitler's mystic adoration of the German "race," against any man's intrinsic values. By "intrinsic values" we signify the goals, beyond mere self-seeking, that animate a human being. If your group, your nation, your "race," your church, is for you a primary attachment, continue to cherish it—give it all you have, if you are so minded. But do not use means that are repugnant to the standards according to which you would have others conduct themselves to you and your values. If your nation were a small one, would you not seethe with indignation if some large neighbor destroyed its independence? Where, then, is your personal integrity if, belonging instead to the large nation, you act to destroy the independence of a small one? You falsify your own values, in the longer run you do them injury, when you pursue them in ways that cannot abide the test of the golden rule.

It follows that while this first principle attacks no intrinsic values, no primary attachments of men to goods that reach beyond themselves, it nevertheless purifies every attachment, every creed, of its accidents, its irrelevancies, its excesses, its false reliance on power. It saves every human value from the corruption that comes from the arrogance of detachment and exclusiveness, from the shell of the kind of absolutism that imprisons its vitality.

At this point a word of caution is in order. The golden rule does not solve for us our ethical problems but offers only a way of approach. It does not prescribe our treatment of others but only the spirit in which we should treat them. It has no simple mechanical application and often enough is hard to apply—what general principle is not? It certainly does not bid us treat others as others *want* us to treat them—that would be an absurdity. The convicted criminal wants the judge to set him free. If the judge acts in the spirit of the golden rule, within the limits of the discretion permitted him as judge, he might instead reason somewhat as follows: "How would I feel the judge ought to treat *me* were I in this man's place? What could I— the man I am and yet somehow standing where this criminal stands— properly ask the judge to do for me, to me? In this spirit I shall assess his guilt and his punishment. In this spirit I shall give full consideration to the conditions under which he acted. I shall try to understand *him*, to do what I properly can for him, while at the same time I fulfill my judicial duty in protecting society against the dangers that arise if criminals such as he go free.''

IV

"Do to others as you would have others do to you." The disease to which all values are subject is the growth of a hard insulation. "I am right: I have the truth. If you differ from me, you are a heretic, you are in error. *Therefore* while you must allow me every liberty when you are in power I need not, in truth I ought not to, show any similar consideration for you." The barb of falsehood has already begun to vitiate the cherished value. While *you* are in power I advocate the equal rights of all creeds: when *I* am in power, I reject any such claim as ridiculous. This is the position taken by various brands of totalitarianism, and the communists in particular have made it a favorite technique in the process of gaining power, clamoring for rights they will use to destroy the rights of those who grant them. Religious groups have followed the same line. Roman Catholics, Calvinists, Lutherans, Presbyterians, and others have on occasion vociferously advocated religious liberty where they were in the minority, often to curb it where in turn they became dominant.

This gross inconsistency on the part of religious groups was flagrantly displayed in earlier centuries, but examples are still not infrequent. Here is one. *La Civilita Catholicâ*, a Jesuit organ published in Rome, has come out as follows:

"The Roman Catholic Church, convinced, through its divine prerogatives, of being the only true church, must demand the right to freedom for herself alone, because such a right can only be possessed by truth, never by error. As to other religions, the church will certainly never draw the sword, but she will require that by legitimate means they shall not be allowed to propagate false doctrine. Consequently, in a state where the majority of the people are Catholic, the Church will require that legal existence be denied to error. . . . In some countries, Catholics will be obliged to ask full religious freedom for all, resigned at being forced to cohabitate where they alone should rightly be allowed to live. . . . The Church cannot blush for her own want of tolerance, as she asserts it in principle and applies it in practice."[1]

Since this statement has the merit of honesty it well illustrates the fundamental lack of rationality that lies behind all such violations of the golden rule. The argument runs: "Roman Catholics know they possess the truth; *therefore* they should not permit others to propagate error." By parity of reasoning why should not Protestants say—and indeed they have often said it—"We know we possess the truth; therefore we should not tolerate the errors of Roman Catholics." Why then should not atheists say: "We know we possess the truth; therefore we should not tolerate the errors of dogmatic religion."

No matter what we believe, we are equally convinced that *we* are right. We have to be. That is what belief means, and we must all believe something. The Roman Catholic Church is entitled to declare that all other religious groups are sunk in error. But what follows? That other groups have not the right to believe they are right? That you have the right to repress them while they have no right to repress you? That they should concede to you what you should not concede to them? Such reasoning is mere childishness. Beyond it lies the greater foolishness that truth is advanced by the

---

[1]Quoted in the *Christian Century* (June 1948).

forceful suppression of those who believe differently from you. Beyond that lies the pernicious distortion of meanings which claims that liberty is only "the liberty to do right"—the "liberty" for me to do what *you* think is right. This perversion of the meaning of liberty has been the delight of all totalitarians. And it might be well to reflect that it was the radical Rousseau who first introduced the doctrine that men could be "forced to be free."

How much do they have truth who think they must guard it within the fortress of their own might? How little that guarding has availed in the past! How often it has kept truth outside while superstition grew moldy within! How often has the false alliance of belief and force led to civil dissension and the futile ruin of war! But if history means nothing to those who call themselves "Christian" and still claim exclusive civil rights for their particular faith, at least they might blush before this word of one they call their Master: "All things therefore whatsoever ye would that men should do unto you, even so do ye also unto them; for this is the law and the prophets."

44 / The Conscience of Huckleberry Finn

JONATHAN BENNETT

I

In this paper, I shall present not just the conscience of Huckleberry Finn but two others as well. One of them is the conscience of Heinrich Himmler. He became a Nazi in 1923; he served drably and quietly, but well, and was rewarded with increasing responsibility and power. . . .

The other conscience to be discussed is that of the Calvinist theologian and philosopher Jonathan Edwards. He lived in the first half of the eighteenth century, and has a good claim to be considered America's first serious and considerable philosophical thinker. . . .

I shall use Heinrich Himmler, Jonathan Edwards, and Huckleberry Finn to illustrate different aspects of a single theme, namely the relationship between *sympathy* on the one hand and *bad morality* on the other.

II

All that I can mean by a "bad morality" is a morality whose principles I deeply disapprove of. When I call a morality bad, I cannot prove that mine is better; but when I here call any morality bad, I think you will agree with me that it is bad; and that is all I need.

There could be dispute as to whether the springs of someone's actions constitute a *morality*. I think, though, that we must admit that someone who acts in ways which conflict grossly with our morality may nevertheless have a morality of his own—a set of principles of action which he sincerely assents to, so that for him the problem of acting well or rightly or in obedience to conscience is the problem of conforming to *those* principles. The problem of conscientiousness can arise as acutely for a bad morality as for any other: Rotten principles may be as difficult to keep as decent ones.

As for "sympathy" I use this term to cover every sort of fellow-feeling, as when one feels pity over someone's loneliness, or horrified compassion over his pain, or when one feels a shrinking reluctance to act in a way which will bring misfortune to someone else. These *feelings* must not be confused with *moral judgments*. My sympathy for someone in distress may lead me to help him, or even to think that I ought to help him; but in itself it is not a judgment about what I ought to do but just a *feeling* for him in his plight. We shall get some light on the difference between feelings and moral judgments when we consider Huckleberry Finn.

Obviously, feelings can impel one to action, and so can moral judgments; and in a particular case sympathy and morality may pull in opposite directions. This can happen not just with bad moralities, but also with good ones like yours and mine. For example, a small child, sick and miserable, clings tightly to his mother and screams in terror when she tries to pass him over to the doctor to be examined. If the mother gave way to her sympathy, that is to her feeling for the child's misery and fright, she would hold it close and not let the doctor come near; but don't we agree that it might be wrong for her to act on such a feeling? Quite generally, then, anyone's moral principles may apply to a particular situation in a way which runs contrary to the particular thrusts of fellow-feeling that he has in that situation. My immediate concern is with sympathy in relation to bad morality, but not because such conflicts occur only when the morality is bad.

Now, suppose that someone who accepts a bad morality is struggling to make himself act in accordance with it in a particular situation where his sympathies pull him another way. He sees the struggle as one between doing the right, conscientious thing, and acting wrongly and weakly, like the mother who won't let the doctor come near her sick, frightened baby. Since we don't accept this person's morality, we may see the situation very differently, thoroughly disapproving of the action he regards as the right one, and endorsing the action which from his point of view constitutes weakness and backsliding.

Conflicts between sympathy and bad morality won't always be like this, for we won't disagree with every single dictate of a bad morality. Still, it can happen in the way I have described, with the agent's right action being our wrong one, and vice versa. That is just what happens in a certain episode in chapter 16 of *The Adventures of Huckleberry Finn*, an episode which brilliantly illustrates how fiction can be instructive about real life.

III

Huck Finn has been helping his slave friend Jim to run away from Miss Watson, who is Jim's owner. In their raft-journey down the Mississippi river, they are near to the place at which Jim will become legally free. Now let Huck take over the story:

> Jim said it made him all over trembly and feverish to be so close to freedom. Well I can tell you it made me all over trembly and feverish, too, to hear him, because I begun to get it through my head that he *was* most free—and who was to blame for it? Why, *me*. I couldn't get that out of my conscience, no how nor no way. . . . It hadn't ever come home to me, before, what this thing was that I was doing. But now it did; and it stayed with me, and scorched me more and more. I tried to make out to myself that *I* warn't to blame, because I didn't run Jim off from his rightful owner; but it warn't no use, conscience up and say, every time: "But you knowed he was running for his freedom, and you could a paddled ashore and told somebody." That was so—I couldn't get around that, no way. That was where it pinched. Conscience says to me: "What had poor Miss Watson done to you, that you could see her nigger go off right under your eyes and never say one single word? What did that poor old woman do to you, that you could treat her so mean? . . ." I got to feeling so mean and miserable I most wished I was dead.

Jim speaks of his plan to save up to buy his wife, and then his children, out of slavery; and he adds that if the children cannot be bought he will arrange to steal them. Huck is horrified:

> Thinks I, this is what comes of my not thinking. Here was this nigger which I had as good as helped to run away, coming right out flat-footed and saying he would steal his children—children that belonged to a man I didn't even know; a man that hadn't ever done me no harm.
>
> I was sorry to hear Jim say that, it was such a lowering of him. My conscience got to stirring me up hotter than ever, until at last I says to it: "Let up on me—it ain't too late, yet—I'll paddle ashore at first light, and tell." I felt easy, and happy, and light as a feather, right off. All my troubles was gone.

This is bad morality all right. In his earliest years Huck wasn't taught any principles, and the only ones he has encountered since then are those of rural Missouri, in which slave-owning is just one kind of ownership and is not subject to critical pressure. It hasn't occurred to Huck to question those principles. So the action, to us abhorrent, of turning Jim in to the authorities presents itself *clearly* to Huck as the right thing to do.

For us, morality and sympathy would both dictate helping Jim to escape. If we felt any conflict, it would have both these on one side and something else on the other—greed for a reward, or fear of punishment. But Huck's morality conflicts with his sympathy, that is, with his unargued, natural feeling for his friend. The conflict starts when Huck sets off in the canoe towards the shore, pretending that he is going to reconnoiter, but really planning to turn Jim in:

> As I shoved off, [Jim] says: "Pooty soon I'll be a-shout'n for joy, en I'll say, it's all on accounts o' Huck I's a free man . . . Jim won't ever forgit you, Huck; you's de bes' fren' Jim's ever had; en you's de *only* fren' old Jim's got now."
>
> I was paddling off, all in a sweat to tell on him; but when he says this, it seemed to kind of take the tuck all out of me. I went along slow then, and I warn't right down certain whether I was glad I started or whether I warn't. When I was fifty yards off, Jim says:
>
> "Dah you goes, de ole true Huck; de on'y white genlman dat ever kep' his promise to ole Jim." Well, I just felt sick. But I says, I *got* to do it—I can't get *out* of it.

In the upshot, sympathy wins over morality. Huck hasn't the strength of will to do what he sincerely thinks he ought to do. Two men hunting for runaway slaves ask him whether the man on his raft is black or white:

> I didn't answer up prompt. I tried to, but the words wouldn't come. I tried, for a second or two, to brace up and out with it, but I warn't man enough— hadn't the spunk of a rabbit. I see I was weakening; so I just give up trying, and up and says: "He's white."

So Huck enables Jim to escape, thus acting weakly and wickedly—he thinks. In this conflict between sympathy and morality, sympathy wins.

One critic has cited this episode in support of the statement that Huck suffers "excruciating moments of wavering between honesty and respectability." That is hopelessly wrong, and I agree with the perceptive comment on it by another critic, who says:

> The conflict waged in Huck is much more serious: He scarcely cares for respectability and never hesitates to relinquish it, but he does care for honesty and gratitude—and both honesty and gratitude require that he should give Jim up. It is not, in Huck, honesty at war with respectability but love and compassion for Jim struggling against his conscience. His decision is for Jim and hell: a right decision made in the mental chains that Huck never breaks. His concern for Jim is and

remains *irrational*. Huck finds many reasons for giving Jim up and none for steal-ing him. To the end Huck sees his compassion for Jim as a weak, ignorant, and wicked felony.[1]

That is precisely correct—and it can have that virtue only because Mark Twain wrote the episode with such unerring precision. The crucial point concerns *reasons*, which all occur on one side of the conflict. On the side of conscience we have principles, arguments, considerations, ways of looking at things:

"It hadn't ever come home to me before what I was doing"
"I tried to make out that I warn't to blame"
"Conscience said 'But you knowed . . .'—I couldn't get around that"
"What had poor Miss Watson done to you?"
"This is what comes of my not thinking"
". . . children that belonged to a man I didn't even know."

On the other side, the side of feeling, we get nothing like that. When Jim rejoices in Huck, as his only friend, Huck doesn't consider the claims of friendship or have the situation "come home" to him in a different light. All that happens is: "When he says this, it seemed to kind of take the tuck all out of me. I went along slow then, and I warn't right down certain whether I was glad I started or whether I warn't." Again, Jim's words about Huck's "promise" to him don't give Huck any *reason* for changing his plan: In his morality promises to slaves probably don't count. Their effect on him is of a different kind: "Well, I just felt sick." And when the moment for fi-nal decision comes, Huck doesn't weigh up pros and cons: he simply *fails* to do what he believes to be right—he isn't strong enough, hasn't "the spunk of a rabbit." This passage in the novel is notable not just for its finely wrought irony, with Huck's weakness of will leading him to do the right thing, but also for its masterly handling of the difference between general moral principles and particular unreasoned emotional pulls.

IV

Consider now another case of bad morality in conflict with human sympa-thy: the case of the odious Himmler. Here, from a speech he made to some S.S. generals, is an indication of the content of his morality:

What happens to a Russian, to a Czech, does not interest me in the slightest. What the nations can offer in the way of good blood of our type, we will take, if necessary by kidnapping their children and raising them here with us. Whether nations live in prosperity or starve to death like cattle interests me only in so far as

[1]M. J. Sidnell, "Huck Finn and Jim," *The Cambridge Quarterly*, vol. 2, pp. 205–206.

we need them as slaves to our *Kultur*; otherwise it is of no interest to me. Whether 10,000 Russian females fall down from exhaustion while digging an antitank ditch interests me only in so far as the antitank ditch for Germany is finished.[2]

But has this a moral basis at all? And if it has, was there in Himmler's own mind any conflict between morality and sympathy? Yes there was. Here is more from the same speech:

I also want to talk to you quite frankly on a very grave matter . . . I mean . . . the extermination of the Jewish race. . . . Most of you must know what it means when 100 corpses are lying side by side, or 500, or 1,000. To have stuck it out and at the same time—apart from exceptions caused by human weakness—to have remained decent fellows, that is what has made us hard. This is a page of glory in our history which has never been written and is never to be written.

Himmler saw his policies as being hard to implement while still retaining one's human sympathies—while still remaining a "decent fellow." He is saying that only the weak take the easy way out and just squelch their sympathies, and is praising the stronger and more glorious course of retaining one's sympathies while acting in violation of them. In the same spirit, he ordered that when executions were carried out in concentration camps, those responsible "are to be influenced in such a way as to suffer no ill effect in their character and mental attitude." A year later he boasted that the S.S. had wiped out the Jews.

without our leaders and their men suffering any damage in their minds and souls. The danger was considerable, for there was only a narrow path between the Scylla of their becoming heartless ruffians unable any longer to treasure life, and the Charybdis of their becoming soft and suffering nervous breakdowns.

And there really can't be any doubt that the basis of Himmler's policies was a set of principles which constituted his morality—a sick, bad, wicked *morality*. He described himself as caught in "the old tragic conflict between will and obligation." And when his physician Kersten protested at the intention to destroy the Jews, saying that the suffering involved was "not to be contemplated," Kersten reports that Himmler replied:

He knew that it would mean much suffering for the Jews. . . . "It is the curse of greatness that it must step over dead bodies to create new life. Yet we must . . . cleanse the soil or it will never bear fruit. It will be a great burden for me to bear."

This, I submit, is the language of morality.

So in this case, tragically, bad morality won out over sympathy. I am sure that many of Himmler's killers did extinguish their sympathies, becoming

[2]Quoted in William L. Shirer, *The Rise and Fall of the Third Reich* (New York, 1960), pp. 937–938. Next quotation: ibid., p. 966. All further quotations relating to Himmler are from Roger Manwell and Heinrich Fraenkel, *Heinrich Himmler* (London, 1965), pp. 132, 197, 184 (twice), 187.

"heartless ruffians" rather than "decent fellows"; but not Himmler himself. Although his policies ran against the human grain to a horrible degree, he did not sandpaper down his emotional surfaces so that there was
no grain there, allowing his actions to slide along smoothly and easily. He
did, after all, bear his hideous burden, and even paid a price for it. He suffered a variety of nervous and physical disabilities, including nausea and
stomach-convulsions, and Kersten was doubtless right in saying that these
were "the expression of a psychic division which extended over his whole
life." . . .

V

In the conflict between sympathy and bad morality, then, the victory may
go to sympathy as in the case of Huck Finn, or to morality as in the case of
Himmler.

Another possibility is that the conflict may be avoided by giving up, or
not ever having, those sympathies which might interfere with one's principles. That seems to have been the case with Jonathan Edwards. I am afraid
that I shall be doing an injustice to Edwards' many virtues, and to his great
intellectual energy and inventiveness; for my concern is only with the worst
thing about him—namely his morality, which was worse than Himmler's.

According to Edwards, God condemns some men to an eternity of uni-
maginably awful pain, though he arbitrarily spares others—"arbitrarily"
because none deserve to be spared:

> Natural men are held in the hand of God over the pit of hell; they have deserved
> the fiery pit, and are already sentenced to it; and God is dreadfully provoked, his
> anger is as great toward them as to those that are actually suffering the executions
> of the fierceness of his wrath in hell . . . ; the devil is waiting for them, hell is gap-
> ing for them, the flames gather and flash about them, and would fain lay hold on
> them . . . ; and . . . there are no means within reach that can be any security to
> them. . . . All that preserves them is the mere arbitrary will, and uncovenanted
> unobliged forebearance of an incensed God.[3]

Notice that he says "they have deserved the fiery pit." Edwards insists that
men ought to be condemned to eternal pain; and his position isn't that this
is right because God wants it, but rather that God wants it because it is
right. For him, moral standards exist independently of God, and God can
be assessed in the light of them (and of course found to be perfect). . . .

Of course, Edwards himself didn't torment the damned; but the question
still arises of whether his sympathies didn't conflict with his *approval* of

---

[3]Vergilius Ferm (ed.), *Puritan Sage: Collected Writings of Jonathan Edwards* (New York, 1953),
p. 370. Next three quotations: ibid., p. 366, p. 294 ("no more than infinite"), p. 372.

eternal torment. Didn't he find it painful to contemplate any fellow-human's being tortured forever? Apparently not:

> The God that holds you over the pit of hell, much as one holds a spider or some loathsome insect over the fire, abhors you, and is dreadfully provoked; . . . he is of purer eyes than to bear to have you in his sight; you are ten thousand times so abominable in his eyes as the most hateful venomous serpent is in ours.

When God is presented as being as misanthropic as that, one suspects misanthropy in the theologian. This suspicion is increased when Edwards claims that ''the saints in glory will . . . understand how terrible the sufferings of the damned are; yet . . . will not be sorry for [them].''[4] He bases this partly on a view of human nature whose ugliness he seems not to notice:

> The seeing of the calamities of others tends to heighten the sense of our own enjoyments. When the saints in glory, therefore, shall see the doleful state of the damned, how this will heighten their sense of the blessedness of their own state. . . . When they shall see how miserable others of their fellow-creatures are . . . ; when they shall see the smoke of their torment, . . . and hear their dolorous shrieks and cries, and consider that they in the mean time are in the most blissful state, and shall surely be in it to all eternity; how they will rejoice!

I hope this is less than the whole truth! His other main point about why the saints will rejoice to see the torments of the damned is that it is right that they should do so:

> Tne heavenly inhabitants . . . will have no love nor pity to the damned. . . . [This will not show] a want of spirit of love in them . . . ; for the heavenly inhabitants will know that it is not fit that they should love [the damned] because they will know then, that God has no love to them, nor pity for them.

The implication that *of course* one can adjust one's feelings of pity so that they conform to the dictates of some authority—doesn't this suggest that ordinary human sympathies played only a small part in Edwards' life?

VI

Huck Finn, whose sympathies are wide and deep, could never avoid the conflict in that way; but he is determined to avoid it, and so he opts for the only other alternative he can see—to give up morality altogether. After he has tricked the slave-hunters, he returns to the raft and undergoes a peculiar crisis:

> I got aboard the raft, feeling bad and low, because I knowed very well I had done wrong, and I see it warn't no use for me to try to learn to do right; a body that

---

4This and the next two quotations are from ''The End of the Wicked Contemplated by the Righteous: Or, The Torments of the Wicked in Hell, No Occasion of Grief to the Saints in Heaven,'' from *The Works of President Edwards* (London, 1817), vol. 4, pp. 507–508, 511– 512, and 509 respectively.

don't get *started* right when he's little, ain't got no show—when the pinch comes there ain't nothing to back him up and keep him to his work, and so he gets beat. Then I thought a minute, and says to myself, hold on—s'pose you'd a done right and give Jim up; would you feel better than what you do now? No, says I, I'd feel bad—I'd feel just the same way I do now. Well, then, says I, what's the use you learning to do right, when it's troublesome to do right and ain't no trouble to do wrong, and the wages is just the same? I was stuck. I couldn't answer that. So I reckoned I wouldn't bother no more about it, but after this always do whichever come handiest at the time.

Huck clearly cannot conceive of having any morality except the one he has learned—too late, he thinks—from his society. He is not entirely a prisoner of that morality because he does after all reject it; but for him that is a decision to relinquish morality as such; he cannot envisage revising his morality, altering its content in face of the various pressures to which it is subject, including pressures from his sympathies. For example, he does not begin to approach the thought that slavery should be rejected on moral grounds, or the thought that what he is doing is not theft because a person cannot be owned and therefore cannot be stolen.

The basic trouble is that he cannot or will not engage in abstract intellectual operations of any sort. In chapter 33 he finds himself "feeling to blame, somehow" for something he knows he had no hand in; he assumes that this feeling is a deliverance of conscience; and this confirms him in his belief that conscience shouldn't be listened to:

It don't make no difference whether you do right or wrong, a person's conscience ain't got no sense, and just goes for him *anyway*. If I had a yaller dog that didn't know no more than a person's conscience does, I would poison him. It takes up more than all of a person's insides, and yet ain't no good, nohow.

That brisk, incurious dismissiveness fits well with the comprehensive rejection of morality back on the raft. But this is a digression.

On the raft, Huck decides not to live by principles, but just to do whatever "comes handiest at the time"—always acting according to the mood of the moment. Since the morality he is rejecting is narrow and cruel, and his sympathies are broad and kind, the results will be good. But moral principles are good to have, because they help to protect one from acting badly at moments when one's sympathies happen to be in abeyance. On the highest possible estimate of the role one's sympathies should have, one can still allow for principles as embodiments of one's best feelings, one's broadest and keenest sympathies. On that view, principles can help one across intervals when one's feelings are at less than their best, i.e. through periods of misanthropy or meanness or self-centeredness or depression or anger.

What Huck didn't see is that one can live by principles and yet have ultimate control over their content. And one way such control can be exercised is by checking of one's principles in the light of one's sympathies. . . .

I don't give my sympathies a blank check in advance. In a conflict between principle and sympathy, principles ought sometimes to win. For example, I think it was right to take part in the Second World War on the allied side; there were many ghastly individual incidents which might have led someone to doubt the rightness of his participation in that war; and I think it would have been right for such a person to keep his sympathies in a subordinate place on those occasions, not allowing them to modify his principles in such a way as to make a pacifist of him.

Still, one's sympathies should be kept as sharp and sensitive and aware as possible, and not only because they can sometimes affect one's principles or one's conduct or both. . . .

45 / Good and the Will of God

EMIL BRUNNER

1. There is no general conception of ethics which would also include the Christian ethic. . . .

It is of course true that even the Christian ethic is concerned with the definition of conduct, which as "right" conduct has to be distinguished from conduct which is accidental or wrong; but this distinction or definition does not take place by means of an ultimate principle, which, as such, would be intelligible and valid. . . . The Christian conception of the Good differs from every other conception of the Good at this very point: that it cannot be defined in terms of principle at all.

Whatever can be defined in accordance with a principle—whether it be the principle of pleasure or the principle of duty—is legalistic. This means that it is possible—by the use of this principle—to pre-determine "the right" down to the smallest detail of conduct. We have already seen how this legalistic spirit corrupts the true conception of the Good from its very roots. The Christian moralist and the extreme individualist are at one in their emphatic rejection of legalistic conduct; they join hands, as it were, in face of the whole host of legalistic moralists; they are convinced that conduct which is regulated by abstract principles can never be good. But equally sternly the Christian moralist rejects the individualist doctrine of freedom, according to which there is no longer any difference between "right" and "wrong." Rather, in the Christian view, that alone is "good" which is free from all caprice, which takes place in unconditional obedience. There is no Good save obedient behaviour, save the obedient will. But this obedience is rendered not to a law or a principle which can be known beforehand, but only to the free, sovereign will of God. The Good consists in always doing what God wills at any particular moment.

This statement makes it clear that for us the will of God cannot be summed up under any principle, that it is not at our disposal, but that so far as we are concerned the will of God is absolutely free. The Christian is therefore "a free lord over all things,"[1] because he stands directly under the personal orders of the free Sovereign God. This is why genuine "Christian conduct"—if we may use this idea as an illustration—is so unaccountable, so unwelcome to the moral rigorist and to the hedonist alike. The moral rigorist regards the Christian as a hedonist, and the hedonist regards him as a rigorist. In reality, the Christian is neither, yet he is also something of both, since he is indeed absolutely *bound* and obedient, but, since he is bound to the *free* loving will of God, he is himself free from all transparent bondage to principles or to legalism. Above all it is important to recognize that even love is not a principle of this kind, neither the love which God Himself *has*, nor the love which He *requires*. Only God Himself defines love in His action. We, for our part, do not know what God is, nor do we know what *love* is, unless we learn to know God in His action, in faith. To be in this His Love, is the Commandment. Every attempt to conceive love as a principle leads to this result: it becomes distorted, either in the rigoristic, legalistic sense, or in the hedonistic sense. Man only knows what the love of God is when he sees the way in which God acts, and he only knows how he himself ought to love by allowing himself to be drawn by faith into this activity of God.

2. "To know God in His action" is only possible in faith. The action of God, in which He manifests Himself—and this means His love—is His revelation. God reveals Himself in His Word—which is at the same time a deed—in an actual event—in Jesus Christ; and He reveals Himself operatively in His living Word, which is now taking place—in the Holy Spirit. Because only conduct which takes place on the basis of this faith (and indeed in this faith in God's Word) can be "good conduct," in the sense of the Christian ethic, therefore, the science of good conduct, of ethics, is only possible within that other science which speaks of the Divine act of revelation, that is, within dogmatics. Reflection on the good conduct of man is only one part of more comprehensive reflection on the action of God in general. For human conduct can only be considered "good" when, and in so far as, God Himself acts in it, through the Holy Spirit. Hence just as this action is connected with the Divine action, so the Christian ethic is connected with dogmatics. . . .

3. The decisive point of view for ethics—even for Christian ethics—is conduct, not being, although even for the Christian ethic it is the being of man,

---

[1]Luther: *Of the Freedom of a Christian Man (Von der Freiheit eines Christenmenschen).*

"the person," which is the decisive point of view for conduct. The new being (*Sein*) of man, in so far as it is regarded only as the work of God, is the "new man" who is based on faith in justification. In so far as in the being of this new man the emphasis is laid on its manifesting itself in a "work," in actions towards others, it forms part of ethics. Yet this ethical element is not a second, independent element alongside of the dogmatic element, but it is simply the emphasis on a special "moment" within it. For just as the Christian Ethic is distinguished from natural ethics by the fact that in it God's action is always regarded as the basis of human action, so it is also characteristic of it that in all action, the *being* of the agent, as that which alone can be really good or evil, is kept in view.

Therefore, in spite of the fact that a uniform division of Christian doctrine into dogmatics and ethics can only take place with the greatest injury to both, there is always an external technical separation, which is forced upon us by necessity, and is indeed justifiable; that is, if this external separation does not denote an inner separation. These considerations may now be summed up in a sentence, in which the special subject of Christian ethics is defined: *Christian ethics is the science of human conduct as it is determined by Divine conduct.*

46 / God and the Good

KAI NIELSEN

I. [INTRODUCTION]

It is the claim of many influential Christian and Jewish theologians (Brunner, Buber, Barth, Niebuhr, and Bultmann—to take outstanding examples) that the *only* genuine basis for morality is in religion. And any old religion is not good enough. The only truly adequate foundation for moral belief is a religion that acknowledges the absolute sovereignty of the Lord found in the prophetic religions.

These theologians will readily grant what is plainly true, namely, that as a matter of fact many nonreligious people behave morally, but they contend that without a belief in God and his Law there is no *ground* or *reason* for being moral. The sense of moral relativism, skepticism, and nihilism rampant in our age is due in large measure to the general weakening of religious belief in an age of science. Without God there can be no objective foundation for our moral beliefs. As Brunner puts it, "The believer *alone* clearly perceives that the Good, as it is recognized in faith, is the sole Good, and all that is otherwise called good cannot lay claim to this title, at least in the ultimate sense of the word." "The Good consists in always doing what God wills at any particular moment." This "Good" can only "take place in unconditional obedience" to God, the ground of our being. Without God life would have no point and morality would have no basis. Without religious belief, without the Living God, there could be no adequate answer to the persistently gnawing questions: What ought we to do? How ought I to live?

Is this frequently repeated claim justified? Are our moral beliefs and conceptions based on or grounded in a belief in the God of Judaism, Christianity, and Islam? More specifically still, we need to ask ourselves three very fundamental questions: (1) Is being willed by God the or even a *fundamental* criterion for that which is so willed being morally good or for its being something that ought to be done? (2) Is being willed by God the *only* criterion for that which is so willed being morally good or for its being something that ought to be done? (3) Is being willed by God the only *adequate* criterion for that which is so willed being morally good or being something that ought to be done? I shall argue that the fact that God wills something—if indeed that is a fact—cannot be a fundamental criterion for its being morally good or obligatory and thus it cannot be the only criterion or the only adequate criterion for moral goodness or obligation.

II. PRELIMINARY MATTERS

By way of preliminaries we first need to get clear what is meant by a "fundamental criterion." When we speak of the criterion for the goodness of an action or attitude we speak of some *measure* or *test* by virtue of which we may decide which actions or attitudes are good or desirable, or, at least, are the least undesirable of the alternative actions or attitudes open to us. A moral criterion is the measure we use for determining the value or worth of an action or attitude. We have such a measure or test when we have some generally relevant considerations by which we may decide whether something is whatever it is said to be. A fundamental moral criterion is (a) a test or measure used to judge the legitimacy of moral rules and/or acts or attitudes, and (b) a measure that one would give up last if one were reasoning morally. (In reality, there probably is no *single* fundamental criterion, although there are fundamental criteria.)

There is a further preliminary matter we need to consider. In asking about the basis or authority for our moral beliefs we are not asking about how we came to have them. If you ask someone where he got his moral beliefs, he should answer that he got them from his parents, parent surrogates, teachers, etc.[1] They are beliefs which he has simply been conditioned to accept. But the validity or soundness of a belief is independent of its origin. When one person naively asks another where he got his moral beliefs, he is most likely not asking how he came by them; he is, in effect, asking: (1) On what authority does he hold these beliefs? or (2) What good reasons or justification does he have for these moral beliefs? He should answer that he does not and cannot hold these beliefs on *any authority*. It is indeed true that many of us turn to people for moral advice and guidance in moral matters, but if we *simply* do what we do because it has been authorized, we cannot be reasoning and acting as moral agents; for to respond as a moral agent, to treat a principle as one's moral principle, it must be something which is subscribed to by one's own deliberate commitment, and it must be something for which one is prepared to give reasons.

With these preliminaries out of the way we can return to my claim that the fact (if indeed it is a fact) that God has commanded, willed, or ordained something cannot, in the very nature of the case, be a fundamental criterion for claiming that whatever is commanded, willed, or ordained ought to be done. . . .*

III. [THE LOGICAL STATUS OF 'GOD IS GOOD': IS IT NON-ANALYTIC?]

To see the rationale for [that claim] we must consider the logical status of "God is good." Is it a nonanalytic and in some way substantive claim, or is it analytic? (Can we say that it is neither?) No matter what we say, we get into difficulties.†

Let us first try to claim that it is a nonanalytic, that is to say, that it is in some way a substantive statement. So understood, God cannot then be by *definition* good. If the statement is synthetic and substantive, its denial cannot be self-contradictory, that is, it cannot be self-contradictory to assert that *x* is God but *x* is not good. It would always *in fact* be wrong to assert this, for God is the Perfect Good, but the denial of this claim is not self-contradictory, it is just false or in some way mistaken. The "is" in "God is

---

[1] P. H. Nowell-Smith, "Morality: Religious and Secular," *The Rationalist Annual* (1961), pp. 5–22.

*[In order to understand the rest of this essay, you must understand two concepts: 'analytic statements' and 'non-analytic (synthetic) statements.' These are defined as follows:

Analytic statement (truth of language): Any statement S is analytic if and only if (a) it is an identity or definition, or (b) it is true solely on the basis of a definition. Examples: (a) 'Puppies are young dogs'; (b) 'Puppies are young.'

Synthetic statement (non-analytic substantive statement): Any statement S is synthetic (substantive) if and only if it is not analytic.—Eds.]

†[See note at the end of section II.—Eds.]

the Perfect Good'' is not the ''is'' of identity, perfect goodness is being predicated of God in some *logically* contingent way. It is the religious experience of the believer and the events recorded in the Bible that lead the believer to the steadfast conviction that God has a purpose or vocation for him which he can fulfill only by completely submitting to God's will. God shall lead him and guide him in every thought, word, and deed. Otherwise he will be like a man shipwrecked, lost in a vast and indifferent universe. Through careful attention to the Bible, he comes to understand that God is a wholly good being who has dealt faithfully with his chosen people. God is not *by definition* perfectly good or even good, but in reality, though not of logical necessity, he never falls short of perfection.

Assuming ''God is good'' is not a truth of language, how, then, do we know that God is good? Do we know or have good grounds for believing that the remarks made at the end of the above paragraph are so? The believer can indeed make a claim like the one we have made above, but how do we or how does he know that this is so? What grounds have we for believing that God is good? Naive people, recalling how God spoke to Job out of the whirlwind, may say that God is good because he is omnipotent and omniscient. But this clearly won't do, for, . . . there is nothing logically improper about saying ''X is omnipotent and omniscient and morally wicked.'' Surely in the world as we know it there is no logical connection between being powerful and knowledgeable, on the one hand, and, on the other, being good. As far as I can see, all that God proved to Job when he spoke to him out of the whirlwind was that God was an immeasurably powerful being; but he did not prove his moral superiority to Job, and he did nothing at all even to exhibit his moral goodness. (One might even argue that he exhibited moral wickedness.) We need not assume that omnipotence and omniscience bring with it goodness or even wisdom.

What other reason could we have for claiming that God is good? We might say that he is good because he tells us to do good in thought, word, and deed and to love one another. In short, in his life and in his precepts God exhibits for us his goodness and love. Now one might argue that children's hospitals and concentration camps clearly show that such a claim is false. But let us *assume* that in some way God does exhibit his goodness to man. Let us assume that if we examine God's works we cannot but affirm that God is good.[2] We come to understand that he isn't cruel, callous, or indifferent. But in order to make such judgments or to gain such an understanding, we must use our own logically independent moral criteria. On our present assumption in asserting ''God is good'' we have of necessity made a moral judgment, a moral appraisal, using a criterion that cannot be based on a knowledge that God exists or that he issues commands. We *call* God ''good'' because we have experienced the goodness of his acts, but in

---

[2]This is surely to assume a lot.

order to do this, in order to know that he is good or to have any grounds for believing that he is good, we must have an independent moral criterion which we use in making this predication of God. So if "God is good" is taken to be synthetic and substantive then morality cannot simply be based on a belief in God. We must of logical necessity have some criterion of goodness that is not derived from any statement asserting that there is a Deity.

IV. [THE LOGICAL STATUS OF 'GOD IS GOOD': IS IT ANALYTIC?]

Let us alternatively, and more plausibly, treat "God is good" as a truth of language. Now some truths of language (some analytic statements) are statements of identity as in "puppies are young dogs" or "a father is a male parent." Such statements are definitions and the "is" is the "is of identity." But "God is good" is clearly not such a statement of identity, for that "God" does not equal "Good" or "God" does not have the same meaning as "good" can easily be seen from the following case: Jane says to Betsy, after Betsy helps an old lady across the street, "That was good of you." "That was good of you" most certainly does not mean "That was God of you." And when we say "conscientiousness is good" we do not mean to say "conscientiousness is God." To say, as a believer does, that God is good is not to say that God is God. This clearly indicates that the word "God" does not have the same meaning as the word "good." When we are talking about God we are not simply talking about morality.

"God is the Perfect Good" is somewhat closer to "a father is a male parent," but even here "God" and "the Perfect Good" are not identical in meaning. "God is the Perfect Good" is like "a triangle is a trilateral" in some important respects. Though something is a triangle if and only if it is a trilateral, it does not follow that "triangle" and "trilateral" have the same meaning. Similarly, something is God if and only if that something is the Perfect Good, but it does not follow that "God" and "the Perfect Good" have the same meaning. When we speak of God we wish to say other things about him as well, though indeed what is true of God will also be true of the Perfect Good. Yet what is true of the evening star will also be true of the morning star for they both refer to the same object, namely Venus, but, as Frege has shown, it does not follow that the two terms have the same meaning if they have the same referent.

And even if it could be made out that "God is the Perfect Good" is in some way a statement of identity, (1) it would not make "God is good" a statement of identity, and (2) we could know that x is the Perfect Good only if we already knew how to decide that x is good. Even on the assumption that "God is the Perfect Good" is a statement of identity, we need some independent way of deciding whether something is good, that is to say, we must have an independent criterion for goodness.

Surely it is more plausible to interpret "God is good" to be analytic in the way "puppies are young," "a bachelor is unmarried," or "unjustified killing is wrong" are analytic. These statements are not statements of identity; they are not definitions, though they all follow from definitions and to deny any of them is self-contradictory.

In short it seems to me correct to argue "God is good," "puppies are young," and "triangles are three-sided" are all truths of language; the predicates *partially* define their subjects. That is to say—to adopt for a moment a Platonic *sounding* idiom—goodness is partially definitive of God-hood, as youngness is partially definitive of puppyhood, and as three sidedness is partially definitive of triangularity.

To admit this is not at all to admit that we can have no understanding of "good" without an understanding of "God," and the truth of the above claim about "God is good" will not show that God is the or even a fundamental criterion for goodness.

Let us first see how it does *not* show that we could not have an understanding of "good" without having an understanding of "God." We couldn't understand the full religious sense of what is meant by "God" without knowing that whatever is denoted by this term is said to be good, but, as "young" or "three-sided" are understood without reference to "puppies" or "triangles," though the converse cannot be the case, so "good" is also understood quite independently of any reference to "God," but again the converse cannot be the case. We can intelligibly say, "I have a three-sided figure here that is most certainly not a triangle" and "Colts are young but they are not puppies." Similarly, we can well say, "Conscientiousness, under most circumstances at least, is good even in a world without God." Such an utterance is clearly intelligible, to believer and nonbeliever alike. It is a well-formed English sentence with a use in the language. But here we can use "good" without implying anything about the reality of God. Such linguistic evidence clearly shows that good is a concept which can be understood quite independently of any reference to the Deity and that morality without religion, without theism, is quite possible. In fact quite the reverse is the case. Christianity, Judaism, and theistic religions of that sort could not exist if people did not have a moral understanding that was, logically speaking, quite independent of such religions. We could have no understanding of the truth of "God is good" or of the concept God unless we had an independent understanding of goodness.

That this is so can be seen from the following considerations. If we had no grasp of the use of the word "young," and if we did not know the criteria for deciding whether a dog was young, we could not know how correctly to apply the word "puppy." Without such a prior understanding of what it is to be young we could not understand the sentence "Puppies are young."

Similarly, if we had no grasp of the use of the word "good," and if we did not know the criteria for deciding whether a being (or if you will, a power or a force) was good, we could not know how correctly to apply the word "God." Without such a prior understanding of goodness we could not understand the sentence "God is good." This clearly shows that our understanding of morality and knowledge of goodness is independent of any knowledge that we may or may not have of the Divine. In fact the very converse is the case. Without a prior and logically independent understanding of "good" and without some nonreligious criterion for judging something to be good, the religious person could have no knowledge of God, for he could not know whether that powerful being who spoke out of the whirlwind and laid the foundations of the earth was in fact worthy of worship and perfectly good.

From the argument we have made so far we can conclude that we cannot decide whether something is good or whether it ought to be done simply from finding out (assuming that we can find out) that God commanded it, willed it, enjoined it, and the like. Furthermore, whether "God is good" is synthetic (substantive) or analytic (a truth of language), the concept of good must be understood as something distinct from the concept of God; that is to say, a man could know how to use "good" properly and still not know how to use "God." In fact quite the reverse is the case. A man could not know how to use "God" correctly unless he already understood how to use "good." An understanding of goodness is logically prior to and is, as such, independent of any understanding or acknowledgment of God. . . .

STUDY QUESTIONS

1. Consider Browne's claim that the total of human happiness would not increase if everyone were unselfish. Can you think of any reason for disagreeing with this claim?

2. In what sense, according to Browne, is each of us the basic source of what is right or wrong? (Is it up to you to say whether the Ten Commandments are to be followed?)

3. Rachels believes that ethical egoism has "monstrous consequences." Do you agree? Be specific.

4. Why does Rachels reject the view that human beings are basically selfish? Can you think of examples of unselfish behavior?

5. Why, according to Taylor, is there a conflict between utilitarianism and justice?

6. Consider a moral problem, for example, abortion or capital punishment. Briefly sketch the differences between a formalistic and a utilitarian approach to this problem. Be specific.

7. According to Bennett, why does Huck Finn, who goes against his morality, turn out to be a better person than Himmler, who follows his morality?

8. Why is Himmler more sensitive to the conflict between sympathy and morality than Huck Finn?

9. How does Bennett's argument cast doubt on the following: (a) If it feels good, it can't be wrong. (b) If you do what morality requires, you can't go wrong.

10. Can we define what is morally right by appeal to what God commands? If so, how and why? If not, why not?

11. In your view, which of the essays in this part provides the best answers to the questions posed in the Preview to Part Nine? Explain and justify your answer.

12. The moral theories in this part assume a conflict between what people want to do and what they ought, morally, to do. Do you think there is such a conflict? If there is, should morality always win?

13. How would each of the following theories define a genuinely worthwhile life: egoism, utilitarianism, ethical formalism, divine command theory?

14. How does MacIver defend the golden rule as the essence of morality?

15. What reasons does Brunner give for a Divine Command theory?

16. Do Nielsen's arguments undermine Brunner's version of the Divine Command Theory?

17. Do Bennett's reflections on sympathy and the limits of formal ethics cast any doubts on MacIver's version of a formalistic ethics?

Further Readings

Brandt, Richard B. "Toward a Credible Form of Utilitarianism." In G. Nakhnikian and H. Castaneda, eds., *Morality and the Language of Conduct*. Detroit: Wayne State University Press, 1963, pp. 107–145. [A sophisticated defense of utilitarianism.]

Glickman, Jack, ed. *Moral Philosophy: An Introduction*. New York: St. Martin's Press, 1976. [An excellent collection of major classics in ethics by Plato, Kant, Hume, and Mill, together with modern articles on each of their philosophies.]

PART TEN

ETHICAL JUDGMENTS

PREVIEW

It seems obvious that there is little, if any, agreement on ethical matters in our society. Ethical controversies involving the pros and cons of abortion, censorship, pornography, and so forth generate lots of heat but little light. This has not always been true. Why is there so much disagreement about ethics today?

This question takes on added significance if we contrast the situation of ethics with that of other areas, for example, science. To some extent, scientists agree on what the facts are, what theories are better than others, what the evidence is, what evidence is irrelevant, and so on. Are scientists luckier or smarter than people who engage in ethical debate? Or is there something about ethics itself which makes disagreement unavoidable?

One way of posing the question about the status of ethical judgments is this: What is ethics (or an ethical theory or judgment) about? Science is about the world. That is, the subject matter of physics is the physical universe. The subject matter of sociology is society. What is the subject matter of ethics?

According to some writers, ethics is about the properties of actions, events, and states of affairs that exist in the world. When, for example, we make ethical judgments about murder, we are saying something about the goodness or badness of taking a human life. The action of killing someone has "objective" properties. Similarly, the table I see has objective properties: It is brown and rectangular, for example.

It is true that we may not have discovered what the properties of any particular moral action, event, or state of affairs are. For example, we may not know whether abortion is good or bad, but it is one or the other whether we know it or not. And of course we may be mistaken in our beliefs about what the ethical properties of any action are; but this only shows that we have not discovered the correct property. According to this view of ethical judgments, we can explain widespread ethical disagreement by saying that we have not discovered which moral properties certain kinds of actions, such as abortions, have.

There are other authors who think that ethical judgments are not about the properties of actions, events, and objects but rather about certain states of mind of human beings. More specifically, ethical subjectivism holds that ethical judgments refer directly to certain feelings, attitudes, and beliefs of individuals or groups, namely, feelings of approval or disapproval with regard to some person or action or quality, etc. (and not to those persons, actions, or questions themselves). Ethical judgments like ''Abortion is immoral'' refer to my own feelings and opinions, or the feelings of many individuals, and not to anything in the act of abortion itself.

There is another view, closely related to but not to be confused with this view. It is the view that ethical judgments are not about anything. And they are not about anything because they are cognitively meaningless. They are mere expressions of feelings, more like a grunt than a judgment.

According to the second and third views, ethical disagreement results from the fact that people have different feelings and attitudes about acts like abortion. If you want ethical agreement on this view, all you have to do is influence people to have the same attitude. For the first view, it is important that ethical agreement be a result of the discovery of what the correct properties of an action are. Here again the analogy with the table is useful. People agree that the table is rectangular because they see that it is. If someone conditioned everybody to believe that circles were rectangles, we would have agreement but it wouldn't count. Similarly, for this view, reaching ethical agreement is not enough. The agreement has to be a result of finding out whether an action is really right or wrong.

Another reason for ethical disagreement is the variety of moral standards, theories, beliefs, and opinions which people hold (implicitly or explicitly). For utilitarians, some abortions may be right and others wrong. For a religious person, all abortions may be wrong. For some people, what's right or wrong, good or bad, differs from one time to another or from one place to another. Their motto might be ''When in Rome do as the Romans do.'' This view holds that there is no one moral standard that is correct or applicable to all people, at all times, and in all places. There are many equally correct standards, depending on where and who you are. Of course, others deny that this is so. They claim that there is only one correct moral standard which is applicable to everyone, everywhere.

This discussion leads us to the two main questions of this part. Before we formulate them, it should be noted that in inquiring about such matters, we are not asking: What sorts of things or acts are good or bad, or which acts are right or wrong? We are not asking for a standard of conduct. That was the subject matter of Part Nine. Rather, in asking such questions, we are asking about the *status* of ethical judgments—that is, assertions of the form 'X is right' and 'X is wrong,' and so on. When anyone utters such a judgment, what is she/he doing? Is she/he making an assertion of fact, or just expressing his/her feelings? Is she/he stating a truth that is meant to apply to everyone? This leads us to the two main questions of this part.

Main Questions

These main questions are:

What is the status of ethical judgments—that is, assertions that something is good or bad, right or wrong?

1. Are ethical judgments objective or subjective? That is, do they assert something about actual actions or states of affairs? Or do they merely assert or express the feelings and tastes of those who utter them?

2. Are ethical judgments absolute or relative? That is, are any ethical judgments (even if not all) meant to be universally applicable? Or are all of them relative to different societies at different times and places?

Answers

We may now explicitly state the answers to our two main questions. These are:

1a. Ethical objectivism: Ethical judgments which employ terms like "good," "bad," "right," "wrong" refer to objective properties of actions, events, and states of affairs.

1b. Ethical subjectivism: Ethical judgments refer directly to certain feelings, attitudes and beliefs of individuals or groups, namely, feelings of approval or disapproval with regard to some person, action or quality—and not to those persons or actions themselves.

1c. Emotivism: Ethical judgments are not about anything; they are mere expressions of feelings, more like a grunt than a judgment, pertaining either to actions or a person's attitude. (Blanshard refers to this view in Essay 48, somewhat misleadingly, as the new subjectivism.)

2a. Ethical absolutism: There is only *one correct* moral standard which is applicable to all people, all times and all places, even if there are, in fact, many conflicting standards which people adhere to.

2b. Ethical relativism: There is no one moral standard that is correct or applicable to all people at all times and in all places. There are many equally correct standards, depending upon where and who you are.

Let us use our abortion example to illustrate these views.

For the objectivist, to say that abortion is wrong is to say something which is either correct or incorrect, just as to say that the table is brown is to say something which is either correct or incorrect.

For the subjectivist, to say that abortion is wrong is to say that some individual or group has certain feelings of disapproval regarding abortion.

For the emotivist, to say that abortion is wrong is merely to express a feeling and not to say anything which has any literal meaning. Thus, uttering the words abortion is wrong is more like grunting (or whatever) than like asserting.

For the absolutist, to say that abortion is wrong is to say that it is wrong for everyone, at all times, in all places, and presumably in all circumstances.

For the relativist, to say that abortion is wrong is to say that some individual or group accepts a moral code or standard according to which it is deemed to be wrong. If some other individual or group accepts a different standard or code, abortion need not be wrong for that individual or group.

Selections

The answers to our main questions are represented as follows:

Question	Answer	Selection
(1)	(1b) Subjectivism	47
(1)	(1c) Emotivism	47*
	(1a) Objectivism [and critique of (1b), (1c)]	48
(2)	(2b) Ethical relativism	49
(2)	(2a) Ethical absolutism [and critique of (2b)]	50

*[The author of selection 47 at certain places seems to advocate subjectivism. But elsewhere he says things which indicate that he really holds the position of emotivism.]

47 / Science and Ethics

BERTRAND RUSSELL

[I. ETHICS AND MORAL RULES]

The study of ethics, traditionally, consists of two parts, one concerned with moral rules, the other with what is good on its own account. Rules of conduct, many of which have a ritual origin, play a great part in the lives of savages and primitive peoples. It is forbidden to eat out of the chief's dish, or to seethe the kid in its mother's milk; it is commanded to offer sacrifices to the gods, which, at a certain stage of development, are thought most acceptable if they are human beings. Other moral rules, such as the prohibition of murder and theft, have a more obvious social utility, and survive the decay of the primitive theological systems with which they were originally associated. But as men grow more reflective there is a tendency to lay less stress on rules and more on states of mind. This comes from two sources—philosophy and mystical religion. We are all familiar with passages in the prophets and the gospels in which purity of heart is set above meticulous observance of the Law; and St. Paul's famous praise of charity, or love, teaches the same principle. . . .

One of the ways in which the need of appealing to external rules of conduct has been avoided has been the belief in "conscience," which has been especially important in Protestant ethics. It has been supposed that God reveals to each human heart what is right and what is wrong, so that, in order to avoid sin, we have only to listen to the inner voice. There are, however, two difficulties in this theory: first, that conscience says different things to different people; secondly, that the study of the unconscious has given us an understanding of the mundane causes of conscientious feelings.

As to the different deliverances of conscience: George III's conscience told him that he must not grant Catholic Emancipation, as, if he did, he would have committed perjury in taking the Coronation Oath, but later monarchs have had no such scruples. Conscience leads some to condemn the spoliation of the rich by the poor, as advocated by communists; and others to condemn exploitation of the poor by the rich, as practiced by capitalists. It tells one man that he ought to defend his country in case of invasion, while it tells another that all participation in warfare is wicked. During the War, the authorities, few of whom had studied ethics, found conscience very puzzling, and were led to some curious decisions, such as that a man might have conscientious scruples against fighting himself, but not against working on the fields so as to make possible the conscription of another man. They held also that, while conscience might disapprove of all war it could not, failing that extreme position, disapprove of the war then in progress. Those who, for whatever reason, thought it wrong to fight, were compelled to state their position in terms of this somewhat primitive and unscientific conception of "conscience."

The diversity in the deliverances of conscience is what is to be expected when its origin is understood. In early youth, certain classes of acts meet with approval and others with disapproval; and by the normal process of association, pleasure and discomfort gradually attach themselves to the acts, and not merely to the approval and disapproval respectively produced by them. As time goes on, we may forget all about our early moral training, but we shall still feel uncomfortable about certain kinds of actions, while others will give us a glow of virtue. To introspection, these feelings are mysterious, since we no longer remember the circumstances which originally caused them; and therefore it is natural to attribute them to the voice of God in the heart. But in fact conscience is a product of education, and can be trained to approve or disapprove, in the great majority of mankind, as educators may see fit. While, therefore, it is right to wish to liberate ethics from external moral rules, this can hardly be satisfactorily achieved by means of the notion of "conscience."

Philosophers, by a different road, have arrived at a different position in which, also, moral rules of conduct have a subordinate place. They have framed the concept of the Good, by which they mean (roughly speaking) that which, in itself and apart from its consequences, we should wish to see existing—or, if they are theists, that which is pleasing to God. Most people would agree that happiness is preferable to unhappiness, friendliness to unfriendliness, and so on. Moral rules, according to this view, are justified if they promote the existence of what is good on its own account, but not otherwise. The prohibition of murder, in the vast majority of cases, can be justified by its effects, but the practice of burning widows on their husband's funeral pyre cannot. The former rule, therefore, should be retained, but not the latter. Even the best moral rules, however, will have *some* exceptions, since no class of action *always* has bad results. We have thus three different senses in which an act may be ethically commendable: (1) It may be in accordance with the received moral code; (2) it may be sincerely intended to have good effects; (3) it may in fact have good effects. The third sense, however, is generally considered inadmissible in morals. According to orthodox theology, Judas Iscariot's act of betrayal had good consequences, since it was necessary for the Atonement; but it was not on this account laudable.

Different philosophers have formed different conceptions of the Good. Some hold that it consists in the knowledge and love of God; others in universal love; others in the enjoyment of beauty; and yet others in pleasure. The Good once defined, the rest of ethics follows: We ought to act in the way we believe most likely to create as much good as possible, and as little as possible of its correlative evil. The framing of moral rules, so long as the ultimate Good is supposed known, is matter for science. For example: Should capital punishment be inflicted for theft, or only for murder, or not at all? Jeremy Bentham, who considered pleasure to be the Good, devoted himself to working out what criminal code would most promote pleasure, and concluded that it ought to be much less severe than that prevailing in his day. All this, except the proposition that pleasure is the Good, comes within the sphere of science.

But when we try to be definite as to what we mean when we say that this or that is "the Good," we find ourselves involved in very great difficulties. Bentham's creed that pleasure is the Good roused furious opposition, and was said to be a pig's philosophy. Neither he nor his opponents could advance any argument. In a scientific question, evidence can be adduced on both sides, and in the end one side is seen to have the better case—or, if this does not happen, the question is left undecided. But in a question as to whether this or that is the ultimate Good, there is no evidence either way; each disputant can only appeal to his own emotions, and employ such rhetorical devices as shall rouse similar emotions in others. . . .

[II. ETHICS AND THE CONCEPT OF GOOD]

Questions as to "values"—that is to say, as to what is good or bad on its own account, independently of its effects—lie outside the domain of science, as the defenders of religion emphatically assert. I think that in this they are right, but I draw the further conclusion, which they do not draw, that questions as to "values" lie wholly outside the domain of knowledge. That is to say, when we assert that this or that has "value," we are giving expression to our own emotions, not to a fact which would still be true if our personal feelings were different. To make this clear, we must try to analyze the conception of the Good.

It is obvious, to begin with, that the whole idea of good and bad has some connection with desire. *Prima facie,** anything that we all desire is "good," and anything that we all dread is "bad." If we all agreed in our desires, the matter could be left there, but unfortunately our desires conflict. If I say "What I want is good," my neighbor will say "No, what I want." Ethics is an attempt—though not, I think, a successful one—to escape from this subjectivity. I shall naturally try to show, in my dispute with my neighbor, that my desires have some quality which makes them more

*[On the face of it.—Eds.]

worthy of respect than his. If I want to preserve a right of way, I shall appeal to the landless inhabitants of the district; but he, on his side, will appeal to the landowners. I shall say "What use is the beauty of the countryside if no one sees it?" He will retort "What beauty will be left if trippers are allowed to spread devastation?" Each tries to enlist allies by showing that his own desires harmonize with those of other people. When this is obviously impossible, as in the case of a burglar, the man is condemned by public opinion, and his ethical status is that of a sinner. . . .

Ethics is an attempt to give universal, and not merely personal, importance to certain of our desires. I say "certain" of our desires, because in regard to some of them this is obviously impossible, as we saw in the case of the burglar. The man who makes money on the Stock Exchange by means of some secret knowledge does not wish others to be equally well informed: Truth (in so far as he values it) is for him a private possession, not the general human good that it is for the philosopher. The philosopher may, it is true, sink to the level of the stock-jobber, as when he claims priority for a discovery. But this is a lapse: In his purely philosophic capacity, he wants only to enjoy the contemplation of Truth, in doing which he in no way interferes with others who wish to do likewise.

To seem to give universal importance to our desires—which is the business of ethics—may be attempted from two points of view, that of the legislator and that of the preacher. Let us take the legislator first.

I will assume, for the sake of argument, that the legislator is personally disinterested. That is to say, when he recognizes one of his desires as being concerned only with his own welfare, he does not let it influence him in framing the laws; for example, his code is not designed to increase his personal fortune. But he has other desires which seem to him impersonal. He may believe in an ordered hierarchy from king to peasant, or from mineowner to black indentured laborer. He may believe that women should be submissive to men. He may hold that the spread of knowledge in the lower classes is dangerous. And so on and so on. He will then, if he can, so construct his code that conduct promoting the ends which he values shall, as far as possible, be in accordance with individual self-interest; and he will establish a system of moral instruction which will, where it succeeds, make men feel wicked if they pursue other purposes than his.[1] Thus "virtue" will come to be in fact, though not in subjective estimation, subservience to the desires of the legislator, in so far as he himself considers these desires worthy to be universalized.

[1]Compare the following advice by a contemporary of Aristotle (Chinese, not Greek): "A ruler should not listen to those who believe in people having opinions of their own and in the importance of the individual. Such teachings cause men to withdraw to quiet places and hide away in caves or on mountains, there to rail at the prevailing government, sneer at those in authority, belittle the importance of rank and emoluments, and despise all who hold official posts." Waley, *The Way and Its Power*, p. 37.

The standpoint and method of the preacher are necessarily somewhat different, because he does not control the machinery of the State, and therefore cannot produce an artificial harmony between his desires and those of others. His only method is to try to rouse in others the same desires that he feels himself, and for this purpose his appeal must be to the emotions. Thus Ruskin caused people to like Gothic architecture, not by argument, but by the moving effect of rhythmical prose. *Uncle Tom's Cabin* helped to make people think slavery an evil by causing them to imagine themselves as slaves. Every attempt to persuade people that something is good (or bad) in itself, and not merely in its effects, depends upon the art of rousing feelings, not upon an appeal to evidence. In every case the preacher's skill consists in creating in others emotions similar to his own— or dissimilar, if he is a hypocrite. I am not saying this as a criticism of the preacher, but as an analysis of the essential character of his activity.

[III. ETHICAL JUDGMENTS]

When a man says "This is good in itself," he *seems* to be making a statement, just as much as if he said "This is square" or "This is sweet." I believe this to be a mistake. I think that what the man really means is: "I wish everybody to desire this," or rather "Would that everybody desired this." If what he says is interpreted as a statement, it is merely an affirmation of his own personal wish; if, on the other hand, it is interpreted in a general way, it states nothing, but merely desires something. The wish, as an occurrence, is personal, but what it desires is universal. It is, I think, this curious interlocking of the particular and the universal which has caused so much confusion in ethics.

The matter may perhaps become clearer by contrasting an ethical sentence with one which makes a statement. If I say "All Chinese are Buddhists," I can be refuted by the production of a Chinese Christian or Mohammedan. If I say "I believe that all Chinese are Buddhists," I cannot be refuted by any evidence from China, but only by evidence that I do not believe what I say; for what I am asserting is only something about my own state of mind. If, now, a philosopher says "Beauty is good," I may interpret him as meaning either "Would that everybody loved the beautiful" (which corresponds to "All Chinese are Buddhists") or "I wish that everybody loved the beautiful" (which corresponds to "I believe that all Chinese are Buddhists"). The first of these makes no assertion, but expresses a wish; since it affirms nothing, it is logically impossible that there should be evidence for or against it, or for it to possess either truth or falsehood. The second sentence, instead of being merely optative, does make a statement, but it is one about the philosopher's state of mind, and it could only be refuted by evidence that he does not have the wish that he says he has. This second sentence does not belong to ethics, but to psychology or biography. The first sentence, which does belong to ethics, expresses a desire for something, but asserts nothing.

Ethics, if the above analysis is correct, contains no statements, whether true or false, but consists of desires of a certain general kind, namely such as are concerned with the desires of mankind in general—and of gods, angels, and devils, if they exist. Science can discuss the causes of desires, and the means for realizing them, but it cannot contain any genuinely ethical sentences, because it is concerned with what is true or false.

The theory which I have been advocating is a form of the doctrine which is called the "subjectivity" of values. This doctrine consists in maintaining that, if two men differ about values, there is not a disagreement as to any kind of truth, but a difference of taste. If one man says "Oysters are good" and another says "I think they are bad," we recognize that there is nothing to argue about. The theory in question holds that all differences as to values are of this sort, although we do not naturally think them so when we are dealing with matters that seem to us more exalted than oysters. The chief ground for adopting this view is the complete impossibility of finding any arguments to prove that this or that has intrinsic value. If we all agreed, we might hold that we know values by intuition. We cannot *prove*, to a color-blind man, that grass is green and not red. But there are various ways of proving to him that he lacks a power of discrimination which most men possess, whereas in the case of values there are no such ways, and disagreements are much more frequent than in the case of colors. Since no way can be even imagined for deciding a difference as to values, the conclusion is forced upon us that the difference is one of tastes, not one as to any objective truth. . . .

[IV. OBJECTIONS AND REPLIES]

Those who believe in "objective" values often contend that the view which I have been advocating has immoral consequences. This seems to me to be due to faulty reasoning. There are, as has already been said, certain ethical consequences of the doctrine of subjective values, of which the most important is the rejection of vindictive punishment and the notion of "sin." But the more general consequences which are feared, such as the decay of all sense of moral obligation, are not to be logically deduced. Moral obligation, if it is to influence conduct, must consist not merely of a belief, but of a desire. The desire, I may be told, is the desire to be "good" in a sense which I no longer allow. But when we analyze the desire to be "good" it generally resolves itself into a desire to be approved, or, alternatively, to act so as to bring about certain general consequences which we desire. We have wishes which are not purely personal, and if we had not, no amount of ethical teaching would influence our conduct except through fear of disapproval. The sort of life that most of us admire is one which is guided by large impersonal desires; now such desires can, no doubt, be encouraged by example, education, and knowledge, but they can hardly be created by the mere abstract belief that they are good, nor discouraged by an analysis of what is meant by the word "good."

When we contemplate the human race, we may desire that it should be happy, or healthy, or intelligent, or warlike, and so on. Any one of these desires, if it is strong, will produce its own morality; but if we have no such general desire, our conduct, whatever our ethic may be, will only serve social purposes insofar as self-interest and the interests of society are in harmony. It is the business of wise institutions to create such harmony as far as possible, and for the rest, whatever may be our theoretical definition of value, we must depend upon the existence of impersonal desires. When you meet a man with whom you have a fundamental ethical disagreement—for example, if you think that all men count equally, while he selects a class as alone important—you will find yourself no better able to cope with him if you believe in objective values than if you do not. In either case, you can only influence his conduct through influencing his desires: If you succeed in that, his ethic will change, and if not, not.

Some people feel that if a general desire, say for the happiness of mankind, has not the sanction of absolute good, it is in some way irrational. This is due to a lingering belief in objective values. A desire cannot, in itself, be either rational or irrational. It may conflict with other desires, and therefore lead to unhappiness; it may rouse opposition in others, and therefore be incapable of gratification. But it cannot be considered "irrational" merely because no reason can be given for feeling it. We may desire A because it is a means to B, but in the end, when we have done with mere means, we must come to something which we desire for no reason, but not on that account "irrationally." All systems of ethics embody the desires of those who advocate them, but this fact is concealed in a mist of words. Our desires are, in fact, more general and less purely selfish than many moralists imagine; if it were not so, no theory of ethics would make moral improvement possible. It is, in fact, not by ethical theory, but by the cultivation of large and generous desires through intelligence, happiness, and freedom from fear, that men can be brought to act more than they do at present in a manner that is consistent with the general happiness of mankind. Whatever our definition of the "Good," and whether we believe it to be subjective or objective, those who do not desire the happiness of mankind will not endeavor to further it, while those who do desire it will do what they can to bring it about.

I conclude that, while it is true that science cannot decide questions of value, that is because they cannot be intellectually decided at all, and lie outside the realm of truth and falsehood. Whatever knowledge is attainable must be attained by scientific methods; and what science cannot discover, mankind cannot know.

48 / The New Subjectivism in Ethics

BRAND BLANSHARD

[I. WHAT IS THE NEW SUBJECTIVISM?]

By the new subjectivism in ethics I mean the view that when anyone says "This is right" or "This is good," he is only expressing his own feeling; he is not asserting anything true or false, because he is not asserting or judging at all; he is really making an exclamation that expresses a favorable feeling.

This view has recently come into much favor. . . . Why is it that the theory has come into so rapid a popularity? Is it because moralists of insight have been making a fresh and searching examination of moral experience and its expression? No, I think not. [It is because a movement in philosophy has put forth a theory of knowledge which had implications for ethics. This movement is logical positivism.] If the new view has become popular in ethics, it is because certain persons who were at work in the theory of knowledge arrived at a new view *there*, and found, on thinking it out, that it required the new view in ethics; the view comes less from ethical analysis than from logical positivism.

As positivists, these writers held that every judgment belongs to one or the other of two types. On the one hand, it may be *a priori* or necessary. But then it is always analytic; i.e., it unpacks in its predicate part of all of its subject. Can we safely say that 7+5 make 12? Yes, because 12 is what we mean by "7+5." On the other hand, the judgment may be empirical, and then, if we are to verify it, we can no longer look to our meanings only; it refers to sense experience and there we must look for its warrant. Having arrived at this division of judgments, the positivists raised the question where value judgments fall. The judgment that knowledge is good, for example, did not seem to be analytic; the value that knowledge might have did not seem to be part of our concept of knowledge. But neither was the statement empirical, for goodness was not a quality like red or squeaky that could be seen or heard. What were they to do, then, with these awkward judgments of value? To find a place for them in their theory of knowledge would require them to revise the theory radically, and yet that theory was what they regarded as their most important discovery. It appeared that the theory could be saved in one way only. If it could be shown that judgments of good and bad were not judgments at all, that they asserted nothing true or false, but merely expressed emotions like "Hurrah" or "Fiddlesticks," then these wayward judgments would cease from troubling and weary heads could be at rest. This is the course the positivists took. They explained value judgments by explaining them away.

Now I do not think their view will do. But before discussing it, I should like to record one vote of thanks to them for the clarity with which they have stated their case. It has been said of John Stuart Mill* that he wrote so clearly that he could be found out. This theory has been put so clearly and precisely that it deserves criticism of the same kind, and this I will do my best to supply. The theory claims to show by analysis that when we say "That is good," we do not mean to assert a character of the subject of which we are thinking. I shall argue that we do mean to do just that.

[II. CRITICISM OF THIS VIEW]

Let us work through an example, and the simpler and commoner the better. There is perhaps no value statement on which people would more universally agree than the statement that intense pain is bad. Let us take a set of circumstances in which I happen to be interested on the legislative side and in which I think every one of us might naturally make such a statement. We come upon a rabbit that has been caught in one of the brutal traps in common use. There are signs that it has struggled for days to escape and that in a frenzy of hunger, pain, and fear, it has all but eaten off its own leg. The attempt failed: The animal is now dead. As we think of the long and excruciating pain it must have suffered, we are very likely to say "It was a bad thing that the little animal should suffer so." The positivist tells us that when we say this we are only expressing our present emotion. I hold, on the contrary, that we mean to assert something of the animal's experience itself, namely, that it was bad—bad when and as it occurred.

[1.] Consider what follows from the positivist view. On that view, nothing good or bad happened in the case until I came on the scene and made my

*[A 19th century British philosopher.—Eds.]

remark. For what I express in my remark is something going on in me at the time, and that of course did not exist until I did come on the scene. The pain of the rabbit was not itself bad; nothing evil was happening when that pain was being endured; badness, in the only sense in which it is involved at all, waited for its appearance till I came and looked and felt. Now that this is at odds with our meaning may be shown as follows. Let us put to ourselves the hypothesis that we had not come on the scene and that the rabbit never was discovered. Are we prepared to say that in that case nothing bad occurred in the sense in which we said it did? Clearly not. Indeed we should say, on the contrary, that the accident of our later discovery made no difference whatever to the badness of the animal's pain, that it would have been every whit as bad whether a chance passer-by happened later to discover the body and feel repugnance or not. If so, then it is clear that in saying the suffering was bad we are not expressing our feelings only. We are saying that the pain was bad when and as it occurred and before anyone took an attitude toward it.

[2.] The first argument is thus an ideal experiment in which we use the method of difference. It removes our present expression and shows that the badness we meant would not be affected by this, whereas on positivist grounds it should be. The second argument applies the method in the reverse way. It ideally removes the past event, and shows that this would render false what we mean to say, whereas on positivist grounds it should not. Let us suppose that the animal did not in fact fall into the trap and did not suffer at all, but that we mistakenly believe it did, and say as before that its suffering was an evil thing. On the positivist theory, everything I sought to express by calling it evil in the first case is still present in the second. In the only sense in which badness is involved at all, whatever was bad in the first case is still present in its entirety, since all that is expressed in either case is a state of feeling, and that feeling is still there. And our question is, is such an implication consistent with what we meant? Clearly it is not. If anyone asked us, after we made the remark that the suffering was a bad thing, whether we should think it relevant to what we said to learn that the incident had never occurred and no pain had been suffered at all, we should say that it made all the difference in the world, that what we were asserting to be bad was precisely the suffering we thought had occurred back there, that if this had not occurred, there was nothing left to be bad, and that our assertion was in that case mistaken. The suggestion that in saying something evil had occurred we were after all making no mistake, because we had never meant anyhow to say anything about the past suffering, seems to me merely frivolous. If we did not mean to say this, why should we be so relieved on finding that the suffering had not occurred? On the theory before us, such relief would be groundless, for in that suffering itself there was nothing bad at all, and hence in its nonoccurrence there would be nothing to be relieved about. The positivist theory would here distort our meaning beyond recognition.

So far as I can see, there is only one way out for the positivist. He holds that goodness and badness lie in feelings of approval or disapproval. And there is a way in which he might hold that badness did in this case precede our own feeling of disapproval without belonging to the pain itself. The pain in itself was neutral; but unfortunately the rabbit, on no grounds at all, took up toward this neutral object an attitude of disapproval, and that made it for the first time, and in the only intelligible sense, bad. This way of escape is theoretically possible, but since it has grave difficulties of its own and has not, so far as I know, been urged by positivists, it is perhaps best not to spend time over it.

[3.] I come now to a third argument, which again is very simple. When we come upon the rabbit and make our remark about its suffering being a bad thing, we presumably make it with some feeling; the positivists are plainly right in saying that such remarks do usually express feeling. But suppose that a week later we revert to the incident in thought and make our statement again. And suppose that the circumstances have now so changed that the feeling with which we made the remark in the first place has faded. The pathetic evidence is no longer before us; and we are now so fatigued in body and mind that feeling is, as we say, quite dead. In these circumstances, since what was expressed by the remark when first made is, on the theory before us, simply absent, the remark now expresses nothing. It is as empty as the word "Hurrah" would be when there was no enthusiasm behind it. And this seems to me untrue. When we repeat the remark that such suffering was a bad thing, the feeling with which we made it last week may be at or near the vanishing point, but if we were asked whether we meant to say what we did before, we should certainly answer Yes. We should say that we made our point with feeling the first time and little or no feeling the second time, but that it was the same point we were making. And if we can see that what we meant to say remains the same, while the feeling varies from intensity to near zero, it is not the feeling that we primarily meant to express.

[4.] I come now to a fourth consideration. We all believe that toward acts or effects of a certain kind one attitude is fitting and another not; but on the theory before us such a belief would not make sense. Broad and Ross have lately contended that this fitness is one of the main facts of ethics, and I suspect they are right. But that is not exactly my point. My point is this: Whether there is such fitness or not, we all assume that there is, and if we do, we express in moral judgments more than the subjectivists say we do. Let me illustrate.

In the novel *The House of the Dead*, Dostoyevski tells of his experiences in a Siberian prison camp. Whatever the unhappy inmates of such camps are like today, Dostoyevski's companions were about as grim a lot as can be imagined. "I have heard stories," he writes, "of the most terrible, the most unnatural actions, of the most monstrous murders, told with the most spontaneous, childishly merry laughter." Most of us would say that in this delight at the killing of others or the causing of suffering there is something very unfitting. If we were asked why we thought so, we should say that these things involve great evil and are wrong, and that to take delight in what is evil or wrong is plainly unfitting. Now on the subjectivist view, this answer is ruled out. For before someone takes up an attitude toward death, suffering, or their infliction, they have no moral quality at all. There is therefore nothing about them to which an attitude of approval or condemnation could be fitting. They are in themselves neutral, and, so far as they get a moral quality, they get it only through being invested with it by the attitude of the onlooker. But if that is true, why is any attitude more fitting than any other? Would applause, for example, be fitting if, apart from the applause, there were nothing good to applaud? Would condemnation be fitting if, independently of the condemnation, there were nothing bad to condemn? In such a case, any attitude would be as fitting or unfitting as any other, which means that the notion of fitness has lost all point.

Indeed we are forced to go much farther. If goodness and badness lie in attitudes only and hence are brought into being by them, those men who greeted death and misery with childishly merry laughter are taking the only sensible line. If there is nothing evil in these things, if they get their moral complexion only from our feeling about them, why shouldn't they be greeted with a cheer? To greet them with repulsion would turn what before was neutral into something bad; it would needlessly bring badness into the world; and even on subjectivist assumptions that does not seem very bright. On the other hand, to greet them with delight would convert what before was neutral into something good; it would bring goodness into the world. If I have murdered a man and wish to remove the stain, the way is clear. It is to cry "Hurrah for murder."

What is the subjectivist to reply? I can only guess. He may point out that the inflicting of death is *not* really neutral before the onlooker takes his attitude, for the man who inflicted the death no doubt himself took an attitude, and thus the act had a moral quality derived from this. But that makes the case more incredible still, for the man who did the act presumably approved it, and if so it was good in the only sense in which anything is good, and then our conviction that the laughter is unfit is more unaccountable still. It may be replied that the victim, too, had his attitude and that since this was unfavorable, the act was not unqualifiedly good. But the answer is plain. Let the killer be expert at his job; let him dispatch his victim instantly before he has time to take an attitude, and then gloat about his perfect crime without ever telling anyone. Then, so far as I can see, his act will be good without any qualification. It would become bad only if someone found out about it and disliked it. And that would be a curiously irrational procedure, since the man's approving of his own killing is in itself just as neutral as the killing that it approves. Why then should anyone dislike it?

It may be replied that we can defend our dislike on this ground that, if the approval of killing were to go unchecked and spread, most men would have to live in insecurity and fear, and these things are undesirable. But surely this reply is not open; these things are not, on the theory, undesirable, for nothing is; in themselves they are neutral. Why then should I disapprove men's living in this state? The answer may come that if other men live in insecurity and fear, I shall in time be infected myself. But even in my own insecurity and fear there is, on the theory before us, nothing bad whatever, and therefore, if I disapprove them, it is without a shadow of ground and with no more fitness in my attitude than if I cordially cheered them. The theory thus conflicts with our judgments of fitness all along the line.

[5.] I come now to a fifth and final difficulty with the theory. It makes mistakes about values impossible. There is a whole nest of inter-connected criticisms here, some of which have been made so often that I shall not develop them again, such as that I can never agree or disagree in opinion with anyone else about an ethical matter, and that in these matters I can never be inconsistent with others or with myself. I am not at all content with the sort of analysis which says that the only contradictions in such cases have regard to facts and that contradictions about value are only differences of feeling. I think that if anyone tells me that having a bicuspid out without an anesthetic is not a bad experience and I say it is a very nasty experience indeed, I am differing with him in opinion, and differing about the degree of badness of the experience. But without pressing this further, let me apply the argument in what is perhaps a fresh direction.

There is an old and merciful distinction that moralists have made for many centuries about conduct—the distinction between what is subjectively and what is objectively right. They have said that in any given situation there is some act which, in view of all the circumstances, would be the best act to do; and this is what would be objectively right. The notion of an objectively right act is the ground of our notion of duty: Our duty is always to find and do this act if we can. But of course we often don't find it. We often hit upon and do acts that we think are the right ones, but we are mistaken; and then our act is only subjectively right. Between these two acts the disparity may be continual; Professor Prichard suggested that probably few of us in the course of our lives ever succeed in doing *the* right act.

Now so far as I can see, the new subjectivism would abolish this difference at a stroke. Let us take a case. A boy abuses his small brother. We should commonly say "That is wrong, but perhaps he doesn't know any better. By reason of bad teaching and a feeble imagination, he may see nothing wrong in what he is doing, and may even be proud of it. If so, his act may be subjectively right, though it is miles away from what is objectively right.'' What concerns me about the new subjectivism is that it pro-hibits this distinction. If the boy feels this way about his act, then it is right in the only sense in which anything is right. The notion of an objective right lying beyond what he has discovered, and which he ought to seek and do, is meaningless. There might, to be sure, be an act that would more gener-ally arouse favorable feeings in others, but that would not make it right for him unless he thought of it and approved it, which he doesn't. Even if he did think of it, it would not be obligatory for him to feel about it in any par-ticular way, since there is nothing in any act, as we have seen, which would make any feeling more suitable than any other.

Now if there is no such thing as an objectively right act, what becomes of the idea of duty? I have suggested that the idea of duty rests on the idea of such an act, since it is always our duty to find that act and do it if we can. But if whatever we feel approval for at the time is right, what is the point of doubting and searching further? Like the little girl in Boston who was asked if she would like to travel, we can answer, ''Why should I travel when I'm already there?'' If I am reconciled in feeling to my present act, no act I could discover by reflection could be better, and therefore why reflect or seek at all? Such a view seems to me to break the mainspring of duty, to destroy the motive for self-improvement, and to remove the ground for self-criticism. It may be replied that by further reflection I can find an act that would satisfy my feelings more widely than the present one, and that this is the act I should seek. But this reply means either that such general satis-faction is objectively better, which would contradict the theory, or else that, if at the time I don't feel it better, it isn't better, in which case I have no mo-tive for seeking it. When certain self-righteous persons took an inflexible line with Oliver Cromwell, his very Cromwellian reply was, ''Bethink ye, gentlemen, by the bowels of Christ, that ye may be mistaken.'' It was good advice. I hope nobody will take from me the privilege of finding myself mistaken. I should be sorry to think that the self of thirty years ago was as far along the path as the self of today, merely because he was a smug young jackanapes, or even that the paragon of today has as little room for im-provement as would be allowed by his myopic complacency.

[III. CONCLUSION]

One final remark. The great problems of the day are international prob-lems. Has the new subjectivism any bearing upon these problems? I think it has, and a somewhat sinister bearing. I would not suggest, of course, that those who hold the theory are one whit less public-spirited than others; surely there are few who could call themselves citizens of the world with more right (if ''rights'' have meaning any longer) than Mr. Russell. But Mr. Russell has confessed himself discontented with his ethical theory, and in view of his breadth of concern, one cannot wonder. For its general acceptance would, so far as one can see, be an international disaster. The assumption behind the old League and the new United Nations was that there is such a thing as right and wrong in the conduct of a nation, a right and wrong that do not depend on how it happens to feel at the time. It is implied, for example, that when Japan invaded Manchuria in 1931 she might be wrong, and that by discussion and argument she might be shown to be wrong. It was implied that when the Nazis invaded Poland they might be wrong, even though German public sentiment overwhelmingly approved it. On the theory before us, it would be meaningless to call these nations mistaken; if they felt approval for what they did, then it was right with as complete a justification as could be supplied for the disapproval felt by the rest of the world. In the present dispute between Russia and our own country over southeast Europe, it is nonsense to speak of the right or rational course for either of us to take; if with all the facts before the two parties, each feels approval for its own course, both attitudes are equally justified or unjustified; neither is mistaken; there is no common reason to which they can take an appeal; there are no principles by which an international court could pronounce on the matter; nor would there be any obligation to obey the pronouncement if it were made. This cuts the ground from under any attempt to establish one's case as right or anyone else's case as wrong. So if our friends the subjectivists still hold their theory after I have applied my little ruler to their knuckles, which of course they will, I have but one request to make of them: Don't make a present of it to Mr. Gromyko.

49 / Anthropology and the Abnormal

RUTH BENEDICT

Modern social anthropology has become more and more a study of the varieties and common elements of cultural environment and the consequences of these in human behavior. For such a study of diverse social orders primitive peoples fortunately provide a laboratory not yet entirely vitiated by the spread of a standardized worldwide civilization. Dyaks and Hopis, Fijians and Yakuts are significant for psychological and sociological study because only among these simpler peoples has there been sufficient isolation to give opportunity for the development of localized social forms. In the higher cultures the standardization of custom and belief over a couple of continents has given a false sense of the inevitability of the particular forms that have gained currency, and we need to turn to a wider survey in order to check the conclusions we hastily base upon this near-universality of familiar customs. Most of the simpler cultures did not gain the wide currency of the one which, out of our experience, we identify with human nature, but this was for various historical reasons, and certainly not for any that gives us as its carriers a monopoly of social good or of social sanity. Modern civilization, from this point of view, becomes not a necessary pinnacle of human achievement but one entry in a long series of possible adjustments.

These adjustments, whether they are in mannerisms like the ways of showing anger, or joy, or grief in any society, or in major human drives like those of sex, prove to be far more variable than experience in any one culture would suggest. In certain fields, such as that of religion or of formal marriage arrangements, these wide limits of variability are well known and can be fairly described. In others it is not yet possible to give a generalized account, but that does not absolve us of the task of indicating the significance of the work that has been done and of the problems that have arisen.

One of these problems relates to the customary modern normal-abnormal categories and our conclusions regarding them. In how far are such categories culturally determined, or in how far can we with assurance regard them as absolute? In how far can we regard inability to function socially as diagnostic of abnormality, or in how far is it necessary to regard this as a function of the culture? . . .

The most spectacular illustrations of the extent to which normality may be culturally defined are those cultures where an abnormality of our culture is the cornerstone of their social structure. It is not possible to do justice to these possibilities in a short discussion. A recent study of an island of northwest Melanesia by Fortune describes a society built upon traits which we regard as beyond the border of paranoia. In this tribe the exogamic groups look upon each other as prime manipulators of black magic, so that one marries always into an enemy group which remains for life one's deadly and unappeasable foes. They look upon a good garden crop as a confession of theft, for everyone is engaged in making magic to induce into his garden the productiveness of his neighbors'; therefore no secrecy in the island is so rigidly insisted upon as the secrecy of a man's harvesting of his yams. Their polite phrase at the acceptance of a gift is, ''And if you now poison me, how shall I repay you this present?'' Their preoccupation with poisoning is constant; no woman ever leaves her cooking pot for a moment untended. Even the great affinal economic exchanges that are characteristic of this Melanesian culture area are quite altered in Dobu since they are incompatible with this fear and distrust that pervades the culture. . . . They go farther and people the whole world outside their own quarters with such malignant spirits that all-night feasts and ceremonials simply do not occur here. They have even rigorous religiously enforced customs that forbid the sharing of seed even in one family group. Anyone else's food is deadly poison to you, so that communality of stores is out of the question. For some months before harvest the whole society is on the verge of starvation, but if one falls to the temptation and eats up one's seed yams, one is an outcast and a beachcomber for life. There is no coming back. It involves, as a matter of course, divorce and the breaking of all social ties.

Now in this society where no one may work with another and no one may share with another, Fortune describes the individual who was regarded by all his fellows as crazy. He was not one of those who periodically ran amok and, beside himself and frothing at the mouth, fell with a knife upon anyone he could reach. Such behavior they did not regard as putting anyone outside the pale. They did not even put the individuals who were known to be liable to these attacks under any kind of control. They merely fled when they saw the attack coming on and kept out of the way. "He would be all right tomorrow." But there was one man of sunny, kindly disposition who liked work and liked to be helpful. The compulsion was too strong for him to repress it in favor of the opposite tendencies of his culture. Men and women never spoke of him without laughing; he was silly and simple and definitely crazy. Nevertheless, to the ethnologist used to a culture that has, in Christianity, made his type the model of all virtue, he seemed a pleasant fellow.

An even more extreme example, because it is of a culture that has built itself upon a more complex abnormality, is that of the North Pacific Coast of North America. The civilization of the Kwakiutl, at the time when it was first recorded in the last decades of the nineteenth century, was one of the most vigorous in North America. It was built up on an ample economic supply of goods, the fish which furnished their food staple being practically inexhaustible and obtainable with comparatively small labor, and the wood which furnished the material for their houses, their furnishings, and their arts being, with however much labor, always procurable. They lived in coastal villages that compared favorably in size with those of any other American Indians and they kept up constant communication by means of sea-going dug-out canoes.

It was one of the most vigorous and zestful of the aboriginal cultures of North America, with complex crafts and ceremonials, and elaborate and striking arts. It certainly had none of the earmarks of a sick civilization. The tribes of the Northwest Coast had wealth, and exactly in our terms. That is, they had not only a surplus of economic goods, but they made a game of the manipulation of wealth. It was by no means a mere direct transcription of economic needs and the filling of those needs. It involved the idea of capital, of interest, and of conspicuous waste. It was a game with all the binding rules of a game, and a person entered it as a child. His father distributed wealth for him, according to his ability, at a small feast or potlatch, and each gift the receiver was obliged to accept and to return after a short interval with interest that ran to about 100 per cent a year. By the time the child was grown, therefore, he was well launched, a larger potlatch had been given for him on various occasions of exploit or initiation, and he had wealth either out at usury or in his own possession. Nothing in the civilization could be enjoyed without validating it by the distribution of this wealth. Everything that was valued, names and songs as well as material objects were passed down in family lines, but they were always publicly assumed with accompanying sufficient distributions of property. It was the game of validating and exercising all the privileges one could accumulate from one's various forebears, or by gift, or by marriage, that made the chief interest of the culture. Everyone in his degree took part in it, but many, of course, mainly as spectators. In its highest form it was played out between rival chiefs representing not only themselves and their family lines but their communities, and the object of the contest was to glorify oneself and to humiliate one's opponent. On this level of greatness the property involved was no longer represented by blankets, so many thousand of them to a potlatch, but by higher units of value. These higher units were like our bank notes. They were incised copper tablets, each of them named, and having a value that depended upon their illustrious history. This was as high as ten thousand blankets, and to possess one of them, still more to enhance its value at a great potlatch, was one of the greatest glories within the compass of the chiefs of the Northwest Coast. . . .

Every contingency of life was dealt with in . . . two traditional ways. To them the two were equivalent. Whether one fought with weapons or "fought with property," as they say, the same idea was at the bottom of both. In the olden times, they say, they fought with spears, but now they fight with property. One overcomes one's opponents in equivalent fashion in both, matching forces and seeing that one comes out ahead, and one can thumb one's nose at the vanquished rather more satisfactorily at a potlatch than on a battle field. Every occasion in life was noticed, not in its own terms, as a stage in the sex life of the individual or as a climax of joy or of grief, but as furthering this drama of consolidating one's own prestige and bringing shame to one's guests. Whether it was the occasion of the birth of a child, or a daughter's adolescence, or of the marriage of one's son, they were all equivalent raw material for the culture to use for this one traditionally selected end. They were all to raise one's own personal status and to entrench oneself by the humiliation of one's fellows. A girl's adolescence among the Nootka was an event for which her father gathered property from the time she was first able to run about. When she was adolescent he would demonstrate his greatness by an unheard of distribution of these goods, and put down all his rivals. It was not as a fact of the girl's sex life that it figured in their culture, but as the occasion for a major move in the great game of vindicating one's own greatness and humiliating one's associates.

In their behavior at great bereavements this set of the culture comes out most strongly. Among the Kwakiutl it did not matter whether a relative had died in bed of disease, or by the hand of an enemy; in either case death was an affront to be wiped out by the death of another person. The fact that one had been caused to mourn was proof that one had been put upon. A chief's sister and her daughter had gone up to Victoria, and either because they drank bad whiskey or because their boat capsized they never came back. The chief called together his warriors. "Now, I ask you, tribes, who shall wail? Shall I do it or shall another?" The spokesman answered, of course, "Not you, Chief. Let some other of the tribes." Immediately they set up the war pole to announce their intention of wiping out the injury, and gathered a war party. They set out, and found seven men and two children asleep and killed them. "Then they felt good when they arrived at Sebaa in the evening."

The point which is of interest to us is that in our society those who on that occasion would feel good when they arrived at Sebaa that evening would be the definitely abnormal. There would be some, even in our society, but it is not a recognized and approved mood under the circumstances. On the Northwest Coast those are favored and fortunate to whom that mood under those circumstances is congenial, and those to whom it is repugnant are unlucky. This latter minority can register in their own culture only by doing violence to their congenial responses and acquiring others that are difficult for them. The person, for instance, who, like a Plains Indian whose wife has been taken from him, is too proud to fight, can deal with the Northwest Coast civilization only by ignoring its strongest bents. If he cannot achieve it, he is the deviant in that culture, their instance of abnormality.

This head-hunting that takes place on the Northwest Coast after a death is no matter of blood revenge or of organized vengeance. There is no effort to tie up the subsequent killing with any responsibility on the part of the victim for the death of the person who is being mourned. A chief whose son has died goes visiting wherever his fancy dictates, and he says to his host, "My prince has died today, and you go with him." Then he kills him. In this, according to their interpretation, he acts nobly because he has not been downed. He has thrust back in return. The whole procedure is meaningless without the fundamental paranoid reading of bereavement. Death, like all the other untoward accidents of existence, confounds man's pride and can only be handled in the category of insults. . . .

These illustrations, which it has been possible to indicate only in the briefest manner, force upon us the fact that normality is culturally defined. An adult shaped to the drives and standards of either of these cultures, if he were transported into our civilization, would fall into our categories of abnormality. He would be faced with the psychic dilemmas of the socially unavailable. In his own culture, however, he is the pillar of society, the end result of socially inculcated mores, and the problem of personal instability in his case simply does not arise.

No one civilization can possibly utilize in its mores the whole potential range of human behavior. Just as there are great numbers of possible phonetic articulations, and the possibility of language depends on a selection and standardization of a few of these in order that speech communication may be possible at all, so the possibility of organized behavior of every sort, from the fashions of local dress and houses to the dicta of a people's ethics and religion, depends upon a similar selection among the possible behavior traits. In the field of recognized economic obligations or sex tabus this selection is as non-rational and subconscious a process as it is in the field of phonetics. It is a process which goes on in the group for long periods of time and is historically conditioned by innumerable accidents of isolation or of contact of peoples. In any comprehensive study of psychology, the selection that different cultures have made in the course of history within the great circumference of potential behavior is of great significance.

Every society, beginning with some slight inclination in one direction or another, carries its preference farther and farther, integrating itself more and more completely upon its chosen basis, and discarding those types of behavior that are uncongenial. Most of those organizations of personality that seem to us most incontrovertibly abnormal have been used by different civilizations in the very foundations of their institutional life. Conversely the most valued traits of our normal individuals have been looked on in differently organized cultures as aberrant. Normality, in short, within a very wide range, is culturally defined. It is primarily a term for the socially elaborated segment of human behavior in any culture; and abnormality, a term for the segment that that particular civilization does not use. The very eyes with which we see the problem are conditioned by the long traditional habits of our own society.

It is a point that has been made more often in relation to ethics than in relation to psychiatry. We do not any longer make the mistake of deriving the morality of our own locality and decade directly from the inevitable constitution of human nature. We do not elevate it to the dignity of a first principle. We recognize that morality differs in every society, and is a convenient term for socially approved habits. Mankind has always preferred to say, "It is a morally good," rather than "It is habitual," and the fact of this preference is matter enough for a critical science of ethics. But historically the two phrases are synonymous.

The concept of the normal is properly a variant of the concept of the good. It is that which society has approved. A normal action is one which falls well within the limits of expected behavior for a particular society. Its variability among different peoples is essentially a function of the variability of the behavior patterns that different societies have created for themselves, and can never be wholly divorced from a consideration of culturally institutionalized types of behavior.

Each culture is a more or less elaborate working out of the potentialities of the segment it has chosen. In so far as a civilization is well integrated and consistent within itself, it will tend to carry farther and farther, according to its nature, its initial impulse toward a particular type of action, and from the point of view of any other culture those elaborations will include more and more extreme and aberrant traits.

Each of these traits, in proportion as it reinforces the chosen behavior patterns of that culture, is for that culture normal. Those individuals to whom it is congenial either congenitally, or as the result of childhood sets, are accorded prestige in that culture, and are not visited with the social contempt or disapproval which their traits would call down upon them in a society that was differently organized. On the other hand, those individuals whose characteristics are not congenial to the selected type of human behavior in that community are the deviants, no matter how valued their personality traits may be in a contrasted civilization. . . .

The problem of understanding abnormal human behavior in any absolute sense independent of cultural factors is still far in the future. The categories of borderline behavior which we derive from the study of the neuroses and psychoses of our civilization are categories of prevailing local types of instability. They give much information about the stresses and strains of Western civilization, but no final picture of inevitable human behavior. Any conclusions about such behavior must await the collection by trained observers of psychiatric data from other cultures. Since no adequate work of the kind has been done at the present time, it is impossible to say what core of definition of abnormality may be found valid from the comparative material. It is as it is in ethics; all our local conventions of moral behavior and of immoral are without absolute validity, and yet it is quite possible that a modicum of what is considered right and what wrong could be disentangled that is shared by the whole human race. When data are available in psychiatry, this minimum definition of abnormal human tendencies will be probably quite unlike our culturally conditioned, highly elaborated psychoses such as those that are described, for instance, under the terms of schizophrenia and manic-depressive.

50 / Ethical Relativism

W. T. STACE

I. [WHAT IS ETHICAL RELATIVISM?]

Any ethical position which denies that there is a single moral standard which is equally applicable to all men at all times may fairly be called a species of ethical relativity.* There is not, the relativist asserts, merely one moral law, one code, one standard. There are many moral laws, codes, standards. What morality ordains in one place or age may be quite different from what morality ordains in another place or age. The moral code of Chinamen is quite different from that of Europeans, that of African savages quite different from both. Any morality, therefore, is relative to the age, the place, and the circumstances in which it is found. It is in no sense absolute.

This does not mean merely—as one might at first sight be inclined to suppose—that the very same kind of action which is *thought* right in one country and period may be *thought* wrong in another. This would be a mere platitude, the truth of which everyone would have to admit. Even the absolutist would admit this—would even wish to emphasize it—since he is well aware that different people have different sets of moral ideas, and his whole point is that some of these sets of ideas are false. What the relativist means to assert is, not this platitude, but that the very same kind of action which *is* right in one country and period may *be* wrong in another. And this, far from being a platitude, is a very startling assertion.

It is very important to grasp thoroughly the difference between the two ideas. For there is reason to think that many minds tend to find ethical relativity attractive because they fail to keep them clearly apart. It is so very obvious that moral ideas differ from country to country and from age to age. And it is so very easy, if you are mentally lazy, to suppose that to say this means the same as to say that no universal moral standard exists—or in other words that it implies ethical relativity. We fail to see that the word "standard" is used in *two different senses*. [1] It is perfectly true that, in one sense, there are many variable moral standards. We speak of judging a man by the standard of his time. And this implies that different times have different standards. And this, of course, is quite true. But when the word "standard" is used in this sense it means simply the set of moral ideas current during the period in question. It means what people *think* right, whether as a matter of fact it *is* right or not. [2] On the other hand when the

*[More commonly called ethical relativism.—Eds.]

absolutist asserts that there exists a single universal moral "standard," he is not using the word in this sense at all. He means by "standard" what is right as distinct from what people merely think right. His point is that although what people think right varies in different countries and periods, yet what actually is right is everywhere and always the same. And it follows that when the ethical relativist disputes the position of the absolutist and denies that any universal moral standard exists, he too means by "standard" what actually is right. But it is exceedingly easy, if we are not careful, to slip loosely from using the word in the first sense to using it in the second sense, and to suppose that the variability of moral beliefs is the same thing as the variability of what really is moral. And unless we keep the two senses of the word "standard" distinct, we are likely to think the creed of ethical relativity much more plausible than it actually is.

The genuine relativist, then, does not merely mean that Chinamen may think right what Frenchmen think wrong. He means that what *is* wrong for the Frenchman may *be* right for the Chinaman. And if one inquires how, in those circumstances, one is to know what actually is right in China or in France, the answer comes quite glibly. What is right in China is the same as what people think right in China; and what is right in France is the same as what people think right in France. So that if you want to know what is moral in any particular country or age, all you have to do is to ascertain what are the moral ideas current in that age or country. Those ideas are, *for that age or country*, right. Thus what is morally right is identified with what is thought to be morally right, and the distinction which we made above between these two is simply denied. To put the same thing in another way, it is denied that there can be or ought to be any distinction between the two senses of the word "standard." There is only one kind of standard of right and wrong, namely, the moral ideas current in any particular age or country.

Moral right *means* what people think morally right. It has no other meaning. What Frenchmen think right is, therefore, right *for Frenchmen*. And evidently one must conclude—though I am not aware that relativists are anxious to draw one's attention to such unsavory but yet absolutely necessary conclusions from their creed—that cannibalism is right for people who believe in it, that human sacrifice is right for those races which practice it, and that burning widows alive was right for Hindus until the British stepped in and compelled the Hindus to behave immorally by allowing their widows to remain alive. . . .

II. [PROPOSED ARGUMENTS FOR ETHICAL RELATIVISM]

I shall now proceed to consider, first, the main arguments which can be urged in favor of ethical relativity; and secondly, the arguments which can be urged against it. . . . [1.] The first [in favor] is that which relies upon the actual varieties of moral "standards" found in the world. It was easy enough to believe in a single absolute morality in older times when there was no anthropology, when all humanity was divided clearly into two groups, Christian peoples and the "heathen." Christian peoples knew and possessed the one true morality. The rest were savages whose moral ideas could be ignored. But all this is changed. Greater knowledge has brought greater tolerance. We can no longer exalt our own morality as alone true, while dismissing all other moralities as false or inferior. The investigations of anthropologists have shown that there exist side by side in the world a bewildering variety of moral codes. On this topic endless volumes have been written, masses of evidence piled up. Anthropologists have ransacked the Melanesian Islands, the jungles of New Guinea, the steppes of Siberia, the deserts of Australia, the forests of central Africa, and have brought back with them countless examples of weird, extravagant, and fantastic "moral" customs with which to confound us. We learn that all kinds of horrible practices are, in this, that, or the other place, regarded as essential to virtue. We find that there is nothing, or next to nothing, which has always and everywhere been regarded as morally good by all men. Where, then, is our universal morality? Can we, in face of all this evidence, deny that it is nothing but an empty dream?

[Criticism /] This argument, taken by itself, is a very weak one. It relies upon a single set of facts—the variable moral customs of the world. But this variability of moral ideas is admitted by both parties to the dispute, and is capable of ready explanation upon the hypothesis of either party. The relativist says that the facts are to be explained by the nonexistence of any absolute moral standard. The absolutist says that they are to be explained by human ignorance of what the absolute moral standard is. And he can truly point out that men have differed widely in their opinions about all manner of topics—including the subject-matters of the physical sciences—just as much as they differ about morals. And if the various different opinions which men have held about the shape of the earth do not prove that it has no one real shape, neither do the various opinions which they have held about morality prove that there is no one true morality.

Thus the facts can be explained equally plausibly on either hypothesis. There is nothing in the facts themselves which compels us to prefer the relativistic hypothesis to that of the absolutist. And therefore the argument fails to prove the relativist conclusion. If that conclusion is to be established, it must be by means of other considerations.

This is the essential point. But I will add some supplementary remarks. The work of the anthropologists, upon which ethical relativists seem to rely so heavily, has as a matter of fact added absolutely nothing *in principle* to what has always been known about the variability of moral ideas. Educated people have known all along that the Greeks tolerated sodomy, which in modern times has been regarded in some countries as an abominable crime; that the Hindus thought it a sacred duty to burn their widows; that trickery, now thought despicable, was once believed to be a virtue; that terrible torture was thought by our own ancestors only a few centuries ago to be a justifiable weapon of justice; that it was only yesterday that western peoples came to believe that slavery is immoral. Even the ancients knew very well that moral customs and ideas vary—witness the writings of Herodotus. Thus the principle of the variability of moral ideas was well understood long before modern anthropology was ever heard of. Anthropology has added nothing to the knowledge of this principle except a mass of new and extreme examples of it drawn from very remote sources. But to multiply examples of a principle already well known and universally admitted adds nothing to the argument which is built upon that principle. The discoveries of the anthropologists have no doubt been of the highest importance in their own sphere. But in any considered opinion they have thrown no new light upon the special problems of the moral philosopher. . . .

[2.] The second argument in favor of ethical relativity . . . consists in alleging that no one has ever been able to discover upon what foundation an absolute morality could rest, or from what source a universally binding moral code could derive its authority.

If, for example, it is an absolute and unalterable moral rule that all men ought to be unselfish, from whence does this *command* issue? For a command it certainly is, phrase it how you please. There is no difference in meaning between the sentence "You ought to be unselfish" and the sentence "Be unselfish." Now a command implies a commander. An obligation implies some authority which obliges. Who is this commander, what this authority? Thus the vastly difficult question is raised of *the basis of moral obligation*. Now the argument of the relativist would be that it is impossible to find any basis for a universally binding moral law; but that it is quite easy to discover a basis for morality if moral codes are admitted to be variable, ephemeral, and relative to time, place, and circumstance. . . .

[Comment /] This argument is undoubtedly very strong. It *is* absolutely essential to solve the problem of the basis of moral obligation if we are to believe in any kind of moral standards other than those provided by mere custom or by irrational emotions. It is idle to talk about a universal morality unless we can point to the source of its authority—or at least to do so is to indulge in a faith which is without rational ground. To cherish a blind faith in morality may be, for the average man whose business is primarily to live right and not to theorize, sufficient. Perhaps it is his wisest course. But it will not do for the philosopher. His function, or at least one of his functions, is precisely to discover the rational grounds of our everyday beliefs— if they have any. Philosophically and intellectually, then, we cannot accept belief in a universally binding morality unless we can discover upon what foundation its obligatory character rests.

[Criticism /] But in spite of the strength of the argument thus posed in favor of ethical relativity, it is not impregnable. For it leaves open one loophole. It is always possible that some theory, not yet examined, may provide a basis for a universal moral obligation. The argument rests upon the [universal] negative proposition that *there is no theory which can provide a basis for a universal morality.* But it is notoriously difficult to prove a [universal] negative. How can you prove that there are no green swans? All you can show is that none have been found so far. And then it is always possible that one will be found tomorrow. . . .

III. [ARGUMENTS AGAINST ETHICAL RELATIVISM]

It is time that we turned our attention from the case in favor of ethical relativity to the case against it. Now the case against it consists, to a very large extent, in urging that, if taken seriously and pressed to its logical conclusion, ethical relativity can only end in destroying the conception of morality altogether, in undermining its practical efficacy, in rendering meaningless many almost universally accepted truths about human affairs, in robbing human beings of any incentive to strive for a better world, in taking the life-blood out of every ideal and every aspiration which has ever ennobled the life of man. . . .

[1.] First of all, then, ethical relativity, in asserting that the moral standards of particular social groups are the only standards which exist, renders meaningless all propositions which attempt to compare these standards with one another in respect of their moral worth. And this is a very serious matter indeed. We are accustomed to think that the moral ideas of one nation or social group may be "higher" or "lower" than those of another. We believe, for example, that Christian ethical ideals are nobler than those of the savage races of central Africa. Probably most of us would think that the Chinese moral standards are higher than those of the inhabitants of New Guinea. In short we habitually compare one civilization with another and judge the sets of ethical ideas to be found in them to be some better, some worse. The fact that such judgments are very difficult to make with any justice, and that they are frequently made on very superficial and prejudiced grounds, has no bearing on the question now at issue. The question is whether such judgments have any *meaning.* We habitually assume that they have.

But on the basis of ethical relativity they can have none whatever. For the relativist must hold that there is no *common* standard which can be applied to the various civilizations judged. Any such comparison of moral standards implies the existence of some superior standard which is applicable to both. And the existence of any such standard is precisely what the relativist denies. According to him the Christian standard is applicable only to Christians, the Chinese standard only to Chinese, the New Guinea standard only to the inhabitants of New Guinea.

What is true of comparisons between the moral standards of different races will also be true of comparisons between those of different ages. It is not unusual to ask such questions as whether the standard of our own day is superior to that which existed among our ancestors five hundred years ago. And when we remember that our ancestors employed slaves, practiced barbaric physical tortures, and burned people alive, we may be inclined to think that it is. At any rate we assume that the question is one which has meaning and is capable of rational discussion. But if the ethical relativist is right, whatever we assert on this subject must be totally meaningless. For here again there is no common standard which could form the basis of any such judgments.

This in its turn implies that the whole notion of moral *progress* is a sheer delusion. Progress means an advance from lower to higher, from worse to better. But on the basis of ethical relativity it has no meaning to say that the standards of this age are better (or worse) than those of a previous age. For there is no common standard by which both can be measured. Thus it is nonsense to say that the morality of the New Testament is higher than that of the Old. And Jesus Christ, if he imagined that he was introducing into the world a higher ethical standard than existed before his time, was merely deluded. . . .

[2.] I come now to a second point. Up to the present I have allowed it to be taken tacitly for granted that, though judgments comparing different races and ages in respect of the worth of their moral codes are impossible for the ethical relativist, yet judgments of comparison between individuals living within the same social group would be quite possible. For individuals living within the same social group would presumably be subject to the same moral code, that of their group, and this would therefore constitute, as between these individuals, a common standard by which they could both be measured. We have not here, as we had in the other case, the difficulty of the absence of any common standard of comparison. It should therefore be possible for the ethical relativist to say quite meaningfully that President Lincoln was a better man than some criminal or moral imbecile of his own time and country, or that Jesus was a better man than Judas Iscariot.

But is even this minimum of moral judgment really possible on relativist grounds? It seems to me that it is not. For when once the whole of humanity is abandoned as the area covered by a single moral standard, what smaller areas are to be adopted as the *loci* of different standards? Where are we to draw the lines of demarcation? We can split up humanity, perhaps—

though the procedure will be very arbitrary—into races, races into nations, nations into tribes, tribes into families, families into individuals. Where are we going to draw the *moral* boundaries? Does the *locus* of a particular moral standard reside in a race, a nation, a tribe, a family, or an individual? Perhaps the blessed phrase "social group" will be dragged in to save the situation. Each such group, we shall be told, has its own moral code which is, for it, right. But what *is* a "group"? Can any one define it or give its boundaries? This is the seat of that ambiguity in the theory of ethical relativity to which reference was made on an earlier page.

The difficulty is not, as might be thought, merely an academic difficulty of logical definition. If that were all, I should not press the point. But the ambiguity has practical consequences which are disastrous for morality. No one is likely to say that moral codes are confined within the arbitrary limits of the geographical divisions of countries. Nor are the notions of race, nation, or political state likely to help us. To bring out the essentially practical character of the difficulty let us put it in the form of concrete questions. Does the American nation constitute a "group" having a single moral standard? Or does the standard of what I ought to do change continuously as I cross the continent in a railway train? Do different States of the Union have different moral codes? Perhaps every town and village has its own peculiar standard. This may at first sight seem reasonable enough. "In Rome do as Rome does" may seem as good a rule in morals as it is in etiquette. But can we stop there? Within the village are numerous cliques each having its own set of ideas. Why should not each of these claim to be bound only by its own special and peculiar moral standards? And if it comes to that, why should not the gangsters of Chicago claim to constitute a group having its own morality, so that its murders and debaucheries must be viewed as "right" by the only standard which can legitimately be applied to it? And if it be answered that the nation will not tolerate this, that may be so. But this is to put the foundation of right simply in the superior force of the majority. In that case whoever is stronger will be right, however monstrous his ideas and actions. And if we cannot deny to any set of people the right to have its own morality, is it not clear that, in the end, we cannot even deny this right to the individual? Every individual man and woman can put up, on this view, an irrefutable claim to be judged by no standard except his or her own.

If these arguments are valid, the ethical relativist cannot really maintain that there is anywhere to be found a moral standard binding upon anybody against his will. And he cannot maintain that, even within the social group, there is a common standard as between individuals. And if that is so, then even judgments to the effect that one man is morally better than another become meaningless. All moral valuation thus vanishes. There is nothing to prevent each man from being a rule unto himself. The result will be moral chaos and the collapse of all effective standards. . . .

[3.] But even if we assume that the difficulty about defining moral groups has been surmounted, a further difficulty presents itself. Suppose that we have now definitely decided what are the exact boundaries of the social group within which a moral standard is to be operative. And we will assume—as is invariably done by relativists themselves—that this group is to be some actually existing social community such as a tribe or nation. How are we to know, even then, what actually is the moral standard within that group? How is anyone to know? How is even a member of the group to know? For there are certain to be within the group—at least this will be true among advanced peoples—wide differences of opinion as to what is right, what wrong. Whose opinion, then, is to be taken as representing *the* moral standard of the group? Either we must take the opinion of the majority within the group, or the opinion of some minority. If we rely upon the ideas of the majority, the results will be disastrous. Wherever there is found among a people a small bag of select spirits, or perhaps one man, working for the establishment of higher and nobler ideas than those commonly accepted by the group, we shall be compelled to hold that, for that people at that time, the majority are right, and that the reformers are wrong and are preaching what is immoral. We shall have to maintain, for example, that Jesus was preaching immoral doctrines to the Jews. Moral goodness will have to be equated always with the mediocre and sometimes with the definitely base and ignoble. If on the other hand we said that the moral standard of the group is to be identified with the moral opinions of some minority, then what minority is this to be? We cannot answer that it is to be the minority composed of the best and most enlightened individuals of the group. This would involve us in a palpably vicious circle. For by what standard are these individuals to be judged the best and the most enlightened? There is no principle by which we could select the right minority. And therefore we should have to consider every minority as good as every other. And this means that we should have no logical right whatever to resist the claim of the gangsters of Chicago—if such a claim were made—that their practices represent the highest standards of American morality. It means in the end that every individual is to be bound by no standard save his own.

The ethical relativists are great empiricists. *What* is the actual moral standard of any group can only be discovered, they tell us, by an examination on the ground of the moral opinions and customs of that group. But will they tell us how they propose to decide, when they get to the ground, which of the many moral opinions they are sure to find there is *the* right one in that group? To some extent they will be able to do this for the Melanesian Islanders—from whom apparently all lessons in the nature of morality are in future to be taken. But it is certain that they cannot do it for advanced peoples whose members have learned to think for themselves and to entertain among themselves a wide variety of opinions. They cannot do it unless they accept the calamitous view that the ethical opinion of the majority is always right. We are left therefore once more with the conclusion that, even within a particular social group, anybody's moral opinion is as good as anybody else's, and that every man is entitled to be judged by his own standards.

[4.] Finally, not only is ethical relativity disastrous in its consequences for moral theory. It cannot be doubted that it must tend to be equally disastrous in its impact upon practical conduct. If men come really to believe that one moral standard is as good as another, they will conclude that their own moral standard has nothing special to recommend it. They might as well then slip down to some lower and easier standard. It is true that, for a time, it may be possible to hold one view in theory and to act practically upon another. But ideas, even philosophical ideas, are not so ineffectual that they can remain for ever idle in the upper chambers of the intellect. In the end they seep down to the level of practice. They get themselves acted on. . . .

IV. [CONCLUSION]

These, then, are the main arguments which the anti-relativist will urge against ethical relativity. And perhaps finally he will attempt a diagnosis of the social, intellectual, and psychological conditions of our time to which the emergence of ethical relativism is to be attributed. His diagnosis will be somewhat as follows.

We have abandoned, perhaps with good reason, the oracles of the past. Every age, of course, does this. But in our case it seems that none of us knows any more whither to turn. We do not know what to put in the place of that which has gone. What ought we, supposedly civilized peoples, to aim at? What are to be our ideals? What is right? What is wrong? What is beautiful? What is ugly? No man knows. We drift helplessly in this direction and that. We know not where we stand nor whither we are going.

There are, of course, thousands of voices frantically shouting directions. But they shout one another down, they contradict one another, and the upshot is mere uproar. And because of this confusion there creeps upon us an insidious skepticism and despair. Since no one knows what the truth is, we will deny that there is any truth. Since no one knows what right is, we will deny that there is any right. Since no one knows what the beautiful is, we will deny that there is any beauty. Or at least we will say—what comes to the same thing—that what people (the people of any particular age, region, society) think to be true is true *for them*; that what people think morally right is morally right *for them*; that what people think beautiful is beautiful *for them*. There is no common and objective standard in any of these matters. Since all the voices contradict one another, they must be all equally right (or equally wrong, for it makes no difference which we say). It is from the practical confusion of our time that these doctrines issue. When all the despair and defeatism of our distracted age are expressed in abstract concepts, are erected into a philosophy, it is then called relativism—ethical relativism, esthetic relativism, relativity of truth. Ethical relativity is simply defeatism in morals.

And the diagnosis will proceed. Perhaps, it will say, the current pessimism as to our future is unjustified. But there is undoubtedly a widespread feeling that our civilization is rushing downward to the abyss. If this should be true, and if nothing should check the headlong descent, then perhaps some historian of the future will seek to disentangle the causes. The causes will, of course, be found to be multitudinous and enormously complicated. And one must not exaggerate the relative importance of any of them. But it can hardly be doubted that our future historian will include somewhere in his list the failure of the men of our generation to hold steadfastly before themselves the notion of an (even comparatively) unchanging moral idea. He will cite that feebleness of intellectual and moral grasp which has led them weakly to harbor the belief that no one moral aim is really any better than any other, that each is good and true for those who entertain it. This meant, he will surely say, that men had given up in despair the struggle to attain moral truth. Civilization lives in and through its upward struggle. Whoever despairs and gives up the struggle, whether it be an individual or a whole civilization, is already inwardly dead.

STUDY QUESTIONS

1. Why, according to Russell, would people with the same morality but different desires fail to agree? What does this tell us about morality? Give an example to illustrate the point.

2. To what extent, in Russell's view, are value judgments outside the realm of knowledge? In what ways can morality be aided by knowledge? Give examples.

3. Why does Russell think it is unhelpful to appeal to conscience in deciding what to do?

4. According to Blanshard, why is the "new subjectivism" popular?

5. Does Blanshard's case of the dead rabbit cast doubt on the new subjectivism? If so, how?

6. According to Blanshard, why can't a "new subjectivist" take moral duty seriously? Give an example.

7. Could a "new subjectivist" engage in a serious moral debate? (What is involved in a serious moral debate?)

8. What is the connection between *cultural* relativity and *ethical* relativity according to Benedict?

9. Is the burden of proof in the absolutist-relativist debate on the relativist or on the absolutist? Why?

10. Is Stace fair to the relativist when he assumes that there is moral progress? How might the relativist respond to this assumption?

11. Stace suggests that if you don't believe in "the one true absolute moral standard" you can't be moral. Do you agree with him?

12. Why do you think it is so difficult to reach agreement on moral issues in our society? What could be done to promote greater agreement on such issues?

13. How might Russell respond to Blanshard? How might Benedict respond to Stace?

14. What are some of the assumptions and presuppositions behind the moral view defended by Stace and Blanshard?

15. Can an ethical outlook like Benedict's explain our desire to criticize our naive beliefs and convictions about morality?

Further Readings

"Anthropology and Ethics," *The Monist*, June 1963. [A good collection of essays on the relations between anthropology and relativism.]

Aristotle. *Nicomachean Ethics*, trans. Sir David Ross. London: Oxford University Press, 1969 reprint. [This classic work spells out the differences between scientific proof and moral reasoning, which has point of contact with many recent authors.]

Foot, Phillippa. "Moral Arguments." *Mind* 67 (1958), 502–513. [Argues that good and bad have some content, so that not anything can be called good or bad.]

Gert, Bernard. *The Moral Rules: A New Rational Foundation for Morality*. New York: Harper & Row, 1970. [A recent attempt to show that moral reasoning is rational.]

Gewirth, Alan. "'Positive' Ethics and 'Normative' Science." *Philosophical Review* 69 (1960), 311–330. [Argues that some of the contrasts between science and ethics defended by subjectivist and relativist theories are incorrect.]

Gifford, N. *When In Rome*. Albany: State University of New York Press, 1981. [A lucid discussion; good for beginners.]

Harman, Gilbert. "Moral Relativism Defended." *Philosophical Review* 84 (1975), 3–23. [Defends moral relativism as a logical thesis about moral judgments.]

Hudson, William Donald. *Modern Moral Philosophy*. Garden City, N.Y.: Anchor Books, 1970. [A useful survey of twentieth-century Anglo-American theories on the status of moral judgments.]

Krausz, M., and J. Meiland, eds. *Relativism: Cognitive and Moral*. Notre Dame: University of Notre Dame Press, 1982. [Advanced readings; important essays.]

Ladd, John. "The Issue of Relativism." *The Monist* 47 (1963), 585–609. [Defends moral relativism as the view that popular opinion defines what's moral and immoral in any given society.]

Montague, Phillip. "Are There Objective and Absolute Moral Standards?" In Joel Feinberg, ed., *Reason and Responsibility*, 4th ed. Belmont, Calif.: Dickenson, 1978, pp. 580–591. [An interesting defense of the view that moral judgments are objective.]

Moore, G. E. *Principia Ethica*. Cambridge: Cambridge University Press, 1903. [A seminal work which really invents the subject of this part of the book.]

Sellars, Wilfrid, and John Hospers, eds. *Readings in Ethical Theory*, 2nd ed. Englewood Cliffs, N.J.: Prentice-Hall, 1970. [Deals with a wide variety of topics related to the issues covered in this part of the book.]

Stevenson, Charles. *Ethics and Language*. New Haven, Conn.: Yale University Press, 1944. [The most sophisticated defense of emotivism.]

Thomson, Judith J., and Gerald Dworkin, eds. *Ethics*. New York: Harper & Row, 1968. [An important collection of essays dealing with the status of ethical judgments.]

PART ELEVEN

THE STATE AND SOCIETY

PREVIEW

Is government a thief or an angel? Is society a group of people who get in your way, or is it like a family, which nurtures and cares for you? Do we want and need father and mother figures, or should we each fend for ourselves, and let others do likewise?

You are now in college. Do you want your life monitored by your dorm counselor, who treats you the way your parents did when you were twelve? Wouldn't it be better if the people in the dorm got together and made up their own visitation policy? And what's going to happen when you graduate and go back to the "real" world? Government and society will tell you what you can and cannot do until you're dead or too old to resist or care. Or maybe this isn't so bad; maybe our leaders know best: maybe freedom and democracy aren't so great. Or maybe we don't have enough freedom, true freedom, until we stop acting selfishly and have a society and government which eliminates all injustices in the world. What do you think?

The questions "What is the best form of government?" and "What should the relations between government and society be?" are two of the most basic and important questions of our society. They have been the concern of almost every major thinker of western culture since Socrates (d. 399 B.C.), yet they are as current and practical as today's newspaper headlines.

In this part, we have gathered essays defending four different political philosophies—four different answers to the above questions—that are, we believe, of most comtemporary significance for political thinking and practice. These are: democracy, libertarianism, (democratic) socialism, and conservativism.

Before proceeding a cautionary note is in order. Each of the above terms has had different and often conflicting meanings or interpretations; and the movements these terms denote have had complex histories, including historical interrelationships with each other. For instance, classical liberalism—nineteenth century capitalist theories of democracy—have more in common with libertarianism and, to some extent, conservativism of today. And socialism, for Cohen, is an extension, not a departure from democratic

[473]

theory—construed broadly enough to include welfare state ideals—and thus is not, as for many Marxists, communists, and socialists, radically different from certain strands of the democratic tradition.

Since it is not possible to survey all the historical and semantic considerations that would be required in a full discussion of the four political philosophies represented in the readings, we shall briefly characterize these views in keeping with the specific interpretation of each of their proponents in this part. This will orient the reader to the selections to follow.

Main Questions

The main questions, then, which this part deals with are:

What is the best form of government?
What should the relations between government and society be?

(These will be treated as parts of a single question.)

Answers

The main answers to our questions are:

a. Democracy: The best form of government is one in which the people, directly or indirectly rule, and in which society allows for the maximum amount of individual freedom together, perhaps, with welfare state measures by which the government plays a role in improving society.

b. Libertarianism: A minimal or nightwatch-person of government is the best; the government is only to protect us from internal or external (foreign) harm or coercion. Society is a voluntary collection of free individuals who relate to each other on a purely voluntary and contractual basis. Government protects this kind of "free market society."

c. Socialism: The best form of government is one in which the government is controlled by the people, who cooperatively own the means of production and distribution, and which provide for the equitable sharing of all labor and benefits by the people's cooperative decisions; society is a cooperative and harmonious community, where goods and benefits are shared equitably by all.

d. Conservatism: The best form of government is one in which the government is a kind of umpire or rule keeper, which preserves the rules, practices, and institutions of a society from generation to generation as little as possible; society consists of the customs that bind a people together from generation to generation.

It will be helpful at this point to make some additional comments on these views, in order to indicate the specific ways in which the writers in this section interpret each of these political philosophies.

a'. Democracy is defined here to mean a form of government in which the citizens elect representatives or themselves have direct control of their government. Democracy is committed to individual freedom, equality of opportunity, legal and social justice—including welfare state measures when justified.

b'. Libertarianism has doubts about the welfare state, and about the emphasis on equality—or at least egalitarianism, the belief that the state should eliminate certain types of social and economic inequalities (e.g., pay differentials) mentioned previously. It places more value on individual freedom, an open market, and limited government to insure freedom for all. Charity is a private voluntary affair, not the business of the state, which has a monopoly on power and, therefore, is dangerous.

c'. Socialism (as defended by Cohen) is a radical and thoroughgoing effort to take the democratic ideals of social justice and equality built into the welfare state brand of democracy and to carry them out in practice on a grand scale. Feeding the hungry, caring for the sick, and so on, should be based upon need. Social justice requires the elimination of all social and economic injustices, which means inequalities based upon such factors as birth, luck, and so on (which libertarians find perfectly justified).

d'. Conservatism about government (as defined by Oakeshott) involves an adherence to a set of shared practices and traditions that bind a group of people together. Government is an umpire, which insures that the rules of the game—the traditions and practices that bind one generation to another— are adhered to, or, when modified, modified in a way that preserves, and not destroys, the ongoing practices and traditions. This is Edmund Burke's (1729–1797) view of society and government as a partnership among generations. The emphasis is, therefore, on continuity and slow change on this view of government and society.

With this background, it is hoped the reader can profitably consider the four views of state and society presented below. This material will pave the way for the issues discussed in Part Twelve (Liberty vs. Authority), as well as be of use in reconsidering some of the issues about morality, religion, science and methods of inquiry that appear in earlier sections of this book.

Selections

The four main answers to our questions of this part are represented as follows:

	Answers	*Selection*
(a)	Democracy	51
(b)	Libertarianism	52
(c)	Socialism	53
(d)	Conservativism	54

51 / Why Choose Democracy?

CHARLES FRANKEL

We have been overexposed to ideologies and political abstractions in this century, and have seen how much men are willing to sacrifice for the sake of ideological certainty. It is not surprising that sensitive men have developed something close to an ideology of uncertainty, and should look with a jaundiced eye on all questions about the justification of political systems. Why choose democracy? Trained in a hard school that has taught us the perils of belief, can we say anything more than that fanaticism is odious and that democracy should be chosen because it asks us to believe in very little?

On the contrary, it asks us to believe in a great deal. I do not believe we can show that the inside truth about the universe, human history, or the human psyche commands us to adopt democratic ideals. Choosing a political ideal is not like demonstrating the truth of a theorem in some geometry, and those who think that democracy needs that kind of justification are indirectly responsible for the uncertainty about it. Despite the semantic inflation from which the current discussion of political ideals suffers, the reasons for choosing democracy are neither mysterious nor difficult. But they are unsettling reasons, and they ask those who accept them to bet a great deal on their capacity to live with what they have chosen.

I. THE SIGNIFICANCE OF THE DEMOCRATIC POLITICAL METHOD

In an area so full of grandiose claims, it is safest to begin by using the word "democracy" in its narrowest sense. So conceived, democracy is the method of choosing a government through competitive elections in which people who are not members of the governing groups participate. Whatever may be said for or against democracy so conceived, it is surely not a supreme ideal of life. It is doubtful that anyone has ever treated the right to cast a ballot once every year or so as an end in itself. A society in which the democratic political method has been consolidated, to be sure, has a tremendous source of reassurance. It possesses a peaceful method for determining who shall hold power and for effecting changes in the structure of power. Yet even peace is only one value among others. It is worth something to have security and order, but how much it is worth depends on the kind of security and order it is. The importance of the democratic political method lies mainly in its nonpolitical by-products. It is important because a society in which it is well established will probably be different in at least four respects—in the conditions that protect its liberties, in the kind of consensus that prevails, in the character of the conflicts that go on within it, and in the manner in which it educates its rulers and citizens.

First, liberties. Construed strictly as a method for choosing governments, democracy does not guarantee the citizen's personal liberties. Democratic governments have attacked personal liberties, as in colonial New England, and undemocratic governments have often protected them, as in Vienna before World War I. Yet competitive elections have their points, and it is only one of their points that they allow a society to choose its government. For in order to maintain competitive elections, it is necessary to have an opposition, the opposition must have some independent rights and powers of its own, the good opinion of some people outside government must be sought, and at least some members of the society must have protections against the vengefulness of the powers that be. And this carries a whole train of institutions behind it—courts, a press not wholly devoted to promoting the interests of those in power, and independent agencies for social inquiry and criticism.

It is these necessitating conditions for elections that give elections their long-range significance. So far as political democracy is concerned, these conditions are only means to ends: they make competitive elections possible. But it is because a system of competitive elections requires and fosters such conditions that it justifies itself. The conditions required for maintaining an honest electoral system are the best reasons for wishing to maintain it. Indeed, a man might value such a system even though he thought all elections frivolous and foolish. He would have as good a reason to do so, and perhaps a better reason, than the man who always finds himself voting happily for the winning side. The outsider and the loser are the peculiar beneficiaries of a political system that creates institutions with a vested interest in liberty.

The democratic political method, furthermore, helps to foster a different kind of social consensus. There have been many kinds of political arrangement that have allowed men to feel that the government under which they live is *their* government. There is no clear evidence that democracy is necessarily superior to other systems in promoting a sense of oneness between rulers and ruled. But the special virtue of a democratic political system is that it permits men to feel at home within it who do not regard their political leaders as their own kind, and who would lose their self-respect, indeed, if they gave their unprovisional loyalty to any human institution. Despite all that is said about democratic pressures towards conformity—and a little of what is said is true—the democratic political system ceremonialized the fact of disagreement and the virtue of independent judgment. If it is to work, it requires an extraordinarily sophisticated human attitude—loyal opposition. The mark of a civilized man, in Justice Holmes' famous maxim, is that he can act with conviction while questioning his first principles. The ultimate claim of a democratic government to authority is that it permits dissent and survives it. In this respect, it dwells on the same moral landscape as the civilized man.

The democratic political method also changes the character of the conflicts that take place in a society. The perennial problem of politics is to manage conflict. And what happens in a conflict depends in part on who the onlookers are, how they react, and what powers they have. A significant fact about political democracy is that it immensely expands the audience that looks on and that feels itself affected and involved. This is why democratic citizens so often find democracy tiring and feel that their societies are peculiarly fragile. Hobbes,* who said that he and fear were born as twins, recommended despotism in the interests of psychological security as well as physical safety.

But to say that democracy expands the scope of a conflict is also to say that democracy is a technique for the socialization of conflict. It brings a wider variety of pressures to bear on those who are quarreling and extends public control over private fights and private arrangements. And it does so whether these private fights are inside the government or outside. The association of democracy with the conception of private enterprise has something paradoxical about it. In one sense, there is more important enterprise that is private—free from outside discussion and surveillance—in totalitarian systems than in democratic systems. The persistent problem in a democratic system, indeed, is to know where to draw the line, where to say that outside surveillance is out of place. That line is drawn very firmly by those who make the important decisions in totalitarian societies.

But the final contribution that the democratic political method makes to the character of the society in which it is practiced is its contributions to education. Begin with the impact of political democracy on its leaders. The democratic method, like any other political method, is a system of rules for governing political competition. And such rules have both a selective and an educational force. They favor certain kinds of men, and make certain kinds of virtue more profitable and certain kinds of vice more possible. From this point of view, the significant characteristic of democratic rules of competition is that the loser is allowed to lose with honor, and permitted to live and try again if he wants. The stakes are heavy but limited. Such a system of competition gives men with sporting moral instincts a somewhat better chance to succeed. Even its typical kind of corruption has something to be said in its favor. The greased palm is bad but it is preferable to the mailed fist.

*[A 17th century English philosopher.—Eds.]

The democratic political method, furthermore, rests on methods of mutual consultation between leaders and followers. There are various ways in which support for the policies of political leaders is obtained in a democracy, but one of the most important is that of giving men the sense that they have been asked for their opinions and that their views have been taken into account. This makes leadership in a democracy a nerve-racking affair. One of the great dangers in a democratic political system, in fact, is simply that leaders will not have the privacy and quiet necessary for serene long-range decisions. But this is the defect of a virtue. In general, power insulates. The democratic system is a calculated effort to break in on such insulation. The conditions under which democratic leaders hold power are conditions for educating them in the complexity and subtlety of the problems for which they are responsible.

And the coin has its other side. "We Athenians," said Pericles,* "are able to judge policy even if we cannot originate it, and instead of looking on discussion as a stumbling-block in the way of action, we think it an indispensable preliminary to any wise action at all." But the fruits of free discussion do not show themselves only in public policy. They show themselves in the attitudes and capacities of the discussants. Democratic political arrangements are among the factors that have produced one of the painful and more promising characteristics of modern existence—men's sense that their education is inadequate, men's assertion that they have right to be educated. And democratic politics help to promote a classic conception of education—it must be social as well as technical, general as well as special, free and not doctrinaire. We can reverse the classic conception of the relation of education to democracy and not be any further from the truth: education is not simply a prerequisite for democracy; democracy is a contribution to education.

II. USES OF DEMOCRACY

But enough of political systems. In any liberal view of men's business, politics is a subordinate enterprise. It has its soul-testing challenges and pleasures, and its great work to do. But like the work of commerce and industry, the work of politics is essentially servile labor. The State is not the place to turn if you want a free commentary on human experience, and governments do not produce science, philosophy, music, literature, or children—or at any rate they do not produce very convincing specimens of any of these things. Politics may achieve its own forms of excellence, but the more important human excellences are achieved elsewhere. And it is from this point of view, I think, that democracy should in the end be considered.

[A 5th century B.C. Athenian statesman.—Eds.]

For the democratic idea is based on the assumption that the important ends of life are defined by private individuals in their own voluntary pursuits. Politics, for liberal democracy, is only one aspect of a civilization, a condition for civilization but not its total environment. That is probably why the air seems lighter as one travels from controlled societies to free ones. One receives an impression of vitality, the vitality of people who are going about their own business and generating their own momentum. They may be going off in more different directions than the members of a centrally organized society, but the directions are their own. The best reasons for choosing democracy lie in the qualities it is capable of bringing to our daily lives, in the ways in which it can furnish our minds, imaginations, and consciences. These qualities, I would say, are freedom, variety, self-consciousness, and the democratic attitude itself.

That democracy is hostile to distinction and prefers mediocrity is not a recent view. And there is an obvious sense in which it is true that democracy makes for homogeneity. Democracy erodes the clear distinctions between classes. It destroys ready-made status-symbols so rapidly that the manufacture of new ones becomes the occupation of a major industry. Most obvious of all, democracy increases the demand for a great many good things, from shoes to education. By increasing the demand, it also puts itself under pressure to cheapen the supply.

Yet certain pertinent facts must be set against these tendencies. First, more good things *are* more generally available in democracies. Second, egalitarianism's twin is the morality of achievement. There is a tension between the democratic suspicion of the man who sets himself apart and the democratic admiration for the man who stands out, but the egalitarian hostility towards ostentatious social distinctions is normally rooted in the belief that each man should be given a chance on his own to show what he can do. And finally, pressures towards uniformity are great in all societies. Is suspicion of the eccentric in egalitarian metropolitan America greater than in an eighteenth-century village? It is difficult to think so. "The fallacy of the aristocrat," Bertrand Russell has remarked, "consists in judging a society by the kind of life it affords a privileged few." Standing alone takes courage anywhere. Usually it also takes money; almost invariably it requires the guarantee that the individual will still retain his basic rights. In these respects modern liberal democracy, despite all the complaints about conformity, has made it easier for the ordinary unprivileged man to stand alone, if he has the will to do so, than any other kind of society known in history.

For however ambiguous some of the facts may be, the official commitment of liberal democracy is to the view that each man has his idiosyncrasies, that these idiosyncrasies deserve respect, and that if the individual does not know what is good for him, it is highly unlikely that a self-perpetuating elite will know better. And this is not just an official commitment. The institutions of liberal democracy go very far in giving it concrete embodiment. Assuming that the members of a democratic society have minimal economic securities, there is a flexibility in their situation which not many ordinary men have enjoyed in the past. If they fall out of favor with one set of authorities, they have a chance to turn around and look elsewhere.

It is unquestionable that there are great constellations of concentrated power in contemporary democratic societies; it is equally unquestionable that there is some freedom in any society. For in dealing with power, bright men learn how to work the angles. But in a democratic society there are more angles to work. Individual freedom of choice is not an absolute value. Any society must limit it; indeed one man's freedom often rests on restricting the next man's. But while freedom of choice is not an absolute value, the democratic doctrine that each man has certain fundamental rights assigns an intrinsic value to his freedom of choice. If it has to be limited, it is recognized that something of value has been sacrificed. Social planning in a democracy is for this reason fundamentally different from social planning in undemocratic environments. The vague phrase "social utility," in a democratic setting, implicitly includes as one of its elements the value of freedom of choice.

What difference does this make? One difference is that variety is promoted; a second is that individuals are educated in self-consciousness. Needless to say, variety, too, has its limits. We do not have to protect dope peddlers in its name. But the full import of variety, of the mere existence of differences and alternatives, is frequently overlooked. It does not merely give us more choices, or offer us a break in the routine. It affects the immediate quality of our experience; it changes our relation to whatever it is that we choose to have or do or be. This is what is forgotten when freedom is defined simply as the absence of felt frustrations, or when it is said that if a man has just what he wants, it makes little difference whether he has any choice or not. A good that is voluntarily chosen, a good which a man is always free to reconsider, belongs to him in a way that a passively accepted good does not. It is his responsibility.

And this means that democratic variety has another use as well. No one can say with assurance that democracy makes people wiser or more virtuous. But political democracy invites men to think that there may be alternatives to the way they are governed. And social democracy, in reducing the barriers of class, caste, and inherited privilege that stand between men, adds to the variety of people and occasions the individual meets and puts greater pressure on his capacity to adapt to the new and different. Political democracy and a socially mobile society thus invite the individual to a greater degree of consciousness about the relativity of his own ways and a greater degree of self-consciousness in the choice of the standards by which he lives. These are conditions for intensified personal experience. The role

of democracy in the extension of these attitudes represents one of its principal contributions to the progress of liberal civilization.

The extension of such attitudes, to be sure, has its risks, which explains
much of our uneasiness about what the democratic revolution means. Fads
and fashions engage and distract larger groups in modern democratic societies. And social mobility, though it gives breadth and variety to men's experience, may well foreshorten their sense of time. Cut loose from fixed
ranks and stations, each with its legends, rationale, and sense of historic
vocation, the citizens of a modern democracy face a peculiar temptation to
live experimentally, with the help of the latest book, as though no one had
ever lived before. But these are the risks not simply of democracy but of
modernity, and they can be controlled. The courts, the organized profes-
sions, the churches, and the universities are storehouses of funded experience. In a society in which they are given independence from the political
urgencies of the moment, they can serve as protections against the dictator-
ship of the specious present. Modernity implies a revolution in human consciousness. Democratic social arrangements reflect that revolution and accept it; but they also provide instruments for guiding and controlling it.
None of democracy's contemporary rivals possess these two qualities to the
same extent.

In the end, indeed, the risks of democracy are simply the risks implicit in
suggesting to men that the answers are not all in. Democracy gives political
form to the principle that also regulates the scientific community—the principle that inquiry must be kept open, that there are no sacred books, that
no conclusion that men have ever reached can be taken to be the necessary
final word. Cant, obscurantism, and lies are of course a good part of the
diet of most democracies. Man is a truth-fearing animal, and it would be a
miracle if any social system could quickly change this fact. But the institutions of liberal democracy are unique in that they require men to hold no ir-
reversible beliefs in anything except in the method of free criticism and
peaceful change itself, and in the ethic on which this method rests. Such a
social system permits men to give their highest loyalty, not to temporary
human beliefs or institutions, but to the continuing pursuit after truth,
whatever it may be. The intellectual rationale of democracy is precisely that
it does not need to make the foolish and arrogant claim that it rests on infal-
lible truths. Men can believe in it and still believe that the truth is larger
than anything they may think they know.

Yet the question that probably gnaws at us most deeply still remains.
Freedom, variety, self-consciousness, a sane awareness of human fallibility,
and loyalty to the principle that inquiry must be kept open—obviously,
these have much in their favor. But they are refined values. Has liberal democracy priced itself out of the competition? Does it have anything to say,
not to those who already know and enjoy it, but to the many more who

must come to want it if human liberties are to be a little more secure in the world than they now are?

One of the debilitating illusions of many Western liberals is that the values of liberal culture are only our own values, that they have little point for those who look at the world differently, and no point at all for those whose lives are poor, mean, brutish, and short. Although colonialists used this view for different purposes, they shared it, and it betrays an inexact understanding of the nature of liberal values. Freedom, variety, self-consciousness, and the chance to seek the truth are all taxing experiences. Their virtues may be hard to conceive by those who have never enjoyed them. Yet in spite of the discomforts these values bring, the evidence indicates, I think, that most men would be happy to have them, and would think their lives enhanced. The difficulty with the most characteristic liberal values is not that they are parochial values. The difficulty is that men have other more imperious wants, like the need for medicines, schooling, bread, release from usurers, or a chance to get out from under corrupt and exploitative regimes. Illiberal programs promise these substantial material improvements and frequently deliver. And liberal programs, if they speak of freedom and leave out the usury and corruption, do not generally bring freedom either.

But let us assume, as there is every reason to assume, that liberal programs, if they are willing to recognize that they, too, must make a revolution, can also improve men's material condition. What can be said to the young man or the young—or old—nation in a hurry? What good reasons can we give, reasons that take account of their present condition and justified impatience, when we try to explain to them—and to ourselves—why the liberal path, despite its meanderings, is preferable to the authoritarian path?

One thing that can be said, quite simply, is that the authoritarian path closes up behind the traveler as he moves. The virtue of liberal democracy is that it permits second thoughts. To choose an authoritarian regime is to bet everything on a single throw of the dice; if the bet is bad, there is no way out save through violence, and not much hope in that direction. To choose a liberal approach, while it does not guarantee against errors, guarantees against the error so fatal that there is no peaceful way out or back. But there is another reason as well. The reason for choosing democracy is that it makes democrats.

Imagine a regime wholly committed to the welfare of those it rules. Imagine, against all the practical difficulties, that it is intelligent, honest, courageous, and that it does not have to enter into any deals with any of the international blocs that dominate the modern scene. And imagine, too, that this regime aims, in the end, to bring democracy and liberal values to the country it rules. But assume only that it claims, for the present, to be the one true spokesman for the public interest, the only group in the society that knows what truth and justice mean. What is the consequence? The consequence is that a democratic attitude is impossible. That attitude has been described in various ways—as a love for liberty, equality, and fraternity, as respect for the dignity of the individual, as a consistent regard for individual rights. The descriptions are not wrong, but they overintellectualize the attitude. At bottom, the democratic attitude is simply an attitude of good faith plus a working belief in the probable rationality of others. And that is what political authoritarianism destroys. Once a society is governed by the doctrine that some one group monopolizes all wisdom, it is divided into the Enlightened and the Unenlightened, and the Enlightened determine who shall be accorded membership in the club. In a modern State this makes almost impossible the growth of that mutual trust between opposing groups which is a fundamental condition for the growth of a strong political community that is also free.

The competition that takes place in a democracy is an instance of cooperative competition. It is a struggle in which both sides work to maintain the conditions necessary for a decent struggle. Accordingly, it rests on the assumption that there are no irreconcilable conflicts, that differences can be negotiated or compromised, if men have good will. Such a system requires men to deal with one another honestly, to make a serious effort to reach agreements, and to keep them after they have been made. It requires them to recognize, therefore, that the other side has its interests and to be prepared to make concessions to these interests when such concessions are not inconsistent with fundamental principles. A democratic ethic does not ask men to be fools. They do not have to assume that their opponents have put all their cards on the table. But democratic competition is impossible if the parties to the competition cannot assume that their opponents will recognize their victory if they win and will cooperate with them afterwards. The intention to annihilate the opposition or to win at all costs destroys the possibility of a regulated struggle. In this sense democracy is an exercise in the ethic of good faith. It is a system that makes it possible for men, not to love their enemies, but at least to live without fearing them. That kind of mutual trust between enemies is what authoritarianism destroys.

No doubt, such an argument may seem pathetically beside the point to men who live in societies that have been torn by distrust for centuries and that have known government only as a name for cruelty and dishonesty. If such men succeed in installing democratic regimes in their countries, they will do so by recognizing their enemies and distrusting them. But the harshness that goes with any deep social revolution is one thing if it is recognized as a bitter and dangerous necessity and is kept within limits. It is another if the violence is doctrinal, and the assumption is made that men can never cooperate unless they have the same interests and ideas. Such an assumption, as all the evidence suggests, encourages the adoption of terror as an official policy and condemns a society to an indefinite period in which power will be monopolistically controlled. In a diversified modern society, indeed in any society that has even begun the movement towards modernity, the doctrine of governmental infallibility trains men in suspiciousness and conspiracy. Perhaps other objectives will be achieved, but under such circumstances their taste will be sour.

Nor does the doctrine of infallibility destroy only good faith. It is also incompatible with a belief in the probable rationality of others. To hold a democratic attitude is to proceed on the assumption that other men may have their own persuasive reasons for thinking as they do. If they disagree with you, this does not necessarily make them candidates for correction and cure. This is the homely meaning of the oft-repeated assertion that democracy has faith in the reasonableness and equality of human beings. The faith does not assert that all men are in fact reasonable, or that they are equal in the capacity to think well or live sensibly. The faith is pragmatic: it expresses a policy. And the policy is simply to credit others with minds of their own, and to hold them responsible for their actions, until there are strong and quite specific reasons for thinking otherwise. Such a policy allows room for the idiosyncrasies of men and permits the varieties of human intelligence to be recognized and used.

In the end, the man who asks himself why he should choose democracy is asking himself to decide with which of two policies he would rather live. One is the policy of normally thinking that his fellows are dangerous to him and to themselves. The other is the policy of thinking that they are reasonable until they show themselves dangerous. To act on either policy has its risks. Why should a man choose one rather than the other? One reason can be found if he asks himself about the consequences the policy he adopts will have for the elementary feelings he will entertain towards his fellows, not in some transfigured world to come, but here and now. The point of the democratic policy is that it makes for democratic feelings. Those who do not wish to see human society divided into exploiters and exploited, those who wish to see each man come into his own free estate, believe that in the ultimate condition men will treat each other with the respect and fellow-feeling that equals show to equals. It is in the name of such moral attitudes that they seek democracy. The final reason for choosing the democratic method is that it provides a training ground, here and now, in just these attitudes.

52 / The Libertarian Manifesto

JOHN HOSPERS

The political philosophy that is called libertarianism (from the Latin *libertas*, liberty) is the doctrine that every person is the owner of his own life, and that no one is the owner of anyone else's life: and that consequently every human being has the right to act in accordance with his own choices, unless those actions infringe on the equal liberty of other human beings to act in accordance with their choices.

There are several other ways of stating the same libertarian thesis:

1. *No one is anyone else's master, and no one is anyone else's slave.* Since I am the one to decide how my life is to be conducted just as you decide about yours, I have no right (even if I had the power) to make you my slave and be your master, nor have you the right to become the master by enslaving me. Slavery is *forced* servitude, and since no one owns the life of anyone else, no one has the right to enslave another. Political theories past and present have traditionally been concerned with who should be the master (usually the king, the dictator, or government bureaucracy) and who should be the slaves, and what the extent of the slavery should be. Libertarianism holds that no one has the right to use force to enslave the life of another, or any portion or aspect of that life.

2. *Other men's lives are not yours to dispose of.* I enjoy seeing operas; but operas are expensive to produce. Opera-lovers often say, ''The state (or the city, etc.) should subsidize opera, so that we can all see it. Also it would be for people's betterment, cultural benefit, etc.'' But what they are advocating is nothing more or less than legalized plunder. They can't pay for the productions themselves, and yet they want to see opera, which involves a large number of people and their labor; so what they are saying in effect is, ''Get the money through legalized force. Take a little bit more out of every worker's paycheck every week to pay for the operas we want to see.'' But I have no right to take by force from the workers' pockets to pay for what I want.

Perhaps it would be better if he *did* go to see opera—then I should try to convince him to go voluntarily. But to take the money from him forcibly, because in my opinion it would be good for *him*, is still seizure of his earnings, which is plunder.

Besides, if I have the right to force him to help pay for my pet projects, hasn't he equally the right to force me to help pay for his? Perhaps he in

[486]

turn wants the government to subsidize rock-and-roll, or his new car, or a house in the country? If I have the right to milk him, why hasn't he the right to milk me? If I can be a moral cannibal, why can't he too?

We should beware of the inventors of utopias. They would remake the world according to their vision—with the lives and fruits of the labor of *other* human beings. Is it someone's utopian vision that others should build pyramids to beautify the landscape? Very well, then other men should provide the labor; and if he is in a position of political power, and he can't get men to do it voluntarily, then he must *compel* them to "cooperate"—i.e. he must enslave them. . . .

3. *No human being should be a nonvoluntary mortgage on the life of another.* I cannot claim your life, your work, or the products of your effort as mine. The fruit of one man's labor should not be fair game for every freeloader who comes along and demands it as his own. The orchard that has been carefully grown, nurtured, and harvested by its owner should not be ripe for the plucking for any bypasser who has a yen for the ripe fruit. The wealth that some men have produced should not be fair game for looting by government, to be used for whatever purposes its representatives determine, no matter what their motives in so doing may be. The theft of your money by a robber is not justified by the fact that he used it to help his injured mother.

It will already be evident that libertarian doctrine is embedded in a view of the rights of man. Each human being has the right to live his life as he chooses, compatibly with the equal right of all other human beings to live their lives as they choose.

All man's rights are implicit in the above statement. Each man has the right to life: any attempt by others to take it away from him, or even to injure him, violates this right, through the use of coercion against him. Each man has the right to liberty: to conduct his life in accordance with the alternatives open to him without coercive action by others. And every man has the right to property: to work to sustain his life (and the lives of whichever others he chooses to sustain, such as his family) and to retain the fruits of his labor.

People often defend the rights of life and liberty but denigrate property rights, and yet the right to property is as basic as the other two: indeed, without property rights no other rights are possible. Depriving you of property is depriving you of the means by which you live. . . .

I have no right to decide how *you* should spend your time or your money. I can make that decision for myself, but not for you, my neighbor. I may deplore your choice of life-style, and I may talk with you about it provided you are willing to listen to me. But I have no right to use force to change it. Nor have I the right to decide how you should spend the money you have earned. I may appeal to you to give it to the Red Cross, and you may prefer to go to prizefights. But that is your decision, and however much I may chafe about it I do not have the right to interfere forcibly with it, for example by robbing you in order to use the money in accordance with *my* choices. (If I have the right to rob you, have you also the right to rob me?)

When I claim a right, I carve out a niche, as it were, in my life, saying in effect, "This activity I must be able to perform without interference from others. For you and everyone else, this is off limits." And so I put up a "no trespassing" sign, which marks off the area of my right. Each individual's right is his "no trespassing" sign in relation to me and others. I may not encroach on his domain any more than he upon mine, without my consent. Every right entails a duty, true—but the duty is only that of *forbearance*—that is, of *refraining* from violating the other person's right. If you have a right to life, I have no right to take your life; if you have a right to the products of your labor (property), I have no right to take it from you without your consent. The nonviolation of these rights will not guarantee you protection against natural catastrophes such as floods and earthquakes, but it will protect you against the aggressive activities *of other men*. And rights, after all, have to do with one's relations to other human beings, not with one's relations to physical nature.

Nor were these rights created by government; governments—some governments, obviously not all—*recognize* and *protect* the rights that individuals already have. Governments regularly forbid homicide and theft; and, at a more advanced stage, protect individuals against such things as libel and breach of contract. . . .

The *right to property* is the most misunderstood and unappreciated of human rights, and it is one most constantly violated by governments. "Property" of course does not mean only real estate; it includes anything you can call your own—your clothing, your car, your jewelry, your books and papers. . . .

"But why have *individual* property rights? Why not have lands and houses owned by everybody together?" Yes, this involves no violation of individual rights, as long as everybody consents to this arrangement and no one is forced to join it. The parties to it may enjoy the communal living enough (at least for a time) to overcome certain inevitable problems: that some will work and some not, that some will achieve more in an hour than others can do in a day, and still they will all get the same income. The few who do the most will in the end consider themselves "workhorses" who do the work of two or three or twelve, while the others will be "freeloaders" on the efforts of these few. But as long as they can get out of the arrangement if they no longer like it, no violation of rights is involved. They got in voluntarily, and they can get out voluntarily; no one has used force.

"But why not say that everybody owns everything? That we *all* own everything there is?"

To some this may have a pleasant ring—but let us try to analyze what it means. If everybody owns everything, then everyone has an equal right to go everywhere, do what he pleases, take what he likes, destroy if he wishes, grow crops or burn them, trample them under, and so on. Consider what it would be like in practice. Suppose you have saved money to buy a house for yourself and your family. Now suppose that the principle, "everybody owns everything," becomes adopted. Well then, why shouldn't every itinerant hippie just come in and take over, sleeping in your beds and eating in your kitchen and not bothering to replace the food supply or clean up the mess? After all, it belongs to all of us, doesn't it? So we have just as much right to it as you, the buyer, have. What happens if we *all* want to sleep in the bedroom and there's not room for all of us? Is it the strongest who wins?

What would be the result? Since no one would be responsible for anything, the property would soon be destroyed, the food used up, the facilities nonfunctional. Beginning as a house that *one* family could use, it would end up as a house that *no one* could use. And if the principle continued to be adopted, no one would build houses any more—or anything else. What for? They would only be occupied and used by others, without remuneration. . . .

How can any of man's rights be violated? Ultimately, only by the use of force. I can make suggestions to you, I can reason with you, entreat you (if you are willing to listen), but I cannot *force* you without violating your rights; only by forcing you do I cut the cord between your free decisions and your actions. Voluntary relations between individuals involve no deprivation of rights, but murder, assault, and rape do, because in doing these things I make you the unwilling victim of my actions. A man's beating his wife involves no violation of rights if she *wanted* to be beaten. *Force is behavior that requires the unwilling involvement of other persons.*

According to libertarianism, the role of government should be limited to the retaliatory use of force against those who have initiated its use. It should not enter into any other areas, such as religion, social organization, and economics.

Government is the most dangerous institution known to man. Throughout history it has violated the rights of men more than any individual or group of individuals could do: it has killed people, enslaved them, sent them to forced labor and concentration camps, and regularly robbed and pillaged them of the fruits of their expended labor. Unlike individual criminals, government has the power to arrest and try; unlike individual criminals, it can surround and encompass a person totally, dominating every aspect of one's life, so that one has no recourse from it but to leave the country (and in totalitarian nations even that is prohibited). Government throughout history has a much sorrier record than any individual, even that of a ruthless mass murderer. The signs we see on bumper stickers are chillingly accurate: "Beware: the Government Is Armed and Dangerous."

The only proper role of government, according to libertarians, is that of the protector of the citizen against aggression by other individuals. The government, of course, should never initiate aggression; its proper role is as the embodiment of the *retaliatory* use of force against anyone who initiates its use.

If each individual had constantly to defend himself against possible aggressors, he would have to spend a considerable portion of his life in target practice, karate exercises, and other means of self-defenses, and even so he would probably be helpless against groups of individuals who might try to kill, maim, or rob him. He would have little time for cultivating those qualities which are essential to civilized life, nor would improvements in science, medicine, and the arts be likely to occur. The function of government is to take this responsibility off his shoulders: the government undertakes to defend him against aggressors and to punish them if they attack him. When the government is effective in doing this, it enables the citizen to go about his business unmolested and without constant fear for his life. To do this, of course, government must have physical power—the police, to protect the citizen from aggression within its borders, and the armed forces, to protect him from aggressors outside. Beyond that, the government should not intrude upon his life, either to run his business, or adjust his daily activities, or prescribe his personal moral code. . . .

What then should be the function of government? In a word, the *protection of human rights*.

1. *The right to life*: libertarians support all such legislation as will protect human beings against the use of force by others, for example, laws against killing, attempting killing, maiming, beating, and all kinds of physical violence.

2. *The right to liberty*: there should be no laws compromising in any way freedom of speech, of the press, and peaceable assembly. There should be no censorship of ideas, books, films, or of anything else by government.

3. *The right to property*: libertarians support legislation that protects the property rights of individuals against confiscation, nationalization, eminent domain, robbery, trespass, fraud and misrepresentation, patent and copyright, libel and slander. . . .

Laws may be classified into three types: (1) laws protecting individuals against themselves, such as laws against fornication and other sexual behavior, alcohol, and drugs; (2) laws protecting individuals against aggressions by other individuals, such as laws against murder, robbery, and fraud; (3) laws requiring people to help one another; for example, all laws which rob Peter to pay Paul, such as welfare.

Libertarians reject the first class of laws totally. Behavior which harms no one else is strictly the individual's own affair. Thus, there should be no laws against becoming intoxicated, since whether or not to become intoxicated is the individual's own decision: but there should be laws against driving while intoxicated, since the drunken driver is a threat to every other motorist on the highway (drunken driving falls into type 2). Similarly, there should be no laws against drugs (except the prohibition of sale of drugs to minors) as long as the taking of these drugs poses no threat to anyone else. Drug addiction is a psychological problem to which no present solution exists. Most of the social harm caused by addicts, other than to themselves, is the result of the thefts which they perform in order to continue their habit— and then the *legal* crime is the theft, not the addiction. The actual cost of heroin is about ten cents a shot; if it were legalized, the enormous traffic in illegal sale and purchase of it would stop, as well as the accompanying proselytization to get new addicts (to make more money for the pusher) and the thefts performed by addicts who often require eighty dollars a day just to keep up the habit. Addiction would not stop, but the crimes would: it is estimated that 75 percent of the burglaries in New York City today are performed by addicts, and all these crimes could be wiped out at one stroke through the legalization of drugs. (Only when the taking of drugs could be shown to constitute a threat to *others*, should it be prohibited by law. It is only laws protecting people against *themselves* that libertarians oppose.)

Laws should be limited to the second class only: aggression by individuals against other individuals. These are laws whose function is to protect human beings against encroachment by others; and this, as we have seen, is (according to libertarianism) the sole function of government.

Libertarians also reject the third class of laws totally: no one should be forced by law to help others, not even to tell them the time of day if requested, and certainly not to give them a portion of one's weekly paycheck. Governments, in the guise of humanitarianism, have given to some by taking from others (charging a "handling fee" in the process, which, because of the government's waste and inefficiency, sometimes is several hundred percent). And in so doing they have decreased incentive, violated the rights of individuals and lowered the standard of living of almost everyone.

All such laws constitute what libertarians call *moral cannibalism*. A cannibal in the physical sense is a person who lives off the flesh of other human beings. A *moral* cannibal is one who believes he has a right to live off the "spirit" of other human beings—who believes that he has a moral claim on the productive capacity, time, and effort expended by others.

It has become fashionable to claim virtually everything that one needs or desires as one's *right*. Thus, many people claim that they have a right to a job, the right to free medical care, to free food and clothing, to a decent home, and so on. Now if one asks, apart from any specific context, whether

it would be desirable if everyone had these things, one might well say yes.
. But there is a gimmick attached to each of them: *At whose expense?* Jobs,
medical care, education, and so on, don't grow on trees. These are goods
and services *produced only by men*. Who then is to provide them, and under
what conditions? . . .

All those who demand this or that as a "free service" are consciously or
unconsciously evading the fact that there is in reality no such thing as free
services. All man-made goods and services are the result of human expenditure of time and effort. There is no such thing as "something for
nothing" in this world. If you demand something free, you are demanding
that other men give their time and effort to you without compensation. If
they voluntarily choose to do this, there is no problem; but if you demand
that they be *forced* to do it, you are interfering with their right not to do it if
they so choose. "Swimming in this pool ought to be free!" says the indignant passerby. What he means is that others should build a pool, others
should provide the material, and still others should run it and keep it in
functioning order, so that *he* can use it without fee. But what right has he to
the expenditure of *their* time and effort? To expect something "for free" is
to expect it *to be paid for by others* whether they choose to or not.

Many questions, particularly about economic matters, will be generated
by the libertarian account of human rights and the role of government.
Should government have no role in assisting the needy, in providing social
security, in legislating minimum wages, in fixing prices and putting a ceil-
ing on rents, in curbing monopolies, in erecting tariffs, in guaranteeing
jobs, in managing the money supply? To these and all similar questions the
libertarian answers with an unequivocal no.

"But then you'd let people go hungry!" comes the rejoinder. This, the
libertarian insists, is precisely what would not happen; with the restrictions removed, the economy would flourish as never before. With the controls taken off business, existing enterprises would expand and new ones
would spring into existence satisfying more and more consumer needs;
millions more people would be gainfully employed instead of subsisting on
welfare, and all kinds of research and production, released from the stran-
glehold of government, would proliferate, fulfilling man's needs and desires as never before. It has always been so whenever government has permitted men to be free traders on a free market. But *why* this is so, and how
the free market is the best solution to all problems relating to the material
aspect of man's life, is another and far longer story.

53 / Socialism

CARL COHEN

$\mathbf{W}$e socialists agree that democracy is necessary and absolutely right. But it is not enough. Democracy is completed, fulfilled, by socialism—which is simply the democratic control of *all* resources in the community by society *as a whole*.

Socialism makes democratic ideals concrete. In it the collective will of the people is put to the service of the people in their daily lives. Through socialism the common interests of all the citizens are protected, their common needs met.

The name "socialism" has—at least to many American ears—a negative, even threatening, connotation. Yet most ordinary people warmly support—under a different name—many activities that are truly socialist in nature. We all know that some things must be done for the community as a whole. And some things can be undertaken *for* the community only *by* the community, acting *as* a community. Constructive collective action in this spirit is socialism.

How, for example, do we "provide for the common defense"? Why, through social action, of course. . . .

How do we make and enforce the criminal law? Collectively, of course. . . .

All democratic experience teaches the need for collective action. Real democracy *is* social democracy, democratic socialism.

While we all practice socialism in many spheres, its applicability to other spheres in which it is equally necessary is widely denied. Sometimes manipulated by the rich and powerful, sometimes blinded by our own slogans, sometimes dreading unreal philosophical ghosts, we fear to take social action where we ought. We fail to complete our democracy.

How can we complete it? Where would collective action have greatest impact on daily life? In the economy, of course. Action as a society is needed most of all in producing and distributing the necessities and comforts of ordinary human life. Socialism is democracy extended to the world of work and money.

All the wealth of the world—the houses and food, the land and lumber and luxuries—is somehow divided and distributed. How is that done? And how should it be done? We socialists try to rethink such fundamental questions: Who gets what? And Why?

Satisfactory answers to these questions must, of course, prove acceptable to the masses. Being democrats above all, we trust the judgment of the people. Their choices, when fully informed, will be rational and fair. We lay it down as a restriction upon ourselves, therefore, that the great changes socialism requires must come only as the honest expression of the will of the citizens, through action by their freely elected representatives. An organic transformation of society can succeed only when genuinely willed by its members. True socialists—unlike some who falsely parade under that banner—never have and never will force their solutions on an unwilling community. Democracies around the world, from India to Sweden, have enthusiastically applied socialist theory to their problems, devising socialist solutions specially suitable to their circumstances. The same basic theory can be applied successfully, with American ingenuity, to American circumstances. Confident that we can prove this to the satisfaction of the citizens concerned, we commit ourselves without reservations to abide by the judgment of the people after the case has been put fairly before them. We compel no one; our socialism is democratic, through and through.

How the wealth of most of the world is now divided is very plain to see. A few people get a great deal, and most people get just barely enough, or a little less than enough, to live decently. Rich and poor are the great classes of society, and everyone knows it well. Early democracies accepted these stark inequities as natural and inevitable. We do not. Some democrats still accept them. Material success (they say) is open to everyone in a system of private enterprise, and rewards properly go to the industrious and the able, those ambitious enough to pull themselves out of poverty by effort and wit. Some succeed, some do not, and most (they conclude) receive their just deserts.

It isn't so. That picture of "free enterprise" is a myth and always has been. In fact, by putting control of industry and finance into private hands, free enterprise results in the ownership of more and more by fewer and fewer, making economic justice unattainable for most. For centuries, wherever capitalism has prevailed, the great body of wealth has rested in the pockets of a tiny fraction of the citizens, while the masses are divided between those who just get by on their wages, and those who are unemployed and poor, inadequately housed, and often hungry. That great division, between those who have and those who have not, is the leading feature of a private enterprise economy, even when democratic. Those who have get more, because money and property are instruments for the accumulation of more money and more property. Economic freedom in such a system, for the vast majority, is only the freedom to work for another. Working men and women are free to sweat for paychecks, free to look for another job, and maybe—if their needs are desperate—free to go on welfare. These are false freedoms, not deserving the name.

Why does it work out that way? Will the poor always be with us? Ought each person to look out only for himself or herself and devil take the hindmost? We deny that this is the spirit of a decent society. We do not accept the inevitability of poverty; we do not think a democracy need be a cut-throat enterprise, and we know that cooperative action by the members of a society in their joint interests can protect both the essential freedoms of each individual and the economic well-being of all. That rational coopera-tion is called socialism. . . .

Every democracy, socialist or not, will seek to protect citizens' political rights—but only socialist democracies protect citizens' *economic* rights. Freedom of speech and assembly are priceless; are not freedom from un-employment and hunger equally so? We think so. The same collective action needed to defend the citizens against aggression from without is needed to organize production rationally and to distribute wealth justly within our own borders. In the economic sphere as much as any other, co-operation and foresight are central. The public ownership of industry is the only way to achieve them. . . .

Socialism is simply economic good sense. The long-term fruits of capital-ism have become too bitter: cycles of boom and bust, unemployment and welfare, personal dissatisfaction and business failure. Inflation steals from everyone (except those who can raise prices and rents quickly); depression demoralizes everyone. Disorder and distress are widespread. Our land it-self is abused, our water poisoned, and our air fouled. When everything is left "up for grabs," the grabbing will be vicious and the outcome chaotic. There can be no intelligent planning for future needs, no rational distribu-tion of products or materials in short supply, no reasonable deployment of human energies, in an economy in which the fundamental rule is dog-eat-dog. Legislation designed to blunt the fangs can do no more than reduce the depth of a serious wound.

Capitalism relies upon the so-called "market economy." The prices asked or offered for raw materials and finished products it leaves entirely to pri-vate parties, individuals or business firms, who enter a supposedly open market. This free market, it is argued, will be self-regulating; supply and demand will rationalize prices, fairness and productivity will be ensured by competition, enterprise encouraged by the hope of profit.

None of this actually works in the way capitalist mythology depicts it. The system relies upon the wisdom and power of economic fairies that never did exist. Nothing in the market is dependable, since everything within it fluctuates in response to unpredictable and uncontrollable factors: the tastes of buyers, the moods of sellers, the special circumstances of ei-ther, accidents causing short supply, or fashions transforming reasonable supply into glut.

Rationality and fairness through competition? No claim could be more fraudulent. In a capitalist market prices depend largely upon the relative strengths (or weaknesses) of the traders. If I own all the orchards, and am therefore the seller of all the cherries in the market, you, dear buyer, will pay my price or eat no cherries. Steel, timber, farm machinery are for sale in the market. Go, dear friend, and bargain with the sellers. Anyone tempted to believe capitalist propaganda about the give and take in the market should put it to the test. Reflect upon your own experiences as a shopper: You were told the price of the item you looked at—a TV set or a can of beans—and you paid that price or left without. That is how the market works for ordinary folks. Giant firms, manufacturers or chain retailers, may bargain with suppliers on occasion—but even then the stronger get the better deals. Those who control resources and money control the market, manipulating it in their own interests. Those who enter the market (either as buyer or seller) with great needs but little power are squeezed and exploited. The weak get twisted, the strong do the twisting. That's free enterprise.

Fairness? Markets do not know the meaning of the word. All's fair in war—and market competition is perpetual war, through guile and threat, on a thousand fronts. Rewards go to the aggressive, the keys to victory are accumulation, possession, control. And rules for fair dealing? They will be evaded, broken surreptitiously, even ignored—just like the rules of war—when it profits the combatants. . . .

Two consequences of capitalist disorder deserve special attention.

The first is unemployment. . . . If unemployment is the cruelest consequence of capitalism, inflation is the most insidious. . . . The little people (whose amassed savings had been used) discover too late that their nest eggs are shrunken, their retirements insecure. The rich get richer and the poor get children.

Reasonable human beings can end all this. Production and distribution can be designed for human service. Cooperation is the key. Society must be organized with mutual service and mutual benefit as its fundamental theme. That theme is not alien to us; it lies at the core of our highest moral and religious ideals. We must realize these ideals in practice.

Economic cooperation entails two practical principles: (1) productive property must be publicly owned; and (2) production and distribution must be planned for the common good. *Public ownership* and *planning*—acting upon both we can readily achieve the substance of democratic socialism.

Public ownership is the base. Public ownership of what? Of the means by which goods are produced and work is carried on. Private persons are not entitled to own the instruments of our common good. A system enabling some to exact profit from the work of others, to wax rich while the glaring needs of others go unmet, is fundamentally corrupt. We would end that corruption by bringing all the elements of the productive economy—the electric utilities and the mines, agriculture and transport, the production of metals and paper and drugs, the airlines and the food chains and the telephone system—under public ownership. . . .

The nationalization of all industry will have two consequences. First, *profit* for some from the work of others will be no more. . . . By eliminating the need for private profit, the public ownership of industry proves itself not only cheaper but more satisfying for all. A nationalized economy can be guided by one overriding purpose—the *general* welfare. The need for service overrules the need for a good return. Some services yield little profit, or none; yet the self-governed community can nevertheless provide such service widely to its own members. . . .

When the railroads (and all other vital industries) are nationalized, the task of striking a balance between wide service and reasonable economy will remain. Public ownership does not provide something for nothing; it distributes essential burdens more fairly. The decisions then to be made about what services are worth what burdens will be made by all of us, through elected representatives. Decisions affecting us all will not be reached in closed board rooms by capitalist magnates motivated by selfish interests. All productive enterprise—the railroads are but one illustration—will be conducted for people, and not for profit. . . .

Two practical principles, we said earlier, comprise the substance of democratic socialism. Public ownership is the first, the foundation of socialism. Planning production and distribution for the common good is the second, and the fruit of socialism. When all members of the community have equal voice in the management of the economy, the elected representatives of those voices will naturally seek to deploy productive powers rationally. The community, then fully in command of its own affairs, will deliberate carefully in choosing its economic goals and in devising the means to attain them. It will make plans. . . .

Two great objections to economic planning must be dealt with. The first is the claim that it does not work. This has been repeatedly proved false.

Every individual, and every community, has experienced successful planning. . . . Good planning is the heart of intelligent policy in every sphere, and it always will be. Without a plan there can hardly be any policy at all. . . .

The second major objection to economic planning is the claim that it will cost us our freedom. This is as false as the claim that it does not work, and more pernicious.

Here lies the nub of the conflict between democratic socialists and our private enterprise critics. Freedom, says the critic, is the paramount social value. The freedom of each individual as an economic agent must be curtailed, they argue, by any large-scale economic plan. Once the goals are set, and the role of each economic element fixed, every private person must be sharply restricted in the use of his own resources. What can be bought and what can be sold or invested will be determined by the plan. The individual will be forced to work where, and when, and as the socialist bureaucrats have decided. Economic planning, they conclude, is but a pretty name for economic slavery.

The complaint is entirely unfounded. It is plausible only because it supposes, falsely, that economic planning under socialism will be imposed from above, by arbitrary authorities over whom we will have no control. Not so. Democratic socialism brings *democratic* planning. In an economy that is publicly owned and managed, *we* are the planners. Long-range designs for the allocation of resources, decisions about what is to be produced and how it is to be distributed, will come not from a secret, all-powerful elite but from *public* bodies, publicly selected, acting publicly, and answerable to the general public. . . .

The critics' picture of socialist planning is a caricature of the real thing. They picture each citizen as a mindless cog in a great machine that grinds on unfeelingly, insensitive to mistakes or changing conditions. But the truly insensitive economy is the *un*planned one, the economy that cannot respond to human needs because it responds to nothing human at all. In that disordered economy the individual is indeed helpless, a bobbing cork on uncontrolled currents. Those currents are brought under control only by giving each citizen a voice in the control of economic as well as political affairs. Democratic planning ensures that voice. The plans will be ours. We can adjust them as we make errors and learn from them; we can refine them as circumstances change. We can scrap bad plans and devise new ones as we develop new needs or new capacities. A planning economy, *honestly* socialized, will not be our master but our servant. Let our critics not forget that our first principle throughout is *self*-government, democracy.

For self-governed citizens liberty is, indeed, a paramount concern. And what is liberty, after all? It consists of the ability and the right of individuals to make choices in determining their own conduct. The greater the range of their choices, the greater their freedom. No one supposes that liberty is absolute, that individuals can be free to do entirely as they please without restriction. Even the best of our laws limit each person's freedom to do some sorts of things in order that all of us may be genuinely free to do many other, more valuable sorts of things. The more complex a society, the more essential are some kinds of self-restriction for the extension of real freedom within it. . . .

Limits on the absolute freedom of private economic agents will be entailed by socialized planning; we make no bones about that. Some of these limits—on the freedom to own, buy, and sell productive resources like factories and farms—will be painful to some, just as universal taxation or compulsory schooling are burdensome now to many. The freedoms gained, from economic insecurity and injustice, will be vastly greater than those given up, and vastly more important.

Socialist restrictions will be felt most keenly by a relatively small number of persons who now enjoy luxury and great economic power. Those who never had investment capital at their disposal, who never were the owners of profit-making wealth, are deprived of nothing in losing economic license. Socialist gains, on the other hand, will be felt directly by every citizen, experiencing steady improvement in the quality of his or her own life, and satisfaction in the increased well-being of others. Never was a wiser bargain struck.

Democracy calls for participation in the important affairs of one's community. One's community is not only his town, or nation, but also his place of work—the factory or office, the restaurant or construction project. Can we make democracy genuine in such places, in the day-to-day lives of ordinary citizens?

Yes, we can, but only under socialism. Where the ownership of the enterprise is private, and profit-oriented, there must be bosses on the job to represent the owners and protect their profits. The workers are hired, whether by the hour or the month, in the owners' interests; they take orders from the bosses or they are fired. Capitalism inevitably produces authoritarianism in labor-management relations. Collective bargaining, of which capitalists make much, does no more than mitigate the severity of worker subordination. . . .

Democracy in the work place does not mean disorder. It does not mean that everyone works when and where and how he or she pleases. It means simply that the members of the work force—knowing themselves as owners as well as consumers and workers—participate with community management in setting work rules, production quotas, hours, and procedures. Of all the ways in which democratic ideals can be realized, this is the most concrete, the most immediate, and the most satisfying. It can be achieved under socialism; on a large scale it can be achieved only under socialism. This by itself is a compelling argument for socialist democracy. . . .

54 / On Being Conservative

MICHAEL OAKESHOTT

How . . . are we to construe the disposition to be conservative in respect of politics? And in making this inquiry what I am interested in is not merely the intelligibility of this disposition in any set of circumstances, but its intelligibility in our own contemporary circumstances.

Writers who have considered this question commonly direct our attention to beliefs about the world in general, about human beings in general,
about associations in general and even about the universe; and they tell us
that a conservative disposition in politics can be correctly construed only
when we understand it as a reflection of certain beliefs of these kinds. It is
said, for example, that conservatism in politics is the appropriate counterpart of a generally conservative disposition in respect of human conduct: to
be reformist in business, in morals or in religion and to be conservative in
politics is represented as being inconsistent. It is said that the conservative
in politics is so by virtue of holding certain religious beliefs; a belief, for example, in a natural law to be gathered from human experience, and in a
providential order reflecting a divine purpose in nature and in human history to which it is the duty of mankind to conform its conduct and departure from which spells injustice and calamity. Further, it is said that a disposition to be conservative in politics reflects what is called an 'organic'
theory of human society; that it is tied up with a belief in the absolute value
of human personality, and with a belief in a primordial propensity of human beings to sin. . . .

Now, setting aside the minor complaints one might be moved to make
about this account of the situation, it seems to me to suffer from one large
defect. It is true that many of these beliefs have been held by people disposed to be conservative in political activity, and it may be true that these
people have also believed their disposition to be in some way confirmed by
them, or even to be founded upon them; but, as I understand it, a disposition to be conservative in politics does not entail either that we should hold
these beliefs to be true or even that we should suppose them to be true. Indeed, I do not think it is necessarily connected with any particular beliefs
about the universe, about the world in general or about human conduct in
general. What it is tied to is certain beliefs about the activity of governing
and the instruments of government, and it is in terms of beliefs on these
topics, and not on others, that it can be made to appear intelligible. And, to
state my view briefly before elaborating it, what makes a conservative disposition in politics intelligible is nothing to do with a natural law or a providential order, nothing to do with morals or religion; it is the observation of
our current manner of living combined with the belief (which from our
point of view need be regarded as no more than an hypothesis) that governing is a specific and limited activity, namely the provision and custody
of general rules of conduct, which are understood, not as plans for imposing substantive activities, but as instruments enabling people to pursue the
activities of their own choice with the minimum frustration, and therefore
something which it is appropriate to be conservative about.

Let us begin at what I believe to be the proper starting-place . . . with
ourselves as we have come to be. I and my neighbors, my associates, my
compatriots, my friends, my enemies and those who I am indifferent
about, are people engaged in a great variety of activities. We are apt to en-

tertain a multiplicity of opinions on every conceivable subject and are disposed to change these beliefs as we grow tired of them or as they prove unserviceable. Each of us is pursuing a course of his own; and there is no project so unlikely that somebody will not be found to engage in it, no enterprise so foolish that somebody will not undertake it. There are those who spend their lives trying to sell copies of the Anglican Catechism to the Jews. And one half of the world is engaged in trying to make the other half want what it has hitherto never felt the lack of. We are all inclined to be passionate about our own concerns, whether it is making things or selling them, whether it is business or sport, religion or learning, poetry, drink or drugs. Each of us has preferences of his own. For some, the opportunities of making choices (which are numerous) are invitations readily accepted; others welcome them less eagerly or even find them burdensome. Some dream dreams of new and better worlds: others are more inclined to move in familiar paths or even to be idle. Some are apt to deplore the rapidity of change, others delight in it; all recognize it. At times we grow tired and fall asleep: it is a blessed relief to gaze in a shop window and see nothing we want; we are grateful for ugliness merely because it repels attention. But, for the most part, we pursue happiness by seeking the satisfaction of desires which spring from one another inexhaustably. We enter into relationships of interest and of emotion, of competition, partnership, guardianship, love, friendship, jealousy and hatred, some of which are more durable than others. We make agreements with one another; we have expectations about one another's conduct; we approve, we are indifferent and we disapprove. This multiplicity of activity and variety of opinion is apt to produce collisions: we pursue courses which cut across those of others, and we do not all approve the same sort of conduct. But, in the main, we get along with one another, sometimes by giving way, sometimes by standing fast, sometimes in a compromise. Our conduct consists of activity assimilated to that of others in small, and for the most part unconsidered and unobtrusive, adjustments.

Why all this should be so, does not matter. It is not necessarily so. A different condition of human circumstance can easily be imagined, and we know that elsewhere and at other times activity is, or has been, far less multifarious and changeful and opinion far less diverse and far less likely to provoke collision; but, by and large, we recognize this to be our condition. It is an acquired condition, though nobody designed or specifically chose it in preference to all others. It is the product, not of 'human nature' let loose, but of human beings impelled by an acquired love of making choices for themselves. And we know as little and as much about where it is leading us as we know about the fashion in hats of twenty years' time or the design of motor-cars.

Surveying the scene, some people are provoked by the absence of order and coherence which appears to them to be its dominant feature; its wastefulness, its frustration, its dissipation of human energy, its lack not merely of a premeditated destination but even of any discernible direction of movement. It provides an excitement similar to that of a stock-car race; but it has none of the satisfaction of a well-conducted business enterprise. Such people are apt to exaggerate the current disorder; the absence of plan is so conspicuous that the small adjustments, and even the more massive arrangements, which restrain the chaos seem to them nugatory; they have no feeling for the warmth of untidiness but only for its inconvenience. But what is significant is not the limitations of their powers of observation, but the turn of their thoughts. They feel that there ought to be something that ought to be done to convert this so-called chaos into order, for this is no way for rational human beings to be spending their lives. Like Apollo when he saw Daphne with her hair hung carelessly about her neck, they sigh and say to themselves: 'What if it were properly arranged'. Moreover, they tell us that they have seen in a dream the glorious, collisionless manner of living proper to all mankind, and this dream they understand as their warrant for seeking to remove the diversities and occasions of conflict which distinguish our current manner of living. Of course, their dreams are not all exactly alike; but they have this in common: each is a vision of a condition of human circumstance from which the occasion of conflict has been removed, a vision of human activity co-ordinated and set going in a single direction and of every resource being used to the full. And such people appropriately understand the office of government to be the imposition upon its subjects of the condition of human circumstances of their dream. To govern is to turn a private dream into a public and compulsory manner of living. Thus, politics becomes an encounter of dreams and the activity in which government is held to this understanding of its office and provided with the appropriate instruments.

I do not propose to criticize this jump to glory style of politics in which governing is understood as a perpetual take-over bid for the purchase of the resources of human energy in order to concentrate them in a single direction; it is not at all unintelligible, and there is much in our circumstances to provoke it. My purpose is merely to point out that there is another quite different understanding of government, and that it is no less intelligible and in some respects perhaps more appropriate to our circumstances.

The spring of this other disposition in respect of governing and the instruments of government—a conservative disposition—is to be found in the acceptance of the current condition of human circumstances as I have described it: the propensity to make our own choices and to find happiness in doing so, the variety of enterprises each pursued with passion, the diversity of beliefs each held with the conviction of its exclusive truth; the inventiveness, the changefulness and the absence of any large design; the excess, the over-activity and the informal compromise. And the office of government is not to impose other beliefs and activities upon its subjects, not to tutor or to educate them, not to make them better or happier in another way, not to direct them, to galvanize them into action, to lead them or to co-ordinate their activities so that no occasion of conflict shall occur; the office of government is merely to rule. This is a specific and limited activity, easily corrupted when it is combined with any other, and, in the circumstances, indispensable. The image of the ruler is the umpire whose business is to administer the rules of the game, or the chairman who governs the debate according to known rules but does not himself participate in it.

Now people of this disposition commonly defend their belief that the proper attitude of government towards the current condition of human circumstance is one of acceptance by appealing to certain general ideas. They contend that there is absolute value in the free play of human choice, that private property, (the emblem of choice) is a natural right, that it is only in the enjoyment of diversity of opinion and activity that true belief and good conduct can be expected to disclose themselves. But I do not think that this disposition requires these or any similar beliefs in order to make it intelligible. Something much smaller and less pretentious will do: the observation that this condition of human circumstance is, in fact, current, and that we have learned to enjoy it and how to manage it; that we are not children *in statu pupillari** but adults who do not consider themselves under any obligation to justify their preference for making their own choices; and that it is beyond human experience to suppose that those who rule are endowed with a superior wisdom which discloses to them a better range of beliefs and activities and which gives them authority to impose upon their subjects a quite different manner of life. In short, if the man of this disposition is asked: Why ought governments to accept the current diversity of opinion and activity in preference to imposing upon their subjects a dream of their own? it is enough for him to reply: Why not? Their dreams are no different from those of anyone else; and if it is boring to have to listen to dreams of others being recounted, it is insufferable to be forced to re-enact them. We tolerate monomaniacs, it is our habit to do so; but why should we be *ruled* by them? Is it not (the man of conservative disposition asks) an intelligible task for a government to protect its subjects against the nuisance of those who spend their energy and their wealth in the service of some pet indignation, endeavouring to impose it upon everybody, not by suppressing their activities in favour of others of a similar kind, but by setting a limit to the amount of noise anyone may emit?

Nevertheless, if this acceptance is the spring of the conservative's disposition in respect of government, he does not suppose that the office of government is to do nothing. As he understands it, there is work to be done which can be done only in virtue of a genuine acceptance of current beliefs simply because they are current and current activities simply because they are afoot. And, briefly, the office he attributes to government is to resolve

*[In state of tutelage.—Eds.]

some of the collisions which this variety of beliefs and activities generates; to preserve peace, not by placing an interdict upon choice and upon the diversity that springs from the exercise of preference, not by imposing substantive uniformity, but by enforcing general rules of procedure upon all subjects alike.

Government, then, as the conservative in this matter understands it, does not begin with a vision of another, different and better world, but with the observation of the self-government practised even by men of passion in the conduct of their enterprises; it begins in the informal adjustments of interests to one another which are designed to release those who are apt to collide from the mutual frustration of a collision. Sometimes these adjustments are no more than agreements between two parties to keep out of each other's way; sometimes they are of wider application and more durable character, such as the International Rules for the prevention of collisions at sea. In short, the intimations of government are to be found in ritual, not in religion or philosophy; in the enjoyment of orderly and peaceable behaviour, not in the search for truth or perfection.

But the self-government of men of passionate belief and enterprise is apt to break down when it is most needed. It often suffices to resolve minor collisions of interest, but beyond these it is not to be relied upon. A more precise and a less easily corrupted ritual is required to resolve the massive collisions which our manner of living is apt to generate and to release us from the massive frustrations in which we are apt to become locked. The custodian of this ritual is 'the government', and the rules it imposes are 'the law'. One may imagine a government engaged in the activity of an arbiter in cases of collisions of interest but doing its business without the aid of laws, just as one may imagine a game without rules and an umpire who was appealed to in cases of dispute and who on each occasion merely used his judgment to devise *ad hoc** a way of releasing the disputants from their mutual frustration. But the diseconomy of such an arrangement is so obvious that it could only be expected to occur to those inclined to believe the ruler to be supernaturally inspired and to those disposed to attribute to him a quite different office—that of leader, or tutor, or manager. At all events the disposition to be conservative in respect of government is rooted in the belief that where government rests upon the acceptance of the current activities and beliefs of its subjects, the only appropriate manner of ruling is by making and enforcing rules of conduct. In short, to be conservative about government is a reflection of the conservatism we have recognized to be appropriate in respect of rules of conduct.

To govern, then, as the conservative understands it, is to provide a *vinculum juris†* for those manners of conduct which, in the circumstances, are

---

*[In an arbitrary manner.—Eds.]
†[Bond of law.—Eds.]

least likely to result in a frustrating collision of interests; to provide redress and means of compensation for those who suffer from others behaving in a contrary manner; sometimes to provide punishment for those who pursue their own interests regardless of the rules; and, of course, to provide a sufficient force to maintain the authority of an arbiter of this kind. Thus, governing is recognized as a specific and limited activity; not the management of an enterprise, but the rule of those engaged in a great diversity of self-chosen enterprises. It is not concerned with concrete persons, but with activities; and with activities only in respect of their propensity to collide with one another. It is not concerned with moral right and wrong, it is not designed to make men good or even better; it is not indispensable on account of 'the natural depravity of mankind' but merely because of their current disposition to be extravagant; its business is to keep its subjects at peace with one another in the activities in which they have chosen to seek their happiness. And if there is any general idea entailed in this view, it is, perhaps, that a government which does not sustain the loyalty of its subjects is worthless; and that while one which (in the old puritan phrase) 'commands for truth' is incapable of doing so (because some of its subjects will believe its 'truth' to be error), one which is indifferent to 'truth' and 'error' alike, and merely pursues peace, presents no obstacle to the necessary loyalty.

Now, it is intelligible enough that any man who thinks in this manner about government should be averse from innovation: government is providing rules of conduct, and familiarity is a supremely important virtue in a rule. Nevertheless, he has room for other thoughts. The current condition of human circumstances is one in which new activities (often springing from new inventions) are constantly appearing and rapidly extend themselves, and in which beliefs are perpetually being modified or discarded; and for the rules to be inappropriate to the current activities and beliefs is as unprofitable as for them to be unfamiliar. For example, a variety of inventions and considerable changes in the conduct of business, seem now to have made the current law of copyright inadequate. And it may be thought that neither the newspaper nor the motor-car nor the aeroplane have yet received proper recognition in the law of England; they have all created nuisances that call out to be abated. Or again, at the end of the last century our governments engaged in an extensive codification of large parts of our law and in this manner both brought it into closer relationship with current beliefs and manners of activity and insulated it from the small adjustments to circumstances which are characteristic of the operation of our common law. But many of these Statutes are now hopelessly out of date. And there are older Acts of Parliament (such as the Merchant Shipping Act), governing large and important departments of activity, which are even more inappropriate to current circumstances. Innovation, then, is called for if the rules are to remain appropriate to the activities they govern. But, as the conservative understands it, modification of the rules should always reflect, and never impose, a change in the activities and beliefs of those who are subject to them, and should never on any occasion be so great as to destroy the *ensemble*. Consequently, the conservative will have nothing to do with innovations designed to meet merely hypothetical situations; he will prefer to enforce a rule he has got rather than invent a new one; he will think it appropriate to delay a modification of the rules until it is clear that the change of circumstance it is designed to reflect has come to stay for a while; he will be suspicious of proposals for change in excess of what the situation calls for, of rulers who demand extra-ordinary powers in order to make great changes and whose utterances are tied to generalities like 'the public good' or 'social justice', and of Saviours of Society who buckle on armour and seek dragons to slay; he will think it proper to consider the occasion of the innovation with care; in short, he will be disposed to regard politics as an activity in which a valuable set of tools is renovated from time to time and kept in trim rather than as an opportunity for perpetual re-equipment.

All this may help to make intelligible the disposition to be conservative in respect of government; and the detail might be elaborated to show, for example, how a man of this disposition understands the other great business of a government, the conduct of a foreign policy; to show why he places so high a value upon the complicated set of arrangements we call 'the institution of private property'; to show the appropriateness of his rejection of the view that politics is a shadow thrown by economics; to show why he believes that the main (perhaps the only) specifically economic activity appropriate to government is the maintenance of a stable currency. But, on this occasion, I think there is something else to be said.

To some people, 'government' appears as a vast reservoir of power which inspires them to dream of what use might be made of it. They have favourite projects, of various dimensions, which they sincerely believe are for the benefit of mankind, and to capture this source of power, if necessary to increase it, and to use it for imposing their favourite projects upon their fellows is what they understand as the adventure of governing men. They are, thus, disposed to recognize government as an instrument of passion; the art of politics is to inflame and direct desire. In short, governing is understood to be just like any other activity—making and selling a brand of soap, exploiting the resources of a locality, or developing a housing estate—only the power here is (for the most part) already mobilized, and the enterprise is remarkable only because it aims at monopoly and because of its promise of success once the source of power has been captured. Of course a private enterprise politician of this sort would get nowhere in these days unless there were people with wants so vague that they can be prompted to ask for what he has to offer, or with wants so servile that they prefer the promise of a provided abundance to the opportunity of choice and activity on their own account. And it is not all as plain sailing as it might appear: often a politician of this sort misjudges the situation; and then, briefly, even in democratic politics, we become aware of what the camel thinks of the camel driver.

Now, the disposition to be conservative in respect of politics reflects a quite different view of the activity of governing. The man of this disposition understands it to be the business of a government not to inflame passion and give it new objects to feed upon, but to inject into the activities of already too passionate men an ingredient of moderation; to restrain, to deflate, to pacify and to reconcile; not to stoke the fires of desire, but to damp them down. And all this, not because passion is vice and moderation virtue, but because moderation is indispensable if passionate men are to escape being locked in an encounter of mutual frustration. A government of this sort does not need to be regarded as the agent of a benign providence, as the custodian of a moral law, or as the emblem of a divine order. What it provides is something that its subjects (if they are such people as we are) can easily recognize to be valuable; indeed, it is something that, to some extent, they do for themselves in the ordinary course of business or pleasure. They scarcely need to be reminded of its indispensability, as Sextus Empiricus tells us the ancient Persians were accustomed periodically to remind themselves by setting aside all laws for five hair-raising days on the death of a king. Generally speaking, they are not averse from paying the modest cost of this service; and they recognize that the appropriate attitude to a government of this sort is loyalty, . . . respect and some suspicion, not love or devotion or affection. Thus, governing is understood to be a secondary activity; but it is recognized also to be a specific activity, not easily to be combined with any other, because all other activities (except the mere contemplation of the scene) entail taking sides and the surrender of the indifference appropriate (on this view of things) not only to the judge but also to the legislator, who is understood to occupy a judicial office. The subjects of such a government require that it shall be strong, alert, resolute, economical and neither capricious nor over-active: they have no use for a referee who does not govern the game according to the rules, who takes sides, who plays a game of his own, or who is always blowing his whistle; after all, the game's the thing, and in playing the game we neither need to be, nor at present are disposed to be, conservative. . . .

STUDY QUESTIONS

1. Why does Frankel "choose Democracy"?

2. What is Hospers' main argument against the welfare state?

3. Does Hospers think government is a thief or an angel?

4. To what extent does Cohen disagree with libertarianism?

5. How, on Cohen's view, is socialism an extension of democracy? To what extent is it a departure from it?

6. Why does Oakeshott think conservatism is a form of government that needs to put an emphasis on the past, rather than the future?

7. Do Hospers and Oakeshott have any doctrines or attitudes about state and society in common?

8. To what extent do Cohen and Frankel have similar ideals of state and society?

9. Are there any forms of state and society that we do not adequately deal with, but which you think are more plausible, e.g., communism, fascism, anarchism? Do some research on one of these views, and write a brief essay, comparing and contrasting it with one of the four answers to our main questions represented in this section.

10. What is the relationship between state and society according to each of the four views represented in this section?

11. What kinds of assumptions about human nature, human happiness and the good life are implicit or explicit in each of the four positions represented in the selections?

12. What kind of notions of freedom, equality and justice do each of the selections implicitly or explicitly endorse?

Further Readings

Berki, R. N. *Socialism*. New York: St. Martin's Press, 1975. [A good survey.]

Cohen, C. *The Four Systems*. New York: Random House, 1982. [A useful survey of democracy, socialism, communism, fascism.]

Held, D., ed. *State and Society*. New York: New York University Press, 1984. [A good collection of essays.]

Hegel, G. W. *Hegel's Philosophy of Right*. Trans. T. M. Knox. New York: Oxford University Press, 1967. [One of the most important and difficult works on political philosophy in the Western tradition.]

Hospers, John. *Libertarianism: A Political Philosophy for Tomorrow*. Los Angeles: Nash Publishing Company, 1971. [A lucid defense of libertarianism by one of its main architects.]

Locke, John. *Second Treatise on Government*. Indianapolis, Ind.: Bobbs-Merrill, Library of Liberal Arts, 1952. [One of the most influential liberal political theories of government in our tradition.]

Manning, D. J. *Liberalism*. New York: St. Martin's Press, 1976. [A lucid account.]

Marx, Karl. *Karl Marx: Selected Writings*, ed. David McLellan. New York: Oxford University Press, 1977. [The best anthology of Marx's writings.]

Nozick, Robert. *Anarchy, State, and Utopia*. New York: Basic Books, 1974. [The most important defense of libertarianism to date; a must reading.]

O'Sullivan, N. K. *Conservatism*. New York: St. Martin's Press, 1976. [A helpful study.]

Plamenatz, John. *Man and Society*, 2 vols. New York: McGraw-Hill, 1963. [A magnificent study of major social and political philosophers from Machiavelli to Marx.]

Plato. *Plato's Republic*, trans. G. M. A. Grube. Indianapolis, Ind.: Hackett, 1974. [Perhaps the most important work in political theory ever written.]

Rawls, John. *A Theory of Justice*. Cambridge, Mass.: Belknap Press, 1971. [Already a classic, this work defends a version of liberal-social contract theory.]

Rousseau, Jean-Jacques. *On the Social Contract*, ed. R. Masters. New York: St. Martin's Press, 1978. [One of the greatest treatises on political philosophy ever written.]

Strauss, Leo. *Natural Rights and History*. Chicago: University of Chicago Press, 1953. [A recent classic which relates political theory, social science, and morality.]

PART TWELVE

LIBERTY VS. AUTHORITY

PREVIEW

Many people believe that freedom leads to happiness, or at least that happiness requires freedom. Others think freedom and happiness are at odds, and that freedom not only leads to unhappiness, but is not really desired by most people, who would prefer authority and social harmony to freedom. In his story of "The Grand Inquisitor," the nineteenth century Russian novelist Dostoyevski tells the story of Christ returning to Earth during the Inquisition of the 14th century in Spain. The Cardinal in charge of the Inquisition—the Grand Inquisitor—has Christ arrested and tries to convince Christ that most people don't want and can't handle freedom, and that freedom and happiness are at odds. At one point the Grand Inquisitor says this: "In the end they most people will lay their freedom at our the Churches feet and say to us 'Make us your slaves, but feed us.' . . . They will be convinced . . . that they can never be free, because they are weak, sinful, worthless and rebellious."[1] If we add: and ignorant, contrary, nonconformist, and so on, we can begin to get some idea of what the conflict between liberty and authority—e.g., the authority of social custom or science—is all about.

Main Questions

The main questions of this part are:

What is freedom?
What is authority? What are the nature and sources of authority?
How are freedom and authority related?

---

[1]Fyodor Dostoyevski, *Notes From Underground / The Grand Inquisitor.* Trans. by R.E. Matton. (New York: Dutton & Co., 1960), p. 127.

These problems boil down to one major problem: What should the relationship be between individual liberty and social authority? That is,

Which is primary: Freedom or authority?

The two main answers to this problem are:

Liberalism: Freedom is primary, and individuals should be able to criticize their customs and pursue their own happiness.

Authoritarianism: Authority is primary, because social harmony is more basic than freedom and is also more necessary or important than personal happiness.

The conflict between these two views takes two forms in modern society. These are:

Freedom vs. authority concerning the binding force of social custom.

Freedom vs. authority concerning the binding force of science, technology and planning by "experts."

With regard to the first form, our main question is:

1. To what extent can society dictate to individuals what they can and cannot do in the name of social cohesion and survival?

With regard to the second form of the conflict between the two views, our main question is:

2. To what extent can modern science (particularly the behavioral sciences) have the right to redesign a culture and eliminate traditional values such as freedom in the name of culture's survival?

Answers

The main answers to these questions are:

1a. Traditionalism: Traditions and customs define what people should and shouldn't do in the name of social harmony.

1b. Anti-traditionalism: Individuals have no obligations to follow the authority of tradition if their reason or conscience finds fault with it.

2a. Scientism: Only the methods and doctrines of modern science are valid; so only a scientifically planned and controlled society is valid.

2b. Anti-scientism: Scientism is wrong, and traditional values such as individual freedom need to be preserved.

Selections

The answers to our two questions in this part are represented as follows:

Question	Answer		Selection
(1)	(1a)	Traditionalism	55
	(1b)	Anti-traditionalism	56
(2)	(2a)	Scientism	57
	(2b)	Anti-scientism	58

55 / Morals and the Criminal Law

LORD PATRICK DEVLIN

What is the connection between crime and sin and to what extent, if at all, should the criminal law of England concern itself with the enforcement of morals and punish sin or immorality as such?

The statements of principle in the Wolfenden Report* provide an admirable and modern starting-point for such an inquiry. . . .

Early in the Report the Committee puts forward:

> Our own formulation of the function of the criminal law so far as it concerns the subjects of this enquiry. In this field, its function, as we see it, is to preserve public order and decency, to protect the citizen from what is offensive or injurious, and to provide sufficient safeguards against exploitation and corruption of others, particularly those who are specially vulnerable because they are young, weak in body or mind, inexperienced, or in a state of special physical, official, or economic dependence.

> It is not in our view, the function of the law to intervene in the private lives of citizens, or to seek to enforce any particular pattern of behavior, further than is necessary to carry out the purposes we have outlined.

The Committee prefaces its most important recommendation

> that homosexual behavior between consenting adults in private should no longer be a criminal offence, [by stating the argument] which we believe to be decisive, namely, the importance which society and the law ought to give to individual freedom of choice and action in matters of private morality. Unless a deliberate attempt is to be made by society, acting through the agency of the law, to equate the sphere of crime with that of sin, there must remain a realm of private morality and immorality which is, in brief and crude terms, not the law's business. To say this is not to condone or encourage private immorality.

Similar statements of principle are set out in the chapters of the Report which deal with prostitution. No case can be sustained, the Report says, for attempting to make prostitution itself illegal. The Committee refers to the general reasons already given and adds: "We are agreed that private immorality should not be the concern of the criminal law except in the special cir-

---

*[The task and recommendations of the committee which wrote this report are explained by the author.—Eds.]

cumstances therein mentioned.'' It quotes with approval the report of the Street Offences Committee, which says: ''As a general proposition it will be universally accepted that the law is not concerned with private morals or with ethical sanctions.'' It will be observed that the emphasis is on *private* immorality. By this is meant immorality which is not offensive or injurious to the public in the ways defined or described in the first passage which I quoted. In other words, no act of immorality should be made a criminal offence unless it is accompanied by some other feature such as indecency, corruption, or exploitation. This is clearly brought out in relation to prostitution: ''It is not the duty of the law to concern itself with immorality as such . . . it should confine itself to those activities which offend against public order and decency or expose the ordinary citizen to what is offensive or injurious. . . .''

If this view is sound, it means that the criminal law cannot justify any of its provisions by reference to the moral law. It cannot say, for example, that murder and theft are prohibited because they are immoral or sinful. The State must justify in some other way the punishments which it imposes on wrongdoers, and a function for the criminal law independent of morals must be found. This is not difficult to do. The smooth functioning of society and the preservation of order require that a number of activities should be regulated. The rules that are made for that purpose and are enforced by the criminal law are often designed simply to achieve uniformity and convenience and rarely involve any choice between good and evil. Rules that impose a speed limit or prevent obstruction on the highway have nothing to do with morals. Since so much of the criminal law is composed of rules of this sort, why bring morals into it at all? Why not define the function of the criminal law in simple terms as the preservation of order and decency and the protection of the lives and property of citizens, and elaborate those terms in relation to any particular subject in the way in which it is done in the Wolfenden Report? The criminal law in carrying out these objects will undoubtedly overlap the moral law. Crimes of violence are morally wrong and they are also offences against good order; therefore they offend against both laws. But this is simply because the two laws in pursuit of different objectives happen to cover the same area. Such is the argument. . . .

I think it is clear that the criminal law as we know it is based upon moral principle. In a number of crimes its function is simply to enforce a moral principle and nothing else. The law, both criminal and civil, claims to be able to speak about morality and immorality generally. Where does it get its authority to do this, and how does it settle the moral principles which it enforces? Undoubtedly as a matter of history, it derived both from Christian teaching. But I think that the strict logician is right when he says that the law can no longer rely on doctrines in which citizens are entitled to disbelieve. It is necessary therefore to look for some other source.

In jurisprudence, as I have said, everything is thrown open to discussion, and, in the belief that they cover the whole field, I have framed three interrogatories addressed to myself to answer:

1. Has society the right to pass judgment at all on matters of morals? Ought there, in other words, to be a public morality, or are morals always a matter for private judgment?

2. If society has the right to pass judgment, has it also the right to use the weapon of the law to enforce it?

3. If so, ought it to use that weapon in all cases or only in some; and if only in some, on what principles should it distinguish?

I shall begin with the first interrogatory and consider what is meant by the right of society to pass a moral judgment, that is, a judgment about what is good and what is evil. The fact that a majority of people may disapprove of a practice does not of itself make it a matter for society as a whole. Nine men out of ten may disapprove of what the tenth man is doing and still say that it is not their business. There is a case for a collective judgment (as distinct from a large number of individual opinions which sensible people may even refrain from pronouncing at all if it is upon somebody else's private affairs) only if society is affected. Without a collective judgment there can be no case at all for intervention. Let me take as an illustration the Englishman's attitude to religion as it is now and as it has been in the past. His attitude now is that a man's religion is his private affair; he may think of another man's religion that it is right or wrong, true or untrue, but not that it is good or bad. In earlier times that was not so; a man was denied the right to practice what was thought of as heresy, and heresy was thought of as destructive of society.

The language used in the passages I have quoted from the Wolfenden Report suggests the view that there ought not to be a collective judgment about immorality *per se*. Is this what is meant by "private morality" and "individual freedom of choice and action"? Some people sincerely believe that homosexuality is neither immoral nor unnatural. Is the "freedom of choice and action" that is offered to the individual, freedom to decide for himself what is moral or immoral, society remaining neutral; or is it freedom to be immoral if he wants to be? The language of the Report may be open to question, but the conclusions at which the Committee arrives answer this question unambiguously. If society is not prepared to say that homosexuality is morally wrong, there would be no basis for a law protecting youth from "corruption" or punishing a man for living on the "immoral" earnings of a homosexual prostitute, as the Report recommends. This attitude the Committee makes even clearer when it comes to deal with prostitution. In truth, the Report takes it for granted that there is in existence a public morality which condemns homosexuality and prostitution. What the

Report seems to mean by private morality might perhaps be better described as private behavior in matters of morals.

This view—that there is such a thing as public morality—can also be justified by *a priori* argument. What makes a society of any sort is community of ideas, not only political ideas but also ideas about the way its members should behave and govern their lives; these latter ideas are its morals. Every society has a moral structure as well as a political one: Or rather, since that might suggest two independent systems, I should say that the structure of every society is made up both of politics and morals. Take, for example, the institution of marriage. Whether a man should be allowed to take more than one wife is something about which every society has to make up its mind one way or the other. In England we believe in the Christian idea of marriage and therefore adopt monogamy as a moral principle. Consequently the Christian institution of marriage has become the basis of family life and so part of the structure of our society. It is there not because it is Christian. It has got there because it is Christian, but it remains there because it is built into the house in which we live and could not be removed without bringing it down. The great majority of those who live in this country accept it because it is the Christian idea of marriage and for them the only true one. But a non-Christian is bound by it, not because it is part of Christianity but because, rightly or wrongly, it has been adopted by the society in which he lives. It would be useless for him to stage a debate designed to prove that polygamy was theologically more correct and socially preferable; if he wants to live in the house, he must accept it as built in the way in which it is.

We see this more clearly if we think of ideas or institutions that are purely political. Society cannot tolerate rebellion; it will not allow argument about the rightness of the cause. Historians a century later may say that the rebels were right and the Government was wrong and a percipient and conscientious subject of the State may think so at the time. But it is not a matter which can be left to individual judgment.

The institution of marriage is a good example for my purpose because it bridges the division, if there is one, between politics and morals. Marriage is part of the structure of our society, and it is also the basis of a moral code which condemns fornication and adultery. The institution of marriage would be gravely threatened if individual judgments were permitted about the morality of adultery; on these points there must be a public morality. But public morality is not to be confined to those moral principles which support institutions such as marriage. People do not think of monogamy as something which has to be supported because our society has chosen to organize itself upon it; they think of it as something that is good in itself and offering a good way of life and that it is for that reason that our society has adopted it. I return to the statement that I have already made, that society means a community of ideas; without shared ideas on politics, morals, and ethics no society can exist. Each one of us has ideas about what is good and what is evil; they cannot be kept private from the society in which we live. If men and women try to create a society in which there is no fundamental agreement about good and evil they will fail; if, having based it on common agreement, the agreement goes, the society will disintegrate. For society is not something that is kept together physically; it is held by the invisible bonds of common thought. If the bonds were too far relaxed the members would drift apart. A common morality is part of the bondage. The bondage is part of the price of society; and mankind, which needs society, must pay its price. . . .

You may think that I have taken far too long in contending that there is such a thing as public morality, a proposition which most people would readily accept, and may have left myself too little time to discuss the next question which to many minds may cause greater difficulty: To what extent should society use the law to enforce its moral judgments? But I believe that the answer to the first question determines the way in which the second should be approached and may indeed very nearly dictate the answer to the second question. If society has no right to make judgments on morals, the law must find some special justification for entering the field of morality: if homosexuality and prostitution are not in themselves wrong, then the onus is very clearly on the law-giver who wants to frame a law against certain aspects of them to justify the exceptional treatment. But if society has the right to make a judgment and has it on the basis that a recognized morality is as necessary to society as, say, a recognized government, then society may use the law to preserve morality in the same way as it uses it to safeguard anything else that is essential to its existence. If therefore the first proposition is securely established with all its implications, society has a prima facie right to legislate against immorality as such.

The Wolfenden Report, notwithstanding that it seems to admit the right of society to condemn homosexuality and prostitution as immoral, requires special circumstances to be shown to justify the intervention of the law. I think that this is wrong in principle and that any attempt to approach my second interrogatory on these lines is bound to break down. I think that the attempt by the Committee does break down and that this is shown by the fact that it has to define or describe its special circumstances so widely that they can be supported only if it is accepted that the law *is* concerned with immorality as such.

The widest of the special circumstances are described as the provision of "sufficient safeguards against exploitation and corruption of others, particularly those who are specially vulnerable because they are young, weak in body or mind, inexperienced, or in a state of special physical, official or economic dependence." The corruption of youth is a well-recognized ground for intervention by the State, and for the purpose of any legislation the young can easily be defined. But if similar protection were to be extended to every other citizen, there would be no limit to the reach of the law. The "corruption and exploitation of others" is so wide that it could be used to cover any sort of immorality which involves, as most do, the cooperation of another person. Even if the phrase is taken as limited to the categories that are particularized as "specially vulnerable," it is so elastic as to be practically no restriction. This is not merely a matter of words. For if the words used are stretched almost beyond breaking-point, they still are not wide enough to cover the recommendations which the Committee makes about prostitution.

Prostitution is not in itself illegal and the Committee does not think that it ought to be made so. If prostitution is private immorality and not the law's business, what concern has the law with the ponce* or the brothelkeeper or the householder who permits habitual prostitution? The Report recommends that the laws which make these activities criminal offenses should be maintained or strengthened and brings them (so far as it goes into principle; with regard to brothels it says simply that the law rightly frowns on them) under the head of exploitation. There may be cases of exploitation in this trade, as there are or used to be in many others, but in general a ponce exploits a prostitute no more than an impresario exploits an actress. The Report finds that "the great majority of prostitutes are women whose psychological makeup is such that they choose this life because they find in it a style of living which is to them easier, freer, and more profitable than would be provided by any other occupation. . . . In the main the association between prostitute and ponce is voluntary and operates to mutual advantage." The Committee would agree that this could not be called exploitation in the ordinary sense. It says: "It is in our view an oversimplification to think that those who live on the earnings of prostitution are exploiting the prostitute as such. What they are really exploiting is the whole complex of the relationship between prostitute and customer; they are, in effect, exploiting the human weaknesses which cause the customer to seek the prostitute and the prostitute to meet the demand."

All sexual immorality involves the exploitation of human weaknesses. The prostitute exploits the lust of her customers and the customer the moral weakness of the prostitute. If the exploitation of human weaknesses is considered to create a special circumstance, there is virtually no field of morality which can be defined in such a way as to exclude the law.

I think, therefore, that it is not possible to set theoretical limits to the power of the State to legislate against immorality. It is not possible to settle in advance exceptions to the general rule or to define inflexibly areas of morality into which the law is in no circumstances to be allowed to enter. Society is entitled by means of its laws to protect itself from dangers, whether

*[Pimp.—Eds.]

from within or without. Here again I think that the political parallel is legitimate. The law of treason is directed against aiding the king's enemies and against sedition from within. The justification for this is that established government is necessary for the existence of society and therefore its safety against violent overthrow must be secured. But an established morality is as necessary as good government to the welfare of society. Societies disintegrate from within more frequently than they are broken up by external pressures. There is disintegration when no common morality is observed, and history shows that the loosening of moral bonds is often the first stage of disintegration, so that society is justified in taking the same steps to preserve its moral code as it does to preserve its government and other essential institutions. The suppression of vice is as much the law's business as the suppression of subversive activities; it is no more possible to define a sphere of private morality than it is to define one of private subversive activity. It is wrong to talk of private morality or of the law not being concerned with immorality as such or to try to set rigid bounds to the part which the law may play in the suppression of vice. There are no theoretical limits to the power of the State to legislate against treason and sedition, and likewise I think there can be no theoretical limits to legislation against immorality. You may argue that if a man's sins affect only himself it cannot be the concern of society. If he chooses to get drunk every night in the privacy of his own home, is any one except himself the worse for it? But suppose a quarter or a half of the population got drunk every night, what sort of society would it be? You cannot set a theoretical limit to the number of people who can get drunk before society is entitled to legislate against drunkenness. The same may be said of gambling. The Royal Commission on Betting, Lotteries, and Gaming took as its test the character of the citizen as a member of society. It said: ''Our concern with the ethical significance of gambling is confined to the effect which it may have on the character of the gambler as a member of society. If we were convinced that whatever the degree of gambling this effect must be harmful we should be inclined to think that it was the duty of the state to restrict gambling to the greatest extent practicable.''

In what circumstances the State should exercise its power is the third of the interrogatories I have framed. But before I get to it I must raise a point which might have been brought up in any one of the three. How are the moral judgments of society to be ascertained? By leaving it until now, I can ask it in the more limited form that is now sufficient for my purpose. How is the law-maker to ascertain the moral judgments of society? It is surely not enough that they should be reached by the opinion of the majority; it would be too much to require the individual assent of every citizen. English law has evolved and regularly uses a standard which does not depend on the counting of heads. It is that of the reasonable man. He is not to be confused with the rational man. He is not expected to reason about anything and his judgment may be largely a matter of feeling. It is the viewpoint of the man in the street or—to use an archaism familiar to all lawyers—the man in the Clapham omnibus.* He might also be called the right-minded man. For my purpose I should like to call him the man in the jury box, for the moral judgment of society must be something about which any twelve men or women drawn at random might after discussion be expected to be unanimous. This was the standard the judges applied in the days before Parliament was as active as it is now and when they laid down rules of public policy. They did not think of themselves as making law but simply as stating principles which every right-minded person would accept as valid. It is what Pollock called "practical morality," which is based not on theological or philosophical foundations but "in the mass of continuous experience half-consciously or unconsciously accumulated and embodied in the morality of common sense." He called it also "a certain way of thinking on questions of morality which we expect to find in a reasonable civilized man or a reasonable Englishman, taken at random."

Immorality then, for the purpose of the law, is what every right-minded person is presumed to consider to be immoral. Any immorality is capable of affecting society injuriously and in effect to a greater or lesser extent it usually does; this is what gives the law its *locus standi*.† It cannot be shut out. But—and this brings me to the third question—the individual has a *locus standi* too; he cannot be expected to surrender to the judgment of society the whole conduct of his life. It is the old and familiar question of striking a balance between the rights and interests of society and those of the individual. This is something which the law is constantly doing in matters large and small. To take a very down-to-earth example, let me consider the right of the individual whose house adjoins the highway to have access to it; that means in these days the right to have vehicles stationary in the highway, sometimes for a considerable time if there is a lot of loading or unloading. There are many cases in which the courts have had to balance the private right of access against the public right to use the highway without obstruction. It cannot be done by carving up the highway into public and private areas. It is done by recognizing that each has rights over the whole; that if each were to exercise its rights to the full, they would come into conflict; and therefore that the rights of each must be curtailed so as to ensure as far as possible that the essential needs of each are safeguarded.

I do not think that one can talk sensibly of a public and private morality any more than one can of a public or private highway. Morality is a sphere in which there is a public interest and a private interest, often in conflict, and the problem is to reconcile the two. This does not mean that it is impossible to put forward any general statements about how in our society the

---

*[or as we would say: The man in the street.—Eds.]
†[standing place.—Eds.]

balance ought to be struck. Such statements cannot of their nature be rigid or precise; they would not be designed to circumscribe the operation of the law-making power but to guide those who have to apply it. While every decision which a court of law makes when it balances the public against the private interest is an *ad hoc* decision, the cases contain statements of principle to which the court should have regard when it reaches its decision. In the same way it is possible to make general statements of principle which it may be thought the legislature should bear in mind when it is considering the enactment of laws enforcing morals.

I believe that most people would agree upon the chief of these elastic principles. There must be toleration of the maximum individual freedom that is consistent with the integrity of society. It cannot be said that this is a principle that runs all through the criminal law. Much of the criminal law that is regulatory in character—the part of it that deals with *malum prohibitum*** rather than *malum in se†*—is based upon the opposite principle, that is, that the choice of the individual must give way to the convenience of the many. But in all matters of conscience the principle I have stated is generally held to prevail. It is not confined to thought and speech; it extends to action, as is shown by the recognition of the right to conscientious objection in war-time; this example shows also that conscience will be respected even in times of national danger. The principle appears to me to be peculiarly appropriate to all questions of morals. Nothing should be punished by the law that does not lie beyond the limits of tolerance. It is not nearly enough to say that a majority dislike a practice; there must be a real feeling of reprobation. Those who are dissatisfied with the present law on homosexuality often say that the opponents of reform are swayed simply by disgust. If that were so it would be wrong, but I do not think one can ignore disgust if it is deeply felt and not manufactured. Its presence is a good indication that the bounds of toleration are being reached. Not everything is to be tolerated. No society can do without intolerance, indignation, and disgust; they are the forces behind the moral law, and indeed it can be argued that if they or something like them are not present, the feelings of society cannot be weighty enough to deprive the individual of freedom of choice. I suppose that there is hardly anyone nowadays who would not be disgusted by the thought of deliberate cruelty to animals. No one proposes to relegate that or any other form of sadism to the realm of private morality or to allow it to be practiced in public or in private. It would be possible no doubt to point out that until a comparatively short while ago nobody thought very much of cruelty to animals and also that pity and kindliness and the unwillingness to inflict pain are virtues more generally esteemed now than they have ever been in the past. But matters of this sort are not determined by

---

*[prohibited evil.—Eds.]
†[evil in itself—Eds.]

rational argument. Every moral judgment, unless it claims a divine source, is simply a feeling that no rightminded man could behave in any other way without admitting that he was doing wrong. It is the power of a common sense and not the power of reason that is behind the judgments of society. But before a society can put a practice beyond the limits of tolerance there must be a deliberate judgment that the practice is injurious to society. There is, for example, a general abhorrence of homosexuality. We should ask ourselves in the first instance whether, looking at it calmly and dispassionately, we regard it as a vice so abominable that its mere presence is an offense. If that is the genuine feeling of the society in which we live, I do not see how society can be denied the right to eradicate it. Our feeling may not be so intense as that. We may feel about it that, if confined, it is tolerable, but that if it spread it might be gravely injurious; it is in this way that most societies look upon fornication, seeing it as a natural weakness which must be kept within bounds but which cannot be rooted out. It becomes then a question of balance, the danger to society in one scale and the extent of the restriction in the other. On this sort of point the value of an investigation by such a body as the Wolfenden Committee and of its conclusions is manifest.

The limits of tolerance shift. This is supplementary to what I have been saying but of sufficient importance in itself to deserve statement as a separate principle which law-makers have to bear in mind. I suppose that moral standards do not shift; so far as they come from divine revelation they do not, and I am willing to assume that the moral judgments made by a society always remain good for that society. But the extent to which society will tolerate—I mean tolerate, not approve—departures from moral standards varies from generation to generation. It may be that overall tolerance is always increasing. The pressure of the human mind, always seeking greater freedom of thought, is outwards against the bonds of society forcing their gradual relaxation. It may be that history is a tale of contraction and expansion and that all developed societies are on their way to dissolution. I must not speak of things I do not know; and anyway as a practical matter no society is willing to make provision for its own decay. I return therefore to the simple and observable fact that in matters of morals the limits of tolerance shift. Laws, especially those which are based on morals, are less easily moved. It follows as another good working principle that in any new matter of morals the law should be slow to act. By the next generation the swell of indignation may have abated and the law be left without the strong backing which it needs. But it is then difficult to alter the law without giving the impression that moral judgment is being weakened. This is now one of the factors that is strongly militating against any alteration to the law on homosexuality.

A third elastic principle must be advanced more tentatively. It is that as far as possible privacy should be respected. This is not an idea that has ever been made explicit in the criminal law. Acts or words done or said in public or private are all brought within its scope without distinction in principle. But there goes with this a strong reluctance on the part of judges and legislators to sanction invasions of privacy in the detection of crime. The police have no more right to trespass than the ordinary citizen has; there is no general right of search; to this extent an Englishman's home is still his castle. . . .

This indicates a general sentiment that the right to privacy is something to be put in the balance against the enforcement of the law. Ought the same sort of consideration to play any part in the formation of the law? Clearly only in a very limited number of cases. When the help of the law is invoked by an injured citizen, privacy must be irrelevant; the individual cannot ask that his right to privacy should be measured against injury criminally done to another. But when all who are involved in the deed are consenting parties and the injury is done to morals, the public interest in the moral order can be balanced against the claims of privacy. The restriction on police powers of investigation goes further than the affording of a parallel; it means that the detection of crime committed in private and when there is no complaint is bound to be rather haphazard, and this is an additional reason for moderation. These considerations do not justify the exclusion of all private immorality from the scope of the law. I think that, as I have already suggested, the test of "private behavior" should be substituted for "private morality" and the influence of the factor should be reduced from that of a definite limitation to that of a matter to be taken into account. Since the gravity of the crime is also a proper consideration, a distinction might well be made in the case of homosexuality between the lesser acts of indecency and the full offense, which on the principles of the Wolfenden Report it would be illogical to do.

The last and the biggest thing to be remembered is that the law is concerned with the minimum and not with the maximum; there is much in the Sermon on the Mount that would be out of place in the Ten Commandments. We all recognize the gap between the moral law and the law of the land. No man is worth much who regulates his conduct with the sole object of escaping punishment, and every worthy society sets for its members standards which are above those of the law. We recognize the existence of such higher standards when we use expressions such as "moral obligation" and "morally bound." The distinction was well put in the judgment of African elders in a family dispute: "We have power to make you divide the crops, for this is our law, and we will see this is done. But we have not power to make you behave like an upright man."

It can only be because this point is so obvious that it is so frequently ignored. Discussion among law-makers, both professional and amateur, is too often limited to what is right or wrong and good or bad for society. There is a failure to keep separate the two questions I have earlier posed—the question of society's right to pass a moral judgment and the question of whether the arm of the law should be used to enforce the judgment. The criminal law is not a statement of how people ought to behave; it is a statement of what will happen to them if they do not behave; good citizens are not expected to come within reach of it or to set their sights by it, and every enactment should be framed accordingly.

The arm of the law is an instrument to be used by society, and the decision about what particular cases it should be used in is essentially a practical one. Since it is an instrument, it is wise before deciding to use it to have regard to the tools with which it can be fitted and to the machinery which operates it. Its tools are fines, imprisonment, or lesser forms of supervision (such as Borstal* and probation) and—not to be ignored—the degradation that often follows upon the publication of the crime. Are any of these suited to the job of dealing with sexual immorality? The fact that there is so much immorality which has never been brought within the law shows that there can be no general rule. It is a matter for decision in each case; but in the case of homosexuality the Wolfenden Report rightly has regard to the views of those who are experienced in dealing with this sort of crime and to those of the clergy who are the natural guardians of public morals.

The machinery which sets the criminal law in motion ends with the verdict and the sentence; and a verdict is given either by magistrates or by a jury. As a general rule, whenever a crime is sufficiently serious to justify a maximum punishment of more than three months, the accused has the right to the verdict of a jury. The result is that magistrates administer mostly what I have called the regulatory part of the law. They deal extensively with drunkenness, gambling, and prostitution, which are matters of morals or close to them, but not with any of the graver moral offenses. They are more responsive than juries to the ideas of the legislature; it may not be accidental that the Wolfenden Report, in recommending increased penalties for solicitation, did not go above the limit of three months. Juries tend to dilute the decrees of Parliament with their own ideas of what should be punishable. Their province of course is fact and not law, and I do not mean that they often deliberately disregard the law. But if they think it is too stringent, they sometimes take a very merciful view of the facts. Let me take one example out of many that could be given. It is an offense to have carnal knowledge of a girl under the age of sixteen years. Consent on her part is no defence; if she did not consent, it would of course amount to rape. The law makes special provision for the situation when a boy and girl are near in age. If a man under twenty-four can prove that he had reasonable cause to believe that the girl was over the age of sixteen years, he has a good defense. The law regards the offense as sufficiently serious to make it one that is triable only by a judge at assizes. "Reasonable cause" means

*[An English reformatory for youths, where traditionally inmates were brutally treated. —Eds.]

not merely that the boy honestly believed that the girl was over sixteen but also that he must have had reasonable grounds for his belief. In theory it ought not to be an easy defense to make out but in fact it is extremely rare for anyone who advances it to be convicted. The fact is that the girl is often as much to blame as the boy. The object of the law, as judges repeatedly tell juries, is to protect young girls against themselves; but juries are not impressed.

The part that the jury plays in the enforcement of the criminal law, the fact that no grave offense against morals is punishable without their verdict, these are of great importance in relation to the statements of principle that I have been making. They turn what might otherwise be pure exhortation to the legislature into something like rules that the law-makers cannot safely ignore. The man in the jury box is not just an expression; he is an active reality. It will not in the long run work to make laws about morality that are not acceptable to him.

This then is how I believe my third interrogatory should be answered— not by the formulation of hard and fast rules, but by a judgment in each case taking into account the sort of factors I have been mentioning. The line that divides the criminal law from the moral is not determinable by the application of any clear-cut principle. It is like a line that divides land and sea, a coastline of irregularities and indentations. There are gaps and promontories, such as adultery and fornication, which the law has for centuries left substantially untouched. Adultery of the sort that breaks up marriage seems to me to be just as harmful to the social fabric as homosexuality or bigamy. The only ground for putting it outside the criminal law is that a law which made it a crime would be too difficult to enforce; it is too generally regarded as a human weakness not suitably punished by imprisonment. All that the law can do with fornication is to act against its worst manifestations; there is a general abhorrence of the commercialization of vice, and that sentiment gives strength to the law against brothels and immoral earnings. There is no logic to be found in this. The boundary between the criminal law and the moral law is fixed by balancing in the case of each particular crime the pros and cons of legal enforcement in accordance with the sort of considerations I have been outlining. The fact that adultery, fornication, and lesbianism are untouched by the criminal law does not prove that homosexuality ought not to be touched. The error of jurisprudence in the Wolfenden Report is caused by the search for some single principle to explain the division between crime and sin. The Report finds it in the principle that the criminal law exists for the protection of individuals; on this principle fornication in private between consenting adults is outside the law and thus it becomes logically indefensible to bring homosexuality between consenting adults in private within it. But the true principle is that the law exists for the protection of society. It does not discharge its function by protecting the individual from injury, annoyance, corruption, and exploitation; the law must protect also the institutions and the community of ideas, political and moral, without which people cannot live together. Society cannot ignore the morality of the individual any more than it can his loyalty; it flourishes on both and without either it dies. . . .

Society cannot live without morals. Its morals are those standards of conduct which the reasonable man approves. A rational man, who is also a good man, may have other standards. If he has no standards at all he is not a good man and need not be further considered. If he has standards, they may be very different; he may, for example, not disapprove of homosexuality or abortion. In that case he will not share in the common morality; but that should not make him deny that it is a social necessity. A rebel may be rational in thinking that he is right, but he is irrational if he thinks that society can leave him free to rebel!. . . .

56 / Immorality and Treason

H. L. A. HART

The Wolfenden Committee on Homosexual Offences and Prostitution recommended by a majority of 12 to 1 that homosexual behavior between consenting adults in private should no longer be a criminal offence. One of the Committee's principal grounds for this recommendation was expressed in its report in this way: "There must remain a realm of private morality and immorality which in brief and crude terms is not the law's business." I shall call this the liberal point of view: for it is a special application of those wider principles of liberal thought which John Stuart Mill formulated in his essay *On Liberty*. Mill's most famous words, less cautious perhaps than the Wolfenden Committee's, were:

> The only purpose for which power can be rightfully exercised over any member of a civilized community against his will is to prevent harm to others. His own good, either physical or moral, is not a sufficient warrant. He cannot rightfully be compelled to do or forbear . . . because in the opinion of others to do so would be wise or even right.

The liberal point of view has often been attacked, both before and after Mill. I shall discuss here the repudiation of it made by Sir Patrick Devlin,* in his recent lecture, which has now been published. This contains an origi-

*[Later, Lord Devlin, the author of the preceding selection.—Eds.]

nal and interesting argument designed to show that "*prima facie* society has the right to legislate against immorality as such" and that the Wolfenden Committee was mistaken in thinking that there is an area of private immorality which is not the law's business. Sir Patrick's case is a general one, not confined to sexual immorality, and he does not say whether or not he is opposed to the Wolfenden Committee's recommendation on homosexual behavior. Instead he gives us a hypothetical principle by which to judge this issue. He says that if it is the genuine feeling of our society that homosexuality is "a vice so abominable that its mere presence is an offense," society has the right to eradicate it by the use of the criminal law.

The publication by Sir Patrick of this lecture is in itself an interesting event. It is many years since a distinguished English lawyer delivered himself of general reasoned views about the relationship of morality to the criminal law. The last to do so with comparable skill and clarity was, I think, the great Victorian judge James Fitzjames Stephen. It is worth observing that Stephen, like Sir Patrick, repudiated the liberal point of view. Indeed his gloomy but impressive book *Liberty, Equality, Fraternity* was a direct reply to Mill's essay *On Liberty*. The most remarkable feature of Sir Patrick's lecture is his view of the nature of morality—the morality which the criminal law may enforce. Most previous thinkers who have repudiated the liberal point of view have done so because they thought that morality consisted either of divine commands or of rational principles of human conduct discoverable by human reason. Since morality for them had this elevated divine or rational status as the law of God or reason, it seemed obvious that the state should enforce it, and that the function of human law should not be merely to provide men with the opportunity for leading a good life, but actually to see that they led it. Sir Patrick does not rest his repudiation of the liberal point of view on these religious or rationalist conceptions. Indeed much that he writes reads like an abjuration of the notion that reasoning or thinking has much to do with morality. English popular morality has no doubt its historical connection with the Christian religion: "That," says Sir Patrick, "is how it got there." But it does not owe its present status or social significance to religion any more than to reason.

What, then, is it? According to Sir Patrick it is primarily a matter of feeling. "Every moral judgment," he says, "is a feeling that no rightminded man could act in any other way without admitting that he was doing wrong." Who then must feel this way if we are to have what Sir Patrick calls a public morality? He tells us that it is "the man in the street," "the man in the jury box," or (to use the phrase so familiar to English lawyers) "the man on the Clapham omnibus." For the moral judgments of society so far as the law is concerned are to be ascertained by the standards of the reasonable man, and he is not to be confused with the rational man. Indeed, Sir Patrick says "he is not expected to reason about anything and his judgment may be largely a matter of feeling."

But what precisely are the relevant feelings, the feelings which may justify use of the criminal law? Here the argument becomes a little complex. Widespread dislike of a practice is not enough. There must, says Sir Patrick, be "a real feeling of reprobation." Disgust is not enough either. What is crucial is a combination of intolerance, indignation, and disgust. These three are the forces behind the moral law, without which it is not "weighty enough to deprive the individual of freedom of choice." Hence there is, in Sir Patrick's outlook, a crucial difference between the mere adverse moral judgment of society and one which is inspired by feeling raised to the concert pitch of intolerance, indignation, and disgust.

This distinction is novel and also very important. For on it depends the weight to be given to the fact that when morality is enforced individual liberty is necessarily cut down. Though Sir Patrick's abstract formulation of his views on this point is hard to follow, his examples make his position fairly clear. We can see it best in the contrasting things he says about fornication and homosexuality. In regard to fornication, public feeling in most societies is not now of the concert-pitch intensity. We may feel that it is tolerable if confined: Only its spread might be gravely injurious. In such cases the question whether individual liberty should be restricted is for Sir Patrick a question of balance between the danger to society in the one scale and the restriction of the individual in the other. But if, as may be the case with homosexuality, public feeling is up to concert pitch, if it expresses a "deliberate judgment" that a practice as such is injurious to society, if there is "a genuine feeling that it is a vice so abominable that its mere presence is an offense," then it is beyond the limits of tolerance, and society may eradicate it. In this case, it seems, no further balancing of the claims of individual liberty is to be done, though as a matter of prudence the legislator should remember that the popular limits of tolerance may shift: The concert-pitch feeling may subside. This may produce a dilemma for the law; for the law may then be left without the full moral backing that it needs, yet it cannot be altered without giving the impression that the moral judgment is being weakened.

If this is what morality is—a compound of indignation, intolerance, and disgust—we may well ask what justification there is for taking it, and turning it as such, into criminal law with all the misery which criminal punishment entails. Here Sir Patrick's answer is very clear and simple. A collection of individuals is not a society; what makes them into a society is among other things a shared or public morality. This is as necessary to its existence as an organized government. So society may use the law to preserve its morality like anything else essential to it. "The suppression of vice is as much the law's business as the suppression of subversive activities." The liberal point of view which denies this is guilty of "an error in jurisprudence": for it is no more possible to define an area of private morality than an area of private subversive activity. There can be no "theoretical limits" to legislation against immorality just as there are no such limits to the power of the state to legislate against treason and sedition.

Surely all this, ingenious as it is, is misleading. Mill's formulation of the liberal point of view may well be too simple. The grounds for interfering with human liberty are more various than the single criterion of "harm to others" suggests: cruelty to animals or organizing prostitution for gain do not, as Mill himself saw, fall easily under the description of harm to others. Conversely, even where there is harm to others in the most literal sense, there may well be other principles limiting the extent to which harmful activities should be repressed by law. So there are multiple criteria, not a single criterion, determining when human liberty may be restricted. Perhaps this is what Sir Patrick means by a curious distinction which he often stresses between theoretical and practical limits. But with all its simplicities the liberal point of view is a better guide than Sir Patrick to clear thought on the proper relation of morality to the criminal law: for it stresses what he obscures—namely, the points at which thought is needed before we turn popular morality into criminal law.

No doubt we would all agree that a consensus of moral opinion on certain matters is essential if society is to be worth living in. Laws against murder, theft, and much else would be of little use if they were not supported by a widely diffused conviction that what these laws forbid is also immoral. So much is obvious. But it does not follow that everything to which the moral vetoes of accepted morality attach is of equal importance to society; nor is there the slightest reason for thinking of morality as a seamless web: one which will fall to pieces, carrying society with it, unless all its emphatic vetoes are enforced by law. Surely even in the face of the moral feeling that is up to concert pitch—the trio of intolerance, indignation, and disgust—we must pause to think. We must ask a question at two different levels which Sir Patrick never clearly enough identifies or separates. First, we must ask whether a practice which offends moral feeling is harmful, independently of its repercussion on the general moral code. Secondly, what about repercussion on the moral code? Is it really true that failure to translate this item of general morality into criminal law will jeopardize the whole fabric of morality and so of society?

We cannot escape thinking about these two different questions merely by repeating to ourselves the vague nostrum: "This is part of public morality and public morality must be preserved if society is to exist." Sometimes Sir Patrick seems to admit this, for he says, in words which both Mill and the Wolfenden Report might have used, that there must be the maximum respect for individual liberty consistent with the integrity of society. Yet this, as his contrasting examples of fornication and homosexuality show, turns out to mean only that the immorality which the law may punish must be generally felt to be intolerable. This plainly is no adequate substitute for a reasoned estimate of the damage to the fabric of society likely to ensue if it is not suppressed.

Nothing perhaps shows more clearly the inadequacy of Sir Patrick's approach to this problem than his comparison between the suppression of sexual immorality and the suppression of treason or subversive activity. Private subversive activity is, of course, a contradiction in terms because "subversion" means overthrowing government, which is a public thing. But it is grotesque, even where moral feeling against homosexuality is up to concert pitch, to think of the homosexual behavior of two adults in private as in any way like treason or sedition either in intention or effect. We can make it *seem* like treason only if we assume that deviation from a general moral code is bound to affect that code, and to lead not merely to its modification but to its destruction. The analogy could begin to be plausible only if it was clear that offending against this item of morality was likely to jeopardize the whole structure. But we have ample evidence for believing that people will not abandon morality, will not think any better of murder, cruelty and dishonesty, merely because some private sexual practice which they abominate is not punished by the law.

Because this is so the analogy with treason is absurd. Of course "No man is an island": What one man does in private, if it is known, may affect others in many different ways. Indeed it may be that deviation from general sexual morality by those whose lives, like the lives of many homosexuals, are noble ones and in all other ways exemplary will lead to what Sir Patrick calls the shifting of the limits of tolerance. But if this has any analogy in the sphere of government it is not the overthrow of ordered government but a peaceful change in its form. So we may listen to the promptings of common sense and of logic, and say that though there could not logically be a sphere of private treason there is a sphere of private morality and immorality.

Sir Patrick's doctrine is also open to a wider, perhaps a deeper, criticism. In his reaction against a rationalist morality and his stress on feeling, he has I think thrown out the baby and kept the bath water; and the bath water may turn out to be very dirty indeed. When Sir Patrick's lecture was first delivered *The Times* greeted it with these words: "There is a moving and welcome humility in the conception that society should not be asked to give its reason for refusing to tolerate what in its heart it feels intolerable." This drew from a correspondent in Cambridge the retort: "I am afraid that we are less humble than we used to be. We once burned old women because, without giving our reasons, we felt in our hearts that witchcraft was intolerable."

This retort is a bitter one, yet its bitterness is salutary. We are not, I suppose, likely, in England, to take again to the burning of old women for witchcraft or to punishing people for associating with those of a different race or color, or to punishing people again for adultery. Yet if these things were viewed with intolerance, indignation, and disgust, as the second of them still is in some countries, it seems that on Sir Patrick's principles no rational criticism could be opposed to the claim that they should be punished by law. We could only pray, in his words, that the limits of tolerance might shift.

It is impossible to see what curious logic has led Sir Patrick to this result. For him a practice is immoral if the thought of it makes the man on the Clapham omnibus sick. So be it. Still, why should we not summon all the resources of our reason, sympathetic understanding, as well as critical intelligence, and insist that before general moral feeling is turned into criminal law it is submitted to scrutiny of a different kind from Sir Patrick's? Surely, the legislator should ask whether the general morality is based on ignorance, superstition, or misunderstanding; whether there is a false conception that those who practice what it condemns are in other ways dangerous or hostile to society; and whether the misery to many parties, the blackmail and the other evil consequences of criminal punishment, especially for sexual offenses, are well understood. It is surely extraordinary that among the things which Sir Patrick says are to be considered before we legislate against immorality these appear nowhere; not even as "practical considerations," let alone "theoretical limits." To any theory which, like this one, asserts that the criminal law may be used on the vague ground that the preservation of morality is essential to society and yet omits to stress the need for critical scrutiny, our reply should be: "Morality, what crimes may be committed in thy name!"

As Mill saw, and de Tocqueville showed in detail long ago in his critical but sympathetic study of democracy, it is fatally easy to confuse the democratic principle that power should be in the hands of the majority with the utterly different claim that the majority, with power in their hands, need respect no limits. Certainly there is a special risk in a democracy that the majority may dictate how all should live. This is the risk we run, and should gladly run; for it is the price of all that is so good in democratic rule. But loyalty to democratic principles does not require us to maximize this risk: Yet this is what we shall do if we mount the man in the street on the top of the Clapham omnibus and tell him that if only he feels sick enough about what other people do in private to demand its suppression by law, no theoretical criticism can be made of his demand.

57 / Designing a Culture

B. F. SKINNER

The social environment of any group of people is the product of a complex series of events in which accident sometimes plays a prominent role. Manners and customs often spring from circumstances which have little or no relation to the ultimate effect upon the group. The origins of more explicit controlling practices may be equally adventitious. Thus the pattern of control exercised by a strong leader, reflecting many of his personal idiosyncrasies, may result in an established governmental classification of behavior as legal or illegal and may even set the pattern for a highly organized agency. The techniques which a saint employs to control himself may become part of the established practices of a religious agency. Economic control is determined in part by the resources available to the group, which are ultimately a matter of geography. Other fortuitous factors are introduced when different cultures intermingle or when a culture survives important changes in the nonsocial environment. A cultural practice is not the less effective in determining the behavior characteristic of a group because its origins are accidental. But once the effect upon behavior has been observed, the source of the practice may be scrutinized more closely. Certain questions come to be asked. Why should the design of a culture be left so largely to accident? Is it not possible to change the societal environment deliberately so that the human product will meet more acceptable specifications?

In many cultural groups we observe practices which might be described as "making changes in practice." The great religious books supply many examples of the deliberate construction of a social environment. The Ten Commandments were a codification of existing and proposed practices according to which, henceforth, behavior was to be reinforced or punished by the group or by the religious agency. The teachings of Christ were more clearly in the nature of a new design. In governmental control, the enactment of a law usually establishes new cultural practices, and a constitution is a similar undertaking on a broader scale. Experimental curricula in schools and colleges and books on child care which recommend substantial changes in family practices are attempts to manipulate important parts of a culture. The social environment is changed to some extent when a new technique of psychotherapy is derived from a theory or from an experimental study of human behavior. Social legislation creates an experimental environment in which behavior is more often reinforced with food, clothing, housing, and so on, and in which certain kinds of deprivation are less likely to occur. Planning the structure of a large industry or governmental agency is an experiment in cultural design. These are all examples of the manipulation of small parts of the social environment; what is called "Utopian" thinking embraces the design of a culture as a whole.

The deliberate manipulation of the culture is therefore itself a characteristic of many cultures—a fact to be accounted for in a scientific analysis of human behavior. Proposing a change in a cultural practice, making such a change, and accepting such a change are all parts of our subject matter. Although this is one of the most complex of human activities, the basic pattern seems clear. Once a given feature of an environment has been shown to have an effect upon human behavior which is reinforcing, either in itself or as an escape from a more aversive condition, constructing such an environment is as easily explained as building a fire or closing a window when a room grows cold. A doctor tells his patient to stop eating a certain food so that he will no longer be troubled by an allergy because he has observed a connection between the food and the allergy. The psychotherapist tells his patient to change to a job to which he is better suited so that he will suffer less from a sense of failure because a similar connection has been established. An economist advises a government to impose heavy taxes in order to check inflation because still another relation has been observed. All these examples involve many detailed steps, many of them verbal, and we should need a more detailed analysis of scientific thinking than can be undertaken here to give a reasonable account of particular instances. But the basic process is clear enough to permit some interpretation.

When we speak of the "deliberate" design of a culture, we mean the introduction of a cultural practice "for the sake of its consequences." But . . . it is never a future consequence which is effective. A change in practice is made because similar changes have had certain consequences in the past. When the individual describes his own behavior, he may speak of past consequences as the "goal" of his current action, but this is not very helpful. We can best understand the cultural designer, not by guessing at his goals or asking him to guess at them for us, but by studying the earlier environmental events which have led him to advocate a cultural change. If he is basing a given proposal upon scientific experiments, we want to know how closely the experimental and practical situations correspond. We may also want to examine other "reasons for making a change" which are to be found in his personal history and in the recorded history of those who have investigated similar areas.

VALUE JUDGMENTS

Such an interpretation of the behavior of the cultural designer brings us to an issue of classical proportions. Eventually, a science of human behavior may be able to tell the designer what kind of culture must be set up in order to produce a given result, but can it ever tell him what kind of result he *should* produce? The word "should" brings us into the familiar realm of the value judgment. It is commonly argued that there are two kinds of knowledge, one of fact and the other of value, and that science is necessarily confined to the first. Does the design of a culture demand the second? Must the cultural designer eventually abandon science and turn to other ways of thinking?

It is not true that statements containing "should" or "ought" have no place in scientific discourse. There is at least one use for which an acceptable translation can be made. A sentence beginning "You ought" is often a prediction of reinforcing consequences. "You ought to take an umbrella" may be taken to mean, "You will be reinforced for taking an umbrella." A more explicit translation would contain at least three statements: (1) Keeping dry is reinforcing to you; (2) carrying an umbrella keeps you dry in the rain; and (3) it is going to rain. All these statements are properly within the realm of science. In addition to this, of course, the word "ought" plays a large part in the control exercised by the ethical group and by governmental and religious agencies. The statement, "You ought to take an umbrella," may be emitted, not as a prediction of contingencies, but to induce an individual to take an umbrella. The "ought" is aversive, and the individual addressed may feel guilty if he does not then take an umbrella. This exhortatory use may be accounted for in the usual way. It is nothing more than a concealed command and has no more connection with a value judgment than with a scientific statement of fact.

The same interpretation is possible when the reinforcing consequences are of an ethical nature. "You ought to love your neighbor" may be converted into the two statements: (1) "The approval of your fellow men is positively reinforcing to you" and (2) "loving your fellow men is approved by the group of which you are a member," both of which may be demonstrated scientifically. The statement may also be used, of course, to coerce an individual into behaving in a fashion which resembles loving his neighbor, and indeed is probably most often used for this reason, but again this is not what is meant by a value judgment.

When a given change in cultural design is proposed primarily to induce people to make the change, we may account for it as in the exhortatory example above. The proposal may also be a prediction of consequences. Sometimes these are easily specified, as when it is said that the group "ought" to approve of honesty because its members will thus avoid being deceived or that it "ought" to disapprove of theft because its members will then avoid the loss of property. Sometimes the implied consequences are less obvious, as when a study of behavior leads someone to propose that we "ought" to deal with criminals in a certain way or that we "ought" to avoid aversive control in education. It is at this point that the classical values of freedom, security, happiness, knowledge, and so on are usually appealed to. We have seen that these often refer indirectly to certain immediate consequences of cultural practices. But the crucial issue concerning value hinges upon another meaning of the word "ought" in which a more remote consequence is implied. Is there a scientific parallel for this kind of value?

THE SURVIVAL OF A CULTURE

We have seen that in certain respects operant reinforcement resembles the natural selection of evolutionary theory. Just as genetic characteristics which arise as mutations are selected or discarded by their consequences, so novel forms of behavior are selected or discarded through reinforcement. There is still a third kind of selection which applies to cultural practices. A group adopts a given practice—a custom, a manner, a controlling device—either by design or through some event which, so far as its effect upon the group is concerned, may be wholly accidental. As a characteristic of the social environment this practice modifies the behavior of members of the group. The resulting behavior may affect the success of the group in competition with other groups or with the nonsocial environment. Cultural practices which are advantageous will tend to be characteristic of the groups which survive and which therefore perpetuate those practices. Some cultural practices may therefore be said to have survival value, while others are lethal in the genetic sense.

A given culture is, in short, an experiment in behavior. It is a particular set of conditions under which a large number of people grow and live. These conditions generate the patterns or aspects of behavior—the cultural character—which we have already examined. The general interest level of members of the group, their motivations and emotional dispositions, their behavioral repertoires, and the extent to which they practice self-control and self-knowledge are all relevant to the strength of the group as a whole. In addition the culture has an indirect effect upon other factors. The general health of the group will depend upon birth rate, hygiene, methods of child care, general living conditions, and hours and kinds of work, upon whether many men and women of talent go into medicine and nursing, and upon what proportion of the wealth of the group goes into the construction of hospitals, public health services, and so on. All these conditions, in turn, depend upon the culture. Cultural practices are also largely responsible for the use which is made of the genetic material born into the group, since they determine whether the individual will be able to develop his talents fully, whether educational institutions will be open to him regardless of class or other distinction, whether educational policies are progressive or reactionary, whether he will be subject to political or economic favoritism in the selection of a profession, and so on. The culture also determines the extent to which the members of the group are preoccupied with food or sex or with escape from minor aversive stimulation in the search for "comfort" or from such major aversive stimulation as hard labor or combat, as well as the extent to which they are subject to exploitation by powerful agencies. In turn, therefore, it determines the extent to which they are able to engage in productive activities in science, art, crafts, sports, and so on. The experimental test of a given culture is provided by competition between groups under the conditions characteristic of a particular epoch.

Is survival, then, a criterion according to which a given cultural practice may be evaluated? Those who are accustomed to appealing to more traditional values are usually not willing to accept this alternative. Survival value is a difficult criterion because it has perhaps even less obvious dimensions than happiness, freedom, knowledge, and health. It is not an unchanging criterion, for what may in this sense be a "good" culture in one period is not necessarily "good" in another. Since survival always presupposes competition, if only with the inanimate environment, it does not appear to define a "good" culture in the absence of competition. There appears to be no way in which we can test the survival value of a culture *in vacuo* to determine its absolute goodness. Conversely, the temporary survival of a culture is no proof of its goodness. All present cultures have obviously survived, many of them without very great change for hundreds of years, but this may not mean that they are better cultures than others which have perished or suffered drastic modification under more competitive circumstances. The principle of survival does not permit us to argue that the status quo must be good because it is here now.

Another difficulty is that survival is often in direct conflict with traditional values. There are circumstances under which a group is more likely to survive if it is not happy, or under which it will survive only if large numbers of its members submit to slavery. Under certain circumstances the survival of a culture may depend upon the unrestricted exercise of sexual behavior, while under other circumstances severely repressive control may strengthen advantageous behavior of other sorts. In order to accept survival as a criterion in judging a culture, it thus appears to be necessary to abandon such principles as happiness, freedom, and virtue. Perhaps the commonest objection to survival is essentially an aversive reaction to the practices which have, thus far in the history of mankind, had survival value. Aggressive action has usually been most successful in promoting the survival of one group against another or of one individual against another.

These difficulties appear to explain why those who are accustomed to the traditional values hesitate to accept survival as an alternative. We have no reason to urge them to do so. We need not say that anyone *chooses* survival as a criterion according to which a cultural practice is to be evaluated. Human behavior does not depend upon the prior choice of any value. When a man jumps out of the way of an approaching car, we may say that he "chooses life rather than death." But he does not jump because he has so chosen; he jumps because jumping is evoked by certain stimulating circumstances. This fact is explained in turn by many earlier contingencies of reinforcement in which quick movement has reduced the threat of impending aversive stimulation or has, . . . avoided aversive consequences. Now, the fact that the individual responds or can be conditioned to respond in this way is not wholly unrelated to the issue of life or death. It is obvious, after the fact, that the behavior has worked to his advantage. But this particular advantage could not have operated before he jumped. Only past advantages could have had an effect upon his behavior. He was likely to jump or to learn to jump because his ancestors were selected from a large population just because they jumped or learned to jump quickly from the paths of moving objects. Those who did not jump or could not learn to jump are probably not represented by contemporary descendants. The "value" which the individual appears to have chosen with respect to his own future is therefore nothing more than that condition which operated selectively in creating and perpetuating the behavior which now seems to exemplify such a choice. An individual does not choose to live or die; he behaves in ways which work toward his survival or death. Behavior usually leads to survival because the behaving individual has been selected by survival in the process of evolution.

In the same sense, the behavior of making a constructive suggestion about a cultural practice does not involve the "choice of a value." A long biological and *cultural* history has produced an individual who acts in a particular way with respect to cultural conditions. Our problem is not to determine the value or goals which operate in the behavior of the cultural designer; it is rather to examine the complex conditions under which design occurs. Some changes in culture may be made because of consequences which are roughly described as happiness, freedom, knowledge, and so on. Eventually, the survival of the group acquires a similar function. The fact that a given practice is related to survival becomes effective as a *prior* condition in cultural design. Survival arrives late among the so-called values because the effect of a culture upon human behavior, and in turn upon the perpetuation of the culture itself, can be demonstrated only when a science of human behavior has been well developed. The "practice of changing practice" is accelerated by science just because science provides an abundance of instances in which the consequences of practices are shown. The individual who is familiar with the results of science is most likely to set up comparable conditions in cultural design, and we may say, if the expression will not be misunderstood, that he is using survival as a criterion in evaluating a practice. . . .

58 / Some Problems for Skinner

MELVIN R. SCHUSTER

I. SKINNER'S TRADITION

Skinner is part of a well-established tradition, extending from the ancient to the modern world, which holds that the function of political society is melioration, that is to say, the improvement of man and the creation of the good life. This conception is essential to Plato's *Republic*,* of course, and serves in the *Gorgias* as the standard in terms of which Socrates denies the greatness of the reputedly great statemen of Athens.[1] Aristotle† gives expression to it when he claims that the state, "originating in the needs of life," continues, "in existence for the sake of the good life",[2] and Skinner continues in the same vein by reaffirming "the doctrine of human perfectibility"[3] and by having the fictional designer of Walden Two‡ criticize our government for refusing to "accept the responsibility of building the sort of behavior needed for a happy state."[4] This tradition is understandably conducive to utopian thinking and to the idea of elitist rule, for if melioration is to have any significance at all, there must exist a good (in some sense), as well as an appropriate means for attaining it, and the good and its means must be knowable. With these ingredients it becomes possible to construct planned worlds of the Platonic or Skinnerian order, and it can then be argued—it seems impossible not to argue—that leadership and authority should reside in those people who possess the knowledge of means and ends required to bring the good life into being. Plato thought that his ideal society would always have to be governed by an intellectual elite because he believed that intelligence was inherited and few men were born with the intellectual potential to rule. Meliorists like Marx§ and Marcuse** on the

[1]Plato, *Gorgias* 515A–517A.

[2]*Politics* 1252b, 28–30. Benjamin Jowett's translation in *The Basic Works of Aristotle*, ed. Richard McKeon (New York, Random House, 1941).

[3]B. F. Skinner, "Freedom and the Control of Man," reprinted in *Utopias* ed. by Peyton E. Richter (Boston: Holbrook Press, Inc., 1971), p. 289. This work will be identified in later references as FCM.

[4]B. F. Skinner, *Walden Two* (Paperback ed.; New York, The Macmillan Co., 1962), p. 166. This book will be identified in later references as WT.

*[Plato was an ancient Greek philosopher. His *Republic* is a model for many utopias.—Eds.]
†[Another ancient Greek philosopher.—Eds.]
‡[A utopian society in the novel *Walden Two* by B.F. Skinner.—Eds.]
§[A 19th century philosopher and political thinker.—Eds.]
**[A 20th century Marxist.—Eds.]

other hand, with a strong humanistic bias, are rather optimistic about the possibilities of man. They consequently regard domination by the few as a transitional device needed to introduce the better world. Elitist rule, becoming unnecessary, is supposed to dissolve. Skinner inclines more toward Plato on this issue, despite his positivist orientation, for he would have rule by experts whose ranks are open to qualified citizens. While his conception of intelligence does not appear to have Plato's general biological rigidity, he does think that there will never be more than a small number of this "exceptional" type, and consequently never more than a few people to do the governing.[5]

It would seem from what has been said that the question concerning the nature of the good at which utopia aims would therefore be fundamental and occupy a central position in all melioristic social thought. Yet this is precisely the kind of question that Skinner condemns and associates with vacuous pedantry; he sees it as an irrelevant puzzle to be played with in university classrooms while the world outside buckles and bends under the problems of population, war, poverty, sickness, insecurity, and misery. Skinner directs his ire at those who are so intellectually meticulous that they will do nothing until every bit of knowledge is dusted and put neatly in its place. But whether or not we know what The Good is, we can surely agree "that health is better than illness, wisdom better than ignorance, love better than hate, and productive energy better than neurotic sloth."[6] A summary of Skinner's concrete utopian goals appears at the end of his last book:

> ". . . a world in which people live together without quarreling, maintain themselves by producing the food, shelter, and clothing they need, enjoy themselves and contribute to the enjoyment of others in art, music, literature, and games, consume only a reasonable part of the resources of the world and add as little as possible to its pollution, bear no more children than can be raised decently, continue to explore the world around them and discover better ways of dealing with it, and come to know themselves accurately and, therefore, manage themselves effectively."[7]

Even with regard to these he is apparently undogmatic. He speaks of an "experimental ethics" that would "profit from experience,"[8] because errors are always possible, and what worked at one time may not at another.[9]

---

[5]*Ibid.* p. 55.

[6]FCM, p. 292.

[7]B. F. Skinner, *Beyond Freedom and Dignity* (New York: Alfred A. Knopf, 1972), p. 214. To be identified in later references as BFD.

[8]WT, p. 174.

[9]B.F. Skinner and Carl Rogers, "Some Issues Concerning the Control of Human Behavior: A Symposium," reprinted in *Humanistic Sociology*, ed. by John F. Glass and John R. Staude (Pacific Palisades, Calif: Goodyear Publishing Co. Inc., 1972), p. 346. This work will be identified in later references as S and R. See also BFD, p. 175–76.

The test is whether it works; the justification he seeks is not speculative but "experimental."[10]

II. SKINNER ON VALUES

To measure workability, Skinner turns to the survival of the culture, and in so doing, and despite his pragmatic drive, faces the problem of ultimate values. Cultural survival does not always harmonize with personal goods, or with the goods of others, but it is the good that Skinner has fixed upon since he thinks it is implied by any attempt to design an entire culture.[11] He offers no further justification of it because he does not believe that one exists.[12] If this is not a very philosophic attitude, it is at least shared by a number of philosophers who also speak of the indefensibility of first principles. At any rate, some may refuse to accept the consequences of Skinner's position since, for example, it would follow that brutality is wrong and justice right merely because of their survival value and, in general, that "those principles which are with us today have been most valuable in this respect."[13] But such a rejection does not constitute grounds for a moral criticism of his utopia. There may be more to ethics than survival, but survival is surely not an unethical goal. Even John Locke's* advocacy of natural rights is qualified by recognition of a "nobler cause" which is "the peace and preservation of all mankind."[14] The survival of mankind may ultimately prove to be in conflict with morality, yet in designing a community it is not unreasonable to proceed on the opposite assumption.

Moreover, when Skinner argues that current values have achieved their status because they have had survival value, he is speculating. It is not the conclusion of an empirical science nor is it a philosophically substantiated position, but simply a reflection of his commitment to the survival of culture. In addition, he recognizes the difficulties of determining in advance whether any specific practice will have survival value.[15] One might ask for the survival value of eating with a fork, and innumerable other folkways. The point is not that Skinner is making the claim that every detail is ultimately explainable in terms of its direct contribution to survival, but that in

---

[10]WT, p. 161. See, too, BFD, p. 153.

[11]BFD, p. 150, 182.

[12]This point is made in BFD, p. 137 and S and R, p. 346. It also appears in B.F. Skinner, *Science and Human Behavior* (Paperback ed: New York: The Free Press, 1965). This latter book will henceforth be referred to as SHB.

[13]SHB, p. 445.

[14]*Second Treatise on Government*, chap. 2, secs. 6,7; in *Social Contract* ed. by Ernest Barker (New York: Oxford University Press, 1962), pp. 5,6.

[15]SHB, p. 434, 436.

*An 18th century British philosopher.—Eds.]

practice—and this is to be stressed—Skinner's ultimate value has virtually no role to play. It lacks both theoretical force, since undefended, and practical force, since too far removed. Thus, in any significant sense, Skinner's morality is really the concrete here-and-now morality discussed earlier; and the experimental validity of those values is, as he argues, obvious to all. It would be "quibbling" to attempt to justify them,[16] as absurd as a "centipede trying to decide how to walk."[17] And presumably it would be just as quibbling and just as absurd to attempt to justify them in terms of ultimate survival value.

In summary, Skinner's goals are actually commonly accepted ones vaguely and almost arbitrarily tied to an ultimate good of cultural survival. The immediate values are hardly unethical, and the ultimate good, though of little functional significance, can itself reasonably be adopted by anyone in a position of social responsibility. Whatever might be unethical about Skinner's world must be located in the means, since it cannot be found in the ends. In fact, the greatest controversy about Skinner has centered upon his manipulation and conditioning of man.

III. MORAL CRITICISMS OF SKINNER'S PROPOSALS

Given, then, Skinner's reasonable and morally praiseworthy immediate and concrete goals for man, and an apparently acceptable principle of influence, the question arises: what is morally wrong with Skinner's proposals? Is it not reasonable and right that mankind should use its available knowledge to control the environment and thereby cure, to the extent possible at the present stage of science, the innumerable and profound ills of the world? Is it not immoral to refuse? And is it not also reasonable, given the goals, to assign the task of achieving them to the people who know best how to do it—the scientist-experts? Skinner's utopian proposals represent an effort to systematize the possibilities for human growth by constructing a total environment wherein problems are resolved by rewarding the good but not the bad. That must be a significant characteristic of any conception of the good society. It is heaven without hell; it is that condition the absence of which accounts for the popular cynical meaning of such terms as "realistic" and "practical." Skinner may be over-optimistic about the possibilities for bringing utopia into existence, but it does not seem reasonable to condemn the vision as unethical.

Many of his critics would agree. As Chomsky* says, Skinner's "libertarian and humanist opponents do not object to 'design of culture,' that is, to

---

[16]FCM, p. 292.
[17]WT, p. 159.
*[A 20th century linguist and critic of Skinner.—Eds.]

creating social forms that will be more conducive to the satisfaction of human needs, though they differ from Skinner in their intuitive perception of what these needs truly are."[18] But what are these needs as Skinner sees them? They are the concrete ones enumerated earlier, and it is hard indeed to imagine a humanist rejecting them. What seems really to be behind the criticism is the fear that Skinner's planned world would destroy the sensitivity, the spirit, and the intelligence of man. Skinner's man would be an automaton, a creature of habit. In reply, something should first be said about habit and rationality. Scientific and philosophic understanding of both appears to be deficient, for most human behavior is, in some sense of the word, habitual, although there are rational and irrational habits. It is surely incorrect narrowly to identify human rationality with the laborious, stumbling, sometimes cramped, deliberate process of thought that is often characteristic of the initial stage in learning. When a man once learns, he may act quickly and spontaneously. Should the learned, the wise, and the accomplished then be denied rationality, intelligence, spirit, and sensitivity, and these qualities be reserved for the fumbling child and the groping novice? The question of habit is obviously a moot point and cannot serve as an adequate basis for a moral criticism of Skinner.

Skinner wants to build rather than destroy intellect, aesthetic sensitivity, creativeness, and flexibility. People, he believes, should be taught how to think,[19] they should not be fed lies and propaganda,[20] and must not be personally stultified.[21] Skinner's educational ideas are directed to turning out a man who can face life with equanimity and confront the unexpected and the different without fear, but with intelligence and an open mind. Operant conditioning is the vehicle for accomplishing this. According to Skinner's understanding of cognitive thought, it, too, follows behavioral rules, so that by proper instruction employing behavioral techniques men's reasoning abilities will be expanded and made more efficient. One should not be upset by the use of the word "conditioning" in this context. As Skinner says, "No theory changes what it is a theory about."[22] What Skinner calls "conditioning," the humanist calls, and would continue to call, "learning" and "responding to reason."

Once the danger of determinism has been removed from conditioning, Skinner's method no longer constitutes a threat. And considering the goals he sets for it—the very reverse of what his critics fear—and his experimental attitude and willingness to change, the charge of mechanical man seems groundless. In fact, neither the ethical, the metaphysical, nor the instru-

---

[18]Noam Chomsky, "The Case Against B.F. Skinner," *The New York Review of Books*, December 30, 1971, p. 24.

[19]ST, p. 119, 121.

[20]WT, p. 207; SHB, p. 443.

[21]WT, p. 209.

[22]BFD, p. 213.

mental areas have provided, upon reflection, a basis for a moral criticism of Skinner's social thought. There remains, then, the fourth and final area, the political.

IV. SKINNER AND THE POLITICAL SPHERE

The charge against it is that Skinner's community is an authoritarian rather than a democratic one. But democratic communities may also be authoritarian (e.g., the tyranny of the majority), and it is not certain that the only legitimate political societies are democracies. Consider the virtues of Skinner's world: it refuses to use the revolutionary and repressive techniques that meliorists like Marcuse support to bring about their better world;[23] membership is entirely voluntary, and even those who are born into it are free to leave; leadership is open to those with the interest and ability; respect is meted out to all and not simply to some on the basis of profession or political position; and people are not socially denounced or held in contempt for not being political activists.[24] Skinner believes that democracy is "almost certainly not the *final* form of government,"[25] and that today its goals can be better attained by using the elitist rule discussed earlier in the paper. But it must not be forgotten that Skinner's elitism, which is the basis of the political criticism, is a consequence of the meliorative hypothesis rather than of his behaviorism. It would be self-defeating to commit society to improvement and then to allow the incapable and the unable to take it from there. If an individual behaved in that way in his personal life, he would be accused of not really having the professed goal, or at least of having other goals that are more important. Plato's old argument has not lost its force and seems unavoidable for any meliorist: that if there is a standard and a commitment to its attainment, then the basis of political authority must be that special knowledge which enables the standard to be achieved. The meliorist hypothesis is humanistic but basically undemocratic.

Consider, further, the possibility of an election in Walden Two. Such a thing would not be,[26] but the people do vote in outside elections, and on those occasions they take the advice of the Political Manager and vote the

---

[23]For Herbert Marcuse's views see, for example, "Ethics and Revolution" in *Ethics and Society* ed. by Richard T. De George (Garden City, New York: Doubleday and Co., Inc., 1966) and "Repressive Tolerance", in Robert Paul Wolff, Barrington Moore, Jr. and Herbert Marcuse, *A Critique of Pure Tolerance* (Boston: Beacon Press, 1969). For Skinner's views on aversive measures, see his chapters on punishment in BFD and SHB. And for his observations on revolution see WT, p. 195, 273.

[24]WT, p. 167. See also chap. 8.

[25]FCM, p. 294. Also, WT, p. 273.

[26]WT, p. 267.

straight "Walden Ticket" as they are told.[27] It is therefore reasonable to suppose that in such a voluntary community, if there were elections, the people would vote as the specialists direct—which would be to vote the specialists into their positions. The notion that the specialists should not give direction or advice would be absurd even in democracy, and it would be utterly destructive not only of Skinner's community but of the meliorative intent upon which it is based.

It must be borne in mind that Skinner's world is a people's world, a voluntary one, and as democratic as a meliorist political order can be. In fact, the community would avoid some of the abuses of which democratic societies are guilty.[28] But it is just this popular, voluntary aspect of Walden Two that is upsetting and that makes it appear dystopian even when it is meant to be utopian. What seems wrong is not the fact that people try to control the environment, improve their lives, influence one another, use conditioning, employ one method of education instead of another, and refuse to punish. The only basis for an ethical criticism is that adult people are being fashioned and their lives molded in accordance with someone else's concept of the good. It becomes more shocking as the control is centralized, massive, and efficient; and the more Skinner depicts its accomplishments— which are significant—the worse it seems, because the greater is its flaw. For people to be controlled against their wills is an affront; but it is frightening and threatening when the role of malleable material is voluntarily, even eagerly adopted. Mill* has said that society has no right to interfere in the life of the individual unless it is "to prevent harm to others. His own good, either physical or moral, is not sufficient warrant."[29] It is this classical, liberal principle that is violated by Walden Two. And when an individual joins the community voluntarily, he violates that responsibility which he has to himself, to lead his own life and not submit to another, even though that other were more competent and the life more commodious. It is the same point that Father Mapple makes in Moby Dick: "Woe to him who would not be true, even though to be false were salvation!"[30]

What is being suggested here is that the ethical criticisms of Skinner are misplaced when they are directed against his goals, or when they become needlessly embroiled in the issue of determinism, or when they panic at the sound of the word "conditioning." The one moral flaw is its very foundation—the meliorative hypothesis. The function of political society cannot be the improvement of man and the creation of the good life; for if it is, then there can be no moral objection to Skinner's world.

---

[27]Ibid., pp. 196–197.
[28]Ibid., pp. 268–269.
[29]John Stuart Mill, On Liberty (New York: Appleton, Century-Crofts, Inc., 1947) p. 9.
[30]Herman Melville, Moby Dick (New York: The Modern Library, 1950), p. 47.
*[A 19th century British philosopher.—Eds.]

STUDY QUESTIONS

1. Why does Devlin maintain that the "average person on the street"—or the "right-minded man on the Clapham omnibus"—should tell you what you can and cannot do?

2. Why, according to Devlin, shouldn't society tolerate everything? Do you agree? If so, give examples of things which society should not tolerate.

3. Why isn't your private life your own business, according to Devlin? Do you agree?

4. According to Devlin, why should society have a right to punish whatever it considers disgusting, intolerable, and immoral?

5. According to Hart, Devlin's view of morality and society were once used to justify burning people at the stake. Explain what Hart means.

6. Is Hart right in maintaining that Devlin confuses "the democratic principle that power should be in the hands of the majority with the . . . claim that the majority, with power in their hands, need respect no limits"? Spell out the differences between these two ideas.

7. Give some examples of the good and bad effects of the role of experts in our society.

8. What does Skinner mean by designing a culture? What are some strengths and weaknesses of his proposals?

9. How do science and method enter into Skinner's programs, and how does this bear on democracy as a form of government?

10. What is Schuster's moral objection to Skinner?

11. What political misgivings does Schuster have against Skinner's program?

12. On what points relating to the survival of a culture would Devlin and Skinner agree and disagree?

13. The essays in this part of the book set up a conflict between autonomy and authority. Is such a conflict inevitable? Are there any examples of societies in which this conflict is minimized or nonexistent? What might such a society be like?

14. Is a society run by experts or by "right-minded" people more or less likely to tolerate criticism of its basic convictions, and more or less likely to foster a sense of wonder about the world, than a society which is not run by experts and "right-minded" people?

Further Readings

Berger, F., ed. *Freedom of Expression*. Belmont, Calif.: Wadsworth, 1980. [A good collection of essays on freedom of speech, censorship, and pornography.]

Bergmann, Frithjof. *On Being Free*. Notre Dame, Indiana: University of Notre Dame Press, 1969. [An original and interesting discussion of freedom, self-development, and education in our society.]

Berlin, Isaiah. *Four Essays on Liberty*. New York: Oxford University Press, 1969. [A spirited and learned defense of classical liberalism.]

Feyerabend, Paul K. *Science in a Free Society*. London: NLB, 1978. [A provocative defense of a free society without the domination of experts.]

Habermas, Jurgen. *Toward a Rational Society*. Boston: Beacon Press, 1970. [An important neo-Marxist discussion of politics and science in advanced industrial societies.]

Kaufmann, Walter. "Are Autonomy and Happiness Compatible? In *Without Guilt and Justice* (New York: Dell, 1973), chap. 8, pp. 203–237. [A stimulating book, in the spirit of Nietzsche's *Beyond Good and Evil*.]

Lyons, David, ed. *Rights*. Belmont, Calif.: Wadsworth, 1980. [Contains important recent papers on rights and justice.]

Machan, Tibor R., ed. *The Libertarian Alternative*. Chicago: Nelson-Hall, 1974. [A collection of essays defending libertarianism on a variety of topics.]

Mill, John Stuart. *On Liberty*. Indianapolis, Ind.: Bobbs-Merrill, Library of Liberal Arts, 1956. [The most important statement and defense of the liberal theory of individual freedom.]

Nietzsche, Friedrich. *Beyond Good and Evil*, trans. Walter Kaufmann. New York: Vintage Books, 1966. [A provocative work by one of the most provocative thinkers in Western history; calls into question the basic beliefs and values of Western culture.]

Popper, Sir Karl Raimund. *The Open Society and Its Enemies*, 4th ed., 2 vols. London: Routledge & Kegan Paul, 1962. [Despite its polemical and one-sided views, a stimulating critique of Plato, Hegel, and Marx.]

Russell, B. *The Scientific Outlook*. New York: W. W. Norton Co., 1939, 1958. [A somewhat dated but still lucid defense of a scientific society.]

Skinner, B. F. *Beyond Freedom and Dignity*. New York: Knopf, 1971. [Advocates the redesign of culture using behavioral engineering and a utilitarian moral outlook.]

GLOSSARY

A posteriori: a statement is a posteriori if one has to appeal to experience in order to find out whether it is true (or false). For example, 'Wolves are carnivores'. 'It is raining'. An a posteriori statement is contingent, rather than necessary. Even if it is true, it could have been false, for example, 'There are 4 chairs in this room'.

A priori: a statement is a priori if one does *not* have to appeal to experience in order to find out whether it is true. For example, 'Bachelors are unmarried', 'It is raining (here and now) *or* it is not raining (here and now)', '2+2=4'. An a priori statement is necessary, rather than contingent. It could not possibly be false. It is necessarily and universally true. (Pronounced ah-pre-or-ee.)

Analytic proposition: any statement S is analytic if and only if either (a) S is an identity or definition ('2+2=4'; 'All fathers are male parents'), or (b) S is true solely on the basis of a definition ('All fathers are male'). The denial of an analytic proposition yields a self-contradiction. For example, if any one denied '2+2=4', then since '2+2' is synonymous with '4', he would be saying '4 does not equal 4'—a self-contradiction.

Argument: a set of statements consisting of a conclusion and one or more premises which purport to provide grounds or reasons for the conclusion, about which it is claimed that the premises imply the conclusion (or the conclusion follows from the premises). Words such as 'for', 'since', 'due to', 'because', 'inasmuch as', etc. usually indicate premises of an argument. Words such as 'thus', 'so', 'hence', 'therefore', 'it follows that', etc. usually indicate the conclusion of an argument (or in some cases, a sub-conclusion if the argument is a complex one).

Contradiction (self-contradiction): (a) a statement which explicitly or implicitly both affirms that something is the case and (simultaneously) denies it—any statement of the form p and not-p. For example, 'This is red all over and not red all over (at the same time)'. Such a statement is necessarily false. (b) The assertion of propositions which are the contradictories of each other. Or more generally, the assertion of two or more propositions which cannot be jointly true. At least one of them must be false.

Contradictories: Two statements are the contradictories of each other if they cannot both be true and cannot both be false. Thus, if one is true, the other must be false; and if one is false, the other must be true. Statements of the following forms are contradictories. (In all cases (A) and (B) are contradictories of each other):

(A) All Xs are Ys.
(B) Some Xs are not Ys.

(A) No Xs are Ys.
(B) Some Xs are Ys.

(A) This is an X.
(B) This is not an X.

Deductive argument: one which claims that the premises provide absolutely conclusive evidence for the conclusion (that the connection between premises and conclusion is a necessary one).

Factual statement: one which purports to say something about some state of affairs in the world, or about kinds of states of affairs, and if true is thus genuinely informative. For example, 'There is beer in the refrigerator'. 'Bodies heavier than air fall when released'.

Formal statement: a non-factual statement.

Inductive argument: one which claims that the premises provide partial or reasonable evidence for the conclusion (that the connection between premises and conclusion is at least probable).

Law of nature: a lawlike statement which is empirically testable and hence established by observations. For example, 'All freely falling bodies falling toward the earth accelerate at a rate of 32 feet per second'.

Lawlike statement: a universal affirmative statement of the form, 'All As are Bs' or 'If X, then Y' (or 'Whenever X, then Y').

Necessary condition: A necessary condition for an event is one in whose absence the event cannot occur. If no condition, then no event. (Some prefer to formulate this as ''. . . does not occur.'') E.g., oxygen is a necessary condition for fire.

Non-verbal question: a question to which proposed answers are nonverbal statements.

Non-verbal statement: (a) a statement which is *not* about words and only words; (b) a statement whose truth does *not* follow solely from the meanings of words. For example, 'All bachelors have an I.Q. of 170 or higher', if true at all, does not follow solely from the meanings of words. The same holds for 'My dog gave birth to puppies yesterday'.

Proposition or statement: an assertion expressed by a complete declarative sentence which is capable of being true or false.

Refutation of law or theory: the finding of a single counter instance to the theory. To refute 'All As are Bs' you don't have to prove or establish that 'No As are Bs'; you merely need to prove or establish that 'Some As are not Bs'. That is, 'There is at least one thing which is A but not B'.

Refuting an argument: the establishing that the conclusion of an argument does not logically follow from the premises. This can be done by various means, both formal and informal.

Self-contradiction: *See* contradiction.

Significant law or theory: one which can be established (as true) on the basis of good evidence (which is objective, open to all, etc.) or good arguments or both. Like all significant factual statements, it must be in principle confirmable and disconfirmable.

Significant (factual) statement: one which can in principle be confirmed or disconfirmed (verified or refuted). For example, 'There are mountains in Tibet'. In order for a statement to be genuine or significant you must be able to specify what counts as evidence for it and what counts as evidence against it.

Sound (deductive) argument: a valid argument with true premises; and hence an argument in which the conclusion must also be true. (If an argument is an inductive one we cannot classify it as either valid or invalid, or sound or unsound. Instead we must classify it as reasonable or unreasonable, correct or incorrect, acceptable or unacceptable, etc.)

Statement: *See* proposition.

Substantive truth: *See* synthetic proposition.

Sufficient condition: A sufficient condition for an event is one in whose presence the event must occur. If condition, then event. (Some prefer to formulate this as ‘“. . . does occur.”’) E.g., rain is a sufficient condition for streets being wet.

Synthetic proposition: a statement which is non-analytic. The denial of a synthetic proposition does *not* yield a self-contradiction.

Tautology: a trivial and non-informative (analytic) statement which is (a) of the form ‘A is A’ (or ‘If p, then p’) or (b) one reducible to that form. For example, ‘Roses are roses’; ‘Sleuths are detectives’. Such an utterance is vacuous.

Theory: a law like statement which *cannot* be empirically tested in any *direct* manner by making observations. For example, ‘Humans have free will’. A theory must be supported by arguments. (Most philosophical claims are theories, in this sense of ‘theory’; but so are the more interesting scientific claims—for example, the kinetic-molecular theory of gases, or the theory of relativity.)

Thesis: the major claim made by an author, or speaker in an essay or lecture, etc. What the author is out to prove or establish. For example, if someone writes an article in which he claims to have evidence that we survive the death of our bodies, then his main thesis is: ‘We (humans) survive the death of our bodies’. An author may of course not only try to defend a certain thesis; he may also attempt to refute others (which compete with it). In much scientific inquiry a thesis (hypothesis, theory) is established or refuted by empirical evidence and testing. In philosophy a thesis (theory or view) is usually established or refuted on the basis of arguments. The thesis then is the conclusion of such argument.

Truth of language: *See* analytic proposition.

Vacuous statement: a statement which purports to be a statement of fact but actually has no factual content whatever. It is empty of content and thus says nothing.

Valid (deductive) argument: one such that *if* the premisses are true, the conclusion *must* be true.

Verbal dispute: a dispute which may appear to be genuine but is not because the disputants are using words in different senses. For example, suppose Ms. A. claims: “No one knows anything.” Mr. B. replies “on the contrary, most of us know lots of things.” Upon probing you find that A uses ‘know’ to mean (among other things) to have absolutely conclusive evidence for; whereas B uses ‘know’ to mean (among other things) to have good reason to believe. The dispute is a verbal one. Note that whereas verbal statements (and questions) are *about* words or follow from (are true or false by virtue of) the meanings of words, a verbal dispute is not necessarily about words. It could have any subject matter. But it is verbal in the sense that it is not a real or genuine dispute because the disputants are talking about different things due to their using words in different senses.

Verbal manipulation: to put forth a claim (as true) which rests on an arbitrary definition of a term or terms; to stipulate your own usage for a term so as to “make” your claim “true”.

Verbal question: a question to which any proposed answer is a verbal statement.

Verbal statement: (a) statement which is *about* words and only words (one which has nothing but words as its subject-matter); (b) a statement whose truth follows from (or is dependent upon) the meanings of words and only the meanings of words. For example, 'All bachelors are unmarried', '"Puppies" means young dogs', 'Puppies are young dogs'.

Note: In ordinary English, the word 'verbal' is *used* in a second sense (as well as the above sense). This second sense is: expressed in words. This is *NOT* the philosophical sense of 'verbal', for obviously all statements are expressed in words (or, at least, in symbols). From this trivial fact, it does not follow that they are verbal in the sense defined above.

Acknowledgments (continued)

"The Humanitarian Theory of Punishment," by C. S. Lewis. From *God in the Dock*. Copyright © 1970 by C. S. Lewis PTE Ltd., reproduced by permission of Curtis Brown, Ltd., London.

"The Mind as Distinct from the Body," by C. E. M. Joad. From *How Our Mind Works*. New York: Philosophical Library, 1947.

"Why I Am a Dualist," by William S. Robinson. Article written for the first edition of this book.

"The Case for Materialism," by Richard Taylor. From *Metaphysics*, © 1963, pp. 42–53. Reprinted by permission of Prentice-Hall, Inc., Englewood Cliffs, N.J.

"Mind Without Matter," by A. A. Luce. From *Sense Without Matter or Direct Perception*. Reprinted by permission of Thomas Nelson and Sons, Ltd., England and Greenwood Press.

"Behaviorism," by John B. Watson. Reprinted from *Behaviorism* by John B. Watson, by permission of W. W. Norton & Company, Inc. Copyright 1924, 1925 by The People's Institute Publishing Company, Inc., 1930 by W. W. Norton & Company, Inc. Copyright renewed 1952, 1953, 1958 by John B. Watson.

"Computing Machinery and Intelligence," by A. M. Turing. From *Mind*, LIX, 1950. Reprinted by permission of Basil Blackwell, Ltd.

"The Imitation Game," by Keith Gunderson. From *Mind* LXXIII, 1964. Reprinted by permission of Basil Blackwell, Ltd.

"The Myth of Immortality," by Clarence Darrow. Originally published in *Forum* 80 (October 1928).

"Is Life After Death Possible?" by C. J. Ducasse. From The Foerster Lecture, University of California, Berkeley (May 1947). Reprinted by permission of the University of California Press.

"Theism and the Existence of God," by Julian Hartt. From J. A. C. Fagginger Auer and Julian Hartt, *Humanism Versus Theism*. Yellow Springs, Ohio: Antioch Press, 1951.

"The Case for Atheism," by Ernest Nagel. In J. E. Fairchild (ed.), *Basic Beliefs*. New York: Sheridan House, Inc., 1959.

"Why I Am Not a Christian," by Bertrand Russell. From *Why I Am Not a Christian* by Bertrand Russell. Copyright © 1957 by Allen and Unwin. Reprinted by permission of Simon & Schuster, Inc.

"Agnosticism," by T. H. Huxley. From *Science and Christian Tradition* by T. H. Huxley. New York: D. Appleton and Co., Inc., 1898, chaps. 7, 9. "Memorial Service," by H. L. Mencken. Copyright 1922 by Alfred A. Knopf, Inc. and renewed 1950 by H. L. Mencken. Reprinted from *A Mencken Crestomathy*, by H. L. Mencken, by permission of Alfred A. Knopf, Inc.

"Theology and Falsification," by Antony Flew, R M. Hare, and Basil Mitchell. From A. Flew and A. MacIntyre, eds. *New Essays in Philosophical Theology*. London: SCM Press Ltd., 1955. Reprinted with permission of Macmillan Publishing Co., Inc. Portion by R. M. Hare appeared first in *University* 1 (1950). Reprinted by permission of the author.

"God and Evil," by H. J. McCloskey. From *The Philosophical Quarterly*, vol. 10 no. 39, 1960. Reprinted by permission of the author and *The Philosophical Quarterly*.

"The Problem of Evil," by John Hick. From *Philosophy of Religion*, 2nd ed., © 1973, pp. 36–43. Reprinted by permission of Prentice-Hall, Inc., Englewood Cliffs, N.J.

"Faith," by Richard Taylor. Reprinted by permission of New York University Press from *Religious Experience and Truth: A Symposium*, ed. by Sidney Hook. © 1961 by New York University.

"Religion, Reason, and Faith," by Richard Robinson. Selections from *An Atheist's Values*. 2nd ed. Oxford: Basil Blackwell, 1975.

"The Dignity of Human Life," by David R. Swenson. From *Kierkegaardian Philosophy in the Faith of a Scholar*. Philadelphia: Westminster Press, 1949, pp. 13–28.

"The Meaning of Life," by Kurt Baier. Inaugural lecture, Canberra University College, 1957. By permission of the author.

"Philosophy and the Meaning of Life," by A. J. Ayer. From "The Claims of Philosophy" in *Polemic*, March 1947, no. 7, pp. 18–33. Reprinted by permission of the author.

"Philosophy and the Meaning of Life," by Kai Nielsen. From "Linguistic Philosophy and 'The Meaning of Life,'" *Cross Currents*, 1964. Reprinted by permission of the author.

"The Morality Trap," by Harry Browne. Reprinted with permission of Macmillan Publishing Co., Inc. from *How I Found Freedom in an Unfree World* by Harry Browne. Copyright 1937 by Macmillan Publishing Co., Inc., renewed 1965 by W. T. Stace.

"Egoism and Moral Skepticism," by James Rachels. From pp. 423–433 of *A New Introduction to Philosophy*, edited by Steven M. Cahn. Copyright © 1971 by Harper & Row, Publishers, Inc. Reprinted by permission of Harper & Row, Publishers, Inc.

"Utilitarianism" by Jeremy Bentham. From *An Introduction to the Principles of Morals and Legislation* by Jeremy Bentham. Oxford: Oxford University Press, 1789, chapts. 1, 2, 4.

"A Problem for Utilitarianism," by Paul W. Taylor. From *Principles of Ethics: An Introduction* by Paul W. Taylor. Copyright © 1975 by Dickenson Publishing Company, Inc. Reprinted by permission of Wadsworth Publishing Company, Belmont, California 94002.

"The Deep Beauty of the Golden Rule," by Robert M. MacIver. From *Moral Principles of Action*, Vol. VI from Science of Culture Series planned and edited by Ruth Nanda Anshen. Copyright 1952 by Harper & Row, Publishers, Inc. Reprinted by permission of Harper & Row, Publishers, Inc.

"The Conscience of Huckleberry Finn," by Jonathan Bennett. From *Philosophy*, vol. 49 (1974), pp. 123–134. Reprinted by permission of Cambridge University Press.

"Good and the Will of God," by Emil Brunner. From *The Divine Imperative*, by Emil Brunner. Copyright © MCMXLVII, by W. L. Jenkins. Used by permission of the Westminster Press.

"God and the Good," by Kai Neilsen. From "God and the Good: Does Morality Need Religion?" in *Theology Today*, vol. 21 (1964). Reprinted by permission of the author.

"Science and Ethics," by Bertrand Russell. From *Religion and Science* by Bertrand Russell (1935). Reprinted by permission of Oxford University Press.

"The New Subjectivism in Ethics," by Brand Blanshard. In *Philosophy and Phenomenological Research*, vol. 9, no. 3 (1949).

"Anthropology and the Abnormal," by Ruth Benedict. In *The Journal of General Psychology* 10 (1934): 59–80, a publication of the Helen Dwight Reid Educational Foundation. Reprinted by permission of Heldref Publications, Washington, D.C.

"Ethical Relativism," by W. T. Stace. Reprinted with permission of Macmillan Publishing Co., Inc. from *The Concept of Morals* by W. T. Stace. Copyright 1937 by Macmillan Publishing Co., Inc., renewed 1965 by W. T. Stace.

"Why Choose Democracy?," by Charles Frankel. From pp. 166–179 of *The Democratic Prospect* by Charles Frankel. Copyright © 1962 by Harper & Row, Publishers, Inc. Reprinted by permission of Harper & Row, Publishers, Inc.

"The Libertarian Manifesto," by John Hospers. From *The Libertarian Alternative*, edited by Tibor R. Machan. Copyright © 1974 by Tibor R. Machan. Reprinted by permission of Nelson-Hall Publishing Company, Chicago.

"Socialism," by Carl Cohen. From *Four Systems* by Carl Cohen. Copyright © 1982 by Random House, Inc. Reprinted by permission of the publisher.

"On Being Conservative," by Michael Oakeshott. From *Rationalism in Politics* by Michael Oakeshott, pp. 182–193. Reprinted by permission of the author.

"Morals and the Criminal Law," by Lord Patrick Devlin. Edited from *The Enforcement of Morals* by Patrick Devlin, © Oxford University Press, 1965, by permission of Oxford University Press.

"Immorality and Treason," by H. L. A. Hart. In *The Listener* (July 30, 1959). Reprinted by permission of the author.

"Designing a Culture," by B. F. Skinner. Reprinted and abridged with permission of Macmillan Publishing Company from *Science and Human Behavior* by B. F. Skinner. Copyright 1953 by Macmillan Publishing Company, renewed 1981 by B. F. Skinner.

"Some Problems for Skinner," by Melvin Schuster. From "Skinner and the Morality of Melioration" in *Utopia/Dystopia* by Peyton E. Richter, ed. is reprinted herewith by permission of the publisher, Schenkman Publishing Co., Cambridge, MA, 1975, parts of pp. 96–99, 103–108. Copyright © 1975 Schenkman Publishing Co.

INDEX

Abnormal, culture defining, 453–459

Abortion, 435–436, 437–438

Absolute morality, 380–381

Absolutism
ethical, 436, 437, 438, 460–469
relativism versus, 17

Aesthetics, 17

Afterimages, sensation of, 165

Agency, theory of. *See* Self-determinism

Agnosticism, 240, 241, 274–279
evil and, 314
See also Skepticism

Antecedent conditions, 98, 99
See also Free will/determinism controversy

Anthropology, ethics and, 453–459

Antipathy
moral values and, 400
principle of sympathy and, 396, 397–399

Anti-scientism, 512, 539–545

Anti-traditionalism, liberty versus authority and, 512, 527–532

A posteriori knowledge, 28–29

A priori knowledge, 28–29

A priori method, for fixing belief, 50–51, 53

Aquinas, Thomas, 330

Arguments, 19–24

Aristotle, 539

Artificial intelligence, 202, 205–216

Ascetisism, principle of, 397–398

Atheism, 240, 241, 252–274, 277–279

Atoms, 83–86

Augustine, 315, 330

Autarchic fiction, 131, 132

Authoritarianism, 483–484

Authority, fixing belief and, 49–50, 52–53
See also Liberty versus authority

Axiology, 15–18
See also Aesthetics; Ethics

Ayer, A. J., 359–369

Bacon, Francis, Sir, 51

Bad morality, 414–423

Baier, Kurt, 348–359

Behaviorism, 156, 190–197

Belief, 14
ethics of, 53–58
fixation of, 46–53
knowing and, 36–38
right to have, 15, 27, 53–64
will and, 59–64
See also Knowledge

Benedict, Ruth, 453–459

Bennett, Jonathan, 414–423

Bentham, Jeremy, 394–401, 441

Berkeley, Bishop, 71, 93

Berlin, Isaiah, 6, 7

Blanshard, Brand, 446–453

Blatchford, Robert, 102–107

Blik, 282–283, 284, 286, 287–288

Brothers Karamazov, 298

Browne, Harry, 378–387

Brunner, Emil, 424–426, 427

Buddha, 271

Burke, Edmund, 326, 475

Butler, Samuel, 271–272

Calvinism, 414, 420–421

Camus, A., 337–338, 367

Capitalism, 494, 495–496

Causation
in science, 82–83

self-determinism and, 124
sense-data and matter and, 187–189
Certainty, faith and, 323–324
Chomsky, Noam, 542–543
Christ
    character of, 268–271
    execution, 321
    morality and, 270–271, 272–273
Christianity, 241, 252–263
    argument against, 262–274
    changes in, 284
    ethics and, 424–426
    evil and, 318, 320
    existence of God and, 241
    faith and, 322–325, 330–334
    meaning of life and, 348–350, 351–359
    reason and, 326–329
Churchill, Winston, 138
Classical liberalism, 473
    See also Democracy
Clericalism, 275–276
Clifford, W. R., 53–58
Cohen, Carl, 473–475, 493–499
Common knowledge, 102–107
Common sense
    free will and, 102–107
    properties of physical objects and, 93–94
Commonsense realism, 68, 73–81
Communism, 474
    See also Socialism
Compatibilism. *See* Soft determinism
Component arguments, 23–24
Computers, thinking and, 205–216
Conclusion, of argument, 20
Conditioned reflex, 193
Conduct
    moral rules of, 439–440
    standards of (*See also* Moral values)
    See also Ethical judgments
Conscience
    deliverances of, 439–440
    Protestant ethics and, 439
    See also Ethical judgments; Moral values

Consciousness, 191
    machine thinking and, 210–211
    See also Mind
Conservatism, 473–475, 499, 507
Contingency arguments, on existence of God, 243
Contingent statements. *See A posteriori* knowledge
Copleston, Father, 367
Cosmological argument, on existence of God. *See* First-cause argument
Crime, 137–138
    See also Punishment
Criminal law, morals and, 514–532
Critique of Pure Reason, 267
Cromwell, Oliver, 452
Culture
    designing, 533–545
    normal and abnormal defined by, 453–459
    survival of, 512, 533–545
    See also Customs, liberty based on
Curiosity, value of, 5–6
Customs, liberty based on, 512, 514–532

Darrow, Clarence, 98, 222–229
Darwin, Charles, 257, 266
Dead hypothesis, 59
Dead option, 59
Death, 13
    See also Immortality
Decision making, moral assessment of. *See* Moral values
Definition, common usage and, 109
Democracy, 473–485, 499
Democratic socialism. *See* Socialism
Descartes, Rene, 25
Descriptions, arguments versus, 21–23
Descriptive statements, 16
Design argument, on existence of God, 243–244, 249, 256–257, 266–267
Determinism. *See* Free will/determinism controversy
Deterrence, punishment and, 100, 114–115, 147

Devlin, Patrick, Lord, 514–531
Divine command theory, moral
    values based on, 376, 377, 423–
    431
Dogmatism, skepticism and, 31–34
Dostoyevski, Fyodor, 298–299, 449–
    450, 511
Doubt, belief and, 46–47
Dualism, mind-body problem and,
    155–156, 178–183, 190
    interactionist dualism, 156
    Platonic dualism, 176–178
    revised dualism, 156, 164–171
    traditional dualism, 156, 158–163
Ducasse, C. J., 229–236

Ecclesiasticism, 275–276
Economics
    capitalism, 494, 495–496
    socialism, 473–474, 475, 493–499
Eddington, Arthur, Sir, 70–72, 74–
    75, 76, 78, 79–81
Edwards, Jonathan, 414, 420–421
Ego, 126–136
Egoism
    ethical, 387, 390 394
    moral values based on, 375, 376,
    378–394
    psychological, 388–390
Einstein, Albert, 84, 265
Emotivism, in ethics, 436–453
Empiricism, 15
Epicurus, 291
Erewhon Revisited, 271–272
Ethical absolutism, 436, 437, 438,
    460–469
Ethical egoism, 387, 390–394
Ethical judgments, 435–438
    emotivism and, 436–453
    ethical absolutism and, 436, 437,
    438, 460–469
    ethical relativism and, 436, 437,
    438, 453–469
    objectivism and, 435–436, 437,
    446–453
    subjectivism and, 436, 437, 438,
    439–453
    See also Moral values
Ethical relativism, 436, 437, 438,

    453–469
Ethics, 17, 407–408, 435
    of belief, 53–58
    Christian, 423–425
    good and, 441–443
    Protestant, 439
    view of life based on religion and,
    344–347, 352–354, 355, 367–368
    See also Ethical judgments; Moral
    values
Evidence
    belief and, 53–58
    knowing and, 38–40
Evil, God and, 291–293
    existence of evil along with God,
    293, 314–321
    incompatibility of evil along with
    God, 293, 295–314
    lack of evil, 319–321
    moral evil, 296, 298–299, 308–313,
    316–318
    physical evils, 296–298, 299–308,
    318–319
Existence. See Meaning of life
Exotic cases, irrationality and,
    31–34
Expectations, human behavior
    influenced by, 160–161
External world, 12, 30–35

Faith. See God, faith in; Religion
Fallacies, religion and, 329–330
Feelings, moral judgments and,
    414, 415, 416–418
Finitude, existence of God and,
    248, 249
Finn, Huckleberry, 414, 415, 416–
    418, 421–422
First-cause argument, on existence
    of God, 243, 247–248, 254–255,
    264
Flew, Antony, 280–282, 283, 286–
    288, 317n
Forced option, 59, 61
Foresight, human behavior influ-
    enced by, 160–161
Formalism, moral values based on,
    377, 407–423
Frankel, Charles, 476–485

Frederick the Great, 346
Freedom
  democracy and, 481
  moral, 316–318
  See also Free will/determinism
    controversy; Liberty versus
    authority
Free enterprise, 494
Free market society, 474
  See also Libertarianism
Free will, moral evil and, 308–313
Free will/determinism controversy,
    13, 97–101, 112–113
  hard determinism, 99, 102–107,
    126–136
  psychoanalysis and, 126–136
  self-determinism, 100, 123–125
  soft determinism, 99–100, 108–
    119, 126–127
  See also Punishment, motive for;
    Responsibility
Freud, Sigmund, 138

Galileo Galilei, 67
Generalizations, phenomenal,
    89–99
Genuine knowledge. *See* Knowl-
    edge
Genuine option, 59, 60
God, 13, 376
  Edwards on, 414, 420–421
  ethics-religious view of life and,
    344–347, 352–354, 355, 367–368
  good and, 423–431, 440
  See also Christianity; Divine com-
    mand theory; Evil, God and;
    God, existence of; God, faith
    in; Religion; Theology
God, existence of, 239–242
  agnosticism and, 240, 241, 274–279
  atheism and, 240, 241, 252–274,
    277–279
  contingency argument on, 243
  design argument on, 243–244,
    249, 256–257, 266–267
  first-cause argument on, 243,
    247–248, 254–255, 264
  moral argument on, 244, 249–250,
    257–258, 267–268

natural law argument on, 244,
    264–266
  non-cognitivism and, 241, 280–
    288
  ontological argument on, 242,
    250–251, 255–256
  religious experience argument
    on, 244, 251–252, 258–259
  remedying injustice argument
    on, 267–268
  theism and, 240, 241, 245–252
God, faith in, 293
  Christian faith and, 322–325
  justifiability of, 293, 322–325
  meaning in life with, 338, 339–347
  meaning in life without, 338, 348–
    359
  unjustifiability of without good
    reasons, 293, 326–334
Gods, 13
  dead, 277–279
Golden rule theory, 375–376, 377,
    407–414
Good, 407, 440–441
  Christian conception of, 423–425
  ethics and, 441–443
  free will and, 308–309, 311–313
  God and the, 423–431, 440
  physical evil resulting in, 303–308
  See also Moral values
Gorgias, 539
Government, 473–475
  authoritarianism, 483–484
  authority of (*See* Liberty versus
    authority)
  conservatism, 473, 474, 475, 499–
    507
  democracy, 473, 474, 475, 476–
    485, 499
  libertarianism, 473, 474, 475, 486–
    492
  socialism, 473–474, 475, 493–499
''*Grand Inquisitor, The*,'' 511
Gravitation, existence of, 84
Greene, Graham, 356
Gunderson, Keith, 216–222

Happiness, 341–344, 363–364
  egoism and, 375, 376, 378–394

liberalism and, 512 (*See also* Liberty versus authority)
utilitarianism and, 375, 376–377, 394–407
Hard determinism, 99, 102–107, 126–136
Hare, R. M., 282–284, 286
Hart, H. L. A., 527–532
Hartt, Julian, 245–252
Heidegger, Martin, 367
Hell, Christ's belief in, 270
Heredity, free will and, 102–107
Hesse, Hermann, 364
Hick, John, 314–321
Himmler, Heinrich, 414, 418–420
Hitler, Adolf, 411
Hobbes, Thomas, 478
Holmes, Oliver W., 478
Homosexuality, law and, 518–519
Hospers, John, 36–45, 126–136, 486–492
House of the Dead, The, 449–450
Humanitarian theory, of punishment, 144–150
Hume, David, 284, 291n, 322, 323
Huxley, T. H., 274–276

Id, 126–136
Idealism, 68, 82–87
    mind-body problem and, 155–156, 183–189
Identity, mind-body problem and, 175–176
Imitation game, on machines as thinking, 205–207, 216–222
Immorality
    criminal law and, 514–532
    moral evil as, 296, 298–299, 308–313
Immortality, 13, 202–203, 204
    affirmative approach to, 229–236
    meaning of life and, 354–355
    negative approach to, 222–229
    theodicy and, 321
Indeterminism, 98, 109, 110
    self-determinism and, 100
    simple, 119–123
    See also Free will/determinism

controversy
Individual liberty. *See* Government; Liberty versus authority
Injustice, God's existence based on argument for remedying of, 267–268
Inquiry, belief and, 46–47
Intelligence, machines and, 205–216
Intelligibility, dualism and, 168–171
Interactionist dualism, 156
Introspective psychology, 190–191
Irrationality, skepticism and, 31–35

James, William, 59–64
Jealousy, as stimulus, 195–197
Jefferson, Professor, 210–211
Jim, Huckleberry Finn and, 416–418, 421–422
Joad, C. E. M., 158–163
Jones, W. T., 11
Journeymen, as philosophers, 359–360
Joyce, G. H., Father, 296, 297, 298, 301, 309, 310
Judaism, evil and, 318
Judas Iscariot, 440
Justice
    God's existence based on argument for maintaining, 267–268
    utilitarianism and, 402–407
Justified-true-belief account, 27

Kant, Immanuel, 249–250, 255, 257, 267
Kepler, Johann, 51
Keynes, John Maynard, 10
Kidd, James, 202–203
Kierkegaard, Soren, 366
Knowing, 36–43
    See also Knowledge; Skepticism
Knowledge, 11, 14, 25, 30, 102, 275
    a posteriori, 28–29
    a priori, 28–29
    definition or criterion of, 14, 26, 27, 36–53
    genuine, 14, 26, 27
    non-skepticism and, 27, 36–53
    skepticism and, 27, 30–35, 240

See also Agnosticism; Belief; Common knowledge; Knowing

Language, 73–81
Lao-tse, 268
Laplace, Marquis de, 261
Law, 514
  criminal, 514–532
  libertarians on, 490–491
  liberty versus, 17
  of nature (*See* Natural law)
Lewis, C. S., 144–150
Lewis, H. D., 327–328
Liberal democracy. *See* Democracy
Libertarianism, 99, 473, 474, 475, 486–492
  See also Soft determinism
Liberty
  custom and, 512, 514–532
  law versus, 17
  libertarianism and, 487, 490
Liberty, Equality, Fraternity, 528
Liberty versus authority, 511–513
  anti-scientism and, 512, 539–545
  anti-traditionalism and, 512, 527–532
  scientism and, 512, 533–538
  traditionalism and, 512, 514–527
Life, 225–226, 227–228
  after death (*See* Immortality)
  dignity and, 339–347
  ethico-religious view of, 344–347, 352–354, 355, 367–368
  libertarianism and, 487, 490
  view of, 339–340
  See also Meaning of life
Linguistic philosophy, meaning of life and, 365–373
Live hypothesis, 59, 60, 61
Living option, 59
Locke, John, 93, 541
Lovelace, Lady, 213–214
Luce, A. A., 183–189

McCloskey, H. J., 295–314
Machines
  persons versus, 202, 203–222
  thinking ability and, 205–216
MacIver, R. M., 407–414

Mackie, J. L., 291, 305, 309, 316n
Man
  meaning of, 179–180
  as mind and body, 177 (*See also* Mind-body problem)
Marcuse, Herbert, 539–540
Market economy, 495
  See also Capitalism
Marriage, society and, 517–518
Marx, Karl, 474, 539–540
Materialism, 156, 165–167
  immortality and, 234–236
  mind-body problem and, 154, 155, 172–183
  sensations and, 167–171
  See also Behaviorism; Dualism, mind-body problem and
Matter, theory of, 183–189
Meaning, mind appreciating, 161–162
Meaning of life, 17–18
  God and, 367–368
  meaninglessness of, 338, 339, 359–371
  nontheistic alternative to, 338, 348–359
  philosophy and, 359–373
  theistic answer to, 338, 339–347
Medieval Christianity, meaning of life and, 348–349, 356–357
Mencken, H. L., 277–279
Menninger, Karl, 137–143
Metaphysical philosophy, 12–14
  a priori method and, 50–51
  proof of, 245–247
  See also Evil; External world; Free will/determinism controversy; God; Immortality; Self
Mill, John Stuart, 2–3, 10, 264, 447, 527, 530, 545
Mind, 203
  See also Immortality; Self
Mind-body problem, 153–157
  behaviorism and, 156, 190–197
  idealism and, 155–156, 183–189
  materialism and, 154, 155, 172–183
  revised dualism and, 156, 164–171

traditional dualism and, 156, 158–163
See also Dualism, mind-body problem and
Mitchell, Basil, 284–286, 287
Momentous option, 60
Moore, G. E., 31
Moral argument, on existence of God, 244, 249–250, 257–258, 267–268
Moral cannibalism, 491
Moral evil, 296, 298–299, 308–313, 316–318
Moral good, 303–308
Morality
  atheism and, 261
  Christ and, 270–271, 272–273
  free will and, 108, 114–115
Morality trap, 378–387
Moral judgment, 514–532
  See also Moral values
Moral questions, 61–62
  objective reasoning and, 368–369, 372
Moral rules, ethics and, 439–441
Moral skepticism, 388–394
Moral values, 375–377
  divine command theory as basis for, 376, 377, 423–431
  egoism as basis for, 375, 376, 378–394
  formalism as basis for, 375–376, 377, 407–423
  utilitarianism as basis for, 375, 376–377, 394–407
  See also Ethical judgments
Motivation, unconscious, 126–136
Murder, as wrong, 356
Murphy, Gardner, 232

Nagel, Ernest, 252–261
Naïve realism, 92–93, 94
Natural law
  evils resulting from, 302
  on existence of God, 244, 264–266
Nazism, 411, 414, 418–420, 453
Negative theodicy, 319
Neurosis, 126–136
Newman, John Henry, 327, 331–332

New subjectivism, 446–453
  See also Emotivism
Newton, Isaac, Sir, 84–85, 109, 264, 265
Nielsen, Kai, 364–373
Nietzsche, Friedrich, 2
1984, 288
Niven, W. D., 304
Non-cognitivism, existence of God and, 241
Non-material, mind as, 155
  See also Mind-body problem
Non-skepticism, 27, 36–53
Nontheistic alternative, meaning of life and, 338, 348–359
Normal, culture defining, 453–459

Oakeshott, Michael, 475, 499–507
Objective requirement, of knowing, 36–37
Objectivism
  ethical, 435–436, 437, 446–453
  subjectivism versus, 16
Objects. *See* Ordinary objects, existence of; Physical objects
Occupancy, mind-body problem and, 178
On Liberty, 527
Ontological argument, on existence of God, 242, 250–251, 255–256
Options, 61
  as decisions between two hypotheses, 59–60
  on gaining or losing, 60–61
Ordinary cases, irrationality and, 34–35
Ordinary objects, existence of. *See* Idealism; Physical objects; Realism
Orwell, George, 288
Overall arguments, 23–24

Pain
  pleasure and, 300
  value of, 395, 400–402
Pascal, Blaise, 328
Peirce, Charles Sanders, 46–53
Perception
  of physical objects, 87–94

synthesized, 162–163
Pericles, 479
Personalist school, evil and, 315
Personal morality, 378–379
Persons, 201
  machines versus, 202, 203–204,
    205–222
  See also Mind-body problem
Phenomenalism, 89–90, 91
Philosophical anthropology, 14
Philosophical atheism, 260
Philosophical questions, 6–10
Physical evils, 296– 308, 318–319
Physical good, 300
  See also Pleasure, value of
Physical objects, 87–94
  immortality and, 235–236
  See also Ordinary objects, exis-
    tence of
Piper, Mrs., 233
Plato, 50–51, 176–178, 539
Platonic dualism, 176–178
Pleasure, value of, 394, 399–401
Politics. See Government
Pontiffs, as philosophers, 359–360,
  361
Possession, mind-body problem
  and, 177
Premise, of arguments, 20
Presuppositions, 3–4
Primary Philosophy, 239
Privacy, state and, 523–524
Property, 487, 488–489, 490
Propositions, knowing and, 36
Prostitution, law and, 518–519
Protestant ethics, 439
Psychical research, immortality
  and, 232–234
Psychoanalysis, free-will and, 126–
  136
Psychological egoism, 388–390
Punishment
  Christ's belief in, 270–271
  criminal law and, 514–532
  physical evil as, 300–301
  See also Law
Punishment, motive for, 98–99
  affirmative approach to, 144–150
  deterrence, 100, 114–115, 147

free will and, 114
  negative approach to, 137–143
  rehabilitation, 100, 145–147
  revenge or retribution, 100, 144
  See also Free will/determinism
    controversy; Responsibility
Pythagoras, 168

Questions
  moral, 61–62
  of personal relations, 62–63
  philosophical, 6–10

Rachels, James, 387–394
Realism, 68, 87–94
  commonsense, 68, 73–81
  naïve, 92–93, 94
  scientific, 68, 70–72
Reality, 11
  See also Metaphysical philosophy
Reason, 333
  faith and, 322–323
  religion and, 325–330
Rehabilitation, punishment and,
  100, 145–147
Relativism, ethical, 436–438, 453–
  469
Relativity-theory, naïve realism
  challenged by, 93
Religion
  acceptance of, 271–272
  defense of, 282–284
  ethico-religious view of life and,
    344–347, 352–354, 355, 367–368
  faith and, 322–325
  fear and, 273
  on living hypothesis, 63–64
  pragmatic fallacy of, 329
  reason and, 325–330
  See also God
Religious experience, God's exis-
    tence based on, 244, 251–252,
    258–259
Republic, 539
Responsibility, 98, 99
  affirmative approach to, 108–125
  determinism and, 114–115
  negative approach to, 137–143
  psychoanalysis and, 133–135

See also Free will/determinism controversy; Punishment, motive for

Retribution, punishment and, 100, 144

Revenge, punishment and, 100

Revised dualism, mind-body problem and, 156, 164–171

Rights, libertarianism and, 486–492
See also Government

Right and wrong, moral assessment of. *See* Moral values

Robinson, Richard, 325–333

Robinson, William S., 164–171

Rules. *See* Moral rules, ethics and

Russell, Bertrand, 258, 262–274, 439–446, 480

Sartre, Jean Paul, 367

Schmidt, Johann Michael, 154

Schuster, Melvin R., 539–545

Science
causation in, 82–86
cultural survival and, 512, 533–545
factitious existences in, 82–86
meaning of life and, 350–351, 352, 355, 358, 359
verification method of, 61

Scientific laws, 84–85

Scientific method, for fixing belief, 51–52

Scientific realism, 68, 70–72

Scientific table, 70–72, 79–81

Scientism, 512, 533–538

Scopes, Thomas, 98

Scriven, Michael, 239

Self, 12–13, 203
body and, 172–173 (*See also* Mind-body problem)
view of life and, 344–347
See also Immortality

Self-determinism, 123–125

Self-interest. *See* Happiness

Sensations
immortality and, 236
materialism and, 167–171
meaning of, 164–165

Sense-data, 184–188

Sense-experiences, 92

Sexual immorality, criminal law and, 518–519, 531

Simple indeterminism, 119–123

Sin, physical evil as God's punishment for, 300–301

Skepticism, 27, 30–45, 240
See also Agnosticism

Skinner, B. F., 97, 533–538

Social conflict, utilitarianism and, 405–406

Socialism, 473–474, 475, 493–499

Society, 17
morality and, 514–532
state and (*See* Government)

Society for Psychical Research, 232, 233, 234

Socrates, 4, 271, 473

Soft determinism, 99–100, 108–119, 126–127

Solidity, physics and, 76–78

Solipsism, 210–211

Soul. *See* Immortality; Mind; Self

Stace, W. T., 83–86, 108–115, 460–469

State, society and. *See* Government

States, revised dualism and, 156, 164–171

Stebbing, Susan, 73–81

Stephen, James Fitzjames, 528

Stimulus, behaviorism and, 194–197

Subjective requirement, of knowing, 37

Subjectivism, ethical, 436, 437, 438, 439–453

Substances, traditional dualism and, 156, 158–163

Substantial table, 70–71

Suicide, as wrong, 356

Super-ego, 126–136

Supernatural maker, 348–350
See also God

Support, for sense data, 186–187

Swenson, David F., 339–347

Sympathy
antipathy and, 396, 397, 398
bad morality and, 414–424

Synthesizing power, mind having, 162–163

Tables, scientific versus substantive, 70–72, 79–81
Taylor, Paul W., 403–408
Taylor, Richard, 115–125, 172–183, 322–325
Teleological argument, on existence of God. *See* Design argument
Tenacity, belief and, 47–49, 51–52
Theism, 240, 241, 245–252, 297
  atheistic critiques, 240, 241, 252–274, 277–279
  evil and, 295–296, 321
  meaning of life and, 338, 339–347
  moral evil and, 305–307, 308
  physical evil and, 299–308
Theodicy, 315–316, 319–321
Theology
  falsification and, 280–288
  machines as thinking and, 209–210
  reason and, 327–328
  See also God; Religion
Therapeutic attitude, 141, 142
Thinking machines and, 205–216
Tolstoy, Leo, Count, 348, 367
Torquemada, Tomas de, 412
Totalitarianism, 489
Traditional dualism, mind-body problem and, 156, 158–163
Traditionalism, liberty versus authority and, 512, 514–527
Treason, immorality and, 527–532
Truth, 36–37, 60
Turing, A. M., 205–222
Twain, Mark, 414, 415, 416–418, 421–423
Two tables, materialism and, 184–185

Unconscious motivation, free will and, 126–136
Unger, Peter, 30–35
Universal morality, 379–380
Unselfishness, 382–383, 384, 388
  See also Egoism
Utilitarianism, moral values based on, 375, 376–377, 394–407
Utopia, 533–538

Value judgments, 16, 356
  culture and, 534–536
  See also Ethical judgments; Moral values
Values, 4–5
  See also Moral values
Verification, method of in science, 61
Voltaire, 266, 300

Walden Two, 97, 539, 545
Watson, John B., 190–197
Welfare state, 474
  See also Democracy
Whiteley, C. H., 87–94
Will
  belief and, 59–64
  of God, 423–425
  See also Free will/determinism controversy
Widsom, John, 280, 303
Worthwhile, meaning of life and, 369–370, 372–373
Wrong, moral assessment of. *See* Moral values
Wundt, Wilhelm, 190–191